Class, Culture,
and the
Agrarian Myth

Studies in Critical Social Sciences Book Series

Haymarket Books is proud to be working with Brill Academic Publishers (www.brill.nl) to republish the *Studies in Critical Social Sciences* book series in paperback editions. This peer-reviewed book series offers insights into our current reality by exploring the content and consequences of power relationships under capitalism, and by considering the spaces of opposition and resistance to these changes that have been defining our new age. Our full catalog of *SCSS* volumes can be viewed at www.haymarketbooks.org/category/scss-series.

CLASS, CULTURE, AND THE AGRARIAN MYTH

TOM BRASS

Haymarket
Books
Chicago, IL

First published in 2014 by Brill Academic Publishers, The Netherlands.
© 2014 Koninklijke Brill NV, Leiden, The Netherlands

Published in paperback in 2015 by
Haymarket Books
P.O. Box 180165
Chicago, IL 60618
773-583-7884
www.haymarketbooks.org

ISBN: 978-1-60846-489-0

Trade distribution:
In the U.S. through Consortium Book Sales, www.cbsd.com
In the UK, Turnaround Publisher Services, www.turnaround-uk.com
In all other countries by Publishers Group Worldwide, www.pgw.com

Cover design by Ragina Johnson.

This book was published with the generous support of Lannan Foundation
and the Wallace Action Fund.

Printed in Canada by union labor.

10 9 8 7 6 5 4 3 2 1

Library of Congress Cataloging-in-Publication Data is available.

MIX
Paper from
responsible sources
FSC® C103567

For Amanda,
Anna, Ned and Miles;
and in memory of my parents

Contents

Acknowledgements   IX
List of Tables and Photographs   XI

Introduction   1

PART 1
Culture, Tradition and Modernity

1 Cultural Struggle 'From Below'   23

2 Cultural Struggle 'From Above'   66

3 Development Caught between Tradition and Modernity   117

PART 2
Screen Images of Rural Struggle

4 Horror, Humour, Fiends and Fools   161

5 Best of Friends, or Worst of Enemies?   203

PART 3
Culture, Class Struggle and Travel

6 The Grand Tour, or from Cosmopolitanism to Nationalism   247

7 Mass Tourism, or the Mob-in-the-Streets Travels Abroad   292

8 Venice – Being There   344

Conclusion   386

Bibliography   395
Subject Index   429
Author Index   441

Acknowledgements

In an age full of ironies, one of the seemingly most inexplicable contradictions is the following. On the one hand, the political left used to advocate economic development, progress, modernity, and internationalism whilst opposing peasant economy, traditional culture and nationalism. On the other, exponents of imperialist ideology used the 'otherness' of ethnicity to oppose democracy, national self-determination and international working class solidarity and mobilization. These positions appear to have been reversed.

Now, therefore, many of those who still regard themselves as leftists are enthusiastic supporters of peasant economy, cultural tradition and nationalist politics (albeit a 'from below' variety), and as such are opposed to economic development, progress and modernity. Exponents of a resurgent imperialism, by contrast, currently endorse the very discourses to which they were originally opposed: modernity, economic development and internationalism, albeit of a 'top down' variety. The question posed in this book is: how did such a contradictory politics emerge, and what kind of discourse underpins and sustains it?

Drawing on articles which have appeared over the past decade in a number of different journals, including *Dialectical Anthropology, Capital and Class, The Journal of Peasant Studies,* and *The Journal of Contemporary Asia,* it is argued here that the root of the problem lies in the resurgence of agrarian myth discourse as the main form of anti-capitalism. At the very moment when many peasants in the so-called Third World were becoming part of a global industrial reserve army of labour, they have been reconstituted – not just at the rural grassroots (the EZLN in Mexico) but also by academic discourse (the 'new' populist postmodernism) and more generally in the sphere of popular culture (film, television, travel writing) – simply as cultural subjects emblematic of ethnic/regional/national identity. Since the latter are historically the preserve of conservatism, it has not been slow politically to reoccupy this traditional ideological ground. The reason for this is the focus of the analysis presented here.

Using examples from a wide range of national/historical contexts – Europe, the Americas and Asia at different points throughout a period covering the sixteenth to the early twenty-first century – this book is divided into three parts. The first examines recent debates about the agrarian myth, modernity, nationalism and populism, with particular reference to the way these inform cultural struggles waged 'from above' and 'from below'. How and why these same themes surface and are reproduced in the domain of popular culture is considered in the second part with respect to film discourse and television images, and in the third with regard to travel literature.

Special thanks are due to the following people. To Professor David Fasenfest, the Series Editor, for encouragement; to Rosanna Woensdregt and Jennifer Obdam of Brill publishers, who guided the book through production; and to my daughter Anna Luisa Brass, who designed and drew the cover illustration. She not only drew the cover for two previous books, *New Farmers' Movements in India* (1995) and *Labour Regime Change in the Twenty-First Century* (2011), but also took the photographs that appear in Chapter 8. By not portraying Venice simply as a location of cultural 'distinction', her photographs show how such images do not always reproduce the stereotypically traditional meanings associated with travel.

As before, this book is dedicated to two sets of kin. To my family: Amanda, and Anna, Ned and Miles. Also, to my parents: my father, Denis Brass (1913–2006), who in addition to his cultural work on music, literature and language, contributed a short book on Portugal (Brass, 1960) to a popular series on travel designed to meet the interest generated by mass tourism; and my mother, Gloria Brass (1916–2012), a Spanish Civil War refugee who became a Labour Councillor in Bristol and wrote a doctorate on El Greco in her ninth decade.

Richmond-upon-Thames
April 2013

List of Tables and Photographs

TABLE   CAPTION

1   Cricket and/as class struggle in *The Go-Between*   230
2   Nationalism, colonialism and imperialism in *The Go-Between*   231
3   European 'self' versus African 'other' in VS. Naipaul   314
4   Classical versus non-classical Greek tradition in Patrick Leigh Fermor   324

PHOTO   CAPTION

1   Albero (Sacca San Girolamo)   351
2   Scuola dei Greci Bricks   356
3   Teschio (San Francesco della Vigna)   361
4   Voga alla Veneta   371
5   Bitta (Chiesa di San Sebastiano)   383

Note: For technical reasons, the five black-and-white photos reproduced in this edition are different from those in colour which appeared in the 2014 edition. As before, however, all were taken by Anna Luisa Brass in Venice.

Introduction
Class, Culture and the Agrarian Myth

During the third and last general election under the Spanish Republic, a lean, underfed Andalusian land-worker was standing in the queue before a polling booth in Granada. A conservative agent who hung about on the lookout for votes to be bought showed him a silver *duro* (or crown) in the hollow of his hand. The worker met the manoeuvre with a blank stare. The agent produced a twenty-five peseta note. Another blank stare. Piqued, he produced a one hundred peseta note, almost a fortune for the poor wretch. Unmoved, the worker out of work let fall a lapidary phrase: "*En mi hambre mando yo.*" I am master of my hunger.[1]

> The recognition by a liberal bourgeois theorist (DE MADARIAGA, 1958: 1–2) of both the existence and the power of class consciousness among the rural workers in 1930s Spain.

• • •

Optimism, n. The doctrine, or belief, that everything is beautiful, including what is ugly, everything is good, especially the bad, and everything right that is wrong. It is held with greatest tenacity by those most accustomed to the mischance of falling into adversity, and is most acceptably expounded with the grin that apes a smile. Being a blind faith, it is inaccessible to the light of disproof – an intellectual disorder, yielding to no treatment but death.

> An observation by AMBROSE BIERCE (1967: 209) during the late nineteenth century that accurately describes the 'new' populist postmodern agenda for plebeian empowerment in the twenty-first

•
• •

---

1 This epigraph is included to make the point that at the rural grassroots consciousness of class not merely exists but is also politically important. Such an observation – which might normally be considered obvious, not to say trite – is currently necessary, because the idea of a consciousness of class has been attacked recently from two directions. First, by the 'new' postmodern populism that dismisses class as 'foundational' and any consciousness thereof as an act of Eurocentric theoretical 'privileging'. And second, by the many ex-Marxists who

It is now clear that the post-war decline in peasant economy has been accompanied in the academic discipline of development studies by a conceptual re-essentialization of the peasantry as a cultural subject by postmodernism. The latter has shifted the analytical focus of the study of peasants away from political economy and history and towards literature and culture, an approach which entailed both the conceptual depriveging of economic development and the political rejection of Marxism, meta-narratives, and European Enlightenment discourse. The profound implications of this change were evident from the emergence and consolidation in the 1990s of the 'new' populist postmodernism, a theory which proclaims the attainment of 'from below' empowerment that has not only reified false consciousness but – in discarding such concepts as rural class formation/struggle/consciousness – has also eroded the emancipatory objectives associated historically with development discourse.[2]

What was at stake, therefore, was not just the form to be taken by economic growth in rural areas of the so-called Third World, but the very fact of development itself. Accordingly, the debate about petty commodity production was to some extent sidetracked down a *cul-de-sac*, where the focus of what remained an economic argument was one about whether or not peasant economy was an obstacle to the development of a capitalist agriculture. In doing so, many in the academy overlooked both the fact and the political significance of an emerging – or re-emerging – discourse in defence of the peasantry, the focus of which was not on its economic viability, but rather on smallholding as a form of cultural empowerment.

Nowhere was this more evident than in the epistemological recuperation by the 'new' populist postmodernism of a specifically cultural dimension of 'peasant-ness'. This was a discourse associated most powerfully with the Subaltern Studies project, formulated initially in the context of Asian historiography and latterly with regard to Latin American history. Reinstatement of the peasant voice as an undifferentiated/pristine subaltern 'other', untainted either by class, by economic development or by the wider capitalist system, was

---

are converts to and enthusiastic supporters of this 'new' postmodern populism. Like the original adherents of the latter, such ex-Marxists now see the rural workforce in any/ every geographical/historical context as incapable of transcending ethnic/national identity, perceived both by them and by 'new' postmodern populists as 'natural', innate and empowering. For details of this dispute, see the exchange between Beverley (2004) and Brass (2002; 2003; 2006).

2   In addition to the subaltern studies project, the components of the 'new' populist discourse include ecofeminism, the new social movements framework, 'everyday forms of resistance' theory, 'post-colonialism', 'post-Marxism', 'post-development', and 'post-capitalism'.

licensed by the dematerialization of discourse, itself an effect of postmodern deconstruction.

At the root of the 'cultural turn' was the privileging by postmodern theory of language, and a corresponding deprivileging of socialism, materialism and class as illegitimate Enlightenment/Eurocentric forms of 'foundationalism' inapplicable to the Third World. Symptomatically, for postmodernism the central epistemological problem is to construct a model that subsumes all kinds/ forms of narrative, a framework that accounts merely for the fact of narrative, not its purpose.[3] No significance is attached to the link between language and the material conditions that give rise to or sustain a particular narrative. Indeed, it is a link the very existence – let alone the efficacy – of which postmodern theory denies.[4] This means that there is no longer a necessary relation between ideological practice and infrastructure, a non-determinate view that the subaltern studies project and postmodernism inherited from structuralism. Nor is there any form of consciousness that – from the point of view of a particular class – can be categorized as false.[5]

That the purpose of postmodern deconstruction is nothing other than a decoupling of language and meaning – a project entailing the negation of concepts such as class, class consciousness and class struggle – was made clear early on by its practitioners in what amounted to a manifesto.[6] However,

---

3   See, for example, Barthes (1977: 79ff.).

4   In short, narrative is decentred, and thereby delinked from a concept of material reality, not least since for postmodern theory language and only language is 'the real'. Hence the view (Barthes, 1977: 123–124, original emphasis) that '[c]laims concerning the "realism" of narrative are therefore to be discounted…"What takes place" in a narrative is from the referential (reality) point of view literally *nothing*; "what happens" is language alone, the adventure of language, the unceasing celebration of its coming'.

5   In ignoring both the fact and effect of the presence of class *within* the ranks of those opposed to colonialism, therefore, the subaltern studies framework overlooked also the degree to which anti-colonial discourse/mobilization was that of small capitalist producers and rich peasants as much as that of poor peasants and agricultural workers. This is among the more damaging Marxist accusations made against the 'new' populist postmodernism.

6   Accepting that what it is proposing constitutes 'a move towards a theory of commentary', an early collection of texts by leading postmodernists (Bloom, de Man, Derrida, Hartman, Hillis Miller, 1979: vii–viii) continues: 'Deconstruction…refuses to identify the force of literature with any concept of embodied meaning and shows how deeply such logocentric or incarnationist perspectives have influenced the way we think about art. We assume that, by the miracle of art, the "presence of the word" is equivalent to the presence of meaning. But the opposite can also be urged, that the word carries with it a certain absence or indeterminacy of meaning. Literary language foregrounds language itself as something not reducible to meaning…'.

this objective, together with its implications for Marxist theory/practice, was overlooked by many engaged in the study of Third World development who endorsed the 'cultural turn'. Consequently, they were unknowingly lured onto the epistemological terrain of the political right, little realizing that the re-essentialization of the peasantry found in the 'new' populist postmodernism that colonized development studies throughout the 1980s and 1990s was prefigured in 1930s reactionary conservatism.[7] Common to the latter and to the 'new' populist postmodernism is discourse about the agrarian myth.

Agrarian Myth Discourse

An historical and contemporary ideology that projects the innateness, immutability and enduring character of socio-economic identity based on Nature, the agrarian myth contains both a discourse-for and a discourse-against.[8] It also consists of two variants, each of which in turn possesses two versions. The peasant or 'from below' version of the agrarian myth is termed here the plebeian, while the second or 'from above' version is the landlord/aristocratic variant. Both variants – the landlord/aristocratic no less than the peasant/plebeian – maintain that the structure of which they are a part is founded on Nature, and thus 'natural'.

Each variant possesses a pastoral and a Darwinian form, amounting respectively to an idyllic vision of the countryside (unequal but harmonious), and a 'red-in-tooth-and-claw' vision, in which the countryside is a site of

---

7 As Marxism has long argued, at the heart of 1930s reactionary discourse – in Germany, Italy and Japan – lay the essentialized concept of peasant as bearer/defender of a similarly innate ethnic or national identity. For those on the political right, therefore, an attack on one necessarily involved an assault on the other.

8 As has been shown elsewhere (Brass, 2000a), the discourse-for of the agrarian myth endorses 'natural'/harmonious rural-based small-scale economic activity (peasant family farming, artisan handicrafts) and culture (religious, ethnic, national, regional, village and family identities, characterized as instinctive because they are derived from Nature). By contrast, the discourse-against of the agrarian myth expresses opposition to urban-based large-scale economic activity (industrialization, finance capital, the city, manufacturing, collectivization, planning, massification, scientificity, rationality) and hostility towards its accompanying institutional/relational/systemic effects (class formation/struggle, revolution, socialism, bureaucracy, the State). All the latter are perceived as non-indigenous/inauthentic/'alien' internationalisms imposed on an unwilling and mainly rural population by 'foreigners', and therefore as responsible for the erosion of a hitherto authentic local culture, traditions and values.

struggle – either by landowners or by peasants – to gain or retain power and/ or property. Both variants depict land/nature as eternal/sacred, an ancient form of existence predicated on (and embodied in) folklore/myth/legend that warn against attempts to change values/identity linked to this. However, it is important to note that such discourse changes in response to class struggle.

What starts out as a pastoral variant of the agrarian myth, embodying either a landlord or a plebeian version, therefore, may be transformed into its Darwinian variant. Conversely, a change from the Darwinian to the pastoral may signal an abeyance in the conflict. For this reason, a number of films and travel accounts combine both forms, the landlord pastoral clashing with the plebeian Darwinian, and vice versa (plebeian pastoral with the landlord Darwinian). Where landlord and plebeian pastoral versions coincide, the intensity of class struggle is likely to be low; alternatively, where Darwinian versions confront one another, class struggle is likely to be acute.

When mobilized ideologically in the domain of popular culture, these con-trasting images of the landlord class are supportive of agrarian populism, which replaces class differences transecting the rural/urban divide with non-class identities based on sectoral difference (the immutability of rural tradi-tion and 'belonging').[9] Because the agrarian myth is centrally about who represents the nation, it is also about the ideologies of nationalism, populism, class, and the State.

Culture against Development

One of the main problems confronting the social sciences generally, and devel-opment studies in particular, concerns an inability to distinguish leftist politics and theory from their right-wing equivalents.[10] During the 1960s development decade, therefore, the failure on the part of the modernization framework to question – and thus to settle ideological accounts with – the politics informing rural culture enabled its subsequent categorization by exponents of the 1980s

---

9   Seen from above, a landlord/peasant relation is not invariably antagonistic. Thus a land-lord can and does approve of peasants as long as they remain tenants or smallholders, and recognize his power, his position in the existing hierarchy, and his property rights. It is when they cease to be 'his' peasants, and instead of remaining subordinates challenge his power, his property rights, or become workers and migrate to the cities, that they are perceived by a landlord as a potential/actual threat.

10 Aspects of this problem not considered here are covered by me elsewhere (Brass, 2000b; 2005; 2013b).

'cultural turn' as a progressive grassroots discourse, one that validated indigenous nationalism. Hence the optimism generated by the 1994 Zapatista uprising in the Mexican state of Chiapas, a political event widely greeted as heralding
a novel and progressive form of anti-capitalist mobilization. By reasserting an
'authentic' cultural otherness, its supporters maintained, peasant smallholders
would form an effective bulwark against globalization threatening their indigenous selfhood.

The populist historiography of James Scott also subscribes to this optimism
about the realization of 'from below' empowerment.[11] Ostensibly consistent
with anarchism, he peoples his Zomia, an upland area in southeast Asia,
with free inhabitants, self-sufficient cultivators exercising self-management
(= 'autonomy') in egalitarian smallscale rural communities beyond the reach
of the State (= State 'avoidance'). However, this is misleading. Despite advancing his resistance-to-the-state theory under the progressive label of an anarchist history, Scott's anti-state discourse has more in common with views of
libertarian philosophers, anarcho-capitalist thinkers, and neoliberal economists.[12] For all the latter, as for Scott, opposition to the state as an institution
remains absolute, and stems principally from its taxation policy, perceived by
libertarians as an illegitimate appropriation, a view which overlooks the redistributive functions linked to this role.

Anarchist political theory opposed to the state as an institution not only
does so mainly on the grounds that historically it has acted on behalf of the
wealthy, in whose interests it has invariably suppressed grassroots movements
opposed to the rich, but also sees virtue in the progressive attempts by the state
committed to public works and welfare programmes, to regulate capital and
rein in the market. This emphasis is very different from that of libertarians generally (and anarcho-capitalists in particular), who seek much rather to prevent
such expenditure, so as to enable the rich to retain more of their wealth that
would otherwise be taken from them by the state in the form of taxation.[13]

Broadly speaking, grassroots agency labelled by Scott as a process of 'resistance' against – or 'avoidance' of – the State frequently entails attempts to get

---

11   See Chapter 3 for the role of Scott's 'everyday-forms-of-resistance' framework in providing
      'new' populist postmodern theory with a form of non-revolutionary grassroots agency
      that leaves intact the wider class structure and its State.

12   Libertarian philosophers include Spencer (1884), Nock (1935) and Nozick (1975), while
      Rothbard (1982) is an example of an anarcho-capitalist thinker, and Hayek (1960) and
      Friedman (1962) are neoliberal economists.

13   For the importance of the political distinction between these forms of libertarianism, see
      Walter (1969: 10), Carter (1971: 28ff.), and Marshall (1992: 559ff.).

the state involved, and thus does not correspond to a wish to 'avoid' this institution. Much rather the opposite, in that agency by slum-dwellers and poor farmers on occasion is designed to make the State pro-active on their behalf, and put into practice its own policies or legislation enforcing minimum wage levels and land reform programmes. Accordingly, his unambiguously all-embracing concept of anti-State agency (= 'avoidance') overlooks the presence of contrary instances.

By putting pressure on the State through class struggle, therefore, workers in urban contexts have managed to secure improvements in pay and conditions, not to mention the franchise, which enabled them to consolidate such gains. It was by stripping away State intervention – the very process Scott endorses – as has occurred in many parts of the world after 1980, that workers have lost this kind of protection, and been left at the mercy of the markets. This is the reason why Marxism has always argued for the capture (*not* the avoidance) of the State, and its subsequent use to implement a socialist programme. Resistance-to-the-State, in other words, also occurs in valley and urban contexts, but of a different kind, by a different subject, and with different objectives. So confining agency to hill populations, as Scott does, is incorrect.

However, resistance by (undifferentiated) peasants in defence of indigenous culture and tradition is now seen as a legitimate part of the struggle against capitalism, a result being that rural struggle is no longer about class but identity politics and thus the national question. Against this it is argued that the recuperation by the 'new' populist postmodernism both of an essentialist peasant culture/economy and of indigenous nationalist agency stems from the idealized concept of popular culture linked to the agrarian myth. Not only does this framework leave intact the existing class structure, and reproduce the populist mobilizing discourse of the political right, but it also (and therefore) undermines international working class solidarity. It is, in short, a conservative form of anti-capitalism.

Paternalism, Populism as 'The Rightness of Things'

As the case of Zomia underlines, the political link between class, populism, resistance and culture is bedevilled by a certain amount of confusion, a difficulty manifested in the populism/paternalism distinction. Some persist in interpreting paternalism not merely as the antithesis of class struggle, but even as evidence for the absence of a class relation itself. Others regard paternalism merely as the benign face of populism, as enabling resource transfers down the hierarchy which mitigate or negate class inequalities.[14] These approaches define paternalism in positive terms, to the benefit of 'those below' as much as 'those above'.[15]

What is involved, however, is not so much a shift from one form to another, more a case of populism complementing – not supplanting – paternalism. As such, the latter was not an alternative to but rather a crucial form of class struggle waged 'from above', deployed not instead of but in conjunction with populist rhetoric and coercion.[16] This underlines why clamping down on dissent by the upper classes was combined with the resort to a populist discourse to achieve their ends. In other words, class struggle taking the form of simple violence against the masses was never by itself going to be enough. To be successful, and ensure the continued rule by those with property and wealth, it needed to be combined with a less directly antagonistic – but no less effective – approach, a pattern realized subsequently in the 'one nation' Toryism of Disraeli.[17]

Paternalism was accordingly part of the carrot-and-stick response by the upper classes in Victorian England to the process of working class formation and struggle occurring throughout the nineteenth century. In the sense that

---

14   In a symptomatically postmodern interpretation, Baaz (2005) explains the paternalistic discourse structuring development aid in terms of an egalitarian link between donors and recipients.

15   As used by some analyses of rural contexts in the so-called Third World – for example Breman (1974) and Gellner and Waterbury (1977) – patronage and paternalism are interchangeable concepts. Each is regarded as a benign arrangement not just linking but to the advantage of those at opposite ends of the class hierarchy.

16   That paternalism was both coercive and an ideological form of class struggle waged 'from above', is evident from the following description (Roberts, 1979: 2): 'Almost all Victorian paternalists held four basic assumptions about society: it should be authoritarian, hierarchic, organic and pluralistic. That it should be authoritarian followed naturally from the very word paternal, which means fatherhood, and which is very nearly synonymous with sovereignty. Fathers command and exact obedience. So do kings, judges, lords lieutenant, magistrates, bishops, archdeacons, squires, parsons, constables, and workhouse governors; their authority is of a paternal nature'. The same text concludes (Roberts, 1979: 275): 'The English governing classes not only had to manage estates, parishes, mills, and quarter sessions but develop a basic social theory, however, rudimentary, that would, in a decade of economic crises, Chartist riots, Irish famines, and burgeoning cities full of crime and disease, assure one of the rightness of things, particularly old things'.

17   For the important role of Disraeli in waging a 'from above' struggle by fostering a populist 'one nation' conservatism in nineteenth century Britain, see Chapter 2. His 'Young England' group was categorized by Marx and Engels (1976: 508) as being exponents of 'feudal socialism', the political object of which was to prevent/pre-empt the emergence of a revolutionary working class.

'we know better than you what is best for you', therefore, the shift from paternalism to populism involved an attempt on the part of landowners to deflect
blame for existing ills and inequalities onto 'the foreigner' thereby establishing
a common identity with plebeian elements based on nationalism.

That these 'from above' strategies operated in tandem is evident, not least
from their co-existence in the texts of liberal bourgeois political economy. On
the one hand, therefore, are found threats that no attempt by trade unions to
oppose the expansion of the industrial reserve army, so as to protect wages/
conditions – and with them living standards – already secured, will be toler-
ated.[18] On the other, however, activity by trade unions analogous to friendly
societies is encouraged, as is more broadly a paternalist approach by the capitalist State. Unlike their present-day equivalents, nineteenth century economic
liberals recognized as fact not only the existence of class struggle between capital and labour, but also the effectiveness of working class organization and
strike action.[19] To avoid revolution, potentially always an outcome of a rising
incidence of 'from below' class struggle, therefore, policies advocated were
those which would create an 'identity of interests' between capital and labour.[20]

---

18   See, for example, the chapter on strikes and trade unions in Fawcett (1876: 240ff.), an
      economic liberal influenced by Bentham, Mill and Darwin. He argued that workers orga-
      nized in combination possessed two functions: one was the equivalent of friendly societ-
      ies (insurance against unemployment or illness), of which he approved; the other, to
      operate a closed shop to protect existing wages/conditions, he condemned. Categorizing
      the withdrawal of labour in pursuit of the latter role as 'vexatious restrictions' and 'social
      terrorism', Fawcett (1876: 243, 244, 245) played the nationalist card and issued a warning
      that can still be heard today: 'If, moreover, these societies [= trade unions] should increase
      in numbers and in power, so as gradually to embrace a large majority of the working
      classes, the industrial prosperity of the nation might be seriously jeopardised, since vari-
      ous branches of industry...might even leave the country. For we cannot compete with
      foreign countries if our manufacturers are to be dictated to by their workmen with regard
      to the use of machinery and the conduct of business'.

19   Observing that 'the bargaining which often goes on in adjusting wages, implies a struggle,
      or a conflict of effort between employers and employed; in this conflict a great advantage
      will be possessed by those who can act in concert, over those who simply act as isolated
      individuals', Fawcett (1876: 249, 250) concedes that 'it appears that strikes are inseparably
      associated with our present economic system. As long as the relations between employers
      and employed continue to be analogous to those between the buyer and seller of a com-
      modity, it must often happen that the one party will refuse to accept the price which is
      offered by the other for labour; if the refusal is persisted in, a strike inevitably ensues'.

20   Fawcett (1876: 251) agreed that, in the context of class struggle, conciliation and arbitra-
      tion procedures were useful, but 'do not provide a completely efficient remedy for strikes.
      These disputes must be regarded as the natural outgrowth of existing relations between

These included not just paternalist government, combining a modicum of regulation with some welfare provision, but also nationalism and populist discourse.[21]

Populism, Culture and Class Struggle

Accordingly, a 'from above' populist discourse takes the form of cultural politics, which become a site of struggle between those at either end of the class hierarchy. Thus, for example, the continuation of monarchy as an institution requires that its subject, and/or those related to its subject, appear to be 'ordinary' by virtue of doing 'ordinary' things. Hence the familiar television images of royals travelling by bicycle, and princes taking an interest in national sporting events. In a similar vein, bourgeois political leaders who have been educated at elite universities and private schools speak with an estuary accent, talk incessantly about football, and cultivate the company of pop stars and members of rock bands.[22]

---

employers and employed. Some plan must be adopted, which will make masters and workmen feel that they have an identity of interest'. He then went on to suggest a purely economic remedy: co-partnerships in industry, whereby the employed would participate in any profits generated by their labour. Fawcett did not consider other – political and ideological – ways in which an 'identity of interests' might be fostered; that is, nationalism and populism. However, Disraeli did.

21   Sir Arthur Helps (1872: 16, 23, 32–33) accepted that '[p]aternal government prevents revolution', whilst insisting that the state retained the right always to resort to physical force when faced with a challenge to its authority. This duality accurately embodies the carrot-and-stick approach of class struggle waged 'from above'.

22   That ruling class continuity depends in some way on fostering plebeian allegiance has long been recognized. Hence the following observation by Mosca (1939: 112): 'In the Middle Ages the first peasant revolts broke out not when feudalism was harshest but when the nobles had learned to associate with one another, when the courts of love – a conscious quest of good manners (the *gai saber*) – had begun to give them polish and alienate them from the rustic ways of the lonely castle'. However, this process has been interpreted in opposing ways. For those like Mosca, who regard aristocratic patronage as benign and economically efficacious, its loss generates antagonism at the rural grassroots among smallholding peasants who wanted nothing more than its restitution. According to this interpretation, the dynamic for the allegiance comes from below. A contrasting view maintains that, because the landowning class feels threatened by actual/potential mobilization on the part of the rural grassroots, the impetus for establishing a politico-ideological allegiance comes from above. The latter interpretation, based as it is on the existence of class struggle, is the one followed here.

Over the past three decades, one consequence of the downgrading or banishment by postmodernism of class as an analytical category has been the conceptual elimination of agency based on this: class struggle. During this period, the focus of much social scientific investigation has shifted to explaining the resurgence of conflict along ethnic and/or national lines, not just in Third World contexts (Africa, Asia, Latin America and the Middle East) but also in Europe. It is clear, however, that not only does class struggle continue, at least as fiercely as in any previous era, but that currently its major impetus comes not 'from below' but rather 'from above'.

Today no socialist needs convincing as to just how 'feral' neoliberal capitalism has become. Having first undermined the ability of workers to oppose politically (anti-strike legislation, union busting, employment outsourcing, the fall of actually-existing communism, the rise of 'New Labour') and ideologically (the promotion of vacuous 'celebrity', the 'cultural turn' replacing materialist analysis), capital shifted its asset-stripping activity from corporations to entire nations (privatization, crisis in the euro zone). Resources that would otherwise be available for investment in education, health, infrastructure, public-sector jobs or welfare programmes were accordingly diverted to off-shore tax havens.

That such a 'from above' class struggle has been waged by capital worldwide is in a sense unsurprising, since this was always inherent in its logic following the globalization process of the last three decades.[23] What does surprise, however, is the ability hitherto of what is now an international capitalist class to get away with this onslaught on the living standards and welfare gains achieved by plebeian components of the global workforce. In part, this is due to a combination of reasons: not just the new international division of labour, but also the displacement of class identity/consciousness/struggle by their ethnic/national/religious

---

23   The fact that capitalists themselves engaged in class struggle 'from above' has long been
      obvious, not just to those on the left. During the 1950s even non-Marxist economists were
      aware of the ability of capital not merely to oppose but to undermine regulation.
      Examining capital flight as a response to government control, therefore, Shonfield (1958:
      221) noted that '[t]he only way to prevent such a movement, once controls are down, is by
      making Britain as attractive place to the owners of capital as any possible alternative
      abroad. This at once sets pretty narrow limits to what Government can do about taxation,
      about social expenditure, about nationalization, and a number of other major political
      issues. Here in fact is the vicarious reassertion of the political power of the owners of
      wealth – not businessmen or people in any active way, but just owners – which the post-
      war social revolution in Britain had set out to prevent'. The full significance of this strug-
      gle, between on the one hand planning/regulation, and on the other *laissez faire* policies
      sought by capital and implemented by its State, emerged three decades later as globaliza-
      tion took hold.

equivalents, and the capacity to persuade large sections of the populations affected that no socialist political alternative to the present economic system is possible.

Any pretence at media objectivity about the latter development has long since vanished, as craven interviewers privilege the opinions of 'markets' (bankers, oligarchs, hedge-fund managers, speculators and financiers), grovelling before multi-millionaire CEOs who advocate yet more deregulation and austerity. The best one can hope for, we are told by media commentators, is to aspire to 'good governance' and a return to an earlier form of capitalism (= 'redemocratization'). This in turn raises the issue of ideology, its formation, role, reproduction and grassroots acceptability. A crucial element accounting for the success of class struggle waged 'from above' has been – and remains – the ownership/control by capitalist enterprises of the mainstream electronic media industries (television, film, radio).

Film and Travel as Class Struggle

There is on the face of it no obvious connection between a peasant movement in Mexico, films the subject of which is the British monarchy, and travel writing about the city of Venice. Not merely does a link exist, however, but the similarity it reveals explains much about conflict involving the changing social structure in each context. Thus the themes encountered in the first part of the book – class struggle waged as much 'from above' as 'from below', the fusion of populism and nationalism, discourse about 'the mob in the streets', progress and development as the 'others' of the agrarian myth – emerge also in the subsequent parts dealing with film and travel writing.

Images on screen have a spurious veracity, whether these are depictions of nation as a specific place (= travel) or of the way class distinctions operate within the latter contexts (monarchy, aristocracy; workers, poor peasants). Hence the crucial role discharged by ideology, and in particular the media and popular culture as these combine in film, television and travel writing. These are sites where capital can and does structure discourse about nation and class, emphasizing the former while downgrading the latter. The importance of film is that it is where populist images – monarch as no different from and thus a legitimate representative of 'the people' and their nation – can be inserted, with all that this implies for the formation and reproduction of working class consciousness.

In political terms, therefore, the antithesis between the internationalism of class and much narrower focus of nationalism gives rise in turn to populism, an ideological synthesis which enables owners of the means of production to claim they are speaking about and for plebeian elements in the same society.[24] Not the least of the many ironies is that the synthesis applies to both ends of the class hierarchy. Discourse informing travel suggests that an initial landlord/ aristocratic cosmopolitanism generated historically by the Grand Tour is displaced by a 'from above' attempt to mobilize the rural grassroots on the basis of the agrarian myth, thereby obtaining support among smallholders and farmers opposed to the effects of industrialization, urbanization and capitalist crisis.

The resulting invocation of anti-foreigner sentiment or town/country divide permits landowners and/or rich peasants to deflect, distort or displace class consciousness by emphasizing loyalties not antagonistic to capital (and thus compatible with the continued process of accumulation). Politico-ideologically, rural identity – which populism claims is culturally innate and unchanging – comes to symbolize the nation itself, and a decline in either smallholding or landlordism becomes synonymous with deculturation and the erosion (or loss) of national identity. It was this task which the populism sought to effect by merging the agrarian myth with popular culture.

Film discourse and travel literature confirm this trend, since each genre combines the negative/positive ideology of the agrarian myth. On the one hand, a disdain for the growth of industrial development, the urban plebeian (= 'the mob in the streets'), and the mass tourist, whilst on the other a sympathetic portrayal of cultural identity – abroad and at home – associated with

---

24   Although the Marxist critique of populism is rightly associated with the work of Lenin and Trotsky, their opposition to this backwards-looking discourse is prefigured in the work of Marx and Engels. Both the latter had attacked agrarian populism half a century earlier, when in the *Communist Manifesto* they considered 'feudal socialism', defined thus (Marx and Engels, 1976: 507ff.): 'The aristocracy, in order to rally the people to them, waved the proletarian alms-bags in front for a banner...so little do they conceal the reactionary character of their criticism that their chief accusation against the bourgeoisie amounts to this, that under the bourgeois regime a class is being developed, which is destined to cut up root and branch the old order of society'. In the sentence that follows, the underlying political fear of landowners who mobilize on the basis of agrarian populism is made clear: 'What they upbraid the bourgeoisie with is not so much that it creates a proletariat, as it creates a *revolutionary* proletariat' (original emphasis). At that same conjuncture, Engels (1976: 355) identified this kind of populist discourse as one which sought 'to establish the rule of the aristocracy', composed of 'adherents of feudal and patriarchal society which has been or is still being daily destroyed by large-scale industry, world trade and the bourgeois society that they have both brought into existence. From the ills of present-day society this group draws the conclusion that feudal or patriarchal society should be restored because it was free from these ills'. His conclusion was that 'it always gives away its real intentions every time the proletariat becomes revolutionary and communist, when it immediately allies itself with the bourgeoisie against the proletarians'.

indigenous and/or rural 'otherness'. The former are perceived as antagonistic to the instinctual, and thus 'natural', elements belonging in the latter category, threatening to overwhelm and destroy them.

Central to this nationalism/populism link, therefore, is the issue of class: not just its formation, but also the struggle it generates.[25] Ostensibly the epistemological link between class, nation, populism and the agrarian myth reveals itself most clearly in relation to debates about economic development over the second half of the twentieth century. More insidious, however, is the continued reproduction of this same link in two less obvious discourses: that about film and, more generally, travel literature. The role within metropolitan capitalist contexts of travel writing – a widely read genre and hugely influential form of 'popular culture' – in reproducing the agrarian myth about rural populations in the so-called Third World should not be underestimated.[26]

Unlike development theory, discussion of which is confined largely to academia, what film and travel literature have to say extends beyond the

---

25   Downgrading the significance of class and class struggle as the motor of social transformation has a long history, not least during the 1960s when much sociological theory insisted that such concepts and processes were redundant. At that conjuncture it was possible for Ralf Dahrendorf (1967: 22) not merely to pose the question that 'by understanding the tone and substance of conflict, we may be able to account for the rate and direction of change', therefore, but to answer as follows: 'Do we know the law of development of modern societies? Marx thought he did, but unfortunately he was wrong. His theory had to be replaced by a new and better one; a process in which many scholars (including myself) have taken part'.

26   Thus the idealized Rousseauesque image of the 'noble savage' (= nomadism as 'natural'/ primitive humanity) which informed the travel writings of Bruce Chatwin was appropriated by him from anthropological texts (Shakespeare, 1999), while a similarly derivative and romanticized account of the Kalahari Bushmen in a correspondingly prelapsarian state structured the equally inaccurate but highly popular narrative in the same genre by Laurens van der Post (Jones, 2001). In the case of the latter writer, this influence not only extended into British ruling class circles but also threatened to have an impact on the shape of the post-apartheid political settlement in South Africa. Dismissing the ANC and Nelson Mandela as 'communists', van der Post (along with the far right in the UK and South Africa itself) championed the separatism of the reactionary Zulu Inkatha movement led by Chief Buthelezi, whose espousal of traditional cultural values represented for the travel writer the embodiment of his own vision of 'natural'/'primitive' man in Africa. From the late 1980s to the early 1990s, van der Post continuously pleaded the Inkatha/ Buthelezi cause to the then conservative prime minister Margaret Thatcher and Prince Charles, with the object of securing their political support for the creation within South Africa of a separate Zulu nation (= KwaZulu-Natal). For a Darwinian interpretation by v.s. Naipaul of 'natural'/'primitive' man in Africa, see Chapter 7 below.

university to reach a much wider audience. Their sphere of operation is the domain of popular culture, and consequently their ideological impact is, it could be argued, somewhat greater. For this reason, a more pervasive and enduring form of influence exercised by the agrarian myth is transmitted ideologically through the realm of film and travel literature.

Why Travel (Writing)?

Despite the fact that travel writing is informed by many of the themes structuring the agrarian myth, not least that of class struggle, it tends to be regarded as innocent politically, and certainly not a worthy object of Marxist scrutiny.[27] Such a view is challenged in this book, since in much the same way as other areas of the social sciences, analysis within academia of travel literature has been colonized by postmodernism. It was as a result of visits abroad that Herder and Herzen both formulated views about the interconnectedness of national identity, class, populism and the agrarian myth.[28] This makes it all the more surprising that travel writing as a genre continues to escape analysis by Marxist theory.

Like film, travel is imbued by 'new' populist postmodernism with a form of original sin, whereby the western self is guilty of constructing images/ideas about the non-western 'other' and his/her culture. The result is an approach which categorizes travel literature simply as a form of 'orientalist' gaze, to be castigated as the handmaiden of domination; initially by colonialism, and latterly by imperialism. Historically, therefore, writing about the culture of a

---

27   Among the useful non-Marxist analyses of travel, that by Fussell (1982) acknowledges the pastoral element, but not the conflict that redefined the mob-in-the-streets as the mass tourist. In common with much of its genre, therefore, the emphasis is on writing-for, not writing-against. That by Withey (1998) focuses on the business of travel, and in particular the important role of Thomas Cook in organizing itineraries. Neither interprets travel in terms of the agrarian myth, nor is the literature generated by foreign journeys linked to a political discourse about nation, class struggle and the 'new' populist postmodernism.

28   For details, see Chapter 6 below. The argument made here about travel accounts contradicts the assertions (Raban, 2011: vii, viii) both that such narratives 'have little in common beyond their shared use of the first person pronoun', and that in the period 1950–1970 'every travel book was so bereft of close relations that it had to make its way through the world as an orphan'. Similarly misplaced is the warning from the same source (Raban, 2011: xvi) that these days 'anyone in search of magic-carpet rides to idyllic, far-flung destinations, should put [travel books] back on the shelf', concluding that '[t]here are no idylls here'. Agrarian myth discourse permeating the genre suggests otherwise.

country becomes for postmodernism – and can only ever be – an exercise in constructing a different identity prior to and as reason for conquest of the place/space inhabited by this 'other'.

A postmodern approach, the focus of which is simply on the 'orientalist' gaze, overlooks a number of things. To begin with, that plebeian rural 'otherness' encountered in a foreign country is viewed positively as long as its subject does not challenge the hierarchy in which s/he is located. Once such quiescence is transcended, and smallholders are transformed into the mob-in-the-streets, travel literature adopts a negative stance towards this subject. In the era of mass tourism, the identity of the 'other' castigated by travel writing shifts yet again, and becomes increasingly the plebeian from home who voyages abroad.

In an important sense, film subjects travel to a process of visual précis, constructing images of an 'other' place that endure, regardless of whether or not they are actually/historically accurate. Generated by film, such perceptions shape what one expects 'to see', both abroad and indeed at home. Thus, for example, Evelyn Waugh recounts how preconceptions formed by cinematic depictions of large rural estates structured what he thought he would see in the course of a journey to Brazil in 1932.[29] The same kind of visual précis operates even when going the other way. Returning from the United States during the late 1940s, therefore, Christopher Isherwood experienced an analogous difficulty in separating the physical reality he encountered on arrival in England – where he was born and educated – from the stereotypical images conveyed by Hollywood films of the country he was now in.[30]

Accordingly, discourse informing both film and travel is not only mutually reinforcing, but as such feeds into the ideological reproduction of all variants –

---

29   'We reached our destination in about two hours and found three sheds and a wired corral.
     It was less than I had expected' confesses Waugh (1951: 221–222), because '[t]hrough the
     influence of cinema, "ranch" had taken on a rather glorious connotation in my mind; of
     solid, whitewashed buildings; a courtyard with a great tree casting its shadow in the centre
     and a balustraded wall, wrought iron gates, a shady interior with old Spanish furniture and
     a lamp burning before a baroque Madonna...I did feel that the word "ranch" had taken a fall'.
30   'Throughout the years I spent in Hollywood', notes Isherwood (1966: 153–154), 'I had
     never tired of protesting against the American film presentation of English life. What
     caricature! What gross exaggeration! But now [the late 1940s] – and increasingly during
     the weeks that followed – I began to reverse my judgment. *Is* it possible to exaggerate the
     Englishness of England? Even the bus which took us from the airport into London seemed
     grotesquely "in character"; one almost suspected that it had been expressly designed to
     amaze foreign visitors...we would pass through an English village complete with a village
     church in a country churchyard; so absurdly authentic that it might have been lifted
     bodily off a movie-lot at MGM...' (original emphasis).

landlord and peasant, red-in-tooth-and-claw and pastoral – constitutive of the agrarian myth. Like film, therefore, travel writing encourages its subject to exorcise poverty, whereby visual 'pretty-fication' overlays (and substitutes for) any evidence about the economic precariousness of rural livelihood experienced by poor peasants and workers. A politically more challenging discourse about what is seen gives way to easier description, generating 'picturesque' images as the economics of poverty shifts to an aesthetic dimension. This transformation is especially true of travel writing that initially registers and is disturbed by the presence of the poor in an 'other' place (beggars, hovels, shanties, etc.).[31]

Themes (and Variations)

Drawing on examples from a wide range of national/historical contexts – Europe, the Americas and Asia at different points throughout a period covering the sixteenth to the early twenty-first century – this book is divided into three parts. The first (Chapters 1 to 3) examines recent debates about the agrarian myth, modernity, nationalism, class struggle waged 'from above' and 'from below', the State and populism, illustrated with reference to peasant movements in Mexico. How and why these same themes surface is considered in the second part (Chapters 4 and 5) with respect to film discourse and television images, and in the third (Chapters 6 to 8) with regard to travel literature.

---

31   This shift is clear, for example, in the case of Nicolas Garland (1983), the cartoonist for the Daily Telegraph, who recorded his impressions of a visit he made to India in 1982. It is a shift, moreover, that is acknowledged (Garland, 1983: 127–128, emphasis added): 'The fields that bordered the road were also busy: farmers ploughed and tilled, and people walked to and fro. I saw thin old ladies carrying huge loads on their heads looking like duchesses practicing advanced deportment exercises. *This was a scene into which words like poverty and hardship were difficult to fit.* Certainly, the people, or many of them, are poor and I have no doubt their lives are hard, but being there and seeing them, at least for me this first time, *I found I could not hold on to such complicated and serious notions.* I gazed unthinking, simply glad to be there'. In much the same vein, Garland (1983: 148, 161, emphasis added) describes village life: 'Evening was falling and people lit fires and candles. The still air was smoky and the scene became more and more pretty. Cows and goats and chickens moved through the streets...All the houses were open and everywhere people sat and talked or strolled about or worked. It was a busy, cheerful place, crowded but not noisy...When I woke up in the morning at about six and looked out of the window the landscape had changed. In the misty light I could see many more palm trees and what I think were paddy fields. The country was criss-crossed by little irrigation canals and there were many ponds or little lakes. The small fields looked neat and well-tended. *The whole aspect was tranquil and pretty'.*

Chapter 1 places the 1994 Zapatista uprising in Chiapas relation to debates on the political left about indigenous autonomy and micro-level nationalist aspirations. When examined in terms of 'from above' and 'from below' variants of *indigenista* discourse, its true precursors are the 1920s Cristeros and 1930s Sinarquistas, both of which were traditional anti-capitalist peasant movements. Belonging to the same agrarian populist lineage, the Zapatista programme (cultural autonomy, human rights, systemically non-specific democracy) leaves the wider class structure and its state intact.

The political origin of populist discourse about the agrarian myth as a long-standing form of class struggle waged 'from above' is traced in Chapter 2. Hence the essentialization of rural identity, culture and resistance has deep roots in European, North American and Latin American history, where it reproduces either a 'from above' or plebeian form of conservative pro-peasant discourse. Because it fails to differentiate the peasantry in terms of class, as well as to decouple Marxism from populism and fascism from capitalism, the subaltern approach overlooks this political lineage.

Chapter 3 examines how the construction of democracy and 'civil society' has been linked by both the political left and right to struggles over property, nation, the market and the State. What conservatives and neoliberals feared, and socialists hoped for, was that 'pure democracy' would enable peasants and workers to capture the State, and thus use the latter to transform existing property and exchange relations. Having relied on the strong State to maintain its socio-economic privileges, the political right first opposed and then endorsed (representative) democracy, thereby combining a populist 'from above' attempt to generate the support of workers and peasants with the idea of a strong capitalist State.

Positioning 'civil society' within the capitalist system, 1960s modernization theory sought to bring peasants and workers into the bourgeois polity without, however, challenging existing traditional rural culture. The latter was the identity mobilized by the 'new' populist postmodernism in the 1980s to construct a concept of a locally-based agrarian 'civil society' outside and against the capitalist State. Resisting – but no longer attempting to capture or control – the State, this seeks merely to establish or re-establish local and systemically non-specific forms of 'natural' identity. This replicates the historical project not of the left but of conservatism and neoliberalism, and as such is politically disempowering for peasants and workers.

Chapter 4 considers how film and television images of landowners, peasants and workers as empowered and hostile correspond to the Darwinian variant of the agrarian myth. Such characterization of its subject as socio-economically strong and engaged in struggle, as a 'fiend' that is dangerous and threatening, suggests that the nation can be represented both by 'those above' and by 'those below'. The humorous portrayal of those belonging to the landowning class which depicts them as 'fools', however, infers that such disempowered elements are 'not worth bothering about', a discourse that removes them from becoming a target in any political struggle waged 'from below'.

A different kind of characterization is examined in Chapter 5, which looks at how powerful-but-friendly film and television images of those at each end of the class structure inform themes dealing with nationalism, imperialism and colonialism. The pastoral version of the agrarian myth, which projects its subject as paternalistic, involves a sympathetic and non-threatening characterization, and is discernible in depictions of aristocracy and – more recently – the British monarchy as 'ordinary', benign and/or disempowered. Royalty, landowner and colonizer are shown to be powerful but well-disposed towards 'those below', whose interests they share, images that licence a populist discourse.

The Grand Tour is the focus of Chapter 6, and in particular its role in enabling the landowning class to acquire a cosmopolitan ideological outlook shared with those occupying the same position in the rural hierarchy elsewhere in Europe. Encountering the revolutionary 'mob-in-the-streets' in the course of visits to France, the travel writing of Herder and Herzen demonstrates how concepts of national identity and populist politics emerged from their experiences abroad. What is at issue, therefore, is not the rise of nationalism *per se*, but the role of travel in this process.

Social difference reproduced by the Grand Tour is not so much in relation to the foreigner encountered in the course of voyages abroad, as that of the aristocratic traveller him/herself in relation to subordinate elements of the population at home. Over the nineteenth century, this underwent a change, as it had to. In order to retain power/property, therefore, it was necessary for landowners to subscribe to an emerging national identity, not one based on a classical/cosmopolitan upbringing. That the class enemy at home was for 'those above' just as much a political concern as the national enemy abroad led to a fusion of nationalism and populism, resulting in an identity that had a plebeian component which could thus be seen by 'those below' – the internal 'other' – as empowering.

Chapter 7 highlights the impact of mass tourism on travel literature, where a twofold fear was expressed by the upper class traveller. On the one hand, the demise of rural 'otherness' abroad, and on the other the arrival there of the mass tourist, the plebeian 'mob-in-the-streets' from home. Each was perceived as a threat to the aristocratic pastoral variant of the agrarian myth reproduced in foreign countries. Of related concern was the encroachment of the 'bush' onto European areas in Africa, interpreted by travel literature as the Darwinian variant of the plebeian version of the agrarian myth.

Accounts of voyages to and foreign residence in Venice are analysed in Chapter 8. Despite its urban character, the city is depicted in travel literature in ways that are consistent with the agrarian myth, combining its two forms of 'otherness'. Epitomizing fears about the loss of traditional rural hierarchy, a pastoral version of the agrarian myth projects the immutability of local cultural identity in the midst of an harmonious rural idll. This is combined with a Darwinian one, which voices anxieties concerning modernizing trends and the intrusion of the mass tourist. The quest for cultural 'authenticity', 'meaning' and 'exclusivity' by 'initiates' is accordingly matched by a corresponding struggle against cultural de-authentication and evidence of modernity.

PART 1

Culture, Tradition and Modernity

••
•

Cultural Struggle 'From Below'

We were exhausted from a long, painful trek; more painful than long, to
tell the truth.... We had lost all our equipment, and had trudged for endless hours through marshlands and swamps. We were all wearing new
boots and by now everyone was suffering from blisters and footsores, but
new footware and fungus were by no means our only enemies. We had
reached Cuba following a seven-day voyage across the Gulf of Mexico
and the Caribbean Sea, without food, plagued by seasickness and aboard
a far-from-seaworthy vessel.

> ERNESTO CHE GUEVARA (1967: 9) on the privations experienced by the guerrilla
> forces prior to the 1959 Cuban revolution

I get up, I give interviews and then it's time to go to bed.

> SUBCOMANDANTE MARCOS (2001: 74), leader of the 1990s Zapatista Movement in
> Chiapas, Mexico, in reply to a question about his average day

Introduction

This chapter focuses on how the discourse of the agrarian myth informed 'from
below' struggle waged by peasant smallholders in the Mexican state of Chiapas
during 1994, led by Subcomandante Marcos and one of the more important
agrarian movements in Latin America. In the course of this mobilization by
the Zapatista Army of National Liberation (the EZLN, or *Ejército Zapatista de
Liberación Nacional*), the spread of neoliberal capitalism was countered ideologically by the reassertion of indigenous cultural nationalism, premised on
what might be termed the long-standing existence of an 'authentic' peasant
nation within the larger social formation. Ethnicity and rural 'otherness' as a
mobilizing discourse, rather than that of class, raises in turn questions about
the political efficacy of traditional cultural identity and national selfhood as
methods of opposing present-day capitalist expansion.

The final two decades of the twentieth century were characterized by three
interrelated global transformations: in terms of dominant discourse about
both economics and ideology, and also of a rural grassroots response to them.
These epistemological shifts – which were also fundamental political ones –
took the form of the rise and the consolidation as practice of *laissez-faire*

economics, postmodern theory, and new social movements. What happened in Chiapas during 1994 and since cannot be understood fully without reference to the impact there of each component – global economic change, ideas about this and how best to oppose it – of what was a single systemic process.

Of interest, therefore, is the nature of the agrarian class structure, and more generally both the debate about this (the *campesinista/descampesinista* positions), and the kind of political conflicts and agency such a class structure generates.[1] Hence the presentation which follows will do two things. First, it will consider the EZLN and Chiapas in terms of a comparative framework (similar kinds of mobilizations elsewhere) and theoretical debates (how is the 1994 episode to be characterized in terms of rural agency). And second, it will place the arguments concerning the causes and objectives of the Zapatista uprising in relation both to those of other agrarian movements, and to discussions about them.

To this end, the first section of this chapter examines the longstanding debate on the political left about indigenous autonomy and nationalism, while the second considers this issue with particular reference to 'from above' and 'from below' variants of *indigenista* discourse. The third section examines the way in which the discourse about indigenous 'otherness' necessarily generates a disempowering intra-class conflict, which is why the fourth looks critically at the broader political economy of *indigenismo*. It is argued that, in many

---

1   Broadly speaking, the *campesinista/descampesinista* divide corresponds to the opposing theoretical positions taken by protagonists in the longstanding (but, in its internationalist form, still relevant) debate on the agrarian question, which concerns the rôle of peasants in providing surpluses for industrial development. Indistinguishable from *indigenismo*, and associated with the work of the Russian populist Chayanov (1966), the *campesinista* position holds that peasant economy, or an homogeneous peasantry composed of self-sufficient petty commodity producers, is a *sui generis* socio-economic category that produces no surplus. Not only does the peasant family farm resist incorporation by wider economic systems (capitalism and socialism), but throughout the countryside of the Third World it constitutes viable alternative (= 'peasantization' or 'repeasantization') to them all. Against this are ranged the adherents of the *descampesinista* position, consisting mainly (but not only) of Marxists who argue that capitalist penetration of agriculture results in 'depeasantization'. What *campesinista* populists regard as an indestructible peasant economy is perceived by *descampesinista* Marxists as being differentiated into a rich, middle and poor peasantry, the top stratum becoming small agrarian capitalists while those from the bottom one join the proletariat. These distinct strata – capital and labour – meet in the market and accumulation takes place, generating a surplus for industrialization. Although there are no *descampesinistas* who think of themselves as agrarian populists, there are currently adherents of the *campesinista* position who nevertheless (and erroneously) believe themselves to be Marxists.

respects, the true precursors of the 1990s Zapatistas are the 1920s Cristeros and 1930s Sinarquistas, each of which constitutes a traditionalist form of anti-capitalist movement belonging to the same agrarian populist lineage. By conceding the modest political objective of democracy, the Mexican State outmanoeuvred the EZLN.

I

The optimism that greeted the 1994 uprising in Chiapas is attributable to the perception – especially on the part of radicals in Western academic circles – of the Zapatistas as a new social movement, and as such as a harbinger of a progressive grassroots politics in the so-called Third World.[2] At times it seemed that, given the relentlessness of the continuing neoliberal onslaught, the mere fact of 'from below' rural agency was in itself a sufficient cause for celebration. Consequently, few in the academy were prepared to question either the political objective or the direction of this grassroots agency, and whether in fact it possessed an agenda that amounted to a programme for change – let alone a viable one. Attention focussed instead on the supposedly novel (= postmodern) demand by smallholding peasants for a return to traditional culture and community authority, and with it the recuperation of an eternal identity emblematic of an authentic process of 'belonging' as embodied in indigenous

---

2   This optimism has generated a large and enthusiastic network of international solidarity with the Zapatistas (Olesen, 2005; Hardt and Negri, 2005), a mainly electronic linkage the mere fact of which is itself frequently invoked in support of claims about the 'newness' of this social movement. This, as de Souza Martins (2003: 331, note 53) has pointed out, is 'due to the simple fact that all previous agrarian movements in Mexico did not have access to the internet', and amounts to the unpersuasive argument that peasant mobilizations are defined largely by the sophistication of their communication technology. Much the same difficulty informs the attempt by De Angelis (2000) to classify the Zapatistas as 'internationalist' purely on the basis of this support network, an interpretation confounded by the indigenous nationalism of EZLN pronouncements. More important in this regard is the precise ideological and political rôle of this international support network. As de León (2007) and Moksnes (2007) attest, not only is its existence conditional on the demobilization of armed struggle in Chiapas, but international supporters visiting the Acteal shrine also reinforce an ensemble of meanings that are politically disempowering. Among them are the significance attached by Roman Catholicism to the innateness of hierarchy, the necessity of obedience to this, hence the notion of passivity and the ennoblement of suffering and martyrdom. In an important sense visiting support – however well intentioned – can also be seen as a form of religious pilgrimage (the benefit of which accrues mainly to the pilgrim).

autonomy. Henceforth cultivators were to be discussed in terms of non-economic agency, that of new social movements.[3]

These new social movements, it was argued, were no longer about class and the desirability of economic development leading to socialism, nor were they aimed at the capture and exercise of state power.[4] The desiderata had changed substantially, securing democracy within the context of capitalism being the sole political objective. Agrarian mobilization was now guided by human rights legislation and the teachings of the church, was more inclusive (particularly of rural women) and based on the valorization of indigenous 'otherness'. Unlike earlier peasant movements – in Mexico itself, as well as in Latin America and elsewhere – new social movements influenced by postmodernism

---

3 One predictably influential variant of this interpretation – or rather re-interpretation – of grassroots agency is the pseudo-sociological notion of 'multitude' informing the fashionable postmodern nostrums of Hardt and Negri (2005). Their attempt to lever the peasantry into this framework (Hardt and Negri, 2005: 115–127) is, unsurprisingly, replete with non-sequiturs, confusions, and simple errors. Thus, for example, the argument about the differentiation of the peasantry into its rich, middle and poor strata is attributed to Mao and not Lenin, whilst the assertion that Marxists generally regarded the peasantry as a class is similarly incorrect. Unlike Guevara, who wished to dissolve nationalism so as to mount a more effective attack on imperialism, Hardt and Negri wish to ban class from this same conflict. Accordingly, their concept 'multitude' erases all economic and property relations linking the individual self to the world, thereby making the struggle against neo-liberalism so inclusive that it is difficult to conceive of any category of 'selfhood' not wholly signed up by them to the defeat of a correspondingly externalized global capitalism. The absence of class trapped between the exclusiveness of individual selfhood on the one hand, and the inclusiveness of being-in-the-world on the other, is evident from the observation (Hardt and Negri, 2005: 127) that 'we are a multiplicity of singular forms of life and *at the same time* share a common global existence' (original emphasis). For them, therefore, no distinction exists between a millionaire and an agricultural labourer, each of whom is simultaneously 'a singular form of life' and both of whom 'share a common global existence'. In other words, between the irreducibility of the self and the sameness of humanity at the global level there is nothing, and the space in which class relations are usually to be found is for Hardt and Negri empty of socio-economic content This is all of a part with their earlier pseudo-conceptual framework, based on the notion of 'Empire' (Hardt and Negri, 2000), the intellectual pretensions of which have been effectively demolished by Petras (2002).

4 On the subject of whether or not a movement that eschews the capture of state power can be considered revolutionary, see the exchanges about Chiapas in the journal *Capital & Class* 85 (Spring, 2005). Marxists insist that any movement which does not attempt to capture the state, or avoids doing this, cannot be regarded as revolutionary, since the state apparatus is not only left intact to rule in the name of the bourgeoisie but – as such – will at some future point move against insurgents who have challenged its power in a specific region of the nation and undermine them, even if it does not crush them militarily.

questioned the desirability of further economic development, not least because of their awareness of environmental issues. The 1994 Zapatista uprising was hailed by many as an example of precisely this 'new' kind of peasant agency (= anti-capitalist but not socialist), invariably categorized as a form of subaltern resistance and accordingly labelled a postmodern rebellion.[5]

Marxism and the National Question

Despite the fact that postmodern concepts of 'the rural' and peasant agency corresponded to the *campesinista* discourse of the agrarian myth, a resurgent populism associated with the subaltern studies project that rose to prominence in the 1980s, many Marxists nevertheless saw in the Zapatista rebellion the prospect of a future politics untainted by pre-1989 forms of actually existing socialism. Hence the call by the EZLN for the autonomy of the indigenous community in Chiapas, plus the challenge mounted there by the Zapatistas to the power of the Mexican State, has been interpreted by some as evidence for the existence in this context of dual power, a central emplacement of Marxist theory. This conceptual and political misrecognition stems from a failure to understand that 'dual power' applies to a revolutionary capture of the State in the course of a transition from democracy to socialism, neither of which objectives are on the political agenda of the EZLN.[6]

---

5   Among those who have claimed that the 1994 Chiapas uprising is the first postmodern rebellion are Burbach (1994), Burbach, Núñez, and Kagarlitsky (1997: 95–96), Rabasa (1997), Holloway and Peláez (1998), Carrigan (2001), Mignolo (2002), Holloway (2002a; 2002b) and Hardt and Negri (2005: 85). Associated with a six-volume series edited by Ranajit Guha (1982–89), the subaltern studies project casts itself as an alternative rural historiography of South Asia, an approach that has spread more recently to Latin American rural historiography (on which see Brass, 2003). Similarly postmodern in its epistemology, the 'everyday forms of peasant resistance' framework is linked to the work of James Scott (1985), and expounded with regard to the 1994 Zapatista uprising by, among others, Castells, Yazawa and Kiselyova (1995/96). In contrast to all these *campesinista* approaches, Marxism confers political legitimacy only on revolutionary struggles for political power undertaken by class categories (a nascent bourgeoisie in the case of a dominant feudalism, a proletariat in the case of a dominant capitalism). For this reason the *descampesinista* position adhered to by Marxists argues that resistance by rich, middle and poor peasants has a different class basis, meaning and objective. It is the exponents of the subaltern/resistance framework, such as Scott and Guha, who maintain the fiction of an undifferentiated peasantry confronting a non-class specific state (a binary opposition which structures the discourse not of Marxism but of agrarian populism, the 'other' of Marxism).

6   The concept 'dual power', central to the analysis by Trotsky of the 1917 Russian Revolution, informs writings by Gilly (1983; 1998) on the subject of Mexican peasants. Initially, he deployed the term in relation to the 1910 Revolution, arguing (Gilly, 1983: 79, 170–171) that the

Perhaps the best illustration of the way some Marxist analysis has metamorphosed into a postmodern 'new' populist one is the endorsement of 'from below' identity politics, a shift that has brought in its train a commitment not just to a non-Marxist discourse about cultural 'otherness' but also – and more problematically – to support for a new upsurge in micro-level ethnic nationalism.[7] The steady economic breakdown of traditional agrarian structures by capitalist development from the 1960s onwards – and especially during the 1980s and 1990s – has been accompanied by a resurgence of the national question, for a long time perceived as a redundant historical legacy of national liberation and colonialism in the Third World. In contrast to the view that, with

---

seizure of land corresponded to dual power, albeit a dual power that did not confront State control in that it remained confined to a particular locality. Gilly (1983: 134) also endorsed the idealized view long associated with the Russian populists: namely, that during the revolutionary era the village (in Mexico) was an egalitarian unit, the inference being that it was untainted by the process of socio-economic differentiation. It comes as no surprise, therefore, that a similar misunderstanding informs his more recent analysis of the Zapatistas in Chiapas. The latter is structured by a subalternist approach combined with Scott's 'everyday forms of resistance' framework (Gilly, 1998: 267, 273, 275, 302, 314), a theoretical blend which is presented as evidence for 'dual power' in Chiapas. (For a similar kind of interpretation, see the concept 'parallel power' utilized by Weinberg, 2000: Chapter 6, in relation to the area of Chiapas controlled by the Zapatistas) Following Ranajit Guha, therefore, Gilly (1998: 294 ff.) identifies eight fundamental characteristics of the 1994 uprising. He then idealizes – as does the EZLN itself – the mere fact of 'standing outside the State', regarding it as evidence for the existence of 'dual power', whereby one of the fundamental characteristics – 'the persistence of ancient community' (Gilly, 1998: 295) – becomes the 'other' of the capitalist State. This contrasts absolutely with the concept as deployed by Trotsky (on which see Brass, 2000a: 72 ff.), for whom it had nothing to do with the perpetuation of 'ancient community' (to which Trotsky was implacably opposed).

7   Writing about the EZLN, therefore, Cleaver (1994: 147) evinces an uncritical approach to Zapatista ideology: 'Among the Indian nations and peoples of the Americas...the affirmation of national identity, of cultural uniqueness, and of linguistic and political autonomy is rooted not only in an extensive critique of the various forms of Western Culture and capitalist organization which were imposed on them through conquest, colonialism and genocide, but also in the affirmation of a wide variety of renewed and reinvented practices that include both social relations and the relationship between human communities and the rest of nature'. Unsurprisingly, this results not only in a corresponding idealization by Cleaver (1994: 153, 154) of the golden age myth ('In traditional Indian society life was not so hard') but also to abandon the notion of class differentiation ('What is unusual and exciting about these developments is how...struggles are not being...subordinated to "class interests"...[and represent instead] a workable solution to the post-socialist problem of revolutionary organization and struggle').

decolonization, Third World nationalism ceased to be a political issue, neoliberal free market policies have given it a new lease of life, albeit in the micro-level form of ethnic autonomy that – in some circumstances – might translate into a separatist movement.[8]

This debate on the political left about the right of indigenous groups to national self determination raises the same issues as those discussed by socialists nearly a century ago.[9] Then it was argued that micro-level nationalist

---

8   That the agrarian mobilization in Chiapas raises difficult questions (the idealization/essentialization of ethnic/peasant identity, the predominance of religious ideology) for those on the left about the political direction of the Zapatistas and Subcomandante Marcos is clear from the analyses by Petras and Vieux (1996), Cunninghame and Ballersteros Corona (1998), and Berger (2001), as well as from the exchange between Hellman (1999; 2000) and Paulson (2000). Nor is it the case that such questions are confined to the domain of theory, about how to interpret Zapatista agency in relation to what is known about peasant movements generally. Just as Maoists in West Bengal recruited Santal tribals for the Naxalite movement during the early 1970s by informing them that there was no difference between what was currently being fought for and what their tribal heroes fought for in 1855 (Brass, 2000a: 126–127 note 30), so the EZLN have mobilized support among indigenous communities in Chiapas by conflating the figure of Emiliano Zapata with Tzeltal deities (Subcomandante Marcos, 2001: 19–21; Stephen, 2002: 164). Rather than utilizing a discourse about class, therefore, those on the political left have tended on occasion to engage in and thereby reinforce a discourse about ethnic identity and indigenous nationalism.

9   Much the same argument about cultural identity and an inherent 'right to self-determination' has been advanced historically by those who were strongly opposed to any concept of socialism. In the late nineteenth century, for example, Bluntschli (1885: 82) made the following claim: '[T]he Germans in the middle ages were at once a people...and a nation...while in the last few centuries they ceased to be a nation, and were rather a people divided into a number of different States, countries, and one may almost say nations. Today [c.1870] the German nation...has come to life again, although individual parts of the German people form parts of non-German nations and States'. In the twentieth century, the same principle informed the creation by the South African apartheid regime of bantustans within the borders of South Africa itself (see below, Chapter 3). These were 'separate nations' based on a cultural/ethnic 'otherness' on the part of the tribal population who, the apartheid regime constantly proclaimed to the outside world, wanted to remain as they had always been, a wish granted to them in the form of a nation of their very own. As many observers pointed out at the time, not only did the majority of the residents of the bantustans reject this arrangement imposed on them from above, but the reason for this was also clear. What the apartheid regime had done was to transform their economically disempowering situation (poverty, oppression, and segregation) into a form of cultural empowerment. Whereas the former invited condemnation and policy initiatives aimed at change, the latter by contrast was a cause for celebration and – as such – a situation that required no further improvement. In short, what was previously a problem had now been turned into a 'solution'.

aspirations led to the fragmentation of working class solidarity, the beneficiary of which would – and could only ever – be imperialism.[10] Led either by a land-owning or nascent capitalist class, such national movements empowered only those belonging to these latter categories, and not workers, whose main interest was best served by links with other members of the same class else-where – that is, horizontal (= international) not vertical (national) ones.[11]

Leftist arguments privileging smallholders also featured in the analysis of nationalism developed in the first decade of the twentieth century by the Austro-Marxist theoretician Otto Baüer.[12] This, 'new' populist postmodernists suggest, is the way forward politically, and hence the model that the left should incorporate into theory and practice because, in the present stage of capital-ism, national difference and not class antagonism is the main contradiction.[13]

---

10   The main proponent of this view was Luxemburg (1976: 251 ff.), who made the following three points. First, that any talk of a-historical and systemically non-specific 'rights' was non-Marxist. Second, that to advocate national self-determination is to leave intact class rule, and thus the oppression and exploitation of workers both within and immediately outside the new nation. And third, those arguments concerning the desirability of national self-determination generally addressed only the political bases of subordination (culture, language), and thus tended to avoid its economic causes (class, exploitation), particularly where these were rooted within the context seeking autonomy. In this connection, it is difficult to disagree with the conclusion arrived at by Nettl (1966: 862) some four decades ago: 'Is it possible to be a Marxist without achieving not only a substitution of class con-sciousness for patriotic consciousness, but an immersion in class *instead* of nation? Have any of the leading Marxists in Russia or China achieved it today? Or is the whole substan-tial return to the national unit as fact and concept the most retrograde step of all? Rosa Luxemburg stands at the apex of the attempt to make operational the Marxist concept of class as the primary social referent, and to break once and for all the old alternative stran-glehold of nation. In this respect her contribution is second to none'. (original emphasis).

11   Arguing against Luxemburg, Lenin (1964) maintained that smaller nations should have the right to secede, but only for two reasons. First, where they formed part not of a nation state but of a larger empire, such as that of Russia under the Tsar. And second, because in his view workers – given the choice – would reject bourgeois or aristocratic rule in a new nation, opting instead to remain within a larger unit that was a workers' state (the USSR). This position was opposed by Luxemburg, who insisted – rightly, as it turned out – that in such contest, *where a politically unspecific notion of 'democracy' circulated*, an indigenous proletariat would always side with an ethnically/culturally similar bourgeoisie to form a separate nation.

12   In Austria a consequence of Baüer's Popular Front reformist politics during the late 1920s and early 1930s was not to strengthen but to *demobilize* working class opposition to fas-cism, and thus in effect to make easier the taking of power by the far right (Kitchen, 1987).

13   The way in which the attempt by Baüer to revise the meaning of socialism, in the process converting it into a discourse about ethics and subjectivity – as did the 'cultural turn' of

Socialism and the National Question

Against this, the crucial distinction informing the Marxist position on nationalism is best summed up by Lenin: 'Combat all national oppression? Yes, of course! Fight *for* any kind of national development, *for* "national culture" in general? – Of course not'.[14] By contrast, and like the prefiguring discourse of Baüer, exponents of the 'new' populist postmodernism eschew this distinction. Consequently, they do indeed end up supporting 'the [f]ight *for* any kind of national development, *for* "national culture" in general'. All of them – Baüer and the 'new' populist postmodernists – regard indigenous peasant nationalism (= 'the unheard voice from below') as a politically desirable goal and historically innate, and as such a positive and an empowering identity. Nationhood as conceptualized by the Austro-Marxist is certainly similar to that of the subaltern studies project.

National identity is linked by Baüer not simply to the fact of a shared language or territory but rather to 'a common history [which] determines and produces [all other components]'.[15] The nation is essentialized as an

---

postmodernism subsequently – was accurately pinpointed during that era (1919–22) by Georg Lukács. In the words of the latter (Lukács, 1971: 38): 'Economic fatalism and the reformation of socialism through ethics are intimately connected. It is no accident that they reappear in similar form in [Eduard] Bernstein, Tugan-Baranovsky and Otto Baüer. This is not merely the result of the need to seek and find a subjective substitute for the objective path to revolution that they themselves have blocked...The "ethical" reformation of socialism is the subjective side of the missing category of totality which alone can provide an overall view'.

14   See Lenin (1964: 35, original emphasis) and also Trotsky (1934: 908 ff.). Earlier, Marx warned that a working class divided along national and/or ethnic lines undermined the solidarity necessary for revolutionary agency. In the late 1860s and early 1870s he (Marx, 1973: 166–171) argued that in Britain 'antagonism [between English and Irish industrial workers] is artificially sustained and intensified by the press, the pulpit, the comic papers, in short, by all the means at the disposal of the ruling classes'.

15   At roughly the same conjuncture, Israel Zangwill, an avowed non-marxist, arrived at a similar definition of national identity. According to him (Zangwill, 1917: 44) nationality 'in its inner or concave aspect, being a form of feeling, can be explained only by psychology. It is – or should be – a section of "the psychology of crowds" [and] springs from the operation of what I propose to call the law of contiguous co-operation'. For both Zangwill and Baüer, therefore, nationalism is a non-transcendent identity that possesses mainly a non-material referent. It is for them simply the accumulated and ever-present product largely of consciousness (history, psychology), an eternal and thus continuous form of being. This suggests two things. First, that the more a definition of identity is structured by non-material aspects (such as language, ethnicity, culture), the more the resulting element of 'community' is likely to be one of nationalism. Conversely, the more such a 'community'

ever-present and thus non-transcendent social form, and he regards the decline of nationhood associated with pre-capitalist social forms (nomadism, rural community, peasant economy) as a loss, to be recuperated under capitalism and fully realized under socialism.[16] For long periods of history, plebeian culture remained regional or local, and only ruling classes were truly nationalist.[17] Under capitalism and socialism, however, the hitherto excluded masses are drawn into and become part of the nation, by virtue of access to an education and a language that have become similarly national in scope. National 'belonging' therefore both precedes and survives capitalism, and in an important sense reaches it apogee in terms of emancipatory potential under socialism.[18]

In a break with all previous Marxist theory about agrarian transformation, Baüer maintained that under socialism not only would private ownership of

---

is defined in specifically *economic* terms, the less likely is it that the resulting identity will be one confined within the boundaries of nationhood. And second, that there is nothing particularly Marxist about the definition of nationalism used by Baüer.

16   That the concepts 'nation' and 'nationhood' are essentialized by Baüer (1978a: 109) is evident from his observation that '[f]or me, history no longer reflects the struggles of nations: instead the nation itself appears as the reflection of historical struggles'. Although he starts out with a premiss that is uncontentious – 'The development of the nation reflects the history of the mode of production and of property' – Baüer (1978a: 108) proceeds on the basis of this to elaborate a theory about nationalism that is problematic. Hence the view that: 'Just as private ownership of the means of production and individual production develops out of the system of primitive communism, and from this, again, there develops co-operative production on the basis of social ownership, so the unitary nation divides into members of the nation and those who are excluded and become fragmented into small local circles; but with the development of social production these circles are again drawn together and will eventually be absorbed into the unitary socialist nation of the future'.

17   According to Baüer (1978a: 109), '[t]he nation of the era of private property and individual production, which is divided into members and non-members, and into numerous circumscribed local groups, is the product of the disintegration of the communist nation of the past and the material for the socialist nation of the future'.

18   In the context of primitive communism and nomadism, 'nation' signified a community based on descent. The sedentarization of agriculture, however, marked a disintegration of that old nationhood, as smallholding peasants became regional/local in terms of culture, while ruling classes maintained a culture that was distinct to them. As capitalism developed, peasants and workers were still excluded, and according to Baüer (1978a: 108) it was only 'when society divests social production of its capitalist integument', under socialism, in other words, that 'the unitary nation as a community of education, work and culture emerges again'. His assumption (Baüer, 1978b: 110) is that 'only socialism will give the whole people a share in the national culture'.

land continue but that the State would ensure the reproduction of peasant economy in a number of crucial ways.[19] Input and output prices for those commodities purchased and sold by peasants would be fixed at a level that guaranteed their subsistence, they would be protected from the impact of lower world market prices for agricultural commodities, a system of marketing cooperatives would be set up, and proprietors would receive debt relief.[20] Baüer equated capitalism simply with finance capital, and that those categorized by him uniformly as 'peasants' might contain rich peasants and/or commercial farmers – potential/actual agrarian capitalists, in other words – was not a possibility that he considered. In essence, this 'socialist' economic programme he drafted for the Austrian Social Democrats in the mid-1920s was no different from that advocated by the neo-populist theorist Chayanov in Russia at that same conjuncture.[21]

Nationalism and Class

The two interrelated difficulties facing the endorsement by Baüer of this a-historical discourse both about national identity and about an economically

---

19 See Baüer (c. 1919: 78–88) and also Pollock (1984: 163 ff.). According to the latter source, in his 1925 Austrian Social Democratic agrarian programme Baüer 'takes over the doctrine of the "eternal peasant," previously rejected bluntly by [Marxist] theory...' Of this Pollock (1984: 168) asks the following two pertinent questions: '[H]ow can one possibly incorporate an explicitly anti-collectivist stratum of the population, which is attached to private property, into a classless society? Is not [the] conception of the small peasantry as an important stratum of the classless socialist society itself a contradiction?'.

20 Because the 'socialist' programme of Baüer was based only on the taxation of existing wealth, and not on the confiscation of property belonging to industrialists and landowners, it was dismissed by Lenin (1965: 361) in the following terms: '...he [Baüer] grew frightened and *began to pour the oil of reformist phrase-mongering on the troubled waters of the revolution*'. (original emphasis) For the same kind of criticisms levelled at Austrian social democrats, see Trotsky (1934: 910 ff.). Significantly, the unwillingness of Baüer to confront the economic power of capital was condemned not just by the Bolsheviks but also by other Austro-Marxists. Thus, for example, even Fischer (1974: 92, 168–169) questioned the willingness of Baüer to compromise with representatives of the political right, the ultra-reactionary *Heimwehr*.

21 According to Baüer, therefore, '[t]he peasant was there before feudal society. He lived through feudal society as well. And in the framework of socialist society too, peasants will live on their own patch of land as a free proprietor' (cited in Pollock, 1984: 165). It was precisely for this reason that he approved of the New Economic Policy in the Soviet Union, described by him as 'a capitulation to capitalism', an endorsement that was condemned by Trotsky (1953: 250). By contrast, Baüer's support for peasant economy was commended by populist writers such as Mitrany (1951: 156–157), according to whom it

undifferentiated peasantry, and those who continue to find this approach relevant today, are simply put. The first is that, once the principal of nationalism has been ceded, then in effect one has also ceded all the elements of 'otherness' – tradition, culture, religion – which compose identity and consciousness of nation, and without which the latter can have neither meaning nor existence. All these forms of 'otherness' can then be deployed by capital to drive a wedge between workers separated by non-class forms of difference (ethnicity, nationality and gender). In short, nationalism is disempowering in terms of building working class consciousness and solidarity. Too often it has been fostered 'from above' in order to undermine 'those below', a view that contrasts absolutely with that of Baüer, for whom nationalism is an incremental 'from below' form of empowerment.

The second difficulty is as important. Because he interpreted nationalism as a positive development, a 'from below' emancipation, Baüer saw the resulting symbolic fusion (peasant = Nature = nation) simply as the best indicator of the way in which a hitherto marginalized peasantry would be drawn into the larger national culture. For him, therefore, the meeting between peasants and nationalism (bringing them into 'the national cultural community') could not be anything other than a progressive and (thus) a politically empowering process, a desirable one leading towards socialism.[22] From the 1920s onwards, however, this same meeting was the driving ideological force behind a very different kind of politics: the 'Green International' (the Vía Campesina of its day), an agrarian populist mobilization and a reactionary form of anti-capitalism

---

'was the most realistic and constructive approach to the peasant problem made by a Socialist in that period', and for whom the views of Baüer 'almost echoed [those of] the Peasant writers [= populists]'.

22   With unintended irony, Baüer (1978b: 110–111) celebrates the meeting between the peasantry and nationalism in the following manner: 'The peasant masses are completely bound by tradition; the household possessions of their ancestors are dear to them, while everything new is hateful. Their love for the values of the past also has political consequences; it is the root of their attachment to the church, their local patriotism, their dynastic loyalty. We have seen the significance of this fact in our investigation of the forces which assure Austria's stability; the peasants who cannot free themselves from the chains of centuries-old tradition are one of the supports of this state. If on the one hand the socialist mode of production integrates the masses for the first time into the national cultural community and thereby strengthens their national consciousness, so on the other hand it destroys their attachment to the ideologies of past centuries which is an obstacle to the full realization of the nationality principle'. Whilst accurate as a description of a process, his concluding observation – 'It not only increases the driving force of the nationality principle, but also clears away the obstacles from its course' – is profoundly wrong in terms of its political direction.

that contributed substantially to the rise in Europe not of socialism but of fascism.[23]

In the case of early twentieth century Europe and North America, therefore, socialists generally opposed the notion of an automatic right to national self-determination, since it not only led to Balkanisation but also enabled an indigenous petty bourgeoisie to make common cause with poor farmers and agricultural labours, to whom in class terms they were opposed.[24] In early twenty-first century Latin America, by contrast, many of those who regard themselves as on the left politically uphold precisely this right to indigenous autonomy on the grounds of ethnic 'otherness', notwithstanding the presence of these same objections (the fragmentation of class unity to the advantage of agribusiness enterprises).[25]

Neoliberalism and the National Question
It is important to stress that the national question does not of itself necessarily advocate the formation here and now of a separate nation state.[26] What it is

---

23   If nothing else, the ominous juxtaposition in Baüer's analysis of the words 'national' and 'socialism' ought to alert one to the presence of a political difficulty. An identical conflation, with similar political consequences, was made by Sombart (1937).

24   In the early 1930s Shachtman (2003) opposed the attempt to create a separate state for the black population in North America, arguing – as Luxemburg had done earlier with reference to Europe – that such a policy would drive a wedge between agricultural labourers and tenants of different ethnic origins. In the case of the United States, he pointed out, 'self-determination for the Black Belt [in the Southern US]' would prevent workers and poor farmers who were black from making common cause with their counterparts who were white.

25   See, for example, the collections edited by Beverley and Oviedo (1993) and also Rodríguez (2001), and more recently the contribution by Beverley (2004). This trend towards a wholesale colonization of peasant studies by postmodern theory has been challenged by Petras (1990), Brass (2000a), and Larsen (2001), all of whom insist on the continuing validity of Marxist theory to an understanding of agrarian transformation in Latin America and elsewhere. Earlier debates about what precisely constituted a Marxist theory and practice for Latin America are contained in the collection edited by Löwy (1992).

26   Although the Zapatistas have expressed no desire for formal nationhood apart from Mexico, many of the political demands they make not only hint at this possibility but contain the kind of powers usually exercised only by a nation state. Thus, for example, their demands include (Zapatista Army of National Liberation, 2002: 640, 642) a 'new pact...which puts an end to centralism and permits regions, indigenous communities, and municipalities to govern themselves with political, economic, and cultural autonomy...', and, further, that: 'We indigenous people must be permitted to organize and govern ourselves autonomously; we no longer want to submit to the will of the powerful,

concerned with, much rather, is both the fact of and components informing a process of 'belonging'. Once established as defining a specific population occupying a given physical space, however, the mere fact of a common language, religion, and set of customs are subject to a twofold dynamic: cultural erosion as a result of capitalist development, the modernity of which is blamed for undermining tradition.[27] As such, the vanishing 'otherness' of cultural identity can then become an impetus fuelling separateness (the object being the protection/recuperation of a pristine culture), especially in contexts where the population concerned has long been subject to exploitation, expropriation and/or oppression. All the latter are, of course, processes that have become more acute as a result of neoliberal policies implemented by many existing nation states over the last two decades of the twentieth century. Given this, the national question can resurface politically, in one of three ways.

First, in the 'from above' form of the view that henceforth cultural identity should be seen as a substitute for economic progress. If rural populations missed out economically, this discourse appears to suggest, they should re-exoticize their poverty, and claim it as part of what made them 'other'. The danger inherent in this, however, is that it creates the ideological space in which micro-nationalisms flourish. Second, therefore, is a 'from below' form that accepts this argument about re-exoticization, but deploys the element of cultural 'otherness' to lay claim to economic resources within the capitalist system (land, inputs from the state). The argument here seems to be: either we get a better economic deal within the existing nation state, or we opt out, in

---

either national or foreign…Justice shall be administered by the same indigenous peoples, according to their customs and traditions, without intervention by illegitimate and corrupt governments…'.

27   Needless to say, where this 'other' identity is also an historically ancient one, chronologically preceding cultural accretions that were established (or implanted) subsequently as a result of foreign conquest and/or colonization, it gives rise to a discourse about prior claims, along the lines of 'we were here before you'. Most of the ethnic conflicts currently taking place throughout the world involve this kind of discourse, which is at root an economic struggle – about property rights to territorially specific resources (land, oil, water, minerals) – that takes the ideological form of a dispute concerning the legitimacy (or illegitimacy) of rival nationalisms. It is perhaps significant that, when making claims to economic resources located within the context over which autonomy is to be exercised, representatives of indigenous movements fail to elaborate on how a shift in ownership patterns will affect urban industrial workers in the wider context whose livelihood is linked to these resources. Whilst claims by sub-nationalisms based on indigenous 'otherness' may indeed be a threat to the existing nation state, they are frequently advantageous to monopoly capitalism, which profits from and thus on occasion encourages (and, indeed, foments) such disputes.

effect declaring ourselves an autonomous nation.[28] And third, in the contrasting 'from below' form that rejects both nationalism and capitalism, arguing instead for a socialist internationalism based on class solidarity that transcends existing borders.[29] Of these three, it is the first and second that have been most enduring in the agrarian history and historiography of Mexico, as the pervasive influence of *indigenista* discourse attests.

II

The epistemology of *indigenismo* is a long one, dating back to the Spanish Conquest, a result of which three interconnected *campesinista* ways of

---

28   That the Zapatista discourse about indigenous grassroots autonomy may eventually translate into calls for territory based on and reflecting this ethnic 'otherness' is a point hinted at in by number of commentators. Thus, for example, Moksnes (2007) outlines the centrality to Maya peasants in Chiapas of Roman Catholic religious teaching generally, and in particular the biblical story about the escape of the Israelites from Egypt under the Pharaohs. As in the case of Israel, therefore, the Exodus narrative deployed by Maya peasants may at some point license a discourse about the formation of a separate nation. The argument made by Harvey (2007) about how adept the indigenous authorities have been in playing the Mexican State off against the Zapatistas also suggests that a fuller sense of autonomy is not wholly fanciful. This possibility is underlined by the strategic location of Chiapas itself, on the border between Mexico and Guatemala, a line that divides peasants belonging to the same ethnic group (a situation informing separatism elsewhere, as the example of the Kurds in the Middle East and the Basques in Spain/France attest). That the EZLN might effect a political transition, and shift from demanding local autonomy for the indigenous population to a separatist movement, has surfaced in the concern expressed by the Mexican State about the integrity of the nation.

29   That socialist internationalism is currently less popular than it used to be scarcely needs mentioning. What is of interest, however, is the way in which erstwhile adherents of this politics are now reinventing themselves. There seems to be a competition involving ex-Marxists now prominent in western academic circles to see who among them is able to denounce socialism in the most vehement terms. A not untypical example is the following (Hardt and Negri, 2005: 255), which resorts to the well-tried but erroneous formula (socialism = fascism) so beloved of cold warriors of old: '...contemporary forms of right-wing populism and fascism are deformed offsprings [*sic*] of socialism – and such populist derivatives of socialism are another reason why we have to search for a postsocialist political alternative today, breaking with the worn-out socialist tradition. It is strange now to have to recall this amalgam of ideological perversions that grew out of the socialist concept of representation, but today we can finally preside over its funeral. The democratic hopes of socialist representation are over. And while we say our farewells we cannot but remember how many ideological by-products, more or less fascist, the great

conceptualizing 'the indigenous subject' came into play. The first of these was the construction 'from below' of a direct link – a hallowed bond, almost – between the colonized indigenous subject at the rural grassroots and the monarch him/herself at the apex of the imperial hierarchy in Europe. At the centre of this discourse was the claim on the part of an indigenous peasantry that, since it was imbued with sacred attributes and ritual practice, land was central to the cultural specificity of ethnic 'otherness'. Consequently, dispossession – an outcome of expropriation – meant the loss of indigenous identity itself.[30] A second strand of *indigenismo* discourse, emanating mainly from North American cultural anthropology and British social anthropology, cast rural inhabitants in many Latin American countries as economically undifferentiated, homogeneous subsistence-oriented smallholders.[31]

Ways of Seeing, Ways of Being Seen

A crucial factor contributing to the ideological reproduction of *indigenismo* discourse, not just in Mexico but throughout the sub-continent, has been the importation by foreign academics and intellectuals of paradigms from domestic or imperial domains elsewhere. Thus, for example, analyses by anthropologists from Chicago of rural society in Mexico from the 1930s onwards were influenced by concepts of 'community' then being applied in the United States itself.[32] From this stemmed, in part, the tendency by US anthropology to

---

historical experiences of socialism were condemned to drag in their wake...There is no longer any possibility of going back to modern models of representation to create a democratic order'. The fact that what passed for socialism was nothing of the sort, and thus the root of the difficulty to which Hardt and Negri allude has more to do with the deployment of non- or anti-socialist ideas/arguments under the guise of socialism, is something which appears to escape them both.

30   The appeal to the monarch in the colonizing nation took the form of a discourse that the latter would him/herself have accepted as legitimate. This was because the claim of royalty to exercise power in a European context was frequently based on many of these same principles (landownership, birthright, lineage, longevity, custom, tradition, ethnicity).

31   In the case of Mexico, an influential example of this view was the study by Redfield (1930) of Tepoztlán, an approach subsequently criticized by Lewis (1951: 428–429) as a 'picture of the village [that] has a Rousseauan quality...[w]e are told little of poverty, economic problems, or political schisms. Throughout his study we find an emphasis upon the cooperative and unifying factors in Tepoztecan society'.

32   Analyses of rural society in Mexico from the 1930s onwards by anthropologists from Chicago include those by Redfield and Rojas (1934), Tax (1952) and Redfield (1956). The focus of anthropological and sociological research undertaken by many of those at Chicago (Stein, 1964: 230 ff.) was the 'decline of community', as migrants to urban areas in the locality shed their rural identity. This same notion – of peasant community in

portray the indigenous community in Mexico generally, and especially in Chiapas, as an a-historical 'cultural isolate'.[33] In much the same vein, the interpretation on the part of British social anthropology of market behaviour in 1940s Mexico as 'non-rational' and guided by the 'lazy native' syndrome drew on functionalist theory about 'primitive culture' in other parts of Empire.[34]

---

decline – was deployed by Chicago anthropologists engaged in Mexican fieldwork, a point conceded by Redfield (1955: 146–147). It should be noted that this particular discourse – by Chicago anthropologists about Mexican peasants – has a long history. Even at the end of the nineteenth century, therefore, the Professor of Anthropology at the University of Chicago, Frederick Starr (1899: 108 ff.) devoted a chapter in a book about Mexican culture to 'Examples of Conservatism', outlining what in his view was an unthinking rejection of modernity on the part of the rural population. In support of this claim he outlined the grassroots rejection of new coins issued by the Mexican State in 1883, That is, in his view the Mexican peasantry had neither the wish for nor an understanding of economic progress.

33   The perception of 'community' as a 'cultural isolate' also derived from anthropological methodology. In focussing his research at the *municipio* level in Chiapas, therefore, the US anthropologist Tax and his Mexican co-fieldworkers triggered a familiar ethnographic bias, whereby the investigation in effect defines the boundaries not just of the unit but of its determinations, all of which are perceived as internal. In a critique of community-based studies conducted in rural Chiapas, Salovesh (1979: 142) makes the following apposite comment: '…municipios, however, are not islands surrounded by unpopulated ocean, nor are they completely autonomous in their internal affairs…as long as we continue to focus exclusively on the municipio as a cultural isolate, we will continue to misunderstand even that which happens within the municipio'. This is an important point, in that – together with notions of 'community' imported from the United States – the internally focussed methodology utilised by US anthropologists reinforced the view of ethnicity not just as a form of 'otherness' outside/apart from Mexico, but also identified this 'difference' as the main – perhaps only – grassroots organizing principle.

34   A case in point is the well-known exchange on this subject between the Mexican anthropologist Julio de la Fuente and the British social anthropologist Bronislaw Malinowski. They disagreed profoundly (Malinowski and de la Fuente, 1982: 178) over the meaning of an episode that occurred in early 1940s Oaxaca, where the two anthropologists were observing peasants selling maize in a local market. About the economic behaviour of a wealthy producer, therefore, Malinowski himself commented: 'At the first shower…he picked up his bags and went home, thus showing that for him comfort was preferable to a few more *almudes* sold…'. This interpretation was rejected by de la Fuente in the following manner: 'I should like to remind you [Malinowski] that [the wealthy producer] on that occasion was more worried by the arrival of more maize than by the water. He commented that there was getting to be a lot of competition, and that it was no longer worth staying'. In other words, the economic behaviour of the wealthy peasant was perfectly rational, its classification by Malinowski as 'irrational' notwithstanding. Prior to

What all these frameworks shared was an idealized perception of rural community as composed of subsistence-oriented cultivators who were culturally pristine, territorially 'ancient', politically egalitarian and economically self-sufficient.[35]

For British and North American anthropology, therefore, those living and working in rural Latin America were autochthonous, the 'noble savages' of myth whose organizational modalities were perceived as innate and unchanging.[36] Unaffected by class divisions (a characteristic, it was claimed, only of urban society), members of the indigenous community inhabited what has been described as an Andean ecosystem enabling them to reproduce themselves economically on a continuous basis as petty commodity producers.[37]

---

conducting fieldwork in Mexico (1940–41), he had carried out research among tribal populations in New Guinea, a British imperial possession where he formulated his influential functionalist theory about 'primitive' culture.

35   This *indigenismo* discourse was also disseminated outside Mexico via the popular culture of Britain and the United States. During the immediate post-war era, for example, popular texts (Toor, 1947; Covarrubias, c. 1946) reproduced images of rural Mexico reducing it to a compendium of cultural 'otherness' (customs, tradition, beliefs, music, dance, myths, tales). It must be emphasized, however, that not all anthropologists have subscribed to this view, as the exchange between Barabas and Bartolomé (1974) and KY and FE (1974) underlines. Whereas the former privilege ethnic 'otherness' in a manner consistent with *indigenismo* discourse, the latter challenge this, and argue against the depiction of an indigenous peasantry as culturally homogenous.

36   That such a view amounted to an *idée fixe* is evident from comments made by the participants in an anthropology seminar (Tax, 1952: 218–219) in 1950 about whether indigenous communities were changing or staying the same ('culture traits', 'acculturation'): 'There is evidence that no matter how far these Indians travel, when they return their horizons aren't extended by personal experience...They're travelling to the US. They're becoming ladinoized when they return...how are we going to explain the ladinoization?...You find this local view of the world even among those who go on commercial trips and come back...But in that case we could predict that the Indian culture is going to last forever...In the US you have a future orientation – "We are making Progress." In the Indian community it is: "Maintain what we used to have"'. What was deemed problematic, in other words, were instances where individuals or groups characterized by anthropologists in terms of a specific culture/ethnicity demonstrated what the latter took to be 'deviant' behaviour – such as wearing non-indigenous clothing, adopting non-indigenous traits, and generally acting 'out of character'. For the importance of the seminar in question, see Cámara Barbachano (1979: 108).

37   This theory is structured by the concept 'verticality' (Murra, 1972), which refers to exchanges between smallholding communities occupying different ecological niches. A result of this culturally determined system of reciprocity, so the argument goes, is that subsistence is guaranteed, capitalist penetration is prevented, and thus no economic differentiation of the Andean peasantry takes place. In this way capitalism remains

This is said to be a tension-free arcadia that some early twentieth century observers in Andean countries identified as either actually or historically socialist formations.[38] During the second half of the twentieth century, both the Trotskyist politics of Hugo Blanco and the Maoist programme of Sendero Luminoso were not only premissed on the recuperation of Andean peasant community, but as such were also presented by their respective adherents as a return to a pre-colonial golden age of Peru. Ironically, each of the latter adhered to the *campesinista* view of agrarian populism, rather than the *descampesinista* position of classical Marxism.[39]

The third strand consists of the endorsement by Latin American writers, intellectuals and politicians of the same *indigenismo* discourse, but with one crucial difference.[40] Unlike the North American and European *campesinista*

---

external to what is as a consequence an eternal form of Andean peasant economy, a specifically Latin American variant of the Chayanovian peasant family farm. Much the same kind of theory operates with regard to Mexico, as is evident from the following analysis by Nash (1967a: 99) of a similar cultural dynamic structuring the economic reproduction of what is also peasant economy in indigenous communities: 'The levelling mechanism keeps the fortunes of the various households nearly equal and serves to ensure the shift of family fortunes from generation to generation. The sanctions behind the operation of the levelling mechanism are generally supernatural, with witchcraft as the means to keep the economic units oriented to the communal drains and claims on their wealth. These economies, then, are market – competitive, free, open – but set into a social structure without corporate units dedicated to and able to pursue economic ends. Working with a cultural pattern forcing the accumulation of wealth into noneconomic channels, and buttressed by a system of supernatural sanctions against those who do not use their wealth, they show a lack of dynamism, a technological conservatism almost equivalent to that of the most isolated communities, and an inability to seize and exploit or create economic opportunity'.

38   In Peru, therefore, Mariátegui (1968) and Castro Pozo (1936) characterized the pre-conquest Inca State as respectively 'communist' and 'socialist', while Reinaga (1960) saw no difference between the soviet programme being carried out in Russia and the indigenist policies his party – the *Partido Indio de Bolivia* – advocated in the case of the rural population in Bolivia.

39   For the details see Brass (2000a: Chapter 2). The persistence of agrarian populist views among peasant movements that claim to be pursuing Marxist or socialist ends, and the inability of those studying and/or writing about them to spot this, is a worrying but not unusual combination. It also suggests that an initial prognosis to the contrary, by Oscar Lewis in the early 1950s, was premature. Writing about Mexico, he accepted (Lewis, 1965: 436 note 1) the 'tendency to view the city as the source of all evil and to idealize rural life', but claimed – wrongly – that such a view 'has been corrected somewhat by the work of rural sociologists in recent years'.

40   On the history of *indigenismo* discourse, see Adams (1967: 475–478), Hewitt de Alcántara (1984), Knight (1990) and Ramos (1998). Latin American literature with an *indigenista*

arguments applied to rural Mexico, therefore, the discourse constructed by Latin Americans placed a central emphasis on the indigenous community as the repository of an authentic non- (or pre-) colonial identity.[41] This positive perception of pre-Hispanic indigenous community as 'natural', almost part of Nature itself, was reinforced by it having 'survived' and 'resisted' colonialism. The latter aspect in turn conferred on the indigenous community an heroic status in past conflicts against European domination, and consequently propelled it to the forefront of *national* struggle, where it has remained.[42] Because of this origin and history, therefore, the epistemology characterizing this particular discourse about *indigenismo* overlaps with a politically far more potent ideology: the foundation myth at the centre of nationalist ideology. In this particular guise, *indigenismo* invokes 'the other' deployed over time in political and – more importantly – ideological battles waged not just against colonialism (of the Spanish and Portuguese), but also against neo-colonialism (of the United States) and imperialism (of international capitalism).[43]

Nationalism, but Whose?

Of the three rival nationalisms circulating in Mexico, only two appear to be politically tainted by their history. Thus *hispanidad* looks to a national identity conferred by the Spanish conquest, and as such is a legacy that is not only colonial but also feudal. By contrast, *Mexicanidad*, or the national identity conferred by independence, is compromised by virtue of its emergence in relation to the modern capitalist State. Unconnected with either of these, and also

---

theme includes well-known texts by Bolivian, Ecuadorian and Peruvian authors (Alegría, 1942; Botelho Gonsálvez, 1967; Lara, 1965; Icaza, 1973), invariably published outside their own country. Writers who deal with the same issue in Mexico include not just Mexicans (Lopez y Fuentes, 1937) but also non-Mexicans. Among the latter are the 'jungle' novels of Traven (1974; 1981; 1982; 1994) about forced labour recruited for work in the mahogany camps of Chiapas during the 1920s.

41   These different strands of *indigenismo* discourse are not mutually exclusive, as the many contributions both by US and by Latin American anthropologists to the collection edited by Nash (1967b) underline.

42   Where the political left in Latin America is concerned, the political dominance of the national struggle (and the peasantry at the forefront of this) may be attributed in part to the continuing influence of Stalinism. From the late 1920s onwards, Stalinist views informing Soviet policy towards the Third World involved the subordination of working class politics to bourgeois nationalist objectives.

43   This is also true of ethnic movements in other Latin American countries, an example being the Confederation of Indigenous Nations of Ecuador (CONAIE) which also rose to prominence during the 1990s (Lucas, 2000).

predating them historically, is the third variant: a specifically indigenous ethnicity. Not only is it premissed on the existence of 'a nation within the nation', and pre-Colombian in origin, therefore, but – and this is an important consideration for those on the left – the peasant community is perceived to be both outside capitalism and also the locus of resistance to it. This is the reason why socialists and even Marxists, who in Europe were opposed to the idealization of peasant community, have in Latin America tended to see this same unit as a politically progressive social force.

In a framework that departs somewhat from this analysis, de la Peña adheres to a different argument.[44] This distinguishes between *indigenismo*, characterized as the 'civilizing project of the West' the object of which over the 1940–70 era was the 'from above' acculturation of the indigenous community in Mexico, and *indianismo*, a 'from below' theory/agency designed to promote the 'liberation of the Indian as a member of an indigenous civilization'. According to this dichotomy, *indigenismo* is the paternalist ideology of an authoritarian State, whilst *indianismo* is the ideology of independent and democratic Indian organizations. As perceived by *indianistas* in Chiapas, this 'from below' project entails the need on the part of indigenous communities to escape from

---

44 See de la Peña (2002). On occasion, and against the trend, anthropologists have noted the contextual specificity of what are usually depicted as eternal 'culture traits', an 'otherness' that indigenous peasants constantly strive to recuperate. Writing in the 1950s about the Maya in Guatemala, Mosk (1965: 168) makes the following observations: 'La Farge did his field study in Santa Eulalia in 1932, when the world was suffering intensely from Depression conditions, and he recorded some effects of the Depression which were called to his attention. The use of Japanese silk blouses by women had been curtailed, and a parallel decline had taken place in the use of European-type clothing by the men of the community. It is interesting, too, that La Farge picked up the opinion from several people that hard times would bring about a revival of pottery making, a craft which, as we have already noted, had been abandoned in the preceding years of good times. Cash, which earlier had been abundant in Santa Eulalia, was very scace in 1932, owing to a reduction in the earnings obtained from labour in the coffee *fincas*, and standards of living had suffered a setback'. In other words, the indigenous cultural 'traditions' that anthropologists invariably cast as enduring because they are much sought after by peasants and workers themselves are much rather contingent phenomena, the existence of which are determined economically. Such cultural erosion as takes place, therefore, occurs 'from below' and is not imposed 'from above'. What capitalist crisis does do, however, is force peasants and workers to adopt once again the 'traditions' they had themselves discarded earlier. That is, it forces them back into the mould of 'otherness', to become 'traditional' once again, not because they want to but because what they would like to do – earn decent wages, make 'non-traditional' purchases, not have to carry out 'traditional' kinds of work – is no longer within their reach economically.

'subjugation within Latin American nation States', in the course of which ethnic groups re-assert their cultural/linguistic/institutional 'otherness', and are
consequently re-valorized as political entities.

However, the distinction between them is not clear-cut, since in the past the
State has frequently endorsed the reproduction of many of the cultural elements which are said – by those both 'above' and 'below' – to be specific to
indigenous identity.[45] Hence the absence of a real distinctiveness between
concepts such as 'ethnic cultural organization', 'ethnic citizenship' and 'socio-
cultural grouping' common to both *indigenista* and *indianista* discourse. The
Mexican State and representatives of indigenous communities might regard
such policy of cultural 'recognition' as progressive, a way of empowering smallholding peasants belonging to particular ethnic groups. A more cynical assessment of this policy would suggest that its object was not just different but a
disempowering one: nothing less than teaching the indigenous population to
'know its place', under the guise of generously recognizing its 'difference'.

The ideological significance in Chiapas of *indigenista* discourse can be illustrated by the way in which Roman Catholic beliefs currently structure Maya
peasant narratives about a pre-colonial golden age. Adopting a stereotypical
good/evil dichotomy, this discourse contrasts an harmonious, egalitarian and
spiritual indigenous past with an impoverished present, in which the Maya are
subordinated to and exploited by a range of non-indigenous (= 'foreign')
oppressors. The presence of the latter is attributed to the Spanish Conquest
and – more generally – colonialism, and is a category that ranges from NAFTA
to local *mestizos*, all of whom are blamed for the poverty and suffering of indigenous communities. This polarity (indigenous = good, non-indigenous = bad)
not only licenses intra-class struggle (see below), but – since it is at the root of
ethnic nationalism – also corresponds to the way in which the foundation
myth overlaps with and reinforces the agrarian myth.[46]

---

45   In 1939, for example, a delegation of Mexican rural teachers was sent by the Ministry of
      Education on an investigative mission to Bolivia, there to study the experimental
      approach to education along indigenous lines (Velasco, 1940). Although the laudable
      objective of this school was to dispel notions of indigenous populations as racially infe-
      rior, by demonstrating to the outside visitor the range of their agricultural and artisan
      skills, the effect of this ethnically specific curriculum was ironically to confirm this very
      perception. Thus the limitation of what was taught to a series of economic activities asso-
      ciated by outsiders with indigenous communities seemingly underlined the innateness of
      'identity' linked to ethnic populations inhabiting these contexts. For a typical example of
      Mexican *indigenismo* at this conjuncture, see Mendieta y Nuñez (1938).

46   Among other things, this suggests that Gilly (1998: 312) is simply wrong when he states
      that 'the [Zapatista] rebellion does not propose a return to a past either distant or near. It

III

Notwithstanding the tendency of the various strands of *indigenismo* discourse to depict the peasantry – both in Mexico and in Chiapas – as socio-economically homogeneous, evidence suggests otherwise. According to one study, an indigenous elite had already emerged in Chiapan peasant communities by the early 1950s.[47] Similarly, between the late 1960s and the early 1980s erstwhile petty commodity producers in Zinacantán were already becoming differentiated in terms of class. Ceasing to be subsistence oriented peasants simply growing maize, these smallholders divided between the majority, whose main source of income came from selling their labour-power, and a minority consisting of accumulators who diversified economically, operating off-farm commercial enterprises (traders, truck owners).[48] Moksnes notes that Maya smallholders work as day labourers or find seasonal employment on coffee plantations in Chiapas, while Saavedra refers to the presence currently in Chiapas of peasant elites and substantial landholders (*finqueros* and *rancheros*), the latter composed of local bosses (*caciques*).[49]

---

suggests instead the possibility of a *nonexcluding modernity...*' (original emphasis). Later in the same analysis, however, he concedes the centrality of indigenous notions about 'timeless myth' to the Zapatista rebellion (Gilly, 1998: 324).

47   Hence the following observation by Rus (1994: 290): 'By 1951–52...Chiapas's ladino elite – the same elite that had perpetrated the conservative reaction of the preceding six years – had already recognized the emergence of a cadre of native leaders with whom it could do business. Such leaders were capable of controlling their communities as *principales* through "tradition," on the one hand, and of negotiating "reasonably," from a position of familiarity, with ladino officials, landowners, and merchants on the other'.

48   These findings emerge from the longitudinal anthropological research conducted in Zinacantan by Cancian (1965; 1987; 1989; 1992). Although by no stretch of the imagination a Marxist, Cancian nevertheless documents the impact of the 1982 debt crisis in terms of an increasing incidence of rural proletarianization, or – where a reduced access to land continues – semiproletarianization. On this he notes (Cancian, 1989: 160): 'Though the process has taken many different forms and has had many different results, I believe that there has been an overall trend towards proletarianization...Populations that were farmers or peasants two or three decades ago [i.e., the early 1960s] have become heavily dependent on wage work in labour markets tied to the world economy'.

49   See Moksnes (2007) and Saavedra (2007). Rus (1994: 268–270) makes much the same point with regard to Tzotzils and Tzeltals, who also worked as migrant labourers on coffee plantations. Of particular interest is his description of the social relations of production and how these were reproduced. Recruited by and subordinated to labour contractors (*enganchadores*), these migrants were trapped in debt peonage, a form of unfreedom familiar throughout rural Latin America. Local indigenous authorities were not only

'Otherness', Identity and Grassroots Agency

Unsurprisingly, therefore, as well as mobilization by peasants on the basis of indigenous identity Chiapas has also been the locus of a specifically rural working class organization and agency.[50] The fact of class differentiation does not, of course, automatically translate into the deployment of either the language or politics of class in any grassroots rural agency.[51] In this kind of situation, there are two reasons why the idioms employed in the course of struggle focus on ethnic identity. First, to deflect from socio-economic divisions within the ranks of ethnic categories, the better-off elements of which deploy non-class discourse in order to generate support from among those who might otherwise not provide this. And second, to establish claims to resources that can be sustained only by virtue of such 'otherness'.[52] Although effective in terms of laying claims to resources, however, struggle conducted on the basis of ethnic identity frequently results in conflict between members of the same class.

---

complicit with this arrangement, but also enforced it. On the use by labour contractors in northern Chiapas of the *enganche* system during the late nineteenth and early twentieth century, see Washbrook (2004).

50   It is important to recall that a specifically working class agency has a history in Chiapas (Rus, 1994: 275 ff.). During the mid-1930s, migrant coffee workers joined a trade union organization, the *Sindicato de Trabajadores Indígenas* (STI), which privileged their identity as mainly that of worker, not an ethnic 'other'. By 1937 some 25,000 Indian labourers were unionized, as a result of which it became impossible to employ non-union workers on the plantations. Additional improvements secured by this unionized indigenous workforce included the elimination of peonage, wage advances and the company store. During the 1940s, however, these specifically working class gains were rolled back, as both labour contractors and traditional authorities fought back. The STI was itself disbanded in 1946 by the governor of Chiapas, who had himself been a labour contractor. What this confirms is that an alternative identity and organizational structure – based on class and trade union membership – is possible, and has existed at the rural grassroots.

51   As is well known, the objective of rural agency that is not socialist is individualist proprietorship: that is, the transformation of a petty commodity producer into a landowning peasant. By contrast, agrarian movements guided by socialist objectives struggle for what might be termed proletarian ends: the common ownership of the means of production, distribution and exchange. In this connection it is important to note that the analytical deployment of the term 'class' does not necessarily mean that the user is describing an agrarian mobilization pursuing socialist/proletarian objectives. Thus, for example, although Warman (1988) applies this concept to the Zapatistas in Morelos during the 1910 Mexican Revolution, what he refers to is a 'peasant class' in opposition to and struggling against landlordism. That is, a populist usage of the term, which is consistent with individualist proprietorship as the object of grassroots agency.

52   Where land is concerned, such claims are made on the basis of usufruct rights enjoyed over generations by a particular peasant community or indigenous group.

The two forms of antagonism occurring in Chiapas described by Harvey confirm this point.[53] Hence the ban imposed on deforestation by the Mexican State for environmental reasons generated strong opposition at the rural grassroots, from peasants engaged in the commercial felling and selling of mahogany trees. These peasants not only formed their own organization, but also supported the Zapatista policy of establishing grassroots autonomy. In a similar vein, the process of remunicipalization in Chiapas was a bid by rival multi-class alliances for access to State resources in the shape of a new municipality. As such, what was essentially an old strategy of clientilism had little to do with the EZLN programme of a new politics. And just as opposition to the ban on logging was couched in terms of an unwarranted interference with indigenous custom, so the rival multi-class groups seeking a municipality deployed their position as *ejidal* authorities and 'the right to customary practices' in support of this. According to Harvey, therefore, the Zapatista threat was simply a pawn in a wider (and older) manoeuvre to gain access to existing resources controlled by the Mexican State.

That the deployment in this fashion of indigenous 'otherness' as a mobilizing discourse generates conflict between different (and sometimes the same) components of the rural poor is also evident. Collier and Collier regard the mobilizing discourse deployed by the Zapatistas as inclusive.[54] They cite the case of women and mestizos, and maintain further that such political inclusivity has been a source of Zapatista strength. This interpretation, however, is challenged by others. Hence the difficulties faced by any grassroots mobilization based on the notion of ethnic cultural 'otherness' is outlined by Leyva and by Moksnes, who note that in Chiapas the targets of a discourse about indigenous empowerment, 'authenticity', 'recognition' and 'victimhood' were *mestizos*, identified as the political enemies to be defeated. Indigenous groups are not uniform in terms of class, any more than are non-indigenous groups. Since the *mestizo* category includes small peasants and agricultural labourers, the struggle for indigenous empowerment is in effect a war between ethnically distinct components of the same class, and involves one set of workers and peasants pitted against another set.[55] That ethnic struggle generates not inter-class

---

53   See Harvey (2007).

54   See Collier and Collier (2007).

55   Nearly three decades ago, one Mexican anthropologist (de la Fuente, 1967: 437) outlined the degree to which – even then – both indigenous and *mestizo* populations were internally differentiated along class lines. Occupational categories such as landowner, agricultural labourer, farmer, artisan, and shopkeeper, were not confined to one group but found in both. He concluded that *mestizos* 'as a group, are richer than the Indians, but generally there are some rich Indians everywhere'.

but intra-class conflict is confirmed by Villafuerte and van der Haar, who point out that the land occupied as a result of invasions by Zapatistas in the Montes Azules area of Chiapas is in fact that of another indigenous group, the Lacandón Indians.[56]

Cultural Autonomy and/as Traditional Authority

According to de León, however, the main support for the EZLN came from middle peasants and small proprietors, migrants who had originally colonized land in Chiapas and who had then proceeded to establish themselves in *ejidos* and producer cooperatives.[57] They were the ones, he argues, who suffered most when the Mexican State began to implement a neoliberal programme, and withdrew agricultural subsidies on which their continued existence as peasants depended. Although this appears to be consistent with the pattern of agrarian mobilization outlined by Wolf – namely, resistance against capitalist encroachment by petty commodity producers struggling to reproduce them-selves as such – there is a crucial difference.[58] Whereas agency in the peasant rebellions covered by Wolf – Russia, China, Vietnam, Algeria and Cuba, as well as the 1910 Mexican revolution – was, he argued, designed to prevent the spread of capitalism and aimed against the state apparatus encouraging this, the pur-pose of the Zapatista uprising by contrast is merely to secure a better deal from the state under the already existing capitalist system. The latter emerges from the analyses of van der Haar and Harvey.[59]

Van der Haar also questions two kinds of received wisdom about the Zapatista uprising in Chiapas: the absence of land reform, and the overarching presence of the Mexican State. The first takes the form of a popular image of Chiapas as a region unaffected by agrarian reform, due principally to the power of the landlord class, until 1994, when the indigenous peasantry took matters into its own hands. Against this view, van der Haar argues that because of land redistribution from the 1930s onwards, *latifundia* no longer exist. Large hold-ings have been broken up, and consequently *ejidos* and peasant communities

---

56   See Villafuerte (2007) and van der Haar (2007).

57   See de León (2007).

58   For this thesis in the now classic study of peasant movements, see Wolf (1971; 2001: 230–240).

59   Like Harvey, de León attributes grassroots discontent on the part of smallholders in Chiapas to the withdrawal of – and hence competition for – resources disbursed by the Mexican State. This discontent, he argues, gathered momentum from 1982 onwards when – following a period (1978–82) of provision/redistribution by the state – free market policies were introduced. Democracy, it is hinted, was seen as a way of regaining access by political means to these economic resources.

now hold much of the land. The second form of received wisdom posits traditional indigenous authorities confronting an all-powerful nation state. The
Zapatista movement, however, gathered support in a rural context where the
Mexican State was historically *weak*, not strong.[60] As a result, indigenous peasant communities in Chiapas were in effect politically autonomous, due to the
virtual *laissez faire* policy adopted towards them by the Mexican State.

For this reason, power at the rural grassroots in Chiapas has been exercised
largely by traditional indigenous authorities.[61] This is consistent with a pattern
found elsewhere in the so-called Third World; in rural Mozambique and
Bolivia, for example, traditional indigenous authorities have reasserted their
political power.[62] It is clear from the analysis by van der Haar both that the
main conflicts over land in Chiapas involve rival claims by individual peasants
or indigenous communities, and also that the antagonism towards the Mexican
State derives from its perceived failure either to intervene in these disputes or
to solve them.[63] From this arises the following intriguing problem. If *de
facto* power lies with traditional indigenous authorities, why have the latter

---

60   This point should perhaps be qualified somewhat, in that the Mexican State was not so
     much weak as ruled *via* traditional indigenous authorities, the latter being the face and
     voice of the former within Chiapan village communities. This kind of indirect rule is a
     process described by Rus (1994: 268) as 'the State enforcing "native traditions" *against the
     natives themselves* to maintain order' (original emphasis). Not only were these authorities
     the better-off elements at the rural grassroots in Chiapas, therefore, but according to the
     same source they also deployed all the symbols and discourse of indigenous 'otherness'.
     This is a common enough phenomenon throughout rural Latin America. In Peru during
     the mid-1970s, for example, both symbols and discourse projecting an image of equality
     (= we-are-all-the-same, we-are-all-peasants) were deployed in a similar fashion by rich
     peasants in an agrarian cooperative located in the eastern lowlands. For an important
     theoretical analysis of the peasant/state relationship in Latin America, and in particular
     how the state routinely co-opts the leadership of peasant movements, see Petras and
     Veltmeyer (2003).
61   This respect for traditional indigenous authorities is also encouraged both by the
     Zapatistas, who co-opt them in order to secure grassroots support (Saavedra, 2007), and
     by the religious teachings of the Roman Catholic church, as adhered to by Mayan peas-
     ants in Chiapas (Moksnes, 2007; Tavanti, 2003).
62   On this point, see Dinerman (2001) and McNeish (2003). The latter attributes a resurgent
     ethnic identity in 1990s Bolivia to the fact that rural trade unions had been undermined
     by the neoliberal structural adjustment policies, creating a political space re-occupied by
     traditional indigenous authority.
63   These involved for the most part small peasants occupying *minifundios* and/or disputed
     holdings cultivated by neighbours, confirming that what was happening amounted in
     some instances to intra-class conflict.

themselves not been able to solve such disputes? Might it be the case, perhaps, that, being unable to solve them, traditional indigenous authorities have dumped this problem in the lap of the Mexican State, and then blamed it for not succeeding where they failed?

Linked to this is the issue of gender, and the extent to which female emancipation is possible within the framework of grassroots power exercised by traditional indigenous authorities in Chiapas.[64] As documented by Olivera, women in the peasant family household continue to experience many of the same kinds of oppression as they have in the past, participation in the EZLN notwithstanding.[65] Not only is the traditional cultural identity of the indigenous female a subordinate one, but community authorities uphold a variety of historical practices (bride price, arranged marriages, domestic violence) that are against the interests of rural women, and strongly opposed by the latter.[66] There is, in short, a basic contradiction in Chiapas between on the one hand the reproduction of cultural 'otherness', the exercise of power by traditional indigenous authorities, and the endorsement of ethnic identity/autonomy by the Zapatistas, and on the other the theory and practice of gender and human rights to which the EZLN is also committed.[67] This underlines the presence

---

64   This is part of a much broader analytical problem, about the extent to which traditional indigenous authorities and institutions are no more than the form taken by capitalist authority and relationships in specific contexts. Not only have traditional indigenous authorities been a central emplacement of the coercive labour regime operating on capitalist plantations in Chiapas, therefore, but evidence from other rural contexts in Latin America suggests that traditional indigenous institutions frequently mask what are in fact production relations between capital and labour. In the case of Peru during the mid-1970s, for example, exchange labour groups based on notionally reciprocal *mink'a* and *ayni* arrangements involved capitalist rich peasants cultivating the profitable coffee crop for export markets. What they swapped with one another in these 'traditional' institutional forms was not their own personal labour-power but that of their kin or neighbouring poor peasants who were their unfree workers (Brass, 1999: Chapter 2).

65   See Olivera (2007).

66   Harvey (2007) notes that because women attribute domestic violence to male consumption of alcohol, they have exerted pressure on municipal authorities in Chiapas to shut down bars on the *ejidos*.

67   In an important sense, the fact that the Zapatistas and their support network attach so much significance to the concept of an institutionally disembodied notion of 'human rights' (Zapatista Army of National Liberation, 2002) is itself an indication of their political weakness. Just how little progress there has been in terms of a theory about human rights – never mind its practice or enforcement – emerges clearly from a comparison of two texts, written a third of a century apart (Raphael, 1967; Owen, 2003). Not only is the conceptual confusion they both reveal palpable, but this problem underlines the

of an incompatibility – and for rural women a disempowering one – at the heart of an agrarian mobilization premissed on a discourse about indigenous empowerment.[68]

IV

It is no exaggeration to say that, one way or another, *indigenismo* has been the principal way in which the identity of rural inhabitants in Central and South America has been constructed – both 'from above' (by monarch, viceroy, colonial and post-colonial State) and 'from below' (by nationalist and/or some socialist intellectuals, and indigenous representatives and communities) – over time. The sole exception to this was a brief period after the Second World War, when for some twenty years during and after the 1960s (the 'development decade') the indigenous subject/community was in effect re-problematized, as an issue of economic backwardness (= underdevelopment).[69] For a relatively

---

inescapable centrality to the concerns of both the EZLN and its supporters of an issue which they continue to evade. Namely, that any notion of legislative protection – 'human rights', as applied to any collectivity and individuals constitutive of this – has no meaning if not upheld and enforced by the State, which in turn necessarily reiterates the political issue posed by Marxist theory. Without struggle aimed at capturing the State, there can be no exercise of the kind of power necessary to provide the Zapatistas with the kind of legislative protection they require.

68   This fact has been routinely overlooked by enthusiastic supporters of the Zapatistas, who fail to question the extent to which the cultural empowerment sought by rural communities on the grounds of their traditions reproduces the historically entrenched disempowerment of indigenous women. An example is the following uncritical observation by Hardt and Negri (2005: 212–213) about the grassroots formation of an unproblematically uniform consciousness (= 'the common'): 'Revolts mobilize the common in two respects... the common antagonism and common wealth of the exploited are translated into common conduct, habits and performativity...These elements of style, however, are really only symptoms of the common dreams, common desires, common ways of life, and common potential that are mobilized in a movement...the EZLN in the Lacandon jungle in Chiapas mixes elements of national history...and forges them together with network relationships and democratic practices to create a new life that defines the movement'.

69   An important aspect of this was the recognition that, in order to survive as petty commodity producers, those classified – by themselves and others – as peasants were required to migrate in search of off-farm income sources to supplement the inadequate economic returns from peasant economy. On the issue of rural outmigration, at this conjuncture and earlier ones, see among others Gamio (1966; 1971), Baird and McCaughan (1979) and Grindle (1988). Whereas adherents to *indigenismo* discourse (such as Gamio) tended to

short time, and to a limited degree, Mexican peasant cultural 'otherness' was de-exoticized, and subordinated to the idea of social and economic progress (= development) as desirable objectives in rural areas of the Third World.[70] To this end, the Mexican State was – together with India – one of the first Third World nations to implement the Green Revolution programme based on high yield varieties. Not only was low-cost credit made available to peasants, but crops destined for the domestic market benefited from a price support system.

Where touched upon, therefore, traditional culture was reconstituted as an obstacle to development. The debate shifted in terms of emphasis, and became one about political economy; whether or not accumulation was taking place in the Mexican countryside, and if so, was the process of capitalist development reproducing or proletarianizing the peasantry.[71] However, many components of *indigenismo* discourse continued to circulate, albeit disguised under the economic rubric of the peasant family farm. Like the indigenous community, peasant economy in Mexico and elsewhere in Latin America was essentialized and said to be capable of reproducing itself independently regardless of the systemic conditions (feudalism, capitalism, socialism) obtaining in the wider society.[72] This *campesinista* or Chayanovian view about the peasantry was itself challenged by the rise and consolidation of neoliberal economic theory (and policies emanating from it) during the 1980s and 1990s.

Land Privatization, Migration and Gender
The 1982 debt crisis in Mexico signalled the end of post-war Keynesianism, and with it the end both of demand management dependent on improving peasant livelihoods and of resource provision to agriculture by the State. Where agriculture was concerned, therefore, market deregulation entailed lower tariff

---

view migration as being by peasants who sold their labour-power in order to remain peasants, those who were not exponents (Baird and McCaughan) perceived the issue rather differently. The latter regarded migrants as proletarians, since their main source of income derived from working for others; these labourers might (or might not) also own a small plot of land, on which they grew crops to supplement their earnings as workers, the principal source of income.

70   See, for example, the texts by García (1967), Gutelman (1971), Hewitt de Alcántara (1976), and Pearse (1980: 185–193).

71   On these debates, see Bartra and Otero (1987) and Bartra (1993).

72   Adherents of this *campesinista* view of the peasantry in Mexico and Colombia include Warman (1980; 1983), Gordillo (1988), and Zamosc (1986). Even when analysed largely in terms of an economic (as distinct from a cultural) dynamic, therefore, peasant smallholding continued to be categorized as 'other' – as external to the national and international economy.

barriers, lower agricultural wages, and – because of the elimination of price controls – a profits squeeze for small agrarian capitalists. *Laissez-faire* policies meant, among other things that the link between State financial provision, peasant agriculture, and domestic consumption was broken, and replaced with policies favouring production for export, debt repayment and land privatization.[73] The *campesinista* response has been to advocate the reconstitution/ protection of peasant economy, a course of action currently pursued by many NGOs with an interest/presence in Chiapas.[74]

By announcing in 1992 the end of the agrarian reform process, plus a future policy of land deregulation and privatization, the Mexican State in an important sense fuelled the rural property seizures that occurred in Chiapas a short time afterwards.[75] In this regard, the land invasions in Chiapas during 1994 appear to have been generated by the same kind of grassroots dynamic that fuelled similar acts of private appropriation that took place in post-1976 China, and Cuba and Russia after 1989, where agrarian collectives and/or cooperatives were in effect dismantled from within.[76] An analogous process occurred

---

73   On this point, see Barkin (1995; 2002) and the collection edited by Randall (1996).

74   Hence the frequently encountered observations on the part of NGOs about the desirability of alternative strategies for small-scale, locally-controlled diversified production, a return to traditional self-sufficiency, programmes to guarantee the survival of peasant communities in the face of market pressures, and the recognition of the vitality of Mexico's indigenous past as essential for a solution to the country's present problems.

75   *Ejido* property rights have become a politically contentious issue after 1992, not least because land registration reveals among other things that those who currently enjoy usufruct rights are not those in whom this right was originally invested. It may these new *de facto* proprietors who feel, perhaps, that their rights might be threatened by the State if they are made public. In other words, registration not only uncovers the presence of rival claims to the same land, but stokes up any conflicts arising from this. It is precisely because a similar registration procedure threatened to reveal who really owned *ejidal* land, and correspondingly who worked the latter but was propertyless, that *ejidatarios* in Atencingo opposed the taking of an agricultural census in the late 1950s (Ronfeldt, 1973: 158–159).

76   In the case of China and Russia (Chossudovsky, 1986: 42 ff.; Allina-Pisano, 2004) this was carried out by better-off producers, who – so as to pre-empt a looming privatization – opportunistically appropriated resources (mainly land) hitherto owned by the State and operated by the members of the agrarian collective. Much the same is true of Cuba (Deere, Pérez and Gonzales, 1994), where the extension/consolidation of private property in land generally, the consolidation of ownership rights within cooperatives, the hiring by the latter of wage labour without property rights, labour market competition with peasant proprietors for workers, and the expansion of the black market all indicate a post-1989 trend towards the privatization of agriculture.

earlier in Mexico itself, where a *de facto* land privatization on some *ejidos* led to the cultivation of what had been common property by the new owners employing hired labourers.[77]

To some degree, this latter pattern was replicated subsequently in Chiapas, but with a difference. One result of market penetration by maize imports, itself a consequence of NAFTA, is that many smallholders in Chiapas are becoming migrants. The latter are males, who travel to the United States in search of work, leaving females in the peasant household to cultivate the family holding. Given the subordinate position of women in the indigenous community, females who remain are frequently dispossessed of family land. This gender disadvantage where indigenous women are concerned is itself compounded by the fact that the privatization of *ejidal* holdings is individualizing landownership in the name of the male household head.[78] Patriarchy and patrilineal inheritance notwithstanding, the historical right of indigenous females to subsistence – enshrined in common ownership of community resources – is as a result undermined. Since husbands frequently sell their holding when they migrate, women in the peasant household are left with no prospect other than to sell their labour-power.

Coffee, Commodification and Class

In the decade following the Zapatista uprising, peasant economy has not fared well. Despite the occupation by Zapatistas of some half a million hectares, of which 200,000 were converted into *ejidal* land, peasant economy in Chiapas

---

77   Although nominally a communal system of landownership, it has according to Bartra (1993: 94–95) always been 'a form that intermingles various types of property: State or nationalized, corporate, communal and private. The *ejido* is, in principle, property of the nation but is granted to a community of peasants in usufruct'. The same source states, unambiguously: 'It has been said that the formation of the *ejido*, as a fruit of the Revolution of 1910, has represented the triumph of communal ownership. If one examines the problem with detachment, this turns out to be a falsehood: *the ejido is not a form of communal property*; rather, it is a disguised form of small private property, or *minifundio*' (original emphasis). *Ejido* land in the Laguna region (Wilkie, 1971) has long been worked by hired workers composed of the landless kin of *ejidatarios*, who worked not only for (or instead of) the latter but also for local landowners and industries.

78   It is for this reason that the presence of class relations inside the *ejido* are so important, since these would cast a more precise light on the connection between on the one hand rural agency in Chiapas, agrarian property relations, and the social division of labour, and on the other issues linked to and arising from gender. On the complex history of the interrelationship between gender and class in rural Mexico, see Fowler-Salamini and Vaughan (1994).

has been eroded and characterized by a continuing situation of crisis. Manifestations of the latter include rural outmigration (to urban centres in Chiapas and elsewhere in Mexico, and to the United States), an increasingly gendered division of labour (women remain in the countryside), and land fragmentation (the spread of the *minifundio*). Crucially, the majority of coffee growers are peasants, and an ending of the quota system – a result of the liberalization of the world market – plus overproduction has led to declining coffee prices and rural incomes linked to them.

The fact that many peasants who supported the EZLN were coffee growers raises the question of the link between class and rural agency that is at the centre of *campesinista/descampesinista* debates, both in Mexico and elsewhere. According to Saavedra, coffee growing peasants joined the Zapatistas almost by default.[79] Confronted on the one hand with declining world market prices for coffee, and on the other with the weakness of existing peasant organizations, *ejidatarios* had no option but to side with the EZLN. Although the insurgents spoke of introducing socialism, it is clear that Zapatista membership had little to do with revolutionary upheaval, and more to do with a desire for higher prices for the sale of the coffee crop. Rank-and-file members equated socialism not only with private property (= ownership of their holdings), a belief fostered by the Zapatistas, but also with 'living like the rich'.

In this respect, the agrarian mobilization in Chiapas is in many ways a classic peasant movement, designed to obtain or reassert the right to individual private property, and thus unconnected with socialist objectives (such as common ownership of the means of production). This was the case during the 1960s, when rural *guerrilla* organizations in Latin America drew support from better-off tenants engaged in conflict with landlords over the ownership of profitable coffee-producing holdings.[80] As agricultural production has become more commercialized and capitalism more pervasive, however, so rural conflict has extended into the realm of commodity prices. The latter was central to the new farmers' movements that emerged in India during the 1980s, when rich peasants who had benefited from earlier land reforms and the Green revolution programme mobilized against the State.[81] Like the Zapatistas, they too mobilized on the basis of an anti-capitalist discourse that was populist and nationalist.

---

79   See Saavedra (2007).

80   On this point, see among others Gott (1971: 15), Paige (1975: 131 ff.), and Fioravanti (1974). Why the coffee crop has long been ecologically suitable for cultivation on peasant smallholdings in Chiapas is outlined in Miranda (1952).

81   For the new farmers' movements in India, see the collection edited by Brass (1995).

That nationalism – and thus the national question – is defined not by the imminence but rather by the immanence of nationhood, and further, that it is fuelled historically by free market policies, has long been conceded.[82] Like their counterparts in Chiapas, therefore, farmers in India campaigned for 'remunerative prices', or lower input costs (of energy, irrigation and credit) plus higher returns for output (crops, livestock). However, again like the Zapatistas, they deployed not an economic but rather a nationalist mobilizing discourse, invoking their 'otherness' as Indian farmers discriminated against by their own State, by the international market, and by rival producers in the

---

82   Not least by English conservatives who supported British imperialism but were opposed to the corrosive impact of the free market on colonial settler loyalty. One such was Richard Jebb (1874–1953), who at the start of the twentieth century warned against the impact of liberal economic policies on nationalist sentiment in self-governing colonies (Australia, South Africa, Canada, New Zealand) of the British Empire. As he saw it, the danger lay in the disintegration of Empire as a result of burgeoning settler nationalism within colonial possessions, where the element of autonomy might easily translate into nationhood. Echoing the Zapatista concern for 'dignity', he defended the grassroots nationalism of white settlers in the following terms (Jebb, 1905: 103–104): 'Its basis is the national sense of self-respect which chafes under the feeling of dependence upon the favour of others. It feels the degradation of living upon sufferance...It abhors the debasing theory that the status of colony is final; or that its only function is to be reproductive in the material sense'. That his endorsement of grassroots nationalism was not just exclusionary but deeply reactionary is evident from the complaint (Jebb, 1926: 329) that, as a result of the 1914–18 war, '[t]he prominent part played by the Japanese at sea and by the Indian troops on land was a new weapon for use in agitation against the settled racial policy which is common to the United States, Canada, Australia and New Zealand and, as regards Asiatics, South Africa. With the encouragement and sometimes the active support of the subversive movement directed from Moscow attempts have been made to organise Asiatic resentment with a view to the overthrow of the British Empire, beginning with India...the higher nationalism [of France contrasts with] the Dominions, where the white man insists on his superior caste'. Having started out as an advocate of free trade, Jebb became an opponent of this. In his view British imperial endorsement of the free market overrode the colonial wish for trade preferences, encouraged settler nationalism in colonies, and ran the risk thereby of converting self-government into a separatist movement. In words (Jebb, 1905: 328) that might find many echoes in the current neoliberal economic climate, he stated that 'the England of unchallenged Cobdenism' presented colonies with a situation where '[t]here was nothing for it but eventual separation'. Although this concern with the territorial integrity and political unity of British imperialism was the mirror image of the problem as perceived by Marxists such as Luxemburg and Lenin, all those who addressed the issue – conservative and socialist alike – were aware of the inherently fissiparous tendencies at work.

US, the EU, and Japan.[83] Where agency involving the deployment by peasants of nationalist and populist anti-capitalist ideology in the context of a free market is concerned, the EZLN possesses clear affinities with two previous agrarian uprisings in Mexico: the Cristeros in the 1920s, and the Sinarquistas of the 1930s.

Cristeros, Sinarquistas...Zapatistas?

To place the Chiapas uprising of 1994 in a lineage that includes not just the 1910 Mexican revolution but also the Cristero movement of the late 1920s and the Sinarquista mobilization a decade later is to do no more than acknowledge the obvious: the continuing importance of rural agency in Mexican history.[84] Although all these agrarian movements were in many respects specific – for example, in terms of social composition and political objectives – they nevertheless share a surprisingly large number of characteristics, not least their agrarian populist discourse. This is particularly true of the lineage extending backwards from Chiapas in 1994, via the Sinarquisatas of the late 1930s to the Cristeros in the late 1920s.

As in the case of Chiapas, therefore, these two earlier uprisings occurred in a period of profound economic crisis, when prices of agricultural commodities were falling sharply. It is clear that in terms of social composition, both the Cristero and the Sinarquista movements involved the mobilization of and support by what were mainly petty commodity producers, regardless of whether they were tenants, sharecroppers and independent proprietors, or whether they also sold their labour-power to others.[85] Accordingly, each uprising can be seen as a reaction in the Mexican context on the part of the peasant family

---

83   Unsurprisingly, in the north Indian state of Uttar Pradesh many of the peasants who were members of the BKU (*Bharatiya Kisan Union*) – one of the most important new farmers' movements – also supported the rise to political power of the BJP, the Hindu chauvinist party (Brass, 1995).

84   The literature on the 1910 Revolution is vast, but see Knight (1986a; 1986b). On the Cristero movement, see Meyer (1973–74; 1976), and on the Sinarquistas see Whetten (1948: 484–522) and Hernández (1999). The Cristero rebellion occurred in the period 1926–29, while the Sinarquista movement emerged in 1937, peaked in 1940/41, and faded in 1944–48. Both were located in the Bajío region, covering the states of Querétaro, Guanajuato, Michoacán, Jalisco and Guerrero.

85   This kind of interpretation has been challenged by Meyer (1976: 85–86) who maintains that – as a result of interviews he conducted with the surviving participants – 'it is possible to reject as false [the view that] the Cristeros were small independent proprietors threatened by agrarian reform...'. He claims that only 14 percent of the combatants were small proprietors, the rest being composed largely of 'farmers or sharecroppers' (15 percent) and those who 'lived by manual labour' (60 percent), a category that included

farm to the Great Depression, the adverse economic effects of which took the familiar form of either declining returns received for crops sold, cutbacks in financial provision by the State, proletarianization resulting from an insufficiency or dispossession of land, or a combination of them all.[86]

Again like Chiapas, religion was central to the mobilizing discourse of both the Sinarquista and the Cristiada movements. Much like the Mayan peasants some sixty years later, the influence on the Sinarquistas of Roman Catholic

---

agricultural workers, muleteers and artisans. However, as Meyer himself accepts, these are not mutually exclusive categories. Hence the admission by him that 'a plurality of occupations was the rule, even among the small proprietors and sharecroppers', so as to be able to argue that peasants accounted for even less than fourteen percent of the combatants, and that the social composition of the Cristeros was far more heterogeneous than his own figures suggest. The problems faced by this methodology are twofold. First, his concept of 'peasant' is restricted to those who already own the land they cultivate, whereas in reality the term extends to include those who operate holdings they may not own: in other words, it is necessary to include 'farmers or sharecroppers' within the category of smallholders. And second, his admission about occupational plurality – which is made to cast further doubt on peasant participation – can in fact be used against him. It is likely, therefore, that the 60 percent who 'lived by manual labour' were actually smallholders – those with conditional access to small plots of land insufficient to meet their economic requirements – who also sold their labour-power to others. The latter, as virtually all analyses of rural agency confirm, see themselves as peasants, regardless of whether they obtain the major portion of their income from cultivating land they own/lease, and – more importantly – it is this individual landowning aspiration that structures their agency. In the case of the Sinarquistas, there is no doubt as to the importance of participation by peasant smallholders, the 'forgotten peasant masses' (Hernández, 1999: 238, 240, 415, 442).

86   In Europe during the 1920s and 1930s, these same processes contributed to the rise of the far right. While the argument that the capitalist crisis of that era had an analogous economic impact in the Mexican countryside is not disputed, the similarity of political outcome is the subject of debate. Hence the following observation by Meyer (1976: 212): 'Some have interpreted [the Cristiada] as a movement similar to that of Salazar or Franco – a precursor of *Sinarchismo*, the Mexican variety of Fascism (1937–45); an attempt at counter-revolution, led by the Church, the big proprietors, and the reactionary pettybourgeoisie'. Meyer denies this link in the case of the Cristeros, but accepts the argument in the case of the Sinarquistas. That the latter were a Mexican variety of fascism is itself challenged by Hernández (1999: 200, 393, 394, 396–397, 453), who nevertheless has difficulty in sustaining this view. His sympathetic account of *Sinarquismo* – its vehement anticommunism, its ultra-nationalism (*hispanidad*), its hankering after a lost golden age, its organizational modalities, its political discourse (admiration for Franco, Mussolini and Hitler), plus the hierarchical and authoritarian structure of the movement – points unambiguously to it having been a fascist mobilization.

teachings meant that they also regarded rural poverty as virtuous.[87] Participants in both the Cristiada and the Sinaquista movements espoused a traditionalist form of Roman Catholicism ('Christ the King') which emerged historically as a reaction against the 1789 French Revolution.[88] On this issue, an analysis sympathetic to the Cristiada observes: 'The religion of the Cristeros was...the traditional Roman Catholic religion, strongly rooted in the Hispanic Middle Ages'.[89] Advocating a return to an earlier form of religious orthodoxy, this strand of Catholicism was strongly opposed not just to rationalism and socialism ('no Catholic can be a socialist') but also to commerce and money.[90]

---

87   Hence the following Sinarquista view (Hernández, 1999: 378): 'Glorification of poverty freely accepted as a means to serve our fellow man [constituted] the ideal basis of Hispanic culture'. Whereas the Sinarquistas endorsed hispanidad but Mayan peasants reject this in favour of a specifically ethnic identity, the celebration of poverty as virtuous by them both is due, ironically, to the same ideological source: the influence of Roman Catholicism.

88   About this Hernández (1999: 469) observes: 'Tradition was glorified, the present rejected; there was a feeling of anti-capitalist nostalgia for an idealised past society....'.

89   On this point, see Meyer (1976: 195).

90   The Sinarquista view regarding the incompatibility between socialism and religion is cited in Hernández (1999: 68). Given the more recent ideological dominance and fashionability of liberation theology, it is easy to forget both that Roman Catholicism has another – and perhaps more authentic – reactionary face, and that during periods of economic crisis it is the latter that has prospered and attracted grassroots support among the poor because of its populist anti-capitalist discourse. During the economic crisis of the 1930s, for example, Belloc (1937) was able to promote Roman Catholic ideas on the grounds that historically the Church condemned liberalism and usury, a protection swept away by the Reformation. His argument was that, no longer held in check by the power of the Church, economic liberalism and usury generated the competition that destroys the virtuous small producer, and unleashes what he maintained were the three un-Godly forces of history – capitalism, the proletariat, and – ultimately – communism. Hence the following view (Belloc, 1937: 152): 'The maleficent activity of excessive competition, of Competition unchecked and uncontrolled, was prevented, because it was regarded as a disease in Society (which it is) and treated as a disease mortal to human dignity and freedom...We have unfortunately in the modern world only too much experience of what unbridled competition will do; there are few who have not come across one or another of its evil effects'. The conservative and hierarchical character of the Church notwithstanding, this anti-capitalist religious discourse permits it to present itself plausibly as part of any solution to the crisis of capitalism. Significantly, the defence advanced by Belloc of the Roman Catholic Church was no different from that of de Maeztu (1941), an ultra-rightwing opponent of the Spanish Republic, who in the same economic crisis of the mid-1930s not only saw religion as a bastion against the global spread of the same unholy

The latter aspect informed the anti-capitalist (= anti-modern) element that structured the nationalism of these earlier peasant movements in Mexico. Nationalism in Sinarquista discourse took the form of a contrast between a rural, pure, spiritual Mexico, and an urban, industrial, capitalist, and thus corrupt United States.[91] Moreover, the latter was seen as eroding the national sovereignty (= pristine rural culture) of the former. This stance led the Sinarquista movement to advocate the colonization and settlement of Lower California, a project designed to prevent its annexation by the United States government.

The nationalism of these two earlier peasant movements adhered to a similar pattern. It was supportive of 'the rural' and especially peasant economy, harmony between classes, religion, and traditional authority, but against 'the urban', politics, the State, big industry, 'foreigners' (capitalist and communist alike), and the notion of class struggle. Not only did the mobilizing discourse of the Cristeros and Sinarquistas in many ways anticipate that of the Zapatistas, therefore, but as in the case of the latter it was emblematic of their agrarian populism.[92]

Like the Cristiada and the Sinarquista movements, the EZLN is also nationalist, but in ways that are contradictory. Opposition by the Zapatistas to NAFTA put them in the vanguard of the struggle against foreign domination (the World Trade Organization, the World Bank, and the International Monetary Fund) in general and US imperialism in particular. Cast in this rôle, therefore, the Zapatistas could be said to have spearheaded national resistance by Mexican society as a whole against the loss of economic, political and cultural sovereignty. At the same time, however, the EZLN was also in the forefront of

---

trinity (finance capital, liberalism, and communism), but also perceived spirituality as a central emplacement of Spanish nationalism, *hispanidad*. The latter, as Hernández (1999: 490 ff.) points out, was an integral component of Sinarquista ideology.

91   Hence the Sinarquista view, expressed in 1941, that (Hernández, 1999: 480): 'The real Mexico does not lie in the cities. It is not in the capital, in any case, alienated, Americanized, false; nor is it in the cities, corrupted by the cinema, the nightclubs, the strident music, where life is faked and simulated. The reality of Mexico, the deep reality, the essence of our authentic being is found in the villages, in the hamlets, on the roads travelled by the Indian alone...'.

92   The populism of the Sinaraquistas is evident from their discourse-for and discourse against, which takes the following form (Hernández, 1999: 393–394): 'the rejection of the Left-Right division; the opposition...to the class struggle, which they viewed as a factor of social dissention; they combated Marxist ideologies because they repudiated nationalism, but they were also opposed to Mexican capitalists, whom they judged timorous and as having sold out to the foreigner. In the Synarchist vision, workers and employers had common interests'.

agency the object of which is to reassert ethnic 'otherness' *within* Mexican society.[93] As well as being an indigenous nation at the forefront of conflict between Mexico and 'foreigners', the ire of the Zapatistas is also turned inwards, against the existing nation state of Mexico.

Shooting the Zapatista Fox

Any peasant movement that eschews capturing state power, but demands local autonomy, necessarily poses an awkward question about the subsequent political relationship between itself and the capitalist state that continues to dominate the wider nation. In short, what kind of future interaction is to occur between the Mexican State and those who challenge its legitimacy to rule over indigenous communities in Chiapas? Here, too, the EZLN faced irreconcilable developments. Democracy has been central to the struggle of the EZLN in Chiapas, an objective that combined electoral reform with breaking the long-standing grip on Mexican politics of the PRI.[94] Together with human rights, democracy was seen by many observers of the Zapatista uprising as a positive outcome wrested by the rural poor from governments and world financial institutions in exchange for accepting the spread of the market. There is, however, a fundamental contradiction between these different strands of the neoliberal project.[95]

---

93   Significantly, Collier and Collier (2007) point out that the attempt by the Zapatistas to recast human rights as economic and social rights failed, and it was only when the latter was replaced by a discourse about indigenous rights to autonomy that EZLN support in Chiapas picked up once again.

94   On democracy as the main object of the 1994 uprising, see Wiener (1994). The EZLN itself (Zapatista Army of National Liberation, 2002: 640) makes this clear: 'We demand truly free and democratic elections, with equal rights and obligations for all the political organizations struggling for power, with real freedom to choose between one proposal and another and with respect for the will of the majority. Democracy is the fundamental right of all peoples, indigenous and non-indigenous'. As has been noted above, the term 'democracy' appears to be synonymous with grassroots indigenous autonomy, and the latter amounts in turn to the continuation of traditional forms of oppression in the name of cultural 'otherness'. When asked about the significance of democracy for indigenous peoples (Lucas, 2000: 106), a leader of the Ecuadorian CONAI replied that 'the term democracy does not exist in the language of indigenous peoples'.

95   For this contradiction, see Reed (2003) and Brittain (2005). There are other contradictions, which nowadays are rarely mentioned, especially by those 'new' postmodern populists committed to a non-specific notion of democracy. One of the most basic antinomies concerns the level at which democracy is to operate, and consequently the resulting incompatibilities between its expression at different levels. This is a problem of which even bourgeois liberal theorists have long been aware. Thus, for example, some fifty years

On the one hand, therefore, the notion of democracy is itself a crucial part of the neoliberal package, since where possible it is desirable for the advocates of *laissez faire* to be able to claim that the market is freely chosen by the rural population which it affects.[96] Bluntly put, ideologically the economics of the market require the kind of grassroots validation that makes the accompanying legitimization conferred by democracy not just optional but necessary. On the other hand, where this kind of acceptance is not forthcoming, the market is nevertheless imposed on its domestic population by the Latin American nation state in a way that negates both democracy and human rights. In other words, not only are political and economic liberalism ultimately incompatible, but for international capitalism the latter strand always supersedes the former.[97]

The modest and self-defeating nature of democracy as a political objective of the uprising in Chiapas is outlined by de León, whose account has the

---

ago de Madariaga (1958: 89–90) acknowledged this difficulty in the following terms: 'There are some liberals who solve the problem of separatism with charming simplicity: a plebiscite. But who does not realise that the mere fact of submitting to a plebiscite, the separation of a country from the whole of which it forms a part, is already conceding separation before the vote even takes place? Who is to designate the territory which will have the vote? Suppose tomorrow Catalonia has to vote on this question and that, by the well-known methods of surprise, exploitation of ignorance, emotions and other electoral forces, two and a half million people vote for a separation and two million for union with the rest of Spain. What does this imply? That Catalonia has voted for separation by a majority of two and a half million out of four and a half million, or that Spain has voted for union by a majority of twenty-five million against two and a half?'. Any attempt within a context of a capitalist national social formation to render ethnic identity downwards – as distinct from rendering class identity upwards (= internationalizing it) – has to confront this dilemma: that of 'nations within the nation', in other words.

96　This is the case not only where a socialist alternative continues to be available, but also where actually-existing socialism has been destroyed. Hence the significance of a discourse about how much better post-1973 Chile and post-1989 Russia were compared with the previous socio-economic system in both these contexts. The need on the part of the market for legitimization is clear, for example, from the deployment in the Thatcherite Britain of concepts such as 'popular capitalism', the inference being that, as everyone benefits from *laissez faire* economic policy, everyone approves of it.

97　As long as they are able to vote, agricultural workers and peasants in Latin America (and elsewhere) will not elect (or re-elect) a government committed simply to a market-led pattern of accumulation, and the implementation of a deflationary economic programme resulting in cutbacks by the State in public expenditure and investment, leading to declining living standards at the rural grassroots. For this reason, monetarists have long recognized the need for a strong State, not just to implement but rather to impose *laissez faire* programmes on an unwilling electorate.

advantage of being that of an 'insider', in that during the mid-1990s he advised the EZLN about the San Andrés accords.[98] He shows how, following military clashes, the objectives of the Zapatistas underwent a change, and shifted to a more limited set of demands: the realization of democracy, of autonomy by indigenous communities, and of global resistance to neoliberalism. Ironically, whilst the latter objectives succeeded in attracting external support (the church, NGOs), they undermined the impact of the Zapatista uprising. In effect, the call for democratization amounted to no more than voting the PRI out of power.

Over the 1994–2004 period, therefore, the EZLN changed from a *guerrilla* organization waging armed struggle against the state to being just another pressure group among the many NGOs operating in Chiapas. The object was no longer to seize state power (if, indeed, it had ever been this), but rather the construction of 'a new cultural hegemony' from below.[99] Hoist by their own petard, the modest demand made by the Zapatistas simply for electoral democracy meant that they were marginalized once this was implemented by the Mexican State, since the latter could argue that the principal claim of the former had now been met.[100] That democracy as an objective of grassroots

---

98   See de León (2007).

99   What form this from below 'cultural hegemony' might take is clear from the analysis by Moksnes (2007), who notes that a central narrative of Mayan peasants in Chiapas is the identification of ethnic 'otherness' with poverty and suffering, a combination encouraged by Roman Catholic teaching. Insofar as the reward for suffering is a spiritual and not a temporal one, found in heaven after death not on earth during life, suffering occasioned by poverty could be seen as promoting the acceptance of the *status quo*. That is, rather than a radical questioning of the existing socio-economic system, with a view to transcending it, religious teaching would appear to counsel what amounts to a celebration of material poverty as virtuous, and as meriting its reward in heaven. As many have pointed out, the danger inherent in such a discourse is that it becomes supportive of the accumulation process, in that it deflects a challenge to this and links redemption to a non-material domain. For this reason, it is a retreat from material reality, and consequently politically disempowering.

100   Part of the problem is that the EZLN failed to specify the content of democracy, as this would apply at the level of the nation state. This is because the issue of democracy remained local (= indigenous autonomy) and general, and was accordingly systemically undifferentiated (=making no distinction between socialist democracy and bourgeois democracy). The amorphous nature of democracy as projected by the Zapatistas is reflected in the unsuccessful attempts by commentators to give it some shape. One such (Esteva, 1999) is reduced to deploying concepts like 'radical democracy', 'radical hope', and 'the transition to hope' [*sic*].

mobilization has yielded few benefits to the rural population of Chiapas is also evident from other sources.[101]

Conclusion

Over the recent past, those having a passing acquaintance with debates about peasants and peasant movements in Latin America might be forgiven for making the assumption that the only analyses of agrarian mobilization were being written by postmodern theorists. Although this assumption is incorrect, it is undeniable that the study of peasants, peasant movements and agrarian transformation in Latin America during the latter part of the twentieth century has undergone a profound change. Like their counterparts in Asia, peasants and rural workers in Latin America are, we are constantly informed, not what they were once thought to be, nor is their agency designed to attain the objectives previously attributed to them. In rural Latin America, just as everywhere else nowadays, new movements are said to be emerging, composed of new rural subjects exercising new forms of agency. In a postmodern framework, therefore, an imposed and disempowering economic backwardness which its rural subjects attempt to transcend is reconfigured as a chosen and empowering form of cultural 'otherness', to be retained/reproduced at all costs.

It is a truism that peasants in many parts of Europe, Asia and Latin America have been equated with 'the nation', an almost universal stereotype reflected by and reproduced in the domain of popular culture everywhere. This kind of multiple association (peasants = Nature = nation) operates regardless of what turn out to be regionally specific cultures within the context of historically constituted nation states. It is perhaps because this peasant/Nature/nation link has been privileged ideologically over time that sub-national units based on the indigenous 'otherness' of peasant culture have a discursive potency denied to most other mobilizing idioms. This ideological power has itself been compounded by the fact that in Latin America the indigenous 'other' was frequently in the forefront of the struggle against colonialism and imperialism, a rôle that privileged yet further the already strong discursive link between 'peasant' and 'nation'.

By eroding cultural 'otherness', neoliberal policies designed to promote market-led global economic development fuelled the re-emergence in Chiapas of what was in essence a sub-nationalism, the indigenous subjects of which privileged the *indigenista/campesinista* view about the desirability of reproducing peasant economy at the rural grassroots. For this reason, the 1994 Zapatista uprising and what has happened since, raise a number of familiar

---

101   See, for example, Villafuerte (2007).

issues relating to the political objective/direction of and agency for change. Framed by rival Marxist/populist theoretical interpretations about the relative importance of class and national identity, these concern the agrarian question plus its 'other', the agrarian myth, as well as human rights, democracy, and – not least – gender. Despite participating in the Chiapas uprising, women are ironically disadvantaged as a result of the EZLN support for traditional indigenous authorities. The latter not only continue to uphold patriarchal relations as part of cultural 'otherness', but also do nothing to prevent female usufruct rights to community land being undermined by its privatization and sale.

Whereas Marxists differentiated the peasantry in order to win its separate class elements for socialism, the 'new' postmodern populism generally – and the subaltern studies project and resistance theory in particular – have reconstituted the peasantry as a unitary category, thereby reinserting it once more into the domain of nationalist discourse. Like the earlier agrarian mobilizations in Mexico, by the Cristeros and Sinarquistas, the 1994 uprising in Chiapas underlines the broader political lesson taught (but not, it seems, learned) by this epistemological shift. In rejecting the nationalism linked to colonialism (*hispanidad*) or capitalist development (*Mexicanidad*), exponents of *indigenismo* discourse – old and new – end up advocating or supporting what is in fact just another form of nationalism. This may be contrasted with the approach of Marxism, which opposes all forms of nationalism in the name of internationalism.

The apparently contradictory endorsement by some Marxists of a resurgent *indigenismo* discourse stems in part from the conflation of internationalism with the existence of an international support network. What the latter provides support for is much rather a narrow form of ethnic nationalism, a politics about the 'otherness' of cultural identity that is the antithesis of internationalism. This antinomy is – or ought to be – unsurprising, not least for Marxism. Now as in the past the dehumanizing and in an economic sense objectifying forces of capitalism have generated a reaction that should be familiar, in the form of a retreat into the ideological subjectivity of indigenous cultural autonomy.

In Chiapas, as elsewhere in the world, this currently takes the form of a reassertion of traditional ethnic identity, an historically ancient and thus (it is claimed) authentic rural grassroots selfhood threatened by neoliberalism. Such calls for re-subjectification, it is argued here, bring in their train a specific ideological consequence. A concept of nationhood as an empowering form of 'from below' plebeian identity creates a political space that can be filled by 'from above' categories belonging to a different class. It permits landowners and/or conservatives to shift discourse from class to nation, thereby targeting external 'others' in a different country as the focus of struggle, a transformation examined in the next chapter.

Cultural Struggle 'From Above'

'...it [is] absurd to suppose that, if the hard-toiled and the needy, the artisan and the agricultural labourer, become the depositories of power, and if they can find agents through whom it becomes possible for them to exercise it, they will not employ it for what...are their own interests'

> The fear expressed by a member of the Victorian ruling class (MAINE, 1885: 44) that, once they have the vote, rural workers in England may exercise it to the benefit of their own class.

Introduction

Much analysis of agrarian struggle written by 'new' populist postmodernists manages to convey one of two impressions: either that 'from below' agency is unproblematically empowering, or that its forcible suppression by the State is the only form of 'from above' struggle. What is overlooked is the presence of another form of 'from above' struggle, also about nationalism which, like that of the EZLN, not only locates at its centre an economically undifferentiated and culturally pristine peasantry but also reasserts the 'authenticity' of rural tradition. However, it is a discourse reproduced as much 'from above' as 'from below', in order to disempower plebeian elements, by pre-empting/preventing the emergence of class consciousness.

Having considered the way in which discourse informing 'from below' struggle by the EZLN in the Mexican state of Chiapas projected rural 'otherness' as empowering, and linked this to indigenous national identity, this chapter examines how the same kind of ideology can be deployed for different ends, by landowners and agrarian capitalists engaged in 'from above' struggle. The object of the latter has been, and in many contexts remains, to obtain the support of peasant smallholders and unite against two social forces, one internal and the other external: on the one hand urban workers opposed to and challenging the authority of employers, and on the other foreign capitalist competitors.

Faced with this twofold opposition, landowners and/or agrarian capitalists seek to unite politically with peasants not on economic issues (where they possess not just different but antagonistic interests), but on cultural grounds (which license claims about the presence of common interests). Hence the political importance to the reproduction by commercial producers and large

proprietors of a discourse about a shared identity of those inhabiting the countryside, an ideology that privileges as 'natural' a rural identity based on traditions, practices and hierarchy linked to agriculture and land, presented in
agrarian myth discourse as enduring and innate as Nature itself.[1]

The focus of this conflict is the State, the object of 'from above' struggle
being to shift discourse about 'belonging', by making the State embody the
interests of 'the people', gathered together in 'the nation' headed by monarchy,
landowners and church, and not of 'class' identity corresponding to that of an
emerging 'mob in the streets'. Across a range of contexts and conjunctures,
therefore, 'from above' struggle taking the form of cultural politics has
attempted to gain acceptance for a specific ideological combination: a fusion
between the aristocratic and plebeian variants informing the pastoral version
of the agrarian myth.

This chapter consists of five sections, the first of which explores the role of
Disraeli in formulating 'from above' struggle over the nation in nineteenth century England. The second and third address the 'from above' struggle over the
State, and charts its populist character. The fourth and fifth sections examine
the role of pro-peasant discourse as a form of populist conservative politics,
both in Europe and the United States, and also in Latin America.

I

In order to ensure the reproduction of their class position, landlords have
increasingly had to project – display – an identity that extended beyond the
class of its bearer.[2] As capitalism developed, populism was the means to this
end. It required landed proprietors to develop a sense of 'self-hood' which
incorporated and defined both 'those above' and simultaneously 'those below',
in the process becoming an identity that was no longer based on cosmopolitan

---

1   As will be seen in Chapters 4–8, these same themes are also present in film discourse and
    travel writing.

2   As one close observer (A Foreign Resident, 1886: 51) of the social order in late nineteenth
    century London indicated, this 'mixture of nobles and nihilists' gave rise to a situation in
    which the 'Tory plutocrat tries to make himself agreeable to the communist, but carefully
    keeps at a little distance as one who is afraid of his pockets being picked...though there is
    upon these occasions...a great blending of elements...there is no real fusion of them'. The
    same source (A Foreign Resident, 1886: 128) concludes by noting 'what are the Conservatives?
    What are their aims and their policy? What their future? Their more active spirits are always
    seeking how they can outbid their opponents, how trump the socialistic card which the radi-
    cal plays...pandering to Demos – the sole King of England'.

'distinction' (see Chapter 6) but rather on existing national elements. It was a shift that enabled a landowning class to identify itself (or to be identified) with the nation, so as to situate itself at the head of any plebeian agency within this context, and thus control its political direction.[3]

Saved from Democracy

Throughout the nineteenth century, the process of turning the focus of working class antagonism in Britain away from the (class) 'enemy within', and towards a (foreign) 'external enemy' was associated with the political career of Disraeli.[4] Such a process depended fundamentally on the ability of landowners to mobilize plebeian support: those above would retain their position, property and power by 'speaking about' and 'speaking to' those below, with the object ultimately of 'speaking for' them politically – the 'people' of whom they now claimed they were a part.[5] Such a role entailed the deployment and

---

3   This shift is evident, for example, in arguments made during the 1870s defending landed property, in which it is claimed that large landowners play a vital national role. Hence the following (Froude, 1877: 281, 301): 'So long as the British nation continues as it is, the landed gentry are as fixed a part of it as the planets of the solar system... Let us have all the talents in Parliament. Let trade, let science, let the learned professions, let wealth, if you like, be represented there, but it will be an ill day when we have no longer in public life the men [= landowners] who represent the historic traditions of Great Britain, who are returned to Parliament with no object of their own gain, and whose services are already pledged to the commonwealth by birth and fortune...'.

4   Details and chronology of Disraeli's political career are contained in Blake (1966). Although it is all too easy to dismiss Disraeli simply as a political opportunist, which in an important sense he was, he nevertheless had the foresight to anticipate the necessity for a populist solution to a central issue facing nineteenth century conservatism. Namely, how to ensure the institutional reproduction of monarchy and aristocracy as capitalism developed. Recognizing that the latter process generated twin threats – from the industrial bourgeoisie and from a nascent working class – Disraeli embarked on a discourse that combined divide-and-rule (landowners as allies of workers struggling against industrial capital) with calls for national unity (against the Irish 'other', for empire and colonization). In this respect, the characterization of Disraeli (Blake, 1972: 2, emphasis added) as the 'founder of *modern* conservatism' is indeed accurate.

5   The effectiveness of this approach – speaking for the people – depends on its acceptability to 'those below', an ideological relation that has been described as 'deference', whereby the right to exercise power is linked to the possession of property, wealth and status. Seen as emblematic of a 'natural superiority', the element of working class 'deference' was still regarded as significant in a later and influential sociological analysis of continuing electoral support for the Conservative Party. Hence the following differentiation of working class Conservatives (McKenzie and Silver, 1968: 242–243): 'One kind (the "deferentials") sees the Conservative elite as the natural rulers of Britain – sensitive to her traditions and peculiarities and uniquely

reproduction of the discourse about *noblesse oblige*; that is, a benign and thus unthreatening image of the landowning class, one that corresponded to the pastoral variant of the agrarian myth (= landlord-as-friend).[6]

In a classic populist fashion, therefore, Disraeli began during the early 1830s – a period of acute class struggle – by going over the heads of Whigs and Tories and appealing directly to 'the people' to unite as a nation (of 'Englishmen').[7] His object was nothing less than to form a national party – a coalition between Tories and Radicals – with the intention of maintaining 'the glory of the Empire and to secure the happiness of the People'.[8] Throughout the nineteenth century, therefore, the formation and consolidation of national 'selfhood' entailed identifying categories of national/ethnic 'otherness', extending from the Irish (see below), via Germans and Americans, to Jews. All the latter are deemed responsible for a diminution in the livelihoods and/or social position of 'the People' who are English: not just of workers and the bourgeoisie, therefore, but also of landowners.[9]

---

qualified to govern by birth, experience and outlook... For another kind of working class Conservative (the "seculars"), the party's elite are judged as the best rulers on more pragmatic grounds...it is a conditional commitment based upon the voter's continuing evaluation of the parties' present performance and prospects of future benefits... In either case, [the Conservative Party] could successfully picture itself as the defender of the national heritage'.

6 In the words of Froude (1877: 291, 304), whose defence of the landowning class emphasized its capacity to look after the well-being of tenants: 'Our landed system is like our political system: it consists of a number of petty monarchies, which are gradually becoming restricted by custom, till the monarch shall remain powerful for good and comparatively powerless to hurt... In such families the old expression Noblesse oblige is a genuine force... There are successive Earls and Dukes [who] have always been true to the people's side through three centuries of political struggle'.

7 Disraeli's words – cited in Blake (1966: 90) – were as follows: 'Englishmen, behold the unparalleled Empire raised by the heroic energies of your fathers; rouse yourselves in this hour of doubt and danger; rid yourselves of all that political jargon and factious slang of Whig and Tory – two names with one meaning, used only to delude you – and unite in forming a great national party which alone can save the country from impending destruction'. This utterance is described by Blake (1966: 90–91) as an attempt to forge 'a Conservative-Radical alliance'; although not identifying it specifically as populist, therefore, such a label nevertheless captures the contradictory element – being of the right, but 'talking' left – that is central to the mobilizing discourse of populism.

8 See Blake (1966: 92, 93).

9 These ethnic/national 'others', against whom 'Englishness' was forged, were paraded in an account (A Foreign Resident, 1886: 43, 47, 49) which began by pointing out that 'the principal forces which sway the social mass, of these the chief is wealth'. The same account

As Disraeli himself acknowledged, the explicit purpose of this appeal for national unity addressed to 'those below' was to ensure the continuation of the monarchical and aristocratic power and wealth.[10] In his 1872 Introduction to the second edition of *The English Constitution*, Bagehot advocated just such a policy, warning against letting the workers exercise their power as a class after having obtained the franchise as a result of the 1867 Reform Act.[11] This practice operated both at home and abroad, thereby combining nationalist ideology linked to empire ('social imperialism') with a populist discourse expressing concern for the domestic working class ('the condition of the people').[12]

---

continues: 'English society, once ruled by an aristocracy, is now dominated mainly by a plutocracy. And this plutocracy is to a large extent Hebraic in its composition. There is no phenomenon more noticeable in the society of London than the ascendancy of the Jews... The second feature to which, in my attempt to present a trustworthy chart of society in London, I should draw attention is the ascendancy of the Teutonic element... Germans elbow Englishmen in all directions, underselling them in commerce, and reducing the increment of the wage-earning classes to a minimum which barely suffices to keep starvation from their doors...in English commercial and professional life [the 'Teuton'] is creating a scare by the manner in which he is displacing the sons of the soil... Not less remarkable than the social organization and authority of the children of Israel and of the fatherland is the place which Americans have won for themselves in the social economy of the English capital. Between the tactics of the Hebrew and the subject of the United States there is a certain similarity; each commences his operations by establishing firmly a centre and a base'.

10   In the words of Disraeli (Blake, 1966: 122), 'I think we may feel that we have some interest in maintaining the prerogative of the Crown and the privileges of the Peers'.

11   Newly-enfranchised workers, Bagehot (1928: 269, 271) feared, 'will have suggested [to them] topics which will bind the poor as a class together; topics which will excite them against the rich... If the first work of the poor voters is to try and create a "poor man's paradise", as poor men are apt to fancy that Paradise, and as they are apt to think they can create it, the great political trial now beginning will simply fail... I can conceive that questions being raised which, if continually agitated, would combine the working-men as a class together'. From this he (Bagehot, 1928: 272) concluded 'in all cases it must be remembered that a political combination of the lower classes, as such and for their own objects, is an evil of the first magnitude; that a permanent combination of them would make them (now that so many of them have the suffrage) supreme in the country... So long as they are not taught to act together, there is a chance of this being averted, and it can only be averted by the greatest wisdom and the greatest foresight in the higher classes'. In the light of all this, recommended Bagehot (1928: 268), the upper classes and their political representatives 'have to guide the new voters in the exercise of the franchise; to guide them quietly, without saying what they are doing, but still to guide them'.

12   McKenzie and Sliver (1968) attribute conservative political dominance in part to the Liberal split in the 1880s, which resulted in Joseph Chamberlain – the most effective

From the mid-1830s, therefore, Disraeli argued for 'a new and more liberal form of Toryism' that would nevertheless defend landed property and its accompanying traditions and institutions.[13] In what was recognizably the landlord pastoral version of the agrarian myth, he linked working class prospects to those of the landowning class, both of which were called upon to uphold a common vision embodying English nationalism, imperialism and political conservatism.[14] Consisting of 'the people', this populist mobilization was aimed at two kinds of enemy: the 'other' abroad and the 'mob-in-the-streets' at home.

Nation = crown + church + people

The immediate targets of this nationalist discourse were the Irish, a ploy designed to rally to the defence of monarchy and landowner – in the name of unity – those plebeian supporters who regarded immigration as a threat to their own employment and livelihoods.[15] Contrary to the view that anti-Irish

---

advocate both of 'social imperialism' and of 'the condition of the people' – joining the Tories.

13   Hence the view (Blake, 1966: 122, 128–129) that at this conjuncture Disraeli's 'contribution to political literature [was] first and foremost a defence of the House of Lords' and further, that he admired Viscount Bolingbroke (1678–1751) as 'the prophet of a reinvigorated Toryism...his deep respect for traditional institutions, and his reverence for landed property and all that goes with it'. On the importance of Bolingbroke for Conservative political theory, see Buck (1975: 35 ff.).

14   '[I]n my opinion', observed Disraeli (Schuettinger, 1970: 239–240), 'the liberty of England depends much upon the landed tenure of England – upon the fact that there is a class which can alike defy despots and mobs, around which the people may always rally, and which must be patriotic from its intimate connection with the soil...the great body of the people of this country [are] "Conservative". When I say "Conservative," I use the word in its purest and loftiest sense. I mean that the people of England, and especially the working classes of England, are proud of belonging to a great country, and wish to maintain its greatness – that they are proud of belonging to an Imperial country, and are resolved to maintain, if they can, their empire – that they believe, on the whole, that the greatness and the empire of England are to be attributed to the ancient institutions of the land...'.

15   Noting that 'Disraeli evinced a virulent racial and religious prejudice towards Ireland', Blake (1966: 131) dismisses this as 'one of the least commendable features of Victorian politics, especially among the unenlightened masses who saw their standards threatened by hordes of alien papist immigrants accepting low wages and living in filthy conditions'. He continues: 'It is, however, surprising to find Disraeli going so far, even though it is true that the attitude fitted with his theory...of Whigs as the anti-national party and the Tories as the party of England'.

racism was for Disraeli an anomaly, this was anything but a departure from the historical pattern of Conservative populism. He was mobilizing those below against the foreign 'other' in order to forge what was a familiar political alliance: between on the one hand aristocrats and landowners, and on the other plebeians, along nationalist lines of 'we are all the same' (= the common identity of 'Englishness').

Although France was designated as the 'other' abroad, in this case it was not so much French nationalism as the French revolutionary tradition which concerned Disraeli. This is evident from his conceptualization of a conservative form of democratic equality. The latter was differentiated between an English type, defined as 'one that elevates and creates', and the French kind, which 'levels and destroys'.[16] Whereas in England 'every man knows or finds his place', a form of equality which Disraeli argued 'calls upon the subject to aspire', in France by contrast the same term means that 'no one should be privileged'.

In formulating this distinction Disraeli anticipated and laid the ideological foundation of twentieth century populist discourse about democratic politics as a form of meritocracy.[17] By claiming that in England workers might aspire to

---

16   This argument, elaborated by Disraeli in his 1835 text *Vindication of the English Constitution*, where his populist concept of Tory democracy took the following form (Buck, 1975: 68–69): 'The English nation, to obtain the convenience of monarchy, have established a popular throne, and, to enjoy the security of aristocracy, have invested certain orders of their fellow-subjects with legislative functions: but these estates, however highly privileged, are invested with no quality of exclusion; and the Peers and the Commons of England are the trustees of the nation, not its masters'. The same populist notion of trusteeship – 'we rule, but we rule for you' (like Canning, a rejection of 'pure democracy') – underwrote British imperialism, for which peasants and workers 'abroad' were no different from agricultural labourers and industrial workers 'at home': not excluded politically, all nevertheless had to be represented by the 'highly privileged' whose sole function was – so Disraeli proclaimed – merely a disinterestedly legislative one. Like the Tories, the Whigs – Gladstonian liberals who supported advocated *laissez faire* policies – also sought to recruit grassroots support by stressing not just free trade but also the necessity of working class enfranchisement and the importance of an egalitarian politics (= freedom of opportunity). The attempt by bourgeois advocates of *laissez faire* policy to enlist the support of workers arose from what was perceived by liberals as a twofold challenge: from the Tories, and from organized labour.

17   This populist discourse advocated by a conservative thinker in the 1830s resurfaced throughout the nineteenth and twentieth centuries, and was adopted by parties not just on the right of the political spectrum. Thus the idea of meritocracy as a solution to inequality structures not just the elite recruitment formulated in the 1870s/80s by Mosca (1939), but also the 1960s/70s Labour governments of Harold Wilson, and latterly the political slogans about inclusiveness proclaimed both by Tony Blair's New 'Labour' (the 'big tent') in the late 1990s and David Cameron's Conservative-led coalition (the 'big society') in 2010.

upward mobility (= join the ranks of the ruling class), while French equality amounted to a levelling downwards (= frustrating plebeian self-improvement), he attempted to reconcile egalitarianism with a class structure that remained intact. A transition to socialism could be avoided, therefore, by changes made not to the class structure but only to its personnel: (democratic) reform displaces (socialist) revolution, and the capitalist system is reproduced.

That Disraeli's nationalism was underwritten by the agrarian myth is evident from his participation in the 'Young England' group during the 1840s. A romantic, backwards-looking movement led by and reflecting landed interests, it was an aristocratic reaction against the industrial bourgeoisie ('Let wealth and commerce, laws and learning die/But leave us still our old Nobility') which looked to 'the people' for support. To this end, 'Young England' discourse condemned the *laissez faire* policies advocated by the bourgeoisie (money, commerce), seeking to obtain backing from those below by claiming that – as peasant farmers and/or tenants – life was better in times past under a benign aristocratic landlord class.[18]

Not only does the fact and importance of this populist element escape historians (such as Blake) who regard 'Young England' as an ineffectual response to industrial capitalism, but they fail to appreciate the full dimension of the 'wider context'.[19] Namely, that the landowning class sought thereby to mobilize

---

18   Disraeli's political views concerning the desirability of an alliance between monarchy and aristocracy on the one hand, and plebeian elements on the other, all under the banner of nationhood (= Crown + Church + People), were projected by means of his fiction: *Coningsby, or The New Generation* (1844), *Sybil, or The Two Nations* (1845), and *Tancred, or The New Crusade* (1847). These views are most succinctly presented in *Sibil*, where Disraeli writes (Blake, 1966: 198–199): 'In the selfish strife of factions, two great existences have been blotted out of the history of England, the Monarch and the Multitude; as the power of the Crown has diminished, the privileges of the People have disappeared; till at length the sceptre has become a pageant and its subject has degenerated into a serf'. In the same vein, he declares that the object of Conservatism is 'to bring back strength to the Crown, liberty to the Subject, and announce that power has only one duty: to secure the social welfare of the PEOPLE'.

19   Opposed to liberal utilitarianism, such paternalistic conservatism is described thus by Blake (1966: 171–172): 'Viewed in its widest context, Young England, like...the Gothic revival, was the reaction of a defeated class to a sense of its own defeat – a sort of nostalgic escape from the disagreeable present to the agreeable but imaginary past... Just as the Oxford Movement set up for its ideal the revival of a pure, uncorrupted, pre-Reformation church which had never existed...So Young England resuscitated a no less mythical benevolent feudal system to set against the radical, centralizing Benthamism which seemed to be carrying all before it in the 1830s and 1840s'. Whilst correct about the nostalgic invocation of an imaginary past, Blake mistakenly perceives 'Young England' as a movement of the defeated. Accordingly, he underestimates the extent to which its object

plebeian support that would off-set bourgeois power whilst at the same time increasing its own. This in turn enabled landowners to do two things: first, to merge with industrial capital, and second to prosper economically and survive politically.

Decline of the Landowning Class?

Why this was necessary can be illustrated by reference to the argument – based on an analysis of the overlapping linkage between large rural properties, wealth, political power and class – about whether or not the British landowning class declined in the century following 1870. A result of on the one hand the economic crisis (1873–1896) during the nineteenth century, when domestic food prices (and rental income) collapsed as a result of imports from the Americas and Australia, and on the other the 'final burgeoning of the fully fledged, large-scale, and highly concentrated industrial economy', plus the concomitant rise of parliamentary democracy, was 'the gradual eclipse [after the 1914–18 war] of the old [aristocratic landowning] order as the dominant force in the legislature and in government'.[20]

This argument, structured by the view that large landholding and industrial capitalist development are incompatible, is faced with three problems. First, it rests on the assumption that, prior to the decline that commenced in the late nineteenth century, the landowning base of aristocracy – and thus its economic power – had been stable, its social composition was correspondingly uniform, and thus the class position of British landlords was crisis-free and subject neither to change nor to threat. Second, even after industrialization reached its apogee, the wealth of this rural class is still equated largely or only with land.[21] And third, the end of aristocratic power is similarly equated with the loss of parliamentary influence. Each of these claims is open to question.

---

was to generate support that would enable the landlord class to reproduce itself politically in a context where *laissez faire* economic theory and policy operated.

20   See Cannadine (1990: 25–26).

21   The centrality to the argument that in Britain landownership is synonymous with aristocratic wealth is evident from the following unambiguous observation (Cannadine, 1990: 16, 17): '[U]ntil the 1870s, there was an exceptionally high correlation between wealth, status, and power, for the simple reason that they were all territorially determined and defined. Land was wealth: the most secure, reliable, and permanent asset. Land was status: its ownership conferred unique and unrivalled celebrity. And land was power: over locality, the county, and the nation.... However the matter is approached, it was land that was the key to riches and status'. Elsewhere, however, the same author (Cannadine, 1994: 165 ff.) provides ample evidence which appears to undermine his original argument. His analysis of the estates owned by the Duke of Devonshire reveals the extent to which

To begin with, even its proponents accept that claims about the demise of landowning wealth and power tend to exaggeration.[22] As important is the fact that landownership and the social composition of landlord class are not fixed historically, as evidenced by the fact that additions to this and subtractions from its ranks were routine occurrences. More significant is the fact that wealth was not necessarily linked to land, the more so as capitalism developed.[23] Even when it was, evidence suggests that the landlord class borrowed in order to invest in extending and/or consolidating their holdings, and agricultural improvements.[24]

---

aristocratic income over the latter part of the nineteenth century was generated by economic investment in industry, so much so that by the 1930s all the debts incurred during the 1890s economic depression had been cleared. The conclusion (Cannadine, 1994: 182–183) emphasizes not merely the survival but the prosperity of the landowning class: 'Like many other nineteenth century aristocratic millionaires, the Devonshires' acres were broad, their income large, and their involvement in non-agricultural ventures extensive.... For the Devonshires, as for many other landed families both super-rich and less wealthy, the pivotal decades were not so much the early Victorian years but the period of and after the great agricultural depression...'.

22   Cannadine (1990: 21, 31) not only accepts that the English landowning class, unlike its European equivalents, survived the revolutions of 1789 and 1848, but also admits that prophesying the demise of the aristocracy is open to exaggeration: 'Despite their gloomy forebodings, there was, during the decades that followed, much vigour and resolution, much resourceful resistance, much outright defiance, much adroit adaptation'. His conclusion (Cannadine, 1990: 700) is that notwithstanding 'the reforms, reverses and retreats of the late nineteenth and early twentieth centuries, it seems that the British patricians survived more tenaciously than some of the European aristocracies...the grandees and gentry of Britain showed substantial staying power'. This was a process that continued beyond the 1914–18 war, the usual point at which the landholding base of this class is said to decline. Hence the caveat issued in this connection by Thompson (1963: 329): 'Such [post-war] sales [of estates] were generally described as "forced", induced by taxation and death duties, but in none of these cases was there a death immediately preceding the sale and it is far more plausible to regard them as a continuation of the pre-war trend towards the contraction of family estates by sale of outlying parts, liberating capital for more profitable uses'.

23   Examples include three of the most important landowning institutions in England: the monarchy, the church, and the universities of Oxford and Cambridge, all of which have diversified economically and managed to retain large holdings (Turner, 2000).

24   See Cannadine (1994: 44 ff.), who comments: 'Not only was land still being bought: it was also still being improved... What was new about this second phase of [post-enclosure activity] was that new sources of finance suddenly became available [from the State] in the mid-Victorian period...it seems that as spending on new land lessened, investment in the improvement of land already held increased, and loans provided much of the finance

However, prosperity and survival in the midst of a capitalist economy depended crucially on who exercised power through the State. What this entailed was not so much that a landlord class should itself exercise such power, only that the State apparatus should be prevented from falling under the control of social forces which might put ownership of large landed property on the political agenda of the nation.

II

The political objections of both conservatives and neoliberals to the State are well known, and stem historically from two main considerations. First, the view that the presence of a nation – based on Nature and embodying 'natural law' – precedes and in an important sense overrides the existence of a State.[25] And second, the fear that the State might at some point fall into plebeian hands (= 'pure democracy'), and be used by 'those below' to implement their economic programme.[26]

In many different contexts and conjunctures, therefore, these objections have underwritten struggles conducted by landlords and agrarian capitalists against poor peasants and workers (= 'the mob-in-the-streets'). The inference is that, whereas the nation is a constant, the State is not. From this, it could be

---

for both types of undertaking... As an aristocratic activity, this was nothing new in the nineteenth century. What was new was the number of families involved, and the scale of their activities' (original emphasis).

25   This is clear from the view expressed by Evola (2002: 127), who belonged to the Italian right, that the 'gap between the political idea of the State and the physical idea of "society" is found...in the opposition that exists between State and nation. The notions of nation, fatherland, and people...essentially belong to the naturalistic and biological plane and not the political one...'. In much the same vein, a member of the French right (Barrès, 1970b: 193) argued at the beginning of the twentieth century that '[n]o Frenchman would ever intend to meddle with the State. But the State that has suffered from the lack of a national consciousness would be mad to neglect that sense of its own identity which every one of our regions has preserved'. For a similar interpretation of the State/nation link held by another influential right-wing theorist, Carl Schmitt, see below.

26   In contrast to 'representative democracy', where voters in effect lose the capacity to control the person mandated the minute the vote is cast, the concept 'pure democracy' broadly speaking refers to a continuing ability on the part of those who mandate to exercise direct control over policy and political programmes. Unlike the mass of voters, individuals elected to represent them in a capitalist system can be and are either bought off or co-opted. This is especially true of the leadership of peasant movements, political parties that espouse parliamentary socialism or social democracy, and trade unions.

argued, stems the significance attached by conservatives both to the agrarian myth and to 'civil society', each of which ideologically validates as innate those identities linked to the nation, ones moreover that can be used to delegitimize and thus challenge those who currently exercise control of the State.[27]

'From above' Struggle Over the State

In an important sense, the structure of 'civil society' has always been of central political concern to those who control the State. This was true even of the mercantilist regime in eighteenth century England, the discourse of which is usually presented as focussed solely on external issues to do with economic rivalries in international trade.[28] Seemingly benign concepts such as the right

---

27   The concept of the nation as prefiguring the State, the latter taking its legal legitimacy from the former, underwrote much of the Catholic/nationalist/conservative theory developed during the 1920s and 1930s by Carl Schmitt about the political necessity of a strong State. Formulated as a reaction to working class mobilization during the 1919 German revolution, his view was that in law sovereignty derives ultimately not from what is written in the constitution but from whoever invokes a state of emergency – termed by him 'the state of exception' – when government is itself challenged 'from below' (Bendersky, 1983: 37). The argument that '(n)orms or laws cannot be sovereign because they cannot decide when a state of exception exists, nor how to counteract it' amounted to a legal justification of a rightwing *coup d'état* ('who rules is right') by a 'sovereign' – the monarch, president or a strong leader – to restore stability/order in the name of 'the people' and (thus) in the interests of the nation (Bendersky, 1983: 25, 58, 122, 224). Supported by a matrix of high-sounding but (when depoliticized) sociologically meaningless concepts – such as the 'friend-enemy' polarity (*freund und feind*) and the 'enemy within' (*staatsfeind*) – Schmitt conferred ideological legitimacy on the capture of State power in Germany during 1933 by the Nazi regime (Bendersky, 1983: 88, 90). Not only did Schmitt declare 'the one-party state to be the state of the twentieth century and...a step toward achieving the unity of the German people', therefore, but he also 'asserted that the *Führer* had the right, in momernts of extreme danger to the nation, to act as the supreme judge, distinguish friend from enemy, and take appropriate measures' (Bendersky, 1983: 204, 216). Significantly, all the legal arguments deployed by Schmitt to justify a *coup d'état* resulting in a strong State constitute a defence of what Trotsky (1975: 451 ff.) categorized as 'Bonapartism'.

28   On this point Furniss (1965: 3–4) notes that 'there is another side to Mercantilism; underlying its international doctrines is a vast body of theory and policy dealing with the domestic economy of the nation and designed as a basis upon which to erect the outstanding structure of foreign policy. This phase of Mercantilism [1660–1775] is of interest because it illustrates the reaction of nationalism upon the class relationships and the life conditions of the people within the nation. It deals primarily with the position of the labourer in the economic organization of the country: with the formation of his rights and duties; with a statement of principles which should govern his standard of living; and, to a smaller extent, with a discussion of how much his wages will, or ought to, be'.

to employment were combined with a requirement on the part of the State legally to enforce a 'duty to labour' on the 'indigent poor', the latter addressing directly the nature of 'civil society'.[29] During an era described by Marx as one of primitive accumulation, therefore, theories proclaiming the 'utility of poverty' to commerce plus legislation about the rural labour market and the necessity of labour were in effect already having an impact on the 'private' domain notionally beyond the purview of the State.[30] This political concern on the part of the ruling class increased as the category of the 'indigent poor' was transformed into a (potentially revolutionary) 'mob-in-the-streets'.

The fear of the revolutionary 'mob-in-the-streets' at the beginning of the nineteenth century was evident among English conservatives who were regarded as more 'moderate'. Even George Canning therefore, whose ideas were seen as prefiguring a politically more inclusive 'one nation' conservatism subsequently associated with Benjamin Disraeli, strongly opposed what he termed 'pure democracy'.[31] He not only delivered warnings against what would

---

29   For details of this, see Furniss (1965: 75 ff., 96 ff.) and Rubin (1979: 35 ff.).

30   '[D]uring the eighteenth century', observes Furniss (1965: 151–152), 'the Justice of the Peace began more and more to assume the position of local autocrat…Decrees frequently partook of the nature of ordinances or laws appertaining to matters of minor importance in the Justice's district. This assumption of legislative function by the Justices made it possible for them to interfere in the social life of the labouring classes, by decreeing that amusements of various kinds would be punished by them as nuisances. Behind these decrees is frequently to be seen the class opinions we have been examining: the belief, namely, that the poor of the country should be obliged to live a life of toil. The fair, the gathering at the alehouse, were denoted as nuisances and suppressed as such, not alone, nor principally, because they bred riot and disturbance but also because they appeared most obviously to relax the industry of the labouring body and entice the workingman away from the "drudgery to which he was born"'. On primitive accumulation in England, see Marx (1976: 873 ff.).

31   For the concept 'pure democracy', see Canning (1820: 21–22), who objected because it would 'sweep away every other branch of the constitution that might attempt to oppose or control it'. It is also clear that what he understood by 'the constitution' was not an accepted form of and set of precepts for government but rather the existing ruling class – the monarchy, church, and aristocratic landowners (Canning, 1820: 21, 32). Invoking the precedent whereby a popular assembly – 'when once that House of Commons should become a direct deputation, speaking the people's will, and that will the rule of Government' – abolished the monarchy during the 1640s Civil War, Canning (1820: 23–24) warned that 'pure democracy' would make it impossible for those with property to resist expropriation by those without ('But to presume to reject an act of the deputies of the whole nation! – by what assumption of right could three or four hundred great proprietors set themselves against the national will?').

happen were the State to come under the control of those who wished to challenge existing property rights, but also advocated and justified violence against agency designed to further this possibility.[32] In the view of Canning, 'pure democracy' would license, if not actually lead to, 'the abolition of property itself'.[33]

The same kind of objection to 'pure democracy', for much the same reasons, was advanced by conservatives over the latter half of the nineteenth century and in the early part of the twentieth. During the late nineteenth century, this argument was advanced in England by Sir Henry Sumner Maine, and in Germany by Albert Schäffle.[34] These conservatives questioned the efficacy of

---

32   Hence the fears listed by Canning (1820: 6–7) as those felt by the 'respectable' elements following the protests that culminated in the 1819 Peterloo massacre, when 'there was not a man of property who did not tremble for his possessions...there was not a man of retired and peaceable habits, who did not tremble for the tranquillity and security of his home... there was not a man of orderly and religious principles, who did not fear that these principles were about to be cut from under the feet of succeeding generations...'.

33   That 'pure democracy' would eventually lead to an attack on existing property rights, a situation that would result in their transformation, was a connection explicitly made by Canning at that conjuncture. 'I hold it frantic to suppose, that from the election of members of Parliament you can altogether exclude, by any contrivance, even if it were desirable to do so, the influence of property, rank, talents, family, connection, and whatever else in the Radical Language of the day is considered as intimidation or corruption', he (Canning, 1820: 28) accepted, 'unless you have found some expedient for disarming property of influence, without (what I hope we are not yet ripe for) the abolition of property itself'.

34   Sir Henry Sumner Maine (1822–88) was a conservative historian of jurisprudence, and Albert Schäffle (1831–1903) a political economist and conservative politician. Both were politically influential in their respective contexts. Although notionally supportive of 'popular government', the success of democracy in America was nevertheless attributed by Maine (1885: xi) to 'have arisen rather from skilfully applying the curb to popular impulses than from giving them the rein'. The United States is extolled much rather for its *laissez faire* and Social Darwinist policies (Maine, 1885: 50–52): 'The United States have justly been called the home of the disinherited of the earth... There could be no grosser delusion than to suppose this result to have been attained by democratic legislation. It has really been obtained through the sifting out of the strongest by natural selection... All this beneficent prosperity is the fruit of recognising the principle of population, and the one remedy for its excess in perpetual emigration. It all reposes on the sacredness of contract and the stability of private property, the first the implement, and the last the reward, of success in the universal competition. These however, are all the principles and institutions which the British friends of the "artisan" and "agricultural labourer" seem not a little inclined to treat as their ancestors did agricultural and industrial machinery. The American are still of opinion that more is to be got for human happiness by private energy

democracy on the grounds that citizenship required a level of competent knowledge about public affairs not only denied to but also unachievable by the voting masses. For them, 'popular government' and democracy opened the doors to socialism, which in their view heralded the irrational rule of 'the mob in the streets', the revolutionary agency of which threatened both property and the State.[35] Limits on democracy in the United States at that conjuncture were

---

than by public legislation'. Complaining that 'Social Democracy owes its political influence to the introduction of universal suffrage, to the now possible procession of the myriad battalions of labour to the ballot box', Schäffle (1892: xiii–xiv) warned that German socialism was 'working zealously to win for itself still greater power by the weapon of universal suffrage: it is carrying on a campaign now in the country districts, and has declared war more fiercely than ever against its chief competitor for power by universal suffrage, namely, the Catholic Church'. He continued (Schäffle, 1892: 126–127): 'I have desired to see a share of political life given to all adult and honest males. But I am also convinced that the political will of a nation needs yet other agents, and must be supplied with counter-poises; that a complete State-Organism can never result from the fluctuating decisions of the majority expressed through universal suffrage alone, and without being associated with any such efficient counterpoise; that the inevitable issue of disregarding this would be that most terrible and desolating of all despotisms, I mean mob-rule'.

35 According to Maine (1885: 24), in France '[t]he mob, which in 1848 overturned the government of the younger Bourbons...had also a leaning to Socialism; and the frightful popular insurrection of June 1848 was entirely Socialistic'. The 'mob' is further characterized (Maine, 1885: 24) as politically 'irreconcileable', in the sense of being composed of plebeians who 'refuse to submit their opinions to the arbitration of any government', which licenses in turn the categorization of such agency as beyond the law (= 'illegal'). Violent suppression by the military, at the behest of the State, of the 'mob' that is 'entirely Socialistic' is thus deemed legitimate. That fear of a 'from below' challenge to existing property relations, as a result of being able to rule via the State, was at the root of the conservative objection to 'popular government' is clear from the following: 'What is to be the nature of the legislation', asks Maine (1885: 44–45), 'by which the lot of the artisan and of the agricultural labourer is to be not merely altered for the better, but exchanged for whatever station and fortune they may think it possible to confer on themselves by their own supreme authority?'. He answers his own question thus (Maine, 1885: 45): '...the belief that government can indefinitely increase human happiness, undoubtedly suggests the opinion, that the stock of good things in the world is practically unlimited in quantity, that it is (so to speak) contained in a vast storehouse or granary, and that out of this it is now doled out in unequal shares and unfair portions... Yet nothing is more certain, than that the mental picture which enchains the enthusiasts for benevolent democratic government is altogether false, and that, if the mass of mankind were to make an attempt at redividing the common stock of good things, they would resemble, not a number of claimants insisting on the fair division of a fund, but a mutinous crew...'. His conclusion (Maine, 1885: 49) demonstrates a willingness – similar to that of neo-liberals

expressed by an advocate of *laissez faire*, William Graham Sumner, who similarly recognized that, as long as control of the State was determined by the
franchise, plebeian control of this apparatus would represent a potential threat
to property relations.[36]

During the 1920s much the same case was made in England by W.H. Mallock,
and in the USA by Walter Lippmann and Albert Jay Nock, also influential conservatives.[37] Just as for Canning the objection was generated by the proximity
of the 1789 French revolution, so for Mallock the same objection made a century later was a consequence of the 1917 Russian revolution, and the main target of his attack was accordingly Marxism.[38] A shift in the discourse of those
on the political right was hinted at in 1923 by Nock, who, in what seems at first
to be a progressive view and an apparent break with earlier conservative fears

---

currently – to countenance the use of coercion to drive 'a mutinous crew' – artisans and
agricultural labourers who dare challenge existing patterns of wealth, division of labour,
and political authority – back to work: 'No later than the end of the last century, large portions of the French peasantry ceased to cultivate their land, and large numbers of French
artisans declined to work, in despair at the vast requisitions of the Revolutionary
Government during the Reign of Terror; and, as might be expected, the penal law had to
be called in to compel their return to their ordinary occupations'.

36   According to William Graham Sumner (Fine, 1956: 86), therefore, 'a democratic state is in
more danger of...interfering with property rights than any other type of state because it is
so sure of itself and so ready to undertake anything. Rights, especially property rights, are
safe only when protected against the exercise of all arbitrary power'.

37   W.H. Mallock (1849–1923), Walter Lippmann (1889–1974) and Albert Jay Nock (1870–1945)
were all writers who gave voice to conservative views. For the objection to 'pure democracy', see Mallock (1924), and on his importance for conservative ideology, see O'Sullivan
(1975: 116–118) and Eccleshall, Geoghegan, Jay, and Wilford (1986: 103–104). In a similar
vein, Lippmann (1955: 34, 41) summarizes his earlier argument (Lippmann, 1922) thus:
'The Western liberal democracies are a declining power in human affairs. I argue that this
is due to a derangement of the functions of their governments which disables them in
coping with the mounting disorder. [...] The conundrum springs from the fact that while
The People as a corporate body are the true owners of the sovereign power, The people, as
an aggregate of voters, have diverse, conflicting self-centred interests and opinions. A plurality of them cannot be counted upon to represent the corporate nation'. Described as
'one of the founders of the renaissance of the political right in America [who provided] a
grounding for later developments in conservatism and libertarianism', Albert Jay Nock
(1991: xxiii, 272) lamented that the 'State was organized in this country [the USA] with
power to do all kinds of things *for* the people, and the people in their short-sighted stupidity, have been adding to that power ever since' (original emphasis).

38   As the example of Seldon (1990) indicates, Marxism remained a target of *laissez faire* conservative discourse even after the fall of the Berlin Wall and the collapse of the Soviet
Union.

about a revolutionary 'mob in the streets', condemns the 'primary function' of the State as being 'the economic exploitation of one class by another'.[39] Nevertheless, the real objection is to what those on the political right refer to as State control over monopolies and 'privileges' (taxation, franchises, tariffs, concessions): that is, the capacity to expropriate and then to redistribute the proceeds of capital accumulation.

In the case of England, it could be argued, this shift confirmed the fusion of populism and nationalism, a process that had been developing over the nineteenth century. By identifying the 'large, propertyless and dependent class' among the victims of the State, a spuriously inclusive discourse conveys the impression that the industrial bourgeoisie, smallholders and the rural working class are no different in a number of significant ways.[40] Each stands to lose in equal measure

---

39   See Nock (1991: 228). Invoking not just the Physiocrats but also Marx, he (Nock, 1991: 222 ff.) characterizes every known historical form of the State as an institution simply for 'economic exploitation'. 'There is no State of which we have a record', he (Nock, 1991: 223) maintains, 'that does not present the phenomenon of two distinct economic classes which have interests directly opposed; a relatively small, owning and exploiting class which lives by appropriating without compensation the labour-products of a relatively large, propertyless and dependent class'.

40   Publications in the Cobden and Free Trade series designed specifically to secure plebeian backing for *laissez faire* included Cobden Unwin [1904], a compilation of oral histories by agricultural workers who had the object of which was to persuade rural labour how much worse off it had been prior to the repeal of the Corn Laws. By ending protection and opening up the domestic market to capitalist competition and thus cheaper foreign grain imports, so the argument ran, the price of bread declined, leaving agricultural workers with more disposable income. Making this connection between *laissez faire* and higher standards of living in the countryside, advocates of free trade attributed low wages, starvation and poverty simply to a wish by landlords and gentry to prevent competition so as to maintain high prices for their agricultural commodities. That it was industrial capitalists who sought to increase the demand for their own output as a result of this populist appeal for plebeian support is clear (Cobden Unwin, 1904: 265, 273–274, original emphasis): '[F]rom the beginning of the French War until the repeal of the Corn Laws, a period of sixty years, this country was in a state of semi-siege. During the whole of that time an underfed people had to buy every article of clothing at the cost of further severe privation in feeding. Everything was bought at the expense of a hard sacrifice elsewhere. It is no wonder, then that the manufacturers of Manchester and Leeds found the home market inelastic, and that when, through improved machinery, they had cheapened the price of textiles, they were not recouped by increased sales. [...] The letters here published, numerous as they are, have been written by a very small portion of English men and women who remember the days of dear bread. To them...the ordinary feeling we associate with all age is reversed. *They* do not look back on their youth as a day of delight which

from State economic regulation and planning (= 'intervention').[41] Moreover, all are united by virtue of a common national identity, which the State in a fundamental sense can be said not to represent. At this conjuncture, therefore, the State apparatus was recast ideologically by those on the political right: as an institution that disadvantaged all in the nation but the very wealthiest.[42] This is a staple of populist discourse, the object of which is to mobilize plebeian support for a bourgeois economic programme based on a multi-class political alliance.

The reason for such an ideological shift is not difficult to discern. Once it became clear that attempts to prevent universal suffrage were going to fail, and that workers and peasants in Europe and elsewhere would indeed be able to

---

they recall with vain regret, but as an Egyptian bondage from which they have been delivered. And just such people are in every village in the land'.

41   The wish to expand the number of landholders – by converting agricultural labourers into tenants – without expropriation of existing property or State intervention emerges clearly in 1890s *laissez-faire* policy on smallholdings (Bear, 1893: 87): 'It is doubtful whether cheap land, either for sale or for letting, will ever be available under the Small Holdings Act, and people, in these times, are not disposed to pay high prices. Land desired by a County Council would be likely to go up in price suddenly, and the authority has no power of compulsory purchase at a valuation – very properly not, in my opinion. For my own part, I fail to see why men should be set up in business as landed proprietors with public funds, and at the risk of the ratepayers. It is highly desirable that small holdings should be available to industrious and thrifty farm-labourers, as stepping stones to a career which would satisfy their reasonable ambition, and thus check an excessive drain of the rural population towards the towns. But, as a rule, the chances of advancement are much greater for men of this class from hiring a holding of moderate size than from purchasing a smaller one'. The same text (Bear, 1893: 93) concludes by formulating policy recommendations along the same lines: 'That the coddling system of manufacturing peasant-proprietors by means of State Funds, and at risk of the ratepayers, is calculated to do a great deal more harm than good, besides being unfair to the ratepayers and to farmers who will be dispossessed of some of their land to make room for new comers'. In other words, by all means provide agricultural labourers with smallholdings, but not acquired on their behalf and paid for by the State.

42   Hence the remedies for the impact on agriculture of trade depression suggested by one exponent of *laissez faire* (Medley, 1885: 31–32) took the following form: 'What is wanted in land is Free Trade. The laws and customs which govern the tenure, devolution, and occupation of land in Great Britain have favoured and stimulated its accumulation in few hands, have conferred on ownership privileges, and exemptions, and powers by way of entail and settlement, which are inimicable to good cultivation, and opposed to the public interest... The community is interested in having the land cultivated so as to give the largest possible return to the capital and labour bestowed upon it; and one of the first steps to be taken is the passing of a measure which shall facilitate the breaking up of encumbered estates, and thus promote the establishment of cultivating ownership'.

vote into government those charged with representing their interests, conservatives were compelled to adopt new strategies in order to continue exercising political power to protect their economic interests.[43] One was a direct 'from above' form of agency: the imposition of a strong State, with or without a democratic mandate.[44] The other was an indirect form: to endorse populist ideology, an attempt to displace class antagonism and conflict by uniting capital and labour along national or ethnic lines.[45]

---

43 Universal suffrage was introduced throughout the twentieth century, especially after the wars of 1914–18 (Canada, USSR, Germany, Hungary, the UK and the USA) and 1939–45 (Italy, Japan, India).

44 The most obvious example being the fascist regimes that came to power in Europe and Asia during the 1920s and 1930s. Even after the defeat of fascism, many on the political right continued to justify their support for it in terms of a bulwark offered by a strong State against the 'chaos' of socialism or a democracy where the proletariat reigned supreme. A case in point is George Santayana, who – like Mallock and Lippmann (see above) – opposed 'pure democracy' on the grounds that 'democracy is power exercised by the proletariat for its own benefit', adding (Santayana, 1952: 348–349) that '"Proletariat" is an ugly modern word for an ugly thing [,a] vast crowd of exiles in their own country whom the lure of industrial wages and town amusements has uprooted from their villages'. During 1950 he justified his support for Italian fascism in the following words (Cory, 1955: 405): 'Of course, I was never a Fascist in the sense of belonging to that Italian party, or to any nationalistic or religious party. But considered…a product of the generative order of society, a nationalist or religious institution will probably have its good sides, and be better perhaps than the alternative that presents itself at some moment in some place. That is what I thought, and still think, Mussolini's dictatorship was for Italy in its home government. Compare with the disorderly socialism that preceded or the impotent party chaos that followed it…Dictatorships are surgical operations, but some diseases require them…'. It should be emphasised, however, that political theory justifying a strong State is neither specifically Prussian nor confined to the 1920s and 1930s, as confirmed by the following observation by a late nineteenth century English theorist (Maine, 1885: 20–21): 'I have now given shortly the actual history of popular government…I state the facts, as a matter neither for congratulation nor for lamentation, but simply as materials for opinion. It is manifest that, so far as they go, they do little to support the assumption that popular government has an indefinitely long future before it. Experience rather tends to show that it is characterised by great fragility…The convinced partisans of democracy care little for instances which show democratic government to be unstable. These are merely isolated triumphs of the principle of evil. But the conclusion of the sober student of history will not be of this kind. He will rather note it as a fact, to be considered in the most serious spirit, that *since the century during which the Roman Emperors were at the mercy of the Praetorian soldiery, there has been no such insecurity of government as the world has seen since rulers became delegates of the community*' (emphasis added).

45 These two forms – strong State and populism – are not of course mutually exclusive; indeed, as fascism attests, a populist discourse can generate the desire for and thus

Hence the attempts made periodically throughout Europe during the nineteenth century by radical liberals and/or conservatives either to maintain or to recruit political support among small farmers and the rural working class. This indirect strategy extended from popular texts published in France and England that sought to persuade agricultural workers as to the 'naturalness' of the market so that they might make common cause with the farmers who employed them, to the Radical Liberal programme in mid-1880s England which advocated what amounted to the extension of peasant economy in the midst of an advanced capitalist nation ('the object of all land reform must be the multiplication of landowners.').[46] The latter in particular marked a political change to

---

legitimize the imposition of a strong State. A strategic need for those on the political right to construct a populist discourse that does not engage with either class or economic issues has long been recognized by conservatives themselves. A case in point is Julius Evola (1898–1974), a fellow-traveller of Italian fascism whose reactionary views – denouncing modernity and advocating a return to ancient 'spiritual values' and hierarchy – have influenced the Italian 'new' right. In order to avoid criticisms from the left, therefore, Evola (2002: 114–115) maintained that it was necessary for those on the right – like himself – to adopt a 'general view of life and of the State that, being based on higher values and interests, definitely transcends the economic plane, and thus everything that can be defined in terms of economic classes'. He added that if 'things were set up in this way, by absolutely refusing to set foot in the field where the Left trains its aim on the *"faux target"*, its polemics would be rendered totally ineffective'. The significance of his concluding words (Evola, 2002: 231, original emphasis) on this subject is unambiguous: 'In the contemporary era it is absolutely important that *the struggle against a degenerate and arrogant Capitalism be waged from above* – in other words, that the State will be the one to assume the initiative of mercilessly fighting this phenomenon and restoring normal conditions, rather than leaving to the Left alone the right of accusation and protest (which then are used to justify subversive actions)'.

46   The popular texts in question were by Marcet (1833) and About (1872), each of which consisted of tracts about political economy aimed at rural workers, designed both to assuage them about laissez faire policies and to undermine support for a socialist programme. In the Radical Liberal programme of the 1880s, reprinted from *The Fortnightly Review* – which advocated 'Free Church, Free Schools, Free Land and Free Labour' – Chamberlain (1885: 9) observed that 'in some purely rural districts, where the condition of the agricultural labourers is worst, it will not be found impossible to run a working man's candidate, who *ex hypothesi*, will be hostile to the vested interests and privileges of landlordism, and, it is plain that even in the counties the chances of the Liberal party will have greatly improved'. The same text went on to note (Chamberlain, 1885: 54, original emphasis): 'It is well that, before relations between the owners and the occupiers of the soil, between proprietor and peasant, are fundamentally readjusted, arrears should be wiped off, but even thus we shall only have arrived at the threshold of the land question. *The object of all land reform must be the multiplication of landowners...it may not be*

the earlier position: the view that the plebeian masses lacked the necessary knowledge for citizenship became instead an acceptance of plebeian citizenship, but under a 'from above' political tutelage.[47]

III

Although it became more marked towards the end of the nineteenth century, this kind of 'from above' development – generating or reproducing grassroots support by means of a populist discourse – emerged before that conjuncture. It could be argued that the stock historical response by the political right to the growth both of a working class and of class consciousness has generally been a populist one, usually involving a call for a mutually reinforcing process of consolidation: national solidarity in the face of a 'foreign' threat combined with cultural reaffirmation.[48]

---

amiss to remind those who object to the multiplication of landowners as a revolutionary step, that its tendencies are distinctly Conservative. The greater the number of those who have an interest in the soil, the deeper will be the popular attachment to it. The conflict of interests will disappear; and our land system, instead of being, as it is now, the symbol of strife – the embodiment of the privileges of the few as opposed to the rights and aspirations of the many – will become a guarantee of class concord and harmony'.

47 This form of conditional access – having a voice in a bourgeois democracy – is recognized in terms such as the 'engineering of consent', and 'manufacturing consent'; or, in Marxist theory, as generating 'false consciousness. The shift in conservative thinking – a coming to terms with the inevitability of 'popular government', but at the same time a desire to place limits on its exercise by 'those below' – is evident, for example, from an initial fear of populist rhetoric ('the Wire-puller'), associated with the power of the 'mob in the streets'. Its potential impact is described by Maine (1885: 30, 32–33) in the following words: 'There is no doubt that, in popular governments resting on a wide suffrage...the leader, whether or not he be cunning, or eloquent, or well provided with commonplaces, will be the Wire-puller. [...] It is through this great natural tendency to take sides that the Wire-puller works. Without it he would be powerless. His business is to fan its flame; to keep it constantly acting upon the man who has once declared himself a partisan; to make escape from it difficult and distasteful...extensions of suffrage, though no longer believed to be good in themselves, have now a permanent place in the armoury of parties, and are sure to be a favourite weapon of the Wire-puller'. Subsequently, however, conservatives saw no reason why they should not themselves take on the role of 'Wire-puller' and utilize this in order to generate plebeian support for their own discourse (nationalism, 'popular' capitalism).

48 The term 'cultural reaffirmation' is preferred to the more usual designation of 'cultural renewal'. The latter involves merely the ideological privileging of cultural identity and discourse in the self-perception of the nation, whereas the former by contrast stipulates

The Most Pardonable Usurpation

Initially, a populist cultural reaffirmation took the form of the Romantic reaction against capitalist development, and the way secularization/urbanization/massification not only undermined the tension-free arcadia that those at the top of the agrarian hierarchy imagined rural society to be, but also generated the radicalization that would usher in socialism. At the centre of this populist discourse was peasant economy, the desirability and viability of which is the subject of a large and important historical debate that has been around since the process of industrialization began.

This populist reaction, which gathered strength as a response by the ancient regime to Enlightenment values/processes and the 1789 French Revolution, structured the rise in Europe of a politically organized conservatism. Its object, to limit the challenge to its economic base, required not just that substantial proprietors mobilize in their own defence but also that they enlist plebeian support in rural areas. Of especial concern to the different components of a European landowning class was a two-stage process. First, the loss of control over their tenants, peasants who would become workers in factories and members of the urban proletariat (that is, the dreaded 'mob in the city'), and second, the subsequent capture by organized labour of the State, which would then be used legislatively to alter property relations in town and countryside alike. This is at the root of the dilemma informing conservative policy on the State.

Although opposed to economic intervention by the State, therefore, conservatives and reactionaries nevertheless recognized that its economic policies required a strong State to enforce them.[49] Hence the apparent ideological contradiction between a simultaneous opposition to yet endorsement of a strong State is a non-existent one, explained ultimately by which class is in control of this apparatus. This twofold and seemingly antinomic role of the State is a consistent and enduring aspect of conservative economic theory from the 1789 French revolution onwards. It is central to the ideas not just of Nassau Senior in the nineteenth century, but also of the political right and of neoliberal economists in the twentieth.[50]

---

    that this culture shall be of a specific kind: emblematic of a traditional and long-standing form of ethnic or national selfhood.

49   Hence the observation (Harris, 1978a: 223): 'There is much misunderstanding...of the classical conception of *laissez-faire*. It may therefore require emphasis that the theory and practice of liberal market economy always envisaged an indispensable role for government'.

50   A bourgeois economist whose defence of capitalism was based on the claim that accumulation was the outcome of 'abstinence' and not surplus extraction, Nassau Senior was

This concern about the impact on the market of regulation conducted in the interests of the working class in control of State is evident in the objections advanced by the economist Nassau Senior to the effects of the 1789 revolution in France.[51] A fear of the kind of power a revolutionary Parisian 'mob-in-the-streets' (= 'the low revolutionary populace') would exercise by virtue of its control over the State apparatus was for him a paramount consideration.[52] His opposition to factory legislation in nineteenth century Britain provided him with an insight to and an understanding of the political role of the State in the economy. Those who controlled the State possessed the capacity not just to regulate the market, but also potentially the ability to expropriate property and redistribute wealth, was it ever to fall under the sway of rural and urban workers.

---

much criticized by Marxists. See, for example, Marx (1971: 30, 353, 506; 1976: 333–334, 613–614, 744 ff.), who described him as 'a mere apologist of the existing order...who opposes the shortening of the working day'. Also Rubin (1979: 320–325), for whom Nassau Senior was 'what one might call the economic barrister of the English factory owners, who found him a faithful assistant in their bitter fight against factory legislation'. Writing in 1842, Nassau Senior (1863: 90) dismissed the opinion that 'the duty of government [is] to regulate production, and promote an equivalent consumption [and that] the minister of commerce ought to direct, by perpetual course of regulations founded on accurate statistical facts, all the proceedings of agriculture and manufactures'. Such views, he concluded approvingly (Senior, 1863: 92), 'explain Bonaparte's contempt'.

51   His words (Senior, 1863: 7) are as follows: '...there was no standard of value. To use, or even possess, metallic money, was a capital crime, and the only legal tender, the assignat, sank to about one four-hundredth part of its nominal value. The seller of a commodity was no longer allowed to fix its price: the price was to be determined by a committee, with reference solely to the ability of purchasers, whether the dealer could afford to sell at that price or not. To discontinue, or even to diminish, any accustomed trade, was to incur the crime of being "suspected"; and to be suspected was to be imprisoned; to be imprisoned was at one period to be massacred, and at another to be guillotined'.

52   For evidence of this fear, see Senior (1863: 131, 150): 'The Parisian populace had the love of tumult and the hatred of authority which belongs to the lowest classes in all great capitals, and the indifference to human life, the readiness to take it and risk it, which is peculiar to the mob of Paris'. Hence the dismissal of the mass support for Robespierre (Senior, 1863: 38, 48): 'His desire of immediate applause led him to flatter the self-love of the Parisian mob, by an adulation of which no man with self-respect could have been guilty; to encourage all their most mischievous prejudices, and to stimulate all their worst passions. In any ordinary State of society such conduct would have been fatal to his prospects as a Statesman; but in a revolution, it gave him unbounded popularity, and popularity was power. [...] Experience has proved the mischiefs and the dangers, both to rulers and to subjects, of what has been called revolutionary government; that is to say, government by a single assembly representing the omnipotence of the people, and exercising or delegating to its own instruments all legislative and executive powers'.

As is clear from what Nassau Senior wrote in the mid-nineteenth century, where democracy results in a 'from below' challenge to existing property relations owners of means of production are justified in resorting to anti-democratic agency and/or discourse, a transformation whereby the State under plebeian control is declared illegitimate, and equated with lawlessness.[53] Legislation enacted by or on behalf of a revolutionary State apparatus under plebeian control is thus deemed to be beyond the law, and attempts to transform property relations or redistribute wealth are in his discourse linked to not just to economic chaos but also to political unaccountability.[54] When this occurs, Manchester liberals no less than reactionaries see virtue in the adoption of anti-democratic (= counter-revolutionary) measures by a strong State – in the words of Nassau Senior 'the most pardonable usurpation that history records' – dedicated to the defence of existing property relations in the name of the nation itself.[55]

Their Whole Emotional Being

Ironically, populist discourse enables conservatives and neoliberals to avoid this 'most pardonable usurpation' whilst simultaneously making the State

---

53   On this Senior (1863: 63) observes: 'Some branches of the legal profession may flourish under a despot...An army or a mob may give power to its chief; but that power cannot be safe until it is supported by legal forms, enforced by legal authorities'.

54   In ideological terms, this discourse licenses a relay in statement whereby all aspects of bourgeois rule are declared 'natural' (bourgeois State + bourgeois economic theory = political and economic wellbeing). On this point see Senior (1863: 49, 52), who observes that in France the 1795 constitution 'provided against the most obvious of the disorders under which the previous governments had fallen. It provided against the dangers of universal suffrage by establishing indirect election... In a country in which the law had been powerless for nearly two years – in which property had been a ground for proscription – in which legal currency had been in a course of daily depreciation, while death was the punishment of those who ventured to refuse it, or even to take it at less than nominal value...the relations of individuals towards one another, and towards the property which had escaped confiscation, required to be ascertained'. For Senior (1863: 53), therefore, the State controlled by plebeians and representing their interests necessarily corresponds to 'a community unsupported by religion, delicacy or morality – in which virtues had so often been declared to be criminal, and crimes to be virtuous, that public opinion had been destroyed...in short, all the misery is exhibited of a society in which mere law is the only restraint'.

55   Hence the view (Senior, 1863: 58, 60) that '[t]he revolution which placed Bonaparte on the consular throne was unquestionably beneficial. The despotism which seems to be the inevitable result of military rule, was more tolerable than that of factions which owed to treason their rise and fall. Even the tyranny of the empire was as great an improvement on

strong. Nowhere is this more the case than in times of inter-imperial struggle, when the political right has been able to mobilize plebeian support for defence of the nation, in the course of which identities linked to property and class are overridden and thus suppressed. Of significance, therefore, is the fact that central to this populist discourse has been – and is – the elision of 'citizenship' with a concept of nationhood, a conflation which underlines their mutual interdependence.[56]

Nationalist ideology, as is well known, was particularly marked among the European working class in the period before the 1914–18 war, when conservatives stressed the link between 'citizenship' and national identity.[57] Rather

---

the intrigues and violence of the Directory, as the Directory was on the anarchy of the Convention'. The reference to treason in the latter quote is most significant, in that it demonstrates how the nation and nationalist sentiments are mobilized against those who challenge property rights.

56   In his theory tracing the emergence of the State, Johann Kaspar Bluntschli (1885: Ch, XIV) maintained that the transformation of 'being' into 'belonging' corresponded also to a process whereby a 'people' became a nation and acquired equated 'citizenship'. The characteristics associated with 'citizenship' – 'the citizen body is felt to be a united and homogeneous class...the guardian of civic freedom, and of the equality of all before the law' – developed historically in the medieval town ('young and pushing societies of free citizens'), but significantly these were also available to 'free cultivators' or 'free peasants' who had escaped servitude or never been unfree. Although this late nineteenth century interpretation of 'being'/'belonging' derived from and was applied by Bluntschli to European (and principally German) history, it has influenced rightwing concepts of nationhood in Germany and India during the twentieth.

57   A symptomatic utterance in this regard is that made by a member of the British ruling class (Roberts, 1912: viii–ix, 14–15) just before the start of the 1914–18 war: 'It is also for my countrymen to decide upon a far mightier issue; for this self-governed, free, and democratic State of England is for all its citizens to assert whether, in this matter of war and preparedness for war... I appeal above all to the young men of this nation, to our young men of every rank and social status, to young men of every trade and profession and calling of any kind... It is they, in a word, who now are England. [...] Much has been said recently of the rights and the power of the workers of this nation. We all, I hope, belong to that class – workers – but the artisan class of the nation has been urged – and to you, the working men of Manchester, I now specifically address myself – you have been urged, I say, to refuse to do your duties in war until your rights in peace are granted. Gentlemen, I say to you, that is not the policy either of Britishers or of men. I will go further: I say to you that it is not by declining or shirking duty that you will extend your rights. He who diminishes the power and vital resources of Great Britain diminishes the power and vital resources of every Britisher. How can you most easily and most securely better yourselves as Britishers – as working men? By making England better, by making it better worth your while to be a citizen of, and a worker in that nation!...I say to you, therefore, assert your

obviously, 'citizenship' is a form of belonging that privileges nationalism, an important political consequence of which is the relative ease with which those on the political right have been able to generate support not just from among workers and peasants of a particular national (or ethnic) identity but also – and ironically from some on the political left.[58] This is as true of newly formed national units that emerge from conquest or decolonization, and what might be termed peasant nations within the nation (such as the Mayas in the Mexican state of Chiapas – see Chapter 1), as it is of social formations long constituted as nations. Underlying the populist discourse in each case is the view that 'we-are-all-the-same', a form of belonging which – when hitched to being (undifferentiated) 'citizens' of a particular nation – avoids (forbids, even)

rights as Britishers by demanding the greatest, the highest of all civic and of all national rights – the right to be taught to defend your country – the right, that is, to defend your own honour as Britons and your liberties as citizens of this Empire. Thus, and thus only, shall you be worthy of that Empire's great past and of the dignity which that past confers upon every man of you, whatever your position in life may be'.

58   This is evident, for example, from the way in which the same Lord Roberts appealed to working class patriotism and invoked the views of socialists when urging the adoption of measures to counter German military strength during 1912. He cites (Roberts, 1912: 4–5, note 1) with approval the chauvinistic words of H.M. Hyndman ('Are the English people mere children thus to be fed on the pap of fatuous pacificism [*sic*]...at one of the most serious crises in the history of our race'.). The impact of this trend at that conjuncture, and especially the way in which nation and State were fused ideologically, was described by another socialist, Belfort Bax (1967: 195–196): 'One of the most striking phenomena of social change in the present generation, the counterpart of the rise and domination of Imperialism in politics, is the installation of imperialistic or patriotic sentiment... This was noticeable enough before the war, but the war, of course, has thrown it into strongest possible relief. In how many thousands of those who have volunteered for the front do we not find the ideal object for which they are prepared to sacrifice themselves to be England or the British Empire. And yet how many of those who profess, and sincerely profess, attachment to England as their ideal object, if they thought a little, would not have to admit that there is much in England, politically, socially, and morally, of which they disapprove! Yet this does not prevent the ideal of nationality from dominating their whole emotional being. [...] For the religion of Patriotism, the national or Imperial State is the *ultima ratio*. It does not recognize any organism or collectivity as object of conduct higher than the State. Humanity is for it a mere phrase. The solidarity, moreover, of those scattered through many existing States, holding like views and like aspirations, never suggests itself to it as perhaps an intrinsically higher object of conduct than any existing State... The only alternative to this erection of imperialistic jingo sentiment, under the name of Patriotism, into a religion, is Socialism'.

reference to class distinctions arising from ownership of property within such national contexts.[59]

An 'Arbitrary Altering of Rewards'

Towards the end of the nineteenth century, exponents of *laissez faire* theory in the United States declared illegitimate any attempt by the State to regulate wages, and equated the receipt by a worker of 'a living wage' with communism.[60] In keeping with this, much of the theory emanating from the political right in the twentieth century, and especially from the mid-1940s onwards, characterizes the State as a source of a new form of unfreedom.[61] Writing towards the end of World War II, neoliberals such as von Mises and H.B. Acton equated State power with fascism, and classified them both as 'totalitarianism', thereby delegitimizing State planning/control and simultaneously licensing the conflation of socialism with fascism that informed subsequent Cold War discourse.[62] Hayek acknowledged the fact that the State did have an economic role, but simply to see that accumulation proceeded smoothly. To some degree, this anticipates and confirms the 'strong State' argument – that the role of the

---

59   This was the sentiment deployed by Lord Roberts (1912: 39–40) in his reply to the interna-
      tionalism of his socialist critics. Democracy, he claimed, meant that plebeian elements
      had replaced the landowning class as rulers of the nation, and as such must now shoulder
      the traditional historical obligation of defending their country. In his words, '[t]he asser-
      tion advanced by Mr Blatchford in criticizing my Manchester speech, that the working
      men of Great Britain will never hear of compulsory [military] service because they dis-
      trust the ruling classes, rests upon a misconception... I shall only observe in this place that
      in a democratic nation the working classes are themselves the ruling classes, and that the
      interests of England and of the Empire are their interests... In former times, when the
      ruling classes of this nation consisted in the very deed of the men of birth and property,
      that class considered it as its sacred right and inalienable privilege to serve the nation in
      war. Now, in the twentieth century, when the working men of this country have by the
      gradual extension of the franchise succeeded to the political influence and supremacy of
      the old aristocratic class, is it too much to hope that, as their condition of life improves,
      they will seek in the same spirit to secure that right and the inalienable privilege – service
      in war? For such service is the only mark of the true and perfect citizenship'.
60   Hence the following view (Fine, 1956: 60) advanced by *laissez faire* theorists in the United
      States: 'The idea that the worker should be paid a living wage, rather than the market
      wage as determined by the laws of the universe, is pure and simple communism...'.
61   This was a trend highlighted in titles such as *The Servile State*, *The Road to Serfdom* and
      1985 – An Escape from Orwell's 1985: A Conservative Path to Freedom, books by, respectively,
      Belloc (1913), Hayek (1944) and Boyson (1975).
62   See von Mises (1945) and the debate between the contributors to Dickinson, Acton,
      Smith, Polanyi and Worswick (1948).

State is not merely accepted by exponents of a *laissez-faire* and conservative political economy, but regarded by them as a necessary aspect of capitalist development and reproduction.

As before, the fear of conservatives was that, once under the control of the working class, the strong (or 'totalitarian') State would through the process of regulation and planning increasingly diminish the ability of capital to maintain, let alone enhance, the profitability on which the accumulation process depended.[63] At stake for conservatives was nothing less than the reproduction of the capitalist system itself.[64] Throughout the 1950s, the 1960s and 1970s, neoliberal political economy contained veiled threats that, was the State to continue with Keynesian demand management policy in order both to solve unemployment and to redistribute income from rich to poor, the resulting economic instability would trigger non-democratic political solutions.[65] Calls for

---

63   For an expression of this conservative fear, see Hutton (1960: 99), who complains: 'Too much State activity, too rapidly, means too much State spending. Too much State spending too fast means a rapid multiplication of State controls to stop private spending: that is, restrictions on production and consumption *plus* higher taxes' (original emphasis). The same source continues (Hutton, 1960: 101): 'In the mythology of the [European] Left... inflation as a policy is treated as a way of expropriating "the capitalists", as well as a way of securing perpetual "full employment" and economic growth by forced savings. Higher taxation of these same capitalists (mainly companies) is then made to yield – among other things – enough to recompense pensioners and other "reputable" receivers of fixed money incomes (e.g., small savers) for the inevitable loss of their purchasing power year by year'. The same point had been made a decade earlier, by Hayek (1967: 270 ff.).

64   Since concern about the future of capitalism in the post-war world centred on the advance of socialism, the latter became the target of this neoliberal counter-attack (Hartwell, 1995: 10, 15). This was effected by means of right-wing think-tanks like the Mont Pelerin Society, which included Hayek and Röpke amongst its membership. Founded in the late 1940s, its task was specifically one of 'discrediting socialism' (Hartwell, 1995: xii, xv). Opposed not just to socialism but also to planning and State intervention, its official history (Hartwell, 1995: xiv) boasts that '[i]t was thirty years before the intellectual tide turned against socialism, and in that period the [Mont Pelerin] Society played an important role in eroding its intellectual foundations'.

65   de Jouvenel (1951), Röpke (1960) and Hutton (1960) – exponents of *laissez faire* linked to neoliberal organizations such as the Institute of Economic Affairs and the Mont Pelerin Society – all attacked the role of the State in fostering income redistribution through taxation and inflation. This was attributed (Hutton, 1960: 51) in turn to the privileged access to the State on the part of organized labour, a result of which was that '[t]herewith came acute bitterness, a sense of inequity and injustice, envy, and much hostility. Therewith, too, came the arbitrary altering of rewards, "differentials" of different trade unions and their members, and social and industrial unrest'. The conclusion was unmistakable: 'Thus within British democracy social tensions and political fissures were developed by

freedom and democracy notwithstanding, it is clear that in order to defend capitalist property and protect capitalist profits – not to say ultimately capitalism itself – those on the political right were prepared to abandon both the former and promote a strong State.[66]

The irony is that, where labour is concerned, unfreedom has been imposed (or re-imposed) not by States under the control or representing the interests of workers – as those on the political right claimed – but rather by States implementing neoliberal programmes and policies. Thus debt peonage and unfree migrant labour has continued to flourish in the agribusiness enterprises of the United States and Latin America, bonded labour in Indian agriculture, and the gangmaster system in many rural economic activities throughout England: all national contexts where *de facto* neoliberal policies are being implemented.[67] In other words, contrary to what the political right insisted would be the case, the curtailment of freedom – and consequently the proliferation of contemporary forms of unfree labour – is the result not of State socialism (where the market has been regulated or eliminated) but rather of the untrammelled market enforced by a capitalist State.

In the name both of *laissez faire* and of restoring what they take to be 'a natural balance', therefore, those on the political right do approve of one particular kind of intervention by the State: that is, *agency designed to reverse earlier gains made by workers and poor peasants*.[68] This is consistent with the view expressed by one prominent Thatcherite in the late 1970s, that '[i]t is not freedom that Conservatives want: what they want is the sort of freedom that will maintain existing inequalities or restore lost ones, so far as political action can do this'.[69] For the contemporary right, therefore, having given the advantage in the class struggle to capital, the State should then give way to

---

inflation akin to those created in the ancient world and in other modern countries: tensions and fissures capable of undoing democratic society itself'.

66   Hence the admission (Hutton, 1960: 132) that 'the modern world in any case does not seem to have much time or much room for democracy, representative government or a free society'. This implicit threat was repeated subsequently by Hayek (1973), Salomon (1983), and the contributors to Harris (1978b).

67   For details and discussion of these instances, see Brass (1999; 2010, 2011).

68   This was the position taken by William Graham Sumner, the principal exponent of *laissez faire* in the period following the American Civil War, of whom Fine (1956: 88) notes that 'in actuality the only type of [State] interference he approved was that designed to undo the work of past reformers and to throw man back upon nature'.

69   The view was that of Cowling (1978: 9), expressed in a collection of essays marking the rise to power on the UK political right of Margaret Thatcher.

'civil society', ensuring that workers remain at a disadvantage.[70] This would be because workers on the one hand no longer had access to State inputs/benefits, and on the other were deprived of the opportunity to influence policy, regain lost ground and – ultimately – capture the State itself.

IV

An important and enduring weapon in the ideological armoury of a ruling class in many different contexts and periods has been the capacity to choose to be 'other', or to have an identity 'different' from that which history confers, both on its own followers/supporters and on those to whom it is opposed.[71] This ideological defence, in which a fear of history leads to and combines with an invocation of 'choice', has at times entailed the mobilization by the class in question of a discourse about Nature and 'the natural', and the application of the latter both to itself and also to the category or class threatening its own

---

70   It is clear that enthusiasts of *laissez faire* policy see 'civil society' as both outside the State and simultaneously an alternative to it, in terms of a 'natural' form of 'voluntary' resource provision that is 'non-political'. Advocating a return to the kinds of 'assistance' extended to the poor in the nineteenth century, neoliberals such as Gray (1992) and Green (1993; 1996) identify 'civil society' as a desirable source of 'welfare without politics', a concept associated with the dubious rubric of 'non-political community'. In this way, not only can individuals in a local community be said to be exercising 'choice' about whether or not to provide less well-off members with subsistence provision, but also – and more significantly from the view of a *laissez faire* approach – how much. The latter can thus be achieved without drawing on State revenues, thereby avoiding the necessity of either taxing or expropriating property belonging to the rich.

71   It could be argued that existentialist claims about 'choice' validated not only the choice-making subject of neo-classical economics but also and subsequently the anti-Enlightenment/anti-foundational framework which underlay the relativistic identity politics of postmodernism. This was perhaps one of the reasons why both existentialism and post-modernism ended up unwittingly occupying the same epistemological ground as conservatism. As pointed out at the time by those on the political right, existentialism was for them a central theoretical emplacement of their own ideology. Jacques Maritain, for example, attempted to claw back from Sartre what he regarded as a Thomist concept of existentialism that legitimized and reasserted the anti-rationalistic act of Christian choice as an method of denying/defying what for those on the right were the unpalatable lessons taught by an historical process unfriendly to his/their cause. Hence the observation (Maritain, 1957: 11–12) that '[a] Thomist who speaks of St. Thomas's existentialism is merely reclaiming his own, recapturing from present-day fashion an article whose worth that fashion itself is unaware of'.

power.[72] It is often forgotten, therefore, that such claims deployed 'from above' about cultural 'difference'/'otherness' refer not just to those who rule but also to those who are ruled, and that the recipients of this act of labelling have usually been peasants. For this reason, claims about the innate 'difference'/'otherness' of what was regarded as an undifferentiated peasantry have been – and remain – central not just to nationalism, to opposition by conservative philosophy to Enlightenment discourse, but also the ideology of the far right.[73] Moreover, such claims can be traced through a common discourse about the agrarian myth shared by the political right in many global contexts.

---

72   The historical potency of a discourse about Nature, and its role in the ideological armoury of any ruling class engaged in struggle with 'those below' is well-known, and was outlined most succinctly in the late 1920s by Vološinov (1976: 11): 'Whenever…a social class finds itself in a state of disintegration and is compelled to retreat from the arena of history, its ideology begins insistently to harp on one theme, which it repeats in every possible variation: *Man is above all an animal.* …The ideology of periods such as these shifts its center of gravity onto the isolated biological organism; the three basic events in the life of all animals – birth, copulation, and death – begin to compete with historical events in terms of ideological significance and, as it were, become a surrogate history. That which in man is nonsocial and nonhistorical is abstracted and advanced to the position of the ultimate measure and criterion for all that is social and historical. It is almost as if people of such periods desire to leave the atmosphere of history, which has become too cold and comfortless, and take refuge in the organic warmth of the animal side of life. That is what happened during the period of the break-up of the Greek city states, during the decline of the Roman Empire, during the period of disintegration of the feudal-aristocratic order before the French Revolution. The motif of the *supreme power and wisdom of Nature* (above all, of man's nature – his biological drives) and of the impotence of history with its much ado about nothing – this motif equally resounds, despite differences of nuance and variety of emotional register, in such phenomena as epicureanism, stoicism, the literature of the Roman decadence (e.g. Petronius's *Satyricon*), the skeptical ratiocination of the French aristocrats in the seventeenth and early eighteenth centuries. *A fear of history, a shift in orientation toward the values of the personal, private life, the primacy of the biological and the sexual in man* – such are the features common to all of these ideological phenomena' (original emphasis).

73   The absurdities arising from this idealization of agrarian custom/practice/tradition can be illustrated from the case of 1930s Germany, where the Nazis presented traditional peasant costume from Bavaria to workers in Northern industrial cities as part of their common national identity, the extent of the cultural gap (and corresponding distinctiveness) between their respective urban/rural backgrounds notwithstanding (Jell-Bahlsen, 1985: 318). The same source concludes that this 'abstraction of "cultural unity" in the shape of folklore aided the Nazi regime in imposing a contrived unity from above onto the people below'.

Pro-peasant European Conservatism

The aristocratic variant of the agrarian myth projecting seigniorial attitudes/values operates even in advanced metropolitan capitalist contexts, where it forms an important ideological component of historical/contemporary conservative discourse that is supportive of smallholding agriculture. In the case of England, for example, early twentieth century imperialist discourse warning against the demise of empire, patriotism and the nation itself attributed this to the economic decline of the small farmer (= the military backbone of nation, colonies and imperial possessions) and a correspondingly inexorable process of rural exodus, urbanization and industrialization.[74]

Not only is this discourse anti-semitic, condemning finance capital (= 'a plutocratic caste') for undermining empire/nation/agriculture, but the traditional landlord class is designated the true defender of the small farmer (and, by inference, the nation itself), the conclusion being that agriculture – both at home and in the colonies – should be encouraged/protected.[75] Significantly, at

---

74 Hence the symptomatic nature of the discourse encountered in White (1901: 95 ff., 101 ff., 256, 312–313), who not only attributes military setbacks in the Boer war to the fact that British soldiers defeated by South African farmers were recruited in towns and cities, but also equates village depopulation and urbanization/industrialization in England with national decline, invokes as ideals both the Russian *mir* and French peasant society ('France is firmly set among the nations by her peasant proprietary'), and concludes on an undeniably fascistic programmatic note ('restore responsibility, enforce it on high and low...[p]atriotism will be taught in our schools, and the gospel of Efficiency will be our national cry').

75 The anti-semitic nature of this discourse is unmistakeable, 'alien'/'foreign'/'materialistic' Jews being identified as a 'cosmopolitan plutocracy' which threatens empire, nation and small farmer alike (White, 1901: 69–70, 74): 'The great and prosperous Jewish nation...is a caste [that] devotes itself mainly to finance...[this] plutocratic caste is a growing menace to our Imperial position. Many of these gentlemen have no roots in the land. They inhabit town houses, and, if they own a place in the country, it is for display. Their investments being mobile, they themselves are cosmopolitan. The influence they bring to bear upon Governments is noxious, because the British Foreign office learns to recognize the interests of rich men as those which alone require attention. Thus it comes to pass that the interests of the rich and the poor are by no means always identical, and the diplomatic, naval, and military forces of the Crown are utilized in the interests of the plutocratic caste – a proceeding which may, and sometimes does, injure the bulk of the people of England. The material side of life is emphasized, the soul of the nation is shrivelled as the fronds of a filmy fern when exposed to the fumes of an acid'. By contrast, the same discourse (White, 1901: 67–68, 74) presents 'authentic' English landlordism in a rather more positive light, as the source of a 'real aristocracy' rooted not in money but in tradition/land/nation, members of which are both the first line of defence against finance capital

the same conjuncture much the same kind of argument structured the plebeian variant of the agrarian myth in the United States of America, where agrarian populists argued that, by proletarianizing yeoman farmers and transforming them into their 'other' (= the 'mob in the streets') finance capital would destroy not only the peasantry (= warriors) which protected its own class power by defending the latter against the proletariat but also and thereby the nation itself.[76]

Discourse about an undifferentiated/a-historical peasantry also circulated in both the aristocratic and the plebeian variants of the agrarian myth in Germany. Thus, for example, the eighteenth century defence of rural tradition and hierarchy against the Enlightenment (*aufklarung*) undertaken by the conservative theoretician Justus Möser did not prevent him from admiring what he regarded as the cultural 'otherness'/'difference' of peasant society, a golden age version of which in his view constituted the authentic and timeless embodiment of German national identity.[77]

---

and also benign protectors of the small farmer: 'The owners of great estates are in a better position to contribute to the welfare of the residents than are the smaller proprietors. They help tenants at a pinch, and assist them to tide over bad times. As a rule, they have more capital than the small owners. They expend it on a system that becomes a family tradition. There is more economy of labour and material. Profit is little, and occasionally, no consideration whatever to the owner of the great estate... The system of land tenure and of primogeniture which have allowed the great estates to descend unimpaired from one generation to another...secures to those dwelling on the soil material and moral advantages greater than any that are promised under any alternative system, and it enables the heads of great families to take part in public affairs without the imputation of interfering in politics for what they can get out of it. To the real aristocracy of the country I look for a remedy for the disease with which our nation has been infected by bad smart society [= the 'plutocratic caste']'.

76   On this point, see Brass (2000a: 255–256).

77   For the details about Justus Möser (1720–1794) see Epstein (1966: Ch. 6). Noting the prefiguring influence of Möser's views on German conservatives such as Adam Müller and Novalis, Epstein (1966: 324, 325) observes that his 'admiration for a society of peasants... has a Jeffersonian flavour; it did not, however, imply any bias towards egalitarianism. On the contrary, Möser explicitly favoured a hierarchic order of society where everybody knew and kept his place...Möser admired a society marked by a great diversity of status, where everybody was content to perform his traditional function for the common good. He looked upon inequality as a positive good, not a necessary evil...'. On the question of a golden age, self-sufficient peasantry as the authentic representatives of German national identity, Möser (cited in Epstein, 1966: 329) observed: 'Where do we find the true German nation? We certainly do not find it at the court of the princes. Our cities today are filled with misshapen and spoiled copies of humanity; ...our countryside with exploited

Much the same is true of twentieth century Germany, where Richard Walther Darré, the Nazi Minister of Agriculture, invoked what he claimed was an unbroken ancient rural lineage – composed of an unchanging/homogeneous peasantry (= a mythical ancestral being closer to Nature, and thus 'more natural') – as evidence for the existence of a pristine nationalism, in terms which were no different from those used by Möser some two hundred years earlier.[78] Such pro-peasant views, moreover, are not of themselves incompatible with a view of Nazism as a form of reactionary modernism bent on carrying through a project of capitalist development and industrialization. Accordingly, those linked to the Nazis who espoused pro-peasant ideology perceived no incompatibility between such views on the one hand, and capitalist development and industrialization on the other.[79] And even where such a specifically

---

peasants. How different was our nation [in the early Middle Ages], when every Franconian or Saxon peasant cultivated and defended in his own person his *paterna rura*, that is his hereditary allodial lands, free of feudal ties or manorial obligations; and when every freeholder went from his homestead to participate in the work of a popular assembly'.

78 Darré's words (cited in Mosse, 1966: 148–150) are as follows: 'First there was the German peasantry in Germany before what is today served up as German history. Neither princes, nor the Church, nor the cities have created the German man. Rather the German man emerged from the German peasantry. Everywhere one will find primordial peasant customs that reach far back into the past. Everywhere there is evidence that the German peasantry, with an unparalleled tenacity, knew how to preserve its unique character and its customs against every attempt to wipe them out...'.

79 The connection between capitalist development and a conservative pro-peasant discourse is clear from the role of peasant economy in the Nazi project. A fascinating insight into the potentially capitalist economic role of smallholding cultivation as envisaged by Nazism, and thus the importance to the latter of reproducing peasant economy, is provided by the arguments advanced by Professor Konrad Meyer (1939). He was the representative of *Stabsamt des Reichsbauernsführers*, who led the German contingent of professional economists attending the 1938 International Conference of Agricultural Economists. Among other things, Meyer (1939: 58, 60, 62, 64) claimed that the growth of peasant economy had effectively refuted Marxist claims about the inexorable nature of land concentration and depeasantization, that the 'internal biological vitality' of the race and nation required material/ideological sustenance by the peasantry, and that the latter formed a solid bulwark in the countryside against the growth in towns of 'class feeling which [originated] in the cities'. The combined economic/political/ideological objectives of fascist pro-peasant discourse, according to Meyer (1939: 58–59), were to kill four particular birds with one stone: first, to retain the political allegiance of the peasantry in a doubly threatening context – from what was perceived to be an external (= 'foreign') menace, and from the unfolding capitalist crisis; second, to prevent the latter from accentuating the process of depeasantization, and consequently the formation of the threatening and much-feared urban 'mob-in-the-streets', which – as an urban proletariat – was the

material incompatibility may have existed, reactionary pro-peasant ideology fulfilled an important mobilizing role in the class struggle.[80]

The Unwieldy Machine of Capitalism

In the case of 1930s Spain, this fear of history manifested itself in the concern of the ultra-right Falange for the effects on the peasantry of the capitalist crisis, a fear that translated into a reactionary and specifically regressive form of anti-capitalist discourse. The result was a conservative pro-peasant programme of agrarian reform, based on a seemingly contradictory ideological combination: an acceptance by the Falange of the Marxist critique of capitalism, but the rejection of its form of transcendence.[81] Like the political right in Germany,

---

traditional bastion of the political left; third, to include small-scale peasant farming *within* the industrialization process, so as to make it more efficient economically, thereby ensuring that smallholding cultivation made a contribution to Germany's requirement for foodstuffs; and fourth, to settle and populate conquered territories (although, for obvious reasons, this is not made explicit by Meyer). In other words, *as a modernized peasant economy that for Nazis simultaneously embodied all the virtues of a 'traditional', rural and specifically German national identity* (= the economically efficient, socially harmonious, culturally enduring, community sustaining activity of family farming), smallholding cultivation could be said to be part of the fascist project of reactionary modernization.

80   Evidence suggests that between 1928 and 1933 rural voting support for the Nazi party increased more dramatically than its urban counterpart, the former rising from 2.8% of all votes cast to 52.4% while the latter rose over the same period from 2.4% to only 39.6% (Knauerhase, 1972: 42, Table 5). The role of petty commodity producers in the rise of German fascism is confirmed for the rural areas of Schleswig-Holstein and Hanover where, in contrast to poor peasants and agricultural labourers who supported the Socialists and Communists, the majority of those who voted for the Nazis in the 1932 elections were peasant family farmers (Loomis & Beegle, 1946).

81   Far from disagreeing with Marx, therefore, it was because they were familiar with his writings, and thought his prognosis historically accurate, that Falangists were vehement anti-Marxists. In short, they detested and feared Marxism not because it was wrong but much rather because it was right. Throughout his writings Primo de Rivera (Thomas, 1972: 160–161, 180) repeats constantly that his anti-Marxism stems from the recognition that Marx was correct in predicting that largescale capitalism would lead to the ruin of small rural producers and through this the nation itself. Much the same is true of fascism elsewhere at that same conjuncture. Hence the observation made by the leader of the British Union of Fascists (Mosley, 1932: 66–67): 'It is now the declared aim of every great nation to have a favourable balance of trade. *Every nation, in fact, seeks to sell more to others than it buys from them – an achievement which, it is clear, all nations cannot simultaneously attain.* So a dog-fight for foreign markets ensues in which the weaker nations go under, and heir collapse in turn reacts upon the victors in the struggle by a further shrinkage of world markets. A continuation of the present world struggle for export markets is clearly the road to

José Antonio Primo de Rivera, founder/leader of the Spanish Falange, endorsed Rousseau's critique of the 'adding-on' inherent in the historical process; that is, the way in which what he regarded as all the 'non-natural' accretions that constitute historical development erode a pre-existing and a-historical 'primitive goodness' and 'natural community'.[82] The solution to the destructive systemic effects on the peasantry of the 1930s capitalist crisis required liberation from these 'non-natural' accretions – from history itself, in other words – so as to return to an ideologically/institutionally 'spontaneous'/('natural') condition: according to Primo de Rivera, this would be the task of the Spanish Falange.

Instead of a progressive, forward-looking 'going-beyond', therefore, Primo de Rivera, sought redemption for rural Spain in the reaffirmation of traditional/feudal values/beliefs embodied 'naturally'/eternally in peasant smallholding agriculture.[83] Because he feared the impact on the latter of the kind of

---

world suicide, as well as a deadly threat to the traditional basis of British trade. These phenomena appear at first sight to support Marxian theory... Some of the Marxian laws do actually operate if mankind is not organized to defeat them, and they are operating today in the inchoate society which they envisage...if we rely on Conservatism to defeat Marxism, we shall be defeated by Marxism' (original emphasis).

82 See Thomas (1972: 98). In attempting to define Spanish nationalism (Thomas, 1972: 98 ff.), however, Primo de Rivera recognized – but did not resolve – the central contradiction facing those on the political right who wished to formulate national identity on the basis of claims to a geographically innate culture that was pristine, traditional and irreducible. Just as it was possible for him to invoke Spanish nationalism as an 'natural' attribute unique to Spain as embodied in the *existing* nation-state, therefore, so others inhabiting specific areas *within* this same national context could in turn invoke an equally distinct set of regional/local characteristics/identity (ethnicity, language, religion, culture, music, folklore, etc.) in order to justify their claim for the creation of a *new* nation-state (Catalonia being the example he cited). In the end, he evaded this problem of separatism, settling instead for the nebulous equation (reminiscent of current postmodernism) nationhood = 'otherness', and then asserting the primacy of an overarching Spanish 'otherness' which in his view subsumed all rival local/regional claims.

83 Hence the view expressed by Primo de Rivera (Thomas, 1972: 209) that Falangists 'do not see agrarian reform as merely a technical and economic problem... Spain is almost entirely rural. *The open country is synonymous with Spain*; if in the Spanish countryside the living conditions imposed on the Spanish sector of agrarian humanity are intolerable, this is not merely an economic problem. It is a total problem, religious and moral' (emphasis added). His idealization of feudalism and regret concerning its passing is contained in Thomas (1972: 21). For Primo de Rivera, peasant farming and individual peasant proprietorship were unconnected with capitalism, the capitalist system and the 1930s crisis: much rather, in his view '[o]ne effect of capitalism was just the annihilation, almost entirely, of private property in its traditional forms' (Thomas, 1972: 158, 178). This was due to the fact that he equated capitalism simply with finance capital (= the usurious

capitalist development that Marx predicted, Primo de Rivera argued that an impoverished peasant family farming – the embodiment of nationalism – had to be rescued by the Falange, both from the Marxist policy of proletarianization that would convert peasants into workers (who would then be 'led astray by Marxism'), a transformation that would result in social chaos/collapse, and also from the clutches of finance capitalism, and made economically viable by means of an agrarian reform programme.[84] The object of the latter would be to 'release small farmers, small industrialists and shopkeepers from the gilt claws of the usurious banks', to restore handicraft production in rural areas, and most importantly to reconstitute and protect the future economic and cultural well-being of the peasant family farm itself.[85]

Claims about the desirability of an innate peasant economy/culture continued to be central to both variants of the agrarian myth from 1945 onwards, its ideological complicity with European fascism notwithstanding. The survival

---

'foreign other'), a conflation which in turn licensed a potent relay in statement decoupling property relations both from the crisis and its solution (peasant economy = private property = non-capitalist = 'natural'/Nature, against which were arraigned all its antagonistic 'others': capitalism = finance capital = foreign other = economic crisis).

84   On these points see Primo de Rivera (Thomas, 1972: 30, 134, 165, 182, 206–207, 234). This was a common theme in the discourse of the European political right during the 1930s, and involved blaming not capital or capitalism but finance capital both for the economic crisis and for the dehumanising impact (= deculturation) of the latter on the peasantry, the embodiment of national identity. In many contexts, this discourse was also ethnicized, and gave rise to a potent ideological opposition between finance capital as the exploitative 'foreign other' (the Jewish 'foreign other' in Nazi Germany) and the exploited peasantry as the national 'self'. For examples of this anti-finance capital stance in the case of the Spanish political right during the 1930s, see Calvo Sotelo (1938) and Primo de Rivera (Thomas, 1972: 29, 159). Socialism was inculpated with the revolutionary destruction of the peasantry and thus by inference of national identity, about which Primo de Rivera (Thomas, 1972: 181) observed the following: 'If we really want to prevent the results foreseen in the Marxist prophecy, we have no choice but to dismantle the unwieldy machine whose turning wheels inevitably bring those results; we must dismantle the unwieldy machine of capitalism, which leads to social revolution, to Russian-style dictatorship'. Similarly, the Republican government to which the Falangists were opposed was accused by Primo de Rivera (Thomas, 1972: 184) of a trend 'towards the collectivisation of agriculture, the transformation of the peasantry into a gregarious mass, just like the workers in the cities'.

85   On these points, see Thomas (1972: 170, 182). For the agrarian reform programme of the Spanish Falange, see Primo de Rivera (Thomas, 1972: 134) who noted that '[t]he state will recognize private property as a valid means of attaining individual, family and social ends and will protect it against being abused by high finance, speculators and moneylenders'.

during the post-war era of a conservative pro-peasant programme was due at least in part to the fact that it circulated now within the discourse of the victorious bourgeoisies, who were ideologically strongly opposed both to socialism and to collectivisation, and – in the context of east European communist revolutions – still feared their own industrial working classes as potentially militant 'mobs in the streets'.

Lamenting the fact that 'the doctrine of progress…still exercises an uncritical and fatalistic influence', therefore, European and North American exponents of this discourse combined the aristocratic and the plebeian variants of the agrarian myth in a symptomatic defence of large landowner and smallholder, both of whom (it was claimed) shared a common rural identity under threat from the urban state and its proletariat.[86] Not only was the post-war

---

86   In the immediate post-war era the concept of an innate 'peasant-ness' was central to the work both of H.J. Massingham, a widely-read writer about the English countryside, and of Wilhelm Röpke, a member of the political right whose ideas influenced European and American conservatism (Abelson, 1988; Hartwell, 1995); for examples of their conservative pro-peasant discourse, see the 'Third Way' ideology propounded by Röpke (1948; 1950), and also the contributions collected in Massingham (1945). Both were vehement anti-communists, and each was influenced by the views of Hayek (see Massingham, 1945: 1–2). Advocating a return to Nature, therefore, Massingham (1945: 7–8) insisted that 'we shall not, in fact begin to understand the meaning of husbandry unless we relate it to the first principles of natural law, which is the earthly manifestation of the eternal law…[t]he pattern of life worked out by pre-industrial rural society was an unconscious obedience to ecological laws'. If Massingham represented the aristocratic variant of the agrarian myth, then the emphasis of Röpke was on the plebeian variant: the significance of his views is that these constitute an epistemological fusion of the agrarian myth, populism, neo-liberal economics and the 'traditional' conservatism of the political right. Hence the centrality to his argument (Röpke, 1950: 201 ff.; 1948: Ch. IX, 'The Peasant Core of Society – Danger of Agrarian Collectivism') of an economically viable smallholding agriculture premissed on the recuperation of an idealized peasant proprietorship was itself linked to the wider political project of the right, incorporating ideological support for smallscale rural production/exchange (artisan, petty trading) and opposition to the largescale (the state, monopolies). For Röpke the importance of peasant family farming was that, since it is immutable and basically individualistic/conservative, it operates as an ever-present economic/political/cultural bulwark against the political dangers represented by economic progress, urbanization, mechanization, class struggle, proletarianization, socialist planning and collectivization. Claiming that smallholding agriculture based on private property 'brings men and nature together' in a way that 'counter-balances the industrial and urban aspects of our civilization with tradition and conservatism, economic independence and self-sufficiency [that derive in turn from a] proximity to nature,…a natural and full existence near the sources of life…', Röpke (1950: 202–203) warned that 'the peasant world together with other small sectors of society, represents today [the early 1940s] a last

trend away from agriculture towards urbanization/industrialization decried as a profanation of Nature and 'natural law', and finance capital blamed for undermining the small farmer, but in some instances this was done in nationalist idioms and barely coded anti-semitic terms (= 'money-power') not so dissimilar to those circulating in the pre-war discourse of the political right (German fascism, British imperialism).[87] By the mid-1960s, the political right in the USA was arguing strongly in favour of the small farmer: this it managed to do because it had executed a populist reappropriation of existing discourse about political freedom, in the process bolstering the claim of conservatives to be disinterestedly plebeian by linking the concept 'freedom' simultaneously to a pro-farmer, pro-market and anti-State ideology.[88]

Pro-peasant ideology continues to inform the discourse of the political right in Europe.[89] In what is currently an almost classic restatement of the

---

great island that has not yet been reached by the flood of collectivization, the last great sphere of human life and work which possesses inner stability and value in a vital sense. It is a priceless blessing wherever this reserve still exists...'.

87   Significantly, among the contributors to the collection edited by Massingham were Edmund Blunden, Rolf Gardiner, and the Earl of Portsmouth, all of whom had been fellow-travellers of the political right in the 1930s (Griffiths, 1983). In what is an astonishing case of denial, and in defiance of evidence to the contrary, however, Massingham (1945: 3, 4) asserts that German fascism was a 'proletarian vice', an instance of 'state absolutism... all urban in origin', and the result of 'the loss...of the timeless rural values in industrialism'. In keeping with the cold war rhetoric of the political right, he then equates German fascism with Russian communism, in order to dismiss them both as examples of industrialized 'totalitarian' states and also to disassociate himself (and his contributors) from pre-war German sympathies. His coded anti-semitism is evident from the following (Massingham, 1945: 6): 'A usurious system was built up round this primary sin of abandoning our native land. It not only maintained itself by ruining our own farmers and pushing those of other lands into debt, but handed over all the power and credit in the community from the primary producer to the dealer. Examine the vested interests of this country, and it will be seen that they are nearly all clustered round the breeding of money...'.

88   Hence the fact that in North America during the mid-1960s, 'Goldwater showed that with liberals in control in Washington, conservatives could appropriate the tradition of antigovernment populism, thus broadening their electoral base and dispelling their traditional image as elitists' (Foner, 1998: 313). Where US agricultural policy was concerned, Goldwater (1964; 38 ff.) united a critique of high taxation and state regulation with claim that only the free market would eliminate surpluses and thus deliver higher prices to the farmer ('[f]arm production, like any other production, is best controlled by the operation of the free market').

89   It is necessary to emphasize that, on the question of economic policy generally, the European political right is not a theoretically homogeneous grouping. In the case of

aristocratic variant of the agrarian myth, therefore, conservative philosophy even now combines a defence of rural hierarchy and tradition based on large landownership with populist concern for the threatened survival of 'natural' forms of rural economy based on small-scale agricultural production.[90] During the period after the second world war, both components of the English pastoral (landlord estate + small family farm) have been continuously undermined by what for populist conservatives are the interconnected and mutually supportive evils of urbanization, taxation and state regulation, all of which have resulted in the appearance of 'that previously unknown and deeply troubling thing: a landscape without boundaries' (that is, no small privately-owned farms), and a loss of the countryside which is now equated with the loss of

---

Britain, the contemporary political right is usually divided into two distinct ideological tendencies: on the one hand the free market economists assembled under the neo-liberal banner, and on the other traditional conservatives less concerned with economic growth than with reasserting ancient privilege. This distinction was accurately delineated in the mid-1980s by David Edgar, who observed that 'an element at least of the impetus behind Thatcherism was to be nothing to do with the release of vital new entrepreneurial energies, but was all about the reassertion of the most ancient of privileges, the most crude and atavistic of class hatreds. That the restitution of seigniorial authority is not the *whole* of New Conservatism shouldn't blind us to the fact that it's a part...' ('Let Them Eat Dirt', *New Statesman*, 26 September 1986, original emphasis).

90 The continuing link between conservatism, the aristocratic variant of the agrarian myth and a pro-peasant ideology is epitomized by the work of Roger Scruton. On the one hand, therefore, the pastoral vision of countryside-as-Englishness he endorses has at its centre an idealized image of the landlord class: hence his acceptance of the view that country house life amounted to 'the conjunction of liberty and liberality that comes about when affluence coincides with a secure and localized social standing', and that 'the country house came to represent an ideal of English civilization – one in which hierarchy was softened by neighbourliness, and wealth by mutual aid' (Scruton, 2000: 237, 239). This benign perception of rural landlordism as seen from above is then attributed to those below: 'Our countryside is inseparable from the country house and its parklands, and expresses the careful integration of villages, farms and vistas that constituted for the gentry, the visible signal of their title. It bears the mark of a mild and deferential despotism, and the nostalgia that people now feel...for the class-divided and deferential [traditional rural] society' (Roger Scruton, 'In Praise of Mild Despotism: Old families, not the National Trust, can save the countryside', *The Business FT Weekend Magazine*, 27 October 2001). Accordingly, this same pastoral vision also requires the inclusion within its ideological framework of a similarly idealized concept of the small family farm: hence the view that in England '[p]rimogeniture, and the abolition of feudal tenures, gave early reality to the small family farm, intact over generations...[i]t is on such farms that the "yeoman stock" celebrated by Macaulay was raised' (Scruton, 2000: 240).

national confidence and identity.[91] Like the plebeian variant invoked by the political right in the United States of the 1960s, therefore, the aristocratic variant of the agrarian myth deployed by late 1990s English conservatism is supportive of the free market, decries State 'interference', and is pro-farmer.[92]

V

Many of these same themes also inform the political discourse of the political right in Latin America. It is the acceptability to landlords and rich peasants

---

91   On these points, see Scruton (2000: 241). Symptomatically, this organic unity of English rural society (landlord + small farmer = 'Englishness', or English national identity) is then contrasted (Scruton, 2001) with the evils of large-scale urban decay ('Many of our inner-city areas are now unviable. Schools are dreadful, drugs and promiscuity threaten the young, and crime levels are soaring'). Among the reasons that England no longer exists (= 'The Forbidding of England'), therefore, is that '[t]he family farm, which maintained the small-scale and diversified production that was largely responsible for the shape and appearance of England, is now on the verge of extinction' (Scruton, 2000: 254). The principal cause of this multiple and inter-related decline – in 'Englishness', English identity, English culture, and the countryside that embodies them all – is the post-war tax system introduced by the Labour government, which destroyed the country house and now threatens the small family farm (Scruton, 2000: 240). The programmatic imperative of this discourse is not difficult to discern. Lamenting that taxation which penalizes inheritance (= 'broken up landed estates') 'now threaten[s] the family farm', Scruton (2001) calls for 'a wholly new and radical conservative policy' that will reverse this process, both by re-establishing family farming ('[t]he family farm is the backbone of the rural economy, and the most important generator of the distinctive British landscapes') and by rolling back European Union and/or British state control ('it is now clear that regulations are killing off small farms'). Small producers, concludes Scruton (2001: 16), must be protected from 'unfair competition'. That pro-farmer views not only continue to resonate within English conservativism but do so in both plebeian and aristocratic forms, underlines both the centrality of the agrarian myth to the populism of the political right, and also the extent to which the discourse of the latter continues to be based on a project of innateness. For this reason, it is necessary to disagree strongly with Cook and Clarke (1990: 140) when they claim that: 'a writer like Scruton is not embarking on a project of innateness but...one of populism'. Much rather, Scruton's populism is not only based on a project of innateness but actually has no meaning outside this ideological framework.

92   A revealing illustration is the trajectory followed by Richard Mabey, currently an influential writer about nature, conservation and farming in England. During the mid-1960s, when the entrenched power in British society of tradition/privilege/hierarchy was being questioned, he (Mabey, 1967) espoused the then commonly-held conservative view that it was the working class, not the bourgeoisie, which objected to attempts to categorize its

alike of the pro-peasant discourse informing the agrarian myth, together with the close link between the latter and the politics of nationality and tradition, that poses difficulties for Latin American subalternists. Because the views of those on the ultra-nationalist political right in 1930s Latin America were from the 1920s onwards influenced strongly by the writings and ideas of their European counterparts (José Ortega y Gasset, José Calvo Sotelo and José Antonio Primo de Rivera among them), many commentators equate reactionary discourse in Latin America simply with a harkening back to European culture and tradition (*Hispanidad*).[93]

Whilst true in part, this argument overlooks the extent to which a specifically *populist* form of rightwing reactionary discourse about rural society locates its nationalism in idealized forms of popular culture and indigenous

---

culture as disempowering. What is of particular interest, however, is the way in which this argument was deployed. Rather than defending tradition/privilege/hierarchy, therefore, the argument took the *opposite* form: *a defence of plebeian cultural 'otherness'*. Hence the view (Mabey, 1967: 15) that 'we shall have class groups forming who share not only different standards for living but different standards *of* living. At this point passing some sort of judgement on class inequalities becomes almost impossibly complex' (original emphasis). The insidiousness and effectiveness of this spuriously democratic kind of discourse should not be underestimated. Conservatives begin by pointing out, uncontentiously, that workers object to attempts by the bourgeoisie to represent their plebeian culture as disempowering; the next step, which is also seemingly uncontroversial, is the conservative claim that, because culture is indeed different, workers are right to make this objection; from this, however, conservatives draw what is palpably a contentious inference. Since cultural formation/reproduction possesses its roots in what one does for a living, conservative political discourse concludes rightly by pointing out that all culture is linked ineradicably to the economics of class. Accordingly, the conservative plea for the innateness of cultural difference becomes in effect a plea also for the retention both of existing class relationships and of the capitalist system itself. It comes as no surprise to learn that Mabey (1980; 1983, 1990), who defended tradition/privilege/hierarchy in this seemingly plebeian fashion during the mid-1960s, was during the 1980s – and is in the late 1990s – not only upholding views about the sacredness of nature, advancing a reactionary form of anti-capitalism, and advocating small-scale subsistence agriculture, but also sharing a platform (Mabey, 2000) with Prince Charles and Vandana Shiva. In other words, over the last three decades Mabey has remained politically consistent, both in his defence of rural tradition/privilege/hierarchy and in his advocacy of small farming: that is, in his espousal of the aristocratic variant of the agrarian myth.

93   See, for example, Rama (1981). Among those on the Latin American political right during the 1930s who were influenced by European fascist ideology, and in particular that of the Spanish *Falange* (see above), were two important Peruvian political leaders: Luis Flores of the *Unión Revolucionaria*, and the Catholic landowner José de la Riva Agüero (see Klaren, 2000: 279–280).

tradition *within* Latin America itself.[94] Not the least of the many difficulties faced by those who attempt to apply a subaltern framework to Latin America, therefore, is the crucial role played by the peasantry in the discourse of the political right, where it takes the form of a specifically plebeian national identity deployed by conservatives and reactionaries as a weapon in their struggle with the left.[95]

Pro-peasant Latin American Conservatism

The difficulty faced by exponents of subalternism is that the agrarian myth is deployed as – or perhaps more – effectively by Latin American conservatives. Like the Spanish Falange and German Nazism, the ultra-nationalist political right in Latin America at the same conjuncture also rooted its claims to and view of a pristine national/cultural identity in an indigenous peasantry.[96] The

---

94 In many ways, these two sources of nationalism – one inside and one outside Latin America – are similar to the two sources of North American rightwing politics: on the one hand the Southern agrarian tradition, linked to visions of European aristocratic culture epitomized by and reproduced in the context of the antebellum plantation system, and on the other an 'authentic' indigenous plebeian version embodied in the frontier myth and its images of family farming.

95 Even those on the political right in 1930s Spain – such as de Maeztu (1937: 203) – evinced a concern for the wellbeing of the indigenous Latin American 'other'.

96 In this connection it is important neither to overlook nor to underestimate the influence of religion on the positions taken by the political right in Latin America (and in Spain). Accordingly, it is significant that, throughout the period from the late nineteenth to the mid-twentieth century, even the reactionary/conservative discourse of the Roman Catholic Church has consistently advocated the protection/survival of peasant small-holding. This is evident from an analysis by Karin Dovring (1956: Ch. 7) of the teachings of Roman Catholicism about land reform, as embodied both in the social Encyclicals of and related pronouncements by the Vatican over a sixty year period – from *De Rerum Novarum* (1891) issued by Pope Leo XIII, through *Quadragesimo Anno* (1931), to the Pentecost message of Pope Pius XII in 1941 and the Vatican-influenced ideas of Christian Democratic politicians in Italy during the early 1950s. Throughout this period, therefore, the official discourse-for and discourse-against of a profoundly conservative Catholic Church was uniform in its views. In keeping with the ideology of those on the political right, the discourse-against of the Roman Catholic Church expressed hostility to the theory, practice and institutions/organizations of the left generally (Bolshevism, socialism, communism, class warfare, class hatred, unionization), and argued against collectivization, asserting that socialism threatened family life and was contrary to natural law; it warned continuously against 'state-interference', condemned socialists and left-wing trade unionists as 'crafty agitators', 'seditious', and 'futile', dismissed equality as 'ridiculous', and insisted that common ownership of property was against workers' interests. Over this same period, by contrast, the official teachings of Roman Catholicism not only endorsed private

latter category was accordingly regarded as 'natural', eternal and homogeneous, all characteristics with which the Latin American political right imbued its nationalism. This was particularly true of the Andean countries, where since independence nationalist discourse had invariably contrasted the exploitative 'foreign other' to the virtuous indigenous self. In addition to the standard right-wing discourse – invocations of organic unity, authority, hierarchy, family, religion and patriotism, combined with opposition to class, class struggle, and the 'foreign other' – the programme for the New Bolivian State (*Nuevo Estado Boliviano*) proposed by the Bolivian Falangists (the fascist FSB, or *Falange Socialista Boliviana*) during the early 1940s invoked and endorsed peasant economy.

Not only was an ethnically-specific peasant identity equated with nationalism (*'El indio es la raíz de nuestra nacionalidad'*), therefore, but this culturally-delineated rural subject was also to be reinforced and guaranteed economically by an agrarian reform (*'Un plan de reforma agraria le dará su liberación económica'*).[97] However, this cultural/economic identity was itself both

---

property in all its forms but especially small and medium peasant family farms: the discourse-for of the Vatican and/or Christian Democratic politicians linked to it continuously stressed the value of small and middle-sized rural landed properties, arguing that Vatican policy was to support 'a society of small owners with farms fit [for] developing family life...', its ideological focus being on the 'care of the individual male farmer, his workplace and land, his home and the raising of his own family' (Karin Dovring, 1956: 302, 305). On this point the same study concludes: 'The concept of the state, the claim for the right of the individual, private property, negativism against the too rich, the stress on the lawful owner and respect for the law...are among the concepts the Vatican made its own. A comparative glance at the different documents will disclose more common symbols which definitely conform to the Vatican ideal for a society: small holdings, small lands where the family can be supported' (Karin Dovring, 1956: 310). Two additional are worthy of note. First, that the two main papal encyclicals reaffirming authority/hierarchy and condemning the left were both issued as ideological guidance during periods of acute economic crisis (1891 and 1931). And, second, that – like the political right generally – the target of Vatican criticism was not the capitalist system *per se* but rather financial capital (= 'greedy capitalist', 'rapacious usury', 'grasping speculators'). This is true of Argentina, where both the discourse-for (upholding authority, hierarchy, nationalism, family farming) and the discourse-against (anti-socialist, anti-Enlightenment, anti-semitic) of the Roman Catholic Church were supportive of – and, indeed, indistinguishable from – the discourse of the political right (Deutsch, 1986; Deutsch and Dolkart, 1993).

97   For the early 1940s political programme of the Bolivian falangists, and the role in this of an indigenous peasantry, see the FSB texts reproduced in Cornejo (1949: 131–138). For the views of its Secretary General, Oscar Unzaga de la Vega, and the attempt by the FSB to reinvent itself politically during the post-war era, see Lora (1970: 271 ff.).

subordinate and fixed, the structural location and immutability of which its subject was expected to recognize and accept: like every other social category in the 'natural' hierarchy which composed the nation, the Bolivian peasantry had in the view of the FSB its own 'natural' economic role in the new corporate order (*'El individuo participará de la unidad orgánica del estado mediante un regimen corporativo en que cada uno desempeñe su función de acuerdo a la calidad y especialización de su trabajo'*).

Even in the southern cone countries of Latin America, where indigenous populations were numerically and economically less significant than in their Andean counterparts, an idealized image of peasant farming still informed the discourse both of nationalism and of the political right. In the case of Argentina, for example, the emergence of the political right at the beginning of the twentieth century was a direct response to the mobilization of the labour movement, and a discourse combining cultural nationalism with anti-modernism, anti-urbanism, and anti-cosmopolitanism was central to the class struggle waged 'from above'.[98] From the 1890s onwards, the political right in Argentina during was not merely anti-semitic but its racism mimicked in every respect that propounded by agrarian populists elsewhere at the same conjuncture, and for much the same reasons.[99] Indeed, it was a twofold desire to rescue an 'authentic' indigenous process of family farming in Argentina from the clutches of ('foreign'/'alien'/'Jewish') finance capital and also to prevent depeasantized

---

98   Hence the observation (Deutsch, 1986: 41–43) that by the start of the twentieth century: 'Some intellectuals blamed foreigners for class conflict [and] urban blight...The gaucho and the Hispanic past found their greatest defenders in the writers whom historians have called the cultural nationalists... The cultural nationalists defined the Argentine character in terms equivalent to traditional society – terms that did not threaten the existing order...the hitherto reviled gaucho now became a model for the masses to follow. Loyal to his employer, content with his station in life, opposed to thrift, rational behaviour, and planning, the idealized gaucho was the antithesis of the successful foreign-born entrepreneur and the labor activist alike'. Such views, the same source notes, 'reflected the extent to which cultural nationalism and intertwined xenophobic and antimodernist sentiments had permeated the upper class'. For the rise of the political right in Argentina, and in particular the role in this from 1919 onwards of the Argentine Patriotic League, see Deutsch (1986; 1999) and Deutsch and Dolkart (1993).

99   In a period of capitalist crisis, therefore, Jews were blamed in the domain of 'popular culture' both for causing the crisis (= finance capitalism) and also for its potential effect (= socialism) (Deutsch, 1986: 35, 44–47, 74–75, 78; Deutsch and Dolkart, 1993: 38–39). This discourse informed widely-read anti-semitic fiction, both in Argentina and in the United States of America: the agrarian populist dystopic book *Caesar's Column* by Ignatius Donnelly (Brass, 2000a: Ch. 6) in the latter context, and in the former the novel *La bolsa* by Julián Martel (Deutsch, 1986: 45–46).

workers from falling into the clutches of ('foreign'/'alien'/'Jewish') socialism that led to the advocacy by the political right of land reform and rural cooperativization.[100]

Fatherland and Order

During the period following the 1914–18 war, the protection of smallholding peasants and/or the reconstitution of a middle peasantry, was central to Argentinian fascism, as represented by the ultra-reactionary policy and discourse of the Argentine Patriotic League (*Liga Patriótica Argentina*).[101] Along with the gaucho, peasant smallholders were considered by those on the political right not just as indigenous and loyal subjects who upheld private property rights and 'knew'/accepted their 'natural' position in the social hierarchy, but also (and therefore) as the embodiment of an 'authentic' rural tradition that contrasted with an 'alien' urban cosmopolitanism represented by a mainly immigrant proletariat which lived/worked in the cities, as the bearer of 'authentic' national identity and consequently as a bulwark against the spread to rural areas of socialist and revolutionary ideas.[102]

---

100   On the cooperative credit unions (*cajas rurales*) set up in the countryside by the Argentine Social League, a forerunner of the political right, in order to provide small farmers with loans so that they would not 'have to turn to foreign sources of financing', see Deutsch (1986: 53).

101   The Argentine Patriotic League was a 'from above' response to labour militancy and mobilization during the 1920s, when the bourgeoisie and petty bourgeoisie feared both that the state would be unable to resist this and that – unchallenged – such working class agency would (as in the case of Russia) lead inevitably to the revolutionary overthrow of the existing socioeconomic order. Its self-professed aims were not just to guard against revolution (= 'to defend the existing socioeconomic order against the left'), but also to maintain national unity ('Fatherland and Order'), to 'help the poor' by 'opposing class hatred', and to protect Argentine nationality and property from 'foreigners', strikes and leftwing ideas/actions. Half its leaders were either themselves landowners or related to members of the landlord class, and many League members had occupations (ranching, commerce) either in agriculture itself or with close links to this (Deutsch, 1983: 66 ff., 80 ff., 102, 104–105, 111).

102   'Land reform was a matter of special interest for the League and a useful example of its ideas. One reason for the importance of this issue was the postwar agrarian disorders. Another was the fact that League members, like cultural nationalists, believed that the countryside was the storehouse of Argentine traditions and virtues, in contrast to the cosmopolitan cities... In formulating their opinions on this topic, some Liguistas followed [the] dictum that order depended not on abolishing property, but on multiplying it... property ownership gave one a sense of self-worth and a stake in the present order; indeed, the worst enemies of Bolshevism were landholding peasants. Dividing large

Throughout the capitalist crisis of the 1920s, the League maintained a pool of strike-breaking workers that was deployed against organized rural labour in every part of the country; these scab workers (*crumiros*) were made available to farmers and tenants who were in dispute with their hired labour.[103] When workers began to organize or withdrew their labour-power, therefore, it was not just large landowners and owners of agribusiness enterprises but also small farmers, ranchers and tenants – many of who were engaged in struggle with their own labourers (over issues such as wage levels, working conditions, and the right to form/join unions) – who called upon the League to come to 'the defence of the cultivator', and it was from these elements of the agrarian petty bourgeoisie that the political right in Argentina received crucial support and recruited much of its membership.

Significantly, pro-peasant ideology continued to be found in the discourse of the bourgeoisie and political right in Latin America throughout the decade and a half after 1945, not least because – like their counterparts in Europe and North America – they were not on the losing side during the war.[104] Thus, for example, an agronomist who was an advisor to the Peruvian landlords' association (*Sociedad Nacional Agraria*, or SNA), and who defended the hacienda system on the grounds that it contributed to the national wealth of Peru, also supported the idea of peasant family farming.[105] When equipped with more advanced forces of production, such independent cultivators could, in his view, operate alongside similarly equipped latifundia.[106]

---

holdings into smaller ones and facilitating their sale to small farmers would create a large antileftist constituency... In one of the rare instances in which a Liguista mentioned Mussolini, Carlés [the Argentine Patriotic League leader] suggested that Argentina follow the example of the Italian Fascists, whose land reforms were enlarging the independent peasantry' (Deutsch, 1986: 168–169).

103   There can be no doubt as to this objective and its long-term political effects. In the view of one commentator (Deutsch, 1986: 112, 152) '[the Argentine Patriotic League] spread anti-leftist publicity, crushed strikes, and replaced unions with [bosses' organizations]. Without serious hinderance from the government, the League helped to weaken the labour movement for decades to come'; unsurprisingly, the number of strikes/strikers declined from 367 and 309,000 in 1919 to an annual average of 90 and 70,000 during the period 1921–1928.

104   That is, in the period *before* the development decade of the 1960s, when peasant economy and the issue of agrarian reform became the central focus of discourse about economic growth and planning (see Chapter 3).

105   The agronomist in question was Gerardo Klinge (1946), who attributed the problems of a minifundist agriculture not to the presence of the *hacienda* system but rather to land fragmentation as a result of inheritance within the context of peasant economy itself.

106   On this point, see Klinge (1946: 369). Much the same is true of India at the same conjuncture, where a report written by representatives of industrial capital (Thakurdas, Tata,

In a similar vein, an important vinyard strike by smallholding tenants in Chile during the early 1950s was organized and led by a member of the Chilean Falange.[107] Like its 1930s Spanish counterpart, the mobilizing discourse used by the Falange in Chile during the course of this strike was that of Roman Catholicism, and in particular the social teachings contained in the papal encyclicals *Rerum Novarum* and *Quadragesimo Anno*, both of which upheld the rights of private property and were against socialism and class struggle, advocating instead class compromise between rural workers and their employers.[108] As the case of peasant smallholders among the indigenous Pewenche population confirms, rightwing political candidates and parties in Chile were still able to draw electoral support from among independent cultivators even in the late 1990s.[109] During the same decade, moreover, elements of the

---

Birla, Dalal, Ram, Lalbhai, Shroff, and Matthai, 1945: 82) similarly advocated 'the establishment of a class of peasant proprietors'. An analogous recommendation was made by yet another capitalist spokesperson (Zinkin, 1956: 209–210), who also supported the idea of an individualist agrarian reform in India on explicitly political grounds, because it 'creates new owners by the million', adding that: 'The difference between a man with two acres and a man with twenty is still great, but it is different in kind as well as in degree from the difference between a man with nothing and a man with two acres'.

107   For a detailed analysis of this strike, see Landsberger (1969).

108   That the vineyard workers' strike was not a success is attributed by Landsberger (1969: 263) to its politically reformist discourse which, by eschewing class struggle, ensured that any 'from below' action undertaken by the strikers stopped short of a challenge to either the property rights of or the power enjoyed by large landowners. An explicitly political objective of undertaking rural grassroots organization in this manner on the part of religious and/or radical rightwing groups was to deny this support to leftwing groups; the latter had been organizing among Chilean vineyard workers since the 1930s.

109   See Fletcher (2001) for evidence of support for the political right by peasant smallholders in the Pewenche indigenous population from the Alto Bío-Bío region of Chile. As this particular case-study makes clear, the opposed views held by the Pewenche regarding their displacement by a hydroelectric dam, and consequent resettlement, were themselves an effect of equally distinct employment histories, or the relative importance of experiences as workers or smallholders in the formation of their political consciousness. Whereas males migrated in search of paid work, Pewenche females remained in charge of cultivating the family smallholding. For the women leading the resistance to Pewenche resettlement, therefore, the importance of 'staying put' was because it permitted them to continue as smallholders on ancestral land. In other words, opposition to dispossession stemmed from their economic identity as peasants, and consequently a stated desire to avoid deculturation was an attempt to present this in a politically more acceptable form, by invoking a discourse about legitimacy rooted in ethnic tradition. As is well documented, this kind of defence has a long history in Latin America, where land rights have been defended by recourse to arguments about ethnicity, tradition, and culture. Its

Argentinian political right shifted their own discourse, from one which emphasized the necessity of temporal (= military) authority exercised 'from above' to
one which invoked the desirability both of religious (= 'natural') and 'from
below' plebeian (= populist) legitimacy.[110]

Conclusion

Historically and currently, both the nation and the State have been – and
remain – central to struggle waged 'from above', the object of which has been
the ideological fusion between aristocratic and plebeian versions of the agrarian myth. In late nineteenth century England, pro-plebeian discourse from the
conservative end of the political spectrum took the form not just of landowner
complaints about factory working conditions, but also aristocratic claims to a
shared victimhood as a result of 'underhand' activity by an external (= non-
English) 'other'. Foreigners – among them Germans, Americans, Jews – were
deemed responsible for all the ills faced by 'the People' who were English: not
just the starvation wages of labour, the undercutting and commercial outcom-
peting of the bourgeoisie, but also the loss of political influence by the
aristocracy.

France was the target of British nationalism advocated by conservatives
during the nineteenth century mainly because of its revolutionary episodes. It
was the latter that conservatism was keen to oppose, and it did so in two ways.
First, by depicting France as the 'other' of the English people, and as such
indissolubly linking its policies – at home and abroad – simply to furthering its
own national interests, thereby deflecting attention from the internationalist
lessons taught by revolution. And second, by building on this difference a populist nationalism at home, a 'we-are-all-the-same' discourse in Britain, thereby
deflecting from the burgeoning class inequalities generated by industrial
capitalism.

---

ideological potency is particularly marked where women are perceived as defenders of a
number of mutually reinforcing 'natural' – and thus immutable – traditional identities: of
Nature, of the family, of subsistence farming, of indigenous culture, and through all the
latter, of the nation itself (female = family = subsistence farming = Nature = nation).

110   As Payne (2000: 74) points out, the political right in Argentina was not only 'unabashed in
its appropriation and adaptation of past cultural symbols', but also 'hired a "cultural
adviser" rather than a political adviser', the object being – as its archenemy, the founder
of the Mothers of the Disappeared, put it – to disguise 'a right-wing agenda with left-wing
discourse to win working-class votes...the demagoguery of working for the lower echelon
of society'.

It is these things that are highlighted in Disraeli's notion of an egalitarian conservative democracy, and the two distinct forms it takes: the one English, the other French. His concept of national identity focuses on differing forms of equality: whereas levelling down in France deprives plebeians of upward mobility, in England by contrast this possibility remains open to them. In this lies the clue both to conservative fears – the emergence of a revolutionary impetus in England similar to that of France – and to attempts to avoid this, by forging an 'other' identity, one that centres on the difference of nation, not the sameness of class across nations. It is clear this kind of conservative strategy has been adopted at other conjunctures in other global contexts.

Hence the political right not only possesses an international dimension to its own ideology, but the latter also allocates similar characteristics and a political role to the peasantry regardless of national context. Against what it categorizes as the 'alien' internationalism of the left (proletariat, class structure, class struggle, socialism), therefore, the right in Germany, Spain, Argentina, and Bolivia during the first half of the twentieth century, and in Europe, North America and parts of Latin America during the second half, counterposed its own 'authentic' form of internationalism: namely, the global existence of peasant economy and culture – the embodiment of nationhood and the repository of cherished rural tradition – threatened with destruction by finance capital and depeasantization. This in turn confers legitimacy on historical and contemporary forms of grassroots resistance conducted by peasant cultivators and farmers in defence of their private property against any ('redistributive') State attempting to change existing social relations of production and thus disrupt what conservatives maintain are organic and harmonious rural communities/ traditions/hierarchy.

This 'from above' concern for those 'from below' characterizes conservative discourse about peasants as populist, a powerful ideology that combines plebeian and aristocratic versions of the agrarian myth. Its object is to disguise the impact of capitalist development in rural contexts by recasting economic inequality as 'natural', and refocusing 'difference' away from class and onto a town/countryside divide. Such a mutually supportive fusion of above and below forms of 'difference'/'otherness' in general, and arguments concerning the innateness of hierarchically-linked-but-socioeconomically-specific rural identities in particular, are found not just in most European, North American and Asian but also in Latin American variants of conservatism. All the latter lament the loss and simultaneously preach the importance of recuperating an historically innate form of (non-class) national/cultural identity that is virtuous, non-conflictive, and rural in origin, and thus unifies the nation, thereby guaranteeing national harmony. For this reason, it is necessary to regard pro-peasant ideology mainly as a *mobilizing* discourse which, by fostering false consciousness among the opponents of capitalism (which include uncompetitive and/or dispossessed peasant proprietors), permits the process of capitalist development to proceed, especially when – as in the case of 1920s and 1930s Europe and Latin America – deployed in a classically populist fashion by groups/parties on the political right.

The whole point about the acceptability to the political right of an idealized image of an undifferentiated, a-historical peasantry is that – once this supposedly homogeneous category is differentiated, and the presence of historically distinct class elements are revealed – it ceases to embody precisely those eternal/a-historical/traditional virtues that make it acceptable to conservatives. As long as the peasantry remains an epistemologically undifferentiated category, however, it licenses a discourse about the agrarian myth that is central to the populist ideology of the political right. Thus the State/nation duality, and the concept of national identity based on this, which informs the search for a pristine grass-roots subaltern 'authenticity' has been – and remains – a polarity that underlies the analyses of agrarian populism and fascism. As the cases not only of Germany and Spain but also Bolivia and Argentina in the period between the 1890s and the 1940s all demonstrate, both agrarian populism and fascism seek to realign what they deem to be a pre-existing indigenous – and thus authentic – national identity with a State apparatus that is deemed to be representative of this.

Of interest, therefore, is why many of the same ideological assumptions informing the agrarian populism and nationalism of the political right re-emerged after the development decade of the 1960s, in debates about the desirability or otherwise of political and economic progress. This is the subject of the next chapter.

CHAPTER 3

Development Caught between Tradition and Modernity

'Subaltern tyrants are ever the most intolerant, and intolerable'

An observation made two centuries ago by J.G.H. ZIMMERMAN 1800: 4

'A system of mal-government begins by refusing man his rights, and ends by depriving him of the power of appreciating the value of that which he has lost'.

Maxim CLXXXIV (COLTON, 1835: 127)

'This is the only way to travel'

Groucho Marx in the film *Duck Soup* (1933), as Rufus T. Firefly, President of Freedonia, sitting on a motorcycle that isn't going anywhere

Introduction: Peasants at the Presidential Palace

Both the relationship between peasants and the State, and the political difficulties it poses, are summed up visually in a celebrated historical image, one familiar to most Latin Americans and Latin Americanists. It is the photograph, taken on 6th December 1914 at the National Palace in Mexico City, of Emiliano Zapata sitting next to Pancho Villa, the latter seated on the presidential throne.[1] Each led a revolutionary force from the north and south of Mexico, composed in Zapata's case of peasants, that had just occupied the national capital. It was this fact that was depicted symbolically in the photographic image of peasant leaders occupying the very seat of power, itself situated within the political domain of the nation State. Yet shortly after this photo was taken, Zapata and his peasant army departed for rural Morelos, never to return to this seat of power, occupied subsequently by others.

In this the agrarian forces led by Zapata were unlike either the Bolsheviks, who in October 1917 stormed the Winter Palace and captured the Russian State, or the guerrillas from the Sierra Maestra who entered and remained in Havana during the 1959 Cuban Revolution. What is common to the strategy pursued by

---

1   The photo is reproduced in Womack (1969: 206ff.) and Casasola (1985: 60).

peasants from Morelos led by Zapata at the start of the twentieth century, and by the Zapatistas of Subcomandante Marcos in Chiapas at its end (see Chapter 1), is the belief that their economic and political difficulties should be addressed and can be solved largely at a local level. The inference is clear: the wider socio-economic system is left intact. As applied to (and by) the peasantry, therefore, 'civil society' operates within its own restricted space, a bounded rural domain – consisting of no more than a particular region, area, or even village – that is the main object of 'from below' agency. This is a view that has once more come back into fashion where current analyses of rural mobilization are concerned.

Thus it is possible to interpret the withdrawal by peasant armies from Mexico City in this fashion in two distinct ways. Marxists (and others) would point to this as evidence of a crucial and debilitating weakness in agrarian movements that have no programme beyond taking over the land in a particular locale and cultivating it on an individual basis. Without capturing the State, not only do peasants lack control over the inputs and economic resources necessary to make their holdings productive, but those dispossessed of their properties (landlords, planters, agribusiness enterprises and commercial farmers) retain the capacity to reverse their expropriation and take back land redistributed.

Anti-Marxist 'new' populist postmodern theorists, by contrast, would see this same act – disengagement from the State – as an indication of the strength of the peasant movement concerned, arguing that its adherents rightly perceive that their interests and a solution to their problems can be addressed only at the rural grassroots, in the communities where they live and work. Taking over the land and redistributing it so as to enable them to meet their own subsistence requirements is, according to 'new' populist postmodernism, doubly empowering. Not only do smallholders demonstrate the efficacy of self-reliance and local autonomy, therefore, but they can imprint their own traditional knowledge and expertise on the redistribution process as well as protecting from the State and 'outsiders' the integrity of the cultural practices that have always structured their livelihoods. For this reason, 'new' populist postmodernists argue, 'civil society' can exist without either transforming property relations in the wider social formation or controlling the State.[2]

---

2 Part of the 'cultural turn' that has bedevilled development studies over the past quarter of a century, the still fashionable 'new' populist postmodernism conjures up nothing so much as the description by Samuel Butler in *Erewhon* of 'The Colleges of Unreason'. Not only did the latter institutions possess 'professorships of Inconsistency and Evasion', where one of the objects of study was 'the Completer Obliteration of the Past', but '[o]ne man was refused a

This approach finds its apogee with reference to 'Zomia', a highland region of southeast Asia, where according to 'new' populist postmodern theory, what is mistakenly categorized as marginality, impoverishment, illiteracy, and a backward culture, are all perceived as 'chosen' by the subjects themselves, and thus empowering.[3] Unlike lowland areas, where State power, class hierarchy and inequality prevail, highland communities are by contrast egalitarian, subsistence-oriented and non-State locations. Those on the periphery choose to be there, in pursuit of which objective they resist-the-State (= 'State evasion'), a form of grassroots agency designed to protect peasant economy.

Of the five sections in this chapter, the first looks at the discourse about 'civil society' and 'citizenship' as this informs left/right political differences, while the second considers the latter distinction in relation to the peasantry and the control/capture of the State. The third section outlines how modernization theory interpreted development simply as the political and economic incorporation of the peasantry, leaving intact a rural culture that was subsequently mobilized against the State by the 'new' populist postmodernism. By reinserting the agrarian myth as an alternative to modernity, the State and its development project, therefore, 'cultural turn' discourse mimicked conservative and neoliberal ideology, a process considered in the fourth section. The fifth examines a theory promoting the allocation to the rural 'other' of its own physical space outside and against the State, in terms of a prefiguring discourse which regards the same outcome as empowering.

I

Granite Hardness, Left and Right

Any consideration of the way in which the political right and left interpret the links between development on the one hand, and property, 'civil society' and the State on the other, must begin by establishing the fact of theoretical consistency informing these different viewpoints.[4] Like that of the political right, the

---

degree for being too often and too seriously in the right, while a few days before I came, a whole batch had been plucked for insufficient distrust of the printed matter' (Butler, 1932: 131–132, 133, 134). Something akin to postmodern aporia is hinted at: 'I ventured feebly to say that I did not see how progress could be made in any art or science, or indeed in anything at all, without more or less self-seeking, and hence unamiability. "Of course it cannot," said the Professor, "and therefore we object to progress." After which there was no more to be said'.

3   On 'Zomia' see below.

4   The theme of ideological consistency – the adherence to an underlying set of principles consistent with a given political philosophy – is one held by those on both right and left. Hence

discourse of the left has to apply and reproduce an underlying set of principles when addressing the impact on those at the rural grassroots – agricultural labourers and poor peasants – of specific forms taken by property relations, the State, the market and 'civil society'. Historically and currently, therefore, advocacy of common ownership of means of production/distribution/ exchange is not encountered in the discourse of the political right, any more than socialists champion either pre-socialist systemic forms (feudalism, capitalism), or private appropriation/ownership of these same resources/ processes.

Although they diverge on some policies, conservatives and neoliberals nevertheless agree that individual property rights – whether of capitalist landlords, commercial farmers or rich peasants – must be upheld by the State, using whatever means necessary (coercion, populist discourse).[5] Accepting this view about the central socio-economic role of the State, those on the political left have by contrast advocated the revolutionary capture/control of this

---

the following observation by the influential right-wing political theorist, Julius Evola (2002: 115): 'For the authentic revolutionary conservative, what really counts is to be faithful not to past forms and institutions, but rather to principles of which such forms and institutions have been particular expressions adequate for a specific period of time and in a specific geographical area… Tradition, in its essence, is something simultaneously meta-historical and dynamic: it is an overall ordering force, in the service of principles that have the chrism of superior legitimacy (we may even call them "principles from above"). This force acts through the generations, in continuity of spirit and inspiration, through institutions, laws and social orders that may even display a remarkable variety and diversity'. From the other end of the political spectrum, the importance of adhering to underlying principles was confirmed by Trotsky (1936: 141, original emphasis): 'It was not flexibility that served (nor should it serve today) as the basic trait of Bolshevism but rather *granite hardness*. It was precisely of this quality, for which its enemies and opponents reproached it, that Bolshevism was always justly proud'. Agreeing about the importance of principle does not, of course, mean agreement as to what those principles advocate.

5 An exception concerns the conditions justifying the expropriation of a landlord class. Such a policy was advocated by neoliberals at the end of the nineteenth century and modernization theorists mid-way through the twentieth on the grounds that national economic development (= capitalism) required this. It is important to note that the object of expropriation was in these situations limited to unproductive landlords – that is to say, taking land from large proprietors who did not (or would not) cultivate it and handing it over to peasants who would. This approach, in which one set of individual property rights gives way to another set of the same, must be distinguished politically from a Marxist programme, where *all* land (not just unproductive holdings) is confiscated by the State, which then becomes its sole owner. The object is the furtherance not of capitalism but of socialism. Similarly, property thus acquired is then made available not to enhance individual units of what are instances of peasant economy, but rather collective enterprises owned/controlled by the State.

apparatus precisely in order not merely to transform both property and production relations, but also to ensure that – once accomplished – such changes
are not reversed. These considerations in turn determine the different shape
taken by concepts such as democracy and 'civil society', neither of which consequently can be said to stand epistemologically outside either politics or
history.

Accordingly, the peasantry, the State, 'civil society' and the nation – plus the
connection between them all – have been and are at the centre of the left/right
political divide, notwithstanding recent theoretical attempts to abolish the left/
right distinction.[6] Historically, the left has always been supportive of the working class, secularism, plus an internationalist outlook based on the existence of
a strong central State and a weak market, and opposed to bourgeois democracy
and a systemically non-specific notion of 'civil society'. The right by contrast has
been supportive not only of decentralised decision-making incorporating any/
all ideological beliefs, 'civil society', religion, and 'primordial loyalties', but also of
nationalism, bourgeois democracy, a weak State and a strong market. Both left
and right have at different times championed the interests of the peasantry, but
under different circumstances, in distinct ways and for very different reasons.

For this reason, of interest is the debate on the political right and left
about the State and the market, and how – despite fundamental differences as
to the weak/strong role of both State and market – conservatives and socialists
have in the past agreed that the form taken by property relations, 'civil
society'/'citizenship', and democracy all depend ultimately on the capture

---

6 Denying the relevance any longer of a left/right political distinction was a mantra uttered by
   many academic supporters of Tony Blair and New Labour. An influential example is Giddens
   (1994), for whom the rejection of this difference gave rise to his espousal of a 'Third Way' that
   transcended political distinctions between left and right. What he forgets, or – more probably – does not know, is that the 'Third Way' concept has long been an emplacement of reactionary discourse. For those on the political right, therefore, the notion of a third way – one
   that is neither capitalist nor socialist – has been a mobilizing ideology informing *nationalist*
   opposition not just to international socialism but also to international capitalism. The latter
   is held as much to blame as the former for undermining the traditional components of a
   specifically *national* culture valued and defended by the political right. That this is still the
   case is evident from mid-1970s Italy, where according to Rao (2006: 267) the slogan of Italian
   neofascists was '*Né destra, né sinistra, Terza Posizione*'. That is, 'neither right, nor left, but a
   Third Way', which is precisely what Giddens himself currently advocates. This is not to say
   that Giddens is a fellow-traveller of the political right – rather obviously he is not. It is to say,
   however, that he has unwittingly reproduced what is in fact a central tenet of rightwing discourse (for evidence of which, see Fiore and Adinolfi, 2004), not least because – appearances
   to the contrary notwithstanding – the history of political theory is for him a closed book.

and/or control of the State. Without effecting and reproducing the latter, and thus enabling the State to plan/regulate the market, claims that poor peasants and agricultural workers in any context and conjuncture have been or are (or indeed could be) empowered necessarily remain unfulfilled.

Yet much current theory about development maintains that rural empowerment and the realization of 'civil society' no longer requires control either of the market or of the State, let alone a fundamental change in agrarian property relations or a revolutionary transition to socialism. Instead, poor peasants and agricultural workers are regarded as empowered by virtue of possessing a specific cultural/ethnic/religious/national identity. Such theory claims, moreover, that the object of rural grassroots agency is limited politically and geographically. Peasants and workers desire no more than to establish or re-establish democracy, frequently within the confines of a particular locality.

II

Just as the political right is in general opposed to State 'interference' in the economy, so historically those on the left have supported intervention/ planning/regulation: the purpose of the latter has been to expropriate means of production – particularly land – so as to facilitate the planning and income redistribution central to the process of development. That a change in the control of State possessed implications for property relations in the countryside has – until recently – always been recognized. This was true of discussions about democracy that followed the English revolution of the 1640s; it also informed debates between Bolsheviks and agrarian populists after the 1917 Russian revolution. The State/property relation was similarly central to much development theory (modernization, post-colonialism) formulated during and after the 1960s.

Over the past half century, the beneficiaries of State intervention in the economies of India and Latin America have to a limited degree included peasants and workers. However, the interventionist role of the State was challenged in the 1980s from two directions. Not just by neoliberal economic theory, therefore, but also by postmodernism, which shifted the development debate away from political economy and class to culture, which as a result became reified, a phenomenon without a material referent.[7]

---

7   It is difficult to convey the extent to which the idea of state intervention and planning in so-called Third World countries was discarded as a result of this twin onslaught (postmodernism, neoliberalism). Perhaps the best way of illustrating the full measure of this

The Left: An Eye to Property

Among those opposed to conservatism, the indissolubility of a link between control of the State, political representation and property relations has long been recognized, and as such has been central to historical disputes over the meaning and structure of democracy itself. This surfaced in the course of the Putney Debates that followed the English Civil War of the mid-seventeenth century, when the question of who controlled the State, and thus had the power to enforce the will of the propertyless once this had been expressed, against

---

epistemological (and political) shift is to cite the words of Doreen Warriner, an earlier and non-Marxist development theorist who made extensive studies of the peasantry. About the link between rural poverty, property relations and culture in the Middle East after the 1939–45 war era, she wrote (Warriner, 1948: 1) as follows: 'Near starvation, pestilence, high death rates, soil erosion, economic exploitation – this is the pattern of life for the mass of the rural population in the Middle East. It is a poverty which has no parallel in Europe, since even clean water is a luxury. Money incomes are low – £5 to £7 per head per year – but money comparisons alone do not convey the filth and disease, the mud-huts shared with animals, the dried fuel dung fuel. There is no standard of living in the European sense – mere existence is accepted as standard. This poverty has become a familiar background in recent years, and as a result of the war in the Middle East area the question of how to raise the standard of living has emerged. In the past students of the Arab world have treated this poverty reverently as a "way of life", as part of an Arab *mystique*, and accepted it as fatalistically as its victims do. By these experts it is believed that to talk of raising living standards is to use criteria which do not apply, and which vitiate the real values of Arab society. This is a natural attitude for those who have found in the Arab world some social values which Western civilization fails to provide, and who are concerned to preserve them. But to emphasize the squalor of life in the Middle East is not necessarily to deny that it has other qualities as well; and if we urge the need of raising the material standard of living, that does not mean that we also urge the general application of the other standards of the West. It is simply to recognize the fact that poverty is an evil in this world as in ours, and that it must be overcome, in order to realize any way of life, as distinct from a sordid struggle for existence'. A decade later, this battle appeared to be won, and in the Preface to a subsequent book Warriner (1957: vii) felt able to note that although '[t]he poverty is not out of date...the perspective has changed. There has been development, far more than seemed possible ten years ago. Then it seemed necessary to justify the belief that poverty was a matter which should concern the Arab countries and the West. Today [= 1956] such justification is no longer needed. It now seems more important to stress the dynamics of change, as they affect the poor, rather than to study underdevelopment as a static condition, the only approach to the region which seemed possible in 1947'. What her comments would have been on current approaches to development, influenced by a postmodern rejection of the concept itself as 'Eurocentric', 'foundational' and 'orientalist', one can only guess. She would most certainly have identified them as a reversion to those very paradigms – 'experts [who] believed that to talk of raising living standards is to use criteria which do not apply' – criticized by her sixty years earlier.

the wishes of those who owned land, quickly became the main concern.[8] What
was to become a recurring theme in the discourse of conservatives – that once
the propertyless had the vote, they would exercise this in order to transform
existing tenure relations and land distribution to their own advantage – was
accordingly voiced at the inception of discussions about the political desirability and economic impact of democracy.

Without addressing the private ownership of land, and how this empowers
those who have it and disempowers those who do not, therefore, any notion of
democracy necessarily lacks substance. At issue is not merely the franchise itself,
but also – and more importantly – its effectiveness in a context where those who
own means of production (including large landholdings) remain unexpropri-
ated and thus retain the capacity to circumvent the mandate of those who are
propertyless. It is, in short, a dispute not merely about political representation
embodying the consent of the governed, but also about its effectiveness and
enforcement by the State. Now, however, this epistemological (and political) link
has been broken, to the extent that it is currently possible to discuss and proclaim the existence of democracy without even mentioning property relations.

---

8   This theme – about the centrality of property relations to the discussion by the Army Council
    of future representative government – is ably summed up by Brailsford (1961: 267ff.) and by
    Foot (2005: 3–44), while the full text of the Putney Debates is contained in Woodhouse (1938).
    The fear on the part of those who owned – and might lose – property was expressed by Ireton
    thus (Brailsford, 1961: 276): 'All the main thing that I speak for is because I would have an eye
    to property. I hope we do not come to contend for victory – but let every man consider with
    himself that he do not go that way to take away all property. For here is the case of the most
    fundamental part of the constitution of the kingdom, which if you take away, you take away
    all by that'. Uttered by Colonel Thomas Rainborough on 29 October 1647, the memorable
    words that encapsulate the radical politics of the Putney Debates are as follows (Woodhouse,
    1938: 53): 'For really I think that the poorest he that is in England hath a life to live, as the
    greatest he; and therefore truly, sir, I think it clear, that every man that is to live under a gov-
    ernment ought first by his own consent to put himself under that government; and I do think
    that the poorest man in England is not at all bound in a strict sense to that government that
    he hath not had a voice to put himself under...' However, as Foot (2005: 35) points out,
    'Rainsborough's "right to live", which he claimed for the "poorest he", referred to political
    rights, not to economic rights. The Levellers were very much for liberty and fraternity. But
    they were not at all sure about equality. They shrank from the conclusions of their contem-
    porary Gerrard Winstanley, who campaigned for a world in which property was held in
    common. The earth, predicted Winstanley in a 1649 pamphlet...would one day become a
    "common treasury". Winstanley, by far the most advanced political thinker of the English
    Revolution, developed his communistic theories into a full-blown political philosophy. He
    argued that true liberty was impossible while property was unequally distributed, and called
    on the common people to take action to create a new egalitarian world'.

The irony is that, historically, even non-Marxists such as Adam Smith and John Ramsey McCulloch also believed that the main purpose of the State was – and could only ever be – to protect existing property relations.[9] From this followed the inference that, if private ownership of land and other means of production, and the corresponding political and ideological power these economic resources confer on their possessors are to be transformed, then control of the State is *ipso facto* a question that has to be addressed. Similarly, any transformation in property relations necessarily entails the capture of and rule through the instrument of the State, both to alter hitherto dominant owner-ship patterns and to ensure that such change is not reversed. This is a political connection that postmodern theory endorsing the efficacy of grassroots resis-tance (conducted there on an 'everyday' basis) that fails to transcend its immediate locale – the site of institutions associated with 'civil society' – is unable to make.

---

9 Accepting that '[c]ivil government supposes a certain subordination', Adam Smith (1812: 74–75) gives as one of the reasons for this 'the superiority of fortune'. He elaborates thus (Smith, 1812: 73–74): 'Wherever there is great property, there is great inequality. For one very rich man, there must be at least five hundred poor, and the affluence of the few supposes the indigence of the many. The affluence of the rich excites the indignation of the poor, who are often driven by want, and prompted by envy, to invade his possessions. It is only under the shelter of the civil magistrate that the owner of that valuable property, which is acquired by the labour of many years, or perhaps of many successive generations, can sleep a single night in security. He is at all times surrounded by unknown enemies, whom, though he never pro-voked, he can never appease, and from whose injustice he can be protected only by the pow-erful arm of the civil magistrate continually held up to chastise it. The acquisition of valuable and extensive property, therefore, necessarily requires the establishment of civil govern-ment. Where there is no property, or at least none that exceeds the value of two or three days labour, civil government is not so necessary'. In a similar vein, McCulloch (1830: 84–85, 88, 288) upholds the principle of *laissez faire* (= 'non-interference') while arguing that the main role of government is to guarantee property relations: 'The finest soil, the finest climate, and the finest intellectual powers, can prevent no people from becoming barbarous, poor, and miserable, if they have the misfortune to be subjected to a government which does not respect and maintain the right of property. This is the greatest of all calamities. [...] let us not, therefore, deceive ourselves by supposing that it is possible for any people to emerge from barbarism or to become wealthy, prosperous, and civilized, without the security of property. [...] It cannot, however, be too strongly or too often impressed upon those in authority, that non-interference ought to be the leading principle of their policy, and interference the excep-tion only; that in all ordinary cases individuals should be left to shape their conduct accord-ing to their own judgment and discretion...The maxim *pas trop gouverner* should never be absent from the recollection of legislators and ministers'.

Strong State, Weak Market

The debate about peasant economy, and whether and why it should be maintained, became more acute towards the end of the nineteenth century, when industrialization spread to new areas (Russia, America). During this period agrarian populism – a plebeian pro-rural politics and philosophy which argued that farmers and peasants were the economic and cultural backbone of the nation – became important in both these contexts. Much the same was true of Austria and Germany, where conservatives insisted that smallholding agriculture should be protected by the State, a position no different from that taken at the same conjuncture by revisionists on the political left.[10] The latter included those – such as von Vollmar, Eduard David, and Otto Hertz – who maintained that socialists should seek to recruit a following among small property owners in rural areas, a view strongly opposed by Kautsky from the 1880s onwards.[11]

It surfaced with a vengeance before, during, and after the 1917 Russian revolution, when the Bolsheviks took issue with agrarian populists over the role of peasants under socialism.[12] Populists maintained both that undifferentiated

---

10   In a programmatic analysis that in many ways anticipates the position taken by Chayanov, the conservative politician and political economist Schäffle (1892: 275–277) argued as follows: 'Propertied labour, at any rate in Germany and Austria, still forms by far the largest portion of the whole of productive labour. It includes the peasantry and the artisans, with almost all their families and belongings. Towards these the State has merely a positive protective task to fulfil, in furthering the private and associated organization of credit... The Social question par excellence is the question of *the retention of the peasant-class.* Popular collective production, as opposed to peasant proprietorship, is open to the very gravest doubts as to whether it would work better industrially, that is, more productively, and, by cheapening the necessities of life, more advantageously for the masses of the people, at the same time securing to each producer and his family the whole result of his labour. It is highly probable...that democratic collective production would be rather less productive than *peasant industry, wherever it is free from a load of unproductive debt.* With the latter important proviso, of keeping free from unproductive debt, the peasant-class has not been and cannot be chained or impoverished by capital. The peasant with his family is proprietor and labourer in one person, and himself draws *the whole of the results of his labour*: property does therefore secure the very thing which Socialism promises but cannot safely guarantee. We are therefore far from having proved that the destruction of the union of property and labour in the peasant-class is inevitable' (original emphases).

11   For this debate over whether or not socialists ought to attempt to seek the support of peasant proprietors, see Salvadori (1979) and Hussain and Tribe (1984). As is clear from the arguments currently advanced by Unger (on which see Petras and Veltmeyer, 2003), this debate continues to be relevant.

12   The most complete account of the 1920s debate in Russia between agrarian populists and Marxists is to be found in Solomon (1977), an important source that has influenced much

peasant economy was an innate organizational form, and that it would continue to exist despite 'external' systemic transformations (from feudalism to
capitalism, and from the latter to socialism). According to populists, therefore,
not only was an egalitarian and innately virtuous smallholding agriculture
unaffected by capitalism, but peasant economy was bolstered by and in turn
reproduced a local version of 'civil society' – based on subsistence cultivation
by the peasant family and household – they thought was already present in the
village (*mir*).[13]

Bolsheviks, by contrast, insisted that the peasantry was differentiated along
class lines in the course of capitalist development, its top stratum (= rich peasants) consolidating means of production and becoming small capitalists, while
its increasingly landless bottom stratum (= poor peasants) joined the ranks of
the proletariat.[14] Instead of private property – the individualist smallholding
economy – supported/advocated by populists, the Bolshevik programme of
agrarian reform was based on collective agriculture, where rural property was
owned/controlled by the State. Among the reasons for this was that the latter
approach facilitated central planning.

The State as Property

Where the Third World was concerned, perhaps the most influential interpretation of the link between control of the State and property relations over
recent decades was that made by Hamza Alavi.[15] More than most, his work
engaged theoretically and politically with colonialism and – before it was appropriated and distorted by postmodernism – the notion of post-colonialism.
The latter concept linked both class and State formation in the so-called Third
World to peasant agency. Because it was allied to the local bourgeoisie and
landlord class, he argued, neo-colonialism continued to flourish by means

---

of the subsequent discussion on the subject. Centrally about the transformation of social
relations in the countryside and the resulting impact on economic growth, this discussion
about the socio-economic differentiation of rural community goes back to debates
between populists (Engel'gardt, Uspenskii, Vorontsov, Chayanov) and Marxists
(Plekhanov, Lenin) in Russia and elsewhere from the 1860s onwards. Then the debate
concerned the future political and economic role of peasants following serf emancipation, and was answered differently by populists and Marxists.

13   Examples of this kind of argument can be found in Shinn (1987) and contributions to the
     volumes edited by Eklof and Frank (1990) and Kingston-Mann and Mixter (1991).

14   The classic Statement of the Bolshevik argument about the socio-economic differentia-
     tion of petty commodity production by capitalism is Lenin (1964).

15   His own social background in Pakistan gave Alavi a unique insight into the significance of
     educated middle class in post-colonial societies, and in particular its crucial political role.

of aid leverage. International capital was thus able to exercise power over newly formed or newly independent Third World States, particularly their army and bureaucracy (termed by him the 'military-bureaucratic oligarchy').

His disagreement with classical Marxist theory was that on account of its colonial experience, the State apparatus of newly independent nations was not, and could not be, an institution through which a single class exercised political power.[16] This was because unlike European countries, where an indigenous bourgeois rose to power economically, in the course of which it shaped the State apparatus in its own image, in post-colonial societies this task had to some degree already been accomplished by a foreign (= metropolitan) bourgeoisie.[17] Hence the State apparatus itself became the crucial site of struggle for economic power exercised in post-colonial contexts, as a result of which the 'bureaucratic-military oligarchy' assumed a relatively autonomous role vis-à-vis competing interests attempting to wrest control over its project and/or resources (the extraction/allocation of economic surplus, who was to benefit from planned development).[18]

Consequently, in erstwhile colonies the indigenous middle class remained economically weak, and had to prosecute a twofold struggle: against on the one hand 'bureaucratic-military oligarchy' in charge of the State apparatus, and on the other the mainly rural masses (to prevent revolution).[19] Rather

---

16   For the details of this, see Alavi (1975).

17   He identified three competing propertied classes struggling for control over the state in Pakistan: an indigenous (= domestic) bourgeoisie, a neo-colonial (= foreign) bourgeoisie, and indigenous landowning class, frequently (and in his view, wrongly) labelled 'feudal' or 'semi-feudal'.

18   On this, see Alavi (1982b).

19   This was linked in turn to his view (Alavi, 1965; 1973a; 1973b) about the revolutionary role of peasants in post-colonial societies. Since no opposition to imperialism could be expected either from an indigenous bourgeoisie or a landowning class, any struggle against capitalism and for socialism in so-called Third World societies would of necessity have to be led by the rural masses in general, and the peasantry in particular. On the basis of his study of agrarian mobilizations in pre-revolutionary Russia, in mid-1920s China (the Hunan movement), and in India during the mid-1940s (the Telegana and Tebhaga movements), Alavi maintained that middle peasants were 'the most militant element of the peasantry'. This theory not only anticipated the 'middle peasant' thesis applied subsequently by Eric Wolf (1971) to peasant movements in other contexts (Mexico, Vietnam, Algeria and Cuba), but also departed from the classic Marxist argument that in the countryside of so-called Third World societies it was the poor peasant who was the main revolutionary subject.

than opposing the continuing economic influence of neo-colonial interests, therefore, the indigenous propertied classes reached an accommodation with imperialism, the outcome being that capitalist development was both dependent and occurred under the aegis of what was misleadingly thought to be 'feudal' landowners utilizing 'pre-capitalist' production relations. That capitalist farming (in the form of the Green Revolution) developed on the basis of supposedly non-capitalist property and production relations meant in turn that it was no longer necessary in such contexts to eliminate 'feudal' structures. These, Alavi concluded, were no longer the obstacles to capitalist development in the so-called Third World that they were once thought to be.[20]

However, the continuing relevance of his views concerning the link between access to property and struggles over the State in the Third World are borne out by the events from the late twentieth century onwards. That the State can be used to release into private ownership once again the valuable economic resources that had been public property is evident from the numerous privatizations that have been effected by neoliberal regimes that came to power during the 1980s and 1990s in erstwhile socialist nations, metropolitan capitalist countries, and Third World contexts alike. Among the lessons taught by such developments is the futility of attempts to ignore State power, by constructing 'civil society' and transforming property relations locally, as though nothing at a level above the rural grassroots mattered.

In the case of Russia after 1989 and China after 1976, therefore, vast personal fortunes were carved out of public assets – including land – following the dissolution of socialism.[21] Although not socialist, much the same happened in the case of the Mexican State: here, too, the privatization of publicly-owned

---

20   Although the view that 'feudal' structures were no obstacle to the growth of capitalist farming has been vindicated, some of his other arguments were challenged by subsequent developments. This was the case with the specificity attached to what was identified as the colonial mode of production. Similarly, the view (Alavi, 1964) that the object of neo-colonialism, or the new imperialism, was not the export of capital to exploit cheap labour in the Third World has difficulties when confronted by what came to be seen as the new international division of labour. What is not open to dispute, however, is the influence of these ideas on those writing at the time about the peasantry and peasant movements. This is especially true of a series of important articles published from the mid-1960s onwards (Alavi, 1964; 1965; 1971; 1975). Their impact during the decade that followed is evident both from the anthologization and translations of his work (Alavi, 1976; 1988a; 1988b), and from its critical application to non-Asian contexts (Saul, 1974).

21   Russian oligarchs such as Roman Abramovich (worth £10.8 billion) made their huge fortunes as a result of the privatization of valuable State assets (oil, industry) during the early 1990s.

utilities generated similarly large amounts of wealth for a few individuals.[22] In the case of Pakistan, it is the military which has benefited from its institutional position vis-à-vis the State: its economic assets – of which rural property is an important component – are valued at around US$10 billion.[23] All these examples confirm that globalization has made the capture of the State more – not less – important politically.

III

Nowhere are the contradictions inherent in politically non-specific notions of State and democracy clearer than in the attempt by modernization theory to construct a concept of 'civil society'. The era following the 1939–45 war was characterized by an ostensibly progressive desire on the part of non-Marxist development theory to bring poor peasants and agricultural workers in the Third World into the capitalist system, not least so as to deny their grassroots agency to socialism in a period of imperial expansion following decolonization.[24] However, this was linked to a restricted concept of change: bringing peasants and workers into the wider society was to be mainly political, not economic. In a context of universal adult suffrage, a process of 'becoming modern' required democratic participation by poor peasants and workers,

22   It is estimated that Carlos Slim, who purchased the State-owned Mexican telecommunications company in 1990, is worth as a result in excess of US$60 billion. See 'Mexican monopolist's fortune leads the world', *Financial Times* (London), 6 July 2007.

23   On this, and in particular the role of senior army officers as the 'new land barons', see Siddiqa (2007).

24   Modernization theorists (Verba, 1989: 399) described 'civic culture' thus: '[It] focused on those political attitudes that would be supportive of a democratic political system. The assumption was that a number of forces led to the development of such attitudes – education; the democratization of nongovernmental authority systems in the family, the school, and the workplace; general trust in one's fellow citizens'. This 'civic culture', observed Almond (1989: 16), was a 'rationalist-activist model of democratic citizenship… conceived in the aftermath of World War II. The events of the 1920s and the 1930s and the reflections of social theorists on those events informed their political theory. The tragic collapse of Italian and particularly German democracy and their subversion into participant-destructive manias…were the powerful historical experiences contributing to this more complex theory of the relationship between political culture and democratic stability'. The irony here is unmissable: the construction of 'civil society' that wished to avoid the fascist mobilizations of the pre-war era nevertheless failed to challenge the very discourse – the enduring *cultural* link between peasant/nation/Nature – which underwrote those reactionary politics.

therefore, but in a way that threatened neither existing property relations, the State nor the wider capitalist system. A corollary was an acceptance that existing grassroots cultural practices and/or ideology – the central emplacements of the agrarian myth – would not just continue as before but were henceforth to be regarded as an indicator of the 'adaptive' success of the modernization process.[25]

Where the study of agrarian transformation was concerned, and in particular how this involved peasants and workers in the Third World, this difficulty – becoming (politically) 'modern' while remaining (culturally) 'ancient' – had two important outcomes. First, it left unchallenged a discourse about peasant/nation/Nature that historically has been the domain of conservatives and the political right (see Chapter 2). And second, much of this same discourse was subsequently taken over wholesale by many of those considered to be on the political left. By the 1980s the latter had metamorphosed into the 'new' populist postmodernists, who mobilized this same discourse in order to challenge not just earlier modernization theory but also current neoliberalism. For these ex-socialists, therefore, the construction of 'civil society' replaced the capture of State power. Similarly, grassroots culture became an alternative to (and substitute for) economic development, an epistemological stance that entailed, among other things, the defence of 'civil society' composed of all those traditional institutions that socialist theory usually criticizes and opposes.

The Right: Becoming Modern, Remaining Ancient

During the Cold war era, advocates of bourgeois democracy were keen to stress the connection between 'civil society' and nation-building, none more so than modernization theory, the then dominant non-Marxist paradigm in development studies.[26] Equating citizenship with bourgeois democracy, and the latter

---

25   In his lengthy and hugely over-optimistic account of democratic 'stability' in India following decolonization, therefore, Wiener (1967: 482ff.) commends the Indian National Congress for its capacity not to transform but to 'adapt' to existing cultural practices. In his words (Wiener, 1967: 15): 'In its efforts to win, Congress adapts itself to the local power structures. It recruits from among those who have local power and influence. It trains its cadres to perform political roles similar to those performed in the traditional society before there was party politics. It manipulates factional, caste, and linguistic disputes...It utilizes traditional methods of dispute settlement to maintain cohesion within the party'.

26   Modernization theory is associated with the work of mainly US political scientists, the most influential of whom – Gabriel Almond, Edward Shils and Samuel Huntingdon – were anti-communist cold warriors intent on formulating an alternative to socialist politics in the Third World (Leys, 1996: 9–11). It assumed a positive correlation between democracy and economic growth: either the former made the latter possible, or

with modernity as projected through national identity, this paradigm allocated a pivotal role to the diffusion of political knowledge via the mass media.[27] As provider of material inputs contributing to accumulation in rural areas, moreover, the State was cast in a similarly positive role. For exponents of modernization theory at that conjuncture, therefore, bourgeois democracy exercised in the context of a benign State apparatus, 'civil society' and nationalism were not just interchangeable concepts but also politically progressive ones.[28] This despite the fact that nationalist discourses invoked cultural identities that were rural, subsistence-oriented, traditional and backwards-looking: or the very ones to which modernization theory was in principle opposed.

The problem confronting modernization theory of the Cold War era is easily discerned. Keen to privilege capitalism so as to combat revolutionary socialism in Third World countries, it exhibited a willingness to endorse any/all anti-Marxist epistemologies, amongst which populism – with its deep roots in the agrarian myth – featured prominently.[29] Signing up the historical enemies of

---

economic growth facilitated a 'deepening' of democracy. In what was a political equivalent of the 'trickle down' theory, the supposition was that economic development would automatically reinforce political democracy, since national 'elites' who delivered higher living standards to the masses would no longer have anything to fear from them in terms of their political parties, the franchise and the secret ballot. In such circumstances, an economically successful 'elite' might expect to remain in power, through its control of the state apparatus, since participatory decision-making would present no threat to capitalist property relations. Among those who have studied the peasantry in Third World countries using this kind of approach are Mair (1963), Rogers (1969), and Huizer (1970).

27   In the Third World where 'villagers are becoming dissatisfied with eating the cake of custom' (Rogers, 1969: 2), (bourgeois) political consciousness formed by (a bourgeois) mass media was perceived as a 'positive good'. Hence catalytic role of mass media and knowledge about politics in the causal link (mass media exposure → greater political participation → national citizen → political modernization) structuring the analysis by Rogers (1969) of the way in which Colombian peasants underwent a transition from tradition to modernity. In his view (Rogers, 1969: 56, 111), 'such political awareness probably indicates...a distinct feeling of being a part of a nation's citizenry, and at least a minimal degree of political modernization... [...] Mass media exposure is positively related to political knowledge...in less developed countries the mass media are powerful transmitters of political news, creators of meaningful citizen interest and participation in politics, and developers of nationalistic spirit. Present findings suggest this belief in the role of the mass media in political modernization may well be justified'.

28   This epistemology underwrote the development model of Lerner (1958), a modernization theorist who influenced the analysis by another such (Rogers, 1969: 44–46) of the Colombian peasantry.

29   That fear of a revolutionary challenge to capitalism, and its replacement with socialism, was uppermost in the minds of modernization theorists during the 1960s is evident from

Marxism and socialism in such circumstances is not without its long-term contradictions, since an anti-modern ideology proclaiming the immutability of traditional cultural 'otherness' is usually also opposed to many aspects of bourgeois democracy itself.[30] Although aware of this possibility, exponents of modernization theory at that conjuncture were nevertheless unable to avoid this trap, given that their primary objective was to deploy any/all discourses opposed to socialism. That such anti-modern discourses emanating from nationalist ideology would then be turned on them, a reversal disseminated via the mass media originally deemed by them to be the bearers of modernity, was an outcome they did not address in any detail.[31]

No Longer Eating the Cake of Custom?

Accordingly, four decades ago (and obviously in ignorance of what was to come), it was possible for modernization theorists to endorse as a positive feature the fact that socialist intellectuals in Yugoslavia combined Marxist theory with a variety of non-modern, long-standing indigenous/folkloric discourses.[32]

---

a concern with what was termed 'revolution and political instability' in rural areas of the Third World. Hence the following observation by one such (Rogers, 1969: 23): 'The political stability of national governments in less developed countries depends in part upon the public opinion of their peasantry...[p]easant attitudes toward government must change in order for the national governments of less developed countries to attain a relative degree of political stability'.

30   This is a lesson that the US is currently being taught yet again in Afghanistan and the Middle East. Characterized as 'blowback', it entails the recognition of the fact that traditional social forces and ideologies mobilized against socialism – armed, financed and supported politically by the US itself – frequently include in their condemnation of modernity (for eroding the cultural 'otherness' specific to a particular ethnicity or nationalism) not just socialism but also neoliberalism and bourgeois democracy.

31   Some modernization theorists were aware of a potential contradiction, but failed to consider the implications of this, let alone give it political importance. Thus, for example, Rogers accepts that regarding nationalism as a positive aspect of modernity may indeed trigger a return to pre-modern ideology. In his view (Rogers, 1969: 378), it 'is possible that nationalism may motivate certain expressions of neo-traditionalization, the process by which individuals change from a modern way of life to a more traditional style of life'.

32   Hence the break with Marxist categories by social scientists in Yugoslavia from the 1950s onwards was praised by Halpern and Hammel (1969: 24) as 'pragmatic eclecticism', in particular the role of intellectuals in recuperating ethnic categories (folk = people = peasant) deployed in the construction of an independent Yugoslavia at the Paris Peace Conference after the end of the 1914–18 war. Despite noting that (Halpern and Hammel, 1969: 18) 'the nation-state sought its ultimate rationalization not so much in literate urban traditions...but in native (folk) institutions and traditions which had survived invasion

The attraction of the latter was not just their anti-Marxist epistemology and nationalistic politics, but also the fact that during the development decade of the 1960s such bourgeois ideology could claim that it, too, had a subject of history that was plebeian: an homogeneous peasantry, undifferentiated by class. Much the same is true of what was then termed 'African Socialism', the adherents of which were similarly commended for their 'considerable pragmatism', a description which accepted as positive the fact that beneath the socialist label there lurked anti-communist, traditionalist and nationalist discourses.[33]

Rather obviously, 1960s modernization theory was culpable of failing to anticipate the return of anti-modern discourses (about the enduring and

---

and foreign political dominance', the populist lineage of this discourse and its reactionary political history are deemed unproblematic. Much the same observations were made subsequently regarding Soviet ethnographic literature, similarly commended by Dunn (1975: 69) as a 'new departure', where 'on the theoretical level, even though the Marxist terminology remains largely intact, important conceptual shifts have taken place...in terms of ideological "culture" and self-awareness and in the recognition that per se it is independent of political or economic factors, or even of the type of social order prevailing in a certain place at a given time'.

33   As the Pan-Africanism of Padmore (1953; 1956) underlines, what passed for 'African Socialism' in the pre-colonial era was invariably nothing more than petty bourgeois nationalism which was strongly antagonistic to Marxist theory and socialist politics. For a discussion of 'African Socialism' at that conjuncture, see the contributions in the volume edited by Friedland and Rosberg (1964). The unwarranted optimism is of modernization theory is evident from the observation (Friedland, 1964: 29) that '[o]ne index is the hostility of modern political leaders toward tribes and tribalism. While political leaders emphasize traditionalism in certain contexts, they are intensely anti-tribal. Tribalism is, of course, an outmoded form of social cohesion, but it remains an important attachment for large numbers of rural Africans unaccustomed to pluralism. Because attachments to traditional institutions impede the attachment of individuals to the new nation-state (via the party), modern political leaders are almost invariably hostile to tribalism. The consequence of their anti-tribalism is to make individuals increasingly dependent upon the single, central focal institution and to undermine the integrity of competing institutions'. A more realistic political assessment was that of Saul (1976: 98), who commented as follows: 'For "tribalism" (the politicization of ethnicity which is all too characteristic a pathology of dependent Africa) does not spring primarily from the bare fact of the existence of cultural differences between people. Rather, it has been teased into life, first by the divide-and-rule tactics of colonialism and by uneven development in the economic sphere that colonialism also facilitates and, second, by the ruling petty-bourgeoisie of the post-colonial period. The latter, too, seek to divide and rule – better from their point of view that peasants should conceive the national pie as being divided, comparatively between regions and tribes, rather than (as is in fact much more clearly the case) between classes'.

valuable character of tradition, ethnicity, peasant identity, nature), their connection with nationalism and the agrarian myth, and the extent to which this was compatible with the interests of capitalism.[34] In a sense this is unsurprising, since nationalist and populist discourses have strong historical links to conservative ideology, especially where peasant/State relations are involved. What is surprising, however, is that some of those on the political left made the same mistake: not just a failure to distance themselves from populism, nationalism and conservative anti-modern discourses, but much rather an endorsement of them.[35]

In part, this failure has its roots in the dualism that structured the mode of production debate conducted in the decades that followed.[36] Conceptualizing an articulation between capitalist and non-capitalist modes within a

---

34   In this connection it is important to differentiate modernity in terms of when, systemically, it can be said to have been accomplished. For this reason, bourgeois modernization theory must be distinguished from an endorsement of a specifically Marxist concept of modernity. The former halts at a capitalist form modernity, signalled by 'choice' as expressed via the market or the ballot box (= democracy), and does not seek to go beyond this. Marxism, by contrast, argues that anti-modern discourses it is necessary to transcend the latter since – in terms of working class empowerment – a politically meaningful kind of modernity can only be achieved under socialism.

35   That some on the political left were just as culpable as modernization theorists of signing up to anti-socialist theoretical positions is evident from the case of Hobsbawm. Not only did he (Hobsbawm, 1981) advance the same argument as postmodernists – about the decline of the working class as the subject of history – but in an essay written in 1966, he confidently made a prognosis about Yugoslavia that was spectacularly wrong. In the latter text, therefore, one encounters the following (Hobsbawm, 1973: 71) confident prediction: 'Belgian capitalism or Yugoslav socialism may well change, perhaps fundamentally; but both are obviously far less likely to collapse at slight provocation than the complex ad hoc administrative formulae for ensuring the coexistence of Flemings and Walloons, or of various mutually suspicious Balkan nationalities'. One wonders whether these episodes and opinions are among the things Hobsbawm had in mind when observing recently (Snowman, 2007: 40) that he 'worries about the incursions of postmodernism into the writing of history, the moral and even factual relativism of some historical writing...[t]he business of the historian...is to remember what others forget'. Others do indeed remember what Hobsbawm seems to have forgotten: his complicity with 1980s anti-foundational views that were in step with the then-emerging postmodernism that he now condemns.

36   The mode of production debate – on which see especially Thorner (1982) – addressed the crucial issue of whether or not capitalism was present in the countryside of Third World nations, and if not, why not. From this central argument there were problematic attempts to construct theories about modes of production that were specific in terms of area (Cardoso, 1975; Coquery-Vidrovich, 1975) or colonialism (Alavi, 1975; 1982a). After the 'development decade' of the 1960s, the Marxist approach to African rural society was in

particular social formation licensed a theoretical dichotomy between urban industrial capitalism and its State on the one hand, and on the other a rural mass of non-capitalist petty commodity producers. Capitalism was externalized, peasants being seen as a *sui generis* class uniformly ranged against the State, rather than internally differentiated along class lines. This in turn gave rise to the defence by a number of those on the political left of peasants engaged in struggles (= 'resistance') against the State and capitalism, in the misplaced belief that such a position was Marxist and furthered the cause of socialism.[37] An inability to distinguish between Marxism and populism led some to espouse the latter, thinking it was the former.[38]

---

the hands of French anthropologists (Terray, 1972, 1975; Rey, 1975), many of whom adhered to the same kind of dualism as neoclassical economists. Thus an indigenous peasantry was said to be part of a lineage mode of production, linked to (= 'articulated with') a wider capitalism, but not actually reproduced by the latter. Others – notably Meillassoux (1981: Part II) – argued that what were taken to be traditional organizational forms at the village level were in fact reproduced by the wider capitalism for its own purposes: as an industrial reserve army of labour, in other words. This view was supported by those who were not anthropologists (Illife, 1983; Stichter, 1985; Swindell, 1985; Sender and Smith, 1986), who argued that a capitalist labour market did indeed emerge in Africa over the twentieth century.

37   As has been argued elsewhere (Brass, 2007b) with regard to 1970s Peru, members of agrarian cooperatives who struggled against the State were usually the better-off peasants, and what they resisted was not the imposition of capitalism – which was already present – but much rather the attempt by the State to regulate the accumulation process. Instead of the strong-State/weak-peasant dichotomy that informed – and continues to inform – much development theory, what the Peruvian case study suggests is the opposite: that is to say, at the rural grassroots it is ironically the better-off peasantry which successfully resists attempts by reformist bureaucrats to prevent both privatization of co-owned means of production and the continued employment of bonded labour.

38   Examples of those who mistook populism for Marxism during the 1970s and 1980s include a rather large number of those writing about the peasantry in Africa (Williams, 1970; 1976; 1977; Bernstein, 1977; 1981; Watts, 1983). A case in point is Williams (1976: 139), for whom the main socio-economic contradiction occurred between State and peasant, a view encapsulated in the following observation: 'It has been assumed that the major source of rural social differentiation is the spread of commodity relations and the emergence of rural capitalists and proletarians out of the peasantry. This ignores the major class divisions between the peasants on the one hand and the state and its beneficiaries on the other'. Another is Bernstein, whose analyses of petty commodity production were not just unambiguously populist then (Gibbon and Neocosmos, 1985) but remain informed by this same theoretical approach – albeit slightly modified – even today (Brass, 2007a). Yet another is Watts (1983; 1984), who initially drew an idealized picture of self-sufficient African rural communities based on the ethos of 'moral economy' that was

Even as an acute left-wing commentator on ideology as Raymond Williams succumbed in the late 1950s to this kind of populist discourse: in his case, it took the form of a defence of plebeian culture just because it was plebeian, seemingly without asking who formed it and why.[39] His assumption then, that all plebeian culture is pristine (= 'authentic' and uncontaminated by capitalism), not only accords ill with his own powerful critiques of the media, but also prefigures the interpretation of peasant society and culture advanced subsequently by postmodern theory in general and the subaltern studies project in particular.

The difficulties generated by the concept of an homogeneous peasantry structuring a this kind of analytical framework emerge most clearly in relation to the issue of political consciousness.[40] Equating 'civil society' with plebeian

---

unambiguously populist. Of late, however, he has become a critic of the 'new' postmodern populism that pervades development theory. Now he argues (Watts, 2007) that 'Saro-Wiwa's political vision invoked Ogoni culture and tradition...demanding a sort of restitution of Ogonia culture based on a quasi-mythic invocation of the past', and that '[f]orms of identity that mattered were irreducibly local [and] social movements from below'. That Watts – like Bernstein – is still confused about quite how populism differs from Marxism is clear from the fact that elsewhere (Nickeon, Watts and Wolford, 2004) he still manages to support the political virtues of grassroots 'peasant resistance', not realizing the link between this process and the 'quasi-mythic invocation of the past' he now criticizes.

39   Hence the following view (Williams, 1958: 79–80): 'There is an English bourgeois culture, with its powerful educational, literary and social institutions, in close contact with the actual centres of power. To say that most working people are excluded from these is self-evident...But to go on to say that working people are excluded from English culture is nonsense; they have their own growing institutions, and much of the strictly bourgeois culture they would in any case not want... The leisure which the bourgeoisie attained has given us much of cultural value. But this is not to say that contemporary culture is bourgeois culture: a mistake that everyone, from Conservatives to Marxists, seems to make. There is a distinct working-class way of life, which I for one value – not only because I was bred in it, for I now, in certain respects, live differently... So, when Marxists say that we live in a dying culture, and that the masses are ignorant, I have to ask them, as I asked them then, where on earth they have lived. A dying culture, and ignorant masses, are not what I have known and see'.

40   A refusal to characterize political consciousness as false, combined with a concept of an undifferentiated peasantry, has (among other things) led to the exculpation of reactionary political regimes in 1920s and 1930s Europe. Hence the critique by Abse (1996) of revisionist accounts of Italian fascism – many of which are based on oral histories collected long after the events addressed – which attempt to argue that it was acceptable to the urban working class. The inference is that, because for them fascism was not disempowering, workers eschewed class struggle. Against this, Abse (1996: 48, 54–55) makes two

culture, either in non-capitalist contexts or under capitalism, is for obvious reasons fraught with difficulty. Defending actually-existing plebeian culture against what is perceived as 'from above' condescension makes it difficult, if not impossible, simultaneously to espouse a concept of consciousness as false, or the view that plebeian culture is not just foisted on the masses but also operates to their disadvantage. This reached its apogee during the 1980s 'cultural turn', when many of the positions held by those on the 'left' became virtually indistinguishable from those historically associated with the political right. Many of those on the left seemed to have forgotten who its political opponents were and are, and thus how to fight them.

IV

Just as neoliberalism was arguing for the withdrawal of the State from economic activity (= 'interference') in the name of *laissez faire* theory, so postmodernism too shifted its analytical gaze in the same way. This was evident in resistance theory, which relocated the site of grassroots agency: away from the State (and its capture in order to exercise political power) and towards variant forms of 'the local' (the region, the village, and the individual peasant smallholder). The existing State apparatus, and its function as the site where a particular class exercised control, was left intact, as struggle was shifted away from these loci of political and economic power and towards 'everyday forms of resistance' confined to the rural grassroots.

In a very real sense, therefore, postmodernists mimicked the advocacy by neoliberal theorists of banishing the State as a site of struggle. In this they also reproduced earlier anti-State discourse, forgetting that those who objected to the plight of rural labour expelled from the land as a result of capitalist penetration of agriculture have all too often presented a contrast between an idealized image of pre-capitalist rural society and an anomic, State-driven urban

---

points. First, that throughout northern and central Italy agency consistent with class struggle (strikes) did continue during the fascist era. And second, that where this kind of struggle was absent, it was because new entrants to the urban working class were recruited from among peasant smallholders, where collective political identities and trade unionization had not existed previously. A case in point was Porto Marghera, in the factories of which no strikes took place throughout the 1920–45 period. This was because the new workforce drawn from the Venetian *terra firma* consisted of part-time workers who were also politically conservative peasant proprietors with no history of agrarian struggles. For the way in which agrarian myth discourse informs the 'meaning' of Venice, see Chapter 8.

capitalism.[41] Seemingly in agreement with neoliberalism, therefore, postmodernism similarly removed the capture of the State from its own political agenda, and with it any real chance of challenging (let alone overcoming and replacing) the class structure on behalf of which this institutional form operated.

The 'Left': Diversity, Variety, Difference

In the analytical framework of the 'new' postmodern populism, the meaning and object of contemporary rural grassroots agency has changed.[42] Instead of attempting to realize the economic fruits and benefits of development by capturing and exercising control of the state apparatus (as Marxists argue), poor peasants and workers in India and Latin America eschew revolutionary agency. Rather, they are said to struggle on a quotidian basis, as subalterns engaged in resistance, and generally only at a local level, merely to retain their existing cultural identity (= 'difference'). It is the latter process and objective, and not class or economic development, which empowers the rural 'other', insists postmodern theory.

Thus, for example, the discourse-against of the agrarian myth deployed by Albó deprivileges class as an analytical category and trade unions as an organizational form, and opts instead for the subaltern category based on the ethnic/cultural identity of what he calls the 'testimonial peoples' of Latin America, composed of 'the modern representatives of old, original civilizations which European expansion demolished'.[43] It is equally clear that Albó also endorses the discourse-for (= 'natural'/harmonious rural community) of the agrarian myth.[44]

---

41   That it is easy to present an idealised image of pre-industrial agrarian society is evident from the description by one late nineteenth century economic historian (Toynbee, 1902: 190) of the 1790s as a period when 'the old warm attachments, born of ancient, local contiguity and personal intercourse, vanished in the fierce contest for wealth among thousands who had never seen each other's faces before'.

42   A characteristic of such theory is that it not only endorses petty commodity production and the ensemble of cultural forms linked to such peasant identity, but then counterposes this to the *class* identity of the rural subject. Ethnicity is perceived by postmodernism as part of peasant identity, and *vice-versa*. Barrès (1970a: 1970b) would no doubt have been heartened to learn that over fifty years after his death academics in France and elsewhere did indeed fulfil their duty as he thought they should, and – having embraced postmodern theory – privileged relativism over universality, advocated cultural 'difference', and supported nationalism any/everywhere.

43   For these points, see Albó (1993: 19).

44   According to Albó (1993: 21), this 'authentic' grass-roots identity is an 'image [in which] one can perceive the unity, born in good measure from a common history [that has] led

As the attempts by Albó and Canclini to reconstruct nations based on traditional ethnicity demonstrate, earlier indigenista views have merely been recy-
cled, and the same arguments now appear under the rubric of Latin American
'subaltern' identity and resistance.[45] For Albó, the 'testimonial peoples' constituting the Latin American subaltern are composed of 'small indigenous
nations' which exist in a 'primordial relationship of culture with cultivation': as
with the Asian subaltern, therefore, the 'testimonial peoples' who form the
'authentic'/indigenous nations of Latin American subalterns, and for whom
'the land is also the fundamental base of their cultural identity', correspond to
a smallholding peasantry.[46]

The irony is unmistakable. Over the past twenty-five years, many of those
writing about the undesirability of further economic development where
peasant smallholders are concerned have done so from a 'new' populist postmodern theoretical framework. In support of this view, they not only invoked
the right of the rural 'other' to his/her own culture, but declared the latter identity innate and thus the ideological and organizational basis for the construction of a local 'civil' society outside and against the neoliberal State. Accordingly,
from the 1980s onwards 'new' populist postmodernism unknowingly deployed
the very same arguments against further economic development in the Third
World countryside as had conservatives half a century earlier.

It was at that conjuncture – 1920s and 1930s Europe – that those such as
Julius Evola and René Guenon invoked against 'Western decadent materialism' what they took to be the timeless and eternal verities of non-Western

---

to a shared language of exchange, to similar systems of beliefs and values, and to many
shared institutions, such as...the *compadrazgo* [fictive kinship] systems and rural community'. As many ethnographic studies conducted in the Andean region confirm (Sánchez
1977, 1982; Brass, 1986), this idealized claim is quite simply incorrect: both Andean rural
community and its institutional forms – such as fictive kinship – have for a very long time
not only been differentiated internally along class lines but also perceived as such by the
poor peasants and agricultural labourers involved.

45   For examples of *indigenista* arguments made by those who are now in the Latin American
subalternist fold, see Albó (1972; 1987; 1988) and Garcia Canclini (2001). For the deep roots
of *indigenismo* in anthropological accounts of the Andean region and Brazil, see Marzal
(1990) and Ramos (1998). For Mexico, see Chapter 1.

46   See Albó (1993: 30–31), where the importance of this nation/culture/land/peasant linkage
to subaltern identity in Latin America is underlined in the following manner: 'Perhaps the
most fundamental point is that, in contrast to the dominant capitalist models, there persists a collective and self-generating development of the productive forces concerned
with maintaining the communal base to a greater or lesser degree in the majority of the
indigenous nations we are referring to'.

traditional religious and aesthetic philosophies and their accompanying socio-economic hierarchies.[47] Significantly, moreover, the desired outcome of their arguments, or the kind of action implied in this conservative discourse, was renunciation (= turning away from the World). Where the continuation of both State and the wider society are concerned, this was a response not dissimilar in effect to the smallscale and systemically unthreatening forms of local resistance currently favoured by postmodern theory.

Not the least problematic aspect of the 'new' postmodern populism, therefore, is that its endorsement of 'difference'/'diversity' fails to differentiate between two antithetical forms of anti-capitalism: one emanating from the political left and another that has its origins in the discourse of the political right. Whereas the former posits socialism as the transcendent 'other' of capitalism, reactionaries invoke a pre-capitalist rural order in which landlord and peasant (= 'the people') live in harmony.[48] The centrality to the latter discourse of notions of cultural innateness rooted in nationhood and pastoral variants of the agrarian myth has been traced in earlier chapters, as has the fact that such epistemology is the same across time and space, to the degree that its core assumptions reappear everywhere and consistently in the ideas of and claims made by conservatives.[49] This is not the first time that a cultural turn

---

47   See Evola (1993) for an endorsement of the pre-modern views, the transcendental phi-
     losophy and traditional conservatism expressed by Guenon in books such as *La crise de
     monde moderne* (Paris, 1927), which the former translated into Italian. 'According to
     Guenon', states Evola (1994: 20–21), 'the sense of tradition has progressively become dim,
     both in the East and in the modern West... This takes place in the context of an absolute
     lack of true principles, of a social and ideological chaos, and of a contaminating mystique
     of becoming which sets a hurried pace for the people to follow. From Europe this cancer
     spreads elsewhere, as a new form of barbarism; anti-tradition penetrates everywhere,
     "modernizing" those civilizations, which, as in the case of India, China or Islam, still pre-
     serve to a certain degree values and rules of life of a different order'. For yet more sup-
     portive references to the anti-modern views of Guenon, see Evola (2003: 142, 209, 210, 215).

48   For the ultra-reactionary Italian aristocrat Julius Evola (1995), therefore, 1930s fascism rep-
     resented the possibility of restoring his ideal of a 'natural' pre-capitalist social order,
     where an equally 'natural' landed elite composed of those like him exercised power. Like
     most of those on the political right at that conjuncture, he opposed modernity and prog-
     ress on the grounds that such processes entailed what for him were undesirable political
     developments. On the one hand, he was antagonistic to the rise of 'the masses' and a
     concomitant advance of materialism and socialism. On the other, he objected to the
     accompanying decline of spirituality, mysticism and religious belief, a loss he character-
     ized as an 'unnatural' desacralization.

49   The following sentiments are ones with which no 'new' postmodern populist could
     disagree, not least because they accurately echo his/her own views: 'The speculative

emanating from that end of the political spectrum has attempted to impose a populist agenda on Marxist political economy.

Beyond the Plain of Real Things

At the first American Writers' Congress held during the mid-1930s, the influential literary critic Kenneth Burke advocated the replacement in the Marxist discourse of 'the proletariat' with 'the people' on the grounds that this would be more inclusive politically.[50] His argument was that such a shift was necessary in order to establish a common unity for change, a strategy not so different from Gramscian hegemony.[51] In the debate which followed, it was pointed out

---

intelligence can envisage a situation of such hatred of the capitalist system that, on the day after the revolution, some kind of standardized collectivism, based on the model appropriate to the most powerful region, would be forced on the whole [nation], not to mention the whole of [the region]. But soon the varied influences of race, custom and climate would come again into their own, and real differences would assert themselves. It is essential that these aspects of human development should be given free reign, so that humanity can affirm the life-giving nature of diversity, of variety, of difference. No single one contains the truth. Only the total diversity approaches that truth'. The nation in question is France and the region is Europe, the year is 1894 and the words are those of Maurice Barrès (1970b: 156), a scion of the French political right.

50   His words were as follows (Burke, 1935: 93): 'I believe the symbol of "the people" makes more naturally for such propaganda by inclusion than does the strictly proletarian symbol (which makes naturally for a propaganda by exclusion, a tendency to eliminate from one's work all that does not deal specifically with the realities of the workers' oppression...)'. Burke (1935: 93) then accepts, with a disarming honesty now rarely encountered, that 'I recognize that my suggestion bears the telltale stamp of my class, the petty bourgeoisie'.

51   Not the least problematic aspect of this attempted shift is that it signals a move onto an epistemological terrain where the political right has long exercised ideological dominance: anti-intellectualism. The inference is that, since discourse about class is 'too complex', a broader and more acceptable populist category of 'the people' will make it easier to recruit political support. By simplifying issues/oppositions/opponents, therefore, the discourse of the political left will cross over into the populist domain of 'commonsense', and become – in Gramscian terms – hegemonic. The difficulty with this is that 'commonsense' – composed precisely of all those discursive elements which the left has to challenge and supplant, not endorse and appropriate – is invariably owned by the political right. The latter asserts that – by arguing for abstract and/or universal concepts that are not in the interests of the specific identity (= national) of 'the people' – intellectuals despise the 'ordinary citizen'. Claiming that '[i]n this as in every other case our wisdom is in agreement with popular opinion which says to those in libraries and laboratories "Let everyone stick to his own skill and the sheep will be well cared for"', Barrès (1970b: 175, 177ff.) complains that intellectuals attempt 'to lay down a rule for man as an abstract

that as 'the people' was a concept deployed by those on the political right, it should be rejected ('The attempt to substitute "people" for "worker" is very dangerous from our point of view').[52] The call by reactionaries for society to reassert a 'pure' cultural identity that was agrarian, and the appeal of this argument to writers, was also recognized as a danger facing Marxists.[53] Because at that conjuncture Marxism was stronger, and the populist threat from the political right more obvious, however, this cultural incursion from literature was consequently resisted successfully.

In many respects, the issues raised in that debate, plus the ground occupied by the protagonists, anticipate the 1980s attack on Marxist development theory by the 'new' postmodern populism. Half a century on, however, the outcome was different; Marxism was weaker, and succumbed for three reasons in particular. First, a rather large number of those regarding themselves as Marxists now had academic positions, where such theory was subject to the whims of intellectual fashion. Second, fascism was no longer perceived by them to be a threat. And third, desirable transformation in the rural Third

---

universal entity. [They do] not consider individual differences...yet what we need are men who are strictly rooted in our soil, in our history and in the national consciousness; men who are fitted to the immediate requirements of the country. The philosophy that at present instructs the state is responsible more than anything else for the belief that the intellectual despises the ordinary citizen and makes intelligence operate at a level of pure abstraction, beyond the plain of real things. [The intellectual] becomes an enemy of society [and is] an agent in the process of uprooting; he belongs to a higher order among those who have no roots'. Accordingly, the anti-intellectualism of the political right serves two purposes: to deprivilege reason (which attacks its own myths) and to reprivilege 'commonsense' (which attracts the support of the plebeian masses). By encroaching on this epistemological territory, with the object of taking it over, socialists risk becoming no different from the political right, which is the dilemma faced by many 'new' populist postmodern theorists.

52   For the debate, see Hart (1935: 165ff.). Opposing the suggestion made by Kenneth Burke, Friedrich Wolf made the following point (Hart, 1935: 167–168): 'A great danger reposes in this formulation of "the people." Hitler and Rosenberg used it. They said, let us not talk any more about the workers, let us talk about the people. In 1918 it was precisely this very same thing that the German reformist leaders utilized. Scheideman and Ebert said we must have a policy that will cover the worker and the small merchant and the middle bourgeoisie. Hitlerism is the continuation of this policy. Hitler knew enough to use this ideological device as a supplement to his blackjacks and machine guns. Utilization of the myth of 'das Volk', the people, is an essential part of the reformist approach'.

53   See, for example, Dahlberg, (1935: 29, 30, 31), who condemns fascism as 'primitivism, a return to medieval culture...the agrarian anti-machine [winning over] intellectual medievalists and agrarians'.

World was now no longer seen as based on class, leading to socialism; instead, the latter has been displaced by a desire to return economically to a 'kinder'/'caring' capitalism and politically to bourgeois democracy (= 'redemocratization').[54] This refusal to transcend capitalism, together with a reaffirmation of 'civil society', nationalism and resurgent micro-level ethnicities, all confirm that, conceptually, 'the people' has indeed displaced 'the worker' as the subject of history.

Subaltern as Citizen?

There is, however, an irresolvable contradiction at the centre of the 'new' postmodern populism as projected via the theoretical framework of the subaltern studies project: the antinomy between on the one hand the anti-modern discourse of agrarian populism and peasant economy, and on the other the equation of 'civil society' and democracy with modernity. This emerges clearly from a comparison of texts on 'civil society' by two long-standing contributors to the subaltern studies series, Partha Chatterjee and Gyanendra Pandey.[55] Whereas one asserts and celebrates the disjuncture between the subaltern and 'civil society', the other seeks to reunite them.

In the subaltern studies project, Gandhian discourse is emblematic of 'authentic' grassroots utterance.[56] The endorsing approach by Chatterjee to

---

54   Examples of current historical analyses written by those who regard bourgeois democracy *per se* as some sort of achievement, the realization or retention of which in Latin America or India is a cause for celebration, include López Alvez (2000) and Guha (2007).

55   The texts in question are by Chatterjee (1984) and Pandey (2006). The postmodern epistemology structuring views about the 'autonomous' grassroots agency undertaken by 'the subaltern' skirts over sociology and politics, and assumes that from-below empowerment is essentially a question of marginal people deciding/defining their own needs. Would that it were this simple! As many analyses of peasant movements bear out, these can contain within their ranks (under the banner of 'we-are-just-peasants') not just poor peasants with a few acres but also much more substantial producers, possessing large amounts of land, capital and political influence. A case in point is the 'new' farmers' movements in India, led by rich producers in Maharashtra, Punjab and UP. Their aim is not to reproduce peasant economy – they are agrarian capitalist producers not family farmers – but to curtail competition from agribusiness enterprises elsewhere. This they do by deploying the old and powerful discourse, to the effect that 'we are all peasants, and as such the backbone of the Indian nation'. Like so many other farmer organizations, what they want is a better deal within the existing capitalist system, not social justice that would empower the landless workers many of them employ.

56   The notion of an undifferentiated peasantry as constitutive both of subaltern and national identity can be traced back most easily to Gandhian discourse. The influence of the latter on Indian nationalism is evident from comments by Jawaharlal Nehru (1938:

this iconic symbol of Indian 'otherness' and peasant resistance is therefore unsurprising. For Gandhi, however, 'civil society' lies not in the institutional matrix of modernity – industry, mechanization, technology, representative democracy – but in earlier, non-modern socio-economic agrarian hierarchy: that of rural India in general, and the village community and peasant family in particular.[57] In his opinion, it is in the latter institutions (= tradition) and not the former (= modernity) that a timeless and unchanging moral order is to be found, based on religion, patriarchy and the absence of material progress and economic development, all dismissed by him as alien 'Western'/colonial impositions on India. It is the very cultural 'difference' of the subaltern that separates him/her from 'civil society', the 'other' of what for Gandhi and Chatterjee is the 'authenticity' of the Indian peasant.

As Chatterjee admits, this view is no different from the backward-looking nineteenth century romanticism of Leo Tolstoy, John Ruskin, Edward Carpenter and the Russian populists.[58] Unlike these last named, who according to

---

476–477) about peasant agency shortly before Independence: 'Mr. Gandhi's contribution to the [Indian National] Congress, his essential contribution about 20 years ago, was to bring the peasantry into the Congress. The whole centre of gravity of the Congress changed. More and more we began to go to the peasants, first of all as persons who thought that they had nothing to learn from the peasants, but to teach them and tell them what to do. But inevitably we found that we had much to learn. We became interested in the peasant problem, which was no part of the nationalist movement. It might almost be said that we wanted to use the peasants in the cause of nationalism. We had started thinking in terms of developing strength to meet British imperialism, but unless the masses supported the cause of nationalism we had no effective strength. Inevitably, therefore, we had to go to the peasants. We organized them on nationalist lines, but the peasant question became more and more an important one to consider. Indeed, the peasant, when he heard talk in terms of "swaraj" or "freedom" or "independence," interpreted it in terms of getting rid of his own burdens. Independence had no other special meaning for him. It was on these lines that the peasantry began to get organized and to become politically conscious, and on the other hand the Congress began to grow peasant-conscious... The workers' problems, therefore, came before the Congress, but it was the peasant problem that essentially occupied it'.

57   That Gandhi regarded not only modernity, democracy, industrialization, secularism, progress, and science but also (and therefore) 'civil society' as impositions on village India of a 'foreign'/Western 'other', to all of which he was as a consequence opposed, is outlined approvingly by Chatterjee (1984: 156ff., 162ff., 170).

58   See Chatterjee (1984: 173ff., 177). Hence the acceptance by Chatterjee (1984: 173) that 'in the *theoretical* sense Gandhian ideology would still be "reactionary," since, as Lenin pointed out in the case of the Russian populists, not only is there simply a romantic longing for a return to an idealized medieval world of security and contentment, there is also

Chatterjee made their criticisms from within 'civil society', he attempts to privilege Gandhian discourse by insisting – implausibly – that it is located outside
history, transcends nationalism, and is in some sense a distinct (= non-
reactionary, non-populist) and thus 'authentic' form of Indian peasant resistance to the State that is 'foreign'.[59] Because he decouples the discourse extolling a culturally pristine undifferentiated peasantry from nationalist ideology
formulated by the urban bourgeoisie, Chatterjee is baffled by the ease with
which the latter 'appropriated' what for him is a seemingly 'other' discourse
about India-as-authentically-rural.[60]

As has been argued in previous chapters, however, there is no contradiction,
since nationalist ideology everywhere has been (and in many contexts still is)
informed by the agrarian myth, which celebrates harmonious 'natural' small-
scale economic activity, and opposes 'foreign' (but not national) capital.[61] Such

---

"the attempt to measure the new society with the old patriarchal yardstick, the desire to
find a model in the old order and traditions, which are totally unsuited to the changed
economic institutions'" (original emphasis).

59   'In its critique of civil society', claims Chatterjee (1984: 176–177), 'Gandhism adopted a
standpoint that lay entirely outside the thematic of post-enlightenment thought, and
hence of nationalist thought as well. In its formulation of the problem of town-country
economic exchanges, of the cultural domination of the new urban educated classes, and
above all of the legitimacy of resistance to an oppressive state, it was able to encapsulate
perfectly the specific political demands as well as the modalities of thought of a peasant-
communal consciousness'.

60   On this point, see Chatterjee (1984: 178, 193–194).

61   The ease with which a combination of the foundation and agrarian myths has been
deployed by those on the political right is evident from the way in which it structured
nationalist discourse in early twentieth century France. Contemplating the graves of
French soldiers who died fighting the Germans in 1870, the ultra-reactionary conservative
Barrès (1970b: 189–193) stressed the covenant those living had with the dead, noting '[it]
poses a moral unity on all. This voice of our ancestors, this lesson of the soil that [these
graves] know so well how to make us understand, is worth more than anything in the
forming the consciousness of a people. The soil gives us the discipline we need: we are the
extension in time of our dead. This is the concept of reality upon which to base our existence. In order to allow the consciousness of a country such as France to free itself, each
person must be rooted in the soil and in the earth...the voice of his blood and the instincts
of the earth'. He continues: 'It is only by drawing your attention to the resources of French
soil, the efforts it demands of us, the conditions, in short, in which our race of foresters,
farmers and winegrowers has developed, that you will come to understand our national
traditions as realities and not mere words'. As used by Barrès, therefore, a potent relay-in-
statement evokes the following connections: nation = nature = soil = peasant = people = ancestors. The latter, moreover, are martyrs for the national cause, buried in the soil

a discourse is acceptable to nationalism precisely because it fails to address two difficulties: that there are capitalist producers in rural areas, and that capitalists in urban areas themselves invest in and own rural property.

Some twenty years later, by contrast, Pandey attempts – unsuccessfully – to redefine the subaltern as part of modernity and 'civil society'.[62] That he has had to try to do this is due, no doubt, to the trenchant critiques levelled at the subaltern studies project by Marxists during the early 1990s: although welcome, his reassessment of what it means 'to be' a subaltern merely exposes its epistemological frailty. Recognizing the contradiction between citizenship-as-modernity and subaltern-as-peasant-located-outside-modernity, Pandey wishes to 'propose the recasting of the figure of the subaltern subject into the deliberately paradoxical, not to say oxymoronic category of subaltern citizen'; in short, he now insists that '[t]he peasant was modern no less than the working class or the insurance agent'.[63] Accepting that the all-embracing category

---

of the nation they died defending. All this, according to Barrès, is the essence of national identity and the dynamic informing nationalism: a fusion of the agrarian and the foundation myths, in other words.

62   Hence the claim (Pandey, 2006: 4737) that '[t]he fact of citizenship, statutory, anticipated or feared, is in my view written into the condition of subalternity'. This claim is itself part of what might be termed a wider project, borne out of desperation. Having seen the political right in India garner electoral advantage from the same kinds of arguments as those made by 'new' postmodern populists such as himself, Pandey is engaged in an attempt to recuperate these arguments/concepts for liberal bourgeois democracy. Hence his futile attempt (Pandey, 1994: 69) to wrest nationhood and nationalism from the BJP and RSS: 'Somewhere along the way [since the 1950s], the question of cultural identity and pride – who "we" are, what it means to be "Indian," what constitutes India's history and culture – is lost, until it re-emerges in the hands of obscurantists and once politically marginal elements. It is as if the entire domain of discourse on culture has been handed over to these groups on a platter... The failure to engage in a continuing debate on the character of the "national" history and culture constitute one of the great failures of left and democratic forces in India since Independence'. Pandey forgets his own role in this process: there has indeed been a debate and a critique of nationalism, but one in which the Subaltern Studies project – of which he was a part – unknowingly *defended* the arguments/concepts about the innateness of culture and peasant society that historically have been no different from those made by the political right.

63   See Pandey (2006: 4736, 4737). He goes so far as to reproduce – almost verbatim – the Marxist critique of the subaltern studies approach, when making the following observation about his colleagues who subscribe to the same project (Pandey, 2006: 4736): 'Looking back at our attempts to rewrite the subaltern experience, and with it the whole colonial construction of history, one might suggest that we have had to contend with an insufficiently acknowledged obstacle. This has to do with a subterranean faith that persists, perhaps even in the writings of many subalternist scholars, in the lack of fit between the

of subaltern can either contain within or have emerge from its ranks those better-off elements who actually belong to a petty bourgeoisie, he recognizes that, once it is accepted that subaltern identity is transected by that of class, the element of 'difference' said to be central to the cultural 'otherness' of subalternity in effect dissolves.[64] As Pandey agrees, 'how is the long-standing struggle [by better-off components] for equality supposed to be folded into this newly asserted right to the recognition of difference?'.[65]

Try as he might, however, Pandey is unable to solve the problem the existence of which he recognizes. The reason for this is not difficult to discern. Hitherto those such as Chatterjee have argued that, in contrast to Marxists, the category of the subaltern was external to the modernity of 'civil society'. Much rather, subalternity was predicated on the primacy of its cultural 'otherness', an identity that preceded modernity and stood outside 'civil society', not least since it overrode that of class. If, as Pandey now accepts, this is no longer the

---

peasantry and industrial bourgeois society, in the "incipience" of peasant political (hence, historical and cultural) consciousness, and the belief that peasants need to advance – towards modernity and full cultural and political citizenship of the modern worlds'. Having in effect declared a *volte face*, he (Pandey, 2006: 4736) nevertheless backtracks, and attempts to rescue the project by maintaining incorrectly that 'the task of subaltern historiography was to recover this underdeveloped figure for history, to restore the agency of the yokel, recognize that the peasant mass was contemporaneous with the modern, part of modernity, and establish the peasant as the maker of his/her own destiny'. That the object of the project was to privilege the agency of petty commodity producers is undeniable; that it also entailed claiming such a subject, identity and agency for modernity is quite simply wrong. Much rather the opposite: the object was to show that precisely in the disjuncture between 'peasant' and 'modernity' lay its very 'authenticity' as an unheard rural voice.

64   This is conceded obliquely, when Pandey (2006: 4739) notes in passing that the category of subaltern in the Southern US – coincident with the black population there – was transected as a result of an emerging 'black middle class'.

65   See Pandey (2006: 4740). 'There is another difficulty', he accepts (Pandey, 2006: 4736): 'Many...modern peasants and agricultural labourers do not wish to remain peasants or agricultural labourers', adding (Pandey, 2006: 4741, note 6) that '[i]t goes without saying that modern capitalist farmers may not only desire these [urban] facilities and comforts, but often enjoy them in full measure, adding the joys of fancy country homes to the resources of the city'. Although no acknowledgement is made of this fact, Pandey thereby takes on board the Marxist criticism made of the subaltern project in 1990 (Brass, 2013a: 153, note 7): 'From the Marxist viewpoint, one of the main objections to the "moral economy" [and subaltern] argument is that it denies the *active* striving of the different components of the rural population as *class* subjects: that is, either by rich peasants to become small agrarian capitalists or by poor peasants and agricultural labourers to improve their position as workers...' (original emphasis).

case, to the extent that subalternity invariably dissolves into class and some subalterns strive for inclusion within 'civil society', then the core defining aspect of subaltern-as-concept (= subaltern difference) ceases to have theoretical efficacy. His desire to resolve this problem fails, and slides inevitably into epistemological incoherence ('[d]ifference as subalternity...[s]ubalternity as difference...[d]ifference is not to be privileged, yet it must not be entirely denied', etc.).[66]

Stated bluntly, in so far as the assertion or reassertion of tradition stops being crucial to what is termed subaltern 'difference' – s/he no longer wishes to remain 'different', and outside history, but wants now to be part of modernity, in other words – this crucial form of backwards-looking populist 'otherness' (= the hankering after an agrarian 'golden age' in which the peasant family farm was able to reproduce itself economically and culturally) cannot be regarded as innate or eternal.[67] The irony is unmistakable: in conceding the critique by Marxism – that historically the essentialist concept of an undifferentiated peasantry central to the subaltern studies framework breaks down into its separate class elements (= rich, middle and poor components) – Pandey in effect acknowledges the epistemological vacuity of this attempt to displace class with ethnic or national identity.

V

In an important sense, the dominance of the 'new' populist postmodernism signals just how far social science discourse has shifted politically since the 1960s development decade. At the latter conjuncture, the main concern of development theory (Marxist and non-Marxist alike) was to end rural socio-economic marginality in the so-called Third World, by bringing peasants and agricultural workers into the wider society. As participants both in the process of economic growth and the political system, the rural poor would then be able

---

66   For these essentially meaningless observations, see Pandey (2006: 4740).

67   Because he is confused about the claims made by populists, Pandey (2006: 4740) mistakenly argues that even the political right is now asserting a universal form of 'sameness'. This is incorrect, since what the populist right asserts is not a universal form but rather a national or ethnic form of 'sameness'. Hence the claim that in France or India the fact of 'being' a French or Indian national overrides other socio-economic identities, such as the fact of being a worker or poor peasant in these same contexts. As has been pointed out elsewhere (Brass, 2000a), not only are these not calls for a universal identity but for the universalization of 'difference', but they are no different from the essentialisms that are central to those of subaltern identity.

to secure better pay/conditions leading to increased living standards. Linked to existing poverty, illiteracy and oppression, therefore, rural marginality was perceived negatively, as an indicator of backwardness and underdevelopment, and thus as a problem to be solved.

From around the 1980s, this approach was not merely abandoned but actually reversed.[68] Henceforth marginality was recast as a form of empowerment, a revision that coincided with and was effected by the rise both of neoliberal economics and of the 'new' populist postmodernism. Peasant/ethnic identity was re-essentialized, and reaffirmed theoretically as an 'authentic' form of selfhood that was eternal due to its culturally indissoluble 'natural' character. Customs, traditions and practices as these already existed at the rural grassroots were now celebrated/endorsed by the 'new' populist postmodernism as forms of cultural 'difference', to be cherished as such.

'New' Populist Postmodernism as Paradigm Shift

To effect this reversal, the same revisionist discourse simultaneously challenged the theoretical approach linked to the 1960s development framework. Declaring the latter a tainted foundational/Eurocentric meta-narrative, the 'new' populist postmodernism dismissed concepts such as class, modernity, development, and progress as inappropriate for an understanding of the rural Third World. Pivotal to this epistemological *volte face* was a specific form of agency, the object of which was no longer the revolutionary capture and control of the state. Just such a non-revolutionary mobilization was provided by

---

68   One of the very few on the left to anticipate this reversal was Baran (1957: 4): 'As long as reason and the lessons to be learned from history were manifestly on the side of the bourgeoisie in its struggle against the obscurantist ideologies and institutions of feudalism, both reason and history were confidently invoked as the supreme arbiters in the fateful contest. There are no more magnificent witnesses to this grand alliance of the ascending bourgeoisie with reason and historical thinking than the great Encyclopaedists of the eighteenth century, than the great realists of the nascent bourgeois literature. But when reason and the study of history began revealing the irrationality, the limitations, and the mere transitory nature of the capitalist order, bourgeois ideology as a whole and with it bourgeois economics began abandoning both reason and history. Whether this abandonment assumed the form of a rationalism driven to its own self-destruction and turning into the agnosticism of modern positivism, *or whether it appeared frankly in the form of some essentialist philosophy contemptuously rejecting all search for and all reliance upon a rational comprehension of history*, the result was that bourgeois thought (and economics as a part of it) turned ever more into a neatly packaged kit of assorted ideological gadgets required for the functioning and preservation of the existing social order' (emphasis added).

James Scott, in the form of his notion of 'everyday-forms-of-resistance', whereby quotidian/smallscale agency undertaken by peasants is said to block every attempt by the state to effect all its 'alien' policies/processes designed to transform the status quo.[69]

In Scott's latest book the 'resistance' model is taken a step further, and is now imbued with a spatial dimension: rural populations are located in upland areas, protecting their autonomy from a malign lowland state. In short, it constitutes ecological determinism, a form of functionalism, one moreover attributed to subjects who, it is claimed, choose to be marginal.[70] Whereas the old functionalism maintained this was good for the wider society, the more recent populist postmodernism insists it is functional for the individuals concerned, who are empowered thereby.

Pristine Nature?

An age-old defence of large property takes the form of the necessity of protecting Nature so as to preserve it for future generations, an argument whereby landowners are constituted – or constitute themselves – as custodians of the environment. Similar in intent to the rejection of an encroaching industrial society that underwrites travel literature, historically this discourse invoked an all-embracing concept of Nature: one incorporating not just the land itself, but also any tribal groups inhabiting it. Hence the claim by landowners to protect both the terrain and its indigenous population from an encroaching urban/ industrial modernity, in the process rescuing 'pristine Nature' and the 'primitive savage'.

Lest it be thought that this discourse – the landlord pastoral variant of the agrarian myth – is now a thing of the past, the same argument about protecting Nature in order to guarantee its 'authenticity' currently enables wealthy capitalists to justify the purchase of large landholdings. Hence the account of Tierra del Fuego at the start of the twentieth century evoked by E. Lucas Bridges (see below, Chapter 7) is being replicated in Patagonia a century later, where a multimillionaire now claims eco-activism as the reason for 'the world's largest private conservation effort, buying vast stretches of wilderness in Chile and Argentina to protect it from development'.[71]

---

69   See Scott (1976; 1985; 1990; 2009).

70   Hence the relay-in-statement whereby 'geographical marginality' = 'cultural choice' = 'zone of resistance' (Scott, 2009: 157).

71   How some 2.2 million hectares have been acquired by a wealthy capitalist who, having made his fortune from the 'outdoor gear' company, has 'quietly poured almost $300 million into reserves and ecological causes through...private San Francisco-registered

As in the case of the earlier project, however, '[t]he idyll of the Patagonia he lives in is deceptive [since] timber companies and cattle breeders are busily harvesting the forests [while] salmon farmers [are] exporting to Japan and Europe'. Another billionaire, 'America's largest landowner' with two million acres in Montana and New Mexico, describes himself as an 'ecologically sensitive' environmentalist.[72] Although claiming his 'acquisitions are part of a project to protect the land and restore native and endangered species', he nevertheless 'combines ecological self-righteousness with a shrewd ability to exploit nature for profit'.[73]

That reserves conceptualized as 'pristine nature' devoted to the protection of their indigenous population currently inform not just landlord but also peasant pastoral versions of the agrarian myth is evident from recent claims made about just such an area in Southeast Asia. According to Scott, 'Zomia' is a new name for the 'largest remaining nonstate space in the world' a vast area extending from northeastern India, via the Central Highlands of Vietnam, to the Chinese provinces of Yunnan, Guizhou, and Sichuan and western Guangxi.[74] Covering some 2.5 million square kilometres and home to a population of one hundred million, 'Zomia' consists of self-governing hill peoples who, Scott insists, must be seen not as remnants of socio-economically more advanced societies, but rather as empowered upland populations living in a 'region of refuge' who chose not to be part of lowland contexts ruled by the State.

---

charitable foundations'. On this, see 'Welcome to My World', *The Observer* (London), 15 February 2009; and also 'Back to nature', *The Financial Times* (London), 11/12 September 2010. For an earlier example of this same discourse, see Bridges (1948: 519–520), who laments that '[m]y hopes that Tierra del Fuego would be the happy home of worthy descendants of their proud, splendid forebears, who had so freely roamed the woods, were not to be realized. With the inrush of civilization into such a small country, the Indian way of life could not prevail against it'.

72   See Wiener (2007).

73   According to Wiener (2007: 201, 204) commercial activity includes bison herds to supply beef for a restaurant chain, hunting, corporate retreats, and the exploitation of coal and methane reserves.

74   For these and the following claims, see Scott (2009). His interpretation is questioned in a review (Brass, 2012) which maintains that it is incorrect to characterize upland Southeast Asia as 'state-repelling' 'zones of refuge/asylum' to which people voluntarily migrate. This is, it is argued, an idealization consistent with the 'new' populist postmodernism, but not supported by ethnographic evidence. The latter suggests that populations neither choose to migrate to upland areas (but go because they are forced off valley land), nor – once there – are they beyond the reach of the lowland State. Consequently, they are anything but empowered and safe in such contexts.

Part of a resurgent populist historiography that has become academically entrenched over the past three decades, it is replacing earlier variants which advocated economic development and modernization, now virtually banished from the intellectual agenda. What Scott opposes, therefore, is any attempt not just to bring such marginal populations into the wider society but also to include them in its development project; namely, those who advocate that hill people and other marginals 'be made the object of development efforts to integrate them into the...economic life of the nation'. The targets of this populist critique are obvious: 1960s modernization theory and – more broadly – Marxism, since each approach endorses systemic change, their political differences notwithstanding.[75] Let the indigenous hill peoples remain as they are, he seems to be saying; indeed, they and their way of life must be protected from any development project generated by the state, a view that has a politically worrying antecedent.

A precursor of Scott's 'Zomia' model, therefore, was advanced eight decades ago with regard to Africa. This argument began, like that of Scott, by supporting the idea of 'tribal cohesiveness', presented as empowering for the indigenous population. From this it went on to propose the adoption of a system of 'separate parallel institutions', one set for Europeans who 'live in the same country' and another for the natives. Its author decried the 'old practice [which] mixed up black with white in the same institutions', presenting this as a form of self-criticism, blaming an over-powerful colonialism for its negative impact on the colonized ('after the native institutions and traditions had been carelessly or deliberately destroyed'). In what was a clever rhetorical device, separateness was presented as a virtuous act undertaken by whites, intent not merely on restoring but protecting traditional African culture the merits of which they had only just recognized.

This virtuous act, it was then revealed, would entail 'segregation' based on 'separate institutions for the two elements...living in their own separate areas'. Since 'institutional segregation carries with it territorial segregation', the policy advocated 'gives the native his own traditional institutions on land which is set aside for his exclusive occupation'. These holdings will be 'adequate' for tribal needs, both now and in the future, and those working in towns will also live apart, again in recognition of their cultural 'otherness'. Like the inhabitants of

---

75   Hence the complaint by Scott (2009: 187–188) that '[a]ny effort to examine the history of social structure and subsistence routines as part of a deliberate political choice runs smack against a powerful civilizational narrative. The narrative consists of a historical series arranged as an account of economic, social and cultural progress...this narrative is profoundly misleading'.

'Zomia' in Southeast Asia, therefore, the African 'other' was to occupy his/her own physical space, a policy which would enable an innate historic identity, together with its cultural traditions/practices and local institutions, to flourish unhindered by the state. Formulated by Jan Christian Smuts for the whole of Africa, this theory of separate development as a benign way of empowering and protecting the native population underwrote the South African apartheid system.[76]

The point is that what was being proposed by Smuts in the 1930s (a policy culminating in the Bantustans), together with the reasons given for it – an empowerment of indigenous cultural 'otherness' in need of protection from an overweening state – are in essence little different conceptually from the defence by Scott of 'zones of refuge' informing his analysis of 'Zomia'. Like Scott in the case of 'non-state' Southeast Asian indigenous hill peoples, more-over, the South African government justified the policy of separate develop-ment on the grounds that it was what the black population wanted. Each chose to live apart, an empowering decision which consequently meant that such a policy should not be seen (by outsiders) as an oppressive exclusionary measure imposed on them.

Unless one is aware of the background to this historiography, the absolute nature of the epistemological about-turn that has occurred in the study of development over the latter part of the twentieth century, the *volte face* is difficult to comprehend. Economic backwardness, criticized from the 1960s onwards on the grounds that it deprived rural populations of basic amenities and improved living standards, was from the 1980s onwards converted by adherents of the 'new' populist postmodernism – Scott among them – into a form of empowerment, actively chosen and defended by its subject.

Conclusion

Historically, the shift in the attitude of the political right – from criticism to the endorsement of working class suffrage – signalled a corresponding emphasis

---

76   This theory is outlined in Smuts (1930: 74–103), whose fear of socialism was the reason for his encouraging African institutions/culture and supporting existing tribal authority. Hence the view (Smuts, 1930: 86, 87) that, if 'the bonds of native tribal cohesion and authority are dissolved, the African governments will everywhere sit with vast hordes of detribalized natives on their hands, for whom the traditional restraints and the discipline of the chiefs and elders will have no force or effect'. If this 'despotic authority of the chiefs' broke down, he feared the emergence of Bolshevism.

on the role of populism in ideological struggle. The aim of the latter was henceforth to gain acceptance at the grassroots (rural and urban alike) of what might be termed the project of capital. Its ideological object was to halt the spread of socialist ideas, and then replace them with bourgeois ones upholding the rights of private property and capitalist ownership menaced by socialism and the class struggle. This involved shaping concepts of and a discourse about forms to be taken by grassroots empowerment – democracy, nationalism, ethnic identity, 'civil society' and the role of the State – that would safeguard (= not fundamentally threaten) existing property relations.

Many aspects of this same project now inform what is wrongly perceived as leftist ideology: the 'new' postmodern populism generally, and in particular current analyses of peasant agency by those belonging to the subaltern studies project or using the 'everyday forms of peasant resistance' framework. 'Civil society' is not only located epistemologically outside and against the capitalist State, thereby mimicking the State/peasant antagonism that informs earlier populism, but also – and again like earlier populism – is where all the 'authentic' cultural forms of a particular nation are said to be present, and where they are reproduced. Like the a-historical village as envisaged by agrarian populism, 'civil society' is the space in which smallscale economic and political activity takes place, community and kinship ties are inherently egalitarian, and a benign traditional culture thrives. In short, 'civil society' is viewed by much development literature influenced by postmodernism as an innately democratic locus beyond the malign agency of the State.

In the period after the second world war, 'civil society' was seen by modernization theory as being part of the State, an interpretation which required that empowerment of poor peasants and workers entailed their political incorporation into the wider society. By contrast, as envisaged by the 'new' populist postmodernism from the 1980s onwards, 'civil society' is seen as the 'other' of the State, an approach which doubly relocates the process of grassroots empowerment: in a specific locality outside and against the State, but leaving the apparatus of national government and its class structure intact. Both conceptually and politically, this latter notion of 'civil society' as a refuge within the wider capitalist system that contains in embryo an alternative organizational and institutional system, is not merely wrong but – unsurprisingly – shares many of the characteristics attributed by earlier populists to rural community and peasant society.

The reason for this shift is linked to the rise of neo-liberalism in the 1980s, when the reproduction of capitalism ceased to depend on the consuming power of peasants in the so-called Third World. What an increasingly international capitalism did require, however, was their labour-power, to produce agricultural commodities that could be exported and consumed elsewhere. No longer the object of development programmes/projects designed to eliminate rural poverty, peasants were in effect reconstituted by much social science discourse as once again 'other'. An important reason that poverty has vanished from the development agenda, therefore, is quite simply that its meaning has been altered. Rather than being categorized as an economic problem, which is what Marxism and much modernization theory did in the 1960s and 1970s, rural poverty has been redefined by postmodernism as part of culture, and thus empowering for its grassroots subjects.

These included notions such as the 'redemocratization' of the State (= neither State nor people are as ideally they should be under capitalism), and the centrality of 'civil society' based on 'citizenship' (= people not as ideally they should be under capitalism). None of these approaches challenge the role of the State in a capitalist world: the only ones who do this, ironically, are positioned at the 'extremes' of the political spectrum. Those on the left, therefore, argue that – initially at least – poor peasants and workers should seek to capture the State, so as to rule through it. By contrast, those who are either no longer Marxists – but still consider themselves to be on the left – or on the right insist that the State ought to be excluded from any transformation. They ensure thereby, in each instance, that those who currently rule through the State continue to do so.

At the start of the twenty-first century, therefore, left and right do indeed appear to have exchanged much of their political content. This apparent exchange of content, however, is due not to a theoretical confluence but to the fact that many of those who claim to be on the political left have abandoned the tenets of socialism. Sections of what is (erroneously) regarded as the left – actually the 'new' populist postmodernism – have abandoned class identity and struggle, and now endorse 'primordial loyalties', decentralised decision-making incorporating any/all ideological beliefs, and see virtue not just in religion and 'civil society' but also in bourgeois democracy, nationalism, a weak State and a strong market. Some of those on the right no longer have difficulty with the concept of class struggle – albeit a 'from above' variant – but now possess an internationalist political outlook and support a strong centralized State.

The issues generated by this are evident from the way grassroots resistance outside and against the State is currently linked to the agrarian myth. Unaware of the extent to which claims about 'Zomia' are rooted in populist historiography, a long-standing discourse championing a rural 'other' opposed to and excluded from development/urbanization/modernization, too much credence is given to the hill communities as 'regions of asylum/refuge', the economic autonomy enjoyed by their inhabitants, as well as to the innate desire on the part of this 'other' always to resist the State and its development project.

To argue, as do exponents of the 'new' populist postmodernism, that rural inhabitants in less-fertile upland areas choose to live and work there (and are consequently empowered by their situation) is rather like saying that hill farmers who scratch a precarious living from poor quality soil choose to do this, as do slum dwellers located on the poorly-resourced fringes of urban conurbations. Such conditions are not chosen by their subjects in preference to all other options; much rather, many of those belonging to marginal populations live/work there only because it is in such peripheral locations that land is available or cheap, rents are low, and they are unable afford the cost of living/ working in better-resourced areas. That rural/urban inhabitants who are marginal make do and mend in these circumstances is self-evident (verging on the tautological), but this is emphatically not the same as their choosing to do so or being empowered thereby.

The reason for the fusion between the agrarian myth on the one hand and both the subaltern/resistance framework and the 'new' populist postmodernism on the other is not difficult to discern. In the epistemology shared by the latter, any/every form of resistance is declared to be legitimate (landlords as well as tenants, the rich as well as the poor). The difficulty with concepts such as 'resistance' and 'power' as deployed by the subaltern framework, therefore, is a political one. By eschewing a politics, resistance theory not only makes no distinction between agency by those occupying antagonistic class positions (commercial farmers, rich peasants, poor peasants and agricultural labourers), but also – with typical postmodern aporia – denies the necessity any longer to have to make such a distinction. The assumption is that all resisters are the same, by virtue of belonging to the same ethnic group, whereas evidence from peasant movements such as the EZLN shows that, in order to understand agrarian resistance/accommodation, such a category must be differentiated along class lines.

Now that economic development, wealth redistribution, progress and modernity are more-or-less off the social scientific agenda, it is unsurprising that 'new' populist postmodern approaches should surface and proclaim that what exists is a form of economic and/or cultural empowerment for 'those below'. Learn to accept what you are (= poor peasants and agricultural labourers) and enjoy what you already have (an 'other' culture, little land, low wages, bleak prospects) is the unspoken sub-text of this kind of resistance linked to the agrarian myth. Verily, it is a tract in keeping with our neoliberal times.

How a similar epistemology, linking nationalism and class struggle to the pastoral and Darwinian variants of the agrarian myth, informs film discourse, is examined in the next two chapters.

PART 2

Screen Images of Rural Struggle

∵

Horror, Humour, Fiends and Fools

I had never seen such a building so lavishly equipped with the instruments of violent death... They seemed, however, ill-adapted to the discreet requirements of twentieth century homicide....

> An observation by Louis Mazzini (TAYLOR, 1974: 250) in the film *Kind Hearts and Coronets*, about the collection of old weapons on the walls of Chalfont Castle, the title of which he was about to inherit.

Laughter, whether conciliatory or terrible, always occurs when some fear passes. It indicates liberation either from physical danger or from the grip of logic.

> THEODOR ADORNO and MAX HORKHEIMER (1977: 364) on why humorous images of the rich and powerful may be advantageous to the latter.

If you laugh at your leaders, you don't cut off their heads.[1]

> A comment by Lord (Kenneth) Baker, Minister in the Conservative governments of Margaret Thatcher during the 1980s, in the course of a radio interview on 2 February, 2006 about the impact on Muslim opinion of cartoons appearing in a Danish newspaper.

Introduction

Previous chapters have outlined the way in which, historically, the landlord class has come under attack from within its own national boundaries, by an indigenous bourgeoisie and/or proletariat. In order to defend itself, and deflect such attacks, it has been necessary for landlords to adopt a threefold strategy. First, to deploy agrarian myth ideology so as to attract support from rural plebeians (smallholders, tenants, sharecroppers). Second, either to project themselves or be represented as being *empowered*: that is to say, as the bearers

---

1   Although the reference was to the contrast between what happened to the French monarchy as a result of the 1789 Revolution, and the capacity of caricaturists such as James Gillray to lampoon royalty in England, Baker was nevertheless making a broader point about the general political rôle of humour.

and/or representatives of national identity, and as such in the forefront of a struggle for the nation. And third, to present themselves or be depicted in a contrasting ideological mode, as *disempowered*: as economically and politically 'not worth bothering about'. The latter kind of ideological defence, it will be argued here, is especially important to the landlord class, since it permits landowners persuasively to deny that they are any longer a power in the realm.

The effectiveness of this landlord defence, however, depends in turn on a number of things. First, the degree to which images conveying disempowerment – for example, humorous depictions of the aristocracy licensing the view that this class is politically and/or economically in decline or actually powerless – are inserted into and reproduced within the domain of popular culture.[2] Second, these primary images must themselves be backed up by secondary ones, extending the conceptual representation of a deprivileged existence to other ruling class institutions (public schools, the military, the church, the state).[3] Third, such an ideological defence on the part of a ruling

---

2   This interpretation of humour as disempowering 'those below' whilst empowering 'those above' contrasts absolutely with the currently fashionable view informing the postmodern conceptualization of laughter as much rather the opposite: that is, disempowering those above' whilst empowering 'those below'. The latter perception stems from the uncritical embrace by postmodernism – see, for example, Stallybrass and White (1986) – of Bakhtinian theory about the political efficacy of carnival, a site of ritual comic/disrespectful discourse (= 'bucolic poetry') that corresponds to Menippean satire aimed at authority by 'those below' (Bakhtin, 1984: 106ff., 112ff., 122ff.). Structured by the 'oral carnival-folkloric' of 'joyful relativity', whereby the world is 'fundamentally changed' and 'all distance between people is suspended', carnivalesque parody and laughter are said by postmodern theory to disempower the ruling class by portraying it as weak. Accordingly, postmodernism accepts at face value the notion that – because of carnivalistic acts such as the 'mock crowning and subsequent decrowning of the carnival king' – the carnival is 'a new mode of interrelationship between individuals' (= landlords, kings and commoners). Since it fails to distinguish between infrastructure and superstructure, however, postmodernism fails consequently to differentiate symbolic opposition from its 'other', an actual challenge to authority. The result is that postmodern theorists reify and thus exaggerate the transformational impact of carnivalesque discourse circulating within the domain of popular culture. What postmodern theory ignores, therefore, is the usual outcome of such transgression: that at the end of the day, when the carnival and all its display of ritual aggression has finished, the agricultural labourer returns to his/her hovel whilst landlord and king remain, respectively, in their manor house and castle. In other words, the existing hierarchy is still intact, and likely to endure until challenged 'from below' not by (forceful) words but by (forceful) deeds.

3   This underlines the *systemic* nature of ruling class power; consequently any struggle undertaken against the latter is likely to fail unless 'those below' are prepared to confront and attack *all* the institutional forms of such power (economic as well as political and ideological).

class must retain an offensive capacity, that is to say a discourse projecting menace or threat (horror mobilized from the domain of the supernatural) should its power be subject to further erosion. And fourth, all this should be accompanied ideally by a parallel discourse proclaiming the existence or achievement of plebeian empowerment.

The inference of the latter is that, were the landowning class and its institutions still efficacious, such 'from below' empowerment would not now exist.[4] This complex and multi-stranded ideological defence, it has been argued, is embodied in contrasting variants belonging to the aristocratic version of the agrarian myth. The latter is differentiated in terms of a pastoral and a Darwinian variant, amounting respectively to an idyllic arcadian vision of the countryside (unequal but harmonious), and a 'red-in-tooth-and-claw' vision, in which the countryside is a site of struggle by landlords to retain their power and/or property.

The continuing efficacy of each relational form considered here – colonialism, nationalism, and landlordism – has been dismissed repeatedly over the latter part of the twentieth century. Colonialism, it was averred, was after 1945 rapidly becoming a thing of the past, as was landlordism in most contexts, not only those in the so-called Third World. Nationalism too was consigned by many observers to the dustbin of history as a nineteenth century relic giving way to larger and more significant economic blocs formed

---

4   This kind of argument structured a response to Genovese (1994: 87) about what would have happened had the southern planter class not lost the American civil war: 'A few years ago I dumped all this on a good friend who ranks among the premier southern historians in the country. "Face it," I said, "notwithstanding all the airy incantations to safe methods of change, and notwithstanding your personal hostility to racism, if you folks had remained in power, black people would still be attending segregated [state] schools and would still be riding in the back of buses." My friend took another swig of Wild Turkey and replied, "Now Gene, if folks like me had actually been in power, there wouldn't have been any [state] schools and buses, and the problem would never have arisen."' The assumption underlying this exchange is that any gains made by 'those below' are substantial, and as such automatically and comprehensively negate all forms of 'from above' power. In reality, however, the changes that do take place in these circumstances are largely cosmetic, the *economic* sources of 'from above' empowerment and 'from below' disempowerment – ownership of or control over means of production (mainly land) – remaining largely in place. What is important from the view of proprietors, however, is that in a discourse about history they should be characterized as losers, not winners. Not only does this invite sympathy – as it clearly does from Genovese – but (more importantly) the subtext is that a transformation involving material assets is complete. In short, no further process of redistribution/reform (= empowerment/disempowerment) is necessary.

as a result of capitalist development (= 'globalization'). The nadir of such claims is represented by the frequent and strident announcements, heard at the end of the twentieth century from exponents of the 'new' postmodern populism, that emancipation had finally been realized by this or that subaltern group. Into this analytical category were slotted on an increasingly regular basis poor peasants and agricultural labourers everywhere, an epistemological procedure accompanied by the abrupt termination of their 'victim' status.[5]

Henceforth, 'new' postmodern populists assured us, such categories – composed for the most part of the rural poor – should be seen more accurately as culturally empowered. A twofold corollary of this declaration of (achieved) emancipation was as follows. First, that systemic transcendence – and all politics and programmatic change in furtherance of this – was immediately classified by 'new' postmodern populists as redundant. And second, by virtue of having declared 'those below' emancipated, the ruling class – and its landowning component – ceased henceforth to be 'a problem'. Not surprisingly, therefore, 'new' postmodern populists quickly labelled theories (like socialism) designed to secure economic and social development an inappropriate Eurocentric imposition based on outmoded Enlightenment grand narratives, and as such demeaning to a rural grassroots already (and sufficiently) empowered by its own existing cultural practices. Among the 'evidence' produced in support of the latter contention was the efficacious nature of widespread and enduring resistance conducted by 'those below', the most prominent form of which has been and is – 'new' postmodern populists claim – laughter projected in carnivalistic acts and the carnivalesque generally.[6]

---

5 Replacing a discourse about economic disempowerment structured by class with one about a grassroots empowered by 'popular' culture was precisely what neoliberals were attempting to do at that conjuncture.

6 Hence the insistence by one exponent of postmodern theory (McHale, 1987: 172) that '[p]ostmodernist fiction is the heir of Menippean satire and its most recent historical avatar'. For a similar view, see Collins (1989). It is necessary to distinguish the more useful component of Bakhtinian theory from its less helpful one. The more useful consists of the observation that all speech is dialogic (Todorov, 1984), in that conversation necessarily leaves unstated much of the context framing its utterances, or that which is understood by participants in order to make sense of what is actually said. The less useful aspect concerns the efficacy attributed by him to the language of carnival. Of these two components, it is unfortunately the second which has been taken up with such enthusiasm by those studying 'from below' rural agency. Thus, for example, carnival and carnivalesque discourse (= 'hidden transcripts') are identified by Scott (1990) as one of the most potent kinds of opposition (= 'everyday forms of resistance') to the existing social order.

That such a thinly-disguised Panglossian discourse has deep roots in conservative political theory is a point made in earlier chapters. However, the presence of an enduring link between on the one hand the discourse of the 'new' postmodern populism, and on the other the kind (and effectiveness) of class struggle waged 'from above' by conservatism in the domain of popular culture, is still deemed by some to be problematic.[7] For this reason, the object of the analysis which follows is to draw out this connection as manifested on film and on television. Since these related themes – the link between popular culture, class struggle, landlordism, colonialism and nationalism – are well represented in films as varied as *Kind Hearts and Coronets*, the *Quatermass* series, *Carleton-Browne of the FO, Carry on Up the Khyber, Raiders of the Lost Ark*, and *Four Weddings and a Funeral*, the common discourse structuring all the latter is examined here.[8]

---

7   There are a number of exceptions to this, in that a specifically political approach to discourses structuring film is evident is the seminal work of Potamkin (Jacobs, 1977), Kracauer (1960) and Richards (1973; 1977; 1989). Unlike Potamkin, for example, Richards is not a Marxist; however, his foregrounding of politics and history when discussing the meaning of a film is useful, more so than the a-historical/a-political 'decentred' framework employed by postmodern theorists (Jameson, 1988, 1994; Connor, 1989; Rutherford, 1990; Bhaba, 1994; Marcus, 1997; Gilroy, Grossberg and McRobbie, 2000; Narayan and Harding, 2000) who currently dominate cultural studies. Perhaps because they eschew the possibility of history and politics, exponents of postmodernism (Metz, 1974, 1982; McCabe, 1985; Collins, 1989; Jameson, 1992; Spivak, 1994) tend to regard film as an hermetically-sealed linguistic discourse (= 'the language of film', or 'film-as-language'), with no easily accessible referent outside of itself. In contrast, Richards examines film through an historian's eyes, in terms of broad political content and historical themes. That said, a difference exists between his approach to the analysis of film and that utilised here. To begin with, Richards (1973) delineates films in terms of distinctive political discourses (American populism, British Imperialism and German Nazism), whereas the following presentation emphasizes the common strands unifying them. As has been argued in previous chapters, conservatism, colonialism and fascism are ruling class ideologies that require a populist mobilizing discourse in order to generate and then sustain a wider politico-ideological acceptability. Moreover, the focus here is both on the specifically rural dimension of these discourses – the agrarian myth, in other words – and on the theme of class rule; of particular interest is how apparently 'innocent' films unexpectedly reproduce images that are ideologically supportive not just of landlordism, but also (and therefore) of colonialism and nationalism. Because of this, the framework adopted here poses the question of the way in which positive/negative film images of landlordism are connected with a discourse about horror/terror and humour/laughter. None of the latter is considered by Richards in his otherwise useful analysis of film.

8   As has been argued elsewhere (Brass, 2001), an important reason why Hollywood film discourse projects both the agrarian myth and populism is the power exercised by directors, producers and/or actors, many of whom either subscribe to the North American nationalist

This chapter is divided into four parts, the first of which explores two diametrically opposed images in popular culture which portray the landlord class
to advantage: as powerful (= the discourse of horror) and as powerless (= the
discourse of humour). The discourse which depicts its subject as powerful is
that of the ghost story, whereby either monarch, aristocrat or plebeian appears
as defender of the nation, is examined in the second part. The third looks at
the way humorous images in popular culture of these same subjects, as weak
and thus 'not worth bothering about', are similarly advantageous politically.
Why the importance of such images continues to elude some of those on the
left is considered in the fourth.

I

To an important extent, the case made here about the advantageous effect
of projecting a powerful landowning institution as disempowered, and thus
'not work bothering about', is the opposite of the one made by Walter Bagehot.
The latter argued that the more the mystery of royalty was dispelled as a result
of increasing exposure to the public gaze, the more disempowered the institution of the monarchy would become.[9] The more public exposure, the more

---

foundation myth (= the small farmer heroically struggling against railroad interests and cattle barons) or are themselves landowners. The significance of this is missed by Drazin (1999)
in an otherwise illuminating analysis of the film *The Third Man* (1949), directed by Carol Reed
and scripted by Graham Greene. About the influence of David Selznick, the producer, Drazin
(1999: 38–39) observes: 'In the conferences Selznick sought to transform Greene's no-hoper
[the character Holly Martins] into an image of unsophisticated but big-hearted pluckiness. It
was a view of themselves that Americans could accept with pride and were familiar with
from the movies – Gary Cooper in *Mr Deedes Goes to Town*, or James Stewart in *Mr Smith Goes
to Washington*...; the simple man reasserting civilized values'. A slightly different explanation
of this intervention would go as follows. The populism of the agrarian myth, as embodied in
the Westerns that Holly Martins writes for a living, and his continuing belief in Harry Limes'
elemental goodness, are undermined by the latter's badness. It was this naivety – the belief
in the reality of life as portrayed in the Westerns he wrote – that the film producer David
Selznick wanted to recast as 'big-hearted pluckiness'. In other words, he wanted to emphasize
the reality of the populist vision to which the Holly Martins character adhered.

9   This view is expressed in the following observation (Bagehot, 1928: 53): 'Above all things our
royalty is to be reverenced, and if you begin to poke about it you cannot reverence it. When
there is a select committee on the Queen, the charm of royalty will be gone. Its mystery is its
life. We must not let in daylight upon magic'. Earlier Bagehot (1928: 35, 40) indicates clearly
the role of monarchy and why it will not in his view withstand close scrutiny: '[S]o long as the
human heart is strong and the human reason is weak, Royalty will be strong because it

'ordinary' the monarch would be perceived as being, the less respect it would get, and consequently the weaker it would become. Against this view, it is argued here that what matters in such a process – which has undoubtedly taken place – is not the fact of exposure to public gaze so much as the *political meaning* conveyed thereby.

Horror, Humour and Class Struggle

Faced with an institution that has been powerful, but is now represented in the domain of popular culture as being disempowered, two responses are possible. One is that, since it no longer has a function, it should be abolished; the other accepts the initial premiss, but maintains by contrast that abolition is unnecessary, as the institution is 'not worth bothering about'.[10] From the same diagnosis, therefore, stem two opposing forms of political resolution: radical (monarchy and/or landlordism ceases) – revolutionary, even (the overthrow of all ruling class institutions) – and reformist (the monarchy and/or landlordism survive). Unsurprisingly, those belonging to ruling class institutions prefer the last outcome, in furtherance of which the dissemination or reproduction of an image of themselves as being de facto 'powerless' in a political or economic sense (preferably both) is helpful.

---

appeals to diffused feeling, and Republics weak because they appeal to the understanding...[hence the function of monarchy] to be a visible symbol of unity to those still so imperfectly educated as to need a symbol'. Since – like all myths – it requires an unquestioning acceptance of a non-rational discourse (= 'feeling') positing the 'naturalness' of hierarchy, the power of the monarchy is ultimately dependent on a corresponding absence of grassroots political consciousness (= 'understanding'). As with conservatism generally, this is only situation in which the reproduction of this ruling class institution is possible.

10   An example of the latter approach is Paxman (2006), a journalist who has a reputation as a radical. The final paragraph of his book encapsulates precisely the contradiction between an acceptance of the anachronistic role of the monarchy and an insistence that the institution is 'not worth bothering about'. Hence the concluding argument (Paxman, 2006: 288): 'Certainly, if we were devising a system of government for the twenty-first century we should not come up with what we have now. The arrangements are antique, undemocratic and illogical. But monarchies do not function by logic. If they work, they do so by appealing to other instincts, of history, emotion, imagination and mythology, and we have to acknowledge that many of the most stable societies in Europe are monarchies, while some of the most unstable and corrupt have presidents. It would theoretically be possible to pull one thread out of the rug woven by history (although we do not know what other threads might then unravel). We could easily pack all of them off to live out their lives in harmless eccentricity on some organically managed rural estate. But why bother?'.

Landlordism and the country house have been and are central to the ruling class in Britain, and significantly form a crucial part of inter-related institutional forms all belonging to the same ancient organizational matrix.[11] This mutually reinforcing network consists of the monarchy, the House of Lords, public school, and Oxbridge, each component of which is not only integral to the reproduction of the others but – more importantly – has thus far managed to escape any fundamental reform, let alone faced abolition.[12] This despite the fact that each component of this network periodically intervenes in the class struggle, either to mount an offensive against or to damp down plebeian mobilization. During the capitalist crisis of the 1930s, for example, the monarchy was one of the three main elements forging a political consensus, presenting itself as an 'above politics' unifier of the nation.[13]

---

11 At the start of his justly famous ghost story 'The Ash-Tree', M.R. James (1931: 54) – the embodiment of this ancient multi-stranded institutional matrix – puts the following declaration of love both for the country-house and for the life of a landowner into the mouth of his narrator: 'Everyone who has travelled over Eastern England knows the smaller country-houses with which it is studded – the rather dank little buildings, usually in the Italian style, surrounded with parks of some eighty to a hundred acres... [P]erhaps most of all I like fancying what life in such a house was when it was first built, and in the piping times of landlords' prosperity, and not least now, when, if money is not so plentiful, taste is more varied and life quite interesting. I wish to have one of these houses, and enough money to keep it together and entertain my friends in it modestly'.

12 The way the components of this institutional matrix interacted during the 1920s and 1930s is chronicled in the fiction of Evelyn Waugh. This world, according to Lodge (2003: 162), was 'inhabited by characters who were for the most part upper-class and in some cases aristocratic, educated at public school and Oxbridge, many of them idle, dissolute,... seldom seen occupied in useful work, their time mostly spent shuttling from party to party or from country house to country house, with occasional adventurous excursions Abroad'.

13 On this see Richards (1983), who argues that – together with the Conservative Prime Minister Stanley Baldwin and the entertainer/film star Gracie Fields – King George V was a major contributor to this political consensus. The King embodied the nation, the Prime Minister the countryside and the entertainer the urban industrial sector. Not the least effective input came from Gracie Fields, a working class female whose public persona radiated optimism (= hope) amidst economic crisis, and whose films projected an unambiguously ('we're all in this together') nationalist sentiment. Because he downplays the element of class struggle during the 1930s, however, Richards fails to identify what each contributor to this consensus had in common: namely, a specifically populist role in deflecting or pre-empting the formation or reproduction of consciousness of class.

In the case of the British aristocracy, this act of institutional survival has involved periodic announcements not so much of its demise as – more subtly – a decline of or diminution in its economic or political influence.[14] The decay of the country house after the 1939–1945 World War not only reproduces images associated historically with Gothic fiction but has also become a metaphor for the loss of economic power on the part of landlordism itself.[15] This discourse about aristocratic ruin (and ruins) entails claims that the source of wealth – land – has been taxed into insignificance or oblivion, and that consequently its role as a landlord class is much reduced or non-existent.[16] When linked to a co-terminous decline of political power traditionally exercised through the House of Lords, the socio-economic base of the British aristocracy – its defenders insist – has been eroded. All that remain are

---

14   Much the same case is made regularly in relation to the monarchy. Hence the recent claim (Paxman, 2006: 281) that '[l]ooked at from a distance, the royal spectacular...looks hardly changed from the days when kings made war and law and had bishops burned at the stake. But it is something of an illusion. Not only does royalty not have the power it once had, it does not live as high off the hog'.

15   This refrain – the demise of large landowners and landownership – is encountered most frequently in the pages of the house journal of the British aristocracy, *Country Life*. Not the least effective part of this discourse is the periodic reproduction in the latter publication of black-and-white or sepia photographs of large country houses (see, for example, Strong 1996), the impression created being that such habitations, together with their owners and acres, are now a thing of the past. This idea is itself reinforced by the frequent absence of landowners and workers from these (seemingly empty) country houses and their surrounding fields.

16   Hence the pessimistic entry in his diary for November 1946 by Evelyn Waugh, a sympathetic chronicler of the pre-war landowning class, 'as to what I should shake off here' by leaving England to live elsewhere. He writes (Davie, 1976: 661): 'The certainty that England as a great power is done for, that the loss of possessions, the claim of the English proletariat to be a privileged race, sloth and envy, must produce increasing poverty; that this time the cutting down will start at the top until only a proletariate [*sic*] and a bureaucracy survive'. In his subsequent entry (Davie, 1976: 662), however, Waugh gives the game away, and recognizes that nothing much has changed or is likely to: 'Why do I contemplate so grave a step as abjuring the realm...? What is there to worry me here...? I have a beautiful house furnished exactly to my taste; servants enough, wine in the cellar. The villagers are friendly and respectful; neighbours leave me alone. I send my children to the schools I please. Apart from taxation and rationing, government interference is negligible'. Later that same month, Waugh nevertheless declares once more his political beliefs (Davie, 1976: 663): 'The French called the occupying German army "the grey lice". That is precisely how I regard the occupying army of English socialist government'.

ritual practices on state occasions conducted by once-powerful but now impoverished landlords, or behaviours amounting to meaningless historical relics that are symbolic only, having been emptied of content.[17]

There is an interesting and politically significant parallel here. As in the case of the monarchy and the British landowning aristocracy, both Oxbridge and the public schools – themselves landowning institutions – have found it necessary to fight a similar rearguard action in order to survive into the twenty-first century.[18] To this end, Oxbridge and the public schools have – like the landlord class – either issued or endorsed periodic reports of their own actual/ imminent demise, not as an institutional form but (more subtly) in terms of the influence they exercise and the ideological role each discharges within the wider ambit of British society. Like those of the landowning aristocracy, both the social values represented by Oxbridge and the public schools, together with their economic and social power, are frequently said to be on the decline, since neither are compatible with modern capitalism. None of this is, of course, true: much rather the opposite.

A perception of a landlord class as weak, and thus 'not worth bothering about' politically informs the decline-of-aristocracy thesis, not just influential

---

17   Such claims were rebutted most effectively by those who were themselves from aristo-
      cratic backgrounds. During the 1830s, for example, Bulwer Lytton (1836a: 24–25), made
      the following observation: 'Without the odium of separate privileges, without the demar-
      cation of feudal rights, the absence of those very prerogatives has been the cause of the
      long establishment of their [= aristocratic] power. *Their authority has not been visible*; held
      under popular names it has deceived the popular eye; – and deluded by the notion of a
      Balance of Power, the people did not see that it was one of the proprietors of the power
      who held the scales and regulated the weights'. (emphasis added). Over a century later
      much the same point was made by Mitford (1959: 47): 'Most people, nowadays, take it for
      granted that the aristocracy is utterly impoverished, a view carefully fostered by the lords
      themselves... There are still many enormous fortunes in the English aristocracy, into
      which income tax and death duties have made no appreciable inroads...'. Significantly,
      it was this aspect, one small part of a much broader argument concerning aristocratic
      'difference', that elicited criticism from defenders (Waugh, 1959: 72) of aristocratic
      privilege.

18   The argument linking the survival both of Oxbridge and of the public schools to the way
      in which such institutions have been depicted in the domain of popular culture has been
      made on a number of earlier occasions, in a celebrated 1939 essay 'Boys' Weeklies' by
      Orwell (1946: 57–82), and more recently by Richards (1988) and Carter (1990). None of the
      latter, however, connect this ability to resist abolition specifically to the humorous por-
      trayal of ruling class institutions as disempowered, and thus in essence as 'not worth
      bothering about' politically.

but also still very much in vogue, notwithstanding evidence to the contrary.[19] Significantly, perhaps, the arguments now deployed in their own defence by large landowners in Britain remains essentially the same as before. Not only does this discourse about landownership remain rooted in nationalist ideology – along the lines of 'we conserve the land for the nation' – but it also presents the landlord class as disempowered politically and economically ('farming doesn't generate sufficient profits to cover the cost of the upkeep required by these grand houses').

The reason why images conveying a weak landlord class 'not worth bothering about' politically are important today is not difficult to discern. Where landowners, Oxbridge and the public schools are concerned, such a discourse serves the same ideological and political end: to act as a populist smokescreen, the purpose of which to protect/defend an institution threatened with reform or abolition by deflecting/disarming criticism, thereby permitting the institution in question to continue to reproduce itself socially and economically.[20]

---

19   Those who subscribe to the decline of aristocracy thesis include Cannadine, on whom see Chapter 2, and Daniels (1994). Symptomatic of this view, for example, is the following observation (Daniels, 1994: 101): 'The Second World War seems to spell the end of aristocratic England. The erosion of the aristocracy's political and economic power had long been under way, notably since the late nineteenth century, but now the very emblems of their culture, their country houses and parks, were visibly disintegrating... The postwar prospects of aristocratic England looked bleak'.

20   One way in which a ruling class institution threatened with abolition deflects/disarms criticism is to claim that it performs a socially useful role, and this is indeed the kind of image which permeates much popular culture. Evidence of this influence is the chivalric code of the landowning class, passed down to the film noir tradition via the unlikely influence of Raymond Chandler, who wrote scripts (or on whose books scripts were based) for classic film noir such as *Murder, My Sweet* (1944), *Double Indemnity* (1944), *The Big Sleep* (1946), *The Blue Dahlia* (1946), *The Brasher Doubloon* (1947), *Lady in the Lake* (1947), *The Long Goodbye* (1973), and *Farewell, My Lovely* (1975). As is well known, the plots of film noir feature a lone and honourable individual – usually a detective (= 'decent cop') – conducting a struggle against invariably unseen forces of evil in a dark and threatening urban landscape. The Hollywood producer John Houseman reports (in Bruccoli, 1976: x) that their enduring friendship was based on 'the surprising premise that he and I...were British public school men – and consequently Gentlemen... [i]t is not always easy to remember that Chandler, whose literary territory was bounded by Malibu on the west, Long Beach on the south, and San Bernadino on the east, and whose writing gave the world some of its most ruthless documentation on the seamier aspects of Southern California society in the twenties and thirties of [the twentieth] century, had spent most of his adolescence in England and had been educated in the classics at Dulwich [and loved] the English public school system...'. The connection between film noir and public

In other words, like the ritual act of the 'mock crowning and subsequent decrowning of the carnival king', a ruling class the power of which depends on the ownership/control of land is able to survive as long as it retains control over its property.

Merely characterizing the monarchy, the aristocracy, the military or the church as weak, inept or useless – by mobilizing the carnivalesque (laughter, parody, satire) against them – without attacking the material basis of such power (land, mineral wealth) in effect leaves their power intact and permits their rule to continue.[21] This is especially true in cases where a second kind of

---

school values is not difficult to discern: Chandler's lone private eye possesses many of the same characteristics as the 'gentleman' heroes, swashbucklers whose values are those of the knightly class. The latter, as Richards (1977: 4, 5) points out, were 'embodied in the chivalric code [which] dates the historical scope of the films from the eleventh to the nineteenth centuries, when this code prevailed... The typical swashbuckling hero is the gentleman hero, well born, comfortably off, a man of breeding and polish, daring and humour, gallantry and charm. He maintains a decent standard of behaviour, fights for King and Country, believes in truth and justice, defends the honour of a lady... The Code is, of course, the Code of the ruling class and its prominence strongly implies an Establishment mentality behind the films'. The specifically populist element – and conservatism – of the knightly code is equally clear: 'The plot-lines of swashbucklers often involve unscrupulous individual members of the aristocracy, who plot to gain power for themselves and who, during the course of the film, perpetuate all kinds of outrages against the people. The monarchy, on the other hand, is seen as embodying fair-minded and disinterested central government... The interests of the monarchy are thus identical with the interests of the people'. And just as swashbucklers protect both kingly authority and the common people against self-seeking and 'unscrupulous' members of the aristocracy, so the lone detective of film noir upholds the rights of the people and – it is inferred – what are the decent values of the existing (capitalist) system against dark forces which threaten to corrupt these.

21   Some long ago recognized that any challenge to aristocratic power which did not at the same time expropriate the material basis of such power – land – would fail. Thus, for example, in his critique of the English landowning class, Bulwer Lytton (1836b: 262–263, original emphasis) noted presciently: 'Believe me then, that if you institute a republic tomorrow, it would be an aristocratic republic... And for one evident reason – namely, the *immense property* of our nobles and landed gentry! Recollect, that in this respect they differ from most other aristocracies, which are merely the shadows of a court and without substance in themselves. From most other aristocracies, sweep away the office and the title, and they themselves are *not*; but banish from court a Northumberland, a Lonsdale, a Cleveland, a Bedford, or a Yarborough; take away their dukedoms and their earldoms, their ribbons or their robes, and they are exactly as powerful, with those broad lands and those mighty rent-rolls, as they were before. In any republic you can devise, men with this property will be *uppermost*; they will be still your rulers...'.

defence – a darker image of an empowered/threatening ruling class – also circulates in the domain of popular culture.

II

These two forms of ideological defence are on the one hand the threat embodied in the ghost story and on the other the deflection implied in the 'not worth bothering about' approach. Where the aristocratic variant of the agrarian myth is concerned, the first of these quite clearly corresponds to the Darwinian version, in that horror/terror emanates from ruling class components the position of which is linked closely to ownership of land (the monarchy, the church, landlords). The second form, whereby these same landowning elements are portrayed humorously, and thus as economically and/or politically disempowered, constitutes the pastoral version.[22]

In terms of 'from above' class struggle, therefore, the literary/filmic images generated are of landlordism as either active/threatening/empowered or, by contrast, passive/non-threatening/disempowered. Either form, moreover, can generate or be accompanied by a populist discourse, in that 'from above'

---

22   Perhaps the best-known examples of a comic portrayal of disempowered English ruling class institutions (aristocracy, public schools, imperialism, colonialism) are those found in the 1930s literary fiction of Evelyn Waugh (1951a; 1951b; 1954; 1962). Significant in this regard is the following observation by the Earl of Birkenhead (1973: 138–139), who was at Oxford with Waugh: 'It was also obvious that Evelyn had formed a withering contempt for the *jeunesse dorée*...(he) saw them as arrogant sciones scions of noble or county families... It was therefore not without amusement that one discovered, as his tastes matured, that when Evelyn began to find pleasure in aristocratic society and the houses these people inhabited, the (*jeunesse dorée*), once objects of his loathing and mauled in his writings, became numbered among his closest friends'. In truth, the mauling (or more accurately 'mauling') by Waugh of the English landowning class – mistakenly reified by Lodge (1973: 215) as 'subtly subversive of upper-class pride and prejudice' – was never anything other than friendly. The same cannot be said of his views about those at the bottom of the social hierarchy. When asked his opinion about the Spanish Civil war, and if he was for or against fascism, Waugh replied (Pryce-Jones, 1973: 3): 'I am not a Fascist nor shall I ever become one unless it were the only alternative to Marxism'. This statement of political belief, widely dismissed as unserious, is in fact much rather the opposite: it encapsulates as accurately as possible the view taken by much of the European bourgeoisie and its organic intellectuals at that conjuncture, who – though not 'natural' allies of the far right – were nevertheless prepared to support reactionary movements in cases where socialism was gaining ground in the class struggle.

agency – or, indeed, the absence of such agency – incorporates plebeian ele-ments in what is a multi-class defence of the nation. Where this defensive struggle to protect the nation is conducted unaccompanied by 'from above' agency, however, the Darwinian version belongs to the plebeian variant of the agrarian myth.

The (Ghostly) Defence of the Realm

The first form of defence deployed in the domain of popular culture by the ele-ments composing this discourse – landlordism, colonialism and nationalism – takes the familiar form of the ghost story. Here, too, there exists a long epistemological lineage, traceable to the Romantic reaction against the Enlightenment, inculpated for the 1789 French Revolution. In contexts where material and political conditions were becoming hostile (a situation marked by the rise of the industrial bourgeoisie and proletariat), the classes whose rule depended historically on ownership of or control over land – the monarchy, the church and the aristocracy – unsurprisingly regarded their political and economic position as increasingly under attack.[23] In addition to shedding the image of cosmopolitan 'distinction' conferred by the Grand Tour (see Chapter 6), therefore, the struggle conducted by the ruling class involved reminding 'those below' challenging their power of its efficacy, longevity and – by inference – its immutability and therefore 'natural' character. Hence the ideological mobilization by Romanticism of a discourse about the supernatu-ral, from which emanates a ghostly menace representing an ancient force.

Deployed in the literature about this non-material 'other' domain are all the ideological pillars structuring the discourse of the *ancien régime*. Among the elements upheld or vindicated by the supernatural are rural tradition and hier-archy, the folkloric, and the power of 'the irrational', all of which are depicted as being under threat from progress, materialism, science, rationality, and intellectual investigation. Hence the centrality to Gothic fiction from the early eighteenth century onwards of a darkened landscape occupied by ruined cas-tles and extinct aristocratic dynasties, metaphors for a declining nation. From this emerges a spectral apparition that not only challenges the rationality of science and scientists, but does so in the name of 'the people' and the nation. It is, moreover, impervious to human agency (particularly that of scientists) and is consequently in an important sense eternal.

Frequently this ghostly force cannot be vanquished, and where it can be the threat it represents is defeated – if at all – only with great difficulty. This kind

---

23   For the details about this process, see Chapter 6.

of symbolic antagonism structured eighteenth century Romanticism, and continued to inform the discourse about the nature of horror and superstition in the late nineteenth century, culminating in what is perhaps the most influential portrayal in popular culture of landlord reaction: Dracula the vampire.[24] It continued into the twentieth century, albeit with a difference: the defence of the nation passes from an ancient ruling class to bourgeois and plebeian components, science itself is absorbed by the supernatural, and the national/colonial aspects of the latter shift to a new imperial power.

Writing at the high point of British imperialism, Kipling unsurprisingly imbues the later nineteenth century supernatural with a colonial hierarchy, and differentiates his ghosts and their efficacy in terms of national identity. For him, therefore, everyone in India is fearful of an English ghost, but no Englishman could possibly be frightened of an Indian (= 'native') ghost.[25] In keeping with the nationalism informing British colonial ideology, therefore, the English characters in Kipling classify Indian coolies with the carriages they pull – as things, in other words. Since only humans generate a ghostly form, by inference neither coolies nor hillmen are regarded as human.[26] The ghost stories of Kipling are accordingly confined to the ranks of the colonizers – about thwarted lovers and long-dead billiard-playing railway workers – and, for the most part, the element of haunting is personal: an *ad hominem* appearance by one individual to another, with the object of avenging a specific wrong done them in the recent past.

To Make the Flesh Creep

A different and politically more significant kind of menace is conveyed by what are perhaps the two most influential examples of this particular genre in the domain of popular culture: the ghost stories of M.R. James and Nigel Kneale.[27] Although the latter similarly recount a return from the past of

---

24   The importance of the vampire story to the discourse of the agrarian myth has been examined by me elsewhere (Brass, 2000a; 2001).

25   Hence the following observation by one of the colonizers (Kipling, 1895: 151): 'No native ghost has yet been authentically reported to have frightened an Englishman; but many English Ghosts have scared the life out of both white and black'.

26   In his story 'The Phantom Rickshaw', Kipling (1895: 131) notes: 'One may see ghosts of men and women, but surely never coolies and carriages. The whole thing is absurd. Fancy a ghost of a hillman'.

27   Accurately described by his biographer (Pfaff, 1980: 425) as 'the best known English writer of ghost stories in [the twentieth] century', and by Graham Greene (1951: 81) as a writer who 'with admirable skill invented ghosts to make the flesh creep [and someone who] astutely used the image which would best convey horror', Montague Rhodes James

someone or something long dead, the object by contrast is to remind those living in the present of ancient forces/powers that cannot be ignored or resisted.[28] Unlike Kipling, for whom the act of haunting is personal, for James it is frequently impersonal: an individual is haunted by something/someone unknown to him, and – again unlike Kipling – the ghost/demon/ghoul represents not another recently dead individual but a primeval force.

Significantly, screen images generated by this discourse have circulated in popular culture, where they have been influential.[29] In the case of M.R. James, a number of these stories were filmed for British television in the 1970s, and repeats were again broadcast in 2004. Moreover, the cult film *Night of the Demon* (1957), directed by Jacques Tourneur, was based on 'Casting the Runes' by James. Where Kneale is concerned, the most influential components of his oeuvre consist of ghost/horror stories written as television plays. First, those in the Quatermass series, broadcast in Britain from the 1950s onwards, culminating in four additional television episodes in 1979, entitled *The Quatermass Conclusion*; and second, *The Stone Tape*, broadcast on British television in 1972.[30] A number of stories in the Quatermass series were subsequently filmed by Hammer Studios for cinema release: these included *The Quatermass Xperiment* (1954) and *Quatermass II* (1956), both directed by Val Guest, and *Quatermass and the Pit* (1967), directed by Roy Ward Baker.

Written at the end of the nineteenth century and beginning of the twentieth, and never out of print since, the ghost stories of M.R. James are about the

---

(1862–1936) was Provost both of Eton and of King's College, Cambridge. Not only was he an impeccably establishment figure in terms of occupation but his political outlook and religious beliefs were undeniably reactionary. Thus, for example, his politics have been described in a sympathetic biography (Pfaff, 1980: 210, 348, 397–398, 420 n86) as conservative and rooted in the eighteenth century (James 'delighted in the old-fashioned mode of life'). In their collected form (James, 1931), these stories have 'remained in print almost continuously ever since, having been reprinted by the original publisher, Edward Arnold, at least twelve times' (Pfaff, 1980: 412; see also 416, n74). His nearest rival over the latter part of the twentieth century was Nigel Kneale (1922–2006).

28   Commentators on the political right – for example, Kingsley Amis (1970: 125–135) – deny that the ghost stories of M.R. James refer to any temporal phenomena, and are certainly not explicable in terms of the socio-economic identity of the protagonists involved.

29   On the influence of the film versions of the Quatermass stories, and their role in consolidating the popularity of films produced by Hammer Studios, see Pirie (1973: 28ff.).

30   For the published versions of these scripts and stories, see *The Quatermass Experiment* (Kneale, 1959), *Quatermass II* (Kneale, 1960a), *Quatermass and the Pit* (Kneale, 1960b), *The Year of the Sex Olympics and Other TV Plays* (Kneale, 1976), and *The Quatermass Conclusion* (Kneale, 1979).

return of an ancient power historically rooted in the soil of the nation, one that is impervious to scientific explanation, should not be challenged, and is best left undisturbed. Where there is an attempt to appropriate symbols and/or resources – a crown, treasure, or land – belonging to this ancient power, retribution follows swiftly, usually in the form of death.[31] This same discourse was deployed to similar effect from the mid-twentieth century onwards by Nigel Kneale. Like James, film and/or television versions of Kneale's highly influential stories about the supernatural posited the continued existence in Britain of the same kind of ancient forces/powers that science was incapable of explaining or resisting.[32]

---

31   This theme informs a number of ghost stories by M.R. James. In 'A Warning to the Curious', for example, a Saxon crown long buried in the soil on the east coast of England is said always to have protected the nation from foreign invasion (James, 1931: 561–587). Its discovery leads to the haunting and death of the individual who finds it, despite the fact that he and friends succeed in restoring the crown to its original hiding place. Hence the 'warning' is clearly aimed at those who interfere with ancient kingly power still engaged in defending the nation. A similar narrative is encountered in 'The Uncommon Prayer-Book' (James, 1931: 490–513), a story about the supernatural power exercised in the present by an edition of the Prayer-Book printed after the execution of Charles I containing a condemnation of Oliver Cromwell. The aristocratic owner of the house and chapel during that epoch was an ardent royalist, even during the Commonwealth, 'one in whom love for Church and King had gradually given place to intense hate of the power that had silenced the one and slaughtered the other' (James, 1931: 503). Most significantly, the victim of this occult force is a book-dealer from London who, it is inferred (James, 1931: 501–503, 506), is Jewish (according to a plebeian voice, 'he weren't a reel Englishman at all'). Once again, therefore, the supernatural is mobilized on behalf of kingship. In 'The Treasure of Abbot Thomas' (James, 1931: 151–179), by contrast, it is wealth accumulated and hidden by the church that is defended, but – as in 'A Warning to the Curious' – the person finding it is similarly compelled to leave it untouched. A longstanding intra-dynastic struggle is depicted in 'The Mezzotint' (James, 1931: 36–53), a conflict resolved by the abduction and murder of the sole surviving heir to the lord of the manor, a ghostly drama enacted in the eponymous mezzotint. Although this particular story appears to be about the revenge of a poacher on a landlord who condemned him to execution, like the latter the former also belongs to a very old family that itself used previously to own the manor. As in the case of the other stories, therefore, this one is also about the class structure in the English countryside, where longstanding and ancient forces still exert their power exercised through the supernatural domain.

32   Significantly, perhaps, whereas in the early Quatermass stories – *The Quatermass Experiment, Quatermass II*, and *Quatermass and the Pit* – the identity of this ancient power is known, in the final story (entitled *The Quatermass Conclusion*) published two decades later it has neither name nor origin. In the latter text, therefore, the ancient power assumes an immanence lacking in the earlier stories, and is only halted, not

Accordingly, both James and Kneale project Darwinian variants of the agrarian myth in their ghost stories.[33] However, those of James embody the aristocratic version, whereas those of Kneale depict the plebeian version. What is defended by the occult as presented in the fictions of M.R. James, therefore, is the old socio-economic order, ruled by and composed of monarchy, church and nobility, all of which combine to represent the nation.[34] The ideological effectiveness of this defence can be attributed to James' researches as an antiquary, and his success in using this knowledge when constructing 'evidence' for the existence of supernatural forces, making the subsequent appearance of the latter all the more plausible.[35] These ancient powers are located by him in

---

destroyed, by science/scientists (Kneale, 1979: 52, 161, 168). Possessing the same kind of characteristics as it has in the earlier stories, the ancient force as depicted in the final story is situated underground, in the earth, where it has been for the past five thousand years (Kneale, 1979: 261). Again like the earlier stories, it returns and destroys gatherings of people (in this case, the young) in particular rural locations. Described as possessing 'hellish powers', this ancient force is regarded as diabolic ('evil', 'satan'), and takes the form of bolts of lighting which strike in (from) places – Neolithic burial grounds, stone circles, and cathedrals – long associated with ritual worship (Kneale, 1979: 52, 96–97, 106, 229, 231, 269). Although this force is described by Quatermass himself as 'a machine', it is never seen, nor (unlike in the earlier stories) is its true identity ever revealed.

33   Kneale comes close to accepting this when he observes of the ghosts in stories by M.R. James that '[o]ften they possess the most basic threat of all...[t]his stirs a dread that must go back to our primitive past...' (Kneale, 1973: x).

34   Thus, for example, one of his less well known ghost stories, 'The Story of a Disappearance and an Appearance' (James, 1931: 439–458), concerns the revenge of a village churchman, a rector murdered by two puppeteers travelling with a Punch and Judy show. The latter were plebeian elements who, it is inferred, objected to his strictures concerning the suitability of their entertainment for the rural inhabitants in the locality. That James should defend the old socio-economic order – monarchy, aristocracy, church, public schools, Oxbridge – is understandable, not just because of his conservative outlook but also in the light of his own very restricted milieu. Hence the following observation by his biographer (Pfaff, 1980: 424): 'Nor is it surprising that, given his personality and background, he moved most easily in the intersecting aristocracies of the bright and the well-placed; the majority of those he influenced most strongly [at Eton and Cambridge] belonged to at least one of these categories, and a person who was in neither was probably not likely to become an intimate friend'. As Provost of King's, James not only took a close interest in the sales and/or rental of land owned by the College but was part of a deputation to the Chancellor of the Exchequer seeking exemption for colleges/universities from land taxation (Pfaff, 1980: 213).

35   Criticism of the discourse informing James' ghost stories should not detract from his very considerable skill in composing them. As his biography notes, the convincing fashion in which he constructs these narratives is due in no small part to 'the brilliance of the

the countryside, where their existence and efficacy is recognized and respected by the plebeian locals, but challenged by visiting academics.[36] James himself was suspicious of social change, particularly that resulting from scientific research, and his stories unsurprisingly endorsed the efficacy of rural tradition dismissed by disbelieving scientists or philosophers, cosmopolitan outsiders who, when confronted with evidence of the supernatural, were subsequently compelled to recant, albeit reluctantly.[37]

---

antiquarian background' (Pfaff, 1980: 415). To this must be added the understated – not to say the restrained – manner in which an apparition finally manifests itself. Hence the effectiveness of unease and disquiet generated by seemingly banal details: for example, the way in which distant ghostly figures move rapidly – 'it's a rustling-like all along the bushes, coming very quick, either towards me or after me' (James, 1931: 526) – and horror is conveyed in 'A Warning to the Curious' and 'Rats' simply by the (skeletal) feet of a ghoul the face of which is never described.

36   Unlike scientists and philosophers, neither of whom believe in the supernatural, those at the top and bottom of the class structure are depicted not only as superstitious but correct in holding to their beliefs. Hence the observation in 'The Tractate Middoth' that 'the country people say he [= a person long dead, has] been seen about there in his old black cloak' (James, 1931: 220), a view that underlines the efficacy of 'from below' rural folk wisdom. Similarly, in 'The Ash-Tree' a Bishop warns the landlord about the dangerous proximity of the tree in question, noting that '[y]ou could never get one of my Irish flock to occupy that room...our Irish peasantry will always have it that it brings the worst of luck to sleep near an ash-tree...' (James, 1931: 69). In the event this superstition held by 'those below' is vindicated. That this view about the efficacy of rural folk wisdom is shared by 'those above' is evident from the story 'Oh, Whistle, and I'll Come to You, My Lad', in which it is the Colonel who rescues the academic when the latter is attacked by a ghost. An emblematic figure of the Victorian establishment, the Colonel is presented as someone who respects tradition and who – in contrast to academics – counsels against questioning ancient forces. Observing that he 'remembered a not very dissimilar occurrence in India', the Colonel endorses rural plebeian belief in the efficacy of the supernatural, commenting 'my experience is, mind you, that there's generally something at the bottom of what these country-folk hold to, and have held to for generations' (James, 1931: 138, 150).

37   For James, therefore, 'Sadducee' is term of disapprobation, attached to disbelieving scientists or philosophers who – initially dismissive of the occult and contemptuous of its exponents – are compelled subsequently to acknowledge both the existence and the efficacy of the supernatural. In his 'My Own True Ghost Story', Kipling (1895: 155) makes a similar allusion, noting that in India the howling of a hyena 'would convince a Sadducee of the Resurrection of the Dead – the worst sort of Dead'. This is because the Sadducees were a Jewish religious group that believed only in the written law, and rejected oral tradition. In their view, the former possessed a validity which the latter did not. James saw no difference between them and Victorian scientists or philosophers who scorned myth, tradition and oral sources. In his story 'The Mezzotint', for example, the power of the

Written for the most part at the end of the nineteenth and beginning of the twentieth century, his ghost stories project Victorian ruling class fears about challenges to its political and economic power, both at home and abroad.[38] Set in Sweden, the story 'Count Magnus' is about a long-dead landowner described as a 'grim old noble' who in the seventeenth century had suppressed peasant rebellions with extreme vigour, punishing or executing the ringleaders. Those tenants who encroached onto his demesne lands were burned in their houses, along with their families. Two centuries later, a visiting scholar investigating this episode is cautioned by local inhabitants against 'over-inquisitiveness', and told of the earlier fate of villagers who – on learning that the noble was dead – hunted on his land, without paying rent. These villagers were attacked and either killed or driven insane by a demonic force: Count Magnus had returned from the dead to protect his property. However, the scholar ignores the warning, and three padlocks binding the dead landowner

---

non-rational is dismissed contemptuously by the 'Sadducean Professor of Ophiology' (James, 1931: 53), while in 'Oh, Whistle, and I'll Come to You, My Lad' the 'Professor of Ontography' maintains similarly that 'I hold that any semblance, any appearance of concession to the view that such things [= ghosts] might exist is equivalent to a renunciation of all that I hold most sacred' (James, 1931: 123). The same character insists subsequently that 'my own views on such subjects are very strong. I am, in fact, a convinced disbeliever in what is called the "supernatural"', to which the reply is that he 'must be little better than a Sadducee' (James, 1931: 138–139). Inevitably, the disbeliever is compelled by subsequent events to reassess his opinions: thus, 'the Professor's views on certain points (= the existence of the supernatural) are less clear cut than they used to be' (James, 1931: 150). The same befalls the disbelieving scientists in 'Casting the Runes' (James, 1931: 235–267), and also the innkeeper in the story 'Number 13', who initially describes himself as an 'educated man [who] has no business with these superstitious notions' (James, 1931: 87). This hostility to those – particularly scientists – who challenged traditional beliefs is borne out by a biographer (Pfaff, 1980: 424), who notes that a criticism levelled at him at Cambridge was that 'James hates thought', and 'he did not like a certain kind of question, especially from a certain kind of person (e.g. a Bloomsburyite asking mockingly about religion)'. Among the 'un-godly' to whom James objected as 'too modern' was the economist John Maynard Keynes and the philosopher Bertrand Russell (Pfaff, 1980: 213–214, 246).

38   An opinion attributed by James (1931: 514–515) to one of his characters is clearly his own: 'Remember, if you please...that I am a Victorian by birth and education, and that the Victorian tree may not unreasonably be expected to bear Victorian fruit. Further, remember that an immense quantity of clever and thoughtful Rubbish is now being written about the Victorian age'. At the time of the First World War, one of his friends wrote to him (Pfaff, 1980: 256) complaining that existing beliefs/certainties were increasingly being dismissed by a 'generation whose loose thinking has been doing immense harm to national life and international politics'.

into his sarcophagus fall off one by one, releasing the Count to pursue and kill him.

The Wild Hunt

Writing half a century later, Kneale adheres to much the same kind of narrative structure, characterization and discourse.[39] Combining the ghost story with science fiction, his television plays and films based on them like M.R. James uphold the veracity of traditional oral sources challenged by scientists and science generally.[40] Again like M.R. James, Kneale depicts a modern world threatened by primeval supernatural forces representing long-established forms of power deeply embedded (sometimes literally) in houses in the English countryside or in the English landscape itself.[41] He takes an unmistakeably Darwinist

---

39   This link is evident from, for example, the fact that Kneale (1973: i–xi) himself provides an introduction to the Folio Society edition of ghost stories by M.R. James.

40   As in the case of the ghost stories by M.R. James, those by Kneale repeatedly depict scientists/academics/intellectuals being wrong footed by local folklore and oral sources. Examples include not just his early stories but also television plays such as *Quatermass and the Pit*, *Quatermass* and *The Stone Tape* (see below), where under the rubric of folkloric wisdom, traditional belief about the supernatural is vindicated. In *Quatermass and the Pit* a librarian wrongly dismisses such information about spectral appearances during the mid-eighteenth century with the following words (Kneale, 1960b: 89): 'street pamphlets are your best source for that sort of thing – nonsense stories and wild rumours. Amazing what they'd believe in those days'. The same is true of the final Quatermass story, where amidst threatening graffiti ('Kill Science', 'Feel Not Think') scientists are challenged – by the masses and political leaders alike – both to 'lay our imperfect intellects aside', to 'unlearn' science, and to 'stop trying to know things' (Kneale, 1979: 34, 79, 111, 197, 253). As is well known, anti-intellectualism is a central emplacement of agrarian populism.

41   This theme surfaces in two of his early stories. One, 'The Pond' (Kneale, 1949: 222–230), concerns an old man, an amateur taxidermist, who hunts frogs in a local pond by imitating their calls, catches and then kills them. All these frogs are skinned, stuffed and arranged by him in 'historical tableaux'. Lured to the pond one night by the mass croaking of (non-existent) frogs, he is himself attacked by an 'elemental' force (of nature) that emerges from deep within the pond. When found next morning, he is not only dead but also stuffed and stitched, in the manner of the frogs he caught. The same is true of his story 'Minuke' (Kneale, 1949: 34–48) where a modern house built on Norse gravestones is also haunted by an 'elemental' force coming up from the ground beneath its foundations. In the highly influential television play *Quatermass and the Pit* (Kneale, 1960b), first broadcast as a six-part series over 1958/59, the atavistic power is located in an ancient cylinder that – like the crown in the M.R. James story 'A Warning to the Curious' – is similarly buried in the ground. It is a sinister object that has throughout history given rise to claims about numerous ghostly apparitions in the locality. Excavation of the site reveals it

view of human nature as rooted in atavistic savagery and myth, his conclusion being that all humanity is essentially 'primitive', a condition which it is unable to transcend.[42] In keeping with the wider political concerns at that conjuncture, these atavistic 'destructive urges' are presented not as the historical outcome of capitalist development but rather as a 'natural' response to population growth and modernity (= 'complexity').[43] Within this conservative discourse

---

to be a spaceship from another planet the original mission of which in the distant past was to colonize Earth. Reactivated as a result of the excavation, this power assumes a diabolic form ('Hob') which threatens both London (= the urban) and the nation. Although the ancient power is in the end destroyed by science, in a subsequent play this situation is reversed. Accordingly, in his 1972 television play *The Stone Tape* (Kneale, 1976), scientists working in a country house long haunted by the ghost of a servant girl believe they have solved the problem of the 'apparition', maintaining it is nothing more than an image given off by the stone walls of the house. Having eliminated this image using electronic equipment, and apparently solved the problem of the house long 'haunted' in this fashion, the scientists turn their attention elsewhere. A more ancient supernatural force then materializes, and kills a female scientist, who in turn becomes a ghostly image. Both symbolically and literally, therefore, the domain of 'the traditional'/'the irrational' has defeated that of 'the modern'/'the rational'.

42   This is especially true of the final Quatermass story (Kneale, 1979), set in a dystopic future where society has disintegrated and England is under the anarchic rule of plebeian gangs, or two kinds of 'mob-in-the-streets'. The first are vigilantes belonging to opposed political hues (socialists and rightwingers), who conduct killing/looting sprees in abandoned urban contexts, and between whom it is inferred no difference exists. The second consist of New Age groups (= 'Planet People') who wander the countryside, and – according to Kneale (1979: 36) – 'are violent in a different way...[t]o human thought'. These New Age people have reverted to a 'primitive' form of existence, and not only subscribe to magic/mythical beliefs, but perceive the violent manifestations of ancient power as positive and redemptive (Kneale, 1979: 34ff.). For them, science is equated with 'sin', the forbidden knowledge that led to the expulsion from the Garden of Eden and the loss of their arcadia (Kneale, 1979: 152ff.).

43   Humanity, it is inferred, is no different from animals, it has an 'animal nature' and is 'naturally' violent. This Darwinist view not only structures *Quatermass and the Pit* but is uttered by characters who are scientists. One of the latter comments on the manifestation of 'primitive' behaviour generated (= 'the Wild Hunt [that] appears in legends the world over... The phantom ride of devils or witches') by the excavated cylinder in the following manner (Kneale, 1960b: 113, 149, 150–151, 178): 'The will to survive...it's an odd phenomenon... I think we may have seen ritual slaughter, to preserve a fixed society – to rid it of mutations. You find something like it on Earth, among certain termites and wasps... I wanted to kill you...Why? Because you're – different. I could feel that – you weren't – one of us. You had to be destroyed. Destroyed'. Significantly, the object of this Darwinian behaviour is a conservative one: 'to preserve a fixed society' – to reproduce the *status quo*, in other words.

of Malthusianism, progress and modernity are portrayed by Kneale as either superficial or unattainable.[44]

There are, however, a number of important contrasts with the fiction of M.R. James. Whereas for James science and the supernatural are antinomies, Kneale depicts scientists as siding with those who believe in the ancient power of the occult.[45] A similar difference is evident in the way gender is presented. Thus, with a few minor exceptions, women are absent from the ghost stories of M.R. James, all the main protagonists of which are male.[46] Female characters not only occupy a central role in the narrative fiction of Kneale but – most significantly – are portrayed by him as 'naturally' in tune with the non-rational, and thus as 'naturally' close to – if not actually an embodiment of – Nature itself.[47] The most crucial divergence, however, concerns the difference in

---

44 The conclusion, uttered again by a scientist (Kneale, 1960b: 188), adopts an unmistakably Darwinian tone: 'the ancient, destructive urges in us, that grow more deadly as our populations [become larger and more complex]... Every war crisis, witch-hunt, race riot, and purge...is a reminder and a warning' of our descent from this ancient power.

45 Thus in *Quatermass and the Pit* when a priest challenges a scientist to account for the ancient power ('I understand you're scientist – are you going to explain all this away in fashionable [= rational] terms?'), the latter replies in the following manner (Kneale, 1960b: 137): '[O]n the contrary, I agree with you...what has been uncovered *is* evil. It's as anciently diabolic as anything ever recorded'. Later the same scientist is depicted as having been affected by the diabolic force unleashed from the buried cylinder – in effect, become 'one of them' (Kneale, 1960b: 177). In short, what occurs is the conversion of a practitioner of 'the rational' into its opposite: an adherent of 'the irrational'.

46 Given the exclusively male society in which M.R. James lived, it is scarcely surprising that female characters are peripheral to his ghost stories. As one of his close friends noted when extolling the virtues of college life (Pfaff, 1980: 216), women were regarded as an intrusion: 'Chapel, Combination Room and the [Provost's] Lodge is a combination nowhere else attained. The club, the country house...all rolled in one with the added freedom – may I say it? we are alone – of a single sex...'.

47 Hence the principal female character in *Quatermass and the Pit* is in the main identified with anti-scientific/anti-modern/'irrational' views. Not only is she the one who investigates the background history to the haunting in the locality, therefore, but she is also the person who presses the efficacy of this explanation on the scientists, arguing that the latter know nothing about what they are doing (Kneale, 1960b: 86–87). The same character also turns out to be the most 'receptive subject' ('a memory stored for millions of years in that hull...and now picked up by the susceptible brain of a young women') when the influence of the ancient power is released from the long buried cylinder (Kneale, 1960b: 146, 149), thereby confirming the link between gender and 'non-rational' explanations and forces. Much the same could be said of the main female character in *The Stone Tape*, who occupies an analogous role in relation to long-standing occult powers. Similarly, the main female character who belongs to the group of surviving scientists in the final

emphasis given to nationalist ideology: for Kneale, the nation is defended against an external 'other' not by its royal or aristocratic components – as it is in the ghost stories of James – but rather by plebeian elements.[48]

In the discourse about the ghostly 'undead', Dracula is the 'foreign' landlord, the (dis-) embodiment of ancient powers located in the countryside of eastern Europe menacing both London (= the urban) and England (= the nation). The same kind of menace in the ghost stories of M.R. James comes from the same kind of class subject, but now at home instead of abroad: the supernatural power is composed of an ancient ruling class defending the nation, and threatening those (scientists) who interfere with this.[49] Not only are the targets of this attack by spectral horror the same in both instances, therefore, but what is defended is similarly the same: the English nation. The latter is in the narrative fiction of Kneale again under attack from an external ancient power, but this

---

Quatermass story (Kneale, 1979: 109, 116–117), is not only depicted stereotypically as an 'earth mother' in charge of subsistence cultivation, but also quickly drawn to the forces of the 'non-rational'.

48   While it is true that both James and Kneale depict plebeian elements as subscribing to a belief in the efficacy of the supernatural, an important difference exists. James portrays them as peripheral to the main story and passively accepting the ancient power confronting them. In *Quatermass and the Pit*, by contrast, Kneale shows plebeians actively engaged in resisting the attempt at recolonizing the nation (a view, however, that changes with the publication in the late 1970s of the final Quatermass story – see below). Similarly, scientists are presented as wanting plebeian support in this struggle. Thus the scientist in charge of excavating the cylinder observes that 'I want the man in the street on my side' (Kneale, 1960b: 18). The co-optation of plebeian elements in the struggle for the nation is also a theme in a film for which Kneale co-wrote the script: *HMS Defiant* (1962), directed by Lewis Gilbert. Set on board a English fighting ship during the Napoleonic wars, its narrative, script, characterization and depiction of life below decks are all much better and more plausible than the gung-ho naval film *Master and Commander* (2003) directed by Peter Weir. What is of particular significance is that when a captured Frenchman attempts to make common cause with the mutinous crew of the English warship by invoking a revolutionary internationalism, the only support he receives is from a villainous/ murderous malcontent ('to hell with England'). Not only is the latter subsequently killed by members of his own crew, but they then make common cause with their captain – who appeals to them in nationalist terms ('if you care for the safety of your country') – in a final battle with the French. This portrayal of plebeian elements mobilized by nationalist sentiment – the displacement of class struggle, in other words – and joining with their rulers in a united front against an 'external' enemy is a populist discourse that Kneale deploys in historical drama, ghost stories and science fiction alike.

49   There are obvious parallels here with the Arthurian legend, which posits the return of the king and his knights to defend the nation at such a time when England is in peril.

time the defence is not only plebeian but also more ambivalent.[50] This is due, perhaps, to the fact that both 'the people' and 'the nation' are themselves descended from that very force which now seeks to colonize – or, rather, to re-colonize – them. In an important sense, therefore, this narrative seeks to establish a lineage between the atavistic power manifested in the domain of the supernatural and all the inhabitants of the nation – the classic discourse of populism.

That this particular discourse about the agrarian myth has come full circle in the domain of popular culture is evident from the film *Raiders of the Lost Ark* (1981) directed by Stephen Spielberg, the first part of the Indiana Jones trilogy. Here, too, the supernatural – in the form of ghosts emanating from the recently discovered Ark of the Covenant – is mobilized in defence of nationalism, this time that of the United States. The hero Indiana Jones, the embodiment of American individualism, is impervious to the malign ancient power unleashed by the Ark.[51] Moreover, the film ends with the inference that science – the Manhatten Project that resulted in the nuclear bomb – is itself nothing more than the activation of an ancient force (= the Ark of the Covenant). As such, supernatural power will henceforth be harnessed discursively to the colonial ambitions of the United States, just as previously it was deployed on behalf of either British colonialism (Kipling), the English ruling classes (M.R. James), or the whole British nation resisting colonization (Kneale).

III

A second method of defence that, it can be argued, corresponds to class struggle conducted 'from above' is one in which humour replaces horror, weakness replaces strength, and landlords or colonialism are presented as disempowered instead of empowered.[52] This 'not-worth-bothering-about' approach, or

---

50   By the final Quatermass story (Kneale, 1979), plebeian elements in general – and the New Age groups in particular – have become complicit with the ancient power itself. Here Kneale inserts a generational divide into the narrative, the old being depicted as thinking repositories of scientific knowledge, while the young by contrast are represented as easy converts to anti-rational/anti-scientific discourse (Kneale, 1979: 231ff.).

51   Indiana Jones persists with his quest, despite being advised by a helper not to pursue his search for the Ark ('it is not of this Earth').

52   This 'not worth bothering about' approach has been influential in the depiction on film of landlordism in India (Brass, 2000a: 284–285). It also informs the humour of Hollywood.

royalty/aristocracy/colonialism as 'paper tiger', whereby comedic depictions of a particular institution, such as landlordism (of the royal or merely aristocratic kind) and colonialism, are said to be subversive politically in that they bring the object of humour into disrepute.

Toffee-Nosed and Useless[53]

The process of rendering the institutional form concerned 'unserious', so the argument goes, corresponds to a process of undermining it.[54] It is almost a cliché, therefore, that over the past two decades the royal princes – and Prince Charles in particular – have for a variety of reasons become the object

---

Woody Allen, whose comedic persona projects the image of a self-deprecating bourgeois intellectual, as someone who – although occupying an elevated position in the class hierarchy – depicts himself as a disempowered 'loser'. That is to say, as being something 'other' than he actually is. The opposite is true of Bob Hope, whose humour similarly inverts the socio-economic position of the subject, but in a different way; in his case, therefore, comedy derives from the over-inflated self-image on the part of a (usually petty-bourgeois) film character – for example, *The Paleface* (1948), directed by Norman Z. McLeod, and *Son of Paleface* (1952), directed by Frank Tashlin – who actually is a 'loser'.

53 'Toffee-nosed and useless' refers to the way servants in the film *Gosford Park* perceive their aristocratic employers.

54 Although the article challenging this kind of argument was started in 2003, when the central thesis – by depicting the politically powerful humorously as weak, inept or useless (= 'not worth bothering about'), the image of politically disempowment in effect contributes to their survival – was already in place, support for its claim came recently from what for the writer is an unexpected source. Going through the papers of my father Denis Brass (1913–2006), I came across the following note: 'Suffocating complacency about [the] risk of Hitler. Seems all inconsistency – lack of study of fascist leaders – Hitler tended to be regarded as a kind of Charlie Chaplin – few politicians read *Mein Kampf*. As a student in Germany during 1935, I became rapidly aware of the danger'. Epitomised in the domain of popular culture by cartoons and caricatures in the 1930s press, fascism and fascist leaders were portrayed humorously, a corollary of this depiction as non-serious being that they were seen as unthreatening. This political complacency about the rise of fascism culminated in the film *The Great Dictator* (1940), directed/scripted by and starring Charlie Chaplin, where even in wartime rightwing European dictators are still depicted as figures of fun. That such images circulated in Germany is evident from the following account (Palmier, 2006: 58–59): 'When [Reck-Malleczwesen] met [Hitler] in a Munich restaurant, together with his friend Friedrich von Mücke, they burst out laughing at his clumsy manners. They were persuaded that a fellow like that could not be dangerous. The same unawareness is shown by Ernest Jünger, who seemed to observe the rise of the Nazis in the 1920s with an amused scepticism'.

of media derision.[55] An effect of this has been that the monarchy is now widely perceived as a politically disempowered institution no longer commanding the public esteem it once enjoyed, and thus in a very real sense an aspect of British society 'not worth bothering about'.

Against this view, it could be said that the effect of acquiring a comedic image is much rather the opposite: in becoming 'unserious', the institution ceases to be projected – and perceived – as a political threat, and thus as a target of political action.[56] By depicting royalty, aristocracy and/or colonialism

---

55   For an example of this view, see Cannadine (1997: 9). The reasons for this derision, it is frequently argued, stem from the institutional demystification of monarchy, as exemplified by the cumulative rendering of its actual/potential incumbents as 'ordinary' (= sociologically non-other). Among the factors contributing to the latter are on the one hand exposure to and active participation in the media (documentaries, game shows, television interviews), and on the other the public expression of fogeyish views (about architecture, medicine and education). Both these combine to dispel the mystique of royalty, by confirming that its members are in their interests and opinions no different from the majority of those they rule. While this is perceived by some to be an advantage, in that it demonstrates the extent to which the monarchy 'represents' the people over whom it is set, such elimination of 'difference' also erodes all the ideological components that are said by its political supporters to justify the 'otherness' of monarchy in the first place. Non-democratic power exercised by those who are in effect no different from those over whom such power is exerted is, in the end, politically indefensible. In this connection, see also the point made by Bagehot (see above).

56   An example of how the 'not worth bothering about' approach defuses a political challenge to a traditional ruling class institution by portraying it humorously as disempowered is the British public school system. The way in which film depicts the educational privilege such institutions confer (and in particular the political, economic and ideological advantages gained thereby) as non-existent is the series made during the late 1950s about a fictional school for girls, St Trinian's, based on the cartoons by Ronald Searle. This comedy series consisted of three films – *The Belles of St. Trinian's* (1954), *Blue Murder at St. Trinian's* (1957) and *The Pure Hell of St. Trinian's* (1960) – all directed by Frank Launder and produced by Sidney Gilliat. It would be easy, but misplaced, to dismiss them as 'merely humorous' – and thus innocent and non-efficacious, particularly since they all adhere to a symptomatic discourse about the advantages/disadvantages associated with the kind of educational institution shown. In each one of the films the school is presented as an institution bereft of efficacy and influence, and as such certainly incapable of conferring advantage of any sort on those attending it. Not only is St. Trinian's ('not one of the better public schools') financially bankrupt, non-functioning educationally, and disconnected from the exercise of political power at the national level, therefore, but its pupils are shown to have the same interests as (and be allied with) plebeian characters. This, to put it no more strongly, is just the kind of 'not worth bothering about' image any traditional ruling class institution under political threat – as at the time was the public school

humorously, they are defused politically, and the fact of landlordism associated with their form of power is itself ejected from the arena of struggle.[57]
Perhaps the best-known literary example of the way Bakhtinian carnivalesque
laughter is linked to hierarchical inversion in a way that licenses the landlord

system – would attempt to project. Of particular interest are two additional aspects: the
position of these films in a similar cinematic lineage depicting ruling class characters, and
the related establishment stereotypes portrayed within the films themselves. Thus
Launder and Gilliat not only scripted *The Lady Vanishes* but also invented its two
characters – Charters and Caldicott – who epitomize upper class 'Englishness'. As is noted
in Chapter 7, the surface appearance of such upper class characters as the object of
humour serves to disguise an underlying courage, ruthlessness and efficiency that
emerges very quickly in times of struggle. In keeping with the effectiveness of this camouflage is the way in which other class stereotypes are deployed in the films about
St Trinian's. The actor Terry-Thomas, who played the main upper class colonial rôle
(Cadogan de Vere Carlton-Browne) in *Carlton-Browne of the FO* (see below) is in *The Pure
Hell of St Trinian's* a similar establishment type but, significantly, down on his luck, an
undischarged bankrupt now operating a dubious travel company. Much the same is true
of another actor, Thorley Walters, who plays incompetent military officers in both films
(Colonel Bellingham, Major Whiteheart). In line with this, the British military in charge of
a colonial outpost in the film *Blue Murder at St. Trinian's* are – laughably – a mobile bath
unit. What all the latter share is the depiction of powerful elements belonging to the
British ruling classes – colonials, officers – as disempowered: as ineffective, straightfor-
wardly risible, or having experienced a decline in social position/influence. In other
words, as politically 'not worth bothering about'.

57   An example of this as applied to royalty is the fictional reconstruction of the memoirs
written in first century Rome by the Emperor Claudius, in which the latter – before becoming Emperor – is warned by friends to 'act dumb' in order to avoid being murdered. The
books by Robert Graves (1960; 1961) formed the basis of the successful 13-episode television series, first broadcast in 1976 and repeated in 2006 and 2013. "'Now listen!", Claudius
is told (Graves, 1960: 112), "'Do you want to live a long busy life, with honour at the end of
it?" "Yes." "Then exaggerate your limp, stammer deliberately, sham sickness frequently, let
your wits wander, jerk your head, and twitch with your hands on all public or semi-public
occasions. If you could see as much as I can see you would know that this was your only
hope of safety and eventual glory."' Claudius does indeed survive the political intrigues
and murder plots within the ranks of the landowning nobility and the imperial family,
eventually to become Emperor. This he does by exaggerating his own physical disabilities,
the object being to portray himself as a fool – in his own words, 'I saved my skin by playing
the imbecile' (Graves, 1961: 389) and 'Instead of keeping quiet about his stupidity, Claudius
explained, in a few short speeches, that it had been a mere mask assumed for the benefit
of Caligula, and that he owed both life and throne to it'. (Suetonius, 1957: 203) – and thus
to be seen by those around him as 'not-worth-bothering-about'. Although in this particular instance the threat comes from members of the same class, and not 'those below', the
principle at work is the same.

pastoral are the characters Jeeves and Wooster in novels (and television series based on them) by P.G. Wodehouse.[58]

These humorous stories are about how a servant – an empowered plebeian – repeatedly comes to the rescue of his master, a disempowered aristocrat.[59] The latter is depicted as benign and thus 'not-worth-bothering-about' politically, whilst his servant not only subscribes to the existing hierarchy but also works hard to reproduce this, and his own subordination within it.[60] What is portrayed, therefore, is the aristocratic pastoral version of the agrarian myth, an arcadian vision of the English countryside as idyllic, where everyone knows (and accepts) his/her place, a rural context that is socio-economically unequal yet harmonious.[61]

---

58   Depicting life in the English country house at the beginning of the twentieth century, these stories outline the extent to which Wooster, an affable but bumbling and ineffective aristocrat, depends on his servant Jeeves, a 'gentleman's gentleman'. Although subordinate to his aristocratic master, Jeeves is nevertheless adroit and knowledgeable, and called upon constantly to rescue Wooster from what are no more than undergraduate pranks (stealing a policeman's helmet, romantic entanglements, etc.). In keeping with this approach, an aristocrat who is leader of a fascist party – Sir Roderick Spode and his 'Blackshorts' – is also depicted humorously, as someone who is similarly 'not-worth-bothering-about' politically.

59   As the example of Don Quijote and Sancho Panza underlines, this theme of a wise servant (= empowered plebeian) coupled with a stupid master (= disempowered aristocrat) is a common one in literature. It informs the film *The Admirable Crichton* (1957) directed by Lewis Gilbert, based on a 1902 play by J.M. Barrie, in which the class hierarchy is inverted as a result of shipwreck, and aristocrats marooned on a desert island become increasingly dependent on their butler and maid for survival. All are eventually rescued, and the class hierarchy is restored once again. A variation on this theme is found in a 1930s novel by Waugh (1954: 18ff.), where retainers and servants are permitted by the landowning family to continue living in the country house long after they have ceased to be employed in service. Here, too, it is the servants, not the landowning family, who are portrayed as empowered (= 'in charge'): for example, one plebeian resents 'the interruption of his "elevenses" – a lavish and ruminative feast which occupied the servants' hall from ten-thirty until noon'.

60   There is a tendency to dismiss the political significance of the comedic way Wodehouse portrays his plebeian and aristocratic characters. This is true of Orwell (1946) in his defence of Wodehouse for having agreed to make propaganda broadcasts for the Nazis during the early 1940s. Accepting that Wodehouse is 'not anti-upper class', Orwell (1946: 164) maintained merely that 'a *harmless* old-fashioned snobbishness is perceptible all through his work' (emphasis added). The harmlessness of this image – of an aristocracy that is disempowered, in other words – is precisely what is questioned here.

61   During the late 1960s, when the aristocratic pastoral version of the agrarian myth was on the ideological defensive, even some conservatives questioned the validity of its

The political insidiousness of comedy, and the degree to which it serves to disarm the viewer by portraying a powerful institution as its political 'other' (= powerless), can be illustrated with reference to a number of films from the latter half of the twentieth century.[62] One of the most important is *Kind Hearts and Coronets* (1949), an Ealing comedy directed by Robert Hamer.[63] It charts the way in which a distant relative of the Duke of Chalfont is snubbed by the aristocratic d'Ascoyne family – because his mother married a commoner ('for love, instead of for rank, or money, or land...') who was also 'foreign' – yet finally inherits the title after having murdered most of the D'Ascoynes that stood between him and the Dukedom.[64]

Superficially, the film appears to be an attack on the concept of aristocracy, by depicting its snobbery, credulity, ineptitude, plus the easy and rapid despatch of its various family members (occupying positions in the church, the military, and in the private banking sector), thereby reinforcing the image of

---

arcadian depiction of rural existence. One such was Angus Wilson, who accepted (Wilson, Smith and Cook, 1971: 17–18) that: 'Until quite lately Englishmen have spent all their emotions in lamenting a lost country Paradise: I am enough traditionalist to believe that such craving for a vanished natural scene is as necessary to spiritual health as is the new urban realism and dandy style that have risen now to redress the excess of nostalgia. Nevertheless, this persistent strain of backward-looking pastoralism has been a weakening drug for England's cultural health in the days of her international decline; and this has been so, I believe, because it has always been based upon a hypocrisy, a refusal until only very recent times to admit to the disgusting social degradation of England's rural poor'.

62   The political significance of humour in relation to film was noted in the mid-1950s by the film director Lindsay Anderson (2004: 226), who objected that 'the adoption [by a film critic] of a tone which enables [him/her] to evade through humour. The fundamental [political] issues are balked'. To dismiss films as escapism, he insisted (Anderson, 2004: 225–226) rightly, was to underestimate their ideological significance, as was the attempt of criticism to adopt an apolitical stance on film ('without politics, without class'). Against those who maintain 'that a critic's function must be restricted to an examination of the aesthetic form of the film under discussion', he argued (Anderson, 2004: 227) – again rightly – that 'I hope I will be pardoned if I say that this distinction between form and content somewhat naïf'. What Anderson detested above all, however, was the use of humour *against film* – to dismiss it as an art form, in other words – and not *within film* (as deployed by me here), as a protective method of camouflaging landlordism. To object to the way humour trivializes art is not the same as pointing out how film comedy disguises the continued exercise of class power.

63   The film script is included in Taylor (1974: 195–264).

64   In the words of of the main protagonist, Louis Mazzini (Taylor, 1974: 218): 'My mother was a member of the D'Ascoyne family. She married, as they thought, beneath her, and from that day, they refused to recognize her or my existence'.

ruling class as both risible and weak. Since it seems also to vindicate the plebeian character undertaking this attack, the outcome is a film ostensibly about a
successful 'from below' challenge by someone of an 'other' nationality to the
British landlord class, the disempowerment of the latter coming about as a
result of an empowered former.

On closer inspection, however, a different kind of politics emerges. Instead
of being a film that not only depicts but justifies the successful struggle waged
by an empowered 'foreign' plebeian against a weak and thus disempowered
landowning family, *Kind Hearts and Coronets* endorses rather than subverts
aristocracy.[65] The story is in fact a thinly disguised neoliberal fable that does
not question the power of the ruling class, but argues only that the wrong people (= the 'less fit') exercise this power, a point of view expressed by the declassé
hero.[66] In this respect the social Darwinist discourse structuring the film is in
fact no different from that found in Shakespearean plays/films such as *Richard
III* (see below) and *Macbeth*, where the object of murder is not to overturn the
institution of monarchy but rather to seize the throne. Although the latter are
tragedies, whilst the film *Kind Hearts and Coronets* is a comedy, they all subscribe to what is essentially the same ideology: one that is supportive of political power exercised of by a landowning ruling class.[67]

---

65   It is evident, therefore, that as Louis Mazzini moves closer to the title, he relishes the
     prospect of becoming a landowner. This is clear from his observation (Taylor, 1974: 250)
     that '[i]t was pleasant to stand on the battlements [of Chalfont Castle], and know that the
     acres, which stretched out as far as the eye could see, would soon be mine'.

66   The main character in the film resents being categorized as a plebeian, and constantly
     proclaims/presses his aristocratic antecedents. As each member of the D'Ascoyne family
     between him and the Dukedom is killed off, and Louis Mazzini succeeds in bettering his
     economic circumstances, he increasingly adopts the hauteur and snobbish views of the
     aristocracy. Hence the description by him of a lover as 'pretty enough in her suburban
     way....[b]ut her face would have looked rather out of place under a coronet' (Taylor, 1974:
     224–225). Similarly, throughout the film he voices the stereotypical disdain of the land-
     owning class for those 'in trade'. Thus trade is referred to as an 'ignominious occupation',
     and shop assistants as 'being commonly regarded as an inferior race who never emerge
     from the other side of the counter'; subsequently he complains that '[w]hen I was a drap-
     er's assistant, and you a rich father's son you showed me no kindness' (Taylor, 1974: 210,
     211, 239).

67   In what remains – rightly – the best analysis of Ealing films, Barr (1977: 119–130) seemingly
     misses this crucial aspect informing the discourse of *Kind Hearts and Coronets*; namely,
     that it is not an attack on English landlordism by dissatisfied plebeian elements, but
     rather a defence of the aristocracy. Hence the argument [Barr, 1977: 128] that '[d]iscount
     his [low] birth and he [Louis Mazzini] is still as good a man as [the D'Ascoynes] – we
     are all sons of Adam. Whatever Louis's motives, whatever his own snobbery, *he acts as*

This kind of film image, not just of the ruling class but also of colonialism, is associated in Britain with the subsequent comedy film *Carleton-Browne of the FO* (1958), directed by John Boulting. When strategically important mineral deposits are discovered on the island of Gaillardia, a British colonial possession, a well-connected but incompetent member of the foreign office is sent as government representative.[68] After being misled and outmaneouvred, he is taken prisoner as the Islanders declare their economic independence by seizing control of their own natural resources. This narrative reflected the view prevailing at the time, just before the Development Decade, when decolonization was in progress; members of the British ruling class are depicted as inept, useless, and easily overwhelmed by cunning and manipulative 'others' in the colonies (= 'foreigners/orientals').[69] In a very real sense, therefore, both

---

    an agent for quite radical class resentments' (emphasis added). This is ironic, since when examining another film in this genre – *Went the Day Well?* (1943), directed by Alberto Calvacanti – the focus is on precisely the betrayal by the village squire of the national cause during wartime, and his subsequent death at the hands of the one of the villagers heroically defending 'rural England/Englishness' against German invaders (Barr, 1977: 29–33). This, Barr (1977: 31) notes, is a situation in which villagers are no longer prepared to 'defer automatically to well-spoken officers', and as such – it could be argued – symbolizes the passing of the pre-war rural social order. This may well be true in terms of cinematic discourse, but – as will be outlined below – this challenge to the power structure in the British countryside was thwarted by the 'from above' struggle conducted by the landlord class, a struggle depicted in other Ealing films like *Kind Hearts and Coronets*.

68   There are many similarities between the film *Carleton-Browne of the FO* and *Scoop*, the 1930s comic novel by Evelyn Waugh (1954). Both project the same kind of benign images, not just of English identity and British imperialism but also of a member of the ruling class charged with upholding colonialism. At the centre of each narrative is an incompetent (and thus 'harmless') son of an old family – a landowning one in the case of *Scoop* – characterized as 'not worth bothering about'. In both cases, this individual accidentally finds himself in an impoverished foreign country (as diplomat or journalist) where rival powers (Russia and Germany in the 1930s, Russia and the United States in the 1950s) contend for control of its mineral wealth. Each emerges as an improbable hero, the epitome of the kind of gentlemen amateur whose achievements reproduce the stereotype of imperial acquisition in a fit of absence of mind.

69   The British colonial ruling class stereotypes in *Carleton-Browne of the FO* – played by actors such as Terry-Thomas, Thorley Walters and Miles Malleson – are all depicted as figures of fun, incompetent and thus non-threatening. The opposite is true of the colonized 'others', who fall into one of two categories. The first is composed of Gaillardian politicians (such as the Prime Minister Amphibulos, played by Peter Sellers) who are uniformly undemocratic, corrupt and self-serving. The second consists of Gaillardian royalty, who by contrast are honest, democratic, represent the true interests of all their people,

colonialism and its main upholders – the British ruling class – are the subject of ridicule, a result of which is that each is projected filmically as 'not worth bothering about'. The image of colonizer as disempowered is itself complemented by that of the colonized as empowered, and – in an authentically populist manner – the anti-colonial revolution by the Island population is led by its young King. Since the latter is Oxford educated and democratic in outlook, however, the 'civilizing mission' of colonialism is itself to some degree seen as justified.

Exhibiting a similar version of the aristocratic variant of the agrarian myth – namely, the 'not-worth-bothering-about' approach – is another film comedy, *Carry on Up the Khyber* (1968), directed by Gerald Thomas. Set in India during 1895, at the high-point of empire, it ridicules not just colonialism and imperial rule by the British upper-class but also the traditions/rituals associated with this kind of power. Hence the aristocratic behaviour and mores of the colonial rulers are parodied, not only in palpably estuary English accents but also in terms of the sang-froid approach to crisis, as brilliantly depicted in the scene of the residency-under-siege.[70] However, much like in *Indiana Jones and the Temple of Doom* (see next chapter), the film *Carry on Up the Khyber* ends with British forces routing the 'natives'; colonialism itself is accordingly vindicated.

Stooping Shoulders and Strained Accents
The epitome of this 'not worth bothering about' approach to colonialism and landlordism, however, is encountered on television in the late 1970s, that most

---

and lead the nation to its independence. In short, a discourse that is doubly populist, by virtue of depicting the British colonial ruling class as disempowered (it wasn't) and the ruling class of the ex-colonial nation as empowered, enlightened and democratic rulers of a Third World country independent of imperial ties (none of which was usually the case).

70   The parody is all the more effective for being carried out by actors who are generally assigned plebeian rôles. This is particularly the case where the principal characters are concerned: thus the colonial ruling caste, Sir Sidney and Lady Ruff-Diamond, are played by Sid James and Joan Sims, actors who are more usually seen in stereotypically working class parts (crooks, taxi drivers, maids, harridans). Perhaps the most perceptive comment in the film on the centrality of *sang-froid* to 'Englishness' comes from Kenneth Williams, who as the local Indian ruler (the Khazi of Kalabar) shrieks in an uncomprehending rage that the colonizers keep their cool under fire but, if a guest pours tea into a cup before the milk, they lose their temper. What disconcerts the invariably unflappable demeanour of the English is a lapse in manners, and certainly not an uprising by the local 'natives', the latter being as a consequence dismissed by the colonizer as trivial.

influential domain of popular culture in Britain.[71] Written by two members of the Monty Python comedy team as part of the 'Ripping Yarns' series, *Roger of the Raj* was an humorous yet affectionate portrayal of ruling class colonial ritual and ideology.[72] This extended from an episode where all the officers of the regiment stationed in India during 1917 in turn break strict codes governing behaviour at the dining table, then apologise before going next door to shoot themselves, to the aristocratic son and heir secretly running off to set himself up in trade, the traditional *bête noir* of the landowning nobility.[73] Depicting members of the landowning aristocracy in this manner, as slightly eccentric but essentially harmless, is not merely the mirror image of colonial rule as portrayed by Kipling, but can amount to a denial or downgrading of an oppressive form of power that continues to be exercised. As such, humour may on occasion much rather be the opposite of subversive, by actually contributing to the reproduction of a class ridiculed in this manner.

This view – that humour reinforces the existing class structure rather than subverts it – goes against the current fashion where much film interpretation is concerned. The conventional wisdom informing the latter approach is that the film comedies of the 1950s challenged establishment institutions by

---

71   Not all such applications of a 'not worth bothering about' approach to the British land-
      lord class at this conjuncture involved a comedic representation. Reviewing the 1981
      television adaptation of the Waugh novel *Brideshead Revisited*, a celebration of the
      British upper classes, Kingsley Amis (1990: 85) observes that an actor portraying one
      aristocrat 'does wonders with the part, arousing pity and concern for a helpless victim',
      thereby suggesting that humour is not necessary for a sympathetic depiction of the
      ruling class.

72   As with many other post-1960s comedians, those who were associated with the Monty
      Python team were themselves establishment products (public school, Oxbridge). The
      objects of their humour not surprisingly reflected this background, in that targets were
      not just those above them socially (the aristocracy) but also those below them (plebeians,
      socialists). Not only are ruling class traditions (associated with colonialism, the aristoc-
      racy and landlordism) all portrayed as absurd, but an additional target of ridicule – most
      famously in the films *Monty Python and The Holy Grail* (1975) and *Monty Python's Life of
      Brian* (1979) – is socialism, the adherents of which are presented as equally risible and
      self-deluding.

73   The final scene (Palin and Jones, 1980) consists of a small shop wedged incongruously into
      the entrance of an imposing aristocratic home surrounded by extensive acres ('Lord
      Bartlesham and the Honourable Miranda Fyffe-Moncrieff, Duchess of Lincoln: Chemists'
      sundries, accessories, douches a speciality'), while the declared aim of its aristocratic
      owners is '[t]o be able to throw off the shackles of wealth and privilege, and live as we'd
      always wanted to live, as simple shopkeepers...'.

satirizing them.[74] In the case of the films directed or scripted by the Boulting brothers, for example, no distinction is made between on the one hand *Carlton-Browne of the FO*, *Brothers in Law* (1957) and *Heavens Above!* (1963), all of which lampoon the ruling class and its institutions (the judicial system, colonialism, the foreign office, the church), and on the other *I'm All Right Jack* (1959), which ridicules trade unions.[75] The assumption is that the object and impact of satire on all these institutions is in all cases the same, and thus the fact of humour does not differentiate between those it targets.

However, the different political structure and object of humour in each case suggests that it is incorrect to identify the presence of an equivalence between them, and thus to conflate all these films under the rubric of an undifferentiated concept of satire.[76] Those belonging to the English ruling class – in

---

74   Significantly, perhaps, this was not the case with regard to threatre at that conjuncture, where the non-threatening aspects of laughter were to some extent recognized by those playwrights labelled 'angry young men'. Hence the observation by one of the latter, John Osborne (1957: 69) that 'I can't go on laughing at the idiocies of the people who rule our lives. We have been laughing at their gay little madnesses, my dear, at their point-to-points, at the postural slump of the well-off and the mentally under-privileged, at the stooping shoulders and strained accents, at their waffling cant, for too long. They are no longer funny, because they are not merely dangerous, they are murderous. I don't think I want to make people laugh at them any more because they are stupid, insensitive, unimaginative beyond hope, uncreative and murderous'. The difficulty with this kind of protest was that, although it accurately identified what it was *against* (broadly speaking, the interlocking components of the British 'establishment' – monarchy, the church, Oxbridge, the BBC, the Conservative Party), it was rather less clear as to what it was *for*. Despite the fact that Osborne (1957: 77ff.) claimed to be a socialist, he avoided both intellectual engagement (beyond generalities) with and political commitment to this kind of politics. Hence the following admissions (Osborne, 1957: 69, 83): 'All art is organized evasion. [...] I am not going to define my own socialism. Socialism is an experimental idea, not a dogma; an attitude to truth and liberty, the way people should live and treat each other. Individual definitions are unimportant'.

75   That these films lampoon everyone, and thus adhere to an undifferentiated concept of satire, is certainly the view held by Roy Boulting (McFarlane, 1997: 79) about the films produced/directed by him and his brother ('...we turned a satirical and jaundiced eye on the pillar institutions of the Establishment – the Army, Law, Foreign Office, City of London and Trades Unions and, finally, the Church...').

76   Hence the following observation by Roy Boulting (McFarlane, 1997: 79) about the even-handedness of the mockery dispensed in *I'm All Right Jack*: 'Both John [Boulting] and I at the time [late 1950s] felt the idea that one particular part of society should be held guilty and responsible for the failures of society at large, and that some other area should be free of blame, was ridiculous. We felt that all areas of society shared some common blame,

Carlton-Browne of the FO, for example – are represented filmically as disempowered, and hence characters without influence or political effect who can
safely be ignored by those around them, and especially 'those below'. Trade
unionists, by contrast, are also portrayed humorously but – unlike their upper-
class counterparts – are shown to be too powerful.[77] The political distinction
between these two comedic images is crucial: whereas characters belonging to
the establishment are weak and thus 'not worth bothering about', those in
trade unions are a danger to the nation whose potency needs to be curbed.[78]

   Where the church is concerned, this 'not worth bothering about' approach
is also true of the humorous way in which the clergy have been depicted on
film and British television. Examples include not just films from the 1950s
and 1960s, like *Father Brown* and *Heavens Above!*, but also television situation comedies such as *All Gas and Gaiters* and – more recently – *The Vicar
of Dibley*.[79] In *Father Brown* (1954), directed by Robert Hamer, the eponymous hero is portrayed as an other-worldly catholic priest interested mainly in

---

and this is what we had to address ourselves to. I do remember that both John and I, at
that time, felt we could see the terrible inadequacy of all those accepted beliefs within
society'.

77   On occasion the image shifts from one to the other, in the sense that a figure of fun
becomes its 'other', as a comedic/'harmless' identity is replaced by a threatening one.
Orwell (1937) noted just such a transformation in the way workers were perceived by
members of what he termed the 'lower-upper-middle class' or the 'shabby-genteel family'
of the 1930s. He describes (Orwell, 1937: 156–157) this shift in the following manner: 'An
attitude of sniggering superiority punctuated by bursts of vicious hatred. Look at any
number of [the humorous magazine] Punch during the past thirty years. You will find it
everywhere taken for granted that a working-class person, as such, is a figure of fun,
except at odd moments when he shows signs of being too prosperous, whereupon he
ceases to be a figure of fun and becomes a demon'.

78   The existence at that conjuncture of 'a danger to the nation' is evident from what is stated
by Roy Boulting, the producer of *I'm All Right Jack* and brother of the director (McFarlane,
1997: 79): 'We shied away from the trite escapism to which pre-war British films had been
wedded. War itself had brought liberation and a national identity to the British film for
the first time in its history. We didn't want to lose that'. That trade unions were considered
to be too powerful also emerges from an interview where Roy Boulting (Sorensen, 1996:
163) reveals that '[w]e worked at Denham [Studios] just after the [1939–1945] war when
things were, in industrial terms, rather difficult. The unions had got completely out
of hand'.

79   This portrayal of the church as a benign and disempowered institution may be contrasted
with the altogether different image of the Roman Catholic church contained in the
German play *The Representative* (Hochhuth, 1963), about the failure of Pope Pius XII to
condemn the Nazi extermination of the Jews.

saving the soul of an art thief who is also a French aristocrat.[80] Similarly, in *Heavens Above!* (1963), directed by John and Roy Boulting, a well-meaning Anglican clergyman who champions the poor and tries to put into effect a programme of wealth redistribution is also portrayed as a figure of fun, a naïve and gullible character. The comedic image of the church in both films is of a benign and largely ineffectual institution whose power is essentially moral: that is, a variation on the theme of 'not worth bothering about'.

The portrayal of establishment characters as disempowered (= 'not worth bothering about'), and thus necessarily positioned outside political discourse, reached its apogee with the film comedy *Four Weddings and a Funeral* (1994), directed by Mike Newell.[81] Not only was it a success financially, but – because of this – it set a pattern for the way in which a benign image of ruling class eccentricity fused with a specifically 'English' national/cultural identity was to be depicted in future films.[82] Regressing to representations both of a disempowered aristocracy and of 'Englishness' projected by P.G. Wodehouse, the focus of the narrative is on a group of friends, most of whom belong to the ruling class, and none of whom seem to have jobs or need to sell their labour-power in order to subsist. Like the character Bertie Wooster, the main focus of their quotidian interests/activity is on how to enter or avoid matrimony, and the sole concessions to modernity are positive film images of homosexual partnerships and disability (deafness). The latter, it could be argued, are politically

---

80   Not only is the theme of religious salvation paramount, but two of the main characters (Flambeau, Lady Warren) depicted sympathetically are members of the French and English upper class.

81   According to Curtis (1994) the film was a runaway box office success, having grossed over US$200 million worldwide. The original budget was no more than US$6 million. Nominated for two oscars, the film won three BAFTA awards in 1995 (for best actor, best actress in a supporting rôle, and best film).

82   One of the main characters, Tom, who is described as a 'very affectionate and very stupid aristocrat', has a castle in the country with 137 rooms and admits to being not 'the richest man in England' but only the seventh richest (Curtis, 1994: 11, 33, 35). He comes close subsequently to conceding the central argument made here (landed aristocracy = 'not work bothering about'), when stating that (Curtis, 1994: 102): 'I think I've fooled them so far – the great advantage of having a reputation for being stupid – people are less suspicious of you'. Another film in the same genre was *Notting Hill* (1999), directed by Roger Mitchell, and for which Curtis also wrote the screenplay. Common to both *Four Weddings and a Funeral* and *Notting Hill* is the pursuit of (dominant) American females by (subordinate) English males, a variation of the relationship depicted in the novels of P.G. Wodehouse (and the *Jeeves and Wooster* television series of the early 1990s), and the 1996 film *Richard III*.

non-threatening, and as such ideological compromises indicative of a populist discourse proclaiming the efficacy of non-class forms of empowerment.

IV

Among the issues raised by the proliferation of media images projecting a dis-empowered aristocracy is what alternative explanations, apart from those advanced by exponents of the 'new' populist postmodernism, are there for the persistence of conservative ideology. On the left of the political spectrum, it seems, there are still those who fail to confront the role of media images in the formation and reproduction of the reactionary discourse that remains even after a national culture has been purged of an overtly aristocratic ideology.

Class, Nation and Populism
What constitutes English culture, and indeed whether – apart from a domi-nant form – it has ever existed, is a much debated and disputed question, not least among those on the left. In the 1960s, for example, this issue was the sub-ject of an exchange between E.P Thompson and Perry Anderson, in which the latter accused the former of 'populist nationalism' for exaggerating the revolu-tionary intent and role of 'the people'.[83] Against the latter view, Anderson maintained that the lack of a 'from below' revolutionary tradition was due to a lack of an authentically indigenous sociological theory capable of challenging this dominant cultural inheritance.[84] In a discourse (doubly patronizing, to native and immigrant alike) the backwardness of English national culture was attributed by him simply – and wrongly – to the influx of 'foreigners' who pro-vided the intellectual components of a national culture that the natives them-selves had somehow been unwilling or unable to supply. The 'foreigner' is, in short, inculpated with the conservatism of national culture in Britain.[85]

---

83   See the exchange between Thompson (1965) and Anderson (1966). For the dismissal as populist nationalism' of Thompson's views about the innate revolutionary disposition of 'the people' in Britain, see Anderson (1966: 33–39).

84   Hence the view (Anderson, 1968: 4): 'A political science capable of guiding the working-class movement to final victory will only be born within a general intellectual matrix which challenges bourgeois ideology in every sector of thought and represents a decisive, hegemonic alternative to the cultural status quo'. The same text continues: 'It is enough to say this, to be reminded that in Britain, at present, there is virtually no organized combat of this kind, anywhere along the front'.

85   Anderson (1968: 56) claimed that historically English society has been a case of 'arrested development' due to the fact that a 'White emigration rolled across the flat expanse of

The ironies here are unmissable. To begin with, Anderson fails to address the way in which pre-existing ideology constitutive of British national culture was formed, and why: in his analysis it has the status of a 'given', something 'already there' that the post-1914 'white' emigration merely reinforced and consolidated. Not only did the elements of this pre-existing ideology form a specifically British national culture, therefore, but the reason for its conservatism stemmed from the way an aristocratic identity fused with its plebeian counterpart. As has been argued in Chapter 2, this was a result of the construction during the nineteenth century of a populist discourse about the existence of a common national 'sameness', a consequence being the formation of a politically conservative ideology to some degree capable of uniting 'those above' with 'those below'. Linked in part to the move *away* from an aristocratic identity formed by the Grand Tour (with its emphasis on cosmopolitanism, a classical background, etc.), and *towards* a more narrowly-focussed plebeian discourse endorsing national selfhood, the popular culture which emerged seemingly precluded the necessity of any further challenge 'from below'.[86]

Because he equates British national culture simply with high culture, however, Anderson misses an important aspect of the way this conservative national ideology was disseminated from the twentieth century onwards.[87] Accordingly, this same populist discourse operated most effectively not in the domain colonized by 'white' emigrés – that is to say, in the academic disciplines of philosophy, literary criticism, political theory, aesthetics, psychoanalysis, and anthropology – but in the realm of popular culture. The influence of the latter – encountered most powerfully in the electronic media, such as cinema, radio and television – is more far-reaching in terms of its impact on the formation and reproduction of a wider British national culture. It is for this reason that the political construction in film of a populist discourse about landowning class empowerment/disempowerment and its relation to nation, state, class and colonialism is considered here to be significant.

While Anderson was right to accuse E.P. Thompson of 'populist nationalism' for the latter's untheorized (= un-sociological) conceptualization of 'the people', therefore, his own advocacy of more/better European theory in order to produce a native sociology capable of formulating opposition to dominant culture is itself vulnerable to the same accusation. Because he is unfamiliar with

---

English intellectual life, capturing sector after sector, until this traditionally insular culture became dominated by expatriates, of heterogeneous calibre'.

86   For the role of the Grand Tour in the formation of national identity, see Chapter 6.

87   This criticism is also true of the argument (Anderson, 1983) about nationalism as 'imagined community'.

the distinction between populism and Marxism, Anderson fails to note that those on the 'left' have been equally at fault in this regard, a point borne out by the subsequent promotion/endorsement of the 'new' populist postmodernism – mistaking it for Marxism – by the journal he himself edited. Moreover, the indigenous sociology that *did* emerge – one has only to think of Giddens – reinforced the very political (not cultural) conservatism to which Anderson objected. The problem lies not with the presence or absence of sociological theory, as Anderson maintains, but rather with its politics: in short, not the fact of sociological 'totality' per se, but rather the kind of dynamic informing its structure and reproduction.[88]

Conclusion

It is argued here and in the chapter to follow that film and/or television images depicting ruling class elements (the monarchy, the church, landlords) whose position is linked closely to ownership of land tend to fall into three categories, all of which portray them in terms that are ideologically advantageous where rural struggle is concerned. Moreover, the focus here is both on the specifically rural dimension of these discourses – the agrarian myth, in other words – and on the theme of class rule. Of particular interest is how apparently 'innocent' films unexpectedly reproduce images that are ideologically supportive not just of landlordism, but also (and therefore) of monarchy, the church, colonialism and nationalism.

The first of these images, which shows them as empowered, and thus as socio-economically strong, tend to emanate from a discourse about horror/terror/revenge. For this reason, this category is labelled 'fiends'. By contrast, the humorous portrayal of these same landowning components as bumbling, silly and ineffectual characters who are dupes, tends to constitute them as 'fools'. Such comedic images convey members of the ruling class as weak: economically and/or politically disempowered, and thus 'not worth bothering about'. Situated ideologically between these contrasting hostile and harmless images

---

88 This somewhat idealised view about the necessarily subversive role of a sociology which addressed the question of a total structure is stated thus (Anderson, 1968: 47): 'British culture never produced a classical sociology largely because British society was never challenged as a whole from within: the dominant class and its intellectuals consequently had no interest in forging a theory of its total structure; for it would necessarily have been an "answer" to a question which to their ideological advantage remained unposed'.

of rural struggle is a liminal category of 'friend' that incorporates aspects of each (see Chapter 5).

Broadly speaking, these three categories as reproduced in film and television appear to be located on a continuum, in terms both of transition and history. The trajectory of 'those above' – monarchy, aristocracy, church, military – goes from an image of empowerment and hostility (= 'fiend') to one of paternalism and noblesse oblige (= 'friend'), culminating finally in one of disempowered harmlessness (= 'fool'), where the subject concerned is depicted in popular culture as 'unserious', no longer a threat and thus 'not worth bothering about'. The opposite trajectory is followed by 'those below'. Whereas plebeian elements who are colonized are initially constituted (by Kipling, Spielberg, and Kneale) as unthreatening, they are subsequently declared (by the Boulting brothers) to be not only empowered but in danger of becoming too powerful.

Equally, film and/or television images of 'fiend' suggest that the nation can be represented both by 'those above' (in the ghost stories of M.R. James) and by 'those below' (in the ghost stories of Nigel Kneale). Although the image of 'friend', conveys a benign landowning class or monarch that continues to represent the nation, these still powerful landowning elements are nevertheless either in the process or in danger of losing this. In film/television images of 'fool', by contrast, 'those above' no longer effectively represent the nation. Depicting landowners as 'fools', and thus 'not worth bothering about', also has advantageous implications for their position in relation to nationalist discourse.

In contrast to the image of 'fiend' and 'friend', therefore, landowners portrayed as 'fools' are absolved from having to lead the nation, since the inference is that they are incapable of doing so through no fault of their own. What is distinctive about this identity as reproduced in popular culture, therefore, is that members of the landlord class thus disempowered are not to blame for this situation. Owners of large rural holdings who are either engaged in hostile action (= 'fiend') or are demobilized (= 'friend'), risk an attack on their property when the crucial link between class and nation is broken. By contrast, proprietors depicted as 'fools' may escape this outcome. In the latter case, therefore, that an ancient landowning institution no longer ideologically represents either nation or people does not necessarily license the next step: political opposition to landlordism per se, culminating in its expropriation.

If one conceptualizes the empowered/disempowered dichotomy structuring the opposition between humour and horror in political terms, it could be said to adhere to the following pattern. Socialists would argue that those who rule by virtue of monarchy/aristocracy/colonialism are indeed powerful, while those who are ruled as a consequence of the existence and reproduction of these relational/institutional/systemic forms cannot be other than disempowered. Film representations which depart from this pattern distort the reality of class power, and as such correspond to an attempt to inculcate false consciousness of class. That an historical progression – Victorian/Edwardian/Post-1945 – seemingly overlaps filmically/televisually with the 'fiend'/'friend'/'fool' images reinforces the impression that in Britain ownership of or control over land is no longer significant economically, and thus of no importance politically.

The following chapter examines the liminal category of 'friend', one that depicts its subject as paternalistic: hence royalty, landowners and (potential) colonizers are shown to be powerful but also benign, 'those above' being friendly towards 'those below', an image of selflessness that corresponds to the concept *noblesse oblige*.

Best of Friends, or Worst of Enemies?

The snobbery of our films is not aristocratic. In British films the aristocracy is generally...treated, though respectfully, as a fine old figure of fun. Similarly, the functions of working class characters are chiefly comic, where they are not villainous. They make excellent servants, good tradesmen, and first-class soldiers.

> The film director LINDSAY ANDERSON (2004: 235) writing in 1956 about the way in which class was represented in British films

At a time when the normal condition of the citizen is a state of anxiety, euphoria spreads over our culture like the broad smile of an idiot.

> An observation made in 1948 by ROBERT WARSHOW (1964: 84) in his influential essay, 'Gangster as Tragic Hero'

As long as you present poverty as something dignified, the establishment will not be disturbed.

> An observation made in 1970 by the Bengali film director, Mrinal Sen (cited in RAJADHYAKSHA and WILLEMEN, 1995: 384)[1]

Introduction

The focus of this chapter is on films projecting the image of its class protagonist as being a powerful-but-friendly subject (= 'friend'), located analytically between the two other categories that featured in the previous chapter, one hostile (= 'fiend') and the other harmless (= 'fool'). These in turn overlapped with two other variables. First, that of pastoral and Darwinian versions of the agrarian myth, the former corresponding to a situation of harmony in the countryside while the latter reflected one of struggle. And second, these two versions each possessed a landlord and plebeian variant, which depicted the class-specific character of the discourse.

---

1 The epigraphs by Warshow and Mrinal Sen are included in order to make the point that not all those formulating or analysing popular culture have succumbed to idealism, and viewed it as a-historical or as unproblematically emancipatory/progressive/empowering.

It could be argued that, where the element of struggle is involved, characterization of 'those above' as 'friends' to 'those below' is more insidious than 'fiend'/'fool' images. Unlike either of the latter, therefore, the portrayal of monarch or aristocrat as a friend-of-the-people seemingly negates the hierarchy at the apex of which such upper class subjects are positioned. In keeping with the discourse of populism, this characterization undermines plebeian consciousness of class. By denying not so much the presence as the efficacy of class, the image of 'friend' permits 'those above' to deflect or suspend references to the existence of a material relation that is unequal, thereby enabling them to be depicted as 'other' than in reality they are: namely, owners of means of production that confer on proprietors such as themselves forms of economic, political, and ideological power not available to 'those below'. What in class terms are enemies can therefore be presented as 'friends' – the central emplacement of populist discourse.

Films with imperialism as a central theme project a combination of versions and variants, and may exhibit opposed forms of the agrarian myth. Those engaged in conquest, for example, will proclaim the desirability of versions of the agrarian myth that are pastoral, resulting in a discourse uniting landlord and/or plebeian of the same national identity. This will be met on the part of the conquered with landlord and/or plebeian versions amounting to Darwinian variants of the agrarian myth.

The recent past has witnessed a resurgence of benign depictions in popular culture of the monarchy and aristocracy, a development evident in films such as *The Queen* (2006) and *The King's Speech* (2011), and television dramas like *House of Cards* (1990–95) and *Parade's End* (2012).[2] All the latter present an image of the British landowning class as benign, adhering to the ideology of noblesse oblige. This is consistent with the self-image projected by Conservative members of the coalition government elected in 2010, one led by politicians from a public school and Oxbridge background, many of whom were old Etonians with considerable wealth and land. The extent to which film depictions reflect or depart from political reality is one of the issues examined here.

As has been noted in the previous chapter, images/narratives that stressed the disempowered and/or politically inefficacious character of aristocracy and

---

2   This approach, focusing as it does on royal and/or aristocratic life in the English country house over a period extending from the late nineteenth century to the first half of the twentieth, also includes the films *Mrs Brown* (1997), directed by John Madden, and *Gosford Park* (2001), directed by Robert Altman, as well as the television series *Downton Abbey* (2010 onwards).

monarchy, it could be argued, contribute to an ideological survival strategy where such institutions are concerned. In addition to film and television images portraying monarchy and/or aristocracy either as empowered and on the offensive (= 'fiends'), or as weak and on the defensive ('fools'), therefore, are those which depict these institutions as not just well-disposed (= 'friends') towards 'those below' but also protective and/or representative of plebeian interests. In this respect, film/television narratives projecting a coincidence of political objectives across the classes adhere to a populist discourse.

This chapter is divided into four parts, the first of which considers how powerful-but-friendly film images of landlord or plebeian structure themes concerned with imperialism, nationalism and colonialism. The second looks at the connection between the pastoral version of the agrarian myth and sympathetic, non-threatening, and thus favourable portrayals on film and television of the British monarchy. How all these themes – imperialism, nationalism, populism, class hierarchy and class struggle – inform the narrative and characterization of one particular film (*The Go-Between*) are examined in the third section. The fourth explores the dissonance between such film images and current political realities.

I

One way in which a powerful subject is depicted advantageously on film replaces the element of horror/terror/revenge with an altogether more benign image. Situated between the hostile horror/terror of the 'fiend' and the harmless ineffectualness of the 'fool', therefore, is an image of rural/colonial/royal dominance disguised as *noblesse oblige*. Into this category come films and/or television series as different as *Indiana Jones and the Temple of Doom, The Man Who Would Be King, The Quiet American, Apocalypse Now Redux, The Go-Between, The Shooting Party, Parade's End, House of Cards, The Queen* and *The King's Speech*.

This powerful-but-friendly characterization is paternalistic, a portrayal which combines the recognition of 'from above' power but its deployment on behalf of 'those below'. A landlord, a monarch or (potential) colonizer is shown to be acting in a selfless manner, displaying concern for and even friendship towards those below him in the socio-economic hierarchy, such as tenants, workers and/or indigenous subjects. As such, it falls within a discourse that is populist. Whilst it is true that the main focus of North American film culture has been on the plebeian variant of the agrarian myth – a frontier composed of 'empty' countryside settled and made productive by smallholders, of which

the most iconic representation is the cowboy – positive images of a landowning aristocracy have also featured prominently.[3]

With Friends like These

The eponymous hero of *Indiana Jones and the Temple of Doom* (1984), directed
by Stephen Spielberg and scripted by George Lucas, is a Davy Crockett figure
consistent with the frontier myth. Under the thin disguise of an academic
archaeologist, Indiana Jones is an adventurer who embodies most of the positive attributes linked ideologically with American individualism.[4] Not only
personally brave and independent, therefore, but – as a 'natural' egalitarian –
he sides with exploited plebeians (Chinese orphans, Indian peasants, child
slaves) against their aristocratic and/or ruling class oppressors (a Maharaja, his
state officials, a high priest).[5] In rescuing the children of the villagers, working

---

3 For the plebeian version of the agrarian myth in America, and in particular how this conflates the foundation myth with agrarian populism, see Hoefle (2003). The most obvious
examples of the aristocratic version of the agrarian myth in the United States are *The Birth of
a Nation* (1915), directed by D.W. Griffiths, and *Gone With the Wind* (1939), directed by Victor
Fleming, both of which presented idealized film images of the Southern planter class. The
former constitutes the Darwinian variant of the aristocratic version of the agrarian myth,
whilst the latter corresponds to the pastoral variant. Writing in 1934, before the appearance
of *Gone With the Wind*, Potamkin (Jacobs, 1977: 263–264) notes rightly that American films
did indeed depict aristocracy – albeit a 'foreign' one – in a positive manner. The nobility
exalted in early US films is that of Tsarist Russia, and the political object was to depict aristocratic virtue threatened by the all its 'others', portrayed negatively: the 1917 Revolution, the
Bolsheviks, and Soviets.

4 The choice by Spielberg of archaeologist-as-hero is also significant in other ways. From the
early nineteenth century onwards, when both the French and the British not only looted
artefacts from Egypt but also inserted Egyptology into a discourse about the historical lineage
of nation and empire, archaeology and archaeologists have been deployed by imperialist
states in two interconnected ways. First, to establish an ideological kinship between nineteenth century empires and their ancient counterparts, in terms of both being examples of
advanced civilizations. And second, to validate conquest as a civilizing project undertaken
by empire-builders for the benefit of colonized populations. Much the same is true of the
kind of antiquarianism practiced by M.R. James and celebrated in his ghost stories (see
Chapter 4), where the object was similarly to reconstitute the ancient past as firmly located
in – and thus part of – the present, the inference being that traditional forms of power are
never vanquished, and as such continue to be efficacious.

5 Such attributes are fairly common in the kind of heroes depicted by Hollywood films. In
many respects, Harry Steele (played by Charlton Heston), the central character in a much
earlier adventure film, *The Secret of the Incas* (1954), directed by Jerry Hopper, prefigures
Indiana Jones. Not only does Steele look like Jones, down to the fedora hat and leather jacket,

as slaves in the mines of the Maharaja, Indiana Jones recasts himself as (and reaffirms the ideological power of) one of the most potent symbols in American political history: the single-handed emancipation of ethnically 'other', unfree plantation workers by an heroic individual. Namely, President Lincoln enforcing the progressive and democratic will of the American masses on an oppressive and aristocratic minority component (cotton planters in the antebellum South) of the nation.

Many aspects of *Indiana Jones and the Temple of Doom* reproduce similar episodes portrayed in earlier fictional discourse about British imperialism, not least those depicted in the film *Lost Horizon* (1937), directed by Frank Capra.[6] The borrowings from the sympathetic chroniclers of British imperialism are difficult to miss. From Kipling, therefore, Spielberg and Lucas recycle the theme of indigenous religious credulity and the incident of the rope-bridge, while from Paul Scott's *Raj Quartet* they take the name of the locality itself (Pankot).[7] As someone with a strong interest in the value of archaeological artefacts as commodities, Indiana Jones also resembles Daniel Dravot and Peachey Carnehan, the two main characters in the film *The Man Who Would be King* (1975), directed by John Houston and based on a story by Kipling. All are adventurers intent on making their fortune, usually at the expense of the indigenous 'other'.

In the work of Kipling these characterizations, episodes and incidents are accompanied by the discourse of imperialism and colonialism (a content from which the form is inseparable), the former licensing a slide into the latter. Significantly, at the centre of English nationalism as portrayed by Kipling and is a fear of the Indian village, the embodiment of grassroots rural 'otherness'

---

but he also exhibits the same cynical and world-weary outlook. Like Indiana Jones, therefore, Steele is an American abroad (in Peru), an individualist adventurer-cum-tomb-robber who is interested only in the exchange-value of archaeological finds. Again like Indiana Jones, having found a valuable relic (= the sacred sunburst of the Incas), he nevertheless returns it to the indigenous peasant farmers in whose cultural system it features centrally.

6   The strong influence on Spielberg of Capra's 1937 classic adventure film is a matter of record. As a biography notes (Baxter, 1996: 19–20), 'Spielberg was drawn even more to the fantasies of the period [and] saw most of Hollywood's imaginative classics, including *Lost Horizon*'.

7   The theme of religious credulity plus the rope-bridge incident are found in the story by Kipling (1895: 193–242). Pankot was the name of the hill station in the highly popular and much acclaimed Granada Television series, *Jewel in the Crown*, based on Scott's *The Raj Quartet*. The fourteen episodes were broadcast on television in the early 1980s, and it is unlikely that they would have escaped the notice of either Spielberg or Lucas, especially as the latter were concurrently engaged in collecting material for and preparing to film *Indiana Jones and the Temple of Doom*, a story set in India at roughly the same conjuncture.

seen by them as potentially threatening.[8] This fear is class specific, since it derives from (and is a reaction to) both the poverty on display at the rural grassroots and its implications for the reproduction of the existing social order. It is also context specific, in that what is feared is the Indian village; where the pastoral idiom is invoked, as it is by Kipling in the case of his fictional kingdom of Kafiristan, villages and their inhabitants are recategorized in terms of national identity, as 'being English' (and thus non-threatening).[9]

This emerges clearly from *The Man Who Would be King*, a film about two adventurers who colonize and rule a Himalayan kingdom (Kafiristan) where they are mistaken for Gods. It consists of the retelling by one of them, Carnehan, of his experiences there, an account that can be interpreted as the history of colonization as told by the colonizer, and the barely disguised theme of which is 'ungrateful natives'. Having been taught by him and his companion Dravot how to improve agricultural production (ploughing, planting and storing crops), to solve disputes and generally how to conduct 'good government', the indigenous tribal population of the Kafiristan region repaid them by killing Dravot and crucifying him. The sub-text is a discourse about a benign intervention on the part of a redeemer, and the Christ-like fate of a deity figure abandoned and persecuted by those ('ordinary mortals') he came to save and believed he had helped.[10]

---

8   Kipling (1895: 165 ff.) expresses these sentiments – but in fictional form – in his sinister tale 'The Strange Ride of Morrowbie Jukes'. The protagonist 'by accident stumbled upon a village [in India] that is well known to exist, though he is the only Englishman who has been there', and finds himself trapped in a crater inhabited by 'a band of loathsome fakirs', a 'terrible village' of the living dead from which he is at first unable to escape. Kipling's Englishman confesses to a 'sensation of nameless terror which I had in vain attempted to strive against', and which now 'overmastered me completely'. The usual colonial hierarchy protecting him had no purchase in this rural context – described as 'a Republic of wild beasts' and 'the hideous Village of the Dead' (Kipling, 1895: 183, 192) – and, after various unsuccessful attempts at escape, the Englishman is finally rescued by his Indian servant.

9   For the 'Englishness' of Kafiristan, see below. Located on the border between the NW frontier of India and Afghanistan, the actual region known as Kafiristan was in the high mountain range of the Hindu Kush, equidistant from Kabul and Peshawar. It is described thus (Munson, 1915: 93): 'The hillsides, thickly wooded with oak and pine, and the green valleys, rich in gardens and orchards and rolling meadows, resemble the Himalayan country, while the people, a pure type of Aryans, are remarkable for their strength and beauty, many of the Kafirs – in strange contrast with their neighbours on every side – being as fair as Europeans, with yellow hair and blue eyes'.

10 This element of betrayal is rendered all the more poignant by the perception of Carnehan and Dravot of the inhabitants of Kafiristan as English, as no different from themselves. Hence their view (Kipling, 1895: 226, 228, original emphasis) that: 'You're

In this kind of discourse – not so much of colonialism but of nationalism and populism – the existing class structure is recuperated. Like Dravot and Carnehan, Indiana Jones is an 'outsider' who comes in (or is brought in) to redeem the local indigenous rural population. Although Indiana Jones is not overtly an imperialist and Empire builder, covertly he is. Unlike Crockett, who in the 1830s extended the internal frontier at the expense of the original indigenous inhabitants (native Americans, Mexicans), Indiana Jones is engaged a century later in extending the *external* frontier (into Asia). In performing the latter task, it could be argued, the character of Indiana Jones is merely anticipating the objectives accomplished subsequently by the US in Vietnam, the Philippines and Korea, and specifically the film roles of fictional characters such as Captain Willard in *Apocalypse Now Redux* and Pyle in *The Quiet American*.

We Stay Forever

By aligning himself – momentarily – with the demonic Kali cult, moreover, Indiana Jones projects horror mobilized from the domain of the supernatural. A menace/threat consistent with the 'fiend' image, it combines the Darwinian and pastoral versions of the plebeian variant of the agrarian myth. Thus the discourse of *Indiana Jones and the Temple of Doom, The Quiet American* and *Apocalypse Now Redux* projects not one but two distinct 'from below' forms: benign powerful-but-friendly elements attributed to an heroic American 'outsider' (Indiana Jones, Pyle, Willard), and a rural grassroots 'other' engaged in struggle (Indian villagers, Vietnamese peasants). Although the class identity of the hero in *Indiana Jones and the Temple of Doom, The Quiet American* and *Apocalypse Now Redux* is plebeian, however, these films nevertheless project American nationalist ideology.

In *Apocalypse Now Redux* and *The Quiet American*, therefore, a preexisting European colonialism is challenged by the main protagonist who is an American.[11] The picture of the decaying plantation and its French owners

---

white people...You are *my* people...I'll make a damn fine Nation of you, or I'll die in the making!...I won't make a Nation...I'll make an Empire! These men aren't niggers; they're English!...They're the Lost Tribes, or something like it, and they've grown to be English'.

11   Set in 1952, when Vietnam was still part of the French colonial empire *The Quiet American* (2002), directed by Philip Noyce, is a story about how Fong, a young Vietnamese girl who is the paramour of an ageing English journalist, Thomas Fowler, is courted by Pyle, a young American who identifies himself as an aid worker. In the course of the film, she shifts her affection (= allegiance) from the former, who represents 'old Europe', to the latter, who embodies the 'young' USA. In one sense this is what 'happened' in the Vietnam war, in that after the defeat of French colonialism at the battle of Dien Bien Phu in 1954,

drawn in *Apocalypse Now Redux* is consonant with the portrayal of landlordism as disempowered.[12] In these films Americans are depicted not just as the
'other' but – more significantly – the democratic 'other'. Even in *Gosford Park*,
a film about English aristocracy, the two American characters are, like the servants, looked down upon by those 'above stairs'. One of these characters is
located physically within – and thus almost a part of – the servants' quarters,
while in *Apocalypse Now Redux*, the process of 'going native' on the part of
Americans is contrasted with the colonial attitudes held by the French planters.[13] The nationalism depicted on screen in such films is that of America,
albeit projected (and none too subtly disguised) as a specifically democratic
form of 'otherness', counterposed in each instance to European landlordism
and/or colonialism.

This discourse aligns the capitalist but 'democratic' United States with
'those below' – servants in *Gosford Park* and the indigenous 'other' in *Apocalypse*

---

the south aligned with the US. Towards the end of the film, after the explosion in the
market-place, Pyle informs Fowler that Fong is 'the mistress of an older European man',
that Europeans cannot prevent communists from taking over, and that he is going to
change all that. Eventually Fong goes back to Fowler and 'old Europe', who because he
cannot obtain a divorce from his wife in London, cannot return there with Fong. So
Fowler announces that he intends to stay in Vietnam with her. In an extended review of
the biographies published since Greene's death, the novelist David Lodge (1996: 40–84)
concurs with the view that Greene was both anti-Communist and anti-American, and
whilst in French Indochina he spied for the British intelligence services. If true, this
underlines the nationalist element involved the contrasting way Greene depicted the tri-
partite struggle for post-War dominance in Asia: on the one hand his sympathetic portrayal of the declining colonial powers (= 'old Europe') and on the other his antagonism to
the other two nationalisms. These corresponded to that of the indigenous Vietnamese
and the United States, the latter presented additionally as the rising new colonial power
(= 'young America').

12   *Apocalypse Now Redux*, directed by Francis Ford Coppola, was reissued in 2002. It has
been re-edited, and contains an additional 49 minutes of previously unseen footage, the
most significant component of which are the scenes set on the French plantation. The
latter is described (Milius and Coppola, 2001: 145) by its French owner as 'our home', and
when asked by Willard 'how long can you possibly stay here?', replies '[w]e stay forever'.
For accounts of the making of the film, see Coppola (1995) and Cowie (2000).

13   In keeping with landlord ideology, the French planter explains (Milius and Coppola, 2001:
153) that 'when my grandfather and my uncle's father came here, there was nothing.
Nothing. The Vietnamese were nothing. So we worked hard, very hard, and brought the
rubber from Brazil, and then plant it here. We took the Vietnamese, work with them,
make something, something out of nothing. So when you ask me why we want to stay
here, Captain, we want to stay here because it's ours, it belongs to us. It keeps our family
together. We fight for that!'

Now Redux – against what it is inferred are feudal remnants (French planters, British aristocracy) of a pre-/non-capitalist regime left over from a by-gone colonial age. Accordingly, the subtext to both *Apocalypse Now Redux* and *The Quiet American* is that the colonial rule over Asia by the old empires has declined, and been supplanted there as the dominant influence by the United States, which is not just democratic but also – and unlike the erstwhile European colonial powers – has a 'natural' affinity with the non-European 'other'. In short, a nationally-specific populist discourse that is not so dissimilar from that which informs the film *Gosford Park*, where both the American characters – the Hollywood movie producer and his valet – are depicted as 'outsiders', 'others' who make common cause with the servants below stairs against the representatives of the old order colonialism/landlordism above stairs.

Populism also informs the way the rural hierarchy is shown in *Indiana Jones and the Temple of Doom*, where the power of the aristocratic landowner, the Maharaja of Pankot, is not challenged but redefined. At the start of the film he is depicted as evil, and ranged alongside other ruling class oppressors. Whereas most of those in the latter category are dead by the end of the film, however, the Maharaja is not: his character is depicted merely as having been misguided, and comes good at the end. Like the British, therefore, Indiana Jones ends up working alongside the representatives of the local rural power structure. The English are portrayed as bumbling incompetents, unaware of the fact that traditional practices opposed and eradicated by colonialism (Thugee, Kali worship, human sacrifice) are resurgent, and once again 'growing powerful'. Both the Indian peasants and Indiana Jones, by contrast, are aware of this development, and are thus shown to be right and 'more knowledgeable' than the existing colonial power.

II

Where the British monarchy is concerned, this same political discourse – the monarch as 'friend' to and representative of 'the people' – informed three influential media portrayals that have appeared over the last quarter of a century: the television series *House of Cards* (1990–95), directed by Paul Seed and Mike Vardy, and two films; *The Queen* (2006), directed by Stephen Frears, and *The King's Speech* (2011), directed by Tom Hooper.[14] The same kind of liminal

---

14   Among the numerous film awards received by *The King's Speech* were many BAFTAs and
     four Oscars. From a budget of US$15 million it generated takings of US$139 million. Its

paternalism – powerful but benign/friendly landowners – informs films such as *The Shooting Party* (1985), directed by Alan Bridges, and *The Go-Between* (1970) directed by Joseph Losey, as well as the television drama *Parade's End* (2012).

I Speak for Them

An acclaimed series broadcast on BBC television, the *House of Cards* trilogy is set in the period after the fall of Margaret Thatcher in the early 1990s, and charts the rise of her fictional successor, an unscrupulous conservative politician who eventually becomes Prime Minister.[15] In pursuit of high office, he murders and smears close rivals and political opponents alike, emerging as party leader; once in office, he implements an unpopular right-wing programme which leads to widespread poverty and deprivation.[16] However, as Prime Minister the most principled and effective resistance he encounters comes neither from the masses nor from the Labour Party opposition but rather from the newly-crowned king, who successfully voices popular

---

success in the United States is unsurprising, given its content, and has been accurately delineated by one film director in the following manner: 'The film industry is divided into two camps. Firstly there is a service industry for America, doing things like special effects for *Harry Potter*. Then there is our indigenous industry dominated by some brilliant film-makers like Ken Loach and Mike Leigh, in the area you might call gritty and realistic. But the world is not looking at gritty and realistic any more. Because the American studios have decided to zero in on the youngest demographic, Ken and Mike still continue to make their films, but for a tiny audience. And when we do succeed, it's with films like *The King's Speech*. That's all America is interested in. It is not interested in council flats'. See 'Interview with Alan Parker', *Financial Times Weekend Magazine*, 24/25 March 2012, p. 32.

15   Convincingly played by Ian Richardson, the main character – Francis Urquhart, the Conservative Party Whip and subsequently Prime Minister – uttered a catchphrase ('You might very well think that; I couldn't possibly comment') signalling plausible deniability that went on to become part of popular culture.

16   Based on the novel by Michael Dobbs, an advisor to Margaret Thatcher and Conservative Party Chief of Staff during the mid-1980s, the trilogy is considered an insider account of how politics and politicians really work and behave. In many respects, *House of Cards* is how the political right sees government – all other considerations are subordinated to the insincerity generated by personal ambition and scheming. *A Very British Coup* (1988) based on a novel by Chris Mullin, a Labour politician, corresponds to a view from the left of the same kind of episode: the ousting by the British ruling class of a socialist Prime Minister. Unlike *House of Cards*, however, the focus of *A Very British Coup* is on scheming to subvert a popular representative with a mandate for political change. The drama concerns collective struggle, between classes, and not individual agency designed to attain personal advancement.

grassroots objections to his rule.[17] When the monarch joins forces with Opposition politicians, he is blackmailed by the Prime Minister and finally compelled to abdicate.[18]

Much the same kind of portrayal informs the film *The King's Speech*, set in late 1930s Britain, about the way in which the future George VI overcomes a speech impediment with the assistance of an Australian therapist. As Duke of York, the main protagonist is a reluctant monarch who becomes king on the abdication of his elder brother, Edward VIII.[19] With the help of a commoner, the speech therapist Lionel Logue, he overcomes his stammer and broadcasts to the nation at the start of the 1939–45 war with Germany.[20] Not only is George VI depicted as a reluctant monarch, a role akin to an indentured labourer, but like the aristocrat in *The Go-Between* (see below) he is an egalitarian (= friend-of-the-people) who accepts – and eventually befriends – the commoner attempting to cure him of his stammer.[21] A sympathetic image of royalty not

---

17   Conflict between the monarch and the Prime Minister is the subject of the second part of the trilogy, *To Play the King*, broadcast on the BBC in 1993.

18   A popular monarch opposing a tyrannical government was also the theme in the play *The Apple Cart* by George Bernard Shaw (1931: 1009–1043). Whereas in the *House of Cards* the Prime Minister outmanoeuvres the king, the reverse is the case in *The Apple Cart*. The latter is described by the author (Shaw, 1934: 323) in his Preface as being about 'a king [who] defeats an attempt by his popularly elected Prime Minister of his right to influence public opinion through the Press and platform'.

19   In what is a telling political contrast, Bertie voices concern about the people, whereas his brother David, as Edward VIII, is depicted as a dissolute character who ignores the national interests and prefers instead to purchase jewellery for his paramour, Mrs Simpson. To his brother, therefore, Bertie complains (Seidler, 2010: 55) that being king 'is a serious business', adding that it is not 'laying off eighty staff at Sandringham [a royal residence] and buying yet more pearls for [Mrs Simpson] while there are people marching across Europe singing "The Red Flag"?'. When discussing the abdication of Edward VIII, the Prime Minister asks Bertie (Seidler, 2010: 63): 'Does the King do what he wants, or does he do what his people expect him to do?'. In other words, the element of self-sacrifice in the name of the people is what his brother lacked, and what he – as George VI – will be required to do.

20   The crucial role of radio broadcasting as a way of talking to the nation, and being heard by the masses, is emphasized by George V when speaking with Bertie. About the BBC microphone, the king observes (Seidler, 2010: 29): 'This devilish device will change everything if you won't [use it]. In the past all a King had to do was look respectable in uniform...Now we must invade people's homes and ingratiate ourselves with them'.

21   Comparing monarchy to indentured servitude (Seidler, 2010: 9), the wife of the Duke of York equates kingship not merely with the lot of a plebeian but also with the most oppressed component of the working class (unfree labour). This comparison is

only beset by but effectively combatting 'ordinary' shortcomings, power is a burden reluctantly assumed but triumphantly discharged by its subject. Personal success in overcoming his speech impediment symbolizes a larger *rite de passage*: from simply being able to speak, to speaking to 'the people' and (ultimately) for the nation.[22]

In each case, the monarch is seen to represent 'the people', on whose behalf he speaks and/or acts: successfully in *The King's Speech*, unsuccessfully in the *House of Cards*. However, success per se is in terms of discourse not as significant as the fact of representation: either way, a sovereign who leads to victory or falls in battle is depicted as doing this at the head of 'the people' and the nation, both of which s/he represents. Precisely the same considerations inform the film *The Queen*, where the monarch is shown to be temporarily at odds with the nation. With the assistance this time of the Prime Minister, the Queen achieves redemption, and secures once more her position as a representative of 'the people' and the country.

Set over a seven day period in September 1997 following the death of Diana, Princess of Wales, the film *The Queen* is a fictional account of meetings between the incoming New Labour Prime Minister Tony Blair and the Queen,

---

supportive of the view that in reality no difference separates monarch from the masses, and licenses the theme that such 'ordinariness' negates the power and wealth of those at the apex of the class hierarchy. Equality between the two main characters, the King and his speech therapist, is embodied in an insistence from the outset (Seidler, 2010: 11, 22) on the part of the latter that first-name terms are adhered to, a form of *lèse majesté* to which royalty strongly objects. When addressed as 'Bertie' by Logue, instead of the usual deferential way ('Your Royal Highness, then Sir after that') the king responds angrily (Seidler, 2010: 24) '...stop calling me that'. Subsequently, the king confesses to Logue (Seidler, 2010: 49) that 'you're the first ordinary [person] I've ever really spoken to. Sometimes, when I ride through the streets and see, you know, the Common Man staring at me, I'm struck by how little I know of his life, and how little he knows of mine'.

22   This element of national unity is stressed by Churchill when speaking with Bertie (Seidler, 2010: 65): 'War with Germany will come, and we will need a King behind whom we can all stand united'. Before addressing the nation just after the declaration of war in September 1939, George VI says to his speech therapist (Seidler, 2010: 87): 'If I am to be king...where is my power? May I form a government, levy a tax or declare a war? No! Yet I am the seat of all authority. Why? Because the Nation believes when I speak, I speak for them. Yet I cannot speak!' In the course of his radio broadcast to the nation, however, the king asserts (Seidler, 2010: 94) that '[i]t is to this high purpose [war against Germany] that I now call my people at home and my peoples across the seas...' He has in effect made the transition to the voice of 'the people', the nation and the empire. The final words of the film, appearing on the screen, emphasize this role (Seidler, 2010: 96): 'Through his broadcasts, George VI became a symbol of national resistance'.

and the formulation of a public response to that event. Not only is it an affectionate depiction of the monarch, depicting her as an 'ordinary' person wounded by the media attacks on the royal family, but central to the narrative is the way in which the Queen ceased to exercise the kind of influence she normally did over such circumstances.[23] Although the representation of power is not comedic in the sense of inviting the audience to laugh at the monarch, the outcome is in effect not so different: the portrayal of the present incumbent of an ancient and otherwise potent landowning institution as 'ordinary' and thus vulnerable elicits sympathy not just for the individual but also (and through this) for the institution itself.[24]

What I Stand for Is Gone

A similarly benign depiction, but this time of the landowning aristocracy, informs two other media portrayals, both located in the Edwardian era. The first is the film *The Shooting Party* that in many respects (conjuncture, context, plot, characterization, and discourse) epitomizes the image of landowner as friend-of-the-people. Based on the novel of the same name by Isabel Colgate, *The Shooting Party* is set in the autumn of 1913 and concerns events occurring in the course of a shooting party – composed mainly of the landed gentry – on a large country estate in England.[25] The central episode involves the accidental shooting and killing by a visiting aristocrat of a local poacher acting as a beater, whom the landowner comforts as he lies dying. Although symbolically this event prefigures the slaughter in the trenches that was to take place in the 1914–18 war, it is also a lament for a paternalistic landlordism

---

23 The sympathetic portrayal of the monarchy is evident from a number of things. For example, from the observation by one film critic (Kemp 2006: 29) that the director 'draws from Helen Mirren [who plays the Queen] a performance that even convinced republicans may feel moved by'. According to the same source, moreover, the 'script digs that carefully constructed façade, showing us the Queen gradually losing control and unable to deal with it'. Collecting the 2007 BAFTA and Oscar awards for that performance, Mirren lost no opportunity to express her own admiration for the monarch and the monarchy.

24 This is in keeping with the critique made elsewhere (Brass, 2000a: 208, 233, notes 94, 95, and 96) of the mistaken interpretation advanced by the majority of commentators – those on the left included – to explain the impact of that episode. For all the latter the reaction of the monarchy to the death of Diana and the funeral oration of Earl Spencer amounted to an attack on the monarchy as an institution, a fundamental change in its fortunes, and thus the dawn of a 'new' political era. As would have been clear to those who examined the discourse structuring that whole episode, it was not a challenge to the monarchy but much rather a defence of it.

25 See Colgate (1980).

to the subjects of whom, it is inferred, the element of *noblesse oblige* was important.

The same kind of nostalgic vision, depicting a benign but soon-to-vanish landlord class, also permeates *Parade's End*, a five-part television dramatization by Tom Stoppard of the novels by Ford Madox Ford.[26] Its central character is Christopher Tietjens, a member of the landowning class, described as 'the last decent man in England', but for whom 'the world ended long ago, in the eighteenth century'.[27] During the 1914–18 war, he not only fights for his country in the trenches but defends the right of ordinary soldiers (= plebeians) under his command to better treatment, given that they too have fought for their country.[28]

For Tietjens, therefore, the class enemy is not plebeian but finance capital: whilst he as landowner is away at the front, together with plebeian elements defending the nation, his banker at home is after his wife and land, and attempts to bankrupt Tietjens as soon as there are insufficient funds to meet his debts.[29] Rejecting the accusation that he doesn't love his country, Tietjens makes it very clear what *his* country is, and what he likes and dislikes about it. It is the countryside he loves, which for him is synonymous with England, and in his view 'was the foundation of order' before money took over. That is, before financial capital established itself, a process he describes as 'handing the country to swindlers and schemers', or the 'Toryism of the pig's trough'.

Asked what his Toryism is, Tietjens delineates clearly all the characteristics associated with *noblesse oblige*: duty, service to 'those below', 'honouring the past' (= maintaining tradition in the countryside), 'frugality' (= not displaying, but nevertheless having, wealth; that is, not being vulgar).[30] To this he adds the

---

26 The tetralogy by Ford appeared between the mid- and late-1920s. In the television drama the demise of the landlord class is depicted symbolically by the felling of the Groby tree that has stood outside the large country house owned by the Tietjens family for many generations.

27 See Stoppard (2012: 21, 136, 171), where the refusal of Tietjens to be provoked by his wife's liaisons with other men generates an anguished observation by her: 'You're such a paragon of honourable behaviour, Christopher, you're the cruellest man I know'. In addition to owning land, his family also owns coal mines (Stoppard, 2012: 297), which suggests it had links to the capitalist economy.

28 See Stoppard (2012: 197).

29 Two cheques bounce, at which point the banker (Stoppard, 2012: 188) cries 'Got you!', despite the fact that they bounce only because Tietjens' army pay arrived late.

30 Central to the aristocratic code of *noblesse oblige* is the following view expressed by Tietjens (Stoppard, 2012: 140): 'Looking after your people, and beggaring yourself if need

discourse of the agrarian myth: Tietjens is 'for agriculture against industry' and 'for the eighteenth century against the twentieth' (= pro-tradition, anti-modern).[31] In *Parade's End*, therefore, England is composed of landowners and their plebeian subordinates united in defence of the nation, a populist alliance that would have been familiar to Disraeli. Since in no other film are these themes – together with their connection to the landlord pastoral version of the agrarian myth – presented in more detail, the narrative and characterization as they appear in *The Go-Between* merits closer examination.

III

The story of *The Go-Between* is well known, and in outline seems to be nothing more than a somewhat banal melodrama. Set in 1900, at the height of Victorian imperialism, it consists of a narrative by Leo Colston, a boy who is almost 13 years old, about his summer holiday spent as a guest of a school friend, Marcus Maudsley, at Brandham Hall, a country house in rural Norfolk leased by the latter's wealthy banking family – the Maudsleys – from its aristocratic landowner, Lord Trimingham. Befriended by Marian Maudsley, the 20-year old sister of Marcus, who is on the point of becoming engaged to the landowner, Leo takes secret messages on her behalf (arranging clandestine assignations) to her lover, Ted Burgess, a tenant farmer on the estate. Leo eventually betrays them, the love affair between Marian and Burgess is made public, and as a result the tenant farmer commits suicide.[32] Trimingham nevertheless marries

---

be before letting duty go hang'. In short, the claim advanced by populist discourse that 'those above' are required to protect the interests of 'those below', to the extent of 'beggaring yourself' (= self-sacrifice in the name of the people). Sympathizing with a private soldier who supports the Bolsheviks (Stoppard, 2012: 312), Tietjens castigates all the 'others' of the agrarian myth that he, as a landowner, would imprison: stockbrokers (= finance capital), Whitehall schemers (= State bureaucrats), 'landowners who don't look after their tenants' (= bad landlords who, unlike him, do not practice *noblesse oblige*), Members of Parliament (= politicians), and 'urban developers' (= modernity, the city). On hearing that the soldier is 'an egalitarian', Tietjens dismisses this as 'the superstition of intellectuals'.

31   Tietjens concludes these views (Stoppard, 2012: 140–142) with the lament that '[w]hat I stand for is gone'.

32   Caute misunderstands the important role of class difference/distance in the public exposure of the affair, when Mrs Maudsley forces Leo to take her to where Marian and Ted Burgess are found having sexual intercourse, thereby guaranteeing humiliation for all concerned, herself included. Describing Leo as being of 'slightly inferior social status, who becomes in Mrs Maudsley's disturbed mind the scapegoat for the whole disaster',

her, and the child to whom she gives birth – fathered by Burgess – eventually succeeds to the title. The story concludes with the visit by the now adult Leo to the place where these events occurred half a century earlier.

We Should Be Nice to Him
What such an outline fails to convey is the extent to which both novel and film accurately depict those symptomatic connections – between class formation/ struggle, landlordism, colonialism and nationalism – under consideration here. Not only do the main characters occupy specific and antagonistic class locations, therefore, but their discourse/agency also embody the kind of struggle associated with these positions.[33] This is not to say that all the characters in *The Go-Between* are mere ciphers for a specific class position, and nothing more. It is nevertheless the case that both film and book versions routinely give voice to opinions and project actions associated with socio-economic locations in the existing agrarian hierarchy.[34] This is (or ought to be) unsurprising,

---

he (Caute, 1994: 272) is doubly wrong, both about their respective class positions, and thus also about the cause of her anger. Because Leo is far beneath Mrs Maudsley in the socio-economic hierarchy, her fury is the same as it would have been had she been defied by one of her servants. It is this defiance by a menial (daring to withhold information concerning the whereabouts of both daughter and lover), not a desire to 'scapegoat', that generates the ire of Mrs Maudsley.

33   Thus, for example, while both components of the ruling class (landed aristocrat, finance capitalist) give voice to nationalist opinions/views, this is not true of either of the two subordinate class elements (urban petty bourgeois and tenant farmer) in the same hierarchy. Both distance based on class, and the efficacy of this divide, between on the one hand members and/or friends of the ruling class (landowner, banker), and on the other the local villagers who work on the estate, is foregrounded in the film script. Thus, for example, Marcus informs Leo (Pinter, 1971: 293) at bedtime: 'When you undress you mustn't fold your clothes and put them on the chair. You must leave them lying wherever they happen to fall. The servants will pick them up. That's what they're for'. Similarly, in the course of the first encounter with Burgess, the tenant farmer, one of those in the party 'at the Hall' observes (Pinter, 1971: 300): 'we don't know him socially, of course, but I think we should be nice to him...'.

34   The fact of class, and the element of difference (social, economic) consequent upon it, are central to the story, which is punctuated with references to and descriptions of the unobtainable 'otherness' of ruling class membership. About the latter, therefore, Leo observes (Hartley, 1985: 39): 'From these resplendent beings, golden with sovereigns (and, I suspected, guineas), arriving, staying, leaving apparently unaffected by any restrictions of work or family ties, citizens of the world who made the world their playground...'. Of his school friend Marcus Maudsley, Leo notes (Hartley, 1985: 16) similarly that he – Marcus – was 'going to Eton, and he was like a premature Etonian, easy, well-mannered, sure of

since it is in fact what a skilful characterization sets out to accomplish, and what a reader/viewer expects to encounter.[35]

The issue therefore concerns not whether such a socio-economic characterization is accurate (necessarily it must be), but rather the manner in which holders of a specific class position are portrayed (negatively, positively), and how they feature (empowered, disempowered) in any outcome. In this respect, *The Go-Between* underlines the fact that for the upper class generally – and the landed aristocracy in particular – marriage has always been an alliance informed by economic considerations. That is, an arrangement that facilitated either the retention or expansion or of its property (effected also through inheritance), or access to external sources of capital.[36] In specifically economic

---

himself'. That Leo feels out place in this situation is evident from his self-criticism (Hartley, 1985: 32): 'Suddenly I caught sight of myself in a glass and saw what a figure of fun I looked. Hitherto I had always taken my appearance for granted; now I saw how inelegant it was compared with theirs; at the same time, and for the first time, I was acutely aware social inferiority. I felt utterly out of place among these smart rich people, and a misfit everywhere'. When he begins to feel more at home, Leo (Hartley, 1985: 75) confesses a liking of the deference accorded him when passing through the surrounding villages: 'Of course I valued the prestige of being with them [Trimmingham and the Maudsleys]; I enjoyed our triumphal progress through the countryside, the passers-by staring at the carriages, the children running to open the gates and scrabbling on the ground for the pennies which the coachman nonchalantly threw them'.

35 Hence the imprimatur of Lord David Cecil in his introduction to the 1968 edition of the collected short stories (Hartley, 1986: vii), where he notes that the 'author of *The Go-Between* is one of the most distinguished of modern novelists...he is also a sharp-eyed chronicler of the social scene'. The latter opinion was presumably one shared by Joseph Losey, the director of the 1971 film, notwithstanding the political gulf – inferred in his claim to be a 'middle-aged Marxist romantic' (Caute, 1994: 275) – between on the one hand the author and on the other both script writer (Pinter) and film director.

36 This is the reason why literary and filmic depictions of love stories set in the first half of the twentieth century that unproblematically cross the boundaries of class – such as *Atonement* (2007) directed by Joe Wright, a film based on the novel by Ian McEwen (2001) – are highly idealized. Set in 1934, *Atonement* is a love story that replicates much of the central theme – an illicit love affair as seen through the eyes of a child – of the *Go Between*. In terms of class, however, the former – unlike the latter – evades what is the central issue of the story: the element of hypergamy. McEwen gets round the obvious difficulty posed by an otherwise forbidden relationship between upper class female and plebeian male by improbably elevating the latter from the ranks, and making him the beneficiary of a 'kind employer' who puts him through Cambridge, thus promoting him to a position where – conceivably – the relationship might not be frowned upon. This contrasts with the far more realistic approach of Hartley in the *Go-Between*, where the relationship is forbidden precisely because it involves a plebeian tenant farmer and an

terms, therefore, such alliances involved – and could only ever involve – an exchange between equals (for example, between a family of a finance capitalist and landowner), and not one that was in class terms asymmetrical (between landowning family and tenant farmer).[37]

Landlord, Capitalist and 'the Trail of Gold'

At the top of the agrarian class structure, and embodying the opinions/interests of the landowning aristocracy, is Lord Trimingham, proprietor of Brandham Hall and its five hundred acres. Not only is he a war hero (having being wounded in the Boer War), who has fought bravely for his country, but he also respects those below him in the class structure who are either armed opponents (South African farmers abroad) or rivals in love (a tenant farmer at home).[38] In contrast to his tenant farmer and his guest Leo (both of whom in their different

---

upper class daughter already betrothed to a landowner who is a war hero. Because he moved in those social circles, Hartley understood that such a relationship was an unforgiveable transgression, and would always be regarded in this light, as much by those below as by those above. McEwan, who wrote much later and had none of the links that had Hartley, tried unsuccessfully to get around this difficulty by engineering an implausible solution: raising the plebeian male from the ranks so as to make him the social equal of the upper class female.

37   That such considerations remained central to the portrayal in literature of love/sex/class even after the 1939–45 war is evident from the following comment by the novelist Anthony Burgess (1984: 64): 'One of the big themes of *Lucky Jim* – and it is a theme to be found in much fiction and drama of the 1950s (John Osborne's *Look Back in Anger*, for instance) – is that of hypergamy – bedding a woman of a social class superior to one's own: this is an aspect of the perennial class motif of British fiction'. Broadly speaking, this is correct, but with one significant distinction: hypergamy refers not to the process of 'bedding' but rather to contracting a marriage with a male occupying a lower socio-economic position. Accordingly, it was the formal act of marriage, not of 'bedding', that was forbidden. Although 'bedding' might itself prefigure marriage, therefore, it was the latter that was in economic terms of more concern to the parties involved.

38   Despite having been disfigured by them, Trimingham's opinion (Hartley, 1985: 134), expressed to Leo, is as follows: '"The Boer's not a bad feller," said Lord Trimingham *tolerantly*. "I don't dislike him personally. It's a pity we have to shoot so many of them but there you are."' (emphasis added). This same view of the Boers – described by Leo as 'tolerant' and 'magnanimous' – is one applied subsequently by the same landed aristocrat to his tenant farmer. When Leo asks Lord Trimingham about Ted Burgess, therefore, the landowner replies 'he's quite a decent feller', about which Leo recalls 'I remembered he [Trimingham] had said this about the Boers...' (Hartley, 1985: 170–171). Although tenant farmer and Boer are his opponents, therefore, the landowner is presented as hating neither, much rather respecting them both.

ways reject nationalism: see below), however, the landowning aristocrat is the embodiment of national virtue: he upholds national identity, fights on behalf of the nation, and has been physically scarred in national combat.[39] All of which merely underlines the extent of his sacrifice on behalf of the nation.[40] As such, he is shown in a doubly positive light: bravely championing the colonial/imperial project outside (and on behalf of) the nation with a benign patrician *noblesse oblige* inside the nation (on behalf of its ruling class).

Socially subordinate to him in the same agrarian hierarchy are the different members of the Maudsley family (Mr and Mrs Maudsley, plus their son Marcus and daughter Marian), who represent the power of financial capital.[41] Although located beneath the aristocratic landowner socially, Maudsley as a wealthy banker was the dominant one economically, a relationship symbolized in their respective contributions to the cricket match (see below).[42] Theirs is a mutual

---

39   As a result of a war wound to his face, Trimingham is 'dreadfully ugly' (Hartley, 1985: 41, 48). This physical deformity, an outcome of battle against the enemies of the nation, puts him at an obvious disadvantage when courting Marian.

40   The importance to the landowner of national identity emerges when he tells Leo the fate of his ancestor who was killed in a duel, and buried in France (Hartley, 1985: 132). The latter was thereby separated not just from 'his people' but also from his own nation, which symbolized in turn the degree to which the ancestor had ceased to embody land and nationhood.

41   That Maudsley is a wealthy banker is evident from the description of him both as being 'of Threadneedle Street' and as directing his financial business 'in the City' (Hartley, 1985: 23, 108). The social subordination of the finance capitalist to the landowner is outlined by Hartley (1985: 98) thus: 'Lord Trimingham often appealed to his host in this way [asking Mr Maudsley's opinion], and it always came as a surprise, for since his lordship's arrival it had seemed as though he, and not Mr Maudsley, was the master of the house'. Elsewhere, this same element of social subordination to the landowning class is put into words by Leo (Hartley, 1985: 72): 'I still have an impression, distinct but hard to analyse, of the change that came over the household with Lord Trimingham's arrival. Before, it had been an air of self-sufficiency...a go-as-you-please gait: now everyone seemed to be strung-up, on tip-toe to face some test...'. Even as a 'guest' in his own house, therefore, the landed aristocrat constitutes a form of class power to which all other forms – including economically substantial ones in their own right, such as the family members of a wealthy banker renting the property – are subservient.

42   Moreover, unlike Leo and Ted Burgess but like Trimingham, the Maudsleys are represented as being nationalist in outlook. Thus Marcus, the school friend of Leo, is said by the latter to be 'a strong patriot' (Hartley, 1985: 85). In an important sense this is a departure from the usual way in which financial capitalists are portrayed in fiction, where there has been a tendency to identify them as perennial ethnic 'others' (stereotypically, the Jewish 'other') whose loyalty is to money and not nation.

interdependence.[43] The inference is that Lord Trimingham needs 'rescuing' by Maudsley money (= 'trail of gold'), a transaction to be effected by his marriage to Marian.[44] It is the economic importance of this political union – between money and land – that prevents Marian from breaking her engagement and marrying beneath her socially. In the class struggle, therefore, finance capital will invariably side with the landowner against the tenant farmer; to side with the latter is in her view unthinkable.[45]

At the other end of the agrarian class structure is Ted Burgess, a tenant farmer on the estate belonging to Lord Trimingham. Although not impoverished, he lives in 'a mean abode', and describes himself as 'a working farmer'.[46] The liaison with the daughter of the banker notwithstanding, his attitude

---

43   The closeness of the link between the two components of the ruling class – the landowning aristocracy and finance capitalists, plus their combined ideological 'otherness' – is acknowledged by Leo at a number of different points. Looking at the battle honours and funerary monuments of the Trimingham family in the local church, therefore, he contemplates the nature of class power (landlord, financier) in the following manner (Hartley, 1985: 55): '...the idea of goodness did attract me...I saw it as something bright and positive and sustaining, like the sunshine, something to be adored, but from afar. The idea of assembled Viscounts contained it for me, and the Maudsleys, as their viceroys, enjoyed it too, not so incontestably, but enough to separate them from other human beings. They were a race apart, super-adults, not bound by the same laws of life as little boys'. On this Leo elaborates (Hartley, 1985: 53) thus: '...it seemed to me that the Maudsleys were the inheritors of the Trimingham renown. It was, I felt, local, and they enjoyed it by right of rent'. This same relationship is the subject of a subsequent exchange between Leo and Lord Trimingham himself (Hartley, 1985: 58). To the observation by the latter that 'Oh, I know everyone around here...', Leo replies: 'Of course it all belongs to you really, doesn't it?...You are a guest in your own house!'. In keeping with his benign image, the landowner answers: And very pleased to be'. About the interdependence of these two ruling class components, Leo then concludes (Hartley, 1985: 60): 'Superimposed on the grandeur of the Maudsleys, was the glory of the Triminghams militant here on earth'.

44   In the book (Hartley, 1985: 129) this fact is put into words by Leo, who comments about the forthcoming engagement: 'Who could not want to get Lord Trimingham? – and by getting him, so Marcus told me, Marian would also get his house. Married to her he could afford to live there. The trail of gold followed her, too'.

45   When Leo asks Marian why she cannot marry the tenant farmer Burgess instead of Trimingham his landlord, she replies (Hartley, 1985: 191) 'I couldn't, I couldn't', adding that 'I must marry him [Trimingham], you [= Leo] wouldn't understand. I *must*. I've *got* to!' (original emphasis).

46   See Hartley (1985: 64), where Burgess tells Leo 'defensively' that 'I'm not what you call a gentleman farmer, I'm a working one'. As tenant farmer, Burgess operates the horse-drawn reaper for harvesting corn, and supervises the 'three or four farm-labourers who were binding the sheaves'.

towards those above him in the agrarian hierarchy is depicted as respectful and deferential, a subordination reciprocated in the form of landlord 'protection'.[47] Like other villagers on the estate, Burgess is categorized by those above him in the class structure in terms of two forms of specifically plebeian 'otherness': he (and they) stinks, and he (and they) dresses 'inappropriately'.[48] Unlike his

---

47   Not only does the tenant farmer describe those at the Hall as 'grand folks' ('I don't have much to do with those grand folks'), but he also salutes Leo, a forelock tugging gesture of respect 'for the Hall' (Hartley, 1985: 64, 92). Coming across Leo in his yard, an angry Burgess threatens to beat him, but – on learning that Leo is 'from the Hall' – 'his [= Burgess'] voice and manner changed completely'. On this change in demeanour (occasioned by class recognition/subordination), Leo himself comments (Hartley, 1985: 63–64): 'I did not despise him for changing his tune when he knew where I came from: it seemed to me right, natural and proper that he should, just as it had seemed right and proper to me to change my tune with Trimingham when I realized that he was a Viscount. I carried my hierarchical principles into my notions of morality, such as they were, and was consciously a respecter of persons'. That Burgess enjoys the 'protection' of his landlord is clear from the first encounter between the former and the Maudsleys who, finding him swimming in 'their' river, do not antagonise the transgressor ('He must know he's trespassing... shall we order him off?') because Trimingham 'wouldn't like it' if they were rude to his tenant farmer (Hartley, 1985: 42).

48   The 'inappropriateness' of both clothing and smell is located with a discourse about the 'otherness' of the uncivilized plebeian, and reproduces thereby the pejorative designation 'the great unwashed'. After the village concert following the cricket match, therefore, Marcus observes to Leo (Hartley, 1985: 124) that '[a]t least don't ask her [Mrs Maudsley]; she feels like I do about the plebs. Anyhow, we've said good-bye to the village for a year. Did you notice the stink in that hall?' More or less the same exchange appears in the film script, where Marcus also tells Leo (Pinter, 1971: 334): 'Well, thank goodness we've said good-bye to the village for a year. Did you notice the stink in that hall?' In a similar vein, Marcus complains (Hartley, 1985: 134) about having to visit his old nanny, who is ill, because 'her house smells!'. Like the farm workers themselves and the nanny's house, the farmyard also stinks. Hence the confession by Leo (Hartley, 1985: 128) that '[n]ow the thought of the farmyard [of Burgess' farm] lost its magic for me:...I had never really relished its strong smells'. The importance of clothing as a marker of class 'belonging'/difference is evident from the disdainful description of plebeian attire after the cricket match (Hartley, 1985: 116): 'Ted [Burgess], who was sitting nearly opposite [Leo was] wearing a lounge suit and a high starched collar [and] looked even less like himself than he did in flannels. The more clothes he put on, the less he looked like himself. Whereas Lord Trimingham's clothes always seemed part of him. Ted's fine feathers made him look a yokel'. Hence the fact of 'being' plebeian is coupled with 'natural smells' and decoupled from clothing (= 'civilized'), the lack of which are deemed more appropriate to such a class location (plebeian = smelly = naked = natural = non-civilized). Significantly, perhaps, the same two markers of class 'belonging'/difference – smell and clothing – were

landlord, however, the tenant farmer is portrayed as unwilling to join the army and go to war in defence of the nation, and thus – in contrast to all those (aristocrat, banker) at the top of the agrarian hierarchy – to be lacking in patriotism.[49] His death – suicide – seemingly underlines this, being a confirmation of the tenant farmer having taken 'a coward's way out'.[50]

Class and Liminality

Between the rulers (landowner and banker) and the ruled (tenant farmer, villagers) is located the central protagonist, the (almost) 13-year old Leo, through whose eyes the events of *The Go-Between* are seen, and by whose voice they are recounted. In many ways, his is the most interesting character in the story, not least because of the twofold liminality of his rôle. On the one

---

also noted by Orwell (1937: 16, 17, 72) in words of scarcely veiled disgust ('[t]he smell of the kitchen was dreadful...the dirt, the smells, the vile food', 'I sometimes think that the price of liberty is not so much eternal vigilance as eternal dirt', etc.). The argument (Orwell, 1937: 159–160, original emphasis) is made most strongly thus: 'But there was another and more serious difficulty. Here you come to the real secret of class distinctions in the West – the real reason why a European of bourgeois upbringing, even when he calls himself a Communist, cannot without a hard effort think of a working man as his equal. It is summed up in four frightful words which people nowadays are chary of uttering, but which were bandied about quite freely in my childhood. The words were: *The lower classes smell.* That was what we were taught – *the lower classes smell*...The smell of their sweat, the very texture of their skins, were mysteriously different from yours'.

49 Having been asked by his landlord to join the army fighting the Boers, Burgess demurs, a situation recounted by Trimingham to Mr Maudsley thus (Hartley, 1985: 171, 172): 'The first time he said he didn't want to, he was quite happy as he was, and let others do the fighting'. When Leo visits the tenant farmer to say goodbye, he asks (Hartley, 1985: 179–180) whether or not it is his intention to enlist in the army ('Is it true you are going to the war?'), to which Burgess answers: 'I don't know that I *am* going...'. About this, Leo states 'I thought this a cowardly speech, and still do'.

50 The suicide of Burgess (Pinter, 1971: 366; Hartley, 1985: 220), who had refused to enlist in the service of his nation, contrasts strongly with the fate of all those characters representing the ruling class. Thus Lord Trimingham, who has not only fought on behalf of the nation but done this heroically, been wounded in the course of this, and risks losing Marian to 'a coward', dies aged only 36 in 1910. His son and heir – actually fathered by Burgess – is killed during the 1939–45 war. The two sons of the wealthy banker – Marcus is one – are both killed in the course of the 1914–18 war. In terms of a military code linked to membership of the ruling class, therefore, the families of the landed aristocrat and the wealthy banker can be said to have fulfilled their duty to the nation. The tenant farmer, however, has not only shirked his duty to the nation, but also died ingloriously by his own hand.

hand, therefore, actually running errands arranging assignments for two lovers; on the other, he himself occupies a pivotal socio-economic position, not just as intermediary between lovers who are themselves situated in different class locations, but also between all the class elements in the story. From an impoverished urban petty-bourgeois background, Leo is in a number of different ways external to the rural context in which he finds himself.[51] He is an outsider in terms of age (a child among adults), economic sector (urban, not rural), in terms of socio-economic position (neither capital nor labour), and misunderstanding what is happening (taken advantage of, a dupe). Yet, in terms specifically of agency, his rôle is central to what is inescapably an unfolding agrarian class struggle.

The socio-economic liminality of Leo – who embodies the 'inbetween-ness' of the urban petty bourgeois – is evident from his unknowing entanglement in an affair that transgresses class boundaries and his oscillating loyalty to those (and others) involved.[52] He is literally caught in the middle of what is symbolically an agrarian struggle between the landed aristocrat (Trimingham) and his tenant farmer (Burgess), each of whom is paying court to finance capital (Marian).[53] In this respect, it is he who is the dupe, since initially Leo is

---

51   Although at the same school as Marcus, the son of the financier, Leo 'lives in a rather small house [in town] with his mother', and his father – now dead – 'worked in a bank [and] was a pacifist' (Pinter, 1971: 291, 295; Hartley, 1985: 15). In other words, Leo comes from an urban lower middle class family, his widowed mother cannot purchase the 'appropriate' summer holiday clothes for him (Hartley, 1985: 21). That his is an impoverished existence – the sort to which Orwell (1937: 157) referred as a 'shabby-genteel family' – is evident from a number of things. Not just the fact that it will be necessary to sell books collected by his father ('Mother said they're quite valuable. We might have to sell them'), therefore, but also that the landowning family has to purchase suitable clothes for Leo during his stay (Pinter, 1971: 295–296; Hartley, 1985: 35).

52   There is a vast literature on the liminal position of the petty bourgeoisie in the class hierarchy – see, among many others, Poulantzas (1975: 191 ff.; 1977: 113–124), Walker (1979), Bechhofer and Elliot (1981), and Abercrombie and Urry (1983). Broadly speaking, it is composed of what are loosely defined as 'middle strata': that is, a sociological category extending from small businesses and family enterprises on the one hand, to non-owning occupations the subjects of which enjoy a semblance of control over the labour process, such as professional and managerial employees. Situated between the two main class positions of capital and labour, in economic and political terms its subjects belong to neither, nor are they said to identify with either. The importance of the petty bourgeoisie, however, lies in its pivotal rôle in the class struggle, and for this reason it is frequently courted by political representatives and/or parties of both left and right.

53   This element of petty bourgeois political ambivalence, caught between landlord and financier on the one hand, and the tenant farmer (and villagers) on the other, extends also

portrayed as an unwitting accomplice of the landowner.[54] This lack of experience is projected in the film (and the book) by recurrent references to the colour green, signifying the extent to which he has been taken advantage of by those around him, and confirming his rôle as a dupe.[55] Having originally shared his allegiance between tenant farmer and landowner, he finally comes down on the side of the latter, and engineers the discovery of the love affair between

---

to nationalism, since he is similarly torn between pro-Boer views, held by his dead father and also embodied by Burgess (Hartley, 1985: 41, 134). Leo confesses (Hartley, 1985: 127) to liking Burgess, 'in a reluctant, half-admiring, half-hating way...when I was away from him I could think of him objectively as a working farmer whom no one at the Hall thought much of. But when I was with him his mere presence cast a spell on me, it established an ascendancy which I could not break. He fitted into my imaginative life, he was my companion of the greenwood, a rival, an ally, an enemy, a friend – I couldn't be sure which'.

54 The twofold characterization central to the unfolding struggle yet peripheral nature of Leo, in terms of not understanding or misunderstanding what is going on, comes out clearly in the book. Hence an unawareness on his part of the description of Burgess as 'a bit of a lad', and why Marian and Burgess would want to exchange messages (Hartley, 1985: 75, 83–84). A similar misinterpretation informs Leo imagining that the reason why Marian visits her old nanny so often is a benign concern for the latter, rather than a method of meeting Burgess (Hartley, 1985: 136). When Leo finally discovers the content of the messages he takes between Marian and Burgess, and realizes that '[t]hey were in love', he confesses 'what a fool I had been!' (Hartley, 1985: 90).

55 Because he lacks suitable summer clothes, Leo is bought a suit, the colour of which is green (Pinter, 1971: 295). Similarly, his birthday present from Marian, a bicycle, is also green (Pinter, 1971: 342–343). In what is a psychologistic reading of the novel, however, Bien (1963: 167 ff.) misinterprets the significance of these constant references to the colour green. According to him, therefore, it represents heat, both of the summer and of Leo's infatuation with Marian. Hence the following (Bien, 1963: 178): 'Heat is connected with green. Originally, heat was his enemy, but with his green suit, it becomes his friend... [Leo] says furthermore that he yearns to achieve a complete corporeal union with the summer.... [In stating that] "Perhaps Marian *was* the heat"...Leo's desire for corporeal union with Marian is established'. In the novel, however, the colour green is not only equated with 'cool' (Hartley, 1985: 37), but also with the innocence/inexperience that characterizes a dupe (= a fool). Thus his friend Marcus teases Leo about the colour of his birthday present, a green bicycle, telling him that that it is because 'you are green yourself, as the poor old English say', and dances around Leo chanting 'green, green, green'. Leo acknowledges the validity of this description, observing (Hartley, 1985: 158): 'For a moment I hated Marcus, and I hated Marian: I saw how green I must look to her and realized how she had taken advantage of me'. Later on, not only does Marcus again call him 'green', but Leo comes to regard the green bicycle as an insult, observing bitterly that 'I have been taken in so often, I have been so green' (Hartley, 1985: 162, 168, 174).

Burgess and Marian.[56] In this, the representation of Leo accurately reflects not only the political ambivalence of the petty bourgeoisie in the wider struggle between capital and labour, but also the inevitability of its betrayal of labour and taking the side of the ruling class.[57]

Struggle consequent on these different positions, involving not just class but also national identity, is joined, famously, in the annual cricket match between the Hall and the village.[58] The symbolic importance of this arena is evident

---

56 Contemplating the mural tablets commemorating long-dead members of the landowner's family, Leo is overwhelmed by the longevity and power of the aristocracy, with which he now identifies. Significantly, this takes place in church, thereby mimicking the act of religious conversion. His thoughts on this are as follows (Hartley, 1985: 53): 'At first I had though of them [members the landed aristocratic lineage] as so much church furniture, utterly dead and gone, more dead, more gone than, than if they had been given proper graves instead of mere wall space. They were something out of a history book; the deeds recorded of them were just like those recorded in a history book: the battles they had fought, the honours they had won, the positions in Government they had held....then the whole [Trimingham] family came to life; it did not belong to history but to today; the church was the citadel of glory; the church and Brandham Hall'. Subsequently, Leo elaborates on the importance to him of longevity, thereby endorsing the discourse about the legitimacy of ancient power (Hartley, 1985: 130): '[T]o me they [the Trimingham family] were immortal...why should the race of the Triminghams ever die out?...The thought of their unbroken line, stretching down the ages, moved me deeply'. That the mere fact of aristocratic 'belonging' has become an important factor in deciding petty bourgeois allegiance emerges (Hartley, 1985: 80) when Marian asks Leo '"Why do you like Hugh [Trimingham] better [than Burgess]? Because he's a Viscount?"', to which Leo replies: '"Well, that's one reason," [he] admitted, without any false shame. Respect for degree was in my blood and I didn't think of it as snobbery..."And Mr Burgess," I went on, "he's only a farmer."'

57 Leo is portrayed as feeling guilty at having 'betrayed' Trimingham by carrying messages arranging assignations between Marian Maudsley and Ted Burgess. In assessing the situation, and allocating blame, Leo alights on Burgess as the culprit; since it was he who 'had enticed Marian into his parlour, his kitchen, and bewitcher her. He had cast a spell on her. That spell I would now break...' (Hartley, 1985: 194). In this way, the urban petty bourgeois finally dissociates himself from the tenant farmer and aligns with landlord and banker. Misunderstanding becomes betrayal, therefore, as Leo deliberately misinforms Marian about the time of the next assignation with Burgess, as a result of which her absence is noticed by her mother and the affair discovered (Pinter, 1971: 358–359, 360–365; Hartley, 1985: 192, 194, 195, 220).

58 The cricket match itself – an account of which is reproduced in a much reprinted anthology of writing about the game (Ross, 1984: 178–190) – occurs roughly at the mid-point of the story (Pinter, 1971: 323–330; Hartley, 1985: 97–116), and occupies a crucial place in delineating class loyalty and alliance, as well as deflecting/expressing class conflict. That

from its being a locus where sports clothing and accessories are equated directly with class, and as such indicate 'belonging' and 'otherness'.[59] Although not initially chosen to play for the Hall, Leo replaces an injured fielder, joining a side composed of landlord, finance capitalist and their servants. The strongest player on the opposing village side is Burgess, the tenant farmer, described as 'a strong hitter [b]ut no sense of culture or discipline', it being noted that 'Trimingham will be far too cunning for him'.[60] Although the landed aristocrat is out for a small score, Mr Maudsley makes a half century, underlining the extent to which landlordism has to be 'rescued' by finance capital.[61] After early

---

the 'us'/'them' division corresponded to one of class is clear from the description of the match by Leo (Hartley, 1985: 113): 'I kept my sense of the general drama between the bowler [Trimingham] and the batsman [Burgess]. Tenant and landlord, commoner and peer, village and hall – these were elements in it'. Early on, when Leo asks Marcus '[i]s there to be a cricket match?', the latter replies (Hartley, 1985: 49): 'Yes, we have it every year. It helps to keep them [= the servants, villagers and tenant farmers] quiet'. Subsequently, Leo learns that 'the Triminghams had always been interested in the game and Mr Maudsley [the banker] carried on the tradition' (Hartley, 1985: 105). The cricket match was thus a proxy struggle, which the aristocratic landowner had always conducted, and a 'tradition' which the finance capitalist was intent on continuing. Not only did Leo like 'existence to be simplified into terms of winning and losing, and I was a passionate partisan' ('I felt the honour of the Hall was at stake and that we could never lift our heads up if we lost'), therefore, but he felt that all the spectators from the surrounding villages – estate tenants and workers – were against 'the Hall' (Hartley, 1985: 105).

59   The centrality of clothing and equipment as markers of class position emerges clearly from the observation by Leo (Hartley, 1985: 104–105) that 'our side [= 'the Hall']' wore white flannels – that is the 'proper' cricket attire – whereas the village team 'distressed me by their nondescript appearance; some wore their working clothes.... we had a score-board, scoring-cards, white sheets [= sight-screens], and a chalk line to mark the boundary. All these correct accessories gave the match the feeling of importance, of mattering intensely, which I required from life...'

60   See Pinter (1971: 328), where it is noted that at cricket Burgess is 'terribly savage'. Asked by Leo what he thinks of Burgess, Trimingham replies (Pinter, 1971: 345–346): 'He's a powerful hitter....'. The danger posed by this occasions a pre-match discussion (Hartley, 1985; 97) between the landed aristocrat and a son of the banker about how best to get the wicket of the tenant farmer ('"We'll get him caught in the deep field," Lord Trimingham said'.).

61   The failure of the landed aristocrat to do well with the bat was a disappointment for the urban petty bourgeois Leo (Hartley, 1985: 105), who saw the former as the rightful standard bearer of ruling class values/identity ('Above all I was anxious that Lord Trimingham should do well [because I] enjoyed the sense of consequence his condescension gave me, and...because the glory of Brandham Hall...centred on him'). Batting success by Mr Maudsley, the banker, is equated with financial acumen ('the quality of judgement'), and elicits from Leo an anti-intellectual response (Hartley, 1985: 106–107): 'It was the

setback, the village side is similarly 'rescued' by Burgess, who makes a big score and threatens to win the match for the opponents of 'the Hall'. Only a few runs short of victory, however, he is finally caught on the boundary by Leo off the bowling of Trimmingham, and 'the Hall' defeats the village and wins the match.[62]

Cricket and/as Class Struggle

Class difference asserts itself in the course of the match, as servants/workers from 'the Hall' and on its team seek out the company of the village side, their opponents on the cricket field.[63] As Table 1 shows, the oppositions deployed in contrasting the innings of banker and tenant farmer merely underline the extent to which the cricket match is a metaphor for agrarian class struggle.[64] The triumph of the financial capitalist, therefore, is attributed to a superior intellect, and represents also the conquest of order/tradition/stability, whereas

---

ascendancy of brain over brawn, of which, like a true Englishman, I felt suspicious'. Symptomatically, this not only avoids mention of the true source of wealth accumulated by financial capital (the extraction of surplus labour), but also reproduces the brain/brawn stereotype legitimizing the division of labour under capitalism.

62 That the victory of 'the Hall' over the village, and inferentially of the ruling class over the assemblage of plebeian elements, is due principally to Leo – thereby underlining the centrality of petty bourgeois agency in the agrarian class struggle – is a point emphasized by both components of the ruling class (landed aristocrat, banker). In the film screenplay (Pinter, 1971: 346), therefore, Trimingham informs Leo that it was he who was responsible for capturing the wicket of Burgess ('...you had the measure of him...[y]ou defeated him'), and thus for the victory over the village team. Similarly, after the cricket match Leo is described by Mr Maudsley (Hartley, 1985: 116) as 'our young David...who slew the Goliath of Black Farm [= Burgess]'. Leo concurs, and muses (Hartley, 1985: 126) that '[i]t was thanks to me that we [= 'the Hall'] had won the cricket match'.

63 Accordingly (Hartley, 1985: 108), 'Tremendous applause greeted Mr Maudsley as he came back, having just made his fifty. He walked alone – the footman, his last companion at the wicket, having joined the fieldsmen, with whom no doubt he felt more at home'.

64 These oppositions are deployed by Leo in his description of the underlying differences between the innings of the tenant farmer and that of the banker. His words (Hartley, 1985: 110) are as follows: 'It was a very different half-century from Mr Maudsley's, a triumph of luck, not of cunning, for the will, and even the wish to win seemed absent from it. Dimly I felt that the contrast represented something more than the conflict between Hall and village. It was that, but it was also the struggle between order and lawlessness, between obedience to tradition and defiance of it, between social stability and revolution, between one attitude to life and another. I knew which side I was on; yet the traitor within my gates felt the issue differently, he backed the individual against the side, even my own side, and wanted to see Ted Burgess pull it off'.

TABLE 1   *Cricket and/as class struggle in* The Go-Between

THE HALL	THE VILLAGE
Mr Maudsley's innings	Ted Burgess' innings
Finance capitalist	Tenant farmer
A triumph of cunning (design, intellect)	A triumph of luck (accident, instinct)
Order	Lawlessness
Obedience to tradition	Defiance of tradition
Social stability	Revolution

SOURCE: COMPILED FROM HARTLEY (1985: 110)

that of the tenant farmer is not just an accident, due simply to luck/instinct, but is inscribed with all the characteristics – lawlessness, defiance of tradition, and potential revolution – of a threatening 'mob-in-the-streets'. These oppositions are reinforced by an accompanying discourse for and against nationalism, colonialism, and imperialism.

Thus the village team is equated with the Boers against whom British imperialism was then waging a colonial war, and dismissed as an ill-clad (= 'motley raiment') team of rustics who celebrated each wicket, much to the delight of the spectators – estate tenants and workers – similarly categorized as a potentially revolutionary 'mob-in-the-streets', enjoying the 'downfall of their betters' (= 'the Hall').[65] Cricket as portrayed in *The Go-Between* is not just a proxy agrarian class struggle, an avoidance mechanism displacing real antagonism onto rivalry expressed in the sporting arena. It also involves a discourse that equates 'the Hall' team of the ruling class with colonialism/imperialism, and

---

65   In the course of the match, Leo oscillates between liking, disliking, and patronizing the village side (Hartley, 1985: 104, 106, 109): 'It was like trained soldiers fighting natives. And then it crossed my mind that perhaps the village team were like the Boers, who did not have much in the way of equipment by our standards, but could give a good account of themselves, none the less; and I looked at them with a new respect'. A subsequent observation by him expressed dislike and fear: 'These Boers in their motley raiment, triumphantly throwing the ball into the air after each kill, how I disliked them! The spectators [villagers, estate tenants and workers] disposed along the boundary...I imagined to be animated by a revolutionary spirit, and revelling in the downfall of their betters'. Finally, he pities them: 'I remember feeling rather sorry for the villagers, as one after another their [bats]men went back, looking so much smaller than when they had walked to the wicket'.

TABLE 2   *Nationalism, colonialism and imperialism in* The Go-Between

THE HALL	THE VILLAGE
The rulers, their servants and clients	The ruled, plebeian estate workforce
Lord Trimingham (landed aristocrat)	
Mr Maudsley (finance capitalist)	Ted Burgess (tenant farmer),
Leo Colston (urban petty bourgeois)	Villagers
Servants	
Anti-Boer	The Boers/'natives'
Colonial power	Colonized
Imperialism	'Revolutionary spirit'
Victorious cricket team	Defeated cricket team

SOURCE: COMPILED FROM HARTLEY (1985: 97–116)

by contrast the rural plebeians of the village team with Boers/'natives', opponents of British nationalism/imperialism (see Table 2).

This Hideous Century We Live In
Notwithstanding the fact that he embodies the same kind of ancient power as that featured in the ghost stories by M.R. James and Nigel Kneale (see previous chapter), the landed aristocrat in The Go-Between is not depicted as threatening (= horror) but much rather as benign, and thus 'not worth bothering about'. In this, his characterization also departs from that outlined above, where members of the ruling class appear as objects of derision (= humour). Although superficially the aristocratic landlord appears to be as much of a dupe as the petty bourgeois, this is deceptive: in this film it is not the former but the latter who is depicted as a fool. Whereas the aristocratic landlord keeps silent about what he knows to be the case (the infidelity of his fiancée), the boy – the petty bourgeois character – remains ignorant of the true meaning of events and relationships.[66] In these respects, the portrayal of the landlordism in The Go-Between is different from the way in which members of the same

---

66   Unlike Leo, who really is a dupe, Trimingham only pretends to be one. As Caute (1994: 271) puts it, 'Edward Fox [who plays Lord Trimingham] effortlessly captures the public-school quality of being a fool yet no fool: of sheltering behind received formulas while knowing what really lurks in the undergrowth'. In other words, Trimingham is neither dupe nor fool, since he is aware of what is going on, and his disempowerment stems from different causes.

class are depicted in the films considered in the previous chapter, where a comedic image renders aristocracy 'unserious', and thereby defuses their political power. In *The Go-Between*, by contrast, the same end is achieved by a rather more sympathetic portrayal of landlordism as benign.

In this lies the clue to the way the agrarian myth features in its narrative. The socio-economic structure of the English countryside under the control of the landed aristocracy is depicted as essentially benign, its element of element of timelessness extending to include tradition and national identity, all of which combine in the person of the landowner.[67] This was the way it had always been and, it is inferred, should remain – the landlord pastoral variant of the agrarian

---

67   That this was a conscious objective is confirmed (Taylor, 1970: 202–203) both by the art director ('What the film needed was a rambling country house which would look as though nothing had been changed for years before the high Edwardian summer in which the action takes place') and by Pinter, who wrote the script ('Looking back at [the first draft of *The Go-Between*], I realised that I had missed a whole aspect, perhaps to me the most important aspect, of the book...the role of time: the annihilation of time...'). Sir Joseph Duveen (1869–1939) who, as an international art dealer, was familiar with the views/opinions expressed in English ruling class circles, accurately captures this sense of timelessness. He writes (Duveen, 1930: 6): 'Looking back at England at the beginning of this century I seem only to see a happy sun-lit landscape; villages unspoilt by hoardings and advertisement signs; a tranquil people whom the topical worry of the Boer War had not seriously upset, a people who had no premonition of the terrific cataclysm awaiting the next generation. Queen Victoria was almost a synonym for immortality'. Although events are situated in the summer of 1900, *The Go-Between* conveys the sense of well-being enjoyed by those at the apex of the rural class structure in Edwardian England. The brief period between the turn of the century and the 1914–18 war is generally depicted, both in literature and films, as a period of 'lost content' – the fact of agrarian class struggle notwithstanding – that vanished in the post-war era. 'My generation of Englishmen', noted John Strachey (1934: 63–64) at the beginning of the 1930s, 'remembers the [pre-1914-18] world...as a vision of childhood; and for a well-circumstanced English child what a golden age of peace, calm, plenty, and security it was! Those who had not lived before 1789, said the French, had never known "la vrai douceur de la vie"'. For me, the word "pre-war" evokes always a memory of midsummer afternoons. A choisa bush grew at the garden door of my parents' big sitting-room in their country house. Brick steps, warm in the sunlight, led down from the wide shady room into the hot garden'. The same kind of sentiments were expressed more recently by the landowning Conservative MP, Alan Clark. In his diaries he laments the passing of and hankers after that same era, when his great-grandparents – also landlords – enjoyed what he accepts was easy living ('What a style!'), described by him thus (Clark, 2002: 135): 'Three large and expensive houses (plus the lodge at Poolewe and the villa at Cap Ferrat), the yatch, hordes and hordes of domestics. My own structure still shadows it...'.

myth, in other words.[68] The overthrow of the existing (= patrician) agrarian hierarchy as a result of a 'from below' challenge to the existing social order by the tenant farmer is therefore presented as a loss also of a systemically benevolent rural community and national identity. By depicting not just landlordism but also those ideological forms (patriotism, colonialism, imperialism) associated with this kind of class power as good-but-defeated, therefore, they are not merely all defused politically, and symbolically expelled from the arena of struggle, but their expulsion has now become a matter for regret.

The fact that *The Go-Between* corresponds to the landlord pastoral variant of the agrarian myth, albeit under threat from below, is also evident from the structure of its resolution. Despite having been vanquished – as evidenced by his defeat in the cricket match, his fruitless pursuit of Marian, and his suicide – it is the tenant farmer who is ultimately victorious, in that he is the father of the heir to the estate. Not only was Lord Trimingham's heir actually the son of his tenant farmer, the blood line so precious to the landed aristocrat having as a consequence died out, therefore, but a half century on Brandham Hall had been 'let to a girl's school'.[69] The inference is that, as undeserved and undesirable as it is, the benign patrician rule exercised by the landowning aristocracy had ceased, and as a class it was as a result now disempowered.[70] The discourse informing *The Go-Between* is, in short, that of the agrarian myth.

That the author of *The Go-Between* espoused the agrarian myth is also clear from what he writes elsewhere.[71] What Hartley approves of in reviewing novels

---

68   This sense of loss, a result of the supercession of the landlord pastoral variant of the agrarian myth, is a lament projected both at the outset of the narrative and repeated at its end. Hence the final words of the book, uttered by a now-aged Marian – 'this hideous century we live in, which has denatured humanity...' (Hartley, 1985: 236) – echo the more famous ones ('The past is a foreign country; they do things differently there') with which the story begins.

69   On this, see Hartley (1985: 229).

70   The dual inference is that the landed aristocracy is not merely disempowered, but has become so as a result of upholding the principled code of *noblesse oblige*. Adherence the latter reinforces the image of Trimingham as a benign landowning aristocrat, for whom honour and rectitude override all other considerations. He goes ahead with his marriage to Marian, despite the fact that the child she now carries is not his, an action designed to show that he 'was as true as steel' (Hartley, 1985: 233).

71   Thus the gender/national/Nature essentialisms that inform the agrarian myth also surface in the short stories by the same writer. In the case of 'The Pampas Clump' (Hartley, 1986: 524–533), therefore, the pampas clump represents a threatening, ancient and 'foreign other' in the midst of a pastoral location, the English country house. Described as a very old shrub that is 'dangerous', 'frightening' and 'sinister', it is equated with the main

written by a friend who attended the same public school and university as he did – that they champion individualism and 'the spirit' against 'collectivism', 'state control', and science – is true also of himself.[72] Other fiction by him reveals many of these same political anxieties, especially his one dystopian novel. The latter depicts the attempt by a (socialist) government after World War III to abolish even facial individuality/'otherness', thereby enforcing physical uniformity in furtherance of an absolute and all-embracing equality, so as to eradicate envy and resentment.[73] Although for the most part unable to match the sort of unease generated by M.R. James and Nigel Kneale, some of the ghost stories of L.P. Hartley nevertheless depict the same kind of symbolic antagonism: a situation where an ancient supernatural power returns to defend rural property/tradition/hierarchy against a variety of modern 'othernesses' (progress, materialism, science).[74]

---

female character (Hartley, 1986: 528), thereby licensing the following relay-in-statement: Nature = pampas clump = ancient power = foreign = threatening = female.

72   About novels of C.H.B. Kitchen, therefore, Hartley (1967: 151) observes: 'Though not a thoroughgoing reactionary Mr Kitchen is a passionate individualist, and as such loathes all forms of collectivism, compulsion and state control, whether Communist, Fascist or simply bureaucratic. With this, as enemies of the spirit, he couples science'. Originally published in the London Magazine during February 1954, just after the appearance of The Go-Between, this review was a thinly-disguised critique of the socialist policies effected by the 1946–51 Labour government of Attlee. Symptomatically, in his own ghost story 'Beauty and the Beast', Kitchen (1931: 139–170) concerns the haunting of the daughter of a land-owning Jewish family that 'had intermarried with the best English blood', the anti-semitic sub-text being punishments inflicted on an ethnically 'other' character who attempted to become part of an aristocracy and a nation that was not theirs.

73   The text in question is Facial Justice by Hartley (1960). This critique of socialism takes the familiar form of caricaturing the extent of uniformity, the object being to present the latter as the inevitable outcome of any attempt to undermine class power/privilege, by expropriating property and redistributing wealth (taxation, planning, extending working class access both to resources such as housing/employment, and to institutions (schools, universities) hitherto dominated by the bourgeoisie. The object is to discredit even moderate reforms, the sub-text being a defence of the existing socio-economic order (capitalism) and its form of property relations against revolutionary impetus aimed at systemic change (socialism). It is a theme encountered in many a dystopian fiction, not only the novel by Hartley (1960) but also the earlier short story 'The New Utopia' by Jerome K. Jerome (1891: 261–279).

74   Hence the ancient power of the church combines with its rôle as a dispossessed landowning class in the story 'Monkshood Manor' (Hartley, 1986: 401–412). It is about a ghost of a monk who was a member of an Abbey dissolved at the Reformation, then on land now occupied by a house constructed with stones taken from the earlier building. He returns

IV

In the United Kingdom, much is heard these days of a collapse of 'deferential culture', the inference being that respect once shown by 'those below' to 'those above' no longer exists. This possesses a subtext doubly advantageous to the landowning class. First, it propagates the myth of an economically and politically disempowered aristocracy and monarchy. Those belonging to the latter categories, it is inferred, are not now in receipt of the same public esteem historically accorded to them; this change is attributed in turn to a decline in their political influence and – consequently – their wealth. And second, it projects the similarly mythological idea of an empowered plebeian, suggesting as it does that not just the ideological distinction but also the political and economic power associated with this is a thing of the past.

---

to revenge himself the present inhabitants and their guests. Much the same kind of narrative structure informs another (and better) ghost story, 'Feet Foremost' (Hartley, 1986: 117–145), but with a more complex and – in terms of a discourse about class – significant *dénoûment*. It too concerns the return of an ancient power, in the ghostly form of the murdered aristocratic wife of an earlier landowner, to wreak revenge on those living in an old manor house reoccupied and restored after one and a half centuries by new owners. 'She comes for vengeance (and) apparently she gets it', the current proprietor informs his guests (Hartley, 1986: 121), '[w]ithin a short time of her appearance, someone in the house always dies [and the ghost exits] with the corpse'. Affronted by the resulting contrast between tradition and modernity – '[The hall] seemed so perfect and new; not only every sign of decay but the very sense of age had been banished' (Hartley, 1986: 118) – the apparition is unknowingly invited into the house by a guest, who becomes ill and is on the point of death, but recovers as the malevolence is itself transferred to a dying stranger. His fiancée discovers in the library the history of a previous haunting, when the then-owner was saved by transferring the vengeance to 'a Body yet nearer Dissolution', a servant girl who was a kitchen maid (Hartley, 1986: 130–131, 142). The moribund guest is saved in the same way, this time the vengeance being transferred to the dying pilot of a crashed aircraft. Like *The Go-Between*, this ghost story is set around the year 1900, and also has a number of obvious affinities with those of M.R. James (see Chapter 4). Not only is the manor house itself located in East Anglia, but it is the servants and not the guests or the owner who recognize and fear the presence of the ghost (Hartley, 1986: 127–128). Of particular interest, however, is the way in which the element of class features in the discourse. Because he is the one who admits the ghost to the manor house, the target of vengeance by an ancient power is himself bourgeois: a businessman who owns a company and lives in London (Hartley, 1986: 134, 137). He survives because – like a previous owner of the manor – revenge is transferred to a plebeian: then a servant girl, now a pilot of the crashed plane. Furthermore, both the bourgeois who survives and the plebeian who dies themselves embody the modernity that is under attack from the ancient landowning aristocratic power.

However, evidence suggests that neither aristocracy nor monarchy is as dis-empowered as 'new' postmodern populists maintain, and consequently laughter directed at a landowning institution is not 'subversive'. As has been argued here, laughter serves instead to deflect attention from the continued political and economic power exercised by those possessing rural property. Both the economic and political power conferred by landownership, together with the kind of ideology such power engenders, is evident from the case of British royalty.

Populist Discourse, from above and from below

A discourse that has its immediate origins in the 1953 novel by L.P. Hartley, *The Go-Between* was written just after World War II, when conservative politicians wanted to display the same kind of benign public image. The political back-drop to the Go-Between is the post-war grassroots political radicalization that followed the 1930s economic depression and culminated in the Labour electoral landslide of 1945.[75] Breaking with the previous *laissez-faire* approach, the Labour Government introduced not just a national health service and compre-hensive education, but also welfare provision advocated by the Beveridge Report. Its programme, which entailed planned state intervention in the econ-omy, nationalization, full employment, progressive taxation and decoloniza-tion, amounted to a situation in which 'an elected Labour Government [threatened] relentlessly to invade the territory of the rich, and occupying it in the interests of the workers and the poor'.[76] Such policies constituted a serious challenge both to unregulated capitalism and to its class hierarchy.

Ostensibly, the political backdrop to the more recent benign (powerful-but-friendly) depictions of monarchy and aristocracy as portrayed in *House of Cards*, *The Queen* and *The King's Speech*, could not be more different. From the 1980s onwards, capitalism became global, resulting in the adoption once

---

75   For the background to the 1945 election, and the subsequent policies introduced by the Labour Government, see Foot (2005: 306 ff.).

76   See Foot (2005: 316). Among those who recognized this potential 'from below' threat to ruling class institutions was the novelist T.H. White (1994: 19–21). Writing at the same time as Hartley, White described the post-1945 era as 'the end of civilization in England', lamenting '[n]ow that glorious palaces like Knowle, Stowe, Wentworth Woodhouse, Bodiam, Montacute, Stourhead, Polesdon Lacey, Blenheim and the rest of them are, or likely to be, "nationalised" for the wonderful proletariat...' He concludes by remarking that 'I have been consoling my old age by running away from [the present], by going back to the grand days of Horace Walpole, and I have written this book in the effort to give one last, loving and living picture of an aristocratic civilization which we shall never see again'.

again of *laissez faire* policies. On the one hand, therefore, the rollback of state intervention in the economy generated reductions in public expenditure, and a decline in welfare provision. This was accompanied by deregulation/casualization of employment, a worsening of pay levels and workplace conditions, outsourcing/relocation of jobs, and rising unemployment levels. On the other, market liberalization and privatization of publicly-owned assets/enterprises were accompanied by increased tax avoidance/evasion on the part of the wealthy, and an ever-expanding gap between the earnings of the rich and poor.

These antithetical processes notwithstanding, both conjunctures – after 1945 and after 1980 – share a common feature in terms of political struggle: each represents a potential crisis for ruling class institutions, albeit for different reasons. One because of an ascendant grassroots mobilization accompanying electoral victory, the other because of grassroots resistance to 'from above' attempts to cutback or eradicate the very gains made earlier. In both instances, images/narratives of ruling class wealth and empowerment could be viewed as ideologically disadvantageous to its survival, inviting as they do a political challenge 'from below'.

Far from being as egalitarian as depicted in dramas like *House of Cards* and *The King's Speech*, therefore, the heir to the throne unsurprisingly holds reactionary views, among them that the masses should not attempt to rise above a place ordained for them by Nature.[77] As regressive is his opinion that religion ought should be deployed in order roll back scientific advances, and the perception that in India slum dwellings are a perfectly acceptable *modus vivendi* for their impoverished inhabitants.[78]

---

77   That he possesses an anti-egalitarian outlook is confirmed not just by an 1985 utterance – 'What I want to know is: what is actually wrong with an elite, for God's sake?' – but also by the following one contained in a confidential memorandum from 2002: 'What is wrong with people nowadays? Why do they all seem to think they are qualified to do things far above their capabilities?...It is a result of social utopianism which believes humanity can be genetically engineered to contradict the lessons of history'. See 'Charles's world', *The Guardian* (London), 19 November 2011. Nor was it the case that his first wife, Princess Diana, widely regarded as the only egalitarian member of the royal family (= 'the people's princess'), was in fact any less so, since 'her treatment of servants was, in its over-familiar way, quite as abusive as the Windsors' and more capricious'. See 'The view from downstairs', *The Guardian* (London), 1 November 2003.

78   On the subject of religion, Prince Charles observed in 1996 that '[d]uring the last three centuries, the western world has seen the growth of a damaging division in the way we see and understand the world around us. Science has tried to assume a monopoly – or rather, a tyranny – over our understanding of the world around us. Religion and science have become separated, and science has attempted to separate the natural world from God,

   In a similar vein, the political power wielded by British royalty is clear from the recently disclosed ability of the monarch to withhold consent to proposed legislation amounts to a veto over laws affecting its economic interests.[79] The latter include a substantial property portfolio, urban real estate as well as farms and timber businesses in rural areas, all of which operate as profitable commercial enterprises.[80] Like many other large capitalist farms in the country, moreover, those owned by Prince Charles utilize the gangmaster system, a

---

with the result that it has fragmented the cosmos and placed the sacred into a separate, and secondary compartment of our understanding, divorced from the practical day-to-day world of man. We are only now beginning to understand the disastrous results of this outlook'. Noting in 2004 that '[i]n Britain we are rapidly losing what is left of our local culture', he elaborates: 'I came across a classic example of "collective intelligence embodied in centuries of tradition" when I visited a shanty town slum in Bombay recently...I was fascinated by the way in which human beings – almost like ants coming together intuitively to create a nest – instinctively coalesce when brought together in large numbers into an "urban form" which enhances that vital sense of community. And it is communities we must create'. For both these comments, see 'Charles's world', *The Guardian* (London), 19 November 2011.

79   For the extent of this power to block legislation, and its secret nature, see 'Twelve draft laws, 650 elected MPs – and one prince with a secret veto', *The Guardian* (London), 31 October 2011; 'Government urged to reveal Charles's input on planning legislation', *The Guardian* (London), 1 November 2011. 'The guidance states that the Queen's consent is likely to be needed for laws affecting hereditary revenues, personal property or personal interests of the Crown, the Duchy of Lancaster or the Duchy of Cornwall...These guidelines effectively mean the Queen and [Prince] Charles both have power over laws affecting their sources of private income. The Queen uses revenues from the Duchy of Lancaster's 19,000 hectares of land and 10 castles to pay for the upkeep of her private homes at Sandringham and Balmoral, while the prince earns 18 m a year from the Duchy of Cornwall'. See 'Secret papers show extent of senior royals' veto over bills', *The Guardian* (London), 15 January 2013.

80   The reported 300 percent rise in the income Prince Charles received over the 1993–2005 period was a result of urban and rural property acquisition, business activity, and tax exemption. 'In a large part', notes the investigation into his wealth, 'Charles' soaring pay has come from the transformation of the [Duchy of Cornwall] into a huge commercial enterprise'. As well as owning rural land in the west of England – 70,000 acres in Devon, 18,000 acres in Cornwall, 15,000 acres in Somerset, and the Isles of Scilly – he also owns office blocks and retail outlets in urban areas. Moreover, the food marketing corporation he owns – Duchy Originals, valued at £460 (widely considered an underestimate) – is a tax exempt operation. See 'The prince of property and his £460 m business empire', *The Observer* (London), 30 January 2005; and 'Charles resists calls for scrutiny of his estates' tax-free privileges', *The Guardian* (London), 25 October 2006.

highly exploitative method of labour contracting involving the recruitment and control of migrant workers.[81]

Another source of income obtained by aristocratic landowners in Britain derives from the Common Agricultural Policy operated by the European Union. Over a two-year period (2002–2004), therefore, the Duke of Westminster received £799,000, the Duke of Marlborough one million, and the Duchy of Cornwall £30,000. The Queen was paid a subsidy of £700,000, the Duke of Bedford obtained £366,000, the Duke of Northumberland got £451,000, and the Prince of Wales received £300,000.[82] These kinds of subsidy have served merely to consolidate already expanding levels of royal and aristocratic wealth.

Thus holdings owned by the Crown Estate doubled in value from £4bn in 2002–2003 to £8bn in 2011–2012, an increase matched (and in some cases exceeded) by the property portfolios of other aristocratic families in Britain.[83] During the same period, the value of the Grosvenor Estate, owned by the Duke of Westminster, went from £2.3bn to £5.8bn, while that of the Cadogan and Howard de Walden Estates went from £1.7bn and £2.4bn respectively to £2.4bn and £3.9 bn. The Duchy of Cornwall is not liable for tax, yet operates as a capitalist enterprise, increasing its purchases of commercial property and expanding its investment portfolio; currently, therefore, 'it competes with other businesses, buying and selling, owning warehouses and holiday cottages, but is exempt from paying for education and healthcare for its workforce'.[84]

---

81   For the use of the gangmaster system on farms owned by Prince Charles, see 'The prince and the gangmaster', *The Guardian* (London), 3 May 2004.

82   These disbursements were greeted with ironic headlines in the British press. See, for example, 'How the CAP helps our poorest farmers', *The Independent* (London), 30 June 2005. See also 'Rich land owners scoop up crock of gold from the EU', 'Royal farms get £1 m from taxpayers', and 'Another countryside', all in *The Guardian* (London), 23 March 2005.

83   See 'Heralding Change – How Britain's landed estates have adapted old business models to prevent the break-up of their property empires', *The Financial Times* (London), 9 June 2013, where the following observations can be found: 'A behemoth of the landed estate world, Grosvenor has transmogrified from stuffy landlord to self-made heavyweight of the international real estate market. The company, which owns most of the homes, offices, shops and restaurants in Mayfair and Belgravia – two of London's most valuable areas – controls property worth almost £6bn and has interests spanning the US, Europe and Asia...The Crown estate has made perhaps the most remarkable transition of all the landed estates. The £8bn portfolio managed on behalf of the monarch has gone from insouciant rent collector just a decade ago to something resembling an ambitious sovereign wealth fund'.

84   See 'Duchy estate rejects dodges and daughters', *The Financial Times* (London), 20–21 July 2013.

Conserving the Land for the Nation

These disbursements and increased wealth notwithstanding, the arguments now deployed in their own defence by aristocratic landowners in Britain remains essentially the same as before. Not only does this aristocratic discourse about landownership remain rooted in nationalist ideology – along the lines of 'we conserve the land for the nation' – but it also presents the landlord class as disempowered politically and economically ('farming doesn't generate sufficient profits to cover the cost of the upkeep required by these grand houses').[85] Despite evincing an image of powerlessness, almost victimhood, the rural landowning class in Britain still appears to exercise considerable power.

The latter is not only political – for example, opposition to right-to-roam legislation plus the demonstrations mounted by the countryside alliance – but also economic. An analysis of property shows how many of the names of those who owned land in the 1890s are still on the lists of those who own land in 2001, and 'old money' based on the inheritance of large rural property still features prominently on lists of the wealthy.[86] Interestingly, in the course of the scandal over the large expenses claimed by members of Parliament during May 2009, the main concern of the Conservative Party leadership stemmed not from the legality or illegality of such claims but rather from the fact that money was spent by Conservative MPs who were already independently wealthy on the upkeep of their rural estates – installing chandeliers, cleaning moats and paying housekeepers. The latter kind of expenditures, it was feared, would raise in the minds of the electorate the very images of privilege and wealth that the Conservative Party had worked so hard to dispel.[87]

---

85   When questioned in the course of a BBC2 television programme – 'Whose Britain is it Anyway?' – broadcast in January 2006, as to how they justified continued ownership of so much rural property, aristocratic landowners responded by deploying precisely these arguments.

86   For a comparison of landowners in the 1890s with those who owned land over a century later, see Cahill (2001). At the turn of the millennium, the continued economic efficacy of landownership in Britain was underlined by the following report: 'The multi-million pound riches of Britain's twenty-something sports stars, entrepreneurs and entertainers are still eclipsed by the enormous inherited wealth of young aristocrats...the really big money is still old money. The fortunes earned through developing computer software, singing in a band [and] importing drugs are dwarfed by the huge sums which will be inherited'. See 'Old money still backs Britain's young rich', *The Observer* (London) 11 April 1999.

87   Hence the anxiety about the effect of 'allegations about [expenditures on] moats, helipads, horse manure, chandeliers and swimming pools, all claimed by some of the most

Film depictions both of an enfeebled European colonialism and of American identity as powerful-but-friendly are also important in terms of a contrast between them and a currently resurgent imperialism. Towards the end of the twentieth century and the beginning of the twenty-first, the United Kingdom, France and the United States – the 'old' and the 'new' imperial powers – joined forces in the pursuit of new conquests in the Middle East and North Africa, designed to establish and maintain control over oil resources vital to capitalist accumulation.

The irony is that, currently, the ideological positions both for and against colonialism, nationalism and imperialism are all informed in turn by populism. This is as true of the 'new' imperialism that has emerged since the 1990s as it is of opposition to its global interventions, based as these are on mobilization under the rubric of new social movements. The difficulty is that such agency, structured as it is by non-class identities, generates a form of anti-capitalism that is spuriously progressive, hiding what is in fact also populist ideology. This underlines yet again the importance of a socialist politics.

Conclusion

How the nostalgia informing films such as *The Go-Between* and *The King's Speech* functions politically is easy to discern. On film, images of a tension-free and/or harmonious past, not only devoid of current anxieties and fears but also projecting 'friendship' that transects class boundaries, generate what amounts to a false hope. This corresponds to a desire on the part of the viewer to return to those times, when – in comparison to the present – society was more ordered, life was more certain, and consequently seemed less difficult. By inculcating this kind of backwards-looking 'solution' – where a better form of existence is to be found in the past, not the future – the nostalgia of such films contribute to and reinforce the anti-modern ideology supportive of conservatism. It is the latter, not socialism, which argues similarly that a return to past values is what needs to be done.

---

senior Conservative squirearchy. The Tory brand had been retoxified overnight...David Cameron's marketing men have worked to freshen his party's "aroma". But the chief smell hanging over it right now is horse manure – merely one of the claims submitted by Tory grandees that have reminded the public how the other half lives. From mole traps to moats, these country life expenses have restored the view of Conservatives as privileged and greedy'. *The Guardian* (London), 16 May 2009.

What is important from the view of wealthy proprietors, therefore, is that in a discourse about history they should on occasion be characterized as losers, not just perpetual winners. Not only does this invite sympathy but (more importantly) the subtext is that a transformation involving material assets is complete. In short, no further process of redistribution/reform (= empowerment/disempowerment) is necessary. The effectiveness of this defence, however, depends in turn on a number of things. First, the degree to which images conveying disempowerment – for example, humorous depictions of the aristocracy licensing the view that this class is politically and/or economically in decline or actually powerless – are inserted into and reproduced within the domain of popular culture.

In this and the previous chapter it has been argued that class identities linked to the agrarian myth fall into one of three categories. That of 'fiend' associated with empowerment and hostility – and projected via horror or ghost stories – represents the Darwinian aristocratic and/or plebeian variant, in which powerful landowning institutions are engaged in struggle with 'those below'. By contrast, the image of 'friend' involving neither horror nor laughter entails that the struggle remain latent. Here depictions of the countryside are mainly of harmony, and as such match the opposite form of the agrarian myth: namely, the pastoral versions of the aristocratic and/or the plebeian variant. The latter also extends to humorous images (= 'fool') projecting a powerful landowning institution as disempowered and thus 'not worth bothering about'.

The image of 'fiend' represents landowners as depicted (by M.R. James) in the late Victorian era, whereas 'friend' corresponds to portrayals (by Losey, Bridges and Stoppard) of aristocracy during the Edwardian period, and 'fool' applies generally to ruling class institutions from the 1950s onwards. In the course of this ideological transition, landowners, church and royalty as depicted in popular culture are presented as no longer a political threat, and seemingly ejected thereby from the arena of struggle. Images of colonialism and imperialism in films and television undergo an analogous transformation from efficacious (colonizer-as-'fiend'), to benign (colonizer-as-'friend') and ultimately to figures of ridicule (colonizer-as-'harmless').

Films considered in these two chapters project what might be termed a symptomatic political discourse, therefore, not just about European landlordism but also about colonialism and nationalism (American as well as European). Images conveying class and/or national empowerment/disempowerment carry over into *Gosford Park*, *Apocalypse Now Redux* and *The Quiet American*, albeit in a different form. In the latter two films especially, the image of European impotence is less humorous and more serious, the argument being that as the old colonial empires are no longer able to stem communism, the United States must step in and do this instead. Much the same is true of the film *Indiana Jones and the Temple of Doom*, except that in this case British imperialism is depicted as unaware of – as well as incapable of dealing with – an indigenous Indian nationalism that similarly draws its support from an 'unthinking mob'.

As projected in films, therefore, the ideological conflict between the United States and Europe over colonialism gives the impression that – having themselves been colonized by the British – America/Americans objected in principle to the existence of colonialism, and take every opportunity to oppose this. However, a closer reading of the films reveals a different subtext: opposition by Americans was not to colonialism per se, but rather to its exercise by Europeans. The real purpose of opposition is not to eliminate colonialism, but to supplant the former colonial power. Hence the discourse is not so much that of colonialism, which in the case of the Europeans is defeated or comes to an end, but rather that of nationalism. The populist element consists of depicting opposition to colonialism as politically 'innocent' – that is to say, without declaring the presence of this 'other' nationalism.

In short, such film and television images are part of the struggle between classes and between nations. Because they deny the conceptual efficacy of class consciousness and struggle, conservatives by contrast would insist that the nominally powerful (landlords, colonial authorities) are in fact weak, while the notionally weak (workers, peasants) are much rather powerful. The central argument made here, therefore, is that by depicting the politically powerful humorously as weak, inept or useless (= 'not worth bothering about'), the image of disempowerment that circulates in the domain of popular culture in effect contributes to their survival.

The remaining three chapters examine travel literature, an area of popular culture that is also influential, and how it too is structured by the discourse of class struggle and the agrarian myth. Of particular significance is the way in which the experience of travel results in a protective fusion between nationalism and populism and a transformation of the 'mob in the streets' into the mass tourist.

PART 3

Culture, Class Struggle and Travel

∴

CHAPTER 6

The Grand Tour, or from Cosmopolitanism to Nationalism

> Travel and travellers are two things I loathe – and yet here I am, all set to tell the story of my expeditions.
>
> An observation by the French anthropologist CLAUDE LÉVI-STAUSS (1961: 17)

Introduction

Previous chapters traced the way in which historically the process of class struggle generated rival versions of the agrarian myth (plebeian; landlord), a discourse about what was claimed to be an innate and enduring rural identity based on Nature. It was the related concept of a place-specific culture that in turn gave rise to the notions of ethnic/indigenous 'otherness' at the root of national selfhood. As capitalism developed, and smallholders were transformed into workers, the political survival of the landowning class was increasingly determined by its capacity to forge an identity that could be shared with peasants and workers in the same context. From this emerged populism, a conservative mobilizing ideology that privileged traditional cultural identity, proclaimed unity among rural proprietors large and small, downplayed class differences in what was depicted as an harmonious countryside, and promoted nationalism.

Populist ideology was most effective politically when accompanied by a fusion of the pastoral version belonging to both the plebeian and the landlord variants of the agrarian myth. In such circumstances, it might be deployed as a form of protection against a variety of non-rural 'others': finance capital (*not* capitalism), the urban proletariat (= 'the mob in the streets'), the foreigner, and socialist ideas/policies. However, where the latter threaten to prevail in the class struggle, the pastoral version is replaced by its Darwinian counterpart, a 'red-in-tooth-and-claw' ideology depicting the countryside as a locus of violent conflict and/or terror. As has been outlined in previous chapters, both versions of the agrarian myth are reproduced in the domain of popular culture, as is evident from their importance in film and television.

In the following three chapters the focus shifts to travel literature, another influential component of popular culture. It is argued that the same themes structuring the agrarian myth as these inform politics and film surface in much writing about travel, both historically and currently. For this reason, this chapter traces the connection between agrarian myth discourse and the Grand Tour. Of interest is how what began as a cosmopolitan ideology espoused by the ruling class, and acquired in the course of European travel, was transformed into nationalism. Although in the case of England this change is generally attributed to the impact of war, and the presence of an external enemy (France), it is argued here that as important was the formation and increasing political significance of an internal enemy: the landless worker in town and countryside, who – as the potential/actual 'mob in the street' – caused much concern among wealthy proprietors and agrarian capitalists.

After the 1789 and subsequent revolutions in France, this fear on the part of 'those above' of class struggle waged by 'those below' licensed the emergence of agrarian populism. As is clear from the travel accounts written by Johann Gottfried Herder and Alexander Herzen, it was as a result of what they saw in the course of journeys to other countries that led them to espouse nationalism and advocate a common cause between landowners and peasants against the urban working class.

This chapter is divided into four parts, of which the first explores the link between travel writing, anthropology and film. The focus of the second is on the Grand Tour and the acquisition by its subject of a cosmopolitan ideological outlook shared with those occupying the same position in the class hierarchy elsewhere in Europe. The third and fourth sections look at the travel writing of Herder and Herzen, and how concepts of national identity and a populist politics emerged from their experiences abroad.

I

Broadly speaking, the concept 'travel literature' incorporates a number of different genres: not just formal accounts of 'other' places visited, designed to be read as such, but also informal accounts – confined to journals or diaries – not usually written with a view to publication. Writings about travel examined here cover both kinds, not least because the informal account frequently contains a 'hidden' discourse revealing opinions/ideas withheld from formal ones destined for publication.[1]

---

1 As is well-known, 'hidden' discourse in travel writing belonging to the informal category may reveal actions/views perceived as unacceptable; for example, sexual encounters or racist opinions. The diaries kept by James Boswell recording his experiences during the mid-1760s

Travel Literature and/as Anthropology

Historically, travel writing has taken many different forms and arisen for different reasons. The latter range from accounts written during or about exile to those explicitly designed to chronicle the act of travel. Thus experiences and/ or information garnered as a result of foreign travel inform many political analyses, Marxist and non-Marxist alike, not least because on occasion the authors of these commentaries have been required to pass on from countries where their presence was deemed unwelcome.[2]

As important is the fact that the term 'travel literature' implies two things. First, that some accounts of travel are written as an extension of literature, by those who have already established reputation as writers about subjects other than travel. And second, that there exists a form of writing about travel that does not fall within the category of literature. The latter designation usually embraces the genre of 'travel guide', comprising a non-literary recitation amounting simply to a descriptive list (= catalogue) of places to be visited, and why. That such a distinction is untenable is clear from admissions made by a number of writers who have contributed to travel literature.[3]

---

when on foreign visits or on the Grand Tour (Pottle, 1952; Pottle, 1953; Brady and Pottle, 1955) detail numerous sexual liaisons. Those kept by Bronislaw Malinowski (1967) when conducting anthropological fieldwork in New Guinea between 1914 and 1918 reveal strongly-held racist attitudes towards the tribals he was studying.

2 The final chapter of his autobiography, entitled by Trotsky (1930: 484–497) 'Planet without a Visa', accurately conveys the extent to which for a political revolutionary exile is a never-ending process of travel, moving reluctantly from place to place. This is also true of Victor Serge (1963; 2004), whose writing is not about travel so much as accounts where travel has been an important feature of an enforced life of exile.

3 'Very taken up with writing an essay on Venice', reads the journal entry by Stephen Spender (1985: 357) for 4 May 1979, adding: 'The usual awful misgivings about my lack of knowledge, experience of Venice, etc. I come out with a few big metaphors and then read Hugh Honour's excellent, at times scintillating, guide book and think facts are what I want and what I lack'. Another writer (Keates, 2011: 3) accepts that '[i]n quest of local colour for my narrative I had found myself ransacking Murray, Baedeker and other travel books of the pre-First World War period'. Similarly, in a letter to his publisher written in 1950 Patrick Leigh Fermor (Cooper, 2012: 249) notes that 'I may retire somewhere to write a chapter or two. Murray's Guide [to Greece]...will be most useful. Do you think you could discover one for Turkey, to cover those parts of Macedonia, Epirus etc. that belonged to the Ottoman Empire till the Balkan Wars?'. Earlier, yet another travel writer (Green, 1936: 96) confessed that, in composing a poem about Venice – a city he had never visited – which won him the 1916 Newdigate Prize, he 'was restricted, for atmosphere, merely to a guide book and a coloured reproduction of one of Turner's incomparable paintings of Venice'. However, this endorsement of the guide book as a literary source does not prevent the same writer from poking fun at one composed by an

In terms of subject matter and methodology, a discernable overlap exists between travel writing and anthropology. The latter entails not merely a visit to but a prolonged stay in – and usually an attempt to become part of – an 'other' society. This compatibility between anthropology and travel writing derives additionally from a common desire to encounter the 'other' in its 'natural' surroundings.[4] Thus anthropology sought out a location inhabited by a 'natural'/untamed subject who – because he/she is untainted by modern development – is said consequently to exist in a state of pristine Nature.

The element of not being tainted by modernity and economic growth also informs much travel writing, the object of which has been – and remains still – to discover a place unspoiled by modern development.[5] Like anthropology, travel writing also gives rise to a proprietorial approach to locations visited or studied. In the case of anthropology, this takes the familiar form along the lines of '*my* village, *my* tribe, which only I understand and know how to interpret to the wider world'. Travel writing on occasion makes a similar claim: to '*my* place, which only I have described, may it long remain so – others (especially mass tourism) keep well away, and don't pollute what I have found'.

Shifting the Gaze from 'Other' to Self

For a number of reasons, the focus of anthropology is now no longer confined to what might be termed 'exotic other places', and has turned towards the society of the ethnographer, and the latter no longer studies either 'primitive' society, tribal groups or peasants in the so-called Third World.[6] One outcome is that the element of novelty which informed fieldwork in what was a hitherto

Italian (Green, 1936: 160–161). Even earlier, in 1842, Thackeray (1906: 19) questioned whether Victor Hugo 'comes into countries with all these facts concerning their history and topography [or] purchases guide-books, like other people, and robs them like other authors do?'.

4   The extent of the overlap between anthropology and travel writing is evident from a comparison of the account by Malinowski (1922: Chapters I and II) of the customs and institutions of the Trobriand Islanders in New Guinea with that by Morand (1928: 111–122) of the 'otherness' of 'magical ceremonies' in Siam. If the former is a case of travel writing by an anthropologist, the latter is one of ethnographic description undertaken by a travel writer.

5   Whereas development theorists – *not* anthropologists – who revisit their research area to undertake a restudy a couple of decades after their initial fieldwork approve of signs of economic advance (building, housing, roads, etc.), travel writers and anthropologists who revisit invariably do so to lament the passing of a way of life.

6   Reasons for this include financial (costs of going/staying abroad for long periods), cut-backs in higher education budgets, and – most importantly – the fact that globalization means that now the 'other' is in purely physical terms systemically part of the same society as the anthropologist him/herself.

'inaccessible' location, the focus of which was on an 'undiscovered' social group (= anthropology-as-exploration), no longer applies.[7] Another is that this shift has been accompanied by an expansion in the domain of travel literature, which in a sense has moved in to occupy and comment on many of those spaces that historically were the preserve of ethnography.

In such instances, the 'other' referred to in disapproving terms in a discourse shared by ethnography and travel writing is the same: not the tribal or ethnic/ indigenous 'other' being studied or described (= revealed to the world), but the 'other' *at home*. That is to say, the people objected to are those who might 'trespass' either on the location occupied by the social group the anthropologist has studied or on the space discovered by the travel writer, and in each case ruin it. The latter kind of transformation follows on from allowing into erstwhile 'pristine' contexts the much feared mass tourist, itself a process giving rise to (and thus is accompanied by) modern development. Notwithstanding this common discourse, a crucial difference exists.

Although both anthropology and travel writing share not just a discourse but also a methodology (= participant/observation), that of most travel writing is based less on long-term residence in another place (as has been anthropology), and frequently amounts to a narrative as a result of 'passing through' a specific location.[8] One consequence of this distinction is that,

---

7 That this aspect of ethnographic practice was shared by the travel writing genre is evident from the following observation by Wilfred Thesiger (1988: 95, emphasis added): 'During this month [spent in Danakil country, in 1930] I led the life for which I had always yearned, hunting big game on my own in the wilds of Africa; but *now I realized that this expedition had meant more to me than just the excitement of hunting. I had been on the borders of a virtually unexplored land inhabited by dangerous, untouched tribes…I had felt the lure of the unexplored, the compulsion to go where others had not been*'. For analogous expressions, see Thesiger (1988: 164–165, 363, 398).

8 This shared methodology extends to the perception concerning the unimportance of acquiring a detailed knowledge about the context to be visited. Thus, for example, Naipaul (2007: 51ff.) maintains that, as he was neither informed about politics, nor did he vote, this was an advantage when he came to travel, since he saw everything with a fresh eye. Such an approach, which proclaims ignorance to be a positive attribute, licenses a slide from travel-as-understanding into travel-as-amusement. Fairly predictably, when presented on current television programmes about travel-as-exploration, this process of 'passing through' has metamorphosed into a branch of entertainment, insofar as its object becomes a form of trial by ordeal (along the lines of 'how far can you go, how much can you endure') that is opened up to a voyeuristic gaze. The extent to which such a shift has been naturalized is evident from a comment by one travel writer, made in the course of the BBC Radio 4 programme 'Crossing Continents' broadcast on 28 April 2012, to the effect that while 'I write about people, in the old days it was all about answers'. That is, an erstwhile analytical approach to an 'other' place

unlike anthropology, the long-term study of which is designed to be nomothetic, travel literature frequently records no more than the fleeting impressions of the author him/herself.[9] Hence the broad distinction between ethnography as – in theory at least – an objective account (writing about the social organization of the place), and travel writing as a largely subjective endeavour (writing about the 'personal experiences' of the author in the place visited).[10]

The privileging of subjectivity, in travel writing as in anthropology, can be attributed to two factors.[11] The first is the rise of postmodern theory, a

---

has been replaced by a descriptive one (= 'about people') in which inhabitants of a foreign country tend to be portrayed as a species of exotic fauna.

9   The account by Malthus (James, 1966) of his Scandinavian travels at the end of the eighteenth century is in many ways nearer to an ethnography, in the sense of gathering much socio-economic data about the places visited. Unlike long-term participant/observation methods structuring anthropological fieldwork, however, his residence in these locations was of short duration. Some authors deny being either a travel writer or an anthropologist. Thus, for example, speaking of his account of the Marsh Arabs in southern Iraq among whom he travelled during the 1950s, Wilfred Thesiger (2005: xiii) comments that '[a]lthough I was almost continuously on the move this is not properly a travel book, for the area over which I travelled was restricted. Nor does it pretend to be a detailed study of the Marshmen among whom I lived, for I am not an anthropologist nor indeed a specialist of any kind'.

10   The approach of travel writers was captured by two of their most respected practioners. When in China during the mid-1930s, Robert Byron (1991: 272) observed that 'it has been very difficult to reformulate all that information [collected during travel], interspersed with personal experiences'. Just over a decade later, Patrick Leigh Fermor (1968: x) noted similarly of travel writing that '[i]t's ultimate purpose, if it must be defined, is to retransmit to the reader whatever interest and enjoyment we encountered. In a word, to give pleasure'. It is these aspects that are crucial; although 'personal experiences' and things of 'interest' are also a feature of ethnographic accounts, travel writing tends to privilege this subjective element rather more than does anthropology. However, such a component is found in diaries compiled during the course of fieldwork (e.g., Malinowski, 1967). Nevertheless, it should be stressed that this emphasis on the 'self' in the course of a travel account is by no means new, and has long been recognized. Hence the endearing admission by Baretti (1770: vi) that 'my only fear upon this occasion, is, that some want of dexterity in the management of my narratives may justly have subjected me to the charge of egotism, as I am convinced that I have passed too frequently from my subject to myself, and made myself much too often the hero of my own story'.

11   In this connection, two caveats should be noted. First, subjectivity has been present in travel writing before the advent of postmodernism. What is new is the degree to which postmodernism has foregrounded the personal narrative. And second, the element of subjectivity is not wholly negative. As used by Henry James, for example, it

development whereby the self has displaced the 'other' as the focus of discussion. This is a consequence of the fact that postmodernism has cast doubt on the capacity of 'otherness' being an identity about which a non-'other' can speak. An inevitable outcome of being in effect forbidden to discuss 'otherness', therefore, was that the emphasis of travel writing shifted from the 'other' back to the self.

As important in this regard has been, secondly, the rise and increasing role of film and television images in conveying meaning about 'other' places, a process which has made comprehensive and 'pure' description less crucial than it used to be.[12] Now what matters in written accounts is how a place appears to the self, and why, the latter displacing the need for providing a comprehensive catalogue as to what can and should be seen in the course of travel. Accordingly, there has been a transformation in writing about travel, whereby the subjective replaces the objective account: the focus has shifted from a disembodied description covering all aspects of another place to those deemed worthy of discussion by the author him/herself.

Class, Travel and Revolution

Historically, the kind of socio-economic information conveyed by an upper class inhabitant to a visitor from the same class about the locality, and in particular its plebeian components, has taken a number of different forms. On the one hand, it was merely an ideological effect of cosmopolitanism.[13] Thus

---

provides insights that enhance his account of a place visited. The accuracy of one of his observations (Kaplan, 1994: 68) – 'The return to Venice [from the Lido] in the sunset is classical and indispensable, and those who, at that glowing hour, have floated toward the towers that rise out of the lagoon, will not easily part with the impression' – is borne out by my own experience.

12   From the outset, cinema has featured in the debate about social change, and especially the way film images have contributed to the erosion of ethnic and/or national 'otherness'. During the 1920s, for example, Paul Morand in his accounts of travel lamented the impact of film on traditional culture. Hence the following comments (Morand, 1928: 119): 'The cinema – that great leveller of all customs – changed all that; ladies of quality now dress in European fashion. [In Siam, King Rama] composed plays, performances [of which] have managed to preserve some of their old lustre. But, even here, there will soon be nothing left...all young Siamese now prefer [Douglas] Fairbanks to Rama'.

13   There are numerous instances in travel accounts of the view 'from above' concerning plebeian elements in a locality being imparted to an upper class visitor. Thus, for example, Malthus recorded (James, 1966: 172–173) that in his 1799 tour of Norway 'Count Smittau is a great farmer, & talked much of the prejudices he had had to encounter among the peasants; but hoped that now some of them were coming over to his opinions'.

meetings abroad with foreigners of a similar class background resulted on occasion in a somewhat idealized account of the living/working conditions of peasants and workers there.[14] In the account of his tour to Scandinavia, therefore, Malthus frequently records the local opinions of landowners, aristocrats, and merchants, regarding the general absence of economic distress due to high wages received by labour and the success of peasant emancipation.[15]

---

14   This ideological reinforcement worked both ways, of course, in that visitors from the European continent tended to mix – and imbibe opinions from – their counterparts when in England. The effect of this is captured in the following description written by Thackeray (1909: 38): 'The German naturalist made a pleasant excursion in England, and having been very hospitably received, not only by his scientific brethren..., but also by many of the gentry, possessors of handsome houses and parks, kind dispensers of good cheer, he has seen the country in its most agreeable aspect, and writes of it with grateful good nature... It is a fine thing to travel, even in the imagination, through the rich inland counties of England in the cheerful summer-time; to go from one fine house to another, where welcome, plenty, elegance, and kindness await you... There is scarcely any foreign traveller that we know of who has not been duly affected by such things; whose records of them are not, by reflection, pleasant'.

15   That local workers were paid high wages, smallholding peasants were emancipated and well-off, and consequently 'the lower classes of people seem to be in a good state', were themes repeated in the course of interviews conducted by Malthus on his travels throughout Scandinavia (James, 1966: 36, 42, 45, 47, 48–49, 59–60, 62, 72, 173). In one sense this is unsurprising, since the answers were to a line of questioning central to his theoretical interests. At the heart of Malthusian epistemology, therefore, was the following relay-in-statement: a strong demand for labour resulted in a higher standard of living, which in turn led to increased population that might exceed food supply. Such a theory took no account of economic mechanisms – such as unfree production relations, debt and coercion – that a rich farmer or landowner could deploy in order to keep wages down even when a labour shortage existed. The travel diary kept by Malthus (James, 1966: 63–64, 80, 117–118, 133, 164–165) does indeed record the prevalence of institutional forms designed to curb wage increases. His account also dispels the oft-heard canard that peasants and workers always preferred to remain in such working arrangements because they provided them with a guaranteed subsistence, the element of unfreedom notwithstanding. The episode is as follows (James, 1966: 63–64): '...we pass'd thro Count Bernstoff's estate, towards the extremity of which is the Pillar erected to him by his grateful peasants for their liberty. He was the first that emancipated his slaves. When he called them together & told them that they were at liberty to go where they pleased it is said that they beg'd he would let them remain in their former state – he replied, that if they continued in the same opinion after five years were elapsed they should have their wish. When the term was expired, he called them together again and asked them if they chose to return to their former state. With earnest entreaties they beg'd that they might not, acknowledged that they did not at first know the value of liberty; but that they were now about to erect a monument to him...'.

On the other, however, such linkages were also contexts where two other kinds of information were exchanged. First, comparisons might be made by the visitor with the cultural, political and/or economic conditions prevailing in his/her own country. Such information either generated or reproduced concepts not just of national 'difference' but also of relative position occupied in the ideological hierarchy of 'civilization'. And second, fears might be expressed to him concerning grassroots discontent and its potential/ actual impact on the existing socio-economic hierarchy and property relations. This was particularly the case after the revolutions of 1789, 1830 and 1848 in France, when travel accounts displayed upper class anxiety – both at home and abroad – lest peasants and workers in other countries follow a similar path.

Uppermost in the minds of local landed proprietors encountered by Malthus during his Scandinavian travels a decade after the French Revolution, therefore, was the fear of a similar kind of uprising in their own Northern European countries.[16] Combined with this was the frequent assertion by them that, although local peasants had had grievances in the recent past, these had now been addressed and there was no longer a danger of revolution. As revealing is the point made by one landowner: having been 'prevailed upon to disperse', peasants were then persuaded that they had nothing to gain from revolution.[17]

Significantly, this same fear of the revolutionary mob-in-the-street is a subtext to Malthusian theory about the dangers (= undesirability) of population

---

16   'We heard' reports Malthus (James, 1966: 42, 73 note 1, 119, 141) that 'the greatest part of the inhabitants are in politics highly averse to the French'; that the assassination of the Swedish King in 1792 had been 'inspired by the French Revolution'; that support for the latter 'could never be thoroughly extinguished'; and that 'Jacobinical' forms of dress were now forbidden.

17   This viewpoint was put to Malthus (James, 1966: 152) in an entry for 14 July 1799: 'From Count Molk after dinner I heard that when he first came to this government which was about 3 years ago, there were many discontents among the peasants, & much disposition towards the French; but that that spirit was nearly over now since they had heard that the lower classes of people in France had gained nothing by the revolution. They now rejoice at the victories of the English. There was at that time also a little difficulty about corn, & the people assembled in parties, & were not without some trouble, prevailed upon to disperse'. In a subsequent entry, for 21 July, Malthus recorded much the same kind of reassurance, this time from another informant. The latter, described (James, 1966: 175) as 'a gentleman who seemed to be a very sensible and intelligent man' observed that peasant farmers 'are at present contented; which was not quite the case at the commencement of the French Revolution'.

increase.[18] His thesis was that demographic growth, unless checked, outstrips food supply; the former in his view could – and should – never be allowed to exceed the latter.[19] The reason for this was that, were food resources to fall behind population growth, the resulting hunger, poverty and social distress would inevitably generate antagonism towards rulers, and thus fuel the discontent leading to revolution.[20]

II

The forging of a specifically British national identity, subsuming 'Englishness', over the period from the eighteenth century to the early nineteenth, has been attributed to the politically unifying role of war with France.[21] Although true in part, this fails to explain a number of significant transformations, and in particular how it was not just war, but more importantly *class* war – both at home and abroad – that informed this emerging British nationalism. That nationalism is reinforced by external threat is a commonplace; what has to be explained

---

18   Information gathered in the course of his 1799 Scandinavian travels was incorporated by Malthus into later editions of his main work on population (Malthus, 1890).

19   Among other things, this thesis led Malthus (1890: 485–486, 552ff.) to oppose Poor Laws: not for a progressive reason – that such legislation was demeaning and oppressive – but rather because in his opinion even the minimal subsistence provided enabled a population to survive beyond the 'natural' limits imposed on it by the accompanying level of food supply. It is hardly surprising that the Malthusian thesis about population dynamics is widely perceived as a thinly-disguised variant of social Darwinism that licenses current *laissez faire* economic theory.

20   The following quotation underlines this connection (Malthus, 1890: 472): 'The pressure of distress on the lower classes of people, together with the habit of attributing this distress to their rulers...is the reason why every free government tends constantly to destruction... While any dissatisfied man of talents has power to persuade the lower classes of people that all their poverty and distress arise solely from the iniquity of government, though, perhaps, the greatest part of what they suffer is unconnected with this cause, it is evident that the seeds of fresh discontents and fresh revolutions are continually sowing... A mob, which is generally the growth of a redundant population goaded by resentment for real sufferings, but totally ignorant of the quarter from they originate, is of all monsters the most fatal to freedom'.

21   This is the argument made by Colley (1992), for whom 'British-ness' emerged from 'the major threats their nation faced from without'. In regarding nationalism *per se* as progressive, Colley is in line with the cultural turn of the 'new' populist postmodernism, which similarly regards ethnic/national identity as progressive/desirable, and thus politically unproblematic.

is the role of class formation and struggle – internal as well as external – in this process, a contributory factor that unfortunately many recent historical analyses of nationalism eschew.[22]

For this reason, such analyses tend to conceptualize nationalist ideology as uniformly empowering or disempowering for this or that national group, rather than particular classes within the latter. Hence the importance of understanding why the ideological formation of the landowning class in Britain, which was initially cosmopolitan and exclusive in outlook, became inwardly focused and thus nationalist and inclusive – that is *populist* – in character.[23] A crucial indicator of this transformation was the Grand Tour, and its role in the construction of aristocratic 'distinction'.[24]

---

22 Recent analyses that conceptualize struggle mainly in national terms as distinct from those of class include not just Colley (1992) but also Anderson (1983), Hobsbawm (1990), Davies (1999), and Miles (2005).

23 The fact of this transformation, together with its remedy (= 'become popular'), is captured by one analysis (Bulwer Lytton, 1836a) of the way in which England and 'Englishness' were changing at the beginning of the nineteenth century. Noting the aloofness of one aristocrat who 'used to carry his eyes and nose in the air, never looking on either side of him', Bulwer Lytton (1836a: 178, original emphasis) remarks that now this same person 'looks round him with a cordial air, casts a frequent glance to the opposite side of the street...stops short, his face beaming with gratulation, shakes them by the hand [and says:] "recollect, my dear sir, I'm entirely at your service." All this is very strange! What can possibly have wrought such a miracle in [the aristocrat]? I will tell you; [he] *has now got constituents*'. The same source continues (Bulwer Lytton, 1836a: 179–180, original emphases): 'It is a profound observation in an Italian historian, that the courtesy of nobles is in proportion to the occasions imposed on them by the constitution, of mixing among the people... The great events that have taken place have shaken the surface of the Aristocratic Sentiment too roughly, to allow it easily to resume its former state. Fashion cannot for many years be what it has been. In political quiet, the aristocracy are the natural dictators of society, and their sentiments are the most listened to...in agitated times, the people rise into importance, and their sentiments become the loudest and most obtrusive; the aggregate of *their* sentiments, as we have seen, is Opinion...the aristocracy unconsciously follow the impulse, and *it becomes the fashion to be popular*'.

24 The concept 'distinction' refers to a range of perceptions and behaviours that confer on a particular class its 'otherness', as recognized both by itself and by those who do not belong. These incorporate practices as various as title (official rank), educational institution(s) attended (school, university), occupation and/or property (especially land), income (size and sources), linguistic codes (gestures, pronunciation, slang), what might broadly be called 'taste' (frequently termed 'cultural preferences'), and any specific 'lifestyle' forms – such as the Grand Tour – that are built into this by custom. For an analysis of 'distinction' as it applies to the French bourgeoisie, see Bourdieu (1986). Samuel Laing accurately captures the extent to which the Grand Tour had by the mid-nineteenth

Civis Romanus Sum, *or Travel and Internationalism*

From its beginnings in Tudor times, the Grand Tour undertaken by members of the English landowning class served – among other things – to establish a sense of affinity with those of an equivalent position in continental Europe.[25]

---

century lost its role in the formation of aristocratic 'distinction'. His observations (Laing, 1850: 1–3) about this change merit quotation at some length: 'What a world of passengers in our steamer! Princes, dukes, gentlemen, ladies, tailors milliners, people of every rank and calling, all jumbled together. The power of steam is not confined to material objects. Its influences extend over the social and moral arrangements of mankind. Steam is the great democratic power of our age; annihilating the conventional distinctions, differences, and social distance between man and man, as well as the natural distances between place and place. Observe that high and mighty Exclusive, sitting all by himself on the bench of the steamer's quarter-deck, wrapped up in his own self-importance and his blue travelling-cloak lined with white, and casting his looks of superiority around him. He is an English gentleman, no doubt, of family and fortune. What a great personage this I-by-myself-I traveller would have been in the days of postchaises-and-four and sailing-packets! Now, in the steam-boat, not a soul, not even the ship-dog, takes the least notice of his touch-me-not dignity. He looks grand, he looks my lord, in vain. Worse than want of respect is this want of notice at all, the being absolutely overlooked. The dinner-bell rings, and down must this great personage scramble with the rest of us; must eat, and drink, and carve, – and ask, and help, or be helped, – and talk, listen, and live, with the other passengers, or go without dinner, and starve; and nobody cares, or puts himself out of the way, for him. His grocer's clerk, perhaps, or his tailor's heir-apparent, outshines him; or, it may be, puts down, in a cavalier tone, his assumption of superiority in the hail-fellow-well-met circle of passengers who are whisked along by this democratic power of steam, at equal pace and equal price, with equal rights and equal consideration'.

25   On this, see Brennan (2004: 9), who attributes this process to a broad desire on the part of the English aristocracy, following religious disputes and schisms, not to be excluded from European 'intellectual and cultural wealth'. 'At the heart of this early Tudor development of a growing belief in the educational and career enhancing efficacy of scholarly peregrination and tourism' observes the same source (Brennan, 2004: 12), 'lay a recognition of the direct links between political power and ostentatious cultural fecundity... To this end, Dudley [Earl of Warwick and Duke of Northumberland] dispatched the architect and artist John Shute on a kind of scholarly fact-finding trip to Italy, with a special brief to examine contemporary Italian interest in classical antiquity and its impact upon continental architectural design'. This periodisation is consistent with the claim by Stoye (1952: 454), that 'the origins of the Grand Tour have been assigned here to a period very considerably earlier than that popularly associated with its heyday, the age of the eighteenth-century oligarchy, because they properly belong to the period when that oligarchy first moved boldly into the centre of the political scene. The usual itinerary of the traveller simply became a means of educating the English gentleman for whatever part he chose to play in later life: he was freeing himself abroad as well as at home and fashioning the convention which suited him best'.

The basis for this was a process of ideological formation influenced in particular by a wider and more general cultural espousal of classical antiquity, regarded as a shared history and educational resource which rulers of separate nation states might legitimately invoke and incorporate into their own discourse.[26] This was one reason why Italy featured so prominently in the itineraries followed by members of the English landowning class.[27] By its very nature (cost, leisure, time), such discourse generated as a result of the Grand Tour was not one in which plebeian elements (peasants, labourers) were either able or expected to participate.[28]

Throughout the sixteenth and seventeenth centuries, this kind of cultural cosmopolitanism was not only the effect of mixing with other foreigners from similar upper-class socio-economic backgrounds, but also crucial to career

---

26   Among the aspects of classical antiquity which formed a common European cultural heritage were its art literature, architecture, customs, traditions, and – not least – its language. These in turn informed the subsequent claims underwriting colonial expansion: namely, the imparting of a civilizing influence to conquered populations. As noted in Chapter 7, it was precisely a shared appreciation of a Latin ode by Horace that established an affinity (= 'mutual belonging') between Patrick Leigh Fermor and General Kreipe, notwithstanding their being enemies during the 1939–1945 war.

27   In answer to his own question '[w]hy were the English so much interested in Italy?', Lytton Sells (1964: 232–233) replies: 'Italy was a land of superior culture and home of the most refined and civilized of peoples. In that land stood the monuments of ancient Rome which evoked in the traveller's mind the heroic days of the Republic and the sensational days of the Empire, the poems of Virgil, Horace and Ovid... The world these studies conjured up...to some travellers seemed more real than the contemporary world'.

28   The extent and form of national ideology among the plebeian elements of the population is difficult to gauge. During the mid-eighteenth century one travel account (Baretti, 1770: 63–64, 65–66) reports that in England '[t]he low people all over the kingdom seem to think that there are but two nations in the world, the English and the French; and he must be a Frenchman who is not an Englishman. Then they know something of a sea-faring people called the Dutch, for whom they have the greatest contempt. But talk to them of other nations; of the Italians for instance: They have heard something of the Italians; but a'n't the 'Talians French? What are they? Have they any bread to eat, or beer to drink, like the English?... Excusing therefore their rudeness to strangers, and their contempt for other countries, (into which contempt they are betray'd by many of their daily scribblers, who are incessantly reviling all other countries;) the populace of England is far from being so hateful as strangers are apt to think a little after their arrival in London'. As at many other historical conjunctures, however, who was deemed 'other', and why, was an identity formed by 'many of their daily scribblers, who are incessantly reviling all other countries'.

advancement in the public/diplomatic service of the nation.[29] Thus, for example, Michel de Montaigne, who came from a wealthy landowning family in France, and visited Italy, Germany and Switzerland during the late sixteenth century, observed that 'I look upon all men as my compatriots, and embrace a Polander with as sincere affection as a French man, preferring the universal and common tye, to all national tyes whatever'.[30]

No less a personage than Francis Bacon, the Lord Chancellor of England, counselled the importance of foreign travel to the educational process, and its necessity for the cultural formation of those among the upper class who could afford to go on the Grand Tour.[31] His advice about the dissemination of such culture, and the way it should bring to bear its influence, is equally significant. Culture acquired as a result of travel abroad was to be adopted on return home, but incrementally; it should be displayed by the traveller in the course

---

29   Hence the observation (Brennan, 2004: 16) that '[b]y the late 1570s…the essential concept of educational tourism for highly privileged young Englishmen was firmly established as a means of training a self-selecting court élite in international affairs and cosmopolitan culture'. This is confirmed for the subsequent era (Stoye, 1952: 25, 26), when 'the Stuarts in due course created in Whitehall an imitation of contemporary European practice…travel often moulded the careers of who rose to greater importance, occasionally becoming high officers of state'.

30   For this view, see Montaigne (1875: 774). It is clear from his account of travel in Switzerland, Germany, and Italy, that he (Montaigne, 1903, I: 14) subscribed to a landlord pastoral version of the agrarian myth, since '[n]othing that Montaigne saw in his travels seems to have given him more pleasure than the sight of exquisite cultivation of the plains and hillsides in Italy and the consequent well-being of the *contadini*'. The account of a tour through north-western Europe at the start of the sixteenth century by Antonio de Beatis is described (Hale, 1979: 42) as 'almost free from national prejudice [and] dispassionate and objective'.

31   This link between travel and the cultural formation of the landowning class is also underlined by Stoye (1952:27): 'From the classes of substantial gentry there were elder brothers and cousins and friends of diplomats and secretaries, who came from and returned to assured properties in the English countryside'. The same source (Stoye, 1952: 456, 460) concludes: 'Travellers abroad naturally take with them impressions of home, and they are what their country has made them; therefore they reflect English social and political development. As travellers returning, they have something positive to contribute. Very simply, they bring Knowledge. It may be a working acquaintance with continental politics, continental languages, continental fashions in dress, music, amusements and building. An impression of these things helps to form an educated public… If English society was very much a local growth at this time, because there had been little immigration except in London and East Anglia, its governing class at any rate managed to acquire a reasonable familiarity with the wider world of Western Europe'.

of discussion and not merely in clothing and gesture, thereby gradually absorbing it into 'the customs of his own country'.[32] In short, members of the English landowning class whose cultural formation was acquired in part as a result of the Grand Tour should not seek to displace existing national identity and discourse, but rather to make what they had learned become part of this.[33]

From the late sixteenth to the mid-seventeenth century, the cultural influence on the English ruling class of themes from classical antiquity acquired in the course of the Grand Tour was displayed most clearly in the development of the landscape garden.[34] Incorporating concepts of Nature drawn from literature and painting, the English garden embodied the pastoral variant of the landlord version of the agrarian myth: a landscape depicted as peaceful, harmonious and unchanging, an image consistent with a discourse about benevolent landed proprietorship.[35] This ideology projecting what was a constructed

---

32   Arguing in 1625 that '[w]hen a traveller returneth home, let him not leave the countries where he hath travelled altogether behind him', Bacon (1755: 55) advised further that 'let his travel appear rather in his discourse, than in his apparel or gesture; and in his discourse let him be rather advised in his answers, than forward to tell stories: and let it appear that he doth not change his country manners for those of foreign parts; but only prick in some flowers of that he hath learned abroad into the customs of his own country'.

33   This was also true of John Evelyn whose diaries recorded his account of European travel during the 1640s and 1650s. According to Brennan (2004: 53), 'Evelyn was also very much concerned with the importation of classical and continental architectural traditions into England...[he] hinted at his own vision of a post-Restoration England which was to be reconstructed in no small measure by those who had travelled widely on the continent, especially in Italy, during the English Civil War...England should remake itself...in the image and likeness of the ancient Roman empire and its modern continental adaptations'. As Stoye (1952: 458) points out, however, this process was grounded ideologically in an earlier period: '...that special quality of life often associated with the Restoration and compounded by historians from the diaries of Pepys and Evelyn...does not owe too much to the new court and the returned cavaliers; it owes even more to the steady stream of travellers over sixty years'.

34   Hence the view (Hunt and Willis, 1975: 11, 12): 'The most powerful literary influence [on theory about landscape] was undoubtedly the celebration of rural life by Virgil and Horace: the *topos* of "*beatus ille*", the happy man, whose contentment was attributed to his rural dwelling and his virtuous, even pious, appreciation of the harmonious scheme of nature and its benevolent creator...the traditions of classical literature came from seventeenth century painting...Claude and Poussin, French artists working in Italy, could be taken as reliable illustrators of Virgil, and their visual authority joined literature as precedent and endorsement of the new gardening'.

35   'Nature's capabilities and potentialities were fully realized in accordance with the rules set by her artistic interpreters in Italy', observe Hunt and Willis (1975: 13, 15, 23), adding

landscape as a 'naturally-occurring' phenomenon served to disguise two things. First, that an additional benefit of the Grand Tour was economic: landlords returned from abroad with knowledge about how to improve agricultural technique. And second, the expansion in rural estates enabling the construction of these landscape gardens was itself dependent on the process of enclosure.[36]

Aristocratic Distinction as 'Fixed Sentiment'

A cosmopolitan ideology drawn from classical antiquity, and acquired as a result of the Grand Tour, was consolidated in the course of the eighteenth century.[37] This took two forms, one negative or exclusionary and the other

---

that 'landscape painting influenced men's thinking about natural scenery; it shaped their responses and gave them a vocabulary with which to articulate their experience of the new gardening... The country estate gave local form to various souvenirs of the Grand Tour. The proprietor of taste repeated the lessons of Europe as best he or his advisers could, prompted by the collections he had made abroad: paintings, engravings, sculpture, views of...famous places, folios on architecture, especially villas and gardens, books on classical antiquity that might contain prints of supposed sites of events first encountered in Roman literature, sketches by visiting Englishmen'. Such classical landscapes included temples and sculptures because 'the authority for much architectural design was antiquity, mediated by Italian Renaissance theory and practice'.

36   'The fortunes of the English landscape garden owed as much to practical matters as to aesthetic pursuits', note Hunt and Willis (1975: 17–18), since 'the English milord also returned from his Grand Tour with trees, flowers and shrubs, and even hints on how to improve agricultural technique. His economic solvency depended on taking agriculture and silviculture seriously...farming methods were radically improved, and drainage, fertilization and crop rotation were introduced. The success, in fact, of the English garden owed much to the fact that in the early 1700s there were huge estates, mainly due to the development of the enclosure system, awaiting exploitation. Evelyn's *Sylva* (1664) had advised landowners to adorn their demesnes "with trees of venerable shade and profitable timber"'.

37   For the importance to the formation of aristocratic discourse in the eighteenth century of a classical education, see Newman (1987: Chapter 1). About the cosmopolitan dimension of aristocratic culture, together with the significance of its consolidation, David Hume (1817: 199) observed that 'where any set of men, scattered over distant nations, maintain a close society or communication together, they acquire a similitude of manners, and have but little in common with the nations amongst whom they live'. Writing in the 1930s, Karl Mannheim (Wolff, 1971: 335) noted similarly that '[a] necessary phase in the acquisition of "cultivation" in the humanistic sense is the "grand tour" or educational trip. One has to go to Italy and Greece to see the monuments of classical antiquity...a practice described unconsciously serves a very definite purpose. This consists of providing a common universe of communication among the different sectors of the cultivated élite as

positive/inclusive. The negative variant entailed the risk of social exclusion from one's position in the class hierarchy, where the relevant cultural formation was deemed insufficient or absent. Whilst on a visit to Italy in 1765, therefore, Boswell – to his obvious chagrin – was frequently chided by the tutor of an aristocrat travelling in the same group with his own lack of knowledge.[38] That Boswell should have been so concerned about this accusation is unsurprising: such cultural deficiency, it was inferred, posed questions about his right to move in these social circles.

By contrast, the inclusive variant – the reproduction of class ideology and behaviours – can also be illustrated with reference to Boswell. In the course of travelling in Prussia a year earlier, he admits to 'a powerful impulse to throw myself at [the] feet' of its King, Frederick the Great.[39] Accepting that 'I am truly the old Scottish baron; I might have said the old feudal baron', Boswell confesses that 'I am haughty towards the tenants on my estate [but] for a superior like the King of Prussia I have prodigious veneration'. He then declares '[d]o not reason with me', adding '[w]hat I am describing…is a fixed sentiment [and] sentiments firmly impressed have much more power than arguments proved to the hilt', concluding that 'it is to sentiments that I always return'. Accordingly, what a landowning aristocrat on the Grand Tour regarded as the 'natural' social order asserted itself abroad, no less than at home: class – both above and below – determined whom he met and how he behaved ('haughty' or 'prodigious veneration'), aspects which for him constituted 'fixed sentiments' beyond rational challenge.[40]

---

differentiated from the mass. To have made the grand tour was the entrance ticket to this select circle'.

38   The words addressed to Boswell by Paul Henri Mallet, the tutor to Lord Mountstuart, were as follows (Brady and Pottle, 1955: 97): 'You know no one branch of learning. You never read. I don't say this to offend you, but of young men who have studied I have never found one who had so few ideas as you…I shall mention among the oddities of my travels that I found a man who had studied little and seen little of the world…' It was a criticism repeated by Mallet subsequently, causing Boswell much annoyance.

39   For this and the following quotations, see the journal entry by Boswell for 31 July 1764 (Pottle, 1953: 43).

40   Newman (1987: 10) observes that Edmund Burke recognized this unifying cosmopolitan discourse as one that stemmed from 'a great range of institutional resemblances between the European states, provided by history and made known through travel…' The same source (Newman, 1987: 12) elaborates: 'In the eighteenth century these unifying tendencies among Europe's upper classes were strengthened into important forces by a marked expansion of international communication and travel, by general acceptance of common standards of genteel speech and manners, and by still other aspects of the aristocratic resurgence which in most countries accompanied these developments. The Grand Tour,

Over the eighteenth century, therefore, a period when landowners increased their wealth by extending their properties at the expense of the commons, foreign travel contributed to the formation and consolidation of a cosmopolitan ideology among the European aristocracy, a process reinforced by a common language (French), code of behaviour, and social networks (friendship, kinship, marriage).[41] The extent to which this was so is revealed by the cargo of a ship, *The Westmorland*, carrying items collected by aristocratic travellers on the Grand Tour, *en route* from Italy to England in 1779.[42] Contents of the armed merchantman, captured by the French, included numerous crates of paintings, prints, statues and books; the latter were marked 'PY', identifying them as part of *Presa Ynglesa* ('The English Prize'), sold on in Madrid to form the core of the Real Academia in the early 1780s.[43]

Such attempts to broaden the culture of the ruling class, however, and make it more cosmopolitan, did not go unchallenged, either in England or in continental Europe.[44] During the seventeenth century, reaction against this process

---

an established feature of English aristocratic education by mid-century, was mirrored in the *"voyage de gentilhomme"* pursued by well-born French, German, Italian, Russian, Spanish and Polish youths as they crisscrossed Europe, often for periods lasting more than three years, spending princely sums, visiting foreign courts, cities, family homes, and salons'.

41 According to Newman (1987: 13): 'The institutionalization of foreign travel, the development of international friendships and marriages, the acceptance of French and the language of international communication, the propagation through the great courts and through dozens of published manuals of a single system of deportment, the tendency to extend formal recognition to foreign noblemen...all of these tendencies [were] working together to promote a single aristocratic civilization throughout Europe'.

42 Hence the observation (Sánchez-Jáuregui and Wilcox, 2012: 27) that '*The Westmorland* presents us with a time capsule from 1779, a window into the art market and the collecting culture of the Grand Tour at a very precise moment. The frequent recurrence in the crates of copies of certain works of art in various painted and printed forms suggests that acquisitions were made according to a tacit canon of masterworks, promoted by the many guidebooks in circulation, popular art treatises, and dealers'.

43 The connection between aristocratic cultural 'distinction' and travel is evident from the description (Sánchez-Jáuregui and Wilcox, 2012: 55) of the cargo as reflecting an 'antiquarian view of art and antiquities [which] linked collecting to the accumulation of expertise'. Despite considerable pressure exercised by their original owners, none of these items were ever returned them.

44 At the English Court, cosmopolitan life was said to have 'upset' conservatives and Puritans (Stoye, 1952: 25). Over time this changed, since those who travelled on the continent were linked to the 'substantial gentry' (Stoye, 1952: 27), and because 'the idea that Experience by Travel completed the process of academic education in school and university, the

on the part of the English conservative gentry – who perceived the influence of foreign travel as 'dangerous, heretical and immoral' – failed to dissuade their offspring from venturing abroad.[45] Similar challenges to the purpose of the Grand Tour, in the name of nationalism, pointing out that what was on offer culturally in other countries was no better than that currently available at home, were evident in eighteenth century France.[46] Why travel abroad to admire the cultural achievements of others, so the argument went, when the equivalents at home were just as good. Significantly, this criticism of the Grand Tour was made by a member of the French aristocracy, suggesting that a nationalist turn – towards a culture that was indigenous in origin – came not 'from below' but rather 'from above'.

A Mere Brute Physical Force

Until the 1789 French revolution, therefore, the Grand Tour was an integral aspect of the cultural formation in Britain of its landowning class.[47] This process involved travel abroad (Paris, Rome, Venice), where a common set of experiences – the appreciation of music, sculpture, architecture, and painting – were accumulated that qualified its subject to participate in

---

sixteenth and seventeenth centuries raised a formidable literature which finally overbore conservative opposition'.

45   'What substitute was there at home for learning and becoming acquainted with the amenities of life in France and Italy?', asks Stoye (1952: 28), who then observes: 'Conservative gentry had a ready answer to such a question: foreign practices were dangerous, heretical and immoral, but in the course of time they spoke with less and less conviction on the point, and their sons were less disposed to believe them'.

46   Hence the following account reported by Lacroix (c.1876: 436): 'The Marquis de Pezay thus condemns what he calls the ridiculous mania of sending new-fledged collegians to travel: "Some schoolboy, who has never looked up at the statues in the Tuileries gardens, posts off to Utrecht to admire some very inferior ones in the gardens of Mme. Termer. Another, who has never seen the King's cabinet, gapes open-mouthed at Bâle before the shop-window of Bernouilli the apothecary, at six pairs of models, two agates, and a piece of coral. A Frenchman ought at least to be acquainted with the Louvre colonnade before he goes to kneel in the squares of St. Peter at Rome and St. Sophia at Constantinople."'.

47   According to Redford (1996: 14) 'the Tour can be seen to fall into four phases: a period of growing popularity, from about 1670 to 1700; a heyday, extending from about 1700 to 1760; a period of gradual decline extending from 1760 to 1790; and a restricted revival, 1815 to about 1835'. The same source attributes its decline at the end of the eighteenth century to a combination of factors. Hence the institutional revival of the public schools and Oxbridge shifted the focus to domestic sources of authority, whilst railways and package tourism enabled the bourgeoisie to travel, and thus deprived the tour of its exclusivity as a marker of cultural 'distinction'.

aristocratic discourse, and thus community.[48] The rural poor encountered in the course of such travel on the European continent were viewed benignly, as impoverished but unthreatening. Its subjects were seen as no more than evidence for an enduring 'natural' order, at the apex of which were located both the local landowner and the traveller from another country.

After the 1789 revolution, however, these same plebeian elements were recast ideologically: from poor and passive to poor and potentially dangerous.[49] This process was itself compounded by the 1848 revolution. In other words, the transformation of the 'cosmopolitan gentleman' into the same class subject whose ideological formation took place 'at home' was in part a response to the making 'at home' as well as abroad of the much-feared mob-in-the-streets.[50] This is one of the reasons why what had been hitherto an identity of

---

48 To this were added a knowledge of history, geography and – in particular – antiquity. The Grand Tour itself is defined (Redford, 1996: 14) thus: '[T]he Grand Tour is not the Grand Tour unless it includes the following: first, a young British male patrician (that is, a member of the aristocracy or the gentry); second, a tutor who accompanies his charge throughout the journey; third, a fixed itinerary that makes Rome its principal destination; fourth, a lengthy period of absence, averaging two to three years'.

49 Of interest was the perceived role of the press in undermining the position of the English aristocracy at that conjuncture (the end of the eighteenth century and the beginning of the nineteenth), by fomenting views (= 'opinion') critical of this class. This was expressed in the following manner (Bulwer Lytton, 1836b: 41–42): 'The influence of the press is the influence of opinion; yet, until very lately, the current opinion was decidedly aristocratic...How has the press become the antagonistic principle of aristocratic power?...By the mere details of vulgar gossip, a great wholesale principle of indignation at the privileged order has been at work; just as in ripening the feelings that led to the [1789] French revolution, the tittle-tattle of the antechambers did more than the works of the philosophers'. This, the same source noted (Bulwer Lytton, 1836b: 43), was because those who wrote for the press did not 'have any dependence on the custom and favour of the great' since they are not 'courted as lions, who, mixing familiarly with their superiors, are...softened by unmeaning courtesies'. An increasing level of political consciousness among those not belonging to the aristocracy meant a change in the balance of political power between classes (Bulwer Lytton, 1836b: 257–258): 'Perfectly right, perhaps, were the statesmen of old in their scoffs and declamations against the people: the people were then uneducated, a mere brute physical force; but the magic of Guttenburg and Füst has conjured a wide chasm between the past and the future history of mankind: the people of one side the gulf are not the people of the other...'. Hence the necessity of the aristocracy having to 'become popular', to court 'the people' and, seemingly, to espouse their concerns and causes.

50 The extent to which the role of the English aristocracy came under political attack during the 1790s, and how this in turn gave rise to a counter-attack, is outlined by Goodrich (2005). Of particular interest is the fact that (Goodrich, 2005: 140–141) 'during the period

class was transformed into an identity of nation; a specifically aristocratic identity based on the acquisition of cosmopolitan 'otherness', a distinctiveness conferred by the Grand Tour, was replaced by an inwardly (= nationally) generated concept of identity. Although not discarded, this cultural distinctiveness, or 'otherness', was relocated and restructured, acquiring thereby an indigenous (= 'English') veneer, important aspects of which could then be said to be shared with plebeian elements in the same context.[51]

1793–1796 one important aim of loyalist writers [defending the aristocracy] was gaining the support of the working people. Many pamphlets were written for a popular audience...fear of revolution at home and invasion from France also prompted loyalists to write pamphlets which attempted to recruit the labouring poor to the loyalist cause. Such fears, together with an abiding fear of French atheism, likewise provoked many Anglican clergymen and evangelical laymen to put pen to paper. Anglican conservative pamphlets, aimed at the people generally, continued to emphasize concepts of political obedience and non-resistance and acceptance of one's place in the social order...'. Others, by contrast, were prepared to sacrifice *a corrupt* aristocracy (*not* aristocracy *per se*) so as to preserve the monarchy, and thus pre-empt a *revolutionary* 'from below' challenge to and overthrow of the whole existing structure. This was the position taken by Bulwer Lytton (1836b: 254–255, 259, original emphasis): 'An aristocracy like ours is, I say, equally hostile to the King's just power and popularity as it is to the welfare of the people...Look again at the history of the states around you; so far from a king deriving strength from an aristocracy, it is the vices of an aristocracy, and not of a monarch, that usually destroy a kingdom; it is the nobles that take popularity from a court...Impatient of the abuses of authority, the people do not examine nicely from *what quarter of authority* the abuses proceed, and they concentrate on the most prominent object the odium which belongs of right to objects more subordinate and less seen. I say that an aristocracy, when corrupted, destroys, and does not preserve a monarchy, and I point to [1790s] France for an example...I deny, then, the assertion of those who term it dangerous to weaken the aristocracy on the ground that by doing so we should weaken the monarchy. [...] Thus, then, neither for the safety of the king nor for that of the people, is it incumbent upon us to preserve undiminished, or rather uncorrected, the Aristocratic power'. What is significant is that both these camps – those defending and those attacking the aristocracy – sought to promote their cause by populist appeals to 'the people', emphasizing how much the political interests of the latter coincided both with their own and with those of the nation.

51   It should be noted that the interpretation adopted here – fear of the plebeian 'mob in the streets' on the part of a landowning aristocracy – is different from the prevailing view accounting for the emergence of a common national identity. Thus Newman (1987: 26ff.) attributes primacy to a process mainly of sanscritization. The latter involved a form of upward cultural mobility on the part of an increasingly wealthy middle class whose access to aristocratic circles was nevertheless blocked. European travel was a method whereby the bourgeoisie sought to emulate those above by acquiring 'distinction'. Whereas emulation locates the impetus for change among the middle classes (= looking

To reproduce their class position, therefore, rural landowners had to develop an identity that transcended that of their own class. This required them to develop a sense of 'self-hood' which incorporated and defined both 'those above' and simultaneously 'those below', in the process becoming an identity that was no longer based on cosmopolitan 'distinction' but rather on existing national elements. It was a shift that enabled a landowning class to identify itself with the nation, so as to position itself at the head of any plebeian agency within this context, and thus control its political direction.

In other words, an unfolding nationalist 'from above' response to the possibility of a 'from below' mobilization that was not only populist but also agrarian in character. Just as it had done for a ruling aristocracy, both the fact of travel and the resulting narratives about this, but now in the domain of popular culture, continued to project 'English-ness', not just 'at home' but increasingly in 'an abroad' that was colonial. In this sense the Grand Tour did not decline, but under the tutelage of a different class subject – the bourgeoisie – continued to play a similar ideological role: the reaffirmation of national identity.

III

Significantly, crucial ideological components of the discourse structuring the agrarian myth – nationalism, populism – were formulated with reference to events and/or circumstances encountered in the course of foreign travel. This can be illustrated with reference to two important travel accounts written either side of the 1789 French Revolution. One is by Johann Gottfried Herder in the late eighteenth century, and the other is by Alexander Herzen in the mid-nineteenth. Of particular interest is the way in which these accounts chart a discursive trajectory, whereby nationalism fuses with populism.[52]

---

upwards), that of populism situates this same dynamic among the landowning class (= looking downwards). The object of emulation is actually an attempt culturally to become like the 'other'; that of populism, by contrast, is seemingly to do so, merely in order to retain the property and wealth that confer 'difference' in class terms.

52 It should be emphasized that a discursive break between nationalism and populism was never absolute, in that many pre-1879 accounts (not necessarily about travel) raised the issue of national sovereignty residing in 'the people' (= king + subjects), while a number of post-1879 ones similarly argued that the monarch should remain the embodiment of national identity (= subjects + king). What was seemingly the element that changed was the relationship between them: as the monarchy appeared to become politically weaker, so 'the people' seemed to become politically stronger. As an historian of nationalism

To Know a Country

Many of the nationalist ideological components that structure the agrarian myth were put in place by Herder, among them the powerful legitimizing discourse about its roots in 'popular culture'. As is clear from his travel diary, Herder formed many of the views about what constituted national 'selfhood' and 'otherness' in the course of a voyage to France undertaken in 1769.[53] The stated object of this journey was to 'win the confidence of the administration, the imperial government and the court, [travelling] through France, England, and Italy with this in mind'.[54] Travel would, Herder argued, enable him to seek ruling class support for his views, and induce the Russian nobility to act on them.[55] In this, he anticipated the cultural nationalism that became

---

(Carr, 1945: 8) has pointed out, a shift of this kind at this particular conjuncture is indeed discernible: 'Frederick the Great still belonged to the age of legitimate monarchy, treated his subjects as instruments of his ambition, despised his native language and culture and regarded Prussia not as a national entity but as his family domain. Napoleon, by posing as the champion and mandatory of the emancipated French nation, made himself the chief missionary of modern nationalism. He was in many senses the first "popular" dictator. Intellectually the transition from Frederick to Napoleon was paralleled by the transition from Gibbon to Burke, or from Goethe and Lessing to Herder and Schiller; the cosmopolitanism of the Enlightenment was replaced by the nationalism of the Romantic movement. The implications of the change were far-reaching. The nation in its new and popular connotation had come to stay. International relations were henceforth to be governed not by personal interests, ambitions and emotions of the monarch, but by the collective interests, ambitions and emotions of the nation'.

53   'During the sea voyage [from Riga to France in 1769] Herder kept a diary, known now as his *Travel Diary (Journal meiner Reise)*, which, however, remained unpublished during his life-time', notes Barnard (1965: xii), adding that '[t]his diary is a most useful documentary source, for it provides the key to his subsequent work'. The *Travel Diary* is reproduced in the collection edited by Barnard (1969: 63–113). Observing that '[t]oday everything is a science', Herder (Barnard, 1969: 88) underlines the importance to him of ideas gained as a result of directly experiencing the 'otherness' of foreign travel: 'I wanted to enlist the aid of travel-books so that I could form an opinion about the countries whose coasts we are passing, as if I had seen the countries themselves; but this too was in vain'. Themes broached in the Travel Diary were explored further in two later essays: his 1770 *Essay on the Origin of Language* (Barnard, 1969: 117–177) and *Yet Another Philosophy of History* (Barnard, 1969: 181–223) in 1774.

54   For this view, see Barnard (1969: 88).

55   Hence the question posed by Herder (Barnard, 1969: 90): 'How would it be possible to persuade the Livonian nobility to support great and good institutions? The nobility of Courland could be approached through Masonic lodges; the Livonians through a sense of honour, the respect due to my cloth, my fame as a scholar, and my usefulness to the province... What a prospect these regions of western and northern Russia will afford, if ever

Slavophilism, and with it makes possible the populist fusion effected later by Alexander Herzen (see below).[56]

Since for him national identity was itself derived from 'the customs of all peoples', Herder condemned the Enlightenment for bringing into question the validity of popular culture.[57] Because elements composing the latter emerge from and are reproduced at the rural grassroots, he argued, and are linked in turn to Nature as it exists in such locations, these aspects of national 'selfhood' are contextually-specific attributes that cannot be imposed on other countries. A corollary of this ideological fix is that these same contextually-specific attributes of a national culture, in turn, cannot be displaced by equivalent grassroots forms of 'selfhood' derived from and constitutive of the cultural 'otherness' in a foreign country.

Accordingly, the theory about national origin as constructed by Herder was necessarily in principle antagonistic to internationalism and its wider identities (law, politics, economics, class, religion) that cut across particular territories. Where a nation existed, so this narrative declared, ideas/institutions/'happiness' derived from a different territory, its people and their culture, had no valid ideological purchase.[58] It is in his travel diary that Herder accurately conveys the sense of the 'otherness' of a country to which he is journeying, and thus of national 'difference' itself, to the extent of disbelieving the evidence of his own eyes.[59]

---

the spirit of culture visits them!... What seeds lie dormant in the spirit of these people [the Slavs] that will give them a mythology, a poetry, a living culture?'.

56   'Would it not prove extremely rewarding', notes Herder (Barnard, 1969: 91), 'to show Russia that she could develop a truly national culture of her own?...Our century is the time for the task...I want to make an attempt in this direction'.

57   'Why', asks Herder (Barnard, 1969: 212), 'finally, drag into every century the story of a partial, derisory lie which ridicules and belittles the customs of all peoples and epochs'.

58   'The general, philosophical, philanthropical tone of our century', notes Herder (Barnard, 1969: 187) disapprovingly, 'wishes to extend "our own ideal" of virtue and happiness to each distant nation, to even the remotest age in history. But can one such single ideal act as an arbiter praising or condemning other nations or other periods, their customs and laws; can it remake them after its own image? Is good not dispersed over the earth?'.

59   According to Herder (Barnard, 1969: 72–73), therefore, 'with what reverence stories are listened to and told on board [ship]! And how strongly a sailor is inclined towards the adventurous element in them! Himself as it were half-adventurer, a man seeking strange new worlds, what fantastic things does he not see at the first startled light? Have I not myself experienced the same on approaching an unfamiliar coast, a new country, or even a particular period in history? How often have I asked myself: is what you saw at first sight actually there?...[w]ith what passion for novelty one approaches the land! How one stares

Such 'otherness' is for him a form of mysteriousness not subject to rational challenge, akin to tales of adventure told by sailors about their sea voyages, the origins of which Herder locates in childhood.[60] Travel animates and reproduces the untutored senses of youth, bringing with it a way of experiencing the world that is 'natural', and in Herder's opinion 'authentic'. Many of his ideas about nationalism, its components and adherents, were redeployed over the nineteenth century by those opposed to the 1789 revolution in France.[61] Nearly a century later, the same kind of arguments surfaced once again, this time embraced by postmodern theorists opposed to Marxist interpretations of economic development. Much like Herder himself, postmodernism not only dismisses the Enlightenment project as Eurocentric and foundational, but also champions indigenous cultural 'otherness' as innate and eternal.

For Herder, therefore, consciousness of what it is to be 'other' is founded on mythical tales (heard in childhood), and as such innate and not open to dispute. From this he draws two conclusions. First, that reason is doomed to failure, since rationality cannot displace the mythological, which is based on 'feeling' as distinct from thinking, and thus privileges the irrational.[62] Hence

---

at the first pilot with his wooden clogs and his great white hat! One thinks that one sees in him the whole French nation... How avid one is for the first face – the first faces – be they only those of old women... How prone one is to form one's first conceptions from a single household, from a few people, and how slowly one reaches the point at which one can claim to know a country!'.

60   'A sailor', observes Herder (Barnard, 1969: 73–74, emphasis added), 'long accustomed to such adventurous tales, believes and spreads them... The result of all this is the emergence of a mentality which finds [these] tales...credible and possible, which repeats such tales, and even believes and recounts them when it no longer finds them possible. Why? Because they were read in youth... *Reason, a later and ephemeral manifestation, cannot destroy the dreams and deepseated beliefs of childhood*'.

61   This took the form of counter-revolutionary support in France for a 'popular monarchy', whereby the king would 'rely on the people rather than on the nobility or the bourgeoisie', a position adopted also by the reactionary Roman Catholic Ultramontane in 1815 (Godechot, 1972: 14, 24). That is, 'making the nation royalist and royalism national', in the words used at that conjuncture by the duc Decazes (Roberts, 1990: 92). Nationalist movements in nineteenth century Europe took their form from popular culture, which linked traditional folklore to concepts of an ethnically homogeneous people residing in a particular territory, and sharing the same language, but also music, crafts, songs, dress, myths, and customs – the whole range of activity that constitutes 'popular culture'.

62   Herder's aim (Barnard, 1969: 74, 80, 82, original emphasis) is nothing less than '[t]o restore the youth of the human mind through true education', an objective possessing 'the germ of a philosophical theory which seeks to explain belief in myths and fictitious stories...it may also discover that all mythologies derive from one common source: the prejudices of

the appeal to him of 'an unspoiled youthful soul, not smothered by abstractions and words'.[63] And second, insofar as national identity is itself rooted in similarly mythological beliefs, it too is not merely innate but also not open to challenge.[64]

The Laws of Crude Primitive Times

In defining what it means to belong to a particular nation, Herder focuses initially on the origin of law (= precedents governing behaviour), and invokes the dichotomy between that based on 'foreign principles' imported from the outside and internal rules deriving from a 'true culture' that consists of indigenous customs.[65] Rejecting the applicability to Russia of 'foreign laws', he argues for regionally-specific codes, reflecting the 'various levels of culture', the 'multiplicity' and 'character' of Russia's nations. This is because some of these 'nations' are 'primitive', a condition to be reflected in their laws; for underdeveloped areas, therefore, codes governing behaviour will be nothing more than 'the laws of crude primitive times'.[66] There can be no universal law, his

---

childhood...one loses one's youth if one *does not use one's senses*'. Recuperating the 'true education' of childhood means privileging 'feeling' over thinking; losing childhood 'feeling', he argues, is to lose also one's senses. This licenses a relay-in-statement whereby youth = myths + stories about travel = the irrational = feeling ≠ rationality.

63   See Barnard (1969: 84, 100), where Herder then laments that with 'our philosophizing about religion, with out too-refined cultivation of reason itself, we are working ourselves into ruin...One must, therefore, refute political thinkers like Diderot...' A principal fear was that Enlightenment discourse would undermine religious belief.

64   Essentializing national identity as a thing-in-itself, Herder (Barnard, 1969: 181, emphasis added) asks 'how then can one survey an ocean of entire peoples, times and countries, comprehend them in one glance, one sentiment or one word, a weak incomplete silhouette of a world? A whole *tableau vivant* of manners, customs, necessities, particularities of earth and heaven must be added to it, or precede it; *you must enter the spirit of a nation before you can share even one of its thoughts or deeds*'.

65   'In what does true culture consist?', asks Herder (Barnard, 1969: 92), and answers: 'Not merely in providing laws but in cultivating morals and customs, especially if the laws are derived from imported foreign principles'.

66   In Herder's opinion (Barnard, 1969: 92–93), 'neither English, nor French, nor German legal minds can legislate for Russia...neither Greece nor Rome can be taken as models...The principles underlying legislation must, moreover, pay heed to the character of Russia's nations, their multiplicity and their various levels of culture: there are regions which are highly developed, but there are also those which are still very primitive or underdeveloped. The laws which the latter need for their development are the basic laws of mankind generally – the laws of crude primitive times. Russia can make excellent use of her underdeveloped peoples...'.

argument continues, because there is no internationally-acceptable philosophy on which to base this.[67] Countering Enlightenment discourse in this manner, Herder laments the passing of a previous 'spirit' (= the 'spirit of valour') and its replacement with a 'commercial spirit', where 'everything is for sale'.[68]

Central to this earlier 'spirit' is language, the origin of which is similarly rooted in small-scale rural communities and a further indicator of the way in which national difference/'otherness' is both innate and specific.[69] According to Herder, language is an effect of sense experience, and thus a natural development which emerges in the context of the kin group, from whence it derives its origin and diversity. As kin groups generate different languages, 'the formation of diverse national languages, therefore, is a natural corollary of human diversity'.[70] The selfhood and 'otherness' which structure national identity are both constituted at the rural grassroots by a process that is doubly 'natural' (= beyond the sphere of rationality): on the one hand by tales heard in childhood, and on the other by language itself, generated from within the kin group.

National identity is for Herder innate, the characteristics of which preceded the Enlightenment era, an earlier period he refers to in ironic mode as a 'primitive age', to be contrasted as such with the achievements claimed by

---

67 Although, like Boswell (see above), Herder held Frederick the Great in high esteem, he nevertheless criticized the King of Prussia for being influenced by French philosophical thought, maintaining (Barnard, 1969: 93–95, 102) that it conferred nothing on the German nation: 'Frederick's and Voltaire's philosophy has spread, but mainly to the detriment of the world... How can the French manner be initiated in German? It cannot...'.

68 Hence the regret expressed by Herder (Barnard, 1969: 95–97) both at the loss in Sweden of 'their very spirit', and at the rise in the Dutch domains of an 'unadulterated commercial spirit which kills or restricts the spirit of valour', adding that 'even now in Holland everything is for sale'.

69 This theme, which emerges towards the end of the travel diary (Barnard, 1969: 107) along the lines of 'the sense and content of speech...what difference there is among nations in their favourite expressions and descriptions, their favourite turns of phrase and their individual modes of thought', is taken up by Herder subsequently in his 1770 essay on language.

70 The causally interrelated laws of Nature are identified by Herder (Barnard, 1969: 158ff.) as follows: first, 'the development of language is as natural to man as his nature'; second, 'Man is by nature a gregarious creature, born to live in society; hence the development of language is both natural and essential for him'; third, this in turn gives rise to 'the formation of a kinship mode of thought'; fourth, '[s]ince the whole human race is not one single homogeneous group, it does not speak one and the same language'; consequently, and finally, '[t]he formation of diverse national languages, therefore, is a natural corollary of human diversity'.

Enlightenment philosophy.[71] The latter, he argued, dismissed all the characteristics of nationalism as 'hatred, hostility towards the foreigner, self-centred parochialism, prejudice, attachment to the soil where one was born and in which one was buried'.[72] Again in ironic mode, Herder labels nationalism as an 'eternal barbarism', and 'national character' as 'native mentality which 'thank God...is no more!'. Continuing in this feigned self-mockery, he seemingly applauds the fact that 'we no longer have a fatherland or kinship feelings', these fundamental aspects of nationalism having been banished by the Enlightenment. Instead, and again in ironic mode, Herder scorns the claim that 'we are all philanthropic citizens of the world', the very cosmopolitanism to which – as an advocate of nationalism – he objects. His final cry, 'National cultures, where are you?', is sarcastic, and aimed directly at Enlightenment discourse.

What Enlightenment philosophy sees as negative traits, however, are for Herder positive ones. Among these are 'prejudice' (see above) and – especially – 'attachment to the soil', an aspect of national identity which unites king and peasant. He defends not only pre-Enlightenment tradition ('the spirit of Nordic chivalry') and religion, but also those forms deemed 'coercive institutions'.[73]

---

71   This point and the following ones – all ironic – are made by Herder thus (Barnard, 1969: 209): 'How wretchedly primitive was the age in which nationality and national character still existed; and with it, hatred and hostility towards the foreigner, self-centred parochialism, prejudice, attachment to the soil where one was born and in which one was buried; a native mentality, a narrow span of ideas – eternal barbarism! With us, thank God, national character is no more!...we no longer have a fatherland or any kinship feelings; instead we are all philanthropic citizens of the world. The princes speak French, and soon everybody will follow their example [in the quest for] the golden age, when all the world will speak with one tongue... National cultures, where are you?'.

72   Taking issue with Voltaire, Herder observes (Barnard, 1969: 191–192): 'We can read of the dark sides of this period in any book. Every classical litterateur who takes our regimented century for the *ne plus ultra* of mankind finds occasion to reproach whole centuries for barbarism, wretched constitutional law, superstition and stupidity... At the same time, he shouts the praises of the light of our century...its warmth in theory... All the books of our Voltaires...are, to the delight of their contemporaries, full of beautiful accounts of how the enlightenment and improvement of the world, philosophy and order, emerged from the bleaker epochs of theism and spiritual despotism'.

73   In what is a panegyric to pre-Enlightenment values and hierarchy, and an attack on the attempt by Enlightenment philosophy to transcend them, Herder (Barnard, 1969: 192) maintains that '[o]ften in these apparently coercive institutions and corporations there was something solid, cohesive, noble and majestic, which we certainly do not feel...with our refined ways...and with our innate cleverness and all-embracing cosmopolitanism. You mock the servitude of these times... You praise nothing so much as the breaking of

This is because, in the opinion of Herder, the 'servitude of [those] times' was 'cohesive, noble and majestic', a situation in which 'master and servant, king and subject, interacted more strongly with one another'. Those described by him as 'men from the North', who despised science but 'respected their gods', adhered to 'good common sense' and 'wild customs', would enter world history in a way that Herder approved.[74] It was these same 'natural' country people and their feudal system who would undermine the cities, by 'providing occupation for men's hands' thereby 'injecting new life into the countryside' and increasing 'happiness'.[75]

Barriers and Turnstiles

Herder makes it clear that one of the main reasons for his critique – if not the main one – is the questioning by Enlightenment discourse of 'authority' and 'the upper classes', a process which in turn has licensed the 'treading under foot' of class and religion.[76] On the question of religious authority, he takes issue with two interrelated Enlightenment challenges: negating the role of God as creator of the world simultaneously denies its cultural diversity, which in turn gives nationalism a theological origin and power. Both Nature and 'natural' humanity are divine creations, therefore, not to be tampered with by the discourse of reason. Maintaining that Enlightenment philosophers who

---

these ties and know of no greater good which ever happened to mankind than when Europe, and with it the world, became free... If only you could realize what these earlier circumstances...did in fact achieve: Europe was populated and built up; generations and families, master and servant, king and subject, interacted more strongly and closely with one another'.

74   Observing that 'a new man was born in the North', Herder elaborated that (Barnard, 1969: 190) 'it was not only human energies, but also laws and institutions, that they [the men from the North] brought on to the stage of world development. To be sure, they despised the arts and sciences...but if they brought nature instead of arts, Nordic common sense instead of sciences, strong and good, though wild, customs instead of elegance, and all of these in a ferment together, what an event it was! Their laws breathed virile courage, dignity, reliance on common sense, honesty and respect for their gods'.

75   'Their feudal system', argued Herder (Barnard, 1969: 190), 'though it undermined the bustling, teeming, wealthy cities, injected new life into the countryside, provided occupation for men's hands, and in doing so, increased their health and happiness'.

76   Herder complains (Barnard, 1969: 219–220): 'How far the genuine, spontaneous esteem for authority, parents and the upper classes has fallen in the world within one century, cannot be expressed. Barriers and turnstiles have been demolished; prejudices, as they are called, of class, education and even of religion have been trodden under foot and even ridiculed to the point of injury: we will all become brothers, thanks to our uniform education,. Agnosticism, enlightenment...'.

cannot understand this project – 'a great divine plan for the whole human race' – nevertheless deny its existence, Herder asks '[w]ho will restore for us the temple of God, which is being built continuously through all the centuries?'.[77]

In his defence of religion, Herder invoked the fact of travel among primitive tribes, which for him confirmed that everywhere people still adhered to religious precepts; for him this constituted evidence for the continuing relevance of religious belief.[78] The target of this argument was Enlightenment philosophy, against which Herder deployed the views advanced by Romanticism. In the name of scepticism (= 'thinking') the discourse of Enlightenment championed internationalism, modernity, rationalism, materialism and secularism. The 'other' of Enlightenment philosophy, Romanticism opposed its espousal of scepticism, rationality, progress, and radicalism; instead, it championed idealism, belief/faith and emotion (= 'feeling'), a discourse supportive both of nationalism and its existing culture and hierarchy (political, religious).[79]

According to Enlightenment philosophy, therefore, rural populations in distant lands were destined to follow a path of development, in the course of which they would discard the kinds of identity Romanticism perceived as unchanging, innate and 'natural'.[80] Along with secularism, it was to this aspect of Enlightenment discourse – not just the desirability but the inevitability of

---

77   For these points, see Herder (Barnard, 1969: 211–212, 214–215, 218), who observes in this connection: 'As a rule, the philosopher is never more of an ass than when he most confidently wishes to play God... He has not considered – this omniscient philosopher that there can be a great, divine plan for the whole human race which a single creature cannot survey, since it is not he, philosopher or monarch of the eighteenth century though he be, who matters in the last resort'.

78   'You will see', proclaims Herder (Barnard, 1969: 218), 'that the bulk of the nations of the earth are still in their childhood, speak the language of childhood, possess its manners and offer examples of its level of culture. Wherever you travel among, and listen to, so-called savages, you hear sounds that illustrate Holy Writ and catch a breath of living commentary upon Revelation'.

79   Privileging feeling and pre-Enlightenment values over thinking and progress, therefore, Herder (Barnard, 1969: 193) maintained both that '[t]he heart and not the head is nourished!', and that '[t]o assume that human destiny is forever marching forward in giant steps...seems to me to be the corollary of our century's pet philosophy'.

80   '[T]he old Gothic structure of freedom, of corporations, of property is cast to the ground and destroyed... Ideas of universal love for humanity, for all nations, and even enemies, are exalted, whilst warm feelings of family and friendship are allowed to decay', observes Herder (Barnard, 1969: 197, 200, 201), continuing: 'A word now about some of the renowned means which are to serve the great creative plan, and the pride of our century: the civilization and enlightenment of mankind'.

social/economic progress, egalitarianism, development and change – that Herder objected. He rejected the view of those who advocated social progress through economic development, arguing that this was not a way of generating more 'happiness'.[81] Progress was neither desirable nor possible, since no change for the better could be effected. Travel was a central emplacement of this case against Enlightenment philosophy, maintained Herder, in that it revealed the innateness and enduring nature of the 'other's difference', and hence confirmed the undesirability and unnaturalness of development/ progress.[82]

Inclinations towards Diversity

Like postmodern theory, which currently labels all forms of actually-existing grassroots discourse as innate and empowering, the 'other' of rationality and Eurocentric foundationalism, Herder perceives the same kind of discourse in much the same way. Because these are part of Nature itself, therefore, rural tradition and culture are perceived as unchanging; as such, this grassroots ideology has to be accepted and indeed celebrated as 'natural'.[83] The political implications, concedes Herder, are that '[a]fter what I have written, I will doubtless be accused of always praising the distant past and of complaining about the present'.[84] His dismissal of Enlightenment philosophy similarly anticipates that currently used by postmodernism: 'I believe the remarks made

---

81   Hence the view (Barnard, 1969: 187) that '[t]hose who have so far undertaken to explain the progress of the centuries have mostly cherished the idea that such progress must lead towards greater virtue and individual happiness. In support of this idea they have... invented the fiction of the "general, progressive amelioration of the world" which few believed, least of all the true student of history and the human heart'.

82   Herder elaborates on this point – travel shows that tribal populations support his case – in the following manner (Barnard, 1969: 218): 'Our travelogues are multiplying and improving: our Europeans find nothing better to do than to run all over the globe in a kind of philosophical frenzy. They collect materials from the four corners of the earth and will someday find what they were least looking for: clues to the history of the most important parts of man's world'.

83   On this point, Herder asks – and answers his own question (Barnard, 1969: 74, 75, 76): 'But is such a credulous person therefore a fool, a stupid ass in every respect? Surely not. Apart from such dreams and delusions, which his occupation, his upbringing, his education and his general habit of thinking have helped to form, he may be a very sensible, capable and intelligent fellow... The common people have a mythology in a thousand things. Is their sense of what is improbable the same as that of the sceptical philosopher or the enquiring scientist?... Every class, every way of life, has its customs'.

84   For this and the following quotation, see Herder (Barnard, 1969: 205).

in this respect are preferable to the gushing, self-congratulatory declamations that one finds in all the books now in vogue'.

Views about the innateness of Nature, and benign but unequal linkages (master and servant, king and peasant) founded on a common 'attachment to the soil' confirm that – like much current postmodern theory – Herder subscribed to the pastoral variant of the agrarian myth. Equally significant in this regard is his endorsement of rural society, because it 'prevented the...unhealthy growth of the cities', combined with an opposition to urbanization ('those slagheaps of human vitality') and economic development.[85] Antagonism to the latter, and support for the former, is expressed in terms both of 'the lack of trade and sophistication prevented the loss of human simplicity', and of an idealization of the pre-Enlightenment class structure (when 'the medieval guilds and baronies engendered pride in the knights and craftsmen').

Locating national origins at the rural grassroots, moreover, validates not just the cultural forms but also the institutional ones encountered there: kinship ideology, peasant family, smallholding agriculture, subsistence economy, social hierarchy are all similarly deemed 'natural' and founded on Nature.[86] That such grassroots forms were regarded by Herder as benign is evident both from the concept 'happiness' applied to them, and from its relativization. Comparison is impossible, he maintains, since individuals occupying different positions in the social hierarchy (monarchs, priests, ploughmen) experience 'happiness' in distinct ways.[87] Much rather such fulfilment is found in the soul/

---

85 Rural society dominated by landlords, avers Herder (Barnard, 1969: 192), 'prevented the luxuriant, unhealthy growth of the cities, those slagheaps of human vitality and energy, whilst the lack of trade and sophistication prevented the loss of human simplicity in such things as sex and marriage, thrift and diligence, and family life generally. The medieval guilds and baronies engendered pride in the knights and craftsmen, self-confidence, steadfastness and manliness in their spheres of activity...'.

86 Hence the view expressed by Herder (Barnard, 1969: 173) that 'nature elected the development of man in society'.

87 For this and the following points, see Barnard (1969: 186–187), where Herder states 'all comparison is unprofitable... Who can compare the shepherd and the Oriental patriarch, the ploughman and the artist, the sailor, the runner, the conqueror of the world? Happiness lies not in the laurel wreath, or in the sight of the blessed herd, in the cargo ship or in the captured field-trophy, but in the soul which needs this, aspires to that, has attained this and claims no more – each nation has its centre of happiness within itself... Mother Nature has taken good care of this. She placed in men's hearts inclinations towards diversity... She has put tendencies toward diversity in our hearts; she has placed part of the diversity in a close circle around us... If, in this development of particular national tendencies towards particular forms of national happiness, the distance between

spirit, which Herder links in turn to national identity: because Nature has made nations different, each one has its own way of finding 'happiness', the realization of which is determined by a people (*volk*) in ways consistent with and inside the boundaries of their own national culture. In keeping with this approach, prejudice is seen by Herder as positive, since it attaches a subject more firmly to the nation.

The cultural nationalism of Herder licensed three political effects: not just opposition to value judgements from outside the nation, and a connection between nation and 'popular' culture, but also the possibility of national sovereignty extending beyond a ruling class. Just who was to compose 'the people', and thus be in a position to participate in the exercise of national sovereignty, therefore became a politically crucial question. The concept of popular sovereignty, in the sense of the right of 'the people' themselves to exercise power, was as yet absent: it would be the next step, formulated by Herzen as the basis of agrarian populism in the mid-nineteenth century.

Like Herzen at a later conjuncture, however, Herder applied the concept 'the people' in an exclusionary manner. For him, therefore, it encompassed only the rural plebeian elements of the nation, its smallholders; excluded from this sense of 'belonging' were the urban proletariat. This in turn gave rise not just to the ideological distinction between peasants (= *Volk*) and workers (= rabble), but also to the insertion of the monarch into the former category ('there is only one class in the State, the *Volk* (not the rabble) and the king belongs to this class as well as the peasant').[88] As 'natural' bearers of the same identity – 'the people' – located in Nature and consecrated by 'popular culture', therefore, King and peasant unite to represent (and defend) the nation. Against

---

nations grows too great, we find prejudices arising... But prejudice is good, in its time and place, for happiness may spring from it. It urges nations to converge upon their centre, attaches them more firmly to their roots, causes them to flourish after their kind, and makes them more ardent and therefore happier in their inclinations and purposes'.

88 On these points see Burke (1981: 217), who argues that in this discourse "'the people" really means "the peasants". As Herder once put it, "[t]he mob in the streets, which never sings or composes but shrieks and mutilates, is not the people". The peasants were seen as the true People because they lived close to Nature and because they were unspoiled by new or foreign ways'. Folksong as a crucial expression of 'popular culture' is outlined by Herder in *Voices of the People in their Songs* (1773). This same folkloric aspect of music, both as the 'voice of the people' and therefore as a way of accessing 'feeling' linked to national 'belonging' was commended by Eduardo Martínez Torner (1924: xiv), a Spanish musicologist, at the start of the twentieth century (*'Es innegable el valor de la música como medio para formación del espíritu'*).

them are deemed to be workers, whose 'otherness' stems from being the 'unnatural' mob-in-the-street (= neither 'the people' nor rooted in Nature).

IV

That the Grand Tour functioned as a site in which the identity of an internal – *not* external – enemy was revealed to the traveller, and further that this process was not confined to Britain, is evident from the case of Alexander Herzen, whose views influenced the development of Russian populism.[89] From a land-owning family, his espousal of Slav nationalism occurred after seeing the effect of the 1848 revolution in Europe, which he did in the course of the Grand Tour. The impact of witnessing such an event on 'people like us, foreign tourists', was for Herzen akin to 'looking idly on while people convulsed by some general madness, run amok and destroy each other in frenzy, while an entire civiliza-tion, a whole world, is collapsing amidst chaos and ruin'.[90]

'Ax-bearing People with Hardened Hands'
Travelling from Berlin to Paris, via Hanover, Cologne and Brussels, the views expressed by Herzen in the course of undertaking the Grand Tour during 1847 reflected his background as a member of the Russian landowning class.[91] Thus, for example, he was pleased that in Germany he was addressed with respect befitting his rank, whilst in France he complained about the lack of deference

---

89   For details of and background to the emergence in nineteenth century Russia of agrarian populism, see among many others the important texts by Hecker (1934), Venturi (1960), Lampert (1965), and Walicki (1969, 1975, 1980).

90   For this description, see Herzen (1956: 71–72, 75). The negative impact of the 1848 revolu-tion on Herzen's optimism about emancipation is noted by Lenin (1963: 26, original emphasis): 'It was this "halt" that caused Herzen's spiritual shipwreck after the defeat of the revolution of 1848. Herzen had left Russia, and observed this revolution at close range. He was at that time a democrat, a revolutionary, a socialist. But his "socialism" was one of the countless forms and varieties of bourgeois and petty-bourgeois socialism of the period of 1848...it was not socialism at all, but so many sentimental phrases, benevolent visions, which were the expression *at that time* of the revolutionary character of the bour-geois democrats...'.

91   Significantly, his earliest letter from Paris in 1847 (Herzen, 1995: 11) records that 'an idle person can have no better life than that of a tourist'. There is a marked contrast between this easy-going attitude borne of his initial stay in pre-revolutionary Paris during the Grand Tour, and his despair at witnessing the events of the 1848 revolution during a later stay in the same city (see below).

shown by servants, 'spoiled' along with workers as result of the emancipatory gains put in place by past revolutions.[92] Parisian workers were regarded by Herzen as benign ('crude plebes') so long as they were quiescent, and did not threaten the existing social order.[93] Nevertheless, his fear was both that 'the mob will remain a mob until it has produced food and leisure for itself', and that conservatives and bourgeois liberals would goad workers into action.[94]

Once in Italy, Herzen's focus shifted, from the potentially revolutionary and therefore dangerous mob-in-the-streets of Paris to pastoral images of the quiescent smallholding peasant proprietor in the countryside.[95] This led him in turn to a comparison with 'our Russian villages, our peasants, whom I used to think about with love in the very South of Italy', and to the conclusion: 'Long live the Russian village, gentlemen – its future is great!'.[96] Like its Italian counterpart, therefore, the Russian peasant was perceived by Herzen as having an 'unbroken strength', a sleeping giant that at some future point might be awakened so as to defend existing property relations in the countryside.[97] The significance of this point emerged subsequently, when Herzen returned to Paris

---

92   On these points, see Herzen (1995: 20, 24–25, 26), who notes: 'Do you know what surprised me most in Paris?...The workers, the seamstresses, and even the servants – in Paris all these common folk are so spoiled...[h]ere it is hard to find a servant who believes in his calling... If you want a foreign servant, take a German; the Germans are willing to serve'.

93   See Herzen (1995: 27, 29, 41). The reason why he approved of workers in Rome was because – unlike their Parisian counterparts – they were seen by him to be non-threatening. Hence the view (Herzen, 1995: 85) that 'the popular movements in Rome have a special character of stately order, of melancholy poetry, like their ruins'.

94   See Herzen (1995: 55ff. 58), who goes on to observe: 'The struggle was obvious and inevitable, its character predictable. The hungry person is savage, but the bourgeoisie defending his property is savage as well'.

95   On entering Italy, therefore, Herzen (1995: 67) notes that '[o]ne thing assaults the eye and makes the Slavonic heart ache – the high stone fences strewn with broken glass...represent a kind of immortalization of exclusive possession, a certain insolent assertion of the right of property'. In keeping with this transformation, he disapproved of the attempt by the French – and in particular French liberalism – to influence the way Italy developed politically after 1789, a move which Herzen (1995: 92–93) noted with satisfaction was rejected by 'people' (= peasants) in Italy.

96   For these views, plus his idealized pastoral images of Italian village life, see Herzen (1956: 17; 1995: 67, 69–70).

97   Once the Russian peasant ceased to be a serf, he would constitute a power in the land which needed guidance and representation (Herzen, 1995: 92, original emphasis): 'The peasant of central Italy is just as unlike a repressed rabble as the Russian muzhik is unlike property...[t]hese peoples have a secret thought or, better, not a thought but an *unbroken strength*'.

in the midst of the 1848 revolution, where his fears about the mob-in-the-streets were realized.[98] It can be argued that, in turn, this lay behind the formulation by him of an alternative path that would avoid the danger of plebeian revolution: agrarian populism.

Herzen's view was that the time of what he termed 'old' Europe was passing, a task that the 1848 revolutions would accomplish.[99] The usual way of interpreting this criticism – by, for example, Isaiah Berlin in his Introduction to the English translation of *From the Other Shore* – is to infer that for Herzen the process of emancipation that he witnessed in 1848 had not gone far enough. The view taken here, by contrast, is that what really concerned Herzen was that it had gone too far, since the combination of the espousal by bourgeois liberals of democratic ideals plus the counter-revolutionary conservative reaction by them and the landowners would open the political door to the urban proletariat and – ultimately – to revolution and socialism.

As an onlooker while the 1848 revolution was taking place in Paris, Herzen recognized the zero-sum nature of class struggle and revolution. Observing that '[t]he slightest concession, act of compassion, mercy, lead back to the past and leave the chains intact', he concluded that '[t]here is no choice – one must either slaughter and go forward or pardon and falter half-way'.[100] It is in the last of his letters, however, that Herzen reveals clearly the identity of the enemy he fears most, together with the reason why the latter must be opposed: '[a]nd here – at the extreme of destruction and calamity – another, domestic, war will begin – the reprisal of the *non-possessing against the propertied*'.[101] A crucial

---

98   This despair is evident from the letter written in June 1848, after having returned to Paris
      (Herzen, 1995: 140): 'More than two months have passed since my last letter. It is difficult
      to continue what I started, for rivers of blood have flowed between that letter and this
      one. Things I never believed could happen in Europe, not even in moments of bitter irrita-
      tion and the blackest pessimism, have become commonplace; they are daily occurrences,
      and no longer surprising'. Following the counter-revolutionary oppression of the Parisian
      workers, Herzen (1995: 143) feared a plebeian mass uprising in revenge: 'I do not know
      whether they will raise the gonfalon of socialism over the Paris stock exchange, but I do
      know that they will take revenge for the June Days... It will be impossible to halt the war
      started by the June Days. All of Europe will be drawn into it'.

99   See Herzen (1956: 167).

100   See Herzen (1956: 49).

101   See Herzen (1995: 198), where this fear of revolution and the urban proletariat is elabo-
      rated in the following cataclysmic manner: 'All Europe will burst its seams, and will be
      drawn into the general devastation; the borders of countries will change, the peoples will
      be united in different groups, nationalities will be broken and assaulted. Cities, taken by
      storm and pillaged, will be impoverished, education will collapse, factories will come to a

aspect of this fear was that an uprising by workers in towns and cities would in turn extend to – and thus 'contaminate' – the countryside, and trigger unrest among the peasantry.[102] As someone from a landowning family, Herzen could not but have been aware of the implications of this possibility for members of his own class.

Bourgeois liberals are blamed by him for having opened Pandora's Box, from which would emerge the much-feared mob-in-the-streets, engaged henceforth in struggle for political supremacy.[103] Conservatives are similarly blamed, but for being unaware that mere physical violence inflicted upon workers would be of itself insufficient to prevent them from taking political power.[104] Neither

---

halt; in the villages it will be empty, the land will remain without hands, as after the Thirty Years War; the weary, driven peoples will submit to everything, military despotism will replace all legality and all administration. Then the conquerors will begin to fight for the spoils. Frightened civilization and industry will flee to England or America, some will carry money with them away from destruction, some science, some the work they had begun'.

102   This concern is expressed in the following manner (Herzen, 1995: 188): 'A heavy storm is rising in the peasant's heart. He knows nothing of the text of the constitution nor of the division of powers, but he looks sullenly at the rich property owner, at the notary, at the usurer; but he sees that no matter how much you work, the profit goes into other hands – and he listens to the worker. Once he has heard him out and understood well, with his ploughman's stubborn firmness, with his fundamental solidity in every action, he will measure his forces, and then will sweep the old social structure from the face of the earth. And this will be the real revolution of the popular masses. It is more than likely that the real struggle of the rich minority and the poor majority will have a sharply communistic character'.

103   On this, see Herzen (1956: 59–60). Elsewhere he describes in apocalyptic terms the struggle that ensues after Pandora's Box has been opened (Herzen, 1995: 194): 'Everything is finished – the representative republic and the constitutional monarchy, freedom of the press and the inalienable rights of man, the public court and the elected parliament... Wherever you look, you sense barbarism: in Paris and in Petersburg, below and above, in palaces and artisans' shops. Who will deal the last blow, complete the affair? The decrepit barbarism of the sceptre or the turbulent barbarism of communism? The bloody sword or the red flag?'.

104   'Revolutionary conservatism', Herzen (1995: 186) argues has a paradoxical outcome: namely, that 'the destruction of the old social forms goes forward thanks to reactionaries and the genuine conservatives'. Where this leads is clear to Herzen (1995: 199): 'Armed communism lifted its head, half jokingly...[t]he proletarian will measure by the same rule as they [the ruling classes] measured him. Communism will rush in stormily, horribly, bloodily, unjustly, quickly. Amid the thunder and lightning, in the glow of burning palaces, on the ruins of factories and offices new commandments will appear, he strongly inscribed features of a new symbol of faith'.

response – democracy espoused by liberals, reaction by conservatives – was in Herzen's opinion an adequate defence against this inevitable outcome: revolutionary upheaval by the urban proletariat, to be followed eventually by a socialist programme and regime.[105]

'Conservatives have Eyes, but they See Not'

Having visited Europe, and seen the impact there of on the one hand liberal democratic ideals, and on the other conservative reaction, Herzen opted instead for a different strategy to pre-empt the emergence of a revolutionary 'mob-in-the-streets'. This took the form of nationalist politics, at the centre of which was an idealized concept of the peasantry based on the agrarian myth.[106] The turn towards the latter, and away from the former, entailed a corresponding negation of cosmopolitanism that had been fostered historically among the upper class by the Grand Tour.[107]

The political role of culture in avoiding the revolutionary seizure of power by an urban proletariat is revealed most clearly when Herzen takes issue with

---

105   According to Herzen, democracy – or 'democratic orthodoxy' (Herzen, 1995: 185) – was no better than reaction, in that both fuelled working class aspirations for political power. 'In some parts of Europe', therefore (Herzen, 1956: 62, original emphasis) people 'cannot be really free, really equal as long as *this* civic framework exists, *this* civilization survives. All intelligent conservatives have known this, and that is why they support the old order with all their strength. Do you imagine for one moment that Metternich and Guizot did not see the injustices of the social order that surrounded them? ...The liberals, on the other hand, have unleashed democracy and yet still want to return to the old order. Which of the two is nearer the truth? In fact, of course, all of them are wrong...' His fear as to what might happen as a result of democracy is made equally clear elsewhere, when he (Herzen, 1995: 186, original emphasis) warns against 'a glimpse of the *red phantom* in the window...the Medusa wearing a Phrygian cap', the result of which would be that 'the arches cracked, and the columns were beginning to sway; arson fires, heads on pikes, ax-bearing people with hardened hands' would appear.

106   'If you were well acquainted with the inner life of France', counsels Herzen (1956: 94–95), 'you would not be surprised that the people want to vote for [Louis-Napoleon] Bonaparte, and you would know that the French people have not the faintest notion of freedom, of the Republic, but they have bottomless national pride'.

107   About following the pattern of European development, therefore, Herzen (1956: 199) expressed the following scepticism: 'Your history...the history of the West, provides us with certain lessons, but no more: we [Slavs] do not consider ourselves the legal executors of your past....[t]he only element of tradition that we accept in is that involved in our organic, our national way of life: and that is inherent in our very being: it is our blood, it acts upon us more like an instinct...' The only aspects from European history that Herzen wants Russia to follow is an instinctual form of nationalism, based on blood.

Donoso-Cortes, a Spanish aristocrat who, as an ultra-conservative, advocated a return to all the values and ideals of a Catholic Europe in the Middle Ages. Noting that Donoso-Cortes 'wants to avert the terrifying future by withdrawing into the impossible past', Herzen agrees with the analysis but not with the solution.[108] The latter, he suggests, involves encouraging the reproduction in the countryside of a somewhat different form of 'otherness' – one the identity of which is national/ethnic/peasant – that would serve to counter the emergence of an urban proletariat and its revolutionary political programme. In order to survive as a landowning class, Herzen seems to be saying, it will be necessary to mobilize peasant smallholders along cultural lines that we do not share, but which will nevertheless ensure our own economic security.[109]

Why Russian peasants were thought by Herzen to be ripe for mobilizing is not difficult to discern. The impending abolition of serfdom – a little over a decade away – meant that the allegiance of emancipated smallholders would soon become a political issue in Russia. It was an attempt to harness this, thereby avoiding a socialist transition effected by the urban plebeian and ensuring their own survival, that explained why members of the landowning class so readily supported agrarian populist ideology.[110] The belief that the

---

108 Donoso-Cortes, agrees Herzen (1956: 154), 'has diagnosed with unusual accuracy the present terrible condition of the European states: he has seen that they are on the edge of an abyss, on the eve of an unavoidable, fatal cataclysm. The picture he draws is terrifying in its truth'. Herzen (1956: 155–156) then criticizes the conclusion drawn by Donoso-Cortes, who 'is convinced that the present forms of social life, as they have developed under the influence of Roman, German, Christian principles, are the only possible ones. As if the ancient world and the contemporary Orient did not present us with examples of social life based on quite different principles, perhaps lower, inferior, but extremely secure!'.

109 Hence the following view (Herzen, 1956: 156–157): 'We agree with Donoso-Cortes that Europe, as she is today, is crumbling away. From their first appearance socialists have constantly said this; on this they all agree. The chief differences between them and the political revolutionaries is that the latter wish to correct and improve the existing order, preserving the old foundations, whereas socialism completely renounces the old order... Such a renunciation is...the death sentence of this society, the premonition of the end... [t]he contemporary state will fall before the protest of socialism'. About this he concludes: 'To stop the fulfilment of a particular destiny is to some degree feasible'.

110 According to Lampert (1965: 14) most landowners in 1860s Russia were 'intensely suspicious of anything that might serve to strengthen the differentiation and industrialization of Russian society, because such tendencies uprooted the peasantry, destroyed primitive simplicity, and snapped the "organic" ties of tradition, deference, and obligation...[in their view] maintenance of "organic" relations between landowner and peasant...would somehow preserve the Russian soul from being corrupted by the disruptive, constricting, and formalizing spirit so powerful in the bourgeois society of western Europe'.

socio-economic distinction between peasant and landowner was anyway insubstantial led Herzen both to think that the former would accept the leadership of the latter, and to declare '[t]he future of Russia lies with the moujik'.[111]

Outside the law, unprotected and thus a passive opponent of the State and 'the existing order of things', the peasant sought 'instinctively' to defend only his locality and the village commune.[112] Furthermore, the latter unit 'has nothing to fear from communist ideas', the inference being that the village commune performed the role of a bulwark against two potential/actual threats: the influence of European 'civilization' (= capitalism) bringing discontent (= revolutionary proletariat) in its wake, and thus a challenge to existing property relations in the countryside.[113]

Building on the views expressed by Herder, and anticipating the ideas of Henri Bergson and Georges Sorel, Herzen stressed both the role and the desirability of instinct – 'the primeval sweetness' – as the determinant of any future grassroots agency in the countryside.[114] Future mobilization of peasants, he argued, should accordingly be guided not by democracy, rationality, intellectuals, politics and 'city-dwellers' (= workers) but rather by a discourse centred on a concept of innate Nature.[115] That is, not the forward-looking Enlightenment

---

111   On this see Herzen (1956: 190, 197), who maintained that the category of aristocracy in Russia 'nowadays includes everyone who is above the level of the people [= peasants]'.

112   'The Russian peasant', argued Herzen (1956: 184), 'has no real knowledge of any form of life but that of the village commune...has no other morality than that which flows quite instinctively and naturally from his communal life; it is profoundly national in character and the little that he knows about the Gospels fortifies him in it'.

113   Hence the view (Herzen, 1956: 189): 'From all this you can see what a blessing it is for Russia that the rural commune has never been broken up...how fortunate it is for the Russian people that they have remained outside all political movements, and, for that matter, outside European civilization, which would undoubtedly have sapped the life of the commune, and which today in Socialism has achieved its own negation'. For his idealized image of the village commune and peasant family farming, see Herzen (1956: 190ff.).

114   'People, the masses, are elemental', observed Herzen (1956: 92), 'their path is the path of nature: they are her nearest heirs, they are led by dark instincts, unaccountable passions, they cling obstinately to what they have achieved...[i]t is absurd the blame the people – they are right because they conform to the circumstances of their past life'. Earlier he states (Herzen, 1956: 76) that 'it is instinct that has led and still leads the masses...we have lost the primeval sweetness of instinct...we have killed in ourselves those natural impulses by means of which history fights its way forward into the future'.

115   His pro-peasant but anti-intellectual, anti-urban and anti-political ideology is difficult for Herzen to disguise. Hence the view (Herzen, 1956: 76) that 'we are, on the whole, city dwellers who have lost both the physical and moral sense – the farmer...can foretell the

project seeking to transform the status quo, but rather a backward-looking ideology seeking to privilege – and thus preserve – an essentialist peasant identity. In an important sense, this was the logical outcome of the argument initially put forward by Herder during the late eighteenth century.

Rooted in popular culture – ancient customs, long-standing tradition, and folkloric beliefs – this pro-peasant ideology sprang from the ensemble of 'dark instincts' and 'unaccountable passions' embodying 'the circumstances of their past life'. Since peasants had as yet no voice, he went on to argue that it was up to us – the landowning class – to represent them.[116] To this end, Herzen dismissed the significance to rural Russia of communism as a unifying force, arguing instead that what united those in the countryside was their identity as Slavs, 'one single race, physiologically and ethnographically homogeneous'.[117] A consequence of having 'managed to preserve for some hundreds of years their nationality, their way of life and their language' was that Slav peoples should 'knit together into an association of free autonomous peoples'.[118]

---

weather, but we cannot'. Maintaining that there is '[n]o real creation in democracy, and that is why it is not the future', Herzen (1956: 89) then advances his views about the desirability of a non-political grassroots agency: 'The future is outside politics, the future soars above the chaos of all political and social aspirations and picks out from them threads to weave into a new cloth which will provide the winding-sheet for the past and the swaddling-clothes for the new-born'. Anti-intellectual and anti-urban discourse is also evident in the criticism (Herzen, 1956: 93–94) that 'men realized the injustice of the times, and tried to redress it bookishly. This tardy repentance on the part of the minority was called liberalism. In a genuine desire to reward the people for thousands of years of humiliation, they declared it sovereign, demanded that every peasant should suddenly become a political person, should grasp the complicated provisions of a half-free, half-servile code of law, abandon his work, that is, his daily bread, and...should concern himself with general issues. [...] Liberals always lived in towns...[t]hey were men of books; they did not know the people at all'.

116   Noting that '[t]he poor Russian people has no one of its own to raise a voice in its defence', Herzen (1956: 165) raises the following question: 'I ask you, then can we, in such circumstances, without gross cowardice, stay silent?' The inference is clear: members of the landowning class, who as rural inhabitants possess a shared identity with smallholding peasants, should step into the breach and represent the latter on the basis of a common agrarian interest.

117   Noting that '[t]he Slav world is moving towards unity', Herzen (1956: 172, 176, 177, original emphasis) rejects emphatically the idea that 'the basis of the life of the Russian people is COMMUNISM', maintaining instead that '[u]nderneath...there is one single race, physiologically and ethnographically homogeneous'.

118   On these points, see Herzen (1956: 176).

Although a seemingly virtuous approach, therefore, Herzen's was actually self-serving, possessing as it does a clearly political discourse-for and a discourse-against. On the one hand, therefore, he was antagonistic to things 'foreign' (= Europe), to the large-scale, to the process of centralization, to the State as institution, to the revolutionary working class, to class struggle and to socialism. On the other, he was supportive of the countryside, of the socio-economically small-scale, and of an instinctive ethnic identity that united peasant and landowner.[119] In short, his was an ideology corresponding to the landlord pastoral variant of the agrarian myth, that in late nineteenth and early twentieth century Russia was to become agrarian populism, and one moreover to which all Marxists were opposed.[120]

Conclusion

Travel literature generally, and historically that connected with the Grand Tour, reveals the extent to which class struggle – at home and abroad – contributed to the formation of national identity. Accounts by those belonging to the landowning class of journeys made throughout Europe confirm the shift from a cosmopolitan ideology shared with other members of the same class abroad to a nationalist one, held in common with subordinate class elements at home. In this the role discharged by the Grand Tour was crucial.

---

119   For an example of this symptomatic discourse-for/discourse-against, see Herzen (1956: 175): 'Centralization is contrary to the Slav genius; federalism, on the other hand, is its natural form of expression. Once the Slav world has become unified, and knit together into an association of free autonomous peoples, it will at least be able to enter on its true historical existence. Its past can be seen only as a period of preparation, of growth, of purification. The heroic form of the State have never answered to the national ideal of the Slavs, an ideal which is vague, instinctive if you like, yet by the same token gives promise for the future of a truly remarkable vitality'.

120   Herzen, noted Lenin (1963: 27, original emphasis), 'is the founder of "Russian" socialism, of "Narodism". He saw "socialism" in the emancipation of the peasants with land, in community land tenure and in the peasant idea of "the right to land". He set forth his pet ideas on this subject an untold number of times. Actually, there is *not a grain* of socialism in this doctrine of Herzen's, as, indeed, in the whole of Russian Narodism...' For a similar view, see Plekhanov (1981). At the root of this disagreement were opposing views about the structure of the village community in Russia. Marxists argued that it was differentiated along class lines (into rich, middle and poor peasant strata), and thus already penetrated by capitalism. Populists, by contrast, regarded its peasant inhabitants as a socio-economically homogenous category, located outside the capitalist system.

European travel enabled the acquisition abroad and the reproduction at home of aristocratic cultural 'distinction', based on classical antiquity. A crucial aspect of this cultural formation was visual, effected as a result of art commissioned or purchased abroad, depicting images captured in the course of the Grand Tour. Paintings fulfilled an important function in reproducing specifically pastoral landscapes in which were frequently embedded themes from classical antiquity. For those undertaking it, therefore, the Grand Tour not only disclosed but also validated the existence of an enduring 'natural' rural social order, Nature and landscape appearing as harmonious and unchanging abroad as at home.

Before the 1789 French revolution, the rural poor encountered during the Grand Tour were perceived as benign; after 1789 they were seen as a potential/actual menace, threatening to become the 'mob in the streets'. It was this as much as anything that occasioned the double transformation: a shift away from an internationally acquired ruling class culture, formed as a result of the Grand Tour, and towards an internally-forged identity that could – it might be claimed – be shared with plebeian elements. The formulation of a nationalist ideology, rather than the internationalism of those who rule, and its subsequent fusion with populism, can be traced to travel accounts by Herder (nationalism) and Herzen (nationalism as populism). In each instance European voyages opened up a comparative dimension, among other things enabling them both not just to observe the 'other' in the latter's own location but also – and perhaps more importantly – to surmise as to the cause and desirability of any differences (or similarities) encountered.

Herder formulates the selfhood of national identity (cultural 'difference', 'otherness') based on discourse of the agrarian myth. Every nation emerges from kinship groups, their place-specific environment, culture, religion and peasant farming; he reasserts the validity of these traditional identities against the universal categories of the Enlightenment. For Herder, any and all concepts of 'happiness' are – and can only be – realized in such national contexts, the inhabitants of which constitute themselves as a 'people'. The latter category subsumes monarch and peasant, but excludes the urban worker, 'the rabble' whose agency is synonymous with the 'mob in the streets'.

The discourse-for/discourse-against of Herder and that of postmodern theory have much in common. All the central and interrelated components (farming, tradition, culture, identity) of their shared epistemology exist outside historical time, unchanging and unchangeable in an eternal present. Each is antagonistic towards Enlightenment philosophy ('Eurocentric', 'foundational'), progress, science, intellectuals (preferring 'good common sense'), and supportive of cultural 'difference', rural tradition ('wild customs'), religion ('respect for

gods'), and pre-capitalist relations (equating serfdom with 'happiness' because
it 'provided occupation for men's hands'). Both subscribe to an idealized vision
of primitive/natural/(unspoiled) humanity, a central emplacement of the
agrarian myth.

Prefiguring postmodernism in this manner is not difficult to understand.
Having privileged the stories of childhood as a 'pure' and enduring influence
on the nature of selfhood, it is but a short step for Herder to claim that indigenous groups in distant lands are emblematic of this pristine identity. Hence
the overlap between on the one hand the postmodern view of rural community in the so-called Third World as the locus of eternal and innate cultural
'difference', and on the other of Herder that the 'noble savage', encountered in
the course of travel, corresponds precisely to the same kind of 'authenticity'
represented by kinship/youth.

Although the components of the agrarian myth are present in Herder, and
like the nationalism of Herzen subsequently to be deployed against the working class, there is still a point of difference between their respective discourses.
Whereas Herder looks upwards for redemption/salvation, towards an enlightened ruling class, Herzen looks downwards for these same political solutions,
towards the peasantry. In the course of his visits to France and Italy around the
middle of the nineteenth century, Herzen chronicled a number of interrelated processes that – as a member of the landowning class – gave him cause
for concern.

First, that by advocating equality, liberals had made it possible for workers
to seek and eventually to assume political power. Second, that conservatives
would find it difficult to oppose such a development. And third, that consequently a different political strategy was required: championing the peasantry
as the defenders of rural tradition, as the embodiment of national identity, as
upholders of property rights, and thus as a bulwark against socialism, regarded
as the inevitable outcome of the urban/industrial development path followed
by European economies.

The revolutionary 'mob in the streets' encountered by Herzen on his visit to
Paris led to the populism that emerged to become part of the 'from above' class
struggle. It signalled what later became a shift in ruling class ideology: from
speaking locally *about* the plebeian subject to speaking nationally *for* him/her.
This discursive slide notwithstanding, landowners still remained apart from
those below in the rural hierarchy, and the 'otherness' of class position/power
continued in place; at times hidden, at times flaunted, but always there and
more often than not economically and politically efficacious. Assurances 'from
above' that all was well with peasants and workers – they were now no longer
unfree, were adequately remunerated, enjoyed security of tenure and improved

living standards – is not just the landlord pastoral version of the agrarian myth but also prepared the ground for the populist approach to politics that emerged subsequently.

It could be argued, therefore, that – generated by what travel revealed to its subject – a twofold process was taking place as a result of the fusion of nationalism and populism. On the one hand, the upper classes acquired components of domestic 'popular culture', hitherto the domain of those below. On the other, plebeian elements acquired 'distinction' by foreign travel, hitherto the domain of those above. It must be emphasized, however, that this was by no means a complete ideological shift, in that the elements of ruling class 'distinctiveness'/'distinction' continued to be important. What changed was that, henceforth, these were *combined* with aspects of plebeian ideology, incorporated by those above into their own discourse.

The next two chapters explore the way in which the mob-in-the-streets that caused such fear in the nineteenth century has in the course of the twentieth been transformed into the plebeian mass tourist. The latter is currently seen by many travel writers as every bit as threatening as was the former.

CHAPTER 7

Mass Tourism, or the Mob-in-the-Streets Travels Abroad

Mrs Rittenhouse: 'And now, my friends, before we start the musical programme, Captain Spaulding has kindly consented to tell us about his trip to Africa...'
Captain Spaulding: 'My friends, I am going to tell you of that great, mysterious, wonderful continent known as Africa. Africa is God's country and he can have it.'

> An exchange between Margaret Dumont and Groucho Marx in the film *Animal Crackers* (1930), directed by VICTOR HEERMAN

This journey has only served to confirm this belief, that the division of America into unstable and illusory nations is a complete fiction. We are one single mestizo race with remarkable ethnographic similarities, from Mexico down to the Magellan Straits.

> ERNESTO CHE GUEVARA (2004) after having travelled round Latin America on a motorcycle during the early 1950s

Introduction

The political and ideological themes emerging from the Grand Tour over the eighteenth and nineteenth centuries also inform travel writing produced during the first half of the twentieth, the era preceding mass tourism. During this period, therefore, upper class travellers find reassurance in far-away places where the kind of socio-economic hierarchy they favour – monarch, nobility, dependent followers of one sort or another – is still intact.[1] When they praise the existence in these contexts of what they refer to as 'natural' man

---

1   Writing at the start of the nineteenth century, William Stewart Rose was initially taken aback at the extent to which the 'system [of inter-class] sociability is almost universal in Italy'. About this he observed (Rose, 1819: 41): 'I recollect passing two days in the family of a gentleman who occupied the principal house in a small town in Tuscany, where, to my great astonishment, I perceived, on returning from an evening walk, the ominous preparations of lights and card-tables. Having asked the meaning of this, I was told that it was my host's turn

(generally rural inhabitants who exhibit the appropriate level of deference), it is their own kind of social system that is being endorsed. The inference is that such hierarchy, itself 'natural', should not be tampered with by 'alien' developments linked to modernity.

This is particularly true of contributions to the literature about travel during the first half of the twentieth century, by – among others – Robert Byron, Evelyn Waugh, Wilfred Thesiger, Georgina Grahame, and E. Lucas Bridges. Their accounts – respectively of journeys undertaken in the Mediterranean area, in Africa and the Middle East, in Italy, and of residence in Tierra del Fuego – epitomize the golden age of foreign travel, and all are structured by the discourse advocating in the main the pastoral variant of the agrarian myth. On the one hand, therefore, they disapprove of modernity, urbanization, industrialization, and socialism. On the other, they approve of the 'otherness' of traditional indigenous identity based on enduring rural culture/customs/crafts, and more generally of small-scale peasant society engaged in subsistence-oriented economic activity.

Received wisdom is that there is a gulf between the way travel was written about in the first half of the twentieth century, before the onset of mass tourism, and travel writing in the second half, when mass tourism had become established.[2] The end of colonialism, the global extension of industrial society and modernity, and the spread of economic development generated huge changes in both the subject and object of travel. Not only in the places and people visited, therefore, but also in the social composition of those who travelled, and in the amount, the way, the frequency and the duration of travel itself.

A result was that foreign travel became less exclusive, a transformation reflected in the discourse structuring this act. Travel ceased to be a process of discovering the cultural 'otherness' of rural inhabitants in a foreign context, and writing about this ceased to be a description and record of such

---

to hold an assembly, solemnized in rotation at the houses of all the *notables* of the place. At this all were present, from the *feudatario* to the apothecary. In some instances, indeed, even common shopkeepers are admitted (and were so formerly) to these county *conversazioni*. Yet, on returning to the city, all have the good sense to fall back into their proper ranks'. Shocked at the seeming dissolution of the 'natural' hierarchy, the writer is relieved to find that subsequently those concerned resume their usual place in the social order ('have the good sense to fall back into their proper ranks'). Normality, as he perceives it, is once again in evidence.

2   This distinction is embodied in the lament (Amis, 1990: 325, 327) about a change in the 'social conditions governing travel writing' from the 1960s onwards, which in his opinion led to the 'demise of the travel-book or the get-there-and-stay-there-book'.

discoveries. Instead, the focus shifted onto the influx of plebeian visitors to hitherto pristine rural spaces/places. Robert Graves, Kingsley Amis, V.S. Naipaul, Patrick Leigh Fermor, and Norman Lewis, all of whom wrote about foreign travel in the second half of the twentieth century, were no longer able to approach this in quite the same way as had Robert Byron, Evelyn Waugh, and Wilfred Thesiger in the early part of the century.

This chapter is divided into six sections, the first three of which examine a number of interrelated themes structuring writing about modern travel: class, the agrarian myth, and nationalism. Equally linked thematically are the issues looked at in the fourth, fifth, and sixth sections: the way in which modernity, mass tourism and socialism feature in the same genre.

I

In keeping with the discourse of the Grand Tour, early twentieth century travel literature subscribed to the agrarian myth. The focus of much of the latter is on the way the upper class subject gazes on those seen, and classifies them as the 'foreign other'. By contrast, the argument here is that, as important, is the way the upper class traveller categorizes as 'other' the visitors to the same place who come from his/her own national context, a contaminating influence to be discouraged and/or avoided at all costs. In other words, the identity giving rise to concern is that of *class* as much as 'foreigner'. Numerous examples suggest that the aristocratic and/or upper class traveller quite likes the foreign 'other', to the extent of lamenting the impact of modern development on traditional rural custom/practice, and blaming this erosion on the malign influence of mass tourism.[3]

Barbarian Invasions
These themes suggest not only that writing about travel is informed by persistent themes, but also that the latter continuities are invariably linked to a discourse about class, both at home and abroad. In each context, therefore, this combines an affinity with those rural elements gazed upon with contempt for the modernizing regime. Both have the same ideological root, in that rural 'otherness' is seen by the traveller and/or travel writer as innate, unchanging and desirable. It is this slide into nostalgia for an ideal-type

---

3   As will be seen below, the exception to this positive depiction of the indigenous 'other' in a foreign land is V.S. Naipaul, who casts such forms of rural plebeian 'otherness' in a negative light.

rural past that inserts (and reproduces) the agrarian myth into accounts of travel.[4]

One theme that constantly reoccurs in travel writing, therefore, is disdain for the 'other'; the latter is accordingly the object of a 'gaze' which is categorized by the travel writer in negative terms. Contrary to prevailing opinion, however, this disdain is not confined to an 'other' that is foreign; its most vehement expression is often directed at the presence in a foreign land of an 'other' from the same country as the visitor.[5] This form of disdain underwrites what is the most commonly encountered dichotomy in travel writing: the difference between the self-as-traveller and the other-as-tourist, a distinction generally overlaid by class.[6] Thus the description 'traveller' is frequently applied to an individual of independent means who makes his way at leisure and by himself in a foreign country, and whose gaze on what he finds there is a discerning one, informed by an understanding/appreciation of what is seen.[7] A foreign

---

4 See, for example, Garland (1983: 161) for a critical but nevertheless symptomatic combination of rural nostalgia and a dislike of modernity and mass tourism: 'One cannot help making, however misleading and silly they may be, and it seems to me that life in India today must in many places be very like life in 18th and 19th-century England. The crafts that still thrive, the traditional ways of life that are still intact, and the great variety of occupation and costume and dialect remind one of accounts of English life of the last two centuries. All that richness has long since vanished from England, except where it has been revived by some local group or organization nostalgically clinging to the past. Seeing it here [in India] is Unforgettable. I would not of course enjoy the hardships of being poor in India, but there's no denying the pleasure to be got from seeing the past in this way. Dickens comes to life before your eyes in the cities; in the country perhaps John Clare is more accurate. It has occurred to me that once India makes it just slightly easier to get about, jet planes will bring half Europe here on holiday trips and the whole thing will in turn become swamped and utterly changed'.

5 This exhibition of class difference is highlighted thus by Stephen Spender (1958: 19): 'English, in his public school accent, sounded even to himself like a subtly aggressive language specially invented for the purpose of insulting compatriots abroad'.

6 Accounts which operate implicitly with this distinction, between self-as-traveller and other-as-tourist, include Michael (1950a,b: 1–19) and Sala (1887: 222), who confesses 'it does not matter whether I am a Philistine or not – I merely wish for the nonce to change minds with the ordinary British travelling Philistine who has never read the *Seven Lamps of Architecture*'.

7 Among those who endorse this concept of traveller is Graves (1969: 160, 164), for whom '[o]ld fashioned tourism was individual...young English milords were expected [to travel] with the object of widening their minds... Where mass-tourism becomes entangled with individual travel, the latter invariably suffers: hotels, planes, ships, beaches, beauty spots, all are monopolized by groups'. Amis (1990: 325–326) holds a similar view about the impact on the 'old fashioned traveller' of mass tourism when he writes: 'One unqualified casualty of these barbarian invasions, as he could hardly have been blamed for calling them, was the old

culture, it is inferred, can only be appreciated by that kind of gaze. This kind of critique emanates also from those foreigners who reside in another country, and see mass tourism as a threat both to its culture and their own lifestyle.[8]

By contrast, 'tourist' is a pejorative term, denoting not just plebeian status, but also a process of rapid transit as part of a much larger group (= mass tourism), permitting no more than a superficial gaze in an undiscerning and uninformed fashion at what is seen. Such disdain translates easily into the kind of fear linked to the agrarian myth: namely, the 'mob-in-the-streets', of which 'mass tourism' becomes a variant. Categorization of the plebeian 'other' as an undiscerning tourist in a foreign country is currently invoked with reference to the way in which foreign destinations cease to be 'exclusive' as a result of being turned into simulacra of the domestic context (= holiday resorts) where the plebeian 'other' resides.[9] In this discourse an 'other' place ceases to be culturally 'other', and becomes instead an extension of the plebeian self, thereby highlighting the extent to which the issue concerns class differences as these occur in the home nation of both the 'traveller' and the 'tourist'.

Drinking at the Same Fountains

Accordingly, ideology linked to and reflecting not just a particular nationalism but also a particular class affected the way in which all 'foreigners' were perceived, those in southern Europe and America no less than the 'other' in the Third World. It informed the way in which travel outside England (= 'the Englishman abroad') was depicted in much popular culture during the first half of the twentieth century, an example of which is the film *The Lady Vanishes* (1938), directed by Alfred Hitchcock.[10] Three aspects are of particular

---

fashioned traveller or travel writer...[t]he fellow knew the place in question, and 'intimately' was the word for how he knew it, an intimacy achieved by means of money, a superior education and, above all, a lot of spare time'.

8   Hence the observation by Graves (1969: 170) about visitors coming to Spain in the mid-1960s, that '[o]nly a very few of each mass-tourist group, of whatever nationality, has sufficient historical or artistic background to appreciate what he is shown; the groups surge into the show places like a football crowd...'

9   As Graves (1969: 162–163) comments, with barely concealed disdain, '[m]ass-tourists ask little except the same sort of food that they eat at home...[b]ut they shy away from any closer approach to the real Spain...[t]he English tourist's most lasting and pleasurable memories are the friendships he has struck up with members of the same group from the same home town'.

10 The story of *The Lady Vanishes* (Hitchcock, 1984) is an adventure involving a number of English passengers on a train journey across the Balkans in which the two main characters (Gilbert and Iris) attempt to find an elderly lady (Miss Froy) who has disappeared.

significance. First, the ease of travel itself, an unmistakeable link with the kind of privileged access and passage that colonialism confers on the colonizer.[11] Second, where and with whom one stayed in the course of such journeys,

Miss Froy, in reality an English spy, is eventually rescued by Gilbert and Iris from her Central European captors, and – together with most of the other English passengers – they all escape safely back to England. What the film demonstrates is the importance when journeying in the Balkans – as Miss Froy notes, 'We're not in England now' – is an Englishness that is solid bourgeois, Oxbridge and monied. Of the train passengers in the film, Charters and Caldicott, played by Basil Radford and Naunton Wayne, constitute the cinematic embodiment of Englishness, and it is how their characters respond to the situation that is of particular significance. The cinematic persona of Radford and Wayne was that of upper class officialdom, an identity they projected in films such as *Night Train to Munich* (1940), *Millions Like Us* (1943), *Whisky Galore* (1949) and *Passport to Pimlico* (1952). In *The Lady Vanishes*, therefore, Charters and Caldicott represent the very essence not just of 'Englishness' but of Englishmen abroad in a potentially hostile/dangerous Central European setting. Their negative perception of the latter as a 'third rate country' with 'rather primitive humour' ('What a country! I don't wonder they have revolutions... After six years in this hole we'd be whimsical') is combined with the expectation of an unhindered passage across the country (told that the train carriages have been uncoupled, their response is disbelief, since '[o]ur bags are in the first class carriage'). Neither knows the language, but both expect everyone to speak English ('The fellow doesn't speak English', 'It's lucky some of you fellows understand English') and to know/understand the cultural importance of cricket ('I'm enquiring about the Test Match in Manchester. Cricket, sir, cricket! What, you don't know?'). Underneath an air of amateurishness (Caldicott: 'My word, I'm glad that it's all over, aren't you? Heaven knows what the [British] Government will say about all this'), however, there is seen to be not only courage but also a ruthless efficiency when it comes to fighting (Charters, of Caldicott: '...he's a damned good shot'; Caldicott: 'You can count on me', Charters: 'me too'). The significance of cricket and Oxbridge emerge clearly in *Night Train to Munich*, where the same two characters travelling by train across Germany just before the outbreak of war encounter someone (played by Rex Harrison) who was at the same Oxford college, but is now dressed as a German officer. That the latter might conceivably be a traitor – actually be a German – is dismissed by Caldicott on the grounds that the person in question had played cricket for the Gentlemen. The German officer turns out to be a British spy on a mission in enemy territory, and – as in *The Lady Vanishes* – Charters and Caldicott save the day. The inference is equally clear. Although seemingly interested only in cricket, therefore, and indeed conveying a humorous air of being 'not worth bothering about', bourgeois stalwarts such as Charters and Caldicott – who project the kind of national identity associated with colonial rule – can be relied upon in times of national crisis.

11   A glimpse of this is provided by a popular guide to rail and sea voyages around the Mediterranean at the beginning of the twentieth century. Hence the tenor of the following observations (Baedeker, 1911: xvii, xxv–xxvi): 'Passports are not absolutely necessary, except in Turkey and Russia;...While the traveller should be both cautious and firm in his

which evinces a similar link not just with colonialism but also between members of the same class in different contexts.[12] And third, even when national conflict supervened, such recognition between actual (or potential) combatants of the same class nevertheless adhered to a specific ideological code.[13]

---

dealings with the natives, he should avoid being too exacting and suspicious. Many of those he meets with are like mere children... [guides] are ignorant and uneducated, and their "explanations" of antiquities or works of art are worthless. When, as sometimes happens, they assume a patronizing or familiar manner, they should be promptly checked and kept in their proper place'. Much the same kind of colonial attitude is found subsequently in a novel by Bradbury (1966: 40), who – significantly – attributes it to a fictional English academic. In the course of visiting the United States during the early 1960s, therefore, this character laments its passing ('The train, indulging all his English nostalgia for the plushy and the genteel... spoke of a time when you could travel over Europe every signal off, and find the whole world not, as you might terrifyingly suppose, all different, but all the same – all service and respect and three-star comfort'.).

12   Perhaps the most telling evidence for an affinity between members of the same class divided not just by nationality but by war is recounted by Leigh Fermor (2003: 85–96). The event occurred during 1944 after the kidnap of General Kreipe, officer commanding the German forces in Crete, by partisans and SOE agents, of whom Leigh Fermor was one (an episode filmed in 1957 as *Ill Met by Moonlight*). His account merits citing in full (Leigh Fermor, 2003: 95–96): 'We woke up among the rocks, just as a brilliant dawn was breaking over the crest of Mount Ida which we had been struggling across for two days. We were all three lying smoking in silence, when the General, half to himself, slowly said: "*Vides ut alta stet nive candidum/Socrate...*" I was in luck. It is the opening line of one of the few odes of Horace I know by heart (*Ad Thaliarchum*, I.ix). I went on reciting where he had broken off: "*...Nec iam sustineant onus/Silvae laborantes, geluque/Flumina constiterint acuto,*" and so on, through the remaining five stanzas to the end. The General's blue eyes swivelled away from the mountain-top to mine – and when I'd finished, after a long silence, he said: "Ach so, Herr Major!" It was very strange. "Ja, Herr General." As though, for a long moment, the war had ceased to exist. We had both drunk at the same fountains long before; and things were different between us for the rest of our time together'. Not only is the common membership of the same class in different national contexts recognized, therefore, but this fact of mutual belonging is revealed by reference to a similar cultural experience, ritually displayed. The result is that the behaviour of each to the other is altered from then on, war notwithstanding.

13   See previous note for a non-fictional example. A fictional depiction of this kind of mutual recognition between members of the same class on the point of being separated by war occurs in the film *The Lady Vanishes*. An enemy officer who boards the train to arrest the English passengers offering armed resistance tells them he was at Oxford University, a coded reference which elicits a positive response from one of the upper class Englishmen present ('So was I'). When the same enemy officer is then knocked unconscious by another of the Englishmen in the carriage, the latter gives as a reason that it was because 'I was at Cambridge'. This reply is humorous and witty to be sure, and always raises a laugh

One celebrated instance of travel writing about this period, therefore, consists of reminiscences on the part of Patrick Leigh Fermor, an associate of the
English upper classes, recording his carefree and easy passage across 1930s
Europe from one landlord estate to another.[14] Not the least important aspect
of this literary genre at this conjuncture – not so long after the 1917 Russian
revolution – was the nostalgic evocation of a lost rural socio-economic order,
and lament for the passing of a landowning class the refined culture of which
was based on the leisure that wealth confers.[15] By inference, therefore, it

---

from the cinema audience. It is also significant, in that antagonism is expressed in terms
not of national identity but rather of institutional rivalries that are specific to the ruling
class at that conjuncture.

14   Leigh Fermor (2003: 40 ff.) admits that his itinerary in mid-1930s Rumania ('Travels in a
Land before Darkness Fell') amounted to 'a stroll from one schloss to another', and that
'my new friends belonged to the scattered Hungarian landowners who had lived for many
generations in the western and densely Rumanian parts'. He is taken by one landowner on
a tour of the local exotic fauna: peasants, their quaint folklore and habitations. Elsewhere
it is noted that (Cooper, 2012: 51) 'the letters [of introduction] written by Baron Liphart-
Ratshoff to his friends opened up an unexpected world of schlosses and country
houses, taking [him] into a landed aristocratic milieu'. In Hungary Leigh Fermor (Cooper,
2012: 65) 'spent every night in comfortable country houses. His hosts were a series of interrelated Hungarian landowners'. The view of the travel writer, therefore, is a 'from above'
one, amounting to an unabashed endorsement of the aristocratic version of the agrarian
myth, or the expression of regret for the good old days of pre-1914 Rumania. In keeping
with this pattern, when on a visit to southern Spain in the 1970s Leigh Fermor (2003:
265 ff.) stays on a large rural estate owned by friends.

15   Hence the following description (Leigh Fermor, 2003: 43): 'Plaster flaked from the columns and pediments, and indoors, room opened into room in vistas of Louis Philippe and
Second Empire furniture... At nightfall...the light caught the chipped gold of an ikon's
halo,...glass cases with the lumpy seals of parchments, the family's two-headed eagle, tall
china stoves, the prisms of chandeliers, stags' antlers, the glass eye of a huge bear's pelt
from the Carpathians, and thousands of books in several languages. The voices would be
talking French rather than Rumanian. The results of this foible (the legacy, as in Russia
and Poland, of several generations) were like the conversations on the first page of War
and Peace, but less silly. Their themes were country ones, crops, timber to be felled, horses
to be bought, sold or shod, and impending shoots: pheasant, waterfowl, bustard, deer,
wolves, wild boar and bears. Although most of these country-dwellers were half-ruined,
life was rich in tales of past extravagance, eccentricity, comedy and intrigue, with a duel
here and there; but literature was the presiding theme; in spite of hard times, books still
arrived from Paris and London'. Like the episode following the kidnap of General Kreipe
in Crete during 1944 (see above), therefore, what this description reveals is the existence
of class affiliation cutting across national boundaries, a mutual recognition effected via
cultural patterns (hunting, reading, speaking) that transcended nationality.

provides testimony about the benign role of the class hierarchy in rural areas, the erosion of which is characterized as a cultural loss experienced by society as a whole. To some degree, this replicates a central theme of the early nineteenth century Grand Tour: namely, both the reaffirmation by an aristocrat travelling in post-1789 Europe of his class position and the validation of his role.[16]

An important consequence of avoiding an intellectual engagement with politics generally, and particularly the class divisions/struggle in the countries through which he travelled, was that on his walk across Germany in 1933 Leigh Fermor misunderstood the meaning of the town/country divide. Hence the perception on his part that rural tradition was in some sense a political, and as such distinct from the town where 'a political ideology forced people to take sides'.[17] Much rather, the strength of rural tradition meant that sides had already been taken in the German countryside, and it was precisely in the

---

16   Such confirmation was provided by a Piedmontese nobleman to the poet Samuel Rogers (1830: 174) during the latter's visit to Italy during the 1820s, when he was told the following story by the former: 'I was weary of life', said the nobleman, 'and, after a day, such as few have known and none would wish to remember, was hurrying along the street to the river, when I felt a sudden check. I turned and beheld a little boy, who had caught the skirt of my cloak in his anxiety to solicit my notice. His look and manner were irresistible. Not less so was the lesson he had learnt. "There are six of us; and we are dying for the want of food." – "Why should I not," said I to myself, "relieve this wretched family? I have the means; and it will not delay me many minutes. But what, if it does?" The scene of misery he conducted me to, I cannot describe. I threw them my purse; and their burst of gratitude overcame me'. In the aftermath of the French revolutionary challenge to the position and role of the landowning class, this episode restores to one of the latter his self-image as a benign dispenser of largesse that is his by right, of coming to the rescue of the impoverished. Not only is there no longer a threat from an 'unthinking mob', therefore, but travel reveals to the nobleman that those who might otherwise belong to that same 'unthinking mob' are now quiescent and grateful for any charitable donation that he as a generous landowner might care to bestow on them. Hence the observation (Rogers, 1830: 171) at that conjuncture: 'Now travel, and foreign travel more particularly, restores to us in a great degree what we have lost'. In short, it reproduces the self-serving ideology of *noblesse oblige*, a central component of the pastoral variant of the aristocratic version of the agrarian myth.

17   Observing that 'I am just living in a pre-war [1914–18] world', Leigh Fermor (Cooper, 2012: 49, 60) was someone for whom 'the countryside was still steeped in tradition, and [he] was far more at ease... There were pitfalls, he realized, in setting up this over-simplified, town-versus-country picture of German politics, but he found it hard to resist. In towns he was confronted by a political ideology that forced people to take sides. In the country he found it easier to surround himself with the beautiful, illusory continuum of history, which connected him to a past that made no demands'.

latter context that Hitler gained mass support from peasant proprietors. The same happened in two other countries through which he travelled at this conjuncture. His idealized image of rural life prevented him from noting the existence of conflict between the Hungarian landlords with whom he stayed and their smallholding Rumanian tenants.[18] Similar clashes between workers and the *Heimwehr* that took place in Austria were also ignored by Leigh Fermor, despite the fact that he was present in Vienna at the very period when this conflict occurred.[19]

The Soft Things of Europe

In a symptomatic observation whilst journeying through the Congo at that period, Evelyn Waugh reproduces two central elements of travel writing discourse: the significance to the self of his/her own class and national identity. It is only in the course of encountering the indigenous 'other', therefore, that one not merely learns to appreciate home comforts, but also recognizes that the latter are in turn an effect of nationality and class position. This twofold ideological consolidation is attributed by Waugh – as by Herder and Herzen at earlier conjunctures (see Chapter 6) – to the fact that in Europe such identities appear less important than when travelling in the domain of the 'other'.[20] It also underscores the importance of class, since the agrarian hierarchy abroad corresponds to what in the opinion of the upper class visitor it should be at home. Hence the confession by Waugh that, 'after so many months it seemed odd and slightly indecent to see white men waiting on each other'; an

---

18   'These tensions [between Hungarians and Rumanians] had little impact on him at the time', notes Cooper (2012: 68), 'and did not seem affect what he saw as the easy relations his Hungarian hosts had with the Rumanian peasants who still worked for them'.

19   See Cooper (2012: 53–54).

20   'In the meantime I worked, rested, and enjoyed the comfort and tranquillity of Elizabethville', noted Waugh (1931: 233), and continues: 'How reassuring are these occasional reconciliations with luxury. How often in Europe, after too much good living, I have begun to doubt whether the whole business of civilised taste is not a fraud put upon us by shops and restaurants. Then, after a few weeks of gross, colonial wines, hard beds, gritty bath-water, awkward and surly subordinates, cigars from savage Borneo or pious Phillipines [*sic*], cramped and unclean quarters, and tinned foodstuffs, one realises that the soft things of Europe are not merely rarities which one has been taught to prefer because they are expensive, but thoroughly satisfactory compensations for the rough and tumble of earning one's living – and a far from negligible consolation for some of the assaults and deceptions by which civilization seeks to rectify the balance of good fortune'.

impression gained as a result of voyaging in Africa was that non-European ethnically 'other' people were – and could only ever be – 'natural' servants.[21]

Robert Byron defines each end of the class hierarchy – upper and plebeian –
largely in terms of taste. Thus in New Delhi, Lady Irwin, the wife of the Viceroy,
is referred to as 'a woman of some taste', and in New York he commends the
upper classes who 'in their behaviour and tastes [are] people like ourselves...
essentially non-vulgar'.[22] Those at the other end of the class hierarchy fall into
two categories: peasants in rural areas, of whom Byron approves, and plebeians inhabiting/working in urban industrial contexts, who incite his disapproval. Smallholders and shepherds in the first category evoke pastoral images,
the emphasis being on the beauty of the landscape plus the enduring character of a traditional culture (clothing, songs, dance) untainted by modernity
and Westernization.[23] These kinds of description are applied by Byron to peasants and village life encountered on his travels not just in the Balkans and Asia,
but also in Russia.[24]

The urban plebeian, however, is perceived negatively by Robert Byron:
either the de-cultured rural 'other', the potentially/actually socialist mob-
in-the-streets, or merely as tourists who are 'vulgar'. Tourists encountered in
the course of travel are described variously as 'beastly countrymen', speakers
with working class accents, or persons with a 'provincial mind [that] makes

---

21   This revealing view is expressed by Waugh (1931: 233–234) en route to Cape Town after
      having visited the Congo.

22   For these descriptions, see Byron (1991: 52, 229). His views about class whilst in America
      during 1935 are particularly revealing: 'What I find here [in New York] which I didn't
      expect, is that there is a very large stratum of purely English people who approximate in
      behaviour and tastes to the English university – educated professional people, to people
      like ourselves – their standard of manners is what ours was before the [1914–18] war. They
      strike one as the real thing...essentially non-vulgar'.

23   Opinions embodied in comments (Byron, 1991: 61, 246) such as '[t]he country of Greece is
      too beautiful for words...shepherds in fustanellas playing pipes among the olive groves,
      groups of peasants doing slow circular dances to their own chants upon the skyline', and
      'I thought how [much the] same villages are all over the world...[i]t was a beautiful
      scene...'

24   Hence the following view (Byron, 1991: 140, emphasis added): 'You have no idea how won-
      derful it is to be in a *huge country* [Tibet] as medieval as Athos...not a wheel in the whole
      country!...this is now the only country where one can see anything of the old China – as
      the modern has become so westernized...' He also likes the Russian countryside and vil-
      lages, perceived as culturally pristine and thus different from the urban centres under
      Bolshevik control (Byron, 1991: 185, 243), places that were 'not unlike England rolling val-
      leys, half wooded'.

one ill'.[25] The fact of poverty and being plebeian – both at home and abroad – is for him simply a matter of aesthetics. At home, therefore, around Oxford one encounters '[s]uch terribly squalid villages and *filthy* children', whilst slum housing is described as 'dramatically squalid'.[26]

Poverty encountered abroad is treated by Byron the same way: in terms not of political economy, as a form of oppression to be abolished, but rather as falling within the realm of aesthetics, as something that offends against good taste. When the poor are encountered abroad in rural areas, a similar aesthetic predominates: that of a picturesque Nature blighted by a non-picturesque poverty.[27] Analogous sentiments are deployed when describing the urban poor of Asia, Russia and the United States. In Asia, therefore, a friend is said to be 'a little deranged by the squalor of the East', while Tibetans resident in Calcutta are 'unutterably filthy'.[28] Significantly, it is deracinated peasants – erstwhile rural inhabitants – who as urban plebeians inspire such disgust.[29] Muscovites queuing to see Lenin's tomb in Red Square during 1932 are labelled 'these hideous uniformed hangdog creatures', and Red army soldiers are said to look 'like goblins'.[30]

Returning there two years later, Byron reports that '[t]he people look uglier than ever – one couldn't believe ugliness on such a scale was possible unless one had seen it...[a]nd how they smell'.[31] In America that same year, Byron

---

25   During 1926, when in Greece, Byron (1991: 69) comes across 'two deliciously common English people...her cockney accent would keep breaking through her refinement'. In a similar vein, he comments (Byron, 1991: 127, original emphasis) that 'we have had such an interesting time and at last *got away* from our beastly countrymen'. A final instance underlines his disdain for fellow nationals abroad, on whom Byron (1991: 135) pronounces the following judgment: 'How vile the English provincial mind can be...it makes one ill'.

26   See Byron (1991: 31, 107, original emphasis).

27   'Anatolia is very picturesque', observes Byron (1991: 75) in 1926, 'camels grazing off willows – storks and cranes in the marshes – women in trousers – everywhere ruined houses and everyone diseased, malformed, more than filthy...without any excuse to exist at all'.

28   Urban Tibetans, states Byron (1991: 132–133), are 'living in the top of a vast house, unutterably filthy, with refuse all over the floors, everyone covered in sores, pockmarked and sweating – utensils lying about with the dregs of yesterday's food and drink'. Elsewhere he observes (Byron, 1991: 154, original emphasis), again of Calcutta: 'What an insight into the occupation of half the world – I can't tell you how I DESPISE it...I never really suspected before how stupendous must be the gulf between oneself and the ordinary man...'

29   On returning to Karachi in 1930, Byron (1991: 160) finds '[t]he ugliness was worse than before'.

30   See Byron (1991: 179, 180).

31   For this description of his return to Moscow in 1935, see Byron (1991: 238, 239). The importance of smell as a way of categorizing the plebeian 'other' and differentiating the latter from the self, is outlined above in Chapter 5, with regard to Orwell's classic 1938 account

notes that '[t]he squalor and filth of all but the centre of New York beats any-thing I have seen since pre-Fascist Naples'.[32] What he approves of about New York, therefore, is the upper class enclave, not the other areas. The rest of the city, inhabited by the urban industrial plebeian, evinces a symptomatic dis-course of disgust (squalor, filth, smell, disease, ugliness).[33]

III

As noted, the agrarian myth divides into a pastoral and Darwinian version. Linked strongly to nationalism and class, for the travel writer the pastoral is differentiated contextually: it can be either at home or abroad, or both at home and abroad. For Norman Lewis, the pastoral is abroad, in Europe generally and Spain in particular. In the case of Robert Byron, therefore, the pastoral version of the agrarian myth is located at home, a result of a position already held in the English class structure. By contrast, for Naipaul the pastoral is related to an aspiration on his part to hold the same position in an adopted country. For Paddy Leigh Fermor and Evelyn Waugh, however, the pastoral is situated both at home (in England) and abroad (in Europe and elsewhere). Vidia Naipaul, and to a lesser extent Wilfred Thesiger, adhere to a Darwinian version of the agrarian myth, whereby a rural 'other' is perceived either as threatening or merely with approval.

---

of English working class life, *The Road to Wigan Pier*. That Byron uses the word 'smelly' as a general term of disapprobation is further suggested by two additional observations (Byron, 1991: 191, 197): that Persians 'sound the most odious race', and that in the course of a journey there during 1933–34 'we travelled by lorry – a hideous experience, shut up in the back with very smelly companions'. The latter negative characteristic, the writer infers, is somehow bound up with – and perhaps no more than an effect of – the former ethnic identity.

32   See Byron (1991: 230, 233), who continues along similar lines that 'I can't tell you how loathsome, how inconceivably disgusting, the landscape is here...the squalor of the millions of little detached houses sitting by themselves, but without any gardens or hedges'.

33   The difference between a largely rural, economically underdeveloped Europe and a rap-idly developing urban industrial America informs the first travel book written by Byron. There he notes (Byron, 1926: 6–7): 'Europe, taken as a whole, is such an unknown quantity to most of her inhabitants, nurtured in the disastrous tradition of the armed and insular state, that they are unable to gauge the contrast between their own corporate civilization, the laborious construction of two thousand years, and the retrograde industrialism sprung up in a night on the other side of the Atlantic'.

The Pastoral, Home and Abroad

The pastoral abroad is exemplified by the description of travel in early twentieth century Italy. This takes the form of 'our route through the lovely pastoral solitudes', in which rural locations are described variously as 'a delightfully unspoilt and unsophisticated place', and 'as yet an absolutely primitive and unspoilt place'.[34] Those belonging to the upper classes who write about travel bring to this a perception based on a shared establishment background. Broadly speaking, they combine one or more of the following identities: public school, Oxbridge, conservative political affiliation, titled, wealthy, and not infrequently from a rural property-owning family.[35] Some travel writers not from this background – for example, Norman Lewis – locate the pastoral abroad but attach little importance to its absence at home.[36]

For this reason, approval of tradition frequently encompassed not just that espoused by the rural 'other' in a foreign context, but extended to include that found at home, as confirmed by the significance for Leigh Fermor of pastoral images from his rural background in England.[37] The existence of a connection

---

34 See Grahame (1909: 179, 183, 216).

35 Most went to public school and Oxbridge, many were/are titled, wealthy and politically conservative, and all moved in an aristocratic milieu. Thus, for example, companions accompanying Robert Byron (1926: 2) on his European journey are identified simply in terms of 'all three had been educated at the same school and at the same university', which disguises the fact that the school was Eton and the university Oxford. Although not themselves wealthy or from the upper class, others were linked by kinship or marriage to European aristocracy.

36 Looking back on his childhood in Enfield at the beginning of the twentieth century, Lewis (1998: 3) recounts how the local squire, Colonel Sir Henry Ferryman Bowles (1858–1943) of Myddelton House 'owned everything down to the last rut in the road and the last tiny cabin perched over the cesspit at the bottom of narrow village gardens'. Reference is also made to the unrelenting presence of the squire and his landowning friends who photographed and 'visited' the estate tenants, concluding (Lewis, 1998: 15) that 'Jesus said of the poor "they are always with you." In Forty Hill it was the rich who were rarely out of sight'. Despite these observations, the account of a context where '[t]he land and its hamlets were owned by...a sporadically benevolent tyrant' (Lewis, 1998: 1) is nevertheless benign and devoid of political criticism. This contrasts with his endorsement of the pastoral abroad, in the shape of an influential account by him of the decline in Latin American indigenous populations (Lewis, 1988), the political impact of which contributed to the formation of Survival International, an NGO dedicated to the preservation of tribal societies.

37 'I spent these important [early] years', confesses Leigh Fermor (Cooper, 2012: 11), 'more or less as a small farmer's child run wild: they have left a memory of complete and unalloyed bliss'. The same pastoral image was reproduced subsequently when he came to write

between adherence to the pastoral at home and abroad is underlined by Thesiger, who linked his own sense of belonging, formed by his public school background, to his subsequent 'respect for tradition and veneration for the past' as found in the places he visited and wrote about.[38] He also saw nothing wrong with slavery as a 'natural' tribal institution, even when it involved its subject in demeaning and/or humiliating acts.[39]

Distant and Barbarous Places

In terms of the agrarian myth, the conservatism and snobbery of Waugh is reflected in his ideological rootedness in country house milieu – a background to which he aspired, although he himself did not come from it.[40] Not merely did he see himself as a country gentleman, but like the latter he also feared modernity/progress which gave rise to the urban 'mob in the streets' and

---

about post-war England (Cooper, 2012: 300): 'The Devon he described is hardly the contemporary Britain of the late 1950s, but a rural vision of ancient walls sunk in damp greenness, with a pervasive smell of earth, rain and wet horse'.

38 At Eton, therefore, Thesiger (1988: 72–73) 'was conscious that here I belonged to a community with roots in the distant past and a distinguished place in British history...[n]o wonder that in this setting, during those impressionable years, I acquired lasting respect for tradition and veneration for the past'. In keeping with the cultural relativism currently embraced by postmodern theory, Thesiger (1988: 202) goes on to explain his own resistance to any/every form of development: 'I also questioned whether it was right to try to impose on the Sudanese the conventions and values of our utterly alien civilization... I could not help feeling that other races were entitled to their own customs and moral standards, however much these might differ from ours. I had witnessed the incessant killing among the Danakil, but accepted it as part of their way of life, and felt no desire to see them administered and civilized'. Curiously, his objection to all things Western does not prevent Thesiger from providing medicines to help cure ailing members of the indigenous groups he travelled amongst.

39 Eating with a tribal chief, he (Thesiger, 1988: 325) notes: 'The slave woman who brought us our food was rewarded with a handful stuffed into her mouth by her master'.

40 That Waugh, who in the 1930s purchased and lived in a country house in Stinchcombe, Gloucestershire, and in the 1950s moved to a large eighteenth century country house in the Somerset village of Combe Florey, saw himself as a country gentleman is clear from an account by a close friend. Describing the traditional way he furnished his first home in the countryside, Penelope Chetwode (1973: 100) concludes: 'In a subtle way, I think he achieved the effect he desired, which was to give the impression of a country house lived in by the same family for generations'. In a letter written in 1984, Kingsley Amis reports (Leader, 2000: 970) that a '[w]oman I met who knew him [= Waugh] a bit said it wasn't so much his rudeness that stuck in your craw as his buttering-up dukes and marquises, praising their marvellous houses and beautiful gardens, lovely daughters & c. He did that to her when she was married to one, then stopped it when she stopped being'.

socialism, whilst admiring rural subordinates – as long as they remained subordinate, rural, and in their place of origin.[41] Waugh was not above criticizing the landowning class for engaging in behaviour that left it vulnerable to political attack by socialists.[42]

Despite appearances to the contrary, the suggestion that Waugh looked down on indigenous culture is mistaken. What he objected to much rather was the attempt to imitate or introduce the political and economic institutions as found in Europe.[43] Traditions and practices encountered by him at the rural grassroots, which he regarded as 'authentic' and emblematic of non-European ethnic 'otherness', elicited his approval precisely because they were 'different'.[44] Hence the view that '[t]he difficulty (and of course the charm) of Abyssinia is the inaccessibility of the interior', which locates the 'authentic'/'other' in a distant rural abode visited by few travellers, to the extent that it confers 'exclusivity' on the ones – such as Waugh – who go there.[45]

---

41   This dichotomy is recognized by Bradbury (1973: 171–172): 'One figure that recurs in his work is that of the jungle or the desert, the dark places of the expanding wilderness; and if it is threatening to him, it is also decidedly attractive...Waugh is very much the novelist of the disillusioned Twenties, in that he shares the prevailing obsession of the decade with barbarism and vitalism as an alternative to rational civilization'. Bradbury is right about Waugh, but wrong to confine his pro-tradition/anti-modern views to his fiction. It is argued here that just such a polarity if found as strongly in Waugh's travel writing, informed by the same kind of discourse.

42   This much is evident from the *mea culpa* spoken by Lord Marchmain in *Brideshead Revisited* (Waugh, 1945: 99): 'It has been my tragedy that I abominate the English countryside. I suppose it is a disgraceful thing to inherit great responsibilities and to be entirely indifferent to them. I am all the Socialists would have me be, and a great stumbling-block to my own party'. What is feared by Waugh is that landowners like Lord Marchmain will make it easier politically for socialists to criticize the aristocracy, and it was for this reason that one of their number is upbraided for not behaving as he ought.

43   Whilst in Zanzibar, therefore, Waugh (1931: 164) observed disdainfully that '[t]he furniture [in the house of a cousin to the Sultan] was a curious medley of pseudo-oriental...and the pseudo-European'.

44   Hence the following confession (Waugh, 1931: 63): 'But no catalogue of events can convey any real idea of these astounding days, of an atmosphere utterly unique, elusive, unforgettable. If in the foregoing pages I have seemed to give undue emphasis to the irregularity of the proceedings, to their unpunctuality, and their occasional failure, it is because this was an essential part of their character and charm. In Addis Ababa everything was haphazard and incongruous; one learned to expect the unusual and yet was always surprised'.

45   See Waugh (1931:92). These distant rural locations are described further as 'the heart of Ethiopia', the monasteries of which have 'for centuries been the centre of Abyssinian spiritual life' (Waugh, 1931: 69, 83).

His admiration for indigenous rural 'otherness' (crafts, religion) indicates that the variant of the agrarian myth to which he subscribes is the pastoral.[46]

In keeping with the agrarian myth, therefore, he approves of the 'other' so long as that 'other' remains in its 'natural' place, both socially (as a subordinate) and physically (1930s Ethiopia and Brazil).[47] This is consistent with landowning ideology, whereby a paternalistic view towards 'those below' stems from their being unthreatening. Accordingly, a conservative such as Waugh can find the tribal/peasant 'other' exotic, admirable even, when such a subject is encountered in its 'natural' habitat, and stays there. However, when evidence of such 'otherness' is encountered where is should not be – at home, on one's own doorstep, so to speak – Waugh takes umbrage.[48] In these circumstances, an encounter with the 'other' – belonging to a different ethnicity or subordinate class – is perceived as potentially/actually threatening.

This is also true of Leigh Fermor, for whom the main object of travel was to search for and locate a pristine subject in the rural society of another country; that is, the Noble Savage of the agrarian myth.[49] This quest extended from gypsies in the Balkans to the indigenous populations of the Caribbean, where his complaint was that much of the Caribbean displayed evidence of modernity, albeit in the usual form of North American colonization (Coca-Cola adverts,

---

46   Hence the endorsement by Waugh (1931: 71) of the following sentiment expressed by a fellow visitor: '[L]ook at the exquisite grace of the basket that woman is carrying. There is the whole character of the people in that plaited straw. Ah, why do we waste our time looking at crowns and canons? I could study that basket all day'.

47   The element of distance between self and other, and its centrality to the act of foreign travel, is expressed clearly when writing in the 1930s about a journey to Brazil. On the subject of this link, therefore, Waugh (1946: 197) observes: 'One does not travel, any more than one falls in love, to collect material. It is simply part of one's life. For myself and many better than me, there is a fascination in distant and barbarous places, and particularly in the borderlands of conflicting cultures and states of development, where ideas, uprooted from their traditions, become oddly changed in transplantation. It is there that I find the experiences vivid enough to demand translation into literary forms'.

48   This is suggested by a diary entry made by Waugh for 3rd September 1963 (Davie, 1976: 791), where he observes: 'Re-reading Robert Byron [the travel writer]. It was fun thirty-five years ago [c. 1930] to travel far and in great discomfort to meet people whose entire conception of life and manner of expression were alien. Now one has only to leave one's gates'.

49   A telling critique by Rodis Ronfos (cited by Cooper, 2012: 289) of Leigh Fermor's wartime role in Crete argued that the latter 'saw only the primitive story-teller [and] had done no service to the Greeks, who appear as "quite nice native servants to the Allied officers they were called upon to serve during the war"'.

racial conflict and political tensions).[50] What he had wanted to see was 'happy natives', which he found in British Honduras.[51] Similarly, on a visit during the late 1980s to Bulgaria, where '[f]arming was still largely unmechanized [Leigh Fermor] was comforted by the sight of so many horses and carts, and people out in the fields with scythes'.[52] An analogous view is expressed by Eric Newby, whose references to peasant superstition in the Mediterranean countries are a way of categorizing rural subjects as always having been the same, mired in the ignorance of a pre-modern age.[53]

Much the same is true of Naipaul, who – like Waugh – also aspired to the position of a country gentlemen, despite not having started out as one, and as such not only came to fear the African 'bush' but also endorsed and defended the English pastoral. The contrast between on the one hand the negative identity Naipaul attributes to rural 'otherness' abroad (Africa, the Caribbean, Latin America), and the hostile way he depicts this, and on the other the positive description of the traditional English landscape, presented in idyllic terms, is absolute.[54] Again like Waugh, Naipaul takes umbrage when the

---

50   Leigh Fermor (Cooper, 2012: 215) 'wandered among the gypsies, trying out his Rumanian with varying degrees of success... For all that, the fair [in 1947] was a disappointment: the gypsies he saw in the Camargue were not as wild as those he had seen in Rumania before the [1939–45] war'. He was equally disappointed on a visit to the Caribbean in the same year (Cooper, 2012: 225), gathering information for his book (Leigh Fermor, 1968: 50–51), to find that '[t]he proximity of the United States to the Antilles is a thing that one constantly feels; perhaps disproportionately so, as it is chiefly apparent in the glittering external symptoms of modern life: Coca-Cola advertisements, frigidaires, wireless sets and motorcars, especially the last'.

51   As reported by Leigh Fermor (Cooper, 2012: 225), therefore, the Indians he met along the river Belize were 'calm, gentle, friendly and laughing easily...there was none of the suspicion on both sides, the touchiness, the banter, the begging, the jeering, the awkwardness' encountered elsewhere in the Caribbean.

52   On this see Cooper (2012: 380).

53   'Like many other peasant communities around the Mediterranean, and also elsewhere', maintains Newby (1984: 91), 'the inhabitants of Kras are still to a great extent governed by the moon in their everyday life'.

54   That Naipaul (1987: 23, 24, 25, 30, 32) subscribes to the English pastoral is evident from the following: 'The solitude of the walk, the emptiness of that stretch of the downs, enabled me to surrender to my way of looking, to indulge my linguistic or historical fantasies; and enabled me, at the same time, to shed the nerves of being a stranger in England. Accident – the shape of the fields, perhaps, the alignment of paths and modern roads, the needs of the military – had isolated this little region; and I had this historical part of England to myself when I went walking. [My] sense of antiquity, my feeling for the age of the earth and the oldness of man's possession of it, was always with me...there was a feeling of continuity. [...] So in tune with the landscape had I become, in that solitude, for

English pastoral is threatened with the urban/industrial 'others' of the agrarian myth, and expresses a strong dislike of the change such development brings to the English countryside.[55]

When espoused by the ruling class, and especially its landowning component, the pastoral version licenses a populist discourse. Why these elements liked and approved of peasants is not difficult to discern: not just their quaintness but their quiescence. Smallholders, whether proprietors or tenants, could be seen as reassuringly non-threatening, as traditional bearers of an authentic and enduring form of cultural 'otherness' in the place visited, an embodiment of national stability that was eternal.[56] For this reason, it is not surprising to encounter travel writing that combines affectionate regard for the plebeian rural 'other' with an admiration for royalty and nobility (foreign and domestic).[57] Where claims about rural harmony and quiescence are contradicted by plebeian agency, however, the pastoral is either undermined or replaced by the Darwinian version of the agrarian myth.

The Inevitable Encroachment of Civilization

The account by E. Lucas Bridges of Patagonia at the start of the twentieth century, which belongs to a genre of travel literature described as a 'get-there-and-stay-there-book', reveals the contradictions structuring the pastoral variant of

---

the first time in England. [...] My feeling for that wide grassy way had grown. I saw it as the old bed of an ancient river, almost something from another geological age; I saw it as the way down which geese might have once been driven to Camelot-Winchester from Salisbury Plain; I saw it as the old stagecoach road. [...] I saw with the eyes of pleasure'. He concludes in a similar vein (Naipaul, 1987: 34): 'Here was an unchanging world – so it would have seemed to the stranger. So it seemed to me when I first became aware of it: the country life, the slow movement of time...' Although he accepts that 'change was constant', his reference to it as encompassing '[m]y own presence in the valley, in the cottage of the manor, was an aspect of another kind of change', confirms that Naipaul sees this as an outsider, wanting to belong – to be a part of what he describes.

55   Observing the intrusion of men, commerce and machines into the countryside, therefore, the main character in the narrative – based clearly on the writer himself – complains (Naipaul, 1987: 44) that 'I didn't like the change. I felt it threatened what I had found and what I had just begun to enter. I didn't like the new busyness, the new machines, the machine-lopping of the hawthorn and the wild rose... And I didn't want that new [asphalt] surface on the farm lane to hold'.

56   'I would recommend people to go to Spain', advised Cyril Connolly (1931: 88–89), 'while the exchange rate is low, and before the last peasants have been metamorphosed into citizens...'

57   See, for example, Grahame (1909: 275, 303, 306), who hopes that England will 'spare our old nobility' and expresses admiration for Italian royalty on the grounds that it will promote much needed agricultural development.

the agrarian myth.[58] In what is a sympathetic portrayal of the Ona tribal inhabitants, Bridges rejects modernity and condemns the spread of industrial civilization as an encroachment that would destroy their way of life ('shatter the age-old silence').[59] Recognizing them as 'the original lords of the land', and as such having a legitimate claim to the space/place that is Tierra del Fuego, he evinces solidarity with a shared rural identity by reiterating his dislike of all things urban.[60] Despite this, when Bridges takes sides in a tribal dispute, the Ona challenge him in the following manner: 'What business is it of yours? What are you doing here in this, our country?'[61]

Why the indigenous population questioned such attempts on the part of Bridges to identify with them is not difficult to discern. During the period from the 1890s until the 1914–18 war, as a result of land grants and purchases from the Argentine government he (and other members of his family) consolidated ownership of large tracts of rural property throughout Tierra del Fuego. Initially, such holdings amounted to some fifty thousand acres on which to

---

58 Since his father, the Rev. Thomas Bridges, was an English missionary posted to Tierra del Fuego in the late nineteenth century (South American Missionary Society, 1890), the classic account by E. Lucas Bridges (1948) of episodes which reveal its socio-economic structure at the beginning of the twentieth conforms to what has been described (Amis, 1990: 327) as a 'get-there-and-stay-there-book'. A foreign national resident in another context becomes an external chronicler of that society, the outcome resembling an ethnography produced by an anthropologist as a result of participant/observation fieldwork. Indeed, Bridges (1948: 529–537) recounts how one particular anthropologist, Frederick Cook, attempted to pass off the Yamana-English Dictionary compiled by the Rev. Thomas Bridges as his own work, an oblique testimony to the value of detailed information compiled by a long-term resident. In this sense, the account by Bridges of Tierra del Fuego is different both from ethnography (Cooper, 1917) and from aristocratic travelogues (Dixie, 1880).

59 Bridges (1948: 336–337) describes a dystopian 'vision of a not far distant future, when the Indian hunter would roam his quiet woods no more; when the light wraith from his camp fire would give place to the smoke from the saw-mills; when the throbbing engines and hooting sirens would shatter forever the age-old silence', adding: 'I share [these] emotions to the full. I was powerless to stop the inevitable encroachment of civilization, but I was determined to do my utmost to soften the blow of it'.

60 Not only does Bridges (1948: 202, 207) aver that 'in my young heart I would have loved to... share their struggle against the advance of so-called civilization into the romantic land that was theirs...[m]y personal sympathies were all with the original lords of the land', therefore, but he (Bridges, 1948: 341–342, 343) also expressed a strong dislike of having to travel periodically to Buenos Aires ('I was glad to get away from the turmoil and rush of the city').

61 See Bridges (1948: 393).

breed and herd sheep. To this was subsequently added a further property – the Estancia Viamonte – on which commercial logging was undertaken, covering in total a quarter of a million acres.[62]

The irony is unmistakeable. Although these acquisitions are justified in terms of preserving the indigenous way of life, it is the capitalist farming of Bridges himself that promotes the dystopian vision he feared would come about.[63] The ambivalence of his relation with the Ona is evident from references to them both as 'my companions' (= friends, equals) or 'my helpers' (= assistants) and as 'my gang of workmen' (= hired labourers, unequals) who clear roads, shear sheep and act as shepherds.[64] A discourse of the landlord pastoral notwithstanding, it is clear that – in terms of beliefs and actions – Bridges follows closely the logic of a capitalist proprietor.

An Inborn Desire to Hunt and Kill

Once 'from below' rural and/or urban agency threatens to establish itself, the emphasis of discourse about the agrarian myth shifts, and either combines with or is displaced by the red-in-tooth-and-claw version. The way in which the pastoral on occasion combines with the Darwinian is evident from the approach of Thesiger and Naipaul.[65] Categorizing the Bedouin of Arabia as an

---

62   From England Bridges (1948: 475) imported steam saw-mill and building materials for the new acquisition, his earlier holdings now being managed by his brother ('the efficient yet benevolent lord of our old domain'). The estate house at Estancia Viamonte possessed 'all modern conveniences' (Bridges, 1948: 475, 481, 483), as well as a cook-house, storage, stables, shearing-shed, and fifteen dwellings 'for the Ona [workers]' who carried out all the stock work of the farm', involving some 120,000 sheep.

63   Hence the declaration by Bridges (1948: 393) that '[i]t was also my intention to make, if possible, a step towards securing as much land as I could...for the benefit of ourselves *and the Ona inhabitants*' (emphasis added). The presentation of land acquisition as being to the benefit of the indigenous population disguises the fact that what he wanted was to have his workers – the Ona – in close proximity, where they would be on call when required by him for his business operations.

64   See Bridges (1948: 339, 356, 359, 405, 460), who reveals the extent to which his relations with the indigenous workers he employed were guided ultimately by commercial objectives. Thus '[f]rom the very beginning I saw the need for them [Ona workers] to learn the use of money...they were paid every evening in cash for their day's work. We paid those who worked well more than the lazy ones and something was discounted from those who habitually turned up unduly late', adding (Bridges, 1948: 483, 501) that 'an even greater incentive than money was pride in their speed and good work'.

65   Although the themes considered here regularly surface in the writings of Naipaul (1981; 1990; 1998; 2010), what follows is based mainly on five sources. Four of these consist of long essays, written during the 1970s, recording impressions gained as a result of visits to

example of 'the noble savage', therefore, Thesiger endorses their Social Darwinist approach to life, in the process justifying his own adherence to the red-in-tooth-and-claw version of the agrarian myth.[66]

The Darwinian version of the plebeian variant of the agrarian myth, incorporating the revenge-of-Nature, which Naipaul equates with the permanence of the 'African bush' and the impermanence of European 'civilization', the former encroaching on what little foothold the latter had managed to obtain in the pre-Independence era.[67] This dichotomy gives rise to the oppositions set out in Table 3. On the one hand, Europe is characterized as the locus of positive attributes (developed, urban, civilized, light) but the values and influence of

---

the Caribbean, Argentina and the Congo: 'Michael X and the Black Power Killings in Trinidad' (Naipaul, 1980: 3–91), 'The Return of Eva Perón' (Naipaul, 1980: 95–170), 'A New King for the Congo: Mobutu and the Nihilism of Africa' (Naipaul, 1980: 173–204), and 'Conrad's Darkness' (1980: 207–228). The fifth is a work of fiction (Naipaul, 1979), although it covers the same ground as the four essays. Since experiences based on time spent in post-Independence Africa also informs his portrayal of an unnamed nation, usually taken to be the Congo, this fiction is included as part of this analysis. Together, these five sources enable a symptomatic reading of views formed by him in the course of travel.

66   'I believe that most men have an inborn desire to hunt and kill and that even today this primitive urge has only been eradicated in a small minority of the human race', observes Thesiger (1988: 115, 399), subsequently elaborating on what precisely this entails: 'Inevitably these Bedu had little veneration for human life. In their frequent raids and counter-raids they killed and were killed, and each killing involved the tribe or family in another blood-feud to be settled without mercy – though in no circumstances would they have tortured anyone. I soon acquired the same attitude, and if anyone had killed one of my companions I would unquestionably have sought to avenge him; I have no belief in the "sanctity" of life'.

67   Describing tribal women as having 'wailed in the forest way' (Naipaul, 1979: 88–89), he cites as cause of their distress the fact that 'it was as though some old law of the forest, something that came from Nature itself, had been overturned'. This reaction is then given anti-modern roots: 'The rage of the rebels was like a rage against metal, machinery, wires, everything that was not of the forest and Africa'. Elsewhere the forest is described (Naipaul, 1980: 179, 181, 186–187) in similarly threatening terms: 'And the bush is close. It begins just outside the city and goes on forever...[it is] the untouched heart of darkness... [s]o little has the vast country been touched: so complete, simple and repetitive appears the African life through which the traveller swiftly passes... About agriculture, as about so many things, as about the principles of government itself, there is confusion. Everyone feels the great bush at his back. And the bush remains the bush, with its own logical life. Away from the mining areas and the decaying towns the land is as the Belgians found it and as they have left it'. The physical and ideological proximity of the 'bush' – the 'real' Africa – is thus just below the surface, not to be suppressed for long, always ready and able to push aside an 'inauthentic' modernity and development.

TABLE 3   *European 'self' versus African 'other' in V.S. Naipaul*

Europe	Africa
Modern	Pre-modern
Light	Dark
Civilized	Primitive
Weak	Powerful
Artificial	Natural
Urban	Nature/forest/'bush'/rural
Secular	Religious
Temporary	Permanent
Colonial	Independent
Developed	Backward
Self	Other

which is seen by Naipaul as frail, transient and destined to vanish ('weak', 'artificial'). On the other, Africa is categorized negatively (dark, the 'bush', forest, rural, backward) but the values of which are eternal and enduring (mysterious, primitive).[68] For Naipaul, therefore, Africa is the negative 'other' of the positive European 'self'. As any/all attempts by Europeans to come to terms with 'the bush' either fail or end in tragedy, the inference is that there is no point even in trying to do this.[69]

---

68   This contrast between 'light' = good and 'dark' = bad is effected thus (Naipaul, 1979: 15) 'In daylight, though, you could believe in that vision of the future. You could imagine the land being made ordinary, fit for men like yourself, as small parts of it had been made ordinary for a short while before independence – the very parts that were now in ruins. But at night, if you were on the river, it was another thing. You felt the land taking you back to something that was familiar, something you had known at some time but had forgotten or ignored, but which was always there. You felt the land taking you back to what was there a hundred years ago, to what had been there always'. Later, a character flying over the country after having visited Europe (Naipaul, 1979: 271) notes the blackness of the forest, thereby reinforcing the theme of Africa = black = the forest = the 'bush'.

69   Thus Fr Huismans, 'a lover of Africa', is murdered by the indigenous population (Naipaul, 1979: 89–90) despite 'his particular kind of dedicated life [which] had made him find human richness where the rest of us saw bush or had stopped seeing anything at all'. As depicted by Naipaul, the death of Fr Huismans in the forest symbolizes the end of Europe seeing positive things in African tradition.

Naipaul maintains that, since the African is at home only in 'the bush', and as such a 'natural' peasant, the benefits of economic development in the town/city are not for him/her.[70] This is confirmed by what he writes about other contexts in the so-called Third World. One is the Caribbean, where in his opinion the black man is always 'performing', being something other than his authentic self, which for Naipaul is – and can only ever be – 'the primitive'.[71] Another is Latin America, where similarly 'inauthentic' non-European 'performances' engaged in 'mimicry' of European 'civilization' are to be found.[72] This is an identity the indigenous subject in all these contexts is incapable of transcending, a fear which haunts Naipaul, who aspires to be – and has succeeded in realizing – that 'otherness' which eludes the former: being non-primitive, being 'civilized'.

Much like an eighteenth century landowner, therefore, Naipaul thinks 'natural' peasants should always remain what they are; pre-modern rural 'primitives' who ought to be satisfied with their lot. That they are not, and in Africa – as in the Caribbean and Latin America – threaten to erase the ideological boundary within which he has confined them, underwrites the Darwinian version of the agrarian myth which informs his writing about travel in 'other' places.[73]

---

70   For the view that the 'real' Africa is to be found in the village, and that all Africans are essentially peasants, see Naipaul (1979: 133, 286). That the same is true of Latin America is clear from his disdain for the Argentinean worker, described (Naipaul, 1980: 159) as being both uneducated (reads comics), being vulgar and without manners (licks fingers to turn pages).

71   The inability of the Caribbean 'other' to transcend his essential rural identity, and the consequent regression to a barbarian savagery of the innately 'primitive, is outlined by Naipaul (1980: 1–91) in relation to the murder of a white female by Black Power adherents in Trinidad.

72   In contrast to the 'civilized' people of Europe and the United States, therefore, in Argentina (Naipaul, 1980: 129) 'the gauchos were very simple-minded barbarians'. In much the same vein (Naipaul, 1980: 139), 'Uruguayans say that they are a European nation, that they have always had their back to the rest of South America. It was their great error, and is part of their failure'.

73   See Naipaul (1979: 286), who complains about 'village people, establishing themselves in town for the first time'. In what is an uncritical introduction to a collection of essays by Naipaul (2002: vii-xv), Pankaj Mishra misinterprets both the position held by the author and the reason for this, wrongly attributing to Naipaul an optimism coupled with 'a well-founded faith in human striving and perfectibility'. As is argued here, the exact opposite is the case, in that from the vantage point of his English pastoral setting Naipaul regards 'human striving' in Africa and elsewhere with ill-disguised horror. Significantly, by 'civilization' Naipaul (2002: 503–517) means only that someone like himself, who travels 'from

IV

In an important sense, the historical connection between on the one hand the act of foreign travel and on the other discourse about national identity and the agrarian myth is – or should be – unproblematic. As long as an individual remained in his/her own country, the distinctiveness of elements composing national/ethnic 'otherness' (language, customs, dress, music, etc.) tended to stay hidden. In such circumstances, the *specifica differentia* of a particular culture may easily be assumed by its subjects to be 'natural' and 'eternal' attributes, adhered to by populations everywhere.[74] This much is clear from the many instances of tribal inhabitants whose self-identity is simply that of being 'the people', or whose remote location is similarly categorized along the lines of 'the centre of the world'. Without an 'other' in order to define what it is precisely that constitutes 'selfhood', the latter has – and can only have – something akin to a solipsistic existence.

Places of the Imagination

Hence the unsurprising nature of the link between foreign travel and the formulation by its subject of ideas and/or concepts about nationalism.[75] What in

---

the margin [= colony] to the centre [= metropolitan capitalism]', is able to earn a living as a writer, nothing more. In other words, he subscribes to the concept of an open-ended individual upward mobility, a veritable bourgeois myth.

74 The extent to which such details, once considered peripheral to politics, have been excluded from important analyses, is evident from the manner and reasons for cutting down the length of a post-war edition of a classic analysis by de Tocqueville (1959). Noting that '[i]n this [1946] edition of *Democracy in America* the text has been reduced to approximately half its original length', the editor, Henry Steele Commager (de Tocqueville, 1959: v), a distinguished historian, justified this in the following way. 'Much that Tocqueville thought necessary to include by way of description and explanation is now quite useless for all practical purposes. There is no need, now, to preserve the rather tiresome account of the geography, native races, colonial history, local and state government of the United States'. He concludes: 'It is hoped, and believed, that the present edition sacrifices nothing that is essential, and presents what is essential in more succinct and palatable form'. It is precisely those aspects – dismissed and consequently excised as 'the rather tiresome account' – which constitute an important insight to how and why a writer from one national context reacts to *all* the features confronting him/her in another.

75 About this connection Liebknecht (1908: 147) writes: '"Patriotism" is a disease by which a sensible man is attacked only in foreign countries; for at home there is so much miserable inadequacy that everybody who is not suffering from paralysis of the brain...is charmed against the bacillus of this political vertigo, also called chauvinism or jingoism, and most dangerous when those attacked by it sanctimoniously turn their eyes upward and carry

national terms is distinctive – or, conversely, the way in which a nation is not, after all, unique – can emerge directly or indirectly. Both stem in part from travel, experienced by the subject in person, or relayed to the latter by someone who has him/herself undergone this. In each case, therefore, concepts of nationhood result from an encounter between the self and a foreign 'other'.[76] Historically such an ideological process cannot but have been generated by travel, an act which fuels what is known or learned about 'other' people inhabiting 'other' places.[77] It is by crossing such boundaries that ideas about nationhood lead cumulatively to the development of national consciousness, the specific form of 'belonging' that corresponds to Herder's *volksgeist*.

This process generates concepts of 'otherness' that are applied both at home and abroad.[78] An outcome of reifying cultural aspects as specific to the

---

God's name on their lips. "In Saxony I praise Prussia, in Prussia I praise Saxony," said Lessing. And this is a sensible patriotism that tries to cure the defects of the home country by the example of the real or imagined good in foreign countries. I had taken advantage of this word of Lessing at an early period and the only drubbing I received since the days of my youth was due to an attack of patriotism while I was abroad'. As a socialist, Liebknecht perceived clearly that what was at issue was not the superiority of one nationalism over another – which is the position taken by postmodernism (privileging grassroots indigenous nationalisms over bourgeois versions) – but of nationalism *per se*.

76   Thus, for example (Barnard, 1965: xiii), '[t]he first time Herder thought of himself consciously as a German was upon his arrival [during 1769] in France. The longer he stayed, the more German he grew in outlook... [He] did not enjoy his stay. He sensed an air of decay; he considered French culture to be on the decline'. Nearly a century later, Herzen reacted in much the same way when visiting Paris, the result in his case being a turn toward Slav identity and Russian nationalism. In a similar vein, Robert Byron reaffirmed his sense of Englishness when travelling abroad over the first half of the twentieth century.

77   This is confirmed by many sources, some of which can surprise. Hence the following: 'I am now travelling in Holland... I assure you, although one is feeling nothing less than national pride, one still feels national shame, even in Holland. The most inferior Dutchman is yet an intelligent citizen compared to the greatest German. And the opinions of foreigners about the Prussian government! There is an awe-inspiring agreement of opinions, nobody is deceived any longer about this system and its simple nature. Some good, then... this is also a revelation, although reversed. It is a truth showing us at least the hollowness of our patriotism, the nature of our administration, and teaching us to hide our faces. You regard me smiling and ask: "What does it avail? You don't start a revolution with shame." I reply: Shame is already a revolution...' These observations were outlined in a letter written by Karl Marx to Ruge in 1843 (Liebknecht, 1908: 17–18).

78   Descriptive and non-analytical, travel writing plays an important role – like anthropology – in defining for a domestic audience the nature of foreign 'otherness'. Morris (2001) decries nationalism and ethnicity, recognizing the deleterious impact of these ideologies in

national/ethnic identity of the self is to license an analogous search for those components which are equally specific to the national/ethnic identity of the 'other'.[79] This twofold essentialization is found in much travel writing, where historically – and currently – a contrast is effected between what are taken to be innate national characteristics. As a number of travel writers have themselves made clear, focussing on what constitutes 'cultural difference', at home and abroad, diverts the gaze away from politics in general and the sameness of politics across nations in particular.[80] It scarcely needs repeating that, in terms of what is to be included/excluded, such an agenda is one that travel writing shares with postmodern theory.

---

neighbouring Yugoslavia, yet his very approach to Trieste – evincing as it does a nostalgia for a lost past – nourishes the roots of these same discourses. Part of this nostalgia entails invoking the agrarian myth, or the view that in the rural areas surrounding Trieste, peasants are all the same and have always done the same kind of things, a view in keeping with the 'natural' seasonal rhythms imposed by Nature on smallholding agriculture.

79   Travelling to India in 1956, Kenneth Clark (1977: 161) observed that '[t]he Indians are in many respects a ridiculous people...'. Comparing Australia to the United States, he notes (Clark, 1977: 150) that the former contains 'thank God, even fewer smart people. What is known as "sophistication" does not suit the Australian character at all...' Nor does he like what he finds in modern Japan, observing (Clark, 1977: 182) that 'I found myself thinking nostalgically of Europe, and wondering how people who are dedicated to these [Japanese] sand gardens could swallow Bernini. Surely he would make them feel sick'. 'Almost everything developed in modern Japan, except in architecture', argues Clark (1977: 183), 'is heartless, inhuman and unsympathetic'.

80   'What was Spain really like? What was the character of Spanish culture and civilization? How did it compare with the French and the English?', asks Gerald Brenan (1950: xi–xii), adding: 'To answer these questions I decided to keep a diary...and it is out of this diary that the present book [about a voyage across southern Spain] has been made... I was tired of politics – especially of the hopeless politics of the Peninsula and wished to give my attention to the more permanent and characteristic features of the country. Regimes, I said to myself, come and go, but what is really important in Spain never changes'. In a similar vein, Patrick Leigh Fermor is reported as saying (Cooper, 2012: 85–86) that 'politics were of little interest to him: he wanted to know what people were like, to learn about their history and what they ate and wore and sang'. He made much the same observation during the 1950s when writing about travel in the Caribbean (Leigh Fermor, 1968: x): 'About the political problems and the economics, which I jettisoned, I feel no such compunction... The scope of the book thus reduces itself to a personal, random account of an autumn and winter spent in wandering through these islands, and it has all the fallibility implicit in such a charter'. Eschewing politics and privileging 'cultural difference' in this manner does not, as will be seen below, prevent these (and other) travel writers from being very critical of socialist regimes while turning a blind eye to right-wing politics.

It might be thought that the impact of writing about foreign travel on the discourse about national identity and the agrarian myth would diminish in the television age, as the electronic image supplanted the word (ethnographic accounts, travel literature) in framing the meaning of 'other' places and peoples. This possibility was recognized early on, in the 1950s, at what might be termed the 'dawn' of the television age, when 'other' places could – and would – be depicted as much by electronic images as by the word.[81] The assumption was that visual access provided a more 'authentic' form of gazing at (= travelling to) another national context and its culture, one that increasingly rivalled – but did not necessarily supplant – written accounts.

Hence the seeming irony in the rise to prominence of writing about travel coinciding with the popularity in metropolitan capitalist countries of television programmes about 'other places' (the 'natural world', travel to 'exotic' locations).[82] There is, however, no contradiction involved, since both image and word project much the same kind of discourse, itself fuelled by the longstanding ideology of the agrarian myth. Notwithstanding changes in the way in which it is transmitted, therefore, this is a discourse about the nature of

---

81   A 1952 editorial in a magazine published under the auspices of the British Council noted (original emphasis): 'It is certain that nothing so readily gives clear impressions of what another country is like as to *see* it and *hear* its sounds. Travel is the best way of getting these impressions, but not everyone can travel. At present films are the principal medium for bringing such sights and sounds to the masses of the people. They may be artificial or false, and therefore diminish rather than increase understanding. Or they may show people as they really are, homes, countryside, wild life – flesh and blood and the human environment'. A Spanish film of *Don Quixote* is commended for providing the viewer with 'an awareness of something that we feel to be in the Spanish tradition which we could not otherwise have had without visiting the Spanish country itself'. It concludes optimistically that 'films have been evolving for half a century with all their realized and unrealized possibilities for providing visual means of communication from country to country. And now television is setting out on the same path...Nothing, it is true, can take the place of reading books and studying the thought of other nations...[b]ut what a fulfilment of our knowledge, or what an introduction to it, if we can actually see people behaving and hear their talk, and observe the scenes amid which they spend their days. This is what films *at their best* can do. This is what television, *at its best*, will do'. See 'Long-Range Vision', *Britain Today*, Number 197 (September, 1952), pp. 6–7.

82   Currently the trend referred to here appears to have reached its apogee in the form of television programmes which combine not just the act of travel to distant locations with a focus on Nature (the Antarctic, the Congo) but also have a 'celebrity' presenter (= a 'personality' from the entertainments industry) who is charged with relaying to the audience his/her experiences about this process.

'otherness' in 'other places' that continues to be reproduced.[83] Thesiger, for example, can approve of the fact that the Abyssinians 'as a race...had not been mongrelized'.[84]

Such continuity is due in part to the political role discharged by this discourse: it permeates the agrarian myth, which in turn is an important component of populism. The latter approach, traceable to an ideological transformation linked historically to the Grand Tour, required that those above would retain their position, property and power by 'speaking about' and 'speaking to' those below, with the object ultimately of 'speaking for' them – the 'people' of whom they now claimed they were a part. In a symptomatic relay-in-statement made during the early 1920s, Robert Byron equates nationalism with aristocracy: England = public school = upper classes = country house, a view elaborated later that same decade when praising the Viceregal Lodge in New Delhi as 'so essentially aristocratic in outlook...none of that stark industrial feeling'.[85] Just as members of the English upper classes defined their identity in relation to the Grand Tour, so for Byron the main purpose of travel abroad was to clarify the meaning of English national identity.[86]

V

Hitherto, a consideration of class, the pastoral version of the agrarian myth, and nationalism reveals them all to contain positive images of rural identity endorsed by those who write about travel. This is not the case with regard to the identities, processes and politics examined in the rest of this chapter.

---

83   Among those recognizing this phenomenon – the persistence of what constitutes 'otherness' – is Henry Miller (1980: 187, emphasis added): 'It is strange that the countries I most wanted to visit I have never seen – India, Tibet, China, Japan, Iceland. *But I have lived with them in my mind.* Once I tried to persuade a British magazine editor to let me make a trip to Lhassa, Timbuctoo and Mecca without any stops between. But I had no luck. All three cities seem like *mysterious places*, and *live in my imagination'.*

84   See Thesiger (1988: 36).

85   Observing that '[t]he 4th of June at Eton is concentrated England', Byron (1991: 23) adds: 'Everything is of the best and stands for all that one cares for in this world, the institutions of the English Upper Classes'. His subsequent endorsement of Lutyens' architectural style as 'so essentially aristocratic' is (Byron, 1991: 151–152) clear: 'I lunched with the Viceroy [Lord Irwin] on Sunday...one was simply lunching in an English country house'.

86   This is evident from the view expressed in 1924 (Byron, 1991: 38) that 'I must travel a little more as all I want to write about is England and the English, and a knowledge of abroad throws them into such high relief – especially seeing English people abroad'.

Equally clear, therefore, is a dislike on the part of travel literature for a symptomatic ensemble of 'others' negating the positive images: modernity and progress, both at home and abroad, since in both contexts economic development erases traditional – and thus 'authentic' – cultural difference.

The result is a pathological disdain, both for the influx of a class-specific domestic 'other' into the country visited (plebeian travellers = tourists), and for its causes. Whereas Leigh Fermor, Waugh and Thesiger object to progress because it intrudes into what for them is a cherished rural pastoral, Naipaul by contrast blames modernity for unjustifiably attempting to 'civilize' the 'primitive' African 'bush'. Castigated for its 'artificiality', progress is deemed by him to be responsible for the 'inauthenticity' of 'half-made' societies in the Third World.

The Rubbish of Our Own Continent

Antagonism to Western modernity on the part of Thesiger arises from his endorsement of Eastern 'otherness', giving rise to the 'pollution' by the former when contrasted with the pristine aspect of the latter ('the authentic Eastern world...remote, beautiful, untamed...as yet totally unaffected by the products and influence of the modern Western world').[87] This was a judgment he made not just about Ethiopia but also about the Druze of Syria and the Marsh Arabs of Iraq, contexts described as a desert pastoral inhabited by 'natural'/untamed indigenous groups outside historical time.[88]

Thesiger was also opposed to educating the indigenous population on the grounds that this opened the door to modern development, of which he

---

87   On this contrast, see Thesiger (1988: 164–165, 434). At Oxford, writes Thesiger (1988: 80),
      'I had little interest in constitutional development, political theory or economic growth,
      none at all in the Industrial Revolution and the technical and scientific achievements that
      ushered in the modern age. I had a romantic, not an objective, conception of history'.
      About the coronation of Emperor Hailie Selassie in 1930, Thesiger (1988: 89, 91) observes
      further that '[h]appily in those days there was no air travel to take us in a few hours to
      Addis Ababa and bring us back a few days later', and that '[t]his was the last time that the
      age-old splendour of Abyssinia was to be on view. Already it was slightly tarnished round
      the edges by innovations copied from the West... However, immensely moved by sights
      reminiscent of my childhood, I ignored what I had no desire to see'.

88   Throughout the 1950s, writes Thesiger (1988: 400), 'the Marshes delighted me with the
      timeless, untroubled beauty of an unspoilt land'. About the Druze in Syria he (Thesiger,
      1988: 361) comments similarly that 'I encountered for the first time a civilized community
      that observed the traditional Arab code of behaviour, but held to their own ancient customs and dress. I found their way of life, little affected by change elsewhere, satisfying as
      a reminder of an Eastern world of fifty years before [c. 1890]'.

strongly disapproved.[89] Most revealingly, he makes clear that his dislike of urban contexts derives from the presence there of 'crowds' which were bereft of 'colour and variety', thereby connecting his anti-urbanism to the 'mob-in-the-streets' which – in aesthetic terms – he deemed wanting (no 'variety' or 'colour').[90] The sole exception was medieval Cairo, described as 'authentic' because of its lack of contact with 'the West'.[91]

Waugh objects to colonization not because it involves exploitation and expropriation, but rather for two different yet interrelated reasons. First, because it presages a transformation of which he disapproves: 'the rubbish of our own continent', by which he means technology, improved transportation, democracy, and trades unions, all changes that conservatism fears.[92] And

---

89   Hence the view (Thesiger, 1988: 196) that 'few of us believed in the benefit of education for these tribal people [in Darfur], none of whom had yet demanded it; the British had brought them security and justice, with which, for the present, they were content. We were well aware of the disruption which must ensue from the wholesale intrusion of an alien education into their society, with the consequent breakdown of family life, drift to the towns, unemployment and discontent'. This is exactly the same reason as that given by Smuts for thinking the apartheid system appropriate in South Africa at the same conjuncture (see Chapter 3).

90   On this see Thesiger (1988: 81): 'The cities I had seen in England and France left me unmoved; their crowds had no interest for me: they lacked the colour and variety for which I craved'. In a similar vein, his observation (Thesiger, 1988: 418) about 1960s Ethiopia notes: 'To me the town typified the least attractive aspects of Abyssinia's recent development: ubiquitous tin roofs, ramshackle modern buildings, noise and fumes of motor transport; its inhabitants forfeited any distinction of appearance by wearing shabby European clothes. I was left with an impression of squalor which would not have been there thirty years earlier [c. 1930]'. This is echoed by Grahame (1909: 270) in the case of Italy, where in 'another quarter...you may pause in something of disgust as you survey the "long, unlovely street" of a rather slummy description, while you stand at its summit, and looking down at a steep declivity, take note of all its unsweptness and the bits of paper and refuse with which its middle gutter is choked'.

91   'In those days', writes Thesiger (1988: 173) of the 1930s, 'modern Cairo was still an attractive town, not yet defaced by shoddy, high-rise buildings: compared with today there was little traffic...' He continues (Thesiger, 1988: 369): 'Of all the Eastern cities I had seen, medieval Cairo impressed me as the most authentic, the least affected by contact with the West'.

92   Writing about his 1930s visit to Africa, Waugh (1931: 202) observes: 'But it is quite certain that, in the expansive optimism of the last century, Africa would not have been left alone. Whether it wanted it or not, it was going to be helped with all the rubbish of our own continent; mechanised transport, representative government, organized labour, artificially stimulated appetites for variety in clothes, food, and amusement were waiting for the African round the corner. All the negative things were coming to him inevitably.

second, because of an affinity with white farmers in Kenya, regarded by Waugh as alienated from Europe on account of its modern trends (industrialization, urbanization, political democracy and worker mobilization), and wishing to do no more than live as country squires.[93] Like him, therefore, these landowners approve of a culturally 'authentic'/traditional Africa from which all progress is as yet absent.

What he wants, in short, is two things. First, for Africa to remain what he thinks it always has been and should for ever remain: the domain of the eternally pristine 'noble savage', untainted by any kind of progress or modernity, the permanent embodiment of an 'authentic' traditional culture as he perceives it to be. And second, that British settlers who have acquired land there should be able to enjoy the kind of life – as country gentry – no longer open to them at home. For much the same reasons, Waugh also disapproves of Indian merchants and traders encountered on a visit to Zanzibar, whom he regards as a disruptive foreign commercial influence eroding the indigenous Arab culture.[94]

As significant in terms of outcome is Leigh Fermor's dislike of modernity and industrial development, two crucial 'others' of the agrarian myth.[95] This kind of reaction emerged in the period after 1939–45 war, when revisiting countries across which he had travelled a decade earlier. Returning to Greece

---

Europe has only one positive thing which it can offer to anyone, and that is what the missionaries brought'.

93 Defending the 'Happy Valley' set he encounters in Kenya, Waugh (1931: 178 ff.) complains that '[a]nother quite inconsistent line of criticism represent the settlers as a gang of rapacious adventurers', but accepts that '[i]t is on the face of it, rather surprising to find a community of English squires established on the Equator'. He then dismisses the argument that British settlers in Africa have no right to land belonging to the indigenous population on the grounds that such occupations ('movements of people') have – and will – always occur. The latter is justified (Waugh, 1931: 181) in terms of being 'an organic process in human life'; in other words, imperialism and colonialism are 'natural' processes that cannot be halted. Eschewing an economic motive for landownership, Waugh (1931: 182–183) insists that settlers acquired property purely for aesthetic reasons: a 'more gentle motive of love for a very beautiful country that they have come to regard as their home, and the wish to transplant and perpetuate a habit of life traditional to them, which England has ceased to accommodate – the traditional life of the English squirearchy...'

94 See Waugh (1931: 166–168).

95 Leigh Fermor (Cooper, 2012: 53) 'liked to think that, if he looked in the right way, he could still see Europe as the Congress of Vienna had left it: a sort of eternal, cultural Europe that lay untouched behind its cities, factories and railway lines; a continent where peasant life was dictated by the round of the seasons and the feasts of the Church, where strange costumes were worn as real clothes and not donned for the tourist trade...'

in 1951, therefore, 'what [Leigh Fermor] feared most [was] Greece losing its ancient identities in an all-pervasive [industrialization]'.[96] This concern is embodied in Table 4, where he effects a contrast between the classical and non-classical elements of Greek tradition, and opts for the latter as the vanishing yet more 'authentic' version.[97]

Not only is there no difference between the classical/non-classical oppositions and those structuring the discourse-against/discourse-for of the agrarian myth, but its characterization in positive/negative terms is endorsed by Leigh Fermor. Like the 'new' populist postmodernism currently, therefore, his travel writing exhibits an antagonism to socialism, industrialization, economic development, and urbanization, and is supportive of traditional rural culture, and its small-scale 'natural'/harmonious activities (peasant family farming) and 'eternal' identities (ethnic/national/village) rooted in Nature. Equally significantly, however, Leigh Fermor recognizes the implications of holding this view: he accepts that it means that 'the poor should be kept in ignorance, poverty and disease to oblige a few romantic travellers'.[98]

TABLE 4   *Classical versus non-classical Greek tradition in Patrick Leigh Fermor*

Classical heritage	Non-classical heritage
Hellene	Romaic
Urban	Rural
Intellectual	Farmer
Progressive	Conservative
Technological	Religious
Modernizing	Backward
Western	Orthodox

SOURCE: COMPILED FROM INFORMATION IN LEIGH FERMOR (2004: 107 FF.) AND COOPER (2012: 332–333)

---

96   For this view, see Cooper (2012: 254).

97   For Leigh Fermor (Cooper, 2012: 333), therefore, 'these two strands are equally valid, equally Greek…but on one point [he] was sure. [Leigh Fermor] was acutely aware that Romiosyne [= non-classical heritage] was in decline, and for him it was a great cause of sadness'.

98   For Leigh Fermor's recognition of the implication of holding this view, see Cooper (2012: 333) and also the author himself (Leigh Fermor, 2004: 122) who writes: 'I can hear some Athenian exclaim at this point "Are we to stop progress for the sake of an occasional

Half-Made Societies

The antagonism felt by Naipaul towards all the 'others' of the agrarian myth emerge with respect to his characterization of the 'new man in Africa', together with the fate of the latter. This identity, embodying as it does modernity, industry, economic development, and urbanization, is represented by the following ensemble: the President of the African country; Raymond, a European who is his adviser; Indar, a visiting lecturer, who is modern, cosmopolitan, urbane, and secular; and the settlement known as 'the Domain', consisting of the new buildings and university that will become 'the new Africa'.[99]

Although initially the Domain corresponds to 'a place of possibility', an artificial creation amounting to 'the merest clearing in the forest, the merest clearing in an immensity of bush and river', it is gradually taken over by the encroaching African 'bush'.[100] This was a process whereby 'Africa, going back to its old ways with modern tools, was going to be a difficult place for some time'.[101] Invoking Conrad's 'heart of darkness' as an enduring truth about

---

eccentric traveller? Undo the work of a hundred-and-fifty years? Bring back piracy and reinstall the brigands, encourage armed faction, civil war, assassination, malaria, illiteracy? What else? Sloth, bribery, dirt, disease, poverty; lawlessness, superstition, stone-age agriculture, the whole wretched inheritance of Ottoman times – all to supply a refreshing change from the sophistication of the West?...Are we to call a halt to industry and tourism?'

99   The background of Indar, together with his attributes and opinions, suggest he corresponds to Naipaul himself. A visiting lecturer from London, staying in the Domain (Naipaul, 1979: 119 ff., 152–167), this character who studied in England observes: 'For someone like me there was only one civilization and one place – London, or a place like it. Every other kind of life was make-believe'.

100 See Naipaul (1979: 129, 130, 134, 149, 170, 186, 277–278), who charts its rise and demise thus: '...in the magical atmosphere of the Domain, among the avenues and new houses, another Africa had been created... [...] And to leave the Domain and drive back to the town, to see the shacks, acres and acres of them, the rubbish mounds, to feel the presence of the river and the forest all around..., to see the ragged groups outside the drinking booths, the squatters' cooking fires on the pavements in the centre of town, to do that drive was to return to the Africa I knew. It was to climb down from the exaltation of the Domain, to grasp reality again. [...] On the other side of the Domain the land for the model farm had become overgrown; all that remained of the project [were] the six tractors standing in a line and rotting. [...]...the Domain had lost its modern "show-place" character. It was scruffier; every week it was becoming more of an African housing settlement. Maize, which in that climate and soil sprouted in three days, grew in many places...' In a non-fictional account (Naipaul, 1980: 189) 'the presidential domain' of Nsele is equated with modernity and progress.

101 See Naipaul (1979: 217).

the innate 'primitiveness' of the indigenous African 'other', Naipaul insists that '[s]eventy years later, at this bend in the river, something like Conrad's fantasy has come to pass'.[102] Such a view is not confined to Africa, since Naipaul also regards the capital cities of both Argentina and Uruguay as 'inauthentic', veneers of European civilization destined to be overwhelmed by the return of the 'bush', the only true identity of the Third World 'other'.[103]

This same trajectory – the urban/modern displaced by the rural/ancient – is followed by the President who, having espoused the 'new Africa' and created the Domain, reverts politically to the 'old'/'real' Africa of the 'bush'.[104] In order to bolster his claim to 'speak to/for the people', therefore, the President – a thinly-disguised Mobutu – uses plebeian idioms to populist effect.[105] Adopting a nationalist/populist discourse, he argues that the 'natural' condition of the

---

102   On this regression to 'primitiveness', described as 'savagery' in a 'wilderness' belonging to the 'earliest ages of man', see Naipaul (1980: 195–196, 215–217).

103   Of Buenos Aires Naipaul (1980: 128) writes: 'Elegance, if in this plebeian immigrant city elegance ever existed outside the vision of expatriate architects, has vanished: there is now only disorder'. Subsequently, this view is elaborated upon (Naipaul, 1980: 161): 'Barbarism, in a city which has thought of itself as European, in a land which, because of that city, has prided itself on its civilization. Barbarism because of that very idea: civilization felt as something far away, magically kept going by others: the civilization of Europe divorced from any idea of an intellectual life and equated with the goods and fashions of Europe: civilization felt as something purchasable, something always there, across the ocean...' Montevideo is similarly described by him (Naipaul, 1980: 134, 137) as 'an artificial metropolis... a 'fabulous city, created all at once, and struck down almost as soon as it had been created'.

104   This contrast is evident from the fact that, initially, the President (Naipaul, 1979: 110) 'was creating modern Africa. He was creating a miracle that would astound the rest of the world. He was by-passing real Africa, the difficult Africa of bush and village, and was creating something that would match anything that existed in other countries'.

105   Hence the President (Naipaul, 1979: 225) 'showed himself again as the friend of the people, the *petit peuple*, as he liked to call them, and he punished their oppressors'. In his non-fictional account of the Congo, Naipaul (1980: 173, 175, 204) makes the same point, noting that 'as [Mobutu] has imposed order on the army and the country so his style changed, and became more African...when the chief [Mobutu] speaks...the modern dialogue stops; and Africa of the ancestors takes over. [...] The kingship of Mobutu has become its own end. The inherited modern state is being dismantled, but it isn't important that the state should work. The bush works; the bush has always been self-sufficient'. Argentina is identified by Naipaul (1980: 105, 114–115) as yet another context where 'they all have native ancestors' and engage in 'ancestor worship': that is to say, are thinly-disguised rural 'primitives'.

African is rural (= the 'bush'), and further that the pre-modern village is the locus of an innate democracy and socialism.[106]

Equally significant is the fact that the implications of this trajectory are misread by Raymond, the European adviser to the President, who – like Fr Huismans – tries and fails to maintain a political focus on the desirability of economic development.[107] He brushes aside the possibility that, beneath the surface appearance of the 'New Africa' lurks the old Africa, the one that continues to espouse traditional beliefs incompatible with modernity. In what is perhaps his most pessimistic observation about the impossibility of development/ progress/modernity, Naipaul labels Africa as a continent of 'half-made societies that seem doomed to remain half-made'.[108]

Not only is this same label ('half-made societies') applied by Naipaul to Argentina and Uruguay, but for him there is little difference between the latter countries and their African counterparts.[109] All are places where a 'primitive' and thus barbarian rural 'other' identity are innate, and cannot be transcended.

---

106   This transition is outlined thus (Naipaul, 1979: 221): 'The African language the President had chosen for his speeches was a mixed and simple language, and he simplified it further, making it the language of the drinking booth and the street brawl, converting himself, while he spoke, this man who kept everybody dangling and imitated the etiquette of royalty and the graces of de Gaulle, into the lowest of the low. And that was the attraction of the African language in the President's mouth'. In the course of the speech, the President talked of 'the need to strengthen the revolution, unpopular though it was with those black men in towns who dreamed of waking up one day as white men; the need for Africans to be African, to go back without shame to their democratic and socialist ways...'

107   When asked about the significance of the fetish the President had on his staff of chiefly office, Raymond answered (Naipaul, 1979: 146): 'I don't know about that. It is a stick. It is a Chief's stick. It is like a mace or a mitre. I don't think we have to fall into the error of looking for African mysteries everywhere'. Despite the extent of his research, therefore, Raymond is unable to comprehend the power of the real/old/traditional Africa, and thus the threat it poses to the continuation of the 'New Africa' (Naipaul, 1979: 195).

108   It was, Naipaul (1980: 216) confesses, 'in the new world I felt that [secure] ground move below me. The new politics, the curious reliance of men on institutions they were yet working to undermine, the simplicity of beliefs and the hideous simplicity of actions, the corruptions of causes, half-made societies that seem doomed to remain half-made; these were the things that began to preoccupy me...'

109   See Naipaul (1980: 104). Of Argentina, therefore (Naipaul, 1980: 167), '[t]he parallel is not with any country in Europe, as Argentine writers sometimes say. The parallel is with Haiti, after the slave rebellion of Toussaint: a barbarous colonial society, similarly made, similarly parasitic on a removed civilization, and incapable of regenerating itself'. The comparison is significant: for Naipaul, therefore, Argentina = Haiti = rural 'other', the country of 'primitive' black slaves, unconnected with European 'civilization'.

In Argentina, therefore, the barbarism of Perón accurately reflected the essential primitiveness of its inhabitants ('He showed the country its unacknowledged half-Indian face'), above which they could not arise, and beyond which they were unable to progress.[110] Modernity, development, civilization – all these were European characteristics and, like the 'imported' culture of their metropolis, not for Argentineans; their self-image as Europeans notwithstanding, such attainments were 'mimicry', and thus beyond their reach.[111]

VI

Even in the mid-nineteenth century, upper class travellers reacted with evident horror at the presence in the country visited of plebeian 'others' from the same nation, regarding this as a 'vulgar' intrusion into the foreign cultural milieu being appreciated.[112] With the development of mass tourism a century later, this antagonism on the part of those writing about travel became more

---

110   See Naipaul (1980: 147).

111   Like the Domain in the Congo, the urban metropolis of Argentina is for Naipaul an 'inauthentic' implantation, a 'mimicry', where its inhabitants 'perform'. In his words (Naipaul, 1980: 153): 'Buenos Aires is such an overwhelming metropolis that it takes time to understand that it is new and has been imported almost whole; that its metropolitan life is an illusion, a colonial mimicry; that it feeds on other countries and is itself sterile... Within the imported metropolis there is the structure of a developed society. But men can often appear to be mimicking their functions'. According to Naipaul (1980: 156), walking along the roads of Buenos Aires 'was to have the sharpest sense of the mimicry and alienness of the great city. It was to have a sense of the incompleteness and degeneracy of these transplanted people who seemed so whole, to begin to understand and fear their violence, their peasant cruelty, their belief in magic, and their fascination with death...' Again like their urban African counterparts, the Argentinean city-dwellers pretend to be what in the opinion of Naipaul they are not and cannot be – civilized, European; they are unable to hide their essential 'primitiveness', and identity that is never far below the surface.

112   This kind of intrusion is evident from the description by Dummond Wolff of an incident when visiting Spain. Admiring Burgos Cathedral, he writes (Dummond Wolff, 1853: 286–287): 'The interior is magnificent...[h]ere I stood thinking on the hero whose chest, the Cofre del Cid, is to be seen in one of the sacristies, – on the glorious destiny of his life, and regretting my departure from the land where, at every step, you behold some relic of chivalry, when what was my horror on hearing the following words: 'Lor!'ow'ansome!' and turning round found two Cockneys...gazing through green spectacles at the Crucifixion by Cerezo. The spasm that struck my heart at the moment was indescribably painful. Here Fleet-street was turned out in the City of El Cid. Fleet-street with its vulgarity untamed by foreign travel...bellowing forth coarse admiration without the use of the letter H'.

pronounced. Spain as the destination of choice for the growth in package tourism from the 1960s onward generated much opprobrium on the part of such commentators, among them Robert Graves, Kenneth Tynan and Kingsley Amis.[113]

Politics Disguised as Aesthetics

In most instances, the 'other' of whom such travel writers disapproved originated not in the place visited, but rather in their own home country. What he terms the 'romantic' element inherent in early twentieth century foreign travel is equated by Waugh, as by others, with its 'exclusivity'; that is, an absence generally of other travellers, and of mass tourism in particular.[114] Echoing the complaint heard from landowners throughout history, Thesiger laments that tourists – ignorant, disruptive elements (= 'mob-in-the-streets') polluting what was for him a sacred place inhabited by 'natural' people outside history – now occupy the spaces he regarded as his preserve.[115] Similarly, for Grahame not only is a desirable location in Italy one where there are 'no British tourists', but 'a certain class of American girl' is also condemned ('we confess that at Siena we would willingly dispense with the presence of the American girl of the type referred to').[116]

---

113 'By the mid-Sixties', complains Amis (1990: 325), 'large parts of the entire [Iberian] peninsula were being seasonally colonized from all over Western Europe'. Although he and Graves accept that mass tourism conferred economic benefits on the inhabitants of resorts, each nevertheless regards the outcome as undesirable (Amis, 1990: 325; Graves, 1969: 168–169).

114 Hence the view (Waugh, 1931: 43) that '[a]part from the officials and journalists who pullulated at every corner, there were surprisingly few visitors. At one time Messers. Thomas Cook and Company were advertising a personally conducted tour, and announcement which took a great deal of the romance out of our expedition'.

115 Hence the view (Thesiger, 1988: 432) that 'Kenya has changed greatly since I first went there. Tourists now swarm on the once-empty beaches and drive all over the game parks'. A similar pessimism informs his view about what has occurred in Ethiopia (Thesiger, 1988: 404): 'Alvares had visited Lalibela [in Abyssinia] in about 1521; Rohlfs, a German explorer, had done so in 1865. since then comparatively few Europeans had been there. I was horrified to hear in Addis Ababa of plans to fly tourists to Lalibela; in such a place large groups of ignorant visitors, with both sexes often dressed alike, would have had a disruptive effect'. Visiting Athens in 1930s, Thesiger (1988: 84) notes and approves of absence of tourists. In keeping with this, the fact that no others were gazing at the same sight enables him (Thesiger, 1988: 363) to maintain the fiction of discovery effected by the self: 'I spent visiting Petra in Trans-Jordan, at a time when, owing to war, there were no tourists to deprive me of my sense of discovery'.

116 For these views, see Grahame (1909: 248, 275, 276–277).

Generally hidden but usually implicit, the upper class view has been (and remains) that, as plebeian taste is 'vulgar', its subjects are incapable of appreciating historic cultures encountered in the course of foreign travel. Moreover, once plebeian travel consolidates itself as mass tourism, it is accompanied by the growth in 'other' contexts of precisely a market that caters to the bad taste of these subjects ('fast food outlets', 'airport art'). Hence, for example, the lament by Gombrich, the art historian, about an inability to appreciate the authentic culture of Austria (= 'real old Austria') due to 'the commercialized simplifications for simpletons that the tourist industry seems to need'.[117] As such, mass tourism is seen as responsible for two developments, neither of which is desirable. It not only degrades traditional culture existing in foreign countries, the aesthetic appreciation of which is itself the main object of upper class travel, but also substitutes for it a simulacrum of plebeian taste as found in the home environment.[118]

Viewed 'from above', therefore, mass tourism appears as a form of cultural pollution consequent upon the arrival in a cherished and hitherto exclusive foreign context of the dreaded 'mob-in-the-streets' from home. It is, in short, perceived by many an upper class traveller as a physical manifestation of a particular kind of 'difference', one largely unconnected with the foreign context in question: namely, the intrusion into these spaces of plebeian socio-economic identities and ideological antagonisms originating from within his own nation. Accordingly, opposition to modernization and industrialization led in turn to antagonism expressed towards the accompanying phenomenon of mass tourism. Hence the lament by Leigh Fermor during the early 1980s of the arrival in hitherto remote areas of Greece of tourists.[119]

---

117   See Gombrich (1965: 14).

118   Of Sicily, Kenneth Clark (1977: 236) observes '[f]ew places have fallen more catastrophically victim to the vulgarities of the present time'. Writing more generally about countries visited, he states (Clark 1977: 178): 'A history of bad taste would be a fascinating subject. Of course it has always existed, but for some mysterious reason its expansion over half the world took place at about the same time in the first years of the nineteenth century...[p]opular taste is bad taste, as any honest man with experience will agree'.

119   'The Mani was no longer as remote as it had been, and even the Leigh Fermors' house was under threat', reports Cooper (2012: 368), adding that they 'were appalled by the prospect of what the [new] road might bring: houses, tavernas, discos, cars, and all the terrors of Greece's burgeoning tourist industry...Tourism was taking root in Kardamyli too. When [he and his wife] had first travelled in the Mani in the early 1950s, hardly anyone had seen a foreigner. Now foreigners came in a seasonal influx...'

Ten Thousand Saw I...

Noting that he had lived in Spain since 1929, the poet Robert Graves warned in 1964 that mass tourism would erode the essential core (*báraka*) of Spanish culture.[120] Identifying mass tourism as an undesirable effect of modernity, the influx of visitors leading to the encroachment of unsightly building, necessarily destroying traditional crafts, and diluting cherished and long-standing customs and tradition, Graves lamented 'what can one do against the so-called Spirit of Progress?'.[121] His conclusion was that '[i]f my village cannot be protected from further exploitation, I may yet find myself retreating to some sheep hut a few hundred feet above my house in the prickly oak belt – this was once used for charcoal burning, but now the charcoal burners have become barmen and their daughters chambermaids in the big Palma hotels – there to end my days'.[122]

A rather more surprising adherent to the same view was Kenneth Tynan, an influential cultural critic regarded by many as holding leftist political views. Like Graves ten years previously, Tynan expressed concerns about the impact of mass tourism, categorizing himself much rather as a 'more selective' visitor (= 'traveller') who wished, most importantly, 'to escape the company of our compatriots'.[123] A decade later, these sentiments were echoed by Kingsley

---

120   Graves (1969: 160) inadvertently reveals that 'the servant problem' – a complaint raised historically by those who approved of traditional rural hierarchy at the apex of which they themselves were positioned – was one of the reasons for going to live in Mallorca, which 'could already boast of a small British colony – retired civil servants from Asian and African dependencies, who had not dared face either the English climate or *the high cost of domestic help at home*'. (emphasis added) There he (Graves, 1969: 161) 'built a house [and] lived like a rich peasant'. Much the same view was expressed by the travel writer Robert Byron (1991: 258) with regard to China in the mid-1930s, where '[o]ne pays a servant 16/- a month, and a head servant 30/-, they feed themselves. When Harold Acton lost all his income...he lived here with a large establishment of servants etc. in a lovely house on 300 dollars a month, which is what he earned as a university teacher...that is to say on £200 a year, and had a little over for collecting. You and father could live like princes...'.

121   See Graves (1969: 172), who went on to observe that 'Anything made by hand has a certain glow of life. Factory-made objects are born dead', adding (Graves 1969: 168): 'Thus for me, the problem of tourism may be reduced to the question of how much *báraka* you are prepared to forfeit for the comforts of modernity'.

122   See Graves (1969: 174).

123   Hence the view (Tynan, 1975: 230, original emphasis): 'The tourist explosion, I believe, is already creating a new breed of European tourist – the anti-tourist, with appetites quite different from those of his predecessors. The traditional holiday-maker goes abroad in search of sun, sea, famous works of art, picturesque scenery and people of his own nationality and kind. The new tourism, of which I am a charter member, is more selective...We

Amis, who equated the physical decline of the place visited (= the shabbiness of Lisbon) with the growth of its urban population.[124] Amis decried the presence of large numbers of tourists in a small fishing village, a location to which he himself had gone a quarter of a century earlier, before the advent of mass tourism.[125]

Much the same view is expressed by Norman Lewis, who – as with many travel writers who see 'their' places despoiled by the subsequent arrival of tourists – is proprietorial, rather like a landowner objecting to peasants occupying portions of his estate. Furthermore, the contrast he draws is instructive: prior to the era of economic growth driven by tourism, the context is depicted in idealized terms as an 'unspoilt' one ('life here [is] devoid of modern stress') where social harmony reigned because class divisions were absent.[126] With the development of mass tourism, however, he laments what he terms the destruction of 'the extraordinary charm' of rural culture by the influx of the plebeian 'other'.[127] The mob-in-the-streets has metamorphosed into the mob-on-the-beaches, an incursion seen by the travel writer as just as threatening to the pastoral version of the agrarian myth.

---

quickly tire of landscape that lacks evidence of human habitation, but we do not want the human beings in question to be fellow-tourists: hence we avoid popular beauty-spots and cultural centres. *Above all, we seek to escape the company of our compatriots, apart from any we may happen to be travelling with'.*

124   'I could find nothing of the Lisbon I remembered from previous visits', he comments (Amis, 1990: 339), 'everything seemed faded, stained or parched. There were more people in the streets than I would have believed possible...[i]n a short time I noticed several cripples and blind persons'.

125   On this point, see Amis (1990: 341): 'When I was there twenty-five years ago [circa 1955] there were two hotels in Portimão – well, more like boarding-houses than hotels. Whereas now...there stretched [on its beach] an irregular band of colour mottled with fawn and medium brown, betokening sand and bodies, ten thousand saw I at a glance'.

126   See Lewis (1998: 54 ff.) for a symptomatic juxtaposition of an idyllic rural life 'before' the incursion of the plebeian mass tourist, and the dystopic 'after' the arrival of the latter. 'Even back in the early Fifties', he observes, 'it was more interesting and usually more pleasant to travel in areas of Europe off the beaten track. In this respect Spain was outstanding... I found Spain as charmingly unspoilt as it had ever been'. Farol, on the Costa Brava, visited periodically by Lewis, is where 'villagers lived in harmony'.

127   'In 1984, after an absence of thirty-four years, I returned to Farol on a visit', notes Lewis (1998: 57–58), adding that 'I had suspected that I should find it unrecognizable and this proved to be the case. What I [encountered] was a *Costa* city stamped out by some industrial process... The fate of Farol is an outstanding example of what was to destroy the extraordinary charm of the villages and towns of the eastern seaboard of Spain...'

For all these writers, therefore, mass tourism is equated not just with the 'mob-in-the-streets', but also the despoilation of the 'natural' landscape, and thus of Nature itself. Graves contemplates 'retreating to some sheep hut', while Tynan and Amis perceive with horror the intrusion of the mass tourist into what was for them a hitherto cherished location (= 'unspoiled'). Namely, a smallscale rural idyll where craft and tradition endured, and from which industry and a foreign plebeian were as yet absent. That is, a situation in which the pristine culture of the rural 'other' remained intact, and thus open to the exclusive gaze (and enjoyment) of the self. Each writer thereby subscribes to a pastoral vision of agrarian myth, embodied in a location abroad where Nature and the 'natural' social order can still be found.[128]

That such views continue to circulate among the British ruling class is evident from comments made by Oliver Letwin, a wealthy old Etonian and Conservative Cabinet Minister, who in April 2011 opposed a new airport development on the grounds that 'we don't want more [working class] people from Sheffield flying away on cheap holidays'. Echoing these sentiments, an introduction to a recent travel literature collection appearing in *Granta* questioned whether it would be possible in future to continue air travel to popular holiday destinations – that is to say, travel by members of the working class – because of its impact on carbon emissions and climate change.[129] With obvious relief,

---

128   It is ironic that Amis subscribes to this idealized notion of rural 'otherness', since he criticized others – not just those who wrote about travel – for holding the same view. One of the latter was accused by him of 'frightful mystique-mongering', and placed (Leader, 2000: 443) in a category of 'chaps who think abroad is mystically fine'. In a letter to Robert Conquest written during 1955 (Leader, 2000: 432) Amis went on to observe: 'What I think I feel about the business...is first I'm all in favour of escapism – but people should realize that that is their motive (very often) for buzzing off down south, and not to try to inflate their pleasure-etc. trips into a spiritual pilgrimage AND THEN COME AND TELL ME ABOUT IT in a travel-book' (original emphasis). The same criticism is levelled at Dylan Thomas, about whom Amis (1991: 133) observes: 'The general picture he draws of the place and the people, in *Under Milk Wood* and elsewhere, is false, sentimentalising...'. That Amis (1991: 137) invokes a similarly nostalgic view (about Swansea) is evident from the confession that 'I miss it constantly and I miss those days. I have a favourite sentimentalized picture of the life there...everything in that picture has disappeared'.

129   'Travel isn't the only cause', notes the editor (Jack, 2006: 12, 13), 'but its contribution to the total of greenhouse gases that warm the world is steadily increasing...[t]ravel no longer seems so innocent or beneficent ('travel broadens the mind') unless one journeys in some pre-industrial carbon-neutral way...' The reference to a return to 'pre-industrial' forms of travel is significant, since this was undertaken only by the better-off elements in society. In other words, what is being advocated is an end to mass tourism, a form of travel by air that – for reasons of cost and time – permits workers to visit other countries.

the editor of *Granta* concluded that '[f]ortunately for the climate, a lot of the world's population is too poor to do much travelling at all', adding 'if that were to change...then a more equitable world...would outlaw or punitively tax all forms of travel which it judged particularly draining of the earth's resources and harmful to the atmosphere'.[130] Aesthetic objections to the 'mob-in-the-streets' on foreign soil are thus bolstered by scientific reasons as to why this kind of plebeian presence (= mass tourism) is no longer feasible.

VII

Following the line adhered to by Herzen after the 1848 revolution, travel writing in the era before the 1939–45 war exhibits a marked antagonism to socialism and socialist politics. 'It is very surprising', admitted Waugh, 'to discover the importance which politics assume the moment one begins to travel'.[131] An ostensibly laudable concern during the first decade of the twentieth century expressed by Grahame for the plight of a poor family from her neighbourhood in rural Italy, on the verge of starvation since the breadwinner had died, turns out to have a different sub-text. It is clear that what she was worried about was the prospect of socialism: that such instances of rural poverty would in the end contribute to the prospect of revolutionary mobilization.[132]

Degraded into a Marxist State
Much the same is true of E. Lucas Bridges in Tierra del Fuego at that conjuncture. He not only insists on control over what is taught to his Ona workers by

---

130   See Jack (2006: 13).

131   On this point see Waugh (1931: 159), who continues: 'Outside Europe one cannot help being a politician if one is at all interested in what one sees; political issues are implicit in everything, and I make no apology for their occasional appearance in these pages. I went abroad with no particular views about empire and no intention of forming any. The problems were so insistent that there was no choice but to become concerned with them'.

132   'Now it must be remembered', writes Grahame (1909: 301), 'that the state of this family was held on all sides to be one of everyday occurrence, and that the neighbourhood in which [they live] is one in which most of the old families of the Tuscan aristocracy have their country seats. Is it any wonder that the Socialist agitator seizes his opportunity to denounce in scathing terms the careless, selfish lives of the Tuscan *"jeunesse dorée"* absorbed as they are in their motor races, their fairs and balls of *"Beneficenze,"* that the whole country is seething with discontent, and that strikes are the order of the day?... Who knows how long these may be on the small scale, and not mount into the forces that make for revolution?'

the church, but also approves of violence to prevent a socialist speaker from teaching them about capitalist exploitation.[133] His objections to modernity and 'civilization' derive as much from a fear lest the influence of urban industrial labour mobilization spread to the indigenous workers on his properties, resulting in trade unionization and strike activity.[134] It was a desire to shield tribal workers from this kind of political 'contagion' that lay behind his wish to protect both their traditional culture and the 'otherness' of their ethnic/ national identity. In this case, therefore, the core elements of the agrarian myth were deployed from above in the form of a populist attempt by the landlord pastoral to establish a shared political identity with the indigenous workers he employed, a discourse the validity of which those below on occasion failed to recognize.

Antagonism to socialism and Bolshevism is difficult for Robert Byron to hide.[135] In a letter home from Athens written in May 1926, he condemns the 1926 General Strike, commenting '[h]ow *dreadful* this is about the coal strike – disastrous', adding that a friend of his 'says that in his family mines...the capital has always paid a Comfortable 10%'.[136] His views about Bolshevism in Russia

---

133 Bridges (1948: 460, 482, 499) is explicit about this element of control over what his workers were allowed to hear. A contract with the priest resident on the estate – who had previously been critical of Bridges' relations with his workforce – 'guaranteed that if at any time we [= landowners] considered his teaching or presence harmful, either to the farm or to the natives, he would, without argument or protest, pack up and leave at once'. Similarly, when 'two well-dressed strangers approached [,] I guessed at once that they were professional agitators and had come on no friendly errand'. Addressing his workers '[o]ne of these two orators waxed eloquent over the crimes of the money-grabbing, capitalistic employers and pointed out the sum each bale of wool was worth in England [finishing] his discourse by saying that their employers were robbing them'. The 'professional agitator' was suddenly attacked by one of the workers, an ex-convict, much to the delight of Bridges, who saw the meeting break up as a consequence. When subsequently he hears of the death of the ex-convict at the hands of the police, Bridges (1948: 500) commends his loyalty to himself as his employer ('Poor wild, faithful Arevalo'). In other words, landlord discourse celebrates both loyalty of the ex-convict and its manifestation on behalf of the employer in the form of violence to disrupt a socialist meeting.

134 'As civilization advanced', lamented Bridges (1948: 498), 'there had been strikes among the workers on some of the farms to the north. These naturally took place at sheep-shearing time, when they were most harmful to the employers'.

135 This critical stance towards the left was not replicated when it came to political regimes of the right. Although he later opposed the Axis powers, initially Byron (1926: 206 ff.) took a sympathetic view of Italian fascism, noting that 'Mussolini, by his internal administration, has fully justified the rule of himself and the enthusiasm of his supporters'.

136 See Byron (1991: 60, original emphasis).

are equally dismissive, alternating between an air of boredom ('too uninterest-ing to bother with') and one of undisguised vehemence and physical disgust ('smelly', 'intellectually blasted population').[137] This is accompanied by an equally vehement condemnation of intellectuals at home for defending social-ism, which Byron maintains can only lead to 'industrial barbarism come true – apes in possession of machines'.[138]

Taken in conjunction with the sentiments about Moscow, the discourse projects the following negative associations: socialism/Bolshevism = ugly, an aesthetic judgment, just as urban poverty is also 'ugly'. That Byron concludes by confessing that '[i]t is an escape to leave Russia', comes as no surprise, except in one particular respect. Whereas the usual way the term 'escape' is deployed in travel literature is in connection with a departure from the home nation, here by contrast it signals leaving the country visited. Byron reveals thereby its ideological dimension: being able to escape not so much a place as a political system which – for whatever reason – is regarded by the writer as undesirable.[139]

Invited by the Ministry of Labour to support a recruitment drive on the eve of the Second World War, Byron declined on the grounds that 'under the pres-ent government England has ceased to mean what I thought it meant'. Informed that the project had the backing of the Trade Unions, he dismissed the signifi-cance of this on the grounds that 'I am not a socialist'.[140] This suggests that the

---

137   'As for Bolshevism and the Five Year Plan and all that', writes Byron (1991: 180) of Russia in
         1932, 'it seems too uninteresting to bother with…[t]here can be no doubt but it is the most
         inefficient, smelly, uncomfortable, obtuse and intellectually blasted population in the
         world'. His contempt for leftist political allegiance is evident from an earlier comment
         about its unserious/misguided nature (Byron, 1926: 5): 'Simon's communism is the misdi-
         rected outcome of sympathy for those less fortunate than himself'.

138   'No more shall I be deceived by English intellectuals who come [to the Soviet Union] on
         conducted tours', insists Byron (1991: 183, original emphasis), since 'by our standards it is
         all *evil*, the sin against the Holy Ghost, the hatred of truth and denial of the spirit'. He
         continues with the warning that '[i]f the five year plan works, it will be the industrial
         barbarism come true – apes in possession of machines…', and expresses (Byron, 1991: 244)
         relief since 'I thought I should have to look at factories here [in Russia], but thank God
         they [the Bolsheviks] don't seem at all anxious for me to do so'.

139   For this point, see Byron (1991: 255).

140   'The Ministry of Labour asked me to join a panel of speakers who would go about the
         country on behalf of National Service', Byron (1991: 299) stated in a 1939 letter, adding:
         'I wrote back: "It seems to me that if you ask people to serve their country, you must be able
         to tell them what this country means. This I cannot do, because under the present govern-
         ment England has ceased to mean what I thought it meant. I regret therefore…" They have

decline he identifies is linked to two processes central to the agrarian myth: on the one hand his dislike of modern industrial development plus a disdain for the urban plebeian; and on the other his approval of all things connected with rural 'otherness'.

Where Thesiger's political sympathies lie is clear from his account of the 1960 coup attempt in Ethiopia, while Haile Selassie was on a visit to Brazil, which failed because the army remained loyal to the Emperor.[141] Thesiger presents this episode from the latter's viewpoint, depicting the attempted coup as *lèse majesté*, despite the fact that Ethiopian historians interpret this in a very different way.[142] The coup leaders were moved by the plight of ordinary Ethiopians under a landlord regime opposed to modernization of any kind.[143] Although the 1960 coup attempt failed, it was a harbinger for the 1974 coup that followed the famine, deposing the Emperor and bringing the left to power. For Thesiger, however, the era of Emperor Haile Selassie corresponds to a golden age, while his ousting 'by clamorous mobs' following the 1974 famine and the subsequent Marxist government are all equated with evil.[144]

In the case of Leigh Fermor, the link between on the one hand where/when he travels, with whom he stays, and what he writes about this and on the other his conservative politics is difficult to disguise.[145] A monarchist who strongly

---

returned to the charge, with a long manifesto from the Trade Unions in favour of National Service. I must explain that I am not a socialist...'

141   For this account, see Thesiger (1988: 429–430).

142   See, for example, Zewde (2001).

143   Thesiger (1988: 420–421) denies both that the Ethiopian peasantry were oppressed by landlordism, and that rural povery was the result, maintaining that 'I gained no impression of a downtrodden peasantry pauperized by feudal landlords...[n]or was I conscious of real poverty'.

144   On this, see especially Thesiger (1988: 434 ff., 438–441), where Haile Selassie is described as a 'benign' reformer. Following the Italian invasion of Abyssinia in 1936, Thesiger (1988: 173) comments: 'Many of my generation were to be passionately concerned with the Spanish Civil War. I felt no such involvement: I detested the anarchists and communists on the Government side...' Of its subsequent history, he (Thesiger, 1988: 433) observes similarly: 'As for Abyssinia, that once proud and independent country with its historic monarchy has now been degraded into a Marxist state'.

145   'Although he was walking through Germany at one of the most significant moments in modern history', therefore, Leigh Fermor described himself (Cooper, 2012: 44–45) as having a 'head...full of the romance of Germany's past. "If only I had had less of a medieval passion, more of a political sense," he admitted in a notebook entry thirty years later, "I would have drunk in, sought out so much more"'. The same source continues: 'He had spent very little time thinking about political ideas [since at] home he had absorbed the

opposed communism, he took part in the military suppression of a republican uprising in Greece, and confessed that his stay with Rumanian landowners 'inoculated me against communism'.[146] Even when conducting wartime operations against the German occupation of Crete in the 1940s, therefore, Leigh Fermor 'was doing his best to neutralize the influence of the Communists [in the resistance]'.[147] It comes as no surprise, therefore, that although resident in Greece at the time he nevertheless felt unable to condemn the colonels' coup of April 1967, his response to this event being 'I don't know what to think'.[148]

Given this antipathy to leftist politics, it is also unsurprising that the changes in the Balkans after the 1939–45 war were met with hostility. Retracing his voyage across the region in the 1930s, Leigh Fermor expressed repugnance about the developments in general and socialism in particular he encountered in 1980s Rumania, Hungary, and Bulgaria.[149] A symptomatically nostalgic utterance notes of the Bulgarian capital Sofia, visited by him in the 1930s, that 'the cheery little Balkan capital [had changed into] the HQ of a dim and remote Soviet province'.[150] Not the least important reason for this hostility was the socialist displacement of rural culture and peasant family farming.

---

middle-class conservatism of his mother, and his ancient school in its rural backwater had given him no reason to question it'.

146 According to his biographer (Cooper, 2012: 338 note), Leigh Fermor 'was known to be pro-monarchist, anti-communist and generally conserative'. An important reason for this (Cooper, 2012: 112) 'was the experience of living with the Cantacuzenes [a landowning family] on the eastern edge of Rumania...that, in his own words, "inoculated me against communism"'. The same source (Cooper, 2012: 113–114) then notes: 'For many of [his] generation, the years 1936 to 1938 were dominated by the Spanish Civil War, but he felt no urge to rush to the aid of the Spanish Republic. The left-wing intellectuals who campaigned passionately on its behalf were not only sympathetic to Communism, but also thought it inevitable. [Leigh Fermor] had been too well inoculated by his years in eastern Europe to trust the Left...' His biographer then adds, without irony, that Leigh Cooper 'did not move in left-wing circles, except at literary cocktail parties'.

147 See Cooper (2012: 157, 197), who observes: 'Given the political turmoil in mainland Greece [Leigh Fermor] was relieved to conclude [in 1944] from the evidence he could gather, that the Communists were not in a very strong position in Crete'.

148 As reported by Cooper (2012: 337–338).

149 Leigh Fermor revisited these countries during the 1980s because, in his view (Cooper, 2012: 370, 379), 'he needed to refresh his memory about Hungary and Rumania. He flew to Budapest, hired a volvo, and drove all over the Great Hungarian Plain [where] "most of my halts were at places I had stayed of old, a series of minor Brideheads really"... [Leigh Fermor] was already well acquainted with the destructiveness of East European communism'.

150 This description is contained in a letter written in December 1985 to the Duchess of Devonshire (Mosley, 2009: 235).

Much the same kind of hostility is expressed by Eric Newby towards 1980s communist regimes in the Balkans (Yugoslavia, Albania), where bureaucratic procedures (of themselves not confined to leftist governments) are castigated and unfavourably contrasted with traditional rural activity, customs and population (= 'quaint') of the pre-communist era.[151] His antipathy extends from dismissing what he is told as mere propaganda, the refrain that nothing works, to the assertion that socialism is an artificial imposition on what is essentially a well-functioning rural society.[152]

The Rage of Primitive Men

A corollary of African and Latin American inhabitants being regarded by Naipaul as 'natural' peasants is that any attempt by them to become 'other' – that is to say, to leave the forest, their 'natural' home and where they belong – is to categorize such an aspiration as an unwarranted search after an identity that is 'inauthentic'. Hence the labelling by Naipaul of this kind of endeavour simply as a 'performance', an act involving the pursuit of an unobtainable object which identifies its subject as nothing more than one of the self-deluding 'mimic men'.[153] From this premise, of not trying to become what is beyond the capacity of the indigenous 'other' to achieve, derives a specific political consequence: the impossibility of socialism.

---

151   About a country house belonging to the landowning Princes Windisch-Graetz, Newby (1984: 96) observes that '[v]ery old retainers, one of whom was pottering about the dilapidated barns and outbuildings in a battered green hat, recall what to them was a happier age before the Second World War'.

152   Characterizing 1980s Albania as 'a sort of communist Tibet', Newby (1984: 115, 120) describes his guide as 'taking the opportunity of which all good communists avail themselves whenever it presents itself to come up with some good news', adding that collective farms he passed while travelling by car 'looked dejected'.

153   For references to 'mimicry' by the inhabitants of Argentina of Europe and the United States, see Naipaul (1980: 105). In this, he echoes the same kind of disapproval as Prince Charles about plebeian aspirations (see Chapter 5). There is an irony in this accusation of mimicry levelled by Naipaul against the black population of Africa and the Caribbean, and the indigenous 'other' more generally, in that not only is it a theme he has examined in fiction (Naipaul, 1957; 1967), but it is a trajectory that in many ways resembles his own. A migrant from Trinidad, and a resident in the UK since 1950, Naipaul initially fulfilled the ideological role of recounting stories about the colonial 'other' for the delectation of the literary bourgeoisie in his adopted nation. Over the years, however, he has transformed himself into an English country gentleman, thereby shifting the element of mimicry from the Caribbean and/or African rural 'other' to the self. As noted by Theroux (1998: 17), 'the hero [of the book The Mystic Masseur] is Ganesh Ramsumair of Trinidad, who turned into G. Ramsay Muir in London' and Naipaul himself are all one and the same person.

Unsurprisingly, therefore, those in erstwhile colonized nations who call for and support ('foreign') revolutionary politics aimed at a socialist transition are for Naipaul also 'fakes'. Such advocates of leftist mobilization ('sentimental hoax') are labelled 'false redeemers' who mislead 'simple people'.[154] Revolution is dismissed as merely one more 'performance' by those defying their 'authentic' identity as 'primitive' inhabitants of the 'bush': those, in short, whom destiny allocates the role of peasants.[155] Serious political thought and struggle consequent on this are not for those in the so-called Third World: for Naipaul, such agency is no more than 'play-acting'. When these 'natural' peasants – in Africa and Latin America alike – discover that, after all, they are only 'primitive men' and not modern, they take a terrible revenge on that which they are not, a reaction Naipaul terms 'African nihilism' and/or guerrilla activity.[156]

Although right about the populism of Mobutu, therefore, Naipaul is wrong to suppose that it is innate to Africa, and to equate it with socialism. The inference that populist idioms are inherent to every kind of from-below mobilization because they embody the interests and aspirations of the rural grassroots

154 In the words of Naipaul (1980: 71), socialists are 'those who continue to simplify the world and reduce other men – not only the Negro – to a cause, the people who substitute doctrine for knowledge and irritation for concern, the revolutionaries who visit centres of revolution with return air tickets...' Elsewhere the identity of 'revolutionaries with return air tickets' emerges (Naipaul, 1994: 107 ff.): the character Lebrun refers to C.L.R. James, also from Trinidad but – unlike Naipaul – a socialist. Pursuing his theme about the 'inauthenticity' of a revolutionary politics in the so-called Third World, Naipaul (1994: 108) states that 'I didn't believe in his character as a revolutionary; didn't believe such a character was possible for a black man from Trinidad...'

155 Like black Africans to try to become modern, therefore, Argentinian guerrillas undertaking revolutionary agency in pursuit of socialist objectives are condemned by Naipaul (1980: 98 ff.) for being 'inauthentic' and engaged in 'performances'. Hence the following view: 'The guerrillas look for their inspiration to the north. From Paris of 1968 there is the dream of students and workers uniting to defeat the enemies of "the people." The guerrillas have simplified the problems of Argentina. Like the campus and salon revolutionaries of the north, they have identified the enemy: the police. And so the social-intellectuals diversions of the north are transformed, in the less intellectually stable south into horrible reality'. His parallel is explicit (Naipaul, 1980: 101): 'Argentine political life is like the life of an...African forest tribe'.

156 On finding themselves unable to sustain modernity, the resentment of those in Africa who aspire to this (Naipaul, 1980: 195) 'can at any time be converted into a wish to wipe out and undo, an African nihilism, the rage of primitive men coming to themselves and finding that they have been fooled and affronted'. Similarly, for Naipaul (1980: 139) '[t]he Tupamaros [guerrillas] were destroyers. They had no programme...'

is incorrect.[157] Much rather, populism is produced and reproduced from above, and reflects the interests of those elements – wealthy merchants, small capitalist producers, their political representatives – unable to unite with plebeian components on the issue of class.[158]

It is, in short, a discourse that is not innate, but rather constructed. Significantly, Naipaul then uses the populist discourse of Mobutu in order to eliminate the possibility for Africa not just of economic development and modernity but also of socialism.[159] All the latter are characterized as inappropriate European impositions on the 'bush', a position that reproduces a central tenet of the 'new' populist postmodern argument that Eurocentric 'foundationalism' is inapplicable to the indigenous rural 'other' in the so-called Third World.

Conclusion

Although eighteenth century cosmopolitanism generated and reproduced an ideological 'exclusivity' among the landed classes, fostered in part by the Grand Tour, this was replaced in the nineteenth century by a nationalism which permitted the upper class to claim a shared identity with plebeian elements in their own country. The struggle continued, since with the emergence of mass tourism, aspects of this same conflict surfaced in the travel writing genre. To the upper class European traveller of the twentieth century, therefore, non-European indigenous 'otherness' encountered abroad was acceptable only so

---

157   When addressing the links between the 'otherness' of the rural grassroots, populist mobilization and issue of ancestors, Naipaul overlooks an important point. Given that people in Europe and the United States also have forebears, where – like Africa – they are also the subject of interest and curiosity, how is having ancestors *per se* an indicator of 'primitiveness', as he infers?

158   According to Naipaul (1980: 177–178), however, it was fear of Mobutu himself that drove populism. Members of the Zairois bourgeoisie were 'anxious only to make it known that they were loyal, and outdone by no one in their "authenticity," their authentic Africanness...' The populist ideology of 'authenticity' (*Authenticité*) introduced by Mobutu entailed the legal requirement to adopt traditional indigenous dress/names, and coincided with the renaming of the Congo itself as the Republic of Zaïre.

159   For Naipaul (1980: 192), therefore, populist discourse invoking an ancient 'authenticity' is the only political option available to an Africa devoid of its European modernity/progress: 'The past has vanished [but] where so little has changed, where bush and river are so overwhelming, another past is accessible, better answering African bewilderment and African religious beliefs: the past as *le bon vieux temps de nos ancêtres*'.

long as it did not reproduce what the European found at home; that is, to imitate European culture (dress, manners, etc.), adopt European politics (democracy, worker organizations, etc.), or follow European economic development (industrialization, urbanization, technology).

Rural 'authenticity' is regarded both with approval and with fear. Since it confirms the 'innateness' of hierarchy as the visitor perceives it ought to be, especially the position within this of peasant and landowner, the pastoral version of the agrarian myth reflects the element of approval. The Darwinian version corresponds to a fear on the part of the travel writer that harmony will be displaced by struggle, resulting either in the de-essentialization or the re-essentialization of what are perceived as enduring, innate and 'natural' rural identities. Such travel accounts are therefore not just writing-for, but also writing-against; not merely the pastoral version of the agrarian myth, but the pastoral devoid of the plebeian urban working class 'other'. They constitute a discourse that is part of the class struggle, in other words.

This is contrary to the way in which postmodern theory categorizes 'difference': as a demeaning method of 'Orientalist' gaze, whereby all European travellers classify non-European ethnic 'otherness' uniformly in negative terms. Against this interpretation, it is argued here that what structures this discourse is not pro-European or anti-non-European identity so much as supportive of a European and non-European identity that is culturally traditional, 'authentic', rural, and in its national location. European and non-European identities to which this same discourse objects are deemed no longer to be culturally 'authentic': the pre-modern giving way to the modern, the village to the town and city, and peasants transformed into workers. Linked to this is element of class determining attitudes towards subjects-out-of-place: on the one hand support for the desire of settler landlords to reproduce an English squirearchy abroad, whilst on the other opposition to the appearance abroad of the plebeian mass tourist.

For Robert Byron, early twentieth-century Europe, Asia and the Middle East are all *loci* of traditional rural 'otherness', the values of which he approves and the existence of which his travels are designed to reveal. By contrast, the United States represents a 'retrograde industrialism' that is capitalist, whilst Soviet Russia constitutes 'industrial barbarism', each of which is the locus of the much-feared plebeian (= the mob-in-the-streets), the outcome of modernity/urbanization and the harbinger of socialism. This suggests that in his case the gaze of the travel writer is informed as much by class (at home and abroad), and not simply – as is generally claimed – by 'orientalism' (= an image of 'the East' as homogeneous).

This disdain for modernity and industrialization led in turn to condemnation of countries where such development had occurred, particularly those with communist governments. For writers about travel such as Patrick Leigh Fermor, Robert Graves, Norman Lewis, Kingsley Amis, and Eric Newby, postwar transformation represented the twin evils associated with economic and political change. Namely, the erosion of national culture and ancient traditions, the alienation of both the peasantry and landowners from their respective 'authentic' identities, and the construction of aesthetically repugnant urban conurbations, all perceived as malign effects of socialist policies and planning.

This kind of approach also informs the travel narratives of V.S. Naipaul, exhibiting as they do a fear about the actual/impending 'encroachment' of the African 'bush' onto areas colonized/developed by Europeans. Here the inference is no longer that advocated by the pastoral variant of the agrarian myth: namely, that so long as the African 'other' remains in the 'bush', where s/he really belongs, such a person is acceptable and non-threatening.

The latter is distinct from the view expressed half a century earlier by Waugh, and as such indicates the presence of two antithetical forms of the agrarian myth. In so far as the indigenous 'other' is regarded as a benign subject, Waugh and others subscribe to the pastoral variant; for Naipaul, by contrast, it is the Darwinian variant that predominates, as embodied in his fears about the encroachment of the African 'bush'. The pastoral variant endorsed by Naipaul is found not in Africa but in England, where his identity is now that of a country squire.

For Waugh, as for Leigh Fermor, Norman Lewis, Wilfred Thesiger, Lucas Bridges and Robert Byron, the danger is that the rural 'other' will change from being a peasant and become a worker. As such, what emerges is the industrial/urban proletariat, the 'mob in the street'. For Naipaul, by contrast, the danger is not that the rural 'other' will change but that, remaining the same, it will as the ethnically-specific 'primitive' invade the town, with the object of reinstating there the African 'bush'. This is consistent with the agrarian myth discourse that takes the form of the revenge-of-Nature, one that in the case of ghost stories and horror films structure the narratives of those such as M.R. James and Nigel Kneale.

The next chapter examines what is simultaneously the apogee and nadir of the travel writing genre. That is, a context seemingly unconnected with agrarian myth, where the discourse about class, the traveller's quest for 'exclusivity', and the resulting struggle against cultural 'de-authentication' all combine: Venice.

CHAPTER 8

Venice – Being There

> The rationalist mind has always had its doubts about Venice...Among
> Venice's spells is one of peculiar potency: the power to awaken the philis-
> tine dozing in the skeptic's breast. People of this kind – dry, prose people
> of superior intelligence – object to feeling what they are supposed to feel,
> in the presence of marvels. They wish to feel something else. The extreme
> position is to feel nothing.
>
> The novelist MARY MCCARTHY (1956: 6) on why the city elicits disdain, overlook-
> ing a different cause: a desire to maintain the cultural 'exclusivity' of what is
> seen there.[1]

Introduction

Ostensibly, the agrarian myth has nothing to do with Venice, an essentially
maritime power widely regarded as the epitome of European urban civilization.[2] Yet many accounts written by those visiting the city suggest otherwise,
the agrarian myth and its attendant concepts (class, culture, nationalism)
being a central aspect of the resulting discourse. Although much of the travel
writing about Venice is descriptive (what the object of the gaze looks like), and
in some instances merely subjective (= personal reactions to the object of the
gaze), this does not mean that Venice has been over-analysed.[3] Nostalgia is a

---

1   That images do not necessarily have to adhere to notions of cultural 'distinction' associated
    with Venice is demonstrated by the photographs 1–5 included here, taken by Anna Luisa
    Brass in the course of visits to the city over the past decade.
2   On the maritime history of Venice, see among many others Lane (1966), Pullan (1968), and
    Davis (1991).
3   The subjective account by Král (2011), for example, does no more than record commonplaces,
    and thus contributes nothing of relevance to an understanding of Venice, consisting for the
    most part of banal observations – 'a man is leaning against an ancient brick wall, as if to see
    how tall he is in comparison' (Král, 2011: 59) – that could be made of any other city at any
    other conjuncture. This contrasts with the approach of Harte (1988), which – although
    descriptive – not only provides important insights, is better written, but also contains fine
    illustrations painted by the author. Whereas the latter text is both informative and about
    Venice, the former is neither, being largely about its author.

common theme in almost every account of the city, Venice being equated with the passing of time, and memories which fade.[4]

In this chapter it is argued that such accounts contain also a threefold subtext, usually implicit but on occasion explicit. First, regret for the loss of traditional rural hierarchy, or the kind of social relations which structured pre-capitalist agriculture. Second, antagonism towards any intrusion into Venetian lagoon society of elements associated with modernity.[5] And third, fear of the urban mob-in-the-streets, or the physical presence in the city of mass tourism.[6] Among the issues considered here, therefore, is the search by travel writing for 'meaning' and 'exclusivity' in Venice.

---

4   Hence the nuanced observation by Horatio Brown (1884: 79): 'Though the true lover of Venice will rejoice at the prosperity which is coming on the place, yet he may be allowed to record, with a certain regret, the beauties that must pass away...' A similar, but more recent, example is Král (2011: 16–18), who writes: 'She [= Venice] shows us...how ephemeral everything is, how essentially ancient, and how any memories they might have are doomed to disappear...it is possible to see Venice herself as a hallucination which soon vanishes. It is at this point that we feel a yearning for the things that slip away from us, especially those whose passing is inevitable'.

5   Thus, for example, Russell Green (1936: 3) equates cars with modernity and extols the absence of both ('Venice is the most unique [city] of all, because wheels are the curse of modernity... and in Venice there are no wheels'). An analogous celebration of the absence of modernity is found earlier, in the travel writing of Henry James. In 1892, therefore, he observes (Kaplan, 1994: 71) that 'the essential present character of the most melancholy of cities resides in its being the most beautiful of tombs. Nowhere else has the past been laid to rest with such tenderness, such a sadness of resignation and remembrance. Nowhere else is the present so alien, so discontinuous, so like a crowd in a cemetery...' The same is true of Paul Morand (2002: 151), who notes that 'were it not for the television aerials, one could be in the eighteenth century', and of Eric Newby (1984: 72) who laments the impact of modernity on villas in the Veneto, noting that 'today [they are] hemmed in by filling stations and windowless factories painted in bilious colours'. An exception in this regard is Raymond Williams, who takes what might be termed a socialist's view on the subject when observing (O'Connor, 1989: 72): 'I remember myself that I saw Mestre and Marghera first, by the normal route. The traffic and oil-tanks weren't a visual experience or a portent of the future: they were what I brought with me – literally how I had come. And since I had come to see Venice I went on through and was glad, and there weren't only the churches and the palaces and the paintings and the gondolas but people reading their papers on the waterbuses on the way to work – "next stop Rialto" – and in the shops and offices, the political posters on the walls, a familiar, interesting, locally beautiful city'.

6   A typical observation in this regard is the one made by Goldring (1913: 88), that 'though the city may be crowded with unsympathetic people one grows entirely oblivious of them'. Symptomatically, perhaps, that Venice – a city 'which we all treasure as one of the gems of World Culture' – should be seen not just by the privileged few but by the masses is a view

These interrelated discourses, emblematic of the agrarian myth, are themselves frequently linked in turn to antithetical political views. In positive terms
to nationalist ideology, similarly emblematic of the agrarian myth, and negatively to socialism, the 'other' of the agrarian myth. Of interest, therefore, is
whether a politically specific meaning has been – and can be – attached to
Venice as a consequence of 'being there'.[7] In short, how does Venice appear to
those positioned at either end of the political spectrum, and is there a pattern
in terms of different judgments as to its 'meaning'. This requires in turn an
examination not of politics and ideology *in* Venice, but rather of the politics
and ideology *of* Venice – what the city and its culture can, does and perhaps
should represent to those visiting it, and why.[8]

This Most Improbable of Cities

Any attempt to address the 'meaning' of Venice necessarily remains daunting, not to say presumptuous, insofar as of all the places examined by
travel writing, it is a location that has perhaps featured more often than

---

(Spender, 1958: 65) put into the mouth of a fictional apparatchik from the Soviet Union.
The inference is that it is only the latter who would contemplate the barbaric act of allowing
the 'mob-in-the-streets' to defile a cultural icon with its presence. Travel guides published
in the late nineteenth and early twentieth century which included quotes about the city
from earlier accounts omitted to provide English translations from French, Italian or
German texts (see, for example, Hare 1900). The inference was that visitors to the city came
from a class background the educational attainment of which rendered such translation
unnecessary.

7   The significance of this aspect – perceptions of the city as historical object linked in turn to
the class position of the viewer, and how the latter deemed what ought to be seen and
remembered, and why – was recognized by, among others, Henry James. In the early 1890s he
wrote (Kaplan, 1994: 93) as follows: 'Venice has ever been a garden of strange social flowers.
It is only as reflected in the consciousness of the visitor from afar – brooding tourist even call
him, or sharp-eyed bird on the branch – that I attempt to give you the little drama [the
arrival]; beginning with the felicity that most appealed to him, the visible, unmistakable fact
that he was the only representative of his class. The whole of the rest of the business was but
what he saw and felt and fancied – what he was to remember and what he was to forget.
Through it all, I may say distinctly, he clung to his great Venetian clue – the explanation of
everything by the historic idea'.

8   Although only one of the five authors from the right and left of the spectrum whose views
about Venice are considered here – Filippo Marinetti, Paul Morand and Evelyn Waugh on the
right; Jean-Paul Sartre and Régis Debray on the left – fall within the category of travel writer
(Waugh is the exception), they have all expressed strong opinions about the *political* meaning of this city. For this reason, therefore, their arguments merit close scrutiny, not least so as
to discern what patterns (if any) inform their respective discourses.

any other.[9] Equally daunting is the fact that its ability to fascinate – for whatever reason – continues undiminished, a point underlined in most accounts,
historical and contemporary.[10] Moreover, such a response is generated from
the very first moment, when one exits from Santa Lucia station after having
arrived in Venice by train.[11] Linked to this is the palpable sense of melancholy

---

9   This particular aspect is best captured by three commentators. The first is Horatio Brown
    (1887: 398–399), in the following observation: 'It is remarkable that the most frequent
    efforts to express the feeling of Venice in words, should have been cast in prose and not in
    verse, and should be the work of foreigners, not Venetians'. Second, Douglas Goldring
    (1913: 100) laments similarly that: 'I suppose one never sees anything in this place which
    some poet or other has not already impeccably described!'. And the third is Evelyn Waugh
    (2003: 137–138), who on a brief visit to the city in 1929 eschewed a detailed analysis, adopt-
    ing instead a somewhat ironical self-effacing approach: 'What can I possibly write, now, at
    this stage of the world's culture, about two days in Venice, that would not be an imperti-
    nence to every educated reader of this book?...No, it seems to me a moment for humility.
    Perhaps if I made my home in Venice for twenty years and attained a perfect command
    [over its language, history, art and culture] I might decently contribute a chapter here to
    what has already been written by those who have mastered all these accomplishments.
    Meanwhile, since there seems no probability of my ever becoming anything more consid-
    erable than one of a hundred globe-trotting novelists, I will pass on to Ragusa'.

10   In the words of Horatio Brown (1887: 396), '[t]he truth is that we must number Venice
    among the "cities of the soul";...she has the fatal gift to touch the imagination, to awaken
    a permanent desire...' For a similar view, projected via fiction, see Waugh (1945: 96–97),
    where the 'incomparable pageant' of Venice defeats the attempt by English visitors not to
    be impressed ('"A bit bleak?" asked Sebastian. "Bleak? Look at that," I led him again to the
    window and the incomparable pageant below and about us. "No, you couldn't call it
    bleak."').

11   This response, characterized by Henry James (Kaplan, 1994: 89) as 'his little first Venetian
    thrill', is a well-attested phenomenon which has a status almost of a cliché. Over a century
    ago, it was described by Horatio Brown (1884: 17, 18) thus: 'The first emotion which is
    awakened in the traveller when he arrives in Venice, will probably be one of delight and
    astonishment, which, if it found expression at all, would take the form of rhapsody, more
    or less incoherent. To emerge from the dust of the railway carriage and the grimy bustle of
    the station, suddenly and without warning upon the borders of the Grand Canal, is a
    transformation so instantaneous and amazing that it catches the breath...During the first
    days after one's arrival in Venice, the mind seems to lose its footing upon fact; the evi-
    dence of the senses falls under doubt. It is only by an effort that the reality of the place is
    assured'. Of a night-time arrival at that same conjuncture, Sala (1887: 212, 217–218) writes:
    'There are to me two delightful ways of entering Venice. The first is to approach it by the
    railway from Mestre, late at night...two miles further, and you know that you have entered
    upon the Lagoons and that the train is putting out to sea...Now you are fairly out on the
    water; and a full ten minutes pass, with total darkness without...Presently you discern the

on leaving the city, a response also encountered in many of those who have written about 'being there'.[12]

Between arrival and departure, what 'being there' involves can take many forms, not least if this has been preceded by earlier visits to Venice.[13] Revisiting the city is itself a process that raises the issue of meaning, and whether or not what is seen/experienced remains the same as before. Much travel writing fails adequately to address this point, the assumption being that, like the place in question, perceptions once formed do not change. An exception in this regard is Henry James, whose account of Venice accurately notes that it is impossible to *re*-experience a first impression of the place, which – in effect – is an

---

horizon bounded by a long line of pale light sending a paler reflex to the sky. Instant by instant the glow grows broader and more brilliant. The train touches land at the island of Santa Lucia [and] then you are in Venice [at] one of the noisiest and most inconveniently crowded railway termini in Italy'. With a slightly different emphasis, but with much the same meaning, Thomas Mann (1940: 88, 89) puts into the mouth of his protagonist von Aschenbach the following words: 'He saw it once more, that landing place that takes the breath away, that amazing group of incredible structures the republic set up to meet the awestruck eye of the approaching seafarer: the airy splendour of the palace and Bridge of Sighs, the columns of lion and saint on the shore, the glory of the projecting flank of the fairy temple, the vista of gateway and clock. Looking, he thought that to come to Venice by the station is like entering a palace by the back door. No one should approach, save by the high seas as he was doing now, this most improbable of cities...Is there any one but must repress a secret thrill on arriving in Venice for the first time – or returning thither after a long absence...' Others who record much the same kind of response extend from Augustus Hare (1900: 11) and Grahame (1909: 200ff.) to Green (1936: 22), Spender (1958: 9) and Morand (2002: 37, 97). At a personal level, the veracity of these descriptions was confirmed when, arriving for the first time at Venice in February 2004, the words spoken by my youngest son (then nine years of age) on emerging from the station in the manner indicated by Horatio Brown, were: 'Daddy, is there a house here that is not famous?'.

12   For example, Thomas Mann (1940: 109), whose main character states: 'The hardest part, the part that more than once it seemed he could not bear, was the thought that he should nevermore see Venice again'. By contrast, Russell Green (1936: 215–216) situates the birth of such melancholy not on leaving the city but on arriving home – the romantic ideal is generated and reproduced once the traveller is no longer in Venice itself.

13   About the capacity of the city to attract and retain the foreign visitor and/or settler from abroad, Henry James (Kaplan, 1994: 106) comments: 'It is a fact that almost everyone interesting, appealing, melancholy, memorable, odd, seems at one time or another, after many days and much life, to have gravitated to Venice by a happy instinct, settling in it and treating it, cherishing it, as a sort of repository of consolations; all of which today [1902], for the conscious mind, is mixed with its air and constitutes its unwritten history'.

episode that remains frozen in time.[14] Seeing it for the second time, and wondering how this would affect his initial reactions to and aesthetic judgments about the city and its culture, James expressed relief at the fact that, on revisiting Venice and seeing what had already been seen once, he had no reason to change his mind. His first impression was confirmed, but not – in terms of the experience itself – reproduced.

The travel writer who lives and works amongst those s/he writes about is in a very real sense involved in an activity akin to participant/observation. Like an anthropologist engaged in long-term fieldwork, such a traveller is not merely a teller-of-stories about – and thus the ideological construction of – the 'other', but rather a chronicler who is seen to possess the added 'authenticity' of having 'been there' on a more substantial basis.[15] From this stems in part the opposition between the 'uninitiated', a term applied by many travel writers to the mass tourist, the infrequent and/or temporary visitor to Venice, and the 'initiate' composed for the most part of those – mainly travel writers – who have resided in the city or on islands in the Venetian lagoon for long periods.[16]

---

14   'I had been curious to see', observed Henry James (Kaplan, 1994: 37) on revisiting Venice in the early 1870s, whether 'I should be disposed to transpose my old estimates – to burn what I had adored and adore what I had burned. It is a sad truth that one can stand in the Ducal Palace for the first time but once, with the...sense of that particular half-hour's being an era in one's mental history; but I had the satisfaction of finding at least – a great comfort in a short stay – that none of my early memories were likely to change places and that I could take up my admirations where I had left them'.

15   The reference in the chapter title is to *Being There*, the book by Jerzy Kosinski (1971) and the 1979 film of the same name directed by Hal Ashby and starring Peter Sellers. A central feature of the book and the film is the power of the media image, and its largely unquestioning absorption by those who see it, aspects which are relevant to much of what has been and still is written about Venice.

16   That the aesthetic and historical impact of Venice is beyond the capacity of the mass tourist to appreciate, particularly those 'uninitiated' coming to the city on a short visit, is a constant refrain in tourist guides and travel writing. A case in point is Augustus Hare, for whom dependence by a visitor on a cicerone for explanations of what to see and where to go is evidence of 'imbecility'. Guides, the reader is informed (Hare, 1900: 3), 'are unusually ignorant, vulgar and stupid at Venice, and all but the most hopelessly imbecile travellers will find them an intolerable nuisance'. Although more sympathetic to the constraints imposed on the traveller by time limits, Russell Green (1936: 5) nevertheless categorizes those able to stay in Venice longer as 'the more sophisticated tourist'. That a brief visit is sufficient to meet the cultural needs of a debased mass tourist is hinted at in many subsequent observations (Green, 1936: 46, 62–63, 191): for example, the reference to tourism generally as the 'contagion of modernity'; that 'all the pleasant but futile needs of modern man'; and that 'the amateur realist is fully satisfied by the dazzling pageant of today'.

Against this dichotomy, it is argued here that there is no reason why those deemed 'uninitiated' may not become 'initiates', whilst the 'initiates' who write about Venice are often themselves unaware of the extent to which their views are influenced by the agrarian myth. An effect of the latter is that (elite/foreign) 'initiate' sources tend to misrepresent the views of the (plebeian/local) inhabitants, depicting as positive and desirable a history and its social relations which locals, by contrast, regard as negative and undesirable.[17] On occasion this takes the form of a condescending attitude, whereby an invariably wealthy foreigner, who has settled in the city patronizes the local Venetian poor, an act of befriending interpreted wrongly as a form of social acceptance.[18]

I

During the mid-1880s, Frederic Eden and his wife Caroline purchased a sizeable plot of land within the city itself, on the Giudecca.[19] Named the Giardini

---

17   Some travel writing from the early part of the twentieth century acknowledges this, albeit in a roundabout way. For example, Karel Čapek, when regretting the mundane residue once the material representation of wealth and power has been subtracted. Hence the observation (Čapek, 1929: 18): 'And now I know why I am so inept to discuss the beauty of Venice. Venice has only palaces and churches, the house of a plain man is simply nothing at all. Bare, narrow, and dark, unprovided with a cornice, or little portal, or a little column, having the odour of a decayed tooth, artistic only through its rabbit-hutch straitness, it does not display the least necessary quality of beauty; you will not, in your rambles, be cheered by the pretty little profile of a cornice or a frame-work entry to greet you with a welcome; poverty, with no trace of virtue. Now then, these one or two hundred palaces do not represent culture but only wealth; no life in beauty but ostentation'.

18   Thus, for example, the tribute written by Henry James (Kaplan, 1994: 104–105) in 1902 to a wealthy American who settled in Venice reproduces the stereotype of an 'outsider' who has been accepted by the local population as one of them. The element of condescension is particularly marked towards the Venetian poor: 'She loved, she had from the first enthusiastically adopted, the engaging Venetian people, whose virtues she found touching and their infirmities but such as appeal mainly to the sense of humour and the love of anecdote...[t]here must have been a multitude of whom it would scarce be too much to say that her long residence among them was their settled golden age'. Further, 'with one of her drawing-rooms permanently arranged as a charming diminutive theatre, she caused to be performed [plays] by the wonderful small offspring of humbler friends, children of the Venetian lower class...'.

19   Brother-in-law of Gertrude Jekyll and the great-uncle of Sir Anthony Eden (British Conservative politician and – briefly – Prime Minister), Frederic Eden (1828–1916)

PHOTO 1   *Albero (Sacca San Girolamo)* (© ANNA LUISA BRASS)

Eden, it is invariably discussed in terms of an aesthetic: the 'English garden' in the midst of Venice.[20] Yet it is clear that it was also, and perhaps more importantly, a commercial enterprise, devoted to the cultivation of cash crops, designed to generate profit for its owners. The same was true also of land purchased by Shirley Guiton at a later date, on the island of Torcello in the Venetian lagoon.

Venetian Pastoral I: Giardini Eden

As owner of the property on the Giudecca, Eden employed seasonal migrant workers to pick and sell fruit from trees on his land (= 'garden'). Observing that '[t]hese mulberries are a source of income', he noted further that '[c]oming back to our vintage we strive to be reconciled for the cutting of our grapes by

---

transformed his purchase of around six acres into what he and others described as 'the largest private garden in Venice'. The latter designation is consistent with the aesthetic she advocated (Jekyll and Weaver, 1913: xvii, xix), with its focus on reproducing the 'natural' and Nature: 'It is upon the right relation of the garden to the house that its value and the enjoyment that is to be derived from it will largely depend...[i]n the arrangement of any site the natural conditions of the place should first be studied. If they are emphatic, or in any way distinct, they should be carefully maintained and fostered...in a place that has some well-defined natural character...it is just that quality that is the most precious'.

20   It attracted the attention of other travel writers, as for example Douglas Goldring (1913: 102) who records walking 'past a lovely example of a Venetian garden (I could divine its beauties from the vivid cascade of greenery pouring over its high crumbling walls)'.

the money they bring in'.[21] Eden invested not only in building ('with very hard labour') a well, in the purchase of commercial livestock the manure of which is used to fertilize his grape vines, but also in buying more land on the nearby Island of Sant'Erasmo, where 'the climate grows for us three crops of hay'.[22] Although 'there is a good deal of trouble in it all', Eden concluded by admitting that 'the return for one's money would surely please an English landlord'.

However, in what is a staple of landowner ideology, and a central emplacement of the aristocratic variant of the agrarian myth, Eden insisted that '[s]hould the reader ask where the profit comes in, the answer is that it is found in the shade and beauty of the pergolas, and is satisfactory and great'.[23] He thereby privileged aesthetic reasons for landownership over purely economic ones, the latter being presented as the by-product of the former. In keeping with the pastoral variant, moreover, Eden also insisted that his workers and the Venetian poor were the main beneficiaries of the productive activity on his land, the economic object of which was to provide them either with employment ('I would not disturb their tenancy') or with subsistence.[24]

His paternalistic (= disdainful) attitude to the workers employed on land he owned was similarly consistent with the aristocratic variant of the agrarian myth.[25] These were referred to as 'aids' (= people-who-help), a description

---

21   See Eden (2003: 44, 71), who in his book devotes Chapter IX, entitled 'The Vintage', to a discussion of the profitability of grape cultivation and yields (Eden, 2003: 77ff.). Stating that 'five tons of grapes are produced annually', Eden (2003: 79) goes on to point out that '[a]t Venice...if table grapes, not grown in too large quantities, can make a price'. However, he (Eden, 2003: 81) then claims that '[w]ith occasional hail-storms, ever-present disease, cost of material, and low prices, the vine-grower's budget is not likely to show a large surplus'. The reason for this complaint is one advanced historically by cultivators everywhere: taxes are too high. Eric Newby (1984: 19ff.) also cultivated vines on land he owned in Tuscany.

22   For these views, see Eden (2003: 95ff., 124, 126).

23   See Eden (2003: 81–82), in what amounts to the oft-heard argument that 'we are in it not for the money but because we take pleasure in Nature'.

24   See Eden (2003: 44). In keeping with this self-image of a benign landowner, he notes (Eden, 2003: 120–121) when discussing payment of his workers that 'the remainder of their wages gives them a larger amount of pocket money than is probably at the disposal of any other people of their class'. That he subscribes to the ideology of *noblesse oblige* is also evident from the following claim (Eden, 2003: 74): 'Our fruit then is abundant and excellent...the price brings it happily within the reach of the poorest'.

25   Such views were not confined to Venetian labourers he employed, since Eden (2003: 86) also thought that British workers who belonged to trade unions were 'lazy'. He thought (Eden, 2003: 102–103) that the British should copy the Italian practice of making prisoners work for employers, lamenting that 'prisoners here [in Italy], instead of living on the rates,

which denies – and thus attempts to defuse the presence of – a wage relation linking owner and labourer.[26] The latter subjects were identified as 'disobedient' and 'lacking discipline', each of which characteristic was attributed to the innate 'racial qualities' of Venetian plebeians.[27] In keeping with this attitude, the espousal by Eden of *noblesse oblige* was evident also in his idealization of rural poverty, a condition not to be eradicated (and therefore 'natural') but to be ameliorated with charity provided by 'those above'.[28]

Venetian Pastoral II: Torcello

Many of these themes are found also in the travel writings of Shirley Guiton. Like the Edens, at an earlier conjuncture and in a different part of Venice, she also purchased a house and land. In her case, on the island of Torcello, during the early 1960s. The resulting experiences there are recounted in two well-received ethnographies, where Guiton described not just how island society in the Venetian lagoon (Torcello, Murano, Burano, Santa Cristina and San Francesco del Deserto) was changing, but also how the land she owned was turned over to commercial agricultural production, locals being employed as workers.[29]

Despite evidence of class formation/struggle (see below), Guiton reproduces without comment the pastoral variant of the agrarian myth when expressed by employers, landholders and proprietors: namely, that 'we are all equal, all family, all the same', sentiments with which it is clear she

---

are taught to earn their polenta', and adding that '[w]e are, let us say it to ourselves, justly proud of British laws and institutions; but sometimes we may perhaps learn something from the polity of others, and surely it is better for society at large, working men included, that the man who is paying the penalty of his wrong-doing should not do so at others' cost'.

26   This form of negation was encountered elsewhere in Italy at this conjuncture. Thus workers employed by Grahame (1909: 110) at her villa in Tuscany are similarly referred to as 'aides'.

27   Hence the view (Eden, 2003: 115–116) that 'our aids are mostly men who, coming to the garden as boys, have grown up in it...[d]isobedience and lack of discipline are, in the lower class of Venetians, racial qualities, and so ingrained'. Similarly negative traits were attributed to her Italian workers by Grahame (1909: 109–112).

28   His benign view of charity (Eden, 2003: 46) handed down by the wealthy is clear not just from a perception of begging as a form of 'subsistence guarantee' but also from sentiments like '[t]he charity of the well-to-do to the poorly-off is great' and the commendation of Queen Elizabeth I for having 'signed a law to prevent the starvation of her meanest subject'.

29   Originally published in the 1970s (Guiton, 1972; 1977), these books have recently been reissued by Faber.

herself agrees.[30] The reason for this is not difficult to discern.[31] Guiton was herself a proprietor who employed workers in order to undertake commercial agricultural production on land she owned. Significantly, the labourer she employed, who worked on her land twenty days a month for a wage and the remainder as a tenant on land leased elsewhere, described her as 'my *padrona*' (= boss).[32]

Of her agricultural labourer, Guiton in turn writes: 'But thanks to their [his family's] hard work, they eat better than most', thereby equating worker well-being simply with 'hard work'.[33] The inference is that workers are responsible for their own situation, for good or ill ('idle' versus 'hardworking'), a distinction which takes no account either of economic relations such as ownership of or separation from means of production or of their systemic effects (rent/wage levels).

This largely uncritical image of the employer/worker relation was itself compounded both by a perception of this link as 'reciprocal' or 'equal', and by an idealization of rural hierarchy as 'natural'.[34] It is an interpretation applied

---

30   For instances of this discourse, see Guiton (1977: 108, 112), who reports employers as saying '[t]here is no question of master (*padrone*) and man here. We are all equal, all one family', and 'we do not have any *signori* (gentry) nor any paupers. We are all of us much the same kind and much the same level financially'. The economic importance of a restaurant on Torcello is attributed (Guiton, 1977: 152) to its owner's 'love and a sense of responsibility for the island and its people'.

31   That she herself endorses such views is evident not just from the concluding section of the ethnography (Guiton, 1977: 201), but also from her sympathetic portrayal of the Venetian nobility. The latter are described by her (Guiton, 1977: 193) in terms of their 'protection and generosity [which] led to the construction of the church and monastery buildings [on the island of San Francesco del Deserto] and the survival of the monastery through many difficult times'. In short, a view of the landlord class as benign/well-meaning that is consistent with the pastoral version of the agrarian myth.

32   'We have always been tenants, never owners', Guiton (1977: 168) was told by her wage labourer, who continued: 'We were not *mezzadri* [sharecroppers]. We did not have to share our harvest with a proprietor or agree with him what crops should be planted or how to market them. We paid rent every year and were free to do what we liked with the land. So we were better off than the *mezzadri*. We are still tenants, those of us who remained on the land'.

33   See Guiton (1972: 145).

34   Observing that Torcello 'has been a dependent society, dependent for its living on patricians, ecclesiastical or lay landowners whom it served', Guiton (1977: 154) then argues that consequently it 'has acquired, because of this past, a softer, gentler outlook…', seeming thereby to approve of grassroots servility inculcated as a result of subordination to members of the landlord class.

by Guiton not just to social relations of production on her own landholding in the Venetian lagoon but also on rural properties throughout Italy; she even laments the passing of a similarly benign working arrangement in England.[35] Subscribing to a Chayanovian view of the never-changing, eternal peasant economy, Guiton characterizes smallholders as fatalistic, no different in their passivity from the livestock they tend, and equates them with Nature itself (peasant = animal = Nature).[36] In keeping with this, she is antagonistic to the intrusion of modernity (technological change, industrialization), particularly where this is effected by a socialist government.[37] The positive/negative characteristics informing the pastoral version of the agrarian myth, in other words.

---

35   Hence the description by Guiton (1972: 146) of the landowner/labourer link as 'the Figaro relationship between master [herself] and man [her worker]'. She continues (emphasis added): 'This depends on a recognition by each of his dependence on the other, combined with a good conceit of himself, and on the sense of equality and respect on both sides arising from this. This relationship was romanticized in many eighteenth-century novels *but it constituted something real...which we in England seem to have lost long since*'.

36   See Guiton (1972: 151–152, 155), and also Horatio Brown (1884: 333) who earlier observed in much the same vein of the Veneto region: 'The road passes several villages occupied by a peasant population – a people who looked as if they had been so long and intimately acquainted with the earth that they had absorbed some of its acquiescence and had accepted the justice of its seasons'. Maintaining that 'the price a *contadino* gets for his produce is the key to the survival of small agriculture, and the lagoon is, necessarily, all small agriculture', but that 'there is no incentive for landowners to find the capital for as long as low prices pertain for agricultural produce', Guiton (1977: 150, 154) advances a central argument made by farmers historically: namely, that economic development has to be based on higher crop prices.

37   For opposition to these aspects of modernity, see Guiton (1972: 126, 187; 1977: 9, 13). Her hostility to leftwing politics generally and communism in particular is evident from various asides. For example, the view (Guiton, 1977: 48) that 'the left wing alliance which now rules the city [Venice] is...much given to gestures of only doctrinaire significance such as parading cultural activities under the heading of whatever horror occupies the forefront of the official party mind'. Similarly, she (Guiton, 1972: 156–157) is dismissive of 'the doctrinaire principles of collectivization', going on to note that in Poland where 'agriculture will become industrialized [constitutes] a long-term danger to the small measure of independence the peasants have preserved'. This approach, embodying a suspicion both of modernity and its accompanying grassroots form of agency, was evident also in the earlier account by Horatio Brown (1884: 143–144) of a strike by gondoliers against the introduction into Venice of what are termed 'hated steamers' – the *vaporettos*. The latter were disliked by Brown, since they represented a break with tradition.

PHOTO 2   *Scuola dei Greci Bricks*   (© ANNA LUISA BRASS)

II

Despite the fact that their accounts were written three-quarters of a century apart, therefore, those by Frederic Eden and Shirley Guiton are both informed by the discourse of the agrarian myth. What was seen by outsiders – such as Eden and Guiton – who subscribed to the agrarian myth in cultural terms – as 'quaintness' and 'tradition', the loss of which was a cause for regret – was seen by the rural population itself mainly in economic terms: as poverty/hardship/insecurity from which to escape, if at all possible.[38]

---

38   A lace-maker told Guiton (1977: 101) that '[b]efore the [1939–45] war there was such poverty here'. Guiton (1977: 38) herself admits that the 'leit-motif of the recollection of the old is poverty and one comes finally to feel that it was poverty which washed out the recollection of other, gentler aspects of life...The poverty of Burano was different from the poverty caused by the depression of the 1930s because it was long-term, ingrained, a normal state of things'.

This Land Eats us All Up

This is clear from the contrast between on the one hand 'the recollection of other, gentler aspects of life' (= agrarian myth, the romanticization of the rural) referred to by Guiton, and on the other the 'recollection of the old' by her informants as being about poverty and its insecurity.[39] The latter notwithstanding, she reaffirms the agrarian myth, invoking the past not in terms of the poverty/insecurity dissipated only by post-1960s economic development as recounted to her in the course of interviews, but rather in terms of a backwards-looking, nostalgic image of idealized pre-industrial rural society in the Venetian lagoon.[40]

Notwithstanding the endorsement by Guiton of the agrarian myth, there is a discernable contradiction between on the one hand her views about the efficacy of this 'golden age' discourse and on the other the views about the past as expressed by her informants. Most of the interviews she conducted with local inhabitants reveal two things which undermine the applicability of the agrarian myth. To begin with, inhabitants pointed out that their living standards and livelihoods improved after the 1960s, as developments in the transportation system within the lagoon area enabled them to find better-paid employment in Venice itself.[41]

As important was the fact that interviews conducted by Guiton indicated that class differentiation and, indeed, struggle, remained a crucial aspect of social relations on the lagoon islands. One well-off informant revealed that, as a result of combining income from fishing with rents from property ownership (land, housing) and profits from shops and commercial agriculture, 'I am very

---

39   Although Guiton (1977: 55) recognizes the agrarian myth – 'that rustic philosophy so much admired by romantic novelists' – she nevertheless overlooks its applicability to her own characterization of socio-economic change in the Venetian lagoon.

40   'Perhaps one of the attractions of Burano in our own troubled erupting industrial societies', concludes Guiton (1977: 198) when contemplating the future of the Venetian lagoon inhabitants, 'is that it is a mirror of ourselves as we were till yesterday. It is a survival of the late nineteenth century, the England of George Bourne, which is just out of reach of our memories, suddenly projected into the third quarter of the twentieth century'.

41   For references by informants to improved job prospects, higher wages, and better living standards after 1960, see Guiton (1977: 19, 25–26, 31, 88, 89, 91–92, 129, 162–163). Before then, according to the description of one informant (Guiton, 1977: 165), '[a] barbarous life it was, a dog's life, that's what'. The latter is consistent with observations contained in earlier accounts of travel to Torcello, as in the following one by Rose (1819: 53): 'Amidst the vestiges of departed grandeur were left some poor and scattered houses...[a]midst these remains glided a few human beings, the miserable tenants of the place'.

comfortable [and] live very well'.[42] Another employer lamented the fact that females no longer wanted to work as lace-makers, insisting that it was a 'tradition' that 'must not be lost', whilst a boat-builder complained about the high cost of wages he now had to pay his labourers.[43] That such gains were the outcome of from-below class struggle was confirmed by a glassmaker, who emphasized that all improvements to pay/conditions had been secured only as a consequence of worker agency and trade union organization.[44] Nevertheless, sharecropping relations still continued in the Venetian lagoon, seen by those trapped in these kinds of arrangement as exploitative and illegal.[45]

Venice, Class and the Agrarian Myth

That there should be a connection between Venice and the aristocratic variant of the agrarian myth is in a sense unsurprising, since historically its

---

42 In the words of the informant himself (Guiton, 1977: 78), 'I am very Comfortable. I do not mean to boast...but I have a number of houses and shops which I let; we'll live very well on the rents...I have one bit of land on the *terraferma* [the mainland] which brings in a good rent and, in addition, enough grapes to make about 350 litres of wine every year. Good red wine. That is what I call good business. I helped to start the fisherman's co-operative here in Burano and I ran it for thirty years...I have always had money coming in from my fishing'.

43 On these points, see Guiton (1977: 72, 113), who also notes in passing the effects of increasing market penetration by capital, albeit not interpreted as such (Guiton, 1977: 55): 'It is the old trades which, at present, are breeding frustration: the fisherman who feels old-fashioned, almost redundant and certainly a failure by any economic yardstick unless he happens to have inherited good equipment...or the small shopkeepers battling with increasing competition'. Earlier accounts, such as that by Grahame (1909: 215–216), extol lace-making in the Veneto region as 'a great boon', since it enabled girls 'in a very poor district to earn their own livelihood'.

44 'See how things change', the informant in question reported (Guiton, 1977: 93), 'bit by bit, thanks to modern advances and fighting for our rights and the growth of the trade unions and by strike action'.

45 One informant who in the 1960s was still a sharecropper, despite the legal abolition of such contracts, provided Guiton (1977: 166) with details about this production relation: 'All this land along the canal and right across the lagoon is *bonifacia*, and there was nothing growing here...when we came. All these vines and all these trees were planted by us... We were one of several families working here and, of course, none of us owned the land we worked. The proprietor divided it up into lots and made a contract with each family. All the families went to work planting potatoes and maize. Then we put in vines and peach trees. Now that everything is bearing, it brings in quite a good return for our work, that is to say it would if it were not a *mezzadria*. And it is still held by us as a *mezzadria*. We get 58 per cent of the crop and the owner gets 42 per cent, and the toil and burden is all ours...this land eats us all up. This was new land here, not belonging to anyone. It was

patrician merchant class not only engaged in trade but also owned land in the surrounding area.[46] Indeed, according to one late nineteenth century account, Venetian patricians regarded the city only 'as a place for a few months' sojourn', having much rather relocated their business activity (livestock rearing, crop farming, viticulture) to the rural mainland where they owned large properties.[47] Equally, Venice generally escapes the anti-urban discourse of much travel writing because it is not modern, and fuels both the cosmopolitanism and then the nationalism of the foreign visitor.[48]

Accordingly, images of plebeian destitution encountered in the Veneto during the Grand Tour served to do two things. Initially, therefore, it furnished evidence for the 'naturalness' of the existing rural social order, abroad as much as at home, thereby reinforcing the cosmopolitanism of visiting aristocrats. Subsequently, however, it contributed to a perception on their part of the good

all acquired by one of these "barons" who know how to fiddle things and here we are all stuck with *mezzadria* contracts. They are absolutely forbidden but the old contracts made before the law was passed are still valid. They should all have been swept away'.

46 The Venetian Republic (the ruler of which styled himself as 'Lord of a Quarter and a Half-Quarter of the Roman Empire'), which replaced Byzantium as the imperial power in the eastern Mediterranean, is one of the best-known instances of an aristocracy reinvesting profits from commerce in land. From the sixteenth century onwards (Woolf, 1968; Braudel, 1982: 284–287), Venetian patrician families and nobles acquired agricultural land in the Po Valley on which to grow crops sold – also profitably – to meet the consumption requirements of the urban population resident in the city. The extent to which Palladian villas built on the terrafirma combined an aesthetic celebration of classical antiquity with the requirements of commercial agriculture (drainage, irrigation, storage, new crops) is outlined by Muraro and Marton (1999). Merging 'the beautiful' with 'the useful', therefore, Palladio's villas for rich landowners both harked back to ancient Rome (= cultural distinction) and simultaneously harmonized this image with the economic objectives (= agricultural production) pursued by his aristocratic Venetian patrons.

47 The account is by Horatio Brown (1884: 155), who notes that 'the noble families [have] come to regard Venice as a place for a few months' sojourn. They go there for the amusements of society; but their heart and their business is no longer there. They have, in many cases, adopted a country life, owning property on the mainland, and devoting all their great and hereditary capacity for commerce, to the rearing of cattle, the growth of crops, the making of wine. They are interested in experiments in silk growing, or ensilage; and spend their money freely on model farmsteads. The government encourages the movement by offering agricultural prizes; and the economy of these Venetian farms is admirable'.

48 The view that, despite its antiquity, the city and its civilization will – unlike Nature – in the end not survive, is expressed by a character in a story by Stephen Spender (1958: 145), in the following terms: 'Venice was an artifact which lay open to destruction with the other remnants of civilization, and Nature would survive, Nature even if there were no life left on the world...'.

fortune to have been born English.[49] This display of foreign poverty made them love their own nation more, it was argued, and prepared them to assume their rightful place in their own society as rulers by providing them with a cultural authority – 'to acquire the style associated with [the Grand Tour] was to possess the time and financial resources available to the very few', in other words – which subordinates were unable themselves either to know or challenge, since they could not afford to go abroad.[50]

That much the same kind of discourse continued towards the end of the nineteenth century is evident from the travel account written by Henry James of his time spent in Venice. His descriptions extend from equating a 'sense of Italy' with 'rural Italy, delightful and quaint', to the observation that 'the poorest Venetian is a natural man of the world' who is 'better company than persons of his class are apt to be among the nations of industry'.[51] Like so many before and since, James approves of the Venetian poor who are 'natural' and – it is inferred – know their subordinate position in relation to upper class foreign visitors (like him), unlike industrial workers in Western capitalist nations who are not similarly deferential.

An analogous endorsement of aristocracy and its hierarchy is evident from the 1930s travel account by Russell Green, who expresses pleasure on encountering in the main square of the city servants looking after the children of its noble families.[52] For him, servants belonging to Venetian aristocracy are no more than a confirmation that ancient traditions 'live on', in much the same way as the continued presence there of old buildings and historic art treasures. As such, it is a view that conforms to the landlord pastoral variant of the agrarian myth, whereby hierarchy (= the socio-economic domain) no less than culture (= the aesthetic domain) appears to be benign, harmonious, eternal and (thus) a 'natural' phenomenon.[53]

---

49   Hence the view (Redford, 1996: 1) that 'gentlemen-in-the-making should engage in... perfecting their Englishness by immersing themselves in the foreign'.

50   On these aspects of the Grand Tour, see Redford (1996: 8, 11). Being able to speak with an authoritative voice as a result of having been on the Grand Tour is not, it should be emphasized, to privilege the 'cultural' over the 'economic'; much rather, it is to understand the crucial importance of being able to exercise the former in order to be able to reproduce the latter, the two combining to secure the continuation of the class position concerned.

51   For these views held by Henry James, see the references in essays about Italy collected in the edition by Kaplan (1994: 58, 106).

52   He notes (Green, 1936: 70) that 'we may observe the brilliantly dressed nurses of aristocratic families...one of the most interesting phenomena of the Piazza'.

53   The conflation of socio-economic and cultural identity is difficult to disguise. 'Venice preserves a certain intimate and familiar concept of the "city-state"', notes Green (1936: 71),

PHOTO 3   *Teschio (San Francesco della Vigna)*   (© ANNA LUISA BRASS)

III

Like many others who write about Venice, Henry James expressed regret about the absence of two kinds of exclusivity: not being able to say anything new about the city, and on occasion not having it all to himself. Recognizing that at the end of the nineteenth century nothing original could be said about looking at Venetian paintings, he celebrated instead the fact that such cultural activity was not on the agenda of the mass tourist.[54] Although the latter sort of

---

'which survives beyond all possible attempts to create a modern mechanical uniformity. The ancient life of Venice lives on imperturbably'. Others allocated a place in this 'natural' hierarchy include the petty commodity producer (Green, 1936: 72–73), a 'figure [which] harmonizes with the background of a medieval city...here, in the still-living Middle Ages which linger on in Venice, we yet can see the itinerant vendor, struggling against the encroachment of the Multiple Store'.

54   On his lack of exclusivity as a cultural commentator, James' lament is as follows (Kaplan, 1994: 58): 'Everything has been said about the mighty painters [Carpaccio, Bellini, Tintoretto, Veronese], and it is of little importance to record that one traveller the more has found them to his taste. "Went this morning to the Academy; was much pleased with Titian's Assumption". That honest phrase has doubtless been written in many a traveller's diary...But it appeals little to the general reader'. Nevertheless, he is pleased that the Scuola di San Rocco is little visited, which confers an exclusivity of a different kind, observing that (Kaplan, 1994: 61–62): 'The interest, the impassiveness, of that whole corner of Venice, however melancholy the effect of its gorgeous and ill-lighted chambers, gives a strange

exclusivity to some degree mitigated the loss of the former kind, the capacity to enjoy it is for James nevertheless under threat from the mere presence of tourism.[55] He disapproves of the *vaporetti* (motor launches) because these enable 'rapid transit', and by conveying the mass tourist about the city, ruined its 'tranquility' for 'knowing ones' like himself.[56]

The Victim of Villainous Improvements

That James subscribes to the anti-development discourse of the agrarian myth is evident from the resentment he exhibits about the way Venice has changed since his first visit. Noting that the Lido has been 'spoiled', he goes on to observe that on his first visit in 1869 it was 'a very natural place'; that is to say, untouched by economic development and mass tourism, and thus still 'quaint'.[57] A decade on, in 1881, the Lido is dismissed by James in terms of a 'victim of villainous improvements'. What the latter consist of is clear: the presence of mass tourists, lower class visitors, and the amenities provided for them ('gas-lamps, lodging-houses, shops'). Put there for the benefit of the lower class, all these 'villainous improvements' defile the 'rural bosom' of the Lido, creating in its place a 'little cockney village'.[58]

---

importance to a visit to the Scuola. Nothing that all travellers go to see appears to suffer less from the incursions of travellers. It is one of the loneliest booths of the bazaar, and the author of these lines has always had the good fortune...of having it to himself'.

55   Henry James makes no attempt to hide his disapproval (Kaplan, 1994: 71), characterizing tourism negatively, 'the everlasting shuffle of these irresponsible visitors in the Piazza is contemporary Venetian life. Everything else is only a reverberation of that'. Elsewhere (Kaplan, 1994: 91, 102) these 'cheap trippers' are described by him as 'the incessant troop of those either bewilderedly making or fondly renewing acquaintance with the dazzling city'.

56   For Henry James (Kaplan, 1994: 85–86, 87), therefore, the 'character' of Venice is embodied in the 'brown plebeian faces', the 'fat undressed women' and 'other simple folk' unaware of the fact that the houses they occupy previously belonged to the aristocracy. The implication is that the former somehow unworthy of now living in the same place as the latter used to occupy, not least because plebeians – unlike James – are the 'unknowing ones of the earth'.

57   'You go to the Lido, though the Lido has been spoiled', complains Henry James (Kaplan, 1994: 67–68), who then proceeds to contextualize his lament thus: 'When I was first in Venice, in 1869, it was a very natural place...Today [c. 1881] the Lido is a part of a united Italy, and has been made the victim of villainous improvements. A little cockney village has sprung up on its rural bosom, and a third-rate boulevard leads from Santa Elisabetta to the Adriatic. There are bitumen walls and gas-lamps, lodging-houses, shops...'.

58   This pejorative description is one that Henry James (Kaplan, 1994: 71) uses again in 1892, when referring to the presence in Venice of 'the cockneyfied Piazzetta'. What he objects to, therefore, is not merely mass tourism but its plebeian aspect.

Such developments, offending as they do the sense of exclusivity and aesthetic taste of Henry James, license in turn a twofold antagonism towards those deemed their cause: the plebeian mass tourist as an 'uninitiated' visitor to the city. The notion of exclusivity informing the concept 'initiate' is used a century later by Král, and conveys the idea of a category composed only of those – like him – capable of appreciating Venice.[59] The masses, 'the average tourist', are not – nor can they ever be – in this category of the 'the elect': they depart, 'leaving the delights of the city untouched for him [= the initiate] alone'. It is these tourists who, 'simply by being here', turn Venice into a gaudy Disneyland; in short, it is they who 'pollute' the city. Merely by being present in a place they can neither understand nor appreciate, the 'uninitiated' are responsible for its resulting cultural degradation.[60]

Much the same applies to Guiton, whose 'uninformed tourist' is the equivalent of James' 'unknowing ones' and Král's 'uninitiated' visitor. Writing about the appeal to the mass tourist of Murano glass, she invokes this as evidence of a 'debased taste' indicative of the 'uninformed'.[61] By contrast, and again like James and Král, Guiton regards herself as one of the 'initiated' where an appreciation of Venice is concerned, on account of having been 'accepted' as a member of the community (= an 'insider') by the inhabitants of Burano.[62]

The reasons behind this ideological duality, whereby the 'insider' is elevated over the 'uninitiated', was perhaps best captured by Horatio Brown, who in the

---

59   For this and the following views, see Král (2011: 14–15).

60   As important aspect of this cultural degradation is the way local traditional crafts – such as glass-making in Murano – have been diluted through the importation of substitutes made more cheaply in China, but still sold in Venice under the label of 'Murano glass'. This change is attributed to the recent expansion in demand for 'authentic' items generated as a result of mass tourism. However, evidence suggests this is not new, and that even a century ago a similar process of substitution was operational. Sala (1887: 213) reports 'the more recent memory of having seen, fluttering from a linen draper's doorpost in the Merceria a number of cotton pocket-handkerchiefs, price...fourpence-halfpenny each, on which were printed in a lively pink pigment bird's-eye views of Venice...possibly printed in Manchester, and decidedly cheap at fourpence halfpenny'. In other words, the dilution of local crafts on cost grounds predates the era of mass tourism. It was this process which Marinetti condemned as 'fakery'.

61   'Anything goes for them [the mass tourist]', Guiton (1977: 56) observes, 'and the average seems steadily to decline and the shops are full of horrors, debased in taste and technique, which sell like hot cakes to the uninformed tourist'.

62   'One knows immediately when one is accepted into the community', she proclaims (Guiton, 1977: 62), continuing that: 'I knew I had been admitted [and] ceased to be a stranger'.

1880s maintained that the issue arose from what was seen as a form of 'trespass' by one kind of traveller on the space considered by another as his/her own private property.[63] This reaction, about how newly-arrived tourists in Venice possess in turn what one has come to regard as one's own property, was recognized subsequently by Max Beerbohm.[64] A variation on this proprietorial attitude is enviousness of visitors who remain in the city as one is about to depart, or who have been there for a much longer period.[65] As will be seen below, this same dichotomy – which projects 'otherness' closely linked to class differences – still underwrites the way Venice is depicted, not just verbally (= travel writing) but also visually (= film, photography, television).

A Dying Glory Smiles

In part, the continued reproduction of the 'insider'/'uninitiated' dichotomy can be seen as a reaction to attempts at making Venice more acceptable to the

---

63   This is clear from the following observation by Horatio Brown (1884: 77): 'There are places which seem marked for public applause, and praise is lavished upon them till it becomes commonplace; there are others which all of us know and love, and yet, for some reason we keep our knowledge to ourselves, and do not go into raptures over them; we even feel a sense of injury, as though a trespass were being committed on our private demesne, should we by accident discover that some one else holds the same appreciative views, which we believed to be peculiar to ourselves'.

64   This form of possessiveness, bordering almost on resentment, is well captured by Beerbohm (1993: 32, original emphasis): 'Silently out of the darkness came a gondola, heading for the steps. There was luggage in the prow, English luggage; and raptly gazing at the terrace there was a party of English people...It was how many days ago that I had arrived, just at this hour? – Days? It seemed years. And I knew that I must have gazed out of the gondola, with just that rapt look, wondering if Venice could be so lovely by day as she was by night, and wondering who was that romantic Venetian leaning against the parapet. For these newcomers *I* was the romantic Venetian, a part of the magical land-sea-scape; and they to me were ordinary English tourists, coming to Venice for the first time, with that in their eyes which had gone from mine...' The return to Venice is informed by the same reaction (Beerbohm, 1993: 36): 'It was a very slow train. My heart outran it a thousand times on the way. No lover was ever more impatient than I. No one had ever been more in love than I was. To think there were people who did not know Venice – people who had never yet lived! And those who did know her – did they know her as I did? No, she had told the secrets of her heart to me alone. She was waiting for me. I was on the way'.

65   This particular sense of property is usually encountered in aspiring or actual 'insiders'. Writing in 1873, Henry James (Kaplan, 1994: 35) makes the following confession: 'Meeting in the Piazza on the evening of my arrival a young American painter who told me that he had been spending the summer just where I found him, I could have assaulted him for very envy'.

plebeian visitor. Although it is true that the tourist appeal of the city has always relied on its history and culture, during the 1940s and 1950s visual depictions aimed at a mass market fell into line with the features of such advertisements. These tended to focus on Venice as a popular seaside holiday resort, projecting images in keeping with this.[66]

To some degree, such images were – and are – reinforced not just by photographs and postcards but also (and perhaps more importantly) by the popularity of the city as film location.[67] Although films wholly or partly set in Venice cover a wide variety of topics and periods, they all have in common the fact that narrative, characterization and even leading actors have to accept a subordinate role to the visual impact made by the location itself. Together with television programmes about Venice, films set in the city cannot but prepare – or confirm – what a visitor sees there and the 'meaning' attached to this.[68] Among the consequences of this visual pre-eminence are, firstly, to fuel the old cliché

---

66   Gender-specific photographic images were accompanied by captions – 'bathing beauties' on Lido beaches, 'a Venetian beauty waits for a gondolier', 'a pretty group of swimmers', and 'tennis, golf, riding, beach games', (Municipality of Venice, 1940: 51, 57, 59; Assessorato al Turismo, c. 1948; Oorthuys and den Doolaard, 1958: 14, 83–85) – designed to appeal to tourists who, it was thought, would not be overly interested in history and culture.

67   The role of the city as a film location of choice for many directors throughout the twentieth century, from the silent cinema onwards, is well documented (Damiani, 2010). Films extend from those based on Shakespeare plays – *Othello* (1952) and *The Merchant of Venice* (2004), directed respectively by Orson Welles and Michael Radford – to historical dramas such as *Giordano Bruno* (1973) and *Casanova* (1976), directed respectively by Giuliano Montaldoa and Federico Fellini. Among the important films directed by Luchino Visconti which use the city as a backdrop are *Senso* (1954) and *Death in Venice* (1971). Nicolas Roeg's *Don't Look Now* (1973) was also set in the city, as was Vittorio De Sica's *Il Viaggio* (1974), while Joseph Losey filmed parts of the opera *Don Giovanni* (1979) there. Other cinematic successes located in Venice include *Summertime* (1955), *Indiana Jones and the Last Crusade* (1989) and *The Talented Mr Ripley* (1999), directed respectively by David Lean, Steven Spielberg and Anthony Minghella.

68   A recent BBC series about the city fronted by Francesco Mosto confirms that television programmes on Venice which combine history and travel are able to generate large viewing audiences. As Raymond Williams pointed out in a 1969 review of an earlier programme about the city, however, the focus of television discourse on pessimism and decline is no different from that examined here. Observing that the presenter on that occasion was 'a travelled and civilized man, humane and reflective', Williams (O'Connor, 1989: 72) then noted that 'now he had the mood of this culture which the BBC selects so regularly: the sad vanishing past, the muddled and hateful present'. In other words, the 'meaning' disseminated *via* other forms of popular culture reinforces that found in much travel writing.

that 'no-one enters Venice as a stranger'. And second, to render more acute the 'insider'/'uninitiated' dichotomy.[69]

Two particular visual aspects connected with modernity attract the opprobrium of observers such as Čapek, Debray, Harte and Král: cameras and clothing. Hence the view expressed by Král that 'dense crowds in whose midst Venice finds herself [composed of tourists equipped with] modern-day extras carrying cameras just like theirs, and wearing identical shorts and T-shirts'.[70] This photo-phobic attitude was echoed by Debray who, like Král, objects to tourists taking photos, much like a tribal who thinks his identity is being stolen by someone who 'takes' his photograph. In an important sense, therefore, an 'initiate' may object that, by capturing a photographic image of the city, the tourist 'other' is taking from him an image of a scene/place that is specific to him, an act tantamount to depriving him of his own particular identity.[71]

Significantly, perhaps, cameras are equated not just with modernity but also with wealth: carried by English tourists before the 1939–1945 war and by Japanese equivalents subsequently.[72] Camera as symbol of modernity also

---

69 Because film images confer on the 'uninitiated' plebeian visitor a form of knowledge about the city, its culture and history, the initiated 'knowing one' is perforce required to immerse him/herself even deeper in Venetian history/culture so as to maintain an ideological distance from the plebeian 'uninitiated' visitor. The significance of the role of film in framing what is seen by the traveller is recognised by Kael (1970: 23, original emphasis), who observes that '[w]hen we travel now, we are not *surprised*, as travellers a century ago must have been; we view so many places in terms of a movie-made *déjà vu*'.

70 See Král (2011: 15).

71 It cannot be entirely accidental that a number of photographic essays about Venice – for example, Fontana (2004), Campigotto (2006), Crovato and Crovato (2008), and Thomas (2012) – depict the city and/or its environs as more-or-less devoid of people, thus succeeding at last in exorcising the 'other' who comes between a subject wanting to capture a personal image and the city itself. Gone, finally, are those around him attempting to do the same, thereby reminding him of his own lack of exclusivity in this context. In order to do this, however, it is necessary to photograph Venice either from the air (Fontana, 2004), by night (Campigotto, 2006), or in the very early morning (Thomas, 2012).

72 In the late 1920s, therefore, opprobrium is expressed by Čapek (1929: 14) towards 'the English [who] sport photographic apparatus'. Chronicling what he terms the Three Ages of Man, spanning the years 1908–1970, Paul Morand similarly rails at mass tourism, its ethnic dimension and the photographic element. Hence the following vision of modernity as inferno, in which all these phenomena are paraded ignominiously in order to effect a contrast with a glorious imperial history (Morand, 2002: 202–203, 204–205): 'The Italian Empire is long past, and the Office of Tourism requires hotels and more hotels... The whole of this Santa Croce districts smokes with gas and carbon monoxide, Cinzano fumes and marijuana. Collapsing suitcases that have just fallen off the top decks of

informed earlier observations which tended to focus not on who was taking a photograph but rather on the aesthetic merits of what the photographic image was able to capture relative to paintings of the same scene.

Photographs of Venice taken by a camera were accordingly deemed to be less 'authentic' than the painted image, a celebration of romanticism (= the unreality of the aesthetic vision) over the technical achievements of the modern (= plain/honest/mechanical, 'the real').[73] Once again, this distinction is both familiar and contemporary: in privileging feeling over thinking, and categorizing the former as the more 'authentic' expression of place, it anticipates the anti-modern/anti-rational discourse of the way the 'new' populist postmodernism endorses the agrarian myth.

The Ethnically 'Other' Tourist

As noted in previous chapters, among those categorized as 'other' by travel writers are locals residing in the place visited. In keeping with this, Venetians themselves have frequently been described in negative terms, as interested only in ways of extracting money from visitors to their city. This takes the form either of being overcharged by traders for items purchased, or of being accosted by beggars seeking alms.[74] Of more concern to travel writers, however, are two

---

buses...the Japanese with their top-heavy Leicas, the 16mm film strewn over the ground... Unlike the Basilica of St Mark's, the Piazzale Roma is a cathedral of drivers. You have to choose between the museum and life'.

73 Hence for Russell Green the visual contrast is between on the one hand the 'authenticity' of images – 'romantic views of Venice' – depicted by Samuel Prout in the 1830s, and on the other the realistic monochromes produced a century later by the camera. Noting that Prout's images 'could not have corresponded with the crude facts', Green (1936: 42ff.,) goes on to observe that: 'The facts? – but the merely external appearance of Venice goes back for so many centuries that, perhaps, the etherealized vision of Mr Prout lies nearer the heart of ultimate truth than the mechanical and pedestrian record of a photograph', concluding (Green, 1936: 59–60) 'But, alas! The monochrome of photography is woefully incapable of rendering that charm [of Venice]'. The distinction is emphasized subsequently (Green, 1936: 86–87, 128ff.) in the following manner: 'We may well compare the exceedingly romantic etching by Mr Samuel Prout...with the record of the realistic camera...how mysteriously does the plain and honest report of the common eye differ from the romanticized vision of the painter'. Nevertheless, Green (1936: 158) opts finally for the latter, insisting 'how much more atmosphere Mr Samuel Prout secures in his drawings than the mechanical eye of the camera can ever obtain'.

74 See, for example, Goldring (1913: 81) who comments that those who sought 'the tourist's cash' consisted not only of 'the Hebrew shopkeepers in the Merceria', but also of the 'ragged horde' spending 'their lives hungrily eying the invader for unconsidered

external kinds of 'other': tourists from their own country, and visitors from other nations.[75] Hence a typical complaint that in Venice there 'were people that one recognized from London or Paris, hordes of every kind of English and American and German tourists – especially Germans, of the loudest type'.[76]

Accordingly, the antagonism felt by travel writers towards the presence in Venice of tourists has a specific ethnic component.[77] Historically, the main targets of this discourse – tourists from Germany, the United States and Japan – have been among the better-off visitors of their day, which in turn raises the issue not so much of nationality as of class.[78] At the end of the nineteenth century and the start of the twentieth, therefore, it is German tourists who annoy. Visitors from that country are described by Henry James in terms of a 'horde', as 'savage', who offend him with their 'uproar'.[79] The same description

---

soldi: beggars, shiftless and downtrodden, hiding in the least savoury parts of the city of their ancestors…'.

75   It is also the case that the nationalism of others is on occasion provoked with regard to the city. Noting that Tchaikovsky had composed his fourth symphony in Venice, Harte (1988: 32) comments that '[i]t is extraordinary how an artist always carries his country in his head'.

76   This is expressed by Goldring (1913: 111), Harte (1988: 136), and Newby (1984). Describing the English tourist as 'strident', Goldring (1913: 79) complained that, on arriving in Venice, he was 'jostled by crowds of English people of the kind I like least – High School marms in spectacles, clergy, and learned persons of both sexes'. Newby (1984: 61) confesses that 'our only preoccupation [was] whether we could find another place to eat, in addition to the few we already knew, which was not infested with, although we hated to admit it, people like ourselves, fellow visitors to Venice…'.

77   Noting that 'there are some disagreeable things in Venice', Henry James (Kaplan, 1994: 48, 49) elaborated that 'there is nothing so disagreeable as the visitors…[I] had not been there for several years, and in the interval the beautiful and helpless city had suffered an increase of injury. The barbarians are in full possession, and you tremble for what they may do. You are reminded, from the moment of your arrival, that Venice scarcely exists any more as a city at all; that it exists only as a battered peep-show and bazaar'.

78   Significantly, the aspect of wealth is rarely identified as such. Antagonism is usually expressed obliquely, and reference is made instead to the preponderance of up-to-date technology (specifically, cameras), a philistine disregard for or an inability fully to appreciate the cultural treasures on display.

79   Using military terms to describe German tourists, Henry James (Kaplan, 1994: 49) compares them to invaders: 'There was a horde of savage Germans encamped in the Piazza, and they filled the Ducal Palace and the academy with their uproar'. Adding that '[t]he English and Americans came a little later', he concludes that the 'months of April and May of the year 1881 were not, as a general thing, a favourable season for visiting the Ducal Palace and the Academy'.

is repeated by Georgina Grahame, for whom the city has 'become the play-ground of Germany, and the northern hordes from Munich and Berlin, which in Autumn fill her steamers and gondolas, make one shudder'.[80]

A similar kind of antagonism is expressed by Douglas Goldring, who complains about 'clumsy Teutons who jostle you, walk on your toes and jabber about the "Marcusplatz"'.[81] The inference of a subsequent objection, by Russell Green, is that German visitors memorize the history, but are incapable of appreciating 'the spirit of the place'.[82] German tourists are accused of privileging rationality/thinking over aesthetics/feeling, thereby reversing the stereotypical response to Venice – that of Romanticism – thought to be appropriate.[83]

For Čapek in the late 1920s, a broad antagonism to 'the terrific mass of tourists' with whom he has to share the city subdivides into a series of ethnic

---

80   See Grahame (1909: 201), who continues in a manner that today would be regarded as offensive: 'The women are not pillars, they are columns of too solid flesh, they make not the slightest effort to soften the hard outlines of their massive forms...and the way in which they bring down their enormous feet on the delicate Opus Alexandrinum pavements of St. Mark's, and the Duomo of Torcello, constitutes a real danger to these fast-vanishing works of art. They scorn ever to avoid trampling on the most beautiful slab tombs in the old churches they visit...[our guide in Egypt] would have quailed before the bulk and the tone of the German, as he is to be seen in Venice in the month of September'.

81   See Goldring (1913: 89, 107) who observes on visiting the Lido that 'Teutonic man was viler than one would have thought possible...If only the Italian Government could be persuaded to pass a law against Germans! (it's all rot to say the English are just as bad, because we simply aren't.)' Much like Georgina Grahame at the same conjuncture, Goldring (1913: 107–108) resorts to description that would now be considered hugely offensive ('trying to avoid noticing the enormously fat and bald Germans of both sexes who sprawled on their backs in long stewing rows...it would have taken more than an army of elderly, middle-class German women, in skin-tight costumes, or of their swollen husbands in tiny striped bathing drawers, to put one out of conceit with such sunlight and such sea'.).

82   Writing in the mid-1930s, Russell Green (1936: 104, original emphasis) comments that 'it is curious that your German traveller will be found to know beforehand even the smallest details of the historic buildings, the sculptures, the most famous paintings...[h]e has already learned it all out of a book...And how easy that is! it needs only the most commonplace of all human gifts – a good memory! But to feel, to grasp, and to express the *spirit* of a place – the *genius loci* – that does, indeed, demand a delicate sensibility and a subtle power of expression which are rarely allied to that more common and mundane faculty of memory'.

83   The affinity Wagner had for Venice, however, is correctly seen by Green (1936: 78–79) as emanating from German Romanticism, a result of the composer having 'discovered his "ruined castle" on the Grand Canal rather than on the Rhine'.

'others' each possessing specific (mostly negative) characteristics.[84] In the case of Waugh, it is American tourists who attracted his opprobrium during 1960.[85] He underlined this anti-Americanism by commending the presence of tourists who were European, contrasting the new and in his view 'inauthentic' culture of the former with what for him was the old and 'authentic' culture of those belonging to the latter category.[86] Europeans, he infers, are not out of place in Venice, whereas Americans are.

At a later conjuncture, however, it is visitors from Japan who arouse particular ire, now of Debray, Harte and Král. The latter all object not just to the Japanese taking photographs, but also to their attire, to their mode of communication ('little tittering groups') and even to their facial expressions ('unpleasant grins on their faces').[87] One suspects that for Debray the presence in Venice of the Japanese is as much an anomaly as would have been the presence there of Mao, which raises in turn the political meaning of the city.

---

84   See Čapek (1929: 13–14), who relates that 'Germans mostly carry rucksacks or wear coarse woollen clothes; the English sport photographic apparatus; Americans are recognizable by their shoulders; and Czechs because they almost resemble Germans and speak in remarkably loud tones...'.

85   When visiting Venice out of season early in 1960, Waugh (1980: 533) expresses relief that there is 'not an American in sight'. Elsewhere he notes that '[n]o one who could afford to go away spent the summer in Venice', adding (Waugh, 1977: 49) '[t]hat is an American craze which began in my lifetime'. A similar view was expressed during the mid-1930s by Russell Green, albeit in a more oblique fashion; commending tourists who spend more time appreciating Venice, and contrasting this with rapid sight-seeing in 'the American fashion'. He writes (Green, 1936: v–vi): 'Nowadays there is an ever-growing host of travellers who possess general culture without the opulent leisure which used to accompany it. They have a fortnight or three weeks in which to cover half Europe. They have not the time (though possibly they have the will) to view and memorize every canvas in the Louvre... Despite their nobler ambitions, they are compelled to tour in the American fashion...'.

86   Identifying an unbridgeable 'Anglo-American impasse – "never the twain shall meet"', Waugh (cited in Bradbury, 1973: 177) justified his anti-Americanism thus: 'There is no such thing as an "American". They are all exiles uprooted, transplanted and doomed to sterility'.

87   'As we gaze at the reflection of the Villa [Pisani] through the water-lillies and dead leaves in the lake', writes Harte (1988: 112), 'a whole party of smartly-overcoated Japanese arrive and begin to photograph themselves in little tittering groups by the statues'. In a similar vein, Král (2011: 82–83) observes that 'we are suddenly surrounded by a crowd of Japanese men in three-piece suits who come out of a building, with fixed, unpleasant grins on their faces, as if they have just bought it...Some more off-spring of the Land of the Rising Sun, this time of a philosophical bent, float past in a boat...going to the window, we are met by a silent barrage of flash bulbs which whiten the dark façade for a moment'.

PHOTO 4   *Voga alla Veneta*   (© ANNA LUISA BRASS)

IV

That Venice should be perceived by those on the political right in terms of aesthetics is unsurprising. Less obvious, however, is the overlap between left and right when it comes to categorizing the 'meaning' of Venice. Equally surprising is the fact that such an approach is not simply an endorsement, but rather divided between positive and negative interpretations. In the ranks of the political right, therefore, are found those who can be defined as being 'for Venice' (Waugh, Morand) and those who are against it (Marinetti). Notwithstanding this difference, all were either complicit with or sympathetic to the far right: Marinetti a co-founder with Mussolini of Italian fascism (*Fasci di combattimento*), Morand an office-holder under the Vichy government, and Waugh a fellow-traveller.[88]

---

88   For these political allegiances, see among others Hamilton (1971) and Lyttelton (1973: 207–221). Much of the writing by Paul Morand (1928; 1929; 1932; 1933; 1937) based on journeys he made during the 1920s and 1930s reveal the extent of the fear about non-European ethnic 'otherness' as this was experienced by an upper-class European traveller. Observing

Venice, Left and Right

The antagonism felt by Marinetti towards Venice at the start of the twentieth century is consistent with modernism, and thus in political terms seemingly progressive.[89] His main objection focused on the contrast between what he saw as its heroic past and its 'servile' present in which Venetians have been reduced to a population of sellers of fake antiques to and waiters on the tourist trade.[90] For this reason, Marinetti advocates the filling-in of its canals, their replacement with roads, and he looks forward to the eventual destruction of historical Venice that will bring an end to the 'illustrious ruins' which people come to see. Ostensibly, therefore, opposition towards Venice expressed by Marinetti, informed as it is by Futurism, has little to do with the agrarian myth discourse espoused by the 'new' populist postmodernism.

Yet many aspects of the latter are in fact endorsed by Futurist ideology: like postmodernism it is populist; it denies the efficacy of history; it is anti-intellectual and anti-rational; opposed to socialism, it privileges instead capitalism, nationalism and ethnic identity.[91] For Marinetti and the Futurists,

---

that as the speed of travel increased, '[t]hen the Chinese and the negro will come to dispute the habitable land with us; there will be race warfare for the best climates', he asked (Morand, 1928: 9, 19) 'will America have to take up arms in the name of us all, and play the last game of the white aristocracy, retreating before the yellow and black races?'. Such fears were especially pronounced in the case of Asian 'otherness', about which Morand (1928: 51, 56, 57) expressed the following sentiments: '[B]ehind those blue bamboos begins the China of the interior where, but yesterday, the White men were masters; whither, perhaps, they will never more return...does she [= China] mean now to push all the White men back to the coast, or clean into the sea? Are the White men, in their turn, their privileges lost or torn from them, to come under the law of might, which they have so often invoked?...To Asiatics all Whites are alike, and form a single nation'. Such views prefigure the ones retailed subsequently about Venice (see below).

89   As is well-known, in 1910 Marinetti proclaimed his opposition to everything that the city represented by throwing copies of his Futurist Manifesto from the Clock Tower onto the crowds gathered below in St. Mark's Square. The critique is contained in two brief pieces: 'Against Past-loving Venice', and 'Speech to the Venetians' (Marinetti, 1972: 54–58). The refusal of the travel writer Douglas Goldring to be impressed by the city is due in part to his sharing the views of Marinetti. Hence the confession (Goldring, 1913: 81) of feeling 'an irresistible longing to...welcome Marinetti with his multi-coloured manifests'.

90   The contrast is made thus (Marinetti, 1972: 57): 'And yet, once you were invincible warriors and gifted artists, audacious navigators, ingenious industrialists, and tireless merchants...And you have become waiters in hotels, ciceroni, pimps, antiquarians, imposters, fakers of old pictures, plagiarists and copyists'.

91   An ethnically-specific, instinctive and aggressive nationalism is evident from the claim by Marinetti (1972: 149, 150, original emphases) that 'Futurist patriotism is an eager

modernity was primarily an aesthetic, not an economic project.[92] This antipathy towards Venetian history led one Futurist and colleague of Marinetti, the painter Carlo Carrà, to exalt the artistic work of Giotto as the first 'authentic expression' of Italian national/ethnic identity in preference to the earlier but 'inauthentic' Byzantine mosaics.[93] The latter, dismissed as 'Oriental/Greek images' (= non-Italian), were found both in Venice itself (St. Mark's Basilica) and its islands (Torcello).[94]

---

passion...for the continuity and development of the race...[y]ou cannot escape these two idea-feelings: *patriotism*, or the active development of the individual and race, and *heroism*, or the synthetic need to transcend human powers, the ascensional force of the race'. That he was a populist is evident not just from his nationalism, and his opposition to socialism and to monarchy in the name of 'the people' (Lyttelton, 1973: 217), but also from the following description (Marinetti, 1972: 254) of fascism in Milan as having 'a conservative revolutionary character that strains to reconcile a harsh progressivism with feelings for a higher charitable justice'.

92   According to Marinetti (1972: 56, 254), locomotives, trams and automobiles represented 'the first outlines of the great Futurist aesthetic', described by him elsewhere as 'an aesthetic of the machine multiplied by gasoline'.

93   Arguing that Giotto is the 'father of Italian painting', whose art 'constitutes one of the most spontaneous efforts of the plastic genius of the Italian people', Carrà (1925: 7, 11, 18) goes on to praise him for the 'abandoning of the rude Byzantine manner and the introduction into his art of grace and naturalness'. More broadly, Carrà (1925: 17) insists that '[t]he Italian painters even before the advent of Giotto tended to have a more spiritual conception than was the case with the Byzantines'. Giotto is commended (Carrà, 1925: 11–12) not only for 'a liberation from the dry Byzantine models', therefore, but – significantly – also for replacing them with 'a direct study from nature'. According to the Futurist Carrà, therefore, '[i]t was by basing itself on these two principles that Italian art began the first great period of its history'. His conclusion (Carrà, 1925: 21) is that '[t]here is barely a trace of direct observation of nature in the Byzantine paintings, while for Giotto this was one of the principal founts of his art...Giotto, son of the people, offers us one of the finest examples of the essentially popular virtue which consists in never losing contact with the earth...the Italians especially have at the bottom of their character such attachment...' For Carrà, therefore, Giotto embodies national virtue (= ethnic identity) that is itself rooted in both the 'people' (= populism) and the Italian soil (= Nature), as such to be differentiated from 'foreign' art (= Byzantine). In other words, a characterization that is consistent with the agrarian myth as interpreted by 'new' populist postmodernist theory.

94   See Carrà (1925: 20, 21), for whom Byzantine art is full of 'maniacal violence' and 'egoism', indicative of 'barbarism'. That the mosaics of Byzantium were in some sense 'other' – and as such an 'alien' intrusion into what was otherwise an authentically Italian artistic tradition – is questionable. 'Much has been said and written about the Byzantine character of St. Mark's architecture and mosaics', observes Vio (2003: 60), adding: 'The style that we call Byzantine was certainly understood by the ancient Venetians as essentially a

The politically reactionary character of a Futurist modernity is evident from the way in which particular categories are depicted in either positive or negative terms. Hence the positive attributes are seen by Marinetti as being a warrior people, engaged both in imperial conquest and in the exploitation/plunder of other nations/peoples (= 'tireless merchants'). Negative ones, by contrast, include socialism, Marxism, workers of one kind or another (waiters, guides, etc., attached to tourism), foreigners and intellectuals (antiquarians). Anti-intellectualism is an explicit aspect of Marinetti's discourse. According to the 1909 Futurist manifesto, its object was to destroy 'museums, libraries, academies of every type [since] we, young and strong Futurists, wish to have nothing to do with the past'.[95] The same is true of his hostility to Marxism and socialism.[96]

As marked is the enthusiasm Marinetti displayed for nationalism and capitalism. The aspect of Venetian subservience which vexed him is clear: it derived not from servility being demeaning in class terms but rather from its being an

---

Roman style. Confirming this, we should recall that Pope Honorius III (1216–1227), through Doge Pietro Ziani, summoned Venetian mosaicists to Rome to execute new mosaics in the apse of San Paolo fuori le Mura, an archetypal Roman church. This can only mean that the Pope took the style of the mosaics in St. Mark's to be Roman. Constantinople was considered, as we know, the second Rome. So the distinction that we draw between Roman and Byzantine does not apply on Italian soil'. However, André Gide appeared to agree with Carrà in regarding Venice as insufficiently 'authentic' in cultural terms. In his Diary entry for 1 May 1914, Gide (1948: 7) observed: 'Constantinople justifies all my prejudices and joins Venice in my personal hell. As soon as you admire some bit of architecture, the surface of a mosque, you learn (and you suspected it already) that it is Albanian or Persian. Everything was brought here, as to Venice, even more than to Venice, by sheer force or by money. Nothing sprang from the soil itself; nothing indigenous underlies the thick froth made by the friction and the clash of so many races, histories, beliefs, and civilizations'.

95   See Marinetti (1972: 42), who a decade later not merely repeats but emphasizes the same point (Lyttelton, 1973: 219): 'We owe nothing to the past'. To the category of history is added those who discuss its meaning, both eliciting his condemnation. 'It is from Italy that we launch through the world this violently upsetting, incendiary manifesto of ours', observes Marinetti (1972: 42), 'because we want to free this land from its...professors, archaeologists, ciceroni, and antiquarians'.

96   Among the 'Associations of ideas must be forcibly broken' listed by Marinetti in 1919 (Lyttelton, 1973: 216), therefore, is the following: 'When you talk of justice, equality, freedom, the rights of the proletariat, of the peasants and of the under-privileged, the struggle against parasites, you immediately think of anti-patriotism, international pacifism, Marxism and collectivism'. A year later he writes (Marinetti, 1972: 148, 150): 'Communism is the exasperation of the bureaucratic cancer that has always wasted humanity... Communism may be realized in cemeteries'.

affront to Italian national identity. Thus his objection was not so much to 'servility' per se as to Venetians 'prostrating' themselves 'before all foreigners'.[97] Urging the inhabitants of the city to 'renounce the Venice of foreigners', he described it as the 'cloaca maxima of passéism'; history is equated with the unwelcome presence in the city of the foreign 'other' (= the tourist), the eradication of the former necessarily resulting in the expulsion of those in the latter category.[98]

Linked to this advocacy of nationalism is the embrace of capitalism. Marinetti argues that, rather than celebrate art and history, Italians should 'prepare a great strong industrial, commercial, and military Venice on the Adriatic Sea, that great Italian lake'.[99] Venetians should in his opinion embrace modern capitalism together with its expansionist militaristic tendencies (= imperial conquest), all in the name of Italian nationalism. Its purpose as seen by him is 'to bring you [Venetians] mountains of goods and a shrewd, wealthy, busy crowd of industrialists and businessmen'.[100] This vision of what Venice is and ought to be is different from that of two other rightwing commentators, Evelyn Waugh and Paul Morand.

False Conversions, Instant Tonsures

Seen by Waugh as the epitome (and thus a repository) of architectural/artistic/cultural achievement in the Mediterranean area, Venice is described by him both as a place of 'melancholy and mystery', and as 'the last glory of Europe'.[101] This is unsurprising, since his enthusiasm for Venice, but his objection to the presence there of American tourists, is in keeping with his more general views about travel, examined in the previous chapter. That is, a like of tradition and

---

97   He chides Venice with wanting 'to prostrate yourself before all foreigners', adding (Marinetti, 1972: 57) that: 'Your servility is repulsive...your humility is boundless'. 'Have you forgotten', asks Marinetti (1972: 57), 'that first of all you are Italians, and that in the language of history this means: builders of the future?'.

98   On this see Marinetti (1972: 55).

99   For this see Marinetti (1972: 58), a view which overlooks the historical fact that, in the Arsenale, Venice possessed not just military capacity but also a naval dockyard run along industrial lines (on which see Davis, 1991).

100   See Marinetti (1972: 56), whose Futurist programme for the city was clear: 'We want to prepare the birth of an industrial and military Venice'.

101   On this and the following points, see Waugh (1977: 48–51). 'If every museum in the New World were emptied', he writes (Waugh, 1977: 49), 'if every famous building in the Old World were destroyed and only Venice survived, there would be enough there to fill a full lifetime with delight. Venice, with all its complexity and variety, is in itself the greatest surviving work of art in the world'.

social hierarchy, a lamentation of their passing, and a distrust of modernity.[102] Although he expresses a dislike of the crowds encountered on his visits to the city, Waugh surprisingly does not adhere to the usual dichotomy ('initiated'/'uninitiated') whereby the travel writer distances him/herself from the mass tourist, arguing instead that '[n]ever believe anyone who tells you he "knows" Venice'. Consistent with his politics, however, is his deferential portrayal of the aristocratic inhabitants in 'one of the few palaces still fully occupied by the original family'.[103]

That for Paul Morand there is more than one Venice suggests a contrast between his version – a cultural one exclusive to people like himself – and the city overrun and thus despoiled by plebeian visitors. Just where an attempt to defend this elitist image of Venice can lead politically is evident from its role in his justification for having collaborated with the rightwing Vichy regime in 1940.[104] Invoking the historical precedent of the 1797 Venetian government, which let in Napoleon so as to preserve the city and its culture, so Vichy in 1940 – argues Morand – collaborated with the invading Germans in order to preserve France and its culture.[105] Hence the plea that not merely should he

---

102   'Waugh's attitude to the United States', notes Bradbury (1973: 170), 'is closely tied to his entire attitude toward the modern world...In the later years of his life, from the end of the [1939–45] war onward, Waugh's bitterness about social evolution and the movement toward equality, welfare and progress was considerable; it was a bitterness about the loss of civilization and hierarchy that maintained and ordered it...'.

103   See Waugh (1977: 50). When considering the latter's contribution to the travel writing genre, Newby (1973: 83) points out that 'Venice he was disinclined to write about and did not until...*Brideshead Revisited*'.

104   Although Morand (2002: 91) claims to have espoused leftist views – 'I have only ever loved peace; though this fidelity has brought me some strangely disloyal strokes of luck; it has taken me from a very advanced left-wing position in 1917 to deposit me in 1940 in a Vichy upheld by the ideas of Charles Maurras' – this is for the following reasons open to question. In a discussion with Marcel Sembat, one of the leaders of the French Socialist Party, during 1917, Morand (2002: 91–92) states that 'I came to understand that we had to overcome our dread of the working man, one of the legacies of 1848 and 1871'. Talking to another socialist leader, Brake-Desrousseaux, in that same year, however, Morand reports that '"I believe in socialism, but I can only think of it as national"', I remarked innocently to Brake-Desrousseaux (I little imagined that, twenty years later, these two words would cause Europe to explode). He replied dryly: "Impossible; socialism is international in its essence"'. Morand's inability to recognize the political difference between internationalism and nationalism on the one hand, and their respective connections to socialism and to fascism on the other, throws doubt on claims about his earlier political allegiance.

105   Morand (2002: 199ff.) undertakes a lengthy consideration of the decision by the government of Venice to allow Napoleon to enter the city in 1797, thereby preventing both its

not be condemned as a collaborator but, much rather, he should be regarded as a far-sighted French patriot.

Travel for Morand is a form of escape, not just from 1920s Paris but from its emerging working class politics, and his search for what he terms an 'authentic' culture leads him to Venice, a journey he refers to as a return home.[106] Hence the longing for Venice, and an equally vehement dislike for others (= tourists) found occupying that space, perceived by Morand as interlopers in a context he now saw as his own. His hope that 'Venice will be saved' requires in turn that first it be 'disinfected of tourists'.[107] In what is a symptomatic declaration of concern at the changes wrought by development, undermining as they do the combined notions of 'exclusivity' and 'authenticity', he condemns the spread and power of modern industry.[108]

---

destruction by cannon and its invasion. The parallel he then draws is clear (Morand, 2002: 200): 'Whether it was 1797 or 1945...Venice has scarcely put up fierce resistance; she wanted to avoid pillage and fire;...the duty of a unique city is to survive'.

106   According to Morand (2002: 109–110), in 1925 'Paris was the city of false life...people were fleeing towards every outlet, every religion, there were false conversions, instant tonsures...Paris lost her moral control of the world, she has never regained it again...[f]rom then on "travelling became my only concern"'.

107   For this discourse of pathology, conjuring up worrying parallels in the history of the political right about the necessity of 'cleansing' a particular group in order to realize national salvation, see Morand (2002: 217, 221). That he still subscribes to the epistemology of this political discourse is clear from the following observations, made in the early 1970s (Morand, 2002: 226, 235, 237, 238): 'In those days, the white race was not ashamed of its hegemony...Seen from Trieste, Venice is the southernmost point of civilization...From Trieste, Stendhal wrote: "Here I confront barbarity." I venture to fall in behind him. The Italian-Yugoslav border divides two worlds; facing one is Asia, and those state-controlled lands that swallow up individuality...you might think that the ebb and flow of the slavic era, spurred on in turn by the Mongol ocean, bides its time; can no one see that it is advancing at the gallop?'.

108   'How many times before the last world war did I take the little road along the banks of the Brenta to return to Venice', laments Morand (2002: 114, 115): 'At that time [pre-1939] there was very little traffic between Venice and the mainland; today [c. 1970] Padua has become an annexe of Venice, extending as far as Verona and Vincenza; buses, coaches and lorries run every half-hour between the Ermetiani and the Piazzale Roma, swallowing up the Lagoon faster than any train; the sleepy, provincial town of Padua is now an important business centre, full of bustle and noise and the sound of gas explosions, and drowning in carbon monoxide fumes that mingle with the foul stench of the Mestre oil refineries...' He continues: 'The Brenta is no longer the summer-time river whose Alpine waters cooled Venice's holidaymakers; tatty huts replace the trees, the water is the colour of olive oil and on its surface float the bloated corpses of dead cats, discarded crates and empty tin cans;

Sympathetic to the idea of Venice as the haven of an ancient European aristocracy, Morand endorses their leisurely lifestyle and – like Paddy Leigh Fermor
in Rumania – expresses sorrow at the dilapidation of their mainland villas.[109]
On his return to the city in 1951 after an absence of twelve years, Morand condemns the lack of exclusivity that now characterized Venice, occupied by a
'throng of foreign peoples' composed of plebeian elements ('hairdressers',
'make-up girls' and 'ticket-holders') previously not seen by him there.[110] Among
those he disapproves of are the post-war *arriviste* elements.[111] By 1964 Venice
was a place Morand no longer recognized as 'authentic', as the *real* Venice of
his youth, a city which in class terms was socially exclusive.[112] It is in relation to

---

pylons and power-lines form the dense vegetation of the new Italy...' En route to India at
an earlier conjuncture, Morand already displayed antipathy to the impact on Venice of
economic development and tourism, coupled with nostalgia for its pre-modern aspects.
'There was a time before the war when only small steamers traveling from Trieste to
Ragusa anchored before Saint George the Greater', he observed (1937: 42), adding: 'The
two pillars of the Piazzetta seemed enormous because no gigantic ship dwarfed them by
comparison; no companion ladder made them look like mere candlesticks. That was
about 1908...Today [the 1930s], from this same window, smoke is seen rising from the
naval dockyards behind the Giardini; aeroplanes arrive hourly from Barcelona or Munich,
from Brindisi or Marseilles...'.

109   On these points see Morand (2002: 116–117), who elaborates thus: 'It is in winter that the
      Venetians of former times used to take refuge in the city, after the hunting season...
      The dances and public life continued until June; then people would return back along the
      Brenta, or go to their Palladian villas in the Euganean hills. It was in the sixteenth century
      that Brenta became fashionable; each patrician family owned one or more villas there...'
      It is clearly a lifestyle with which he feels an affinity, observing (Morand, 2002: 152) that
      the 'pleasures of life in the twenties were uninhibited, but one had to be well dressed and
      come from a good family'.

110   'I would not see Venice again for another twelve years', wrote Morand (2002: 171, 176) about
      June 1939, adding that 'from the moment I arrived [in Venice in September 1951] I knew
      that I was coming to say farewell to a certain world...In St Mark's Square, there was what
      a Venetian Montaigne would call "the throng of foreign peoples". It wasn't a matter of
      hairdressers or make-up girls having missed their trains or planes, or of "ticket-holders"
      jeopardised by last-minute defections – local politics, the American press, left-wing puri-
      tanism and the resentment of those who had been excluded were all blended together'.

111   According to Morand (2002: 179) these included 'oil-rich Asians, bored Americans, kings
      from *Candide*, the jet-setters and a sea of ship-owners'.

112   Distressed at the passing of an 'authentic' upper class lifestyle represented by the Palazzo
      Labia, as its contents are sold off, Morand (2002: 186, 189) comments in 1964: 'I look upon
      that world of yesteryear without resentment, nor regret; quite simply, it no longer exists;
      for me, at least, since it continues, without any bother or fuss, in a universe that is a little
      more brutal, a little more doomed...[i]t is merely that its ways are no longer mine'.

this change, in this place, that his reactionary politics reassert themselves: Morand now reveals a disdain not just for modernity but also for democracy, equality, female emancipation and revolution, all of which he rejects.[113]

Che Sprawled in a Gondola?
Turning to the meaning of Venice as seen from the political left, here – despite an expectation to the contrary – there is a discernable overlap both with travel writing generally, and also with accounts by those on the political right. Like Marinetti, therefore, neither Jean-Paul Sartre nor Régis Debray value what the Futurist terms the 'passéism' of the city and its history.[114] Purporting to be an 'inexpert tourist', Sartre unsuccessfully searches for the 'real' Venice, and pronounces it an elusive object: for him the city remains 'always the *Other*', and in the end 'Venice is wherever I am not'.[115] This same category of 'otherness' is

---

113   'We are seeing the dawn of a primitive matriarchy, a post-nuclear one, it occurs to me', notes Morand (2002: 195), who continues that 'democracy, the blackmailer of the weak, brackets the Female with those who were once subjugated, the Blacks, servants, the working class, children and all those liberated people who have become the masters. The composition of the masses will change, but the masses will remain; that is what is meant by "revolution"'.

114   Given that neither Sartre nor Debray approve of things Venetian, the question to ask is: can – should – a socialist like Venice? Leftist connections to and writings about Venice take many forms. Thus, for example, the Peruvian Marxist José Carlos Mariategui was in Venice in September 1920, and wrote about it in 'Los Amantes de Venecia' ('*En una estancia de un hotel del Lido, con las ventanas abiertas al panorama de Venecia y a la música de góndolas de la Laguna, he leído esta novísima edición de la obra de Maurras*'.). Participation by Sartre in a 1956 conference held in Venice has been satirized by Spender (1958). During the early 1960s, Antonio Negri, who still lives in the city, helped organize political activity among the working class in nearby Marghera (Calia, 2011).

115   For these views, see Sartre (2000: 24–25, 28, emphasis added), where he elaborates: 'Wherever you happen to be, the real Venice is always to be found elsewhere. At least, that's how it is for me. Normally, I'm pretty much contented with what I have, but in Venice, I fall prey to a sort of jealous madness. If I did not restrain myself, I should be constantly on this bridge, or that gondola, insanely searching for the secret Venice on the far side. Needless to say, as soon as I step down, everything withers. I turn around: the quiet mystery has reappeared on the other side. I have long been resigned to this fact: Venice is wherever I am not...One evening when I was coming back from Murano, my boat was the only object as far as the eye could see: no more Venice...There is something provocative about this maidenly reserve. And this, what is this opposite me? Is it the *Other* pavement in a residential street or the *Other* bank of a river? In any event, it is always the *Other*...I see the smooth walls of a retreating human world; a little world, so limited, so enclosed, rising up conclusively like a thought in the midst of a desert. I am not in it'.

then located outside Venice itself, in a double form: the 'strangeness' on the one hand of its local inhabitants, 'distant as those Arab women whom I saw from Spain bowing down upon the soil of Africa'; and on the other, of the visitor from overseas ('disquieting as the savages in horror films').[116]

Sartre's response adheres to a pattern that is familiar: the 'real' Venice that eludes his search for it can be seen as no more than a variant of the desire for an exclusive access to the city and its culture. One form of 'otherness' – the local, the tourist – stands between Sartre and his access to another kind of 'otherness' (the city itself), in the process rendering both unknowable (= 'strange'). This alienation stems, as in so many other cases, from an inability to say anything new about the experience of visiting the city.[117]

That the latter response on occasion structures writing about travel by those on the political left is also evident from a similar kind of aristocratic disdain informing the recent critique by Régis Debray aimed at Venice.[118] Finding that the number of those visiting the city have sullied it by their very presence, in

---

116   'The *Other* Venice is overseas', asserts Sartre (2000: 26–27, original emphasis), adding: 'Two women in black are coming down the steps of Santa Maria della Salute...They are suspect and wonderful. Of course, they are women, but as distant as those Arab women whom I saw from Spain bowing down upon the soil of Africa. *Bizarre*: they inhabit those untouchable houses, Holy Women from Across the Sea. And there is another untouchable, that man who has taken up position in front of the church they have just left, so that he can look at it...How awful, he is...holding the Blue Guide in his left hand with a Rolleiflex slung over his shoulder. What can be less shrouded in mystery than a tourist? Well, this one, let me tell you, frozen in suspect immobility, is as disquieting as the savages in horror films who hold apart the rushes, then disappear, after looking, with shining eyes, as the heroine walking through the swamp. He is the tourist from the Other Venice and I shall never see what he does...The tourist goes off with his mystery. He steps on to the little bridge and vanishes, leaving me alone above the motionless Canal. Today, the far bank seems still more inaccessible'.

117   Hence the following lament (Sartre, 2000: 29): 'From the depths of some ancient gaze my eyes try to fish out sunken palaces, but only bring up generalities. Am I observing or recalling? I see what I know. Or, rather, what another person knows already. Some Other memory is haunting mine...the remembrances of Another rise up before me....everything has the weary air of what is already past, already seen'.

118   For this critique, see Debray (2002), whose aristocratic disdain is in a sense unsurprising, given his political trajectory. From an advocate of armed struggle in Latin America to overthrow capitalism (Debray, 1967), who in the late 1960s joined Che Guevara's guerrilla band in Bolivia, was captured and imprisoned there for four years (Debray, 1973), he became in the early 1980s an adviser to President Mitterand of France (Debray, 2007). This familiar political transition, from revolutionary to reformist, helps explain in part the views held by Debray about the 'meaning' of Venice.

the process making it impossible for him to bask in the 'exclusivity' of a Proustian/Jamesian contemplation, Debray declares Venice to be an 'experience' no longer worth having.[119] The source of his annoyance surfaces quickly: it is that 'Venice requires an education', the inference being that the common tourist (='unthinking mob') not only lacks this but – more significantly – can never attain it.[120]

His contempt, as expressed in numerous observations, echoes the reasons that a late eighteenth century landowner might have given for abandoning the Grand Tour ('the industrialization of travel, charter flights').[121] For the ex-Marxist Debray, therefore, Venice is no longer as exclusive as it once was, and accordingly no longer confers distinction on those who gaze upon it. Like Amis, Graves, Morand, and others, therefore, he exhibits the disdain of those who dislike the crowd because it has invaded space hitherto regarded as culturally 'authentic' and de-authenticated it (= sacrilege) merely by being present in an otherwise 'exclusive' location. Again like others who write about Venice, Debray has also come to regard the city in proprietorial terms.[122]

In an attempt to disguise the reactionary political discourse structuring his critique, however, Debray adopts what he accepts is a populist view, and contrasts the 'naturalness' of Naples (= 'the volcano town, shrieking with vulgarity,

---

119   'There are no visions in Venice anymore, just confirmations', he states (Debray, 2002: 50, 64), adding '[it is] the miracle [that] works on all the common run of men'.

120   See Debray (2002: 24).

121   These observations by Debray (2002: 42, 43, 44) are as follows: 'Everyone loves Venice in order to be different from everyone else...the vulgar *arrivisme*...entered the realms of utter ridicule back in the [nineteen] sixties, with the industrialization of travel, charter flights...a hundred thousand anaesthetised aesthetes in tee-shirts, crammed into an area the size of a handkerchief, ankle deep in greasy food wrappers and beer cans, hunting in packs for the crucial tiny difference in the same shot through the viewfinder of the same Japanese camera'.

122   An exception in this regard is Mary McCarthy, who earlier accepted not merely the necessity of having to share the city with tourists but also the consequent loss by her of 'exclusivity'. Agreeing that 'the tourist Venice *is* Venice', she commented (McCarthy, 1956: 16, 19, 20, original emphasis): 'Contrary to popular belief, there are no back canals where a tourist will not meet himself, with a camera, in the person of the other tourist crossing the little bridge...Sophistication, that modern kind of sophistication that begs to differ, to be paradoxical, to invert, is not a possible attitude in Venice. In time, this becomes the beauty of the place. One gives up the struggle and submits to a classic experience. One accepts the fact that what one is about to feel or say has not only been said before by Goethe or Musset but is on the tip of the tongue of the tourist from Iowa who is alighting in the Piazzetta with his wife in her furpiece and jewelled pin. Those Others, the existential enemy, are here identical with oneself...'.

[where] the common people project an air of distinction') with the 'artificiality' of Venice (= 'The island city...used as a drawing room by the whole planet... a place where "people of quality" display common behaviour').[123] Similarly, his dismissive observation that '[h]ow much more than comic, how *painful*, would have been a [camera] shot of...Che [Guevara] sprawled in a gondola' ignores two things.[124] First, whilst Guevara may not have 'sprawled in a gondola', he certainly sprawled in the ruins of Machu Picchu, a city to which apply many of the same criticisms that Debray makes of Venice. And second, it was precisely in the course of this experience – as a tourist, in other words – that Guevara consolidated his political views, and thus began on a path which led to the 1959 Cuban revolution.[125]

Conclusion

Unsurprisingly, accounts of voyages to and/or residence in Venice, from the era of the Grand Tour to that of the mass tourist, follow the general pattern established by the travel writing genre. More surprising, particularly given its urban character, trading economy and maritime history, is the fact that this similarity extends to the agrarian myth, not least in combining its two forms of 'otherness': a pastoral version (the immutability of local cultural identity in an harmonious rural idyll) and a Darwinian one (the threatening proximity of industry; the intrusion of the mass tourist, the 'mob-in-the-street').

---

123   See Debray (2002: 29). Overlooking the fact that from the physical proximity of the basilica, the ducal palace and the prisons one can learn more about the nature and interlocking structure of political power than from a library of textbooks, he endorses (Debray, 2002: 33, 53, 63) the presence in Naples of religious 'feeling' and excoriates Venice for its absence ('Travelling from the Campania to the Veneto is a regression from African animism to cultural animation'). The endorsement in 1987 by Edmund White (2006: 210) of Istanbul in preference to Venice follows along much the same kind of lines: ' And yet I find Istanbul vastly more *sympathique* than Venice. Whereas Venice is a museum, Istanbul is a humming hive, a living, thriving metropolis. Venice has turned its back on the Orient and become one of the choicest resorts for Europeans and Americans. In Istanbul, however, Jewish businessmen brush shoulders with Kurdish peasant women in seven layers of skirts'.

124   For this, see Debray (2002: 37, original emphasis).

125   The visit by Che Guevara to Machu Picchu and his views about this are recorded by Granado (2003: 85ff.) and by Guevara himself (2004). This hints at the possibility of a return to the cosmopolitanism of the Grand Tour, albeit by a different class subject; confirming a plebeian internationalism (and perhaps even a revolutionary politics) instead of the aristocratic ideology reproduced historically as a result of travel abroad.

PHOTO 5   *Bitta (Chiesa di San Sebastiano)*   (© ANNA LUISA BRASS)

Nationalism and class, two components of the agrarian myth, feature prominently in travel writing about Venice. It is nationalist, in that the presence of
Europeans is preferred to that of Americans or Japanese, and also about class,
in that the better-off and/or aristocratic components (= traveller) of any
nationality are preferable to the plebeian elements (= mass tourist) of any
nationality. The exception is itself also in keeping with the discourse of the
agrarian myth: for those better-off visitors who settle in the city, the rural
inhabitant from the Venetian lagoon employed as their workforce is regarded
through paternalist lens, as part of the local traditional culture, almost in terms
of an enduring aesthetic that is the city itself (= salt-of-the-earth). Idealizing
rural poverty in this manner, such travel writing about Venice is no different
from that about other places.

Class also surfaces in the distinction that pervades travel literature about
Venice, between the 'initiate' and 'non-initiated' visitor. Whereas the former is
applied to the more discerning traveller, one from a socio-economic background that permits an understanding and appreciation of what Venetian history/culture means, the latter category by contrast refers to the plebeian mass
tourist devoid of such knowledge. Linked to this dichotomy is the issue of

'exclusivity', whereby this capacity to enjoy the history/culture of the city is itself threatened by the presence there of mass tourists.

Lamentations about the impact of modernity on the loss of traditional rural hierarchy also raise the issue of class. Spanning the period from the 1880s to the 1960s, this theme informed the pastoral version of the agrarian myth present in the accounts of Eden and Guiton. In an important sense, their accounts of Venice represent not just a continuation of an old discourse about the agrarian myth in the midst of an urban setting, but also a fusion between travel writing and anthropology. In each case, therefore, an outsider 'passing through' a specific location settles in it – as a proprietor – and produces what amounts to an ethnography based on participant/observation.

In both instances, the aesthetic disguises commercial reasons for land purchases. Eden and Guiton display a nostalgia for pre-modern rural society, and their accounts are informed by a paternalistic approach to locals employed as workers, whereby rural hierarchy is idealized as reciprocal and 'natural'. This contrasted with views expressed by locals themselves, who saw these same 'quaint' and traditional jobs (lacemakers, sharecroppers) as oppressive sources of their own poverty and economic insecurity.

The core elements of an ideology about class and class struggle are therefore present in the agrarian myth as this applies to Venice and the Venetian lagoon. A 'from above' perception of working arrangements as 'benign' and enduring, and thus acceptable to locals, was negated by a contrasting 'from below' perception of these same relational forms as oppressive and undesirable. Eden and Guiton, however, adhere to a pastoral discourse that denies plebeian antagonism by reversing the categories involved: actual property (land, gardens; labour-power) is recast as culture, whilst culture itself is depicted as private property. This discursive shift, and particularly its latter strand – culture as private property conferring 'exclusivity'– is in keeping with much travel writing about the city, not least by those holding opposing political views.

Aesthetics and 'exclusivity' are central to the divergent approaches of those belonging to the political right. Objections by Marinetti to Venice derive from his Futurist ideology which – like postmodernism – rejected history and argued that the past was irrelevant (= 'the cloaca maxima of passéism'). Again like postmodernism, Futurism was an aesthetic movement, dazzled by the present – in its case, the beautiful shapes of speeding motor cars and machine-guns. The rejection by Marinetti of Venice on account of its 'passéism' seemingly contrasts absolutely with the nostalgic embrace of the city by Waugh and Morand, precisely because it represents the past. Like Marinetti, Morand is considered a modernist, and again like Marinetti, his modernism lies in the form, not the content, of what is written. In common with Herzen and Herder, both of whom encountered in Paris a future they disliked, Morand regarded historic Venice as a refuge from the French capital, and for much the same reason.

The mob-in-the-streets that frightened Herzen and Herder in late eighteenth and nineteenth century Paris reappears in mid-twentieth century Venice as the plebeian mass tourist. Here the same kind of mass presence threatens to appropriate a different form of property: to 'de-authenticate' culture, and the 'exclusivity' this confers in terms of class. Even those on the political left, such as Sartre and Debray, succumb to this discourse about the meaning of Venice, and – like Morand – perceive mass tourism as an undesirable form of 'from below' cultural appropriation. Photography and film enable the mass tourist to access the visual image of Venice, an aspect of modernity whereby the 'uninitiated' plebeian visitor not merely gains entry to a culture/history that confers 'exclusivity' on the upper class traveller but also appropriates (= 'steals') this form of property that hitherto has bestowed distinction on its possessor/owner. The camera in Venice symbolizes not just modernity, therefore, but also a way in which the plebeian mass tourist captures what has been regarded hitherto as cultural property.

Conclusion

A politically conservative discourse about the culturally innate and unchanging nature of rural identity, the agrarian myth replaces the socio-economic process of becoming with an eternal situation of systemically non-transcendent being. It challenges or reverses the polarity informing development, whereby modernity = good and tradition = bad. Not only is there no past in such a discourse, but – more importantly – there is no future that is different from the present, an approach that privileges stasis over transformation, and thus cannot but result in the conceptual essentialization of the peasantry. Rural tradition and identity symbolize the nation itself, and a decline in either smallholding or landlordism becomes synonymous with deculturation and the erosion (or loss) of national identity.

Ironically, at the end of the twentieth century and into the twenty-first, it is this very same discourse that has been given a new lease of life by a theoretical framework its supporters perceive as not merely radical but leftist: the 'new' populist postmodernism. Peasant essentialism re-emerged during the 1960s, in the shape of populist claims about a socio-economically undifferentiated smallholder (= the rural 'other') in so-called Third World countries resisting the development of a capitalist agriculture there on the basis of a non-transcendent economic and/or cultural identity. It currently structures the postmodern variants of the 'new' populism that have come to dominate the social sciences. Opposed to Eurocentric metanarratives premised on Enlightenment rationality, and to Marxist theory/practice in particular, the 'new' populist postmodern theory endorses instead a process of 'resistance'/' empowerment' based on non-class identities/agency that celebrate 'diversity', 'difference', and 'choice' within the existing capitalist system.

For this reason, the focus of the critique made here is on the way in which 'new' populist postmodern theory has reasserted the analytical validity of agrarian myth discourse, and how this has not just negated but reversed the desirability of economic development. Following in the footsteps of their South Asian counterparts, exponents of the Latin American subaltern framework are currently engaged in a quest for evidence of an authentic and thus empowering rural consciousness/agency, a discourse about 'popular culture' linking peasant 'otherness' to the reproduction of smallholding agriculture and a return to ancient/indigenous nationhood.

Among the issues not addressed by sub-nationalisms is the continued impact on them of capital and the nation state. Similarly absent, and symptomatic of their populism, is the failure on the part of the Zapatistas and their support networks to confront the link between class and democracy. Simply to call for the adherence on the part of the Mexican social formation to a systemically non-specific form of democracy, as the EZLN have done, without simultaneously calling into question the class structure which gives expression to the way in which (and for whom) political democracy operates within this wider context, negates their own demand for social justice in Chiapas. Leaving the class structure intact ensures that those with wealth will continue as before to privilege their own political interests within the confines of any democratic system that does not expropriate them. This they will do either directly – where a conservative government is elected – or indirectly, by subverting any non-conservative government with a popular mandate for change. Such is the (really rather obvious) risk facing calls for the implementation of a systemically non-specific form of democracy.

Along with democracy, human rights are regarded as one of the main benefits gained as a result of the struggle conducted by the Zapatistas. Few, however, tend to question precisely what this means, and consequently to ask how much of a political achievement such a framework – based on human rights – can really ever be. In one sense, the concept of human rights is a meaninglessly nebulous set of 'motherhood and apple pie' conventions (= 'the righting of wrongs'), a series of a-political (or more accurately de-politicized) international legislative ordinances more honoured in the breach than in the observance. In another and more important sense, however, the necessity of having to invoke a 'safety net' principle like human rights – against the possibility of military attack or State oppression – represents not so much a political achievement as the nadir of politics.

In a similar vein, what does indigenous cultural 'autonomy' actually mean? If not a formal transition to the politics of and struggle for national self-determination, then it can only be an attempt informally to capture and retain the timeless suspension in aspic of the indigenous community within the wider Mexican social formation. This kind of situation cannot be anything other than one in which indigenous culture becomes a celebration of rural poverty, recast by all those involved as empowering for the peasants concerned. In other words, indigenous culture is re-exoticized in a fashion that would be familiar to those anthropologists engaged in constructing *indigenista* images of rural ethnic 'otherness' in 1940s Mexico.

Examining the current impact of the agrarian myth, therefore, necessarily involves tracing the way the State and the market have featured in the discourse of the political left and right, and in particular how conservatives feared and socialists hoped that 'pure' democracy would threaten property relations. That such fears and hopes were borne out is evident from their respective political strategies. In the case of conservatives, this took a dual form: a populist 'from above' attempt to generate the support of workers and peasants was combined with the idea of a strong capitalist State. Those on the left of the political spectrum argued that the redistribution of landed property and other economic resources was central to any notion of democracy. Historically, capture and control of the State was also seen by socialists as the instrument necessary for the realization of such policy.

Marxism confers political legitimacy only on revolutionary struggles for political power undertaken by class categories (a nascent bourgeoisie in the case of a dominant feudalism, a proletariat in the case of a dominant capitalism). Accordingly, socialists argue that the peasantry is not homogeneous, and that consequently resistance by rich, middle and poor peasants has a different class basis, meaning and objective. It is the exponents of postmodernism who maintain the fiction of an homogeneous peasantry resisting – or avoiding – a non-class specific State (a binary opposition which structures the discourse not of Marxism but of populism, the 'other' of Marxism). Instead of a transformation in which some peasants become small capitalists and others de facto workers, rural change is said by populism to involve an absolute opposition, between a uniform body of commodity producers and the State.

Failure to address this left/right divide, and in particular the presence of class, was at the root of the contradictions informing modernization theory, which sought the democratic participation of peasants and workers but without challenging traditional cultural and ideological values/beliefs circulating at the rural grassroots. Incomplete political incorporation paved the way for the 'cultural turn', when opposition to the State and socialist development – a discourse associated with conservatism and *laissez faire* – was taken up by the 'new' populist postmodernism. Capture/control of the State by workers and poor peasants gave way analytically to subaltern resistance and empowerment inside capitalism, in the form of political 'citizenship' exercised within 'civil society'.

Like democracy and 'redemocratization', the term 'civil society' is one of those currently fashionable concepts invoked in an a-historical and virtually content free way to signal the presence/absence of progress by a similarly amorphous socio-economic category, composed of 'the subaltern' or 'the people'. In many respects, 'civil society' is depicted as the desired 'other' of the State, and all too often its epistemological function seems to be to avoid engagement with the impact on poor peasants and workers of the accumulation process. Along with bourgeois property relations, therefore, the capitalist system itself appears to have been sanctified analytically as a 'natural' and thus non-transcendent phenomenon. Instead of undertaking class struggle leading to the common ownership of means of production/distribution/exchange, we are told, smallholders and agricultural labour now seek only to establish 'civil society' as a space of refuge within an economic context dominated by the market.

What postmodernism overlooked, therefore, is that 'from below' mobilization based on culture opens the door not just to nationalism, and ultimately conservatism, but also to populism. In nineteenth century England the shift from 'speaking about' and 'speaking to' the plebeian subject, to 'speaking for' the latter was facilitated by paternalism and its overlap with populist discourse. Landowners, tenants and workers were subsumed under the all-embracing label of 'the People', thereby forming the nation ruled over by the monarchy. In other words, an unfolding nationalist 'from above' response to the possibility of a 'from below' mobilization that was not only populist but also agrarian in character. Just as it had done for a ruling aristocracy, both the fact of travel and the resulting narratives about this, but now in the domain of popular culture, continued to project 'English-ness', not just 'at home' but increasingly in 'an abroad' that was colonial.

Insofar as the economic power of the landlord class merges with and becomes part of that of capital generally, this underlines the fallacy of treating the former as separate from – and indeed opposed to – the latter, to the degree of attempting to mobilize 'progressive' capitalists against reactionary landlords. The argument about separate entities (landlord, capitalist) holds good only as long as capitalism has not developed. Once it has, landlords can – and do – invest in non-agricultural activities, while capitalists for their part purchase rural estates. For this reason, it is no longer possible to insist categorically on their economic distinctiveness, and consequently to locate them on different sides in the class struggle. Whilst it is true there may indeed be a turnover as regards social composition – erstwhile merchants and/or financiers become landowners – the class position and interest, which stems from property rights, stays the same.

During the twentieth century, the agrarian myth appears on film, where landowners are depicted in one of three ways. As empowered-but-hostile, engaged in a 'from above' struggle to defend their property; as empowered-but-benign-or-populist, in that they retain their source of wealth, but chose either not to exercise their power against those below (= 'benign') or to exercise this on behalf of those below (= populist). And as wholly disempowered, and thus 'not worth bothering about'. The contrasting variants of the agrarian myth structuring film and television images of the landowning class give rise to a discourse about 'fiends', friends' and 'fools'. When portrayed as empowered and hostile in a discourse projecting horror/terror/revenge (= 'fiends'), film/television images are those of the aristocratic Darwinian version. Pastoral versions depict members of that class either as ineffectual 'fools' or as paternalistic 'friends'; landowners are represented as disempowered or benign. In their different ways, all these images can be regarded as a form of class struggle waged 'from above', in that landowners appear on the one hand as too powerful to be opposed by 'those below', and on the other as weak, and thus harmless or non-threatening.

The element of *noblesse oblige* which informs the landlord pastoral variant of the agrarian myth is structured by the same kind of discourse as monarchs and aristocrats who appear as characters in twentieth century films and television serials. This form of populist conservatism is consistent with a favourable image of landowning aristocrat – or monarch – as a 'friend' of workers and peasants. Those belonging to the landowning class (monarch, church, aristocracy) are depicted as empowered-but-benign, in that they retain their source of wealth, but chose either not to exercise their power against those below (= "benign") or to exercise this on behalf of those below (= populist).

Just as film permits the self to experience another space at another time, so travel writing conveys to the self that same experience recounted by another. For this reason, the focus on travel literature, another influential form of 'popular culture', reveals that an analogous shift occurs in discourse about the plebeian subject. Nationalism fuses with populism over the eighteenth and nineteenth centuries, while in the twentieth the much feared 'mob in the streets' metamorphoses into the mass tourist. As long as the 'other' encountered abroad remains traditional/rural/quiescent, the foreign plebeian attracts an approving gaze on the part of the upper class traveller. Once this subordination is challenged, and the plebeian becomes the 'mob in the streets', this subject ceases to be viewed positively. In keeping with this kind of transformation, the 'other' objected to by travel writers, particularly in the era of mass tourism, is increasingly the plebeian from home who journeys abroad, threatening to despoil the pastoral there.

By its very nature, the variant of the agrarian myth that pervades travel literature is the aristocratic/landlord version, which generally speaking, adheres to the following historical pattern. The initial epoch was that of the Grand Tour, which lasted in one form or another until the early nineteenth century. Throughout this era there was almost a formal requirement on the part of those belonging to the better-off components to travel, an undertaking effected in the company of a tutor and retinue, to destinations throughout Europe. It was a period that coincided with a position of landowner/aristocratic dominance at home, in the course of which a cosmopolitan ideology acquired during the Grand Tour embraced and celebrated rural 'otherness' both at home and abroad.

The century that followed corresponded to what might be termed the epoch of the lone upper class traveller. Although no longer a formal requirement, travel was undertaken largely by 'gentlemen amateurs', to destinations in and beyond Europe. Such visits, frequently linked to imperial adventures (or indeed conquest), coincided with the emergence at home of national identity and a populist politics, in response to the development of industrial capitalism and its plebeian workforce. The latter process generated concern among the upper class, and travellers from this stratum lamented the loss of rural 'otherness' at home, but as yet not abroad, where it could still be found (and celebrated).

From the landlord pastoral informing much writing about the Grand Tour, which depicts peasants not just as 'quaint' and 'traditional' but also as passive inhabitants of the harmonious countryside, there is a discernable change to Darwinian plebeian images. This is accompanied by what might be termed a defensive shift in the political ideology of the landowning class, from a cosmo-politan (= exclusive) to a nationalist (= shared) outlook. In an attempt to repro-duce a sense of cultural distance, the upper class traveller seeks 'exclusivity' abroad. However, the mid-twentieth century onwards is, in terms of travel lit-erature, the epoch of mass tourism.

On the one hand, although no longer unchallenged, the landlord/aristo-cratic variant of the agrarian myth struggles to reproduce itself in a context where an urban industrial working class has emerged as a political force. Travel literature registers this fact by lamenting the continuing demise of rural 'other-ness', as embodied in cultural tradition/custom, not only at home but now also abroad, and especially in Europe. This is combined with a dislike of modern industrial development and/or communist regimes in places visited, and in particular a resentment of the intrusive presence abroad of plebeian mass tourism. Darwinian plebeian images encountered in travel writing accordingly incorporate mass tourism into the discourse of class struggle, whereby cul-tural distinction conferred by 'exclusivity' (home and abroad) is threatened by the presence and numbers of plebeian visitors. In doing so, the aristocratic/landlord variant of the agrarian myth invokes two kinds of nationalism: that of the travel writer (his/her home abode), and that of the place visited. The essential – and rural – cultural identity of each context, this discourse infers, is under threat from the urban 'mob-in-the-streets'.

On occasion the seamless transition between travel writing and political commentary displays all the characterizations associated with the landlord version of the agrarian myth. Claiming that people from the 'bush' are 'natural peasants' who will always be 'primitives' at heart, and thus remain impervious and resistant to – and even destructive of – modernity/development/progress, such travel literature reproduces the central argument of the Darwinian version of the agrarian myth. Africans are – and always will be – happy peasants, primitives from 'the bush'; progress, modernity, and development generally are thus 'inauthentic' objectives, not for them. When advocated, therefore, such discourse is merely a 'performance', and always no more than a display of 'inauthenticity'. The view that modern economic development is not an appropriate model for the so-called Third World rural 'other' to follow becomes a fear lest the encroachment by this same kind of plebeian rural 'other' threatens to overrun not just European influence in Africa but also – and ultimately – a cherished version of the landlord pastoral in Europe itself.

Discourse about the agrarian myth projects two distinct concepts of Nature: an empowered one, or Nature-on-the-attack, and a disempowered version, or Nature-under-attack. This active/passive dichotomy, which corresponds to the Darwinian/pastoral duality structuring the agrarian myth, informs much of the writing about travel considered here. In the case of the pastoral, therefore, the lament of travel writers concerns the encroachment of modernity on an 'harmonious' rural context inhabited by culturally pristine smallholders. By contrast, in the case of the Darwinian version, the lament derives from the return of the 'primitive' rural 'other' from the 'bush', threatening thereby a fragile and 'artificial' European modernity that has managed to establish itself. The latter in turn is blamed for misleading the innately rural 'other' as to his/her true identity: that of a peasant, and not as s/he thought – or was led to believe – 'civilized'.

Either way, in these opposed versions of the agrarian myth the identity of the non-European 'other' is perceived as immutable: the indigenous subject is fixed, conceptually, as culturally 'primitive', a destiny that precludes any form of political and economic development. In many respects, such an interpretation coincides with that advanced subsequently by those endorsing the 'cultural turn'. Exponents of the 'new' populist postmodernism recuperated core elements of the agrarian myth, not least the perception of the Third World peasant identity as unchanging and unchangeable. Rural identity was declared innate, and a traditional form of cultural 'otherness' deemed empowering; consequently, this discourse asserted, its subjects had no need of material benefits associated with 'Eurocentric' concepts such as progress, modernity, and economic development.

The difficulty with the re-exoticization of indigenous 'otherness', therefore, is that under the guise of cultural nationalism, it projects an idealized view about the economic feasibility of petty commodity production under capitalism. Notwithstanding the claim that small producers have been undermined largely by intrigue and corruption (that is, the present socio-economic system would be fine if only it were permitted to function properly by government and business), there is a strong argument – which 'new' populist postmodern theory avoids confronting – to the effect that it is in the nature of capitalism, national as well as international, to undermine petty commodity production. Accordingly, since there would seem to be little prospect for rural population to reproduce itself economically simply as a self-sufficient peasantry under capitalism, this would appear to suggest that alternatives have to transcend the latter rather than be found within it.

Bibliography

A Foreign Resident, 1886, *Society in London*, London: Chatto & Windus, Piccadilly.

Abelson, Edward (ed.), 1988, *A Mirror of England: An Anthology of the Writings of H.J. Massingham (1888–1952)*, Devon: Green Books.

Abercrombie, Nicholas, and John Urry (eds.), 1983, *Capital, Labour and the Middle Classes*, London: George Allen & Unwin.

About, Edmund, 1872, *Handbook of Social Economy, or the Worker's ABC*, London: Strahan & Co., 56 Ludgate Hill.

Abse, Tobias, 1996, 'Italian Workers and Italian Fascism', in Richard Bessel (ed.), *Fascist Italy and Nazi Germany: Comparisons and Contrasts*, Cambridge: Cambridge University Press.

Adams, Richard N., 1967, 'Nationalization', in Manning Nash (ed.) [1967b].

Adorno, Theodor, and Max Horkheimer, 1977, 'The Culture Industry: Enlightenment as Mass Deception', in James Curran, Michael Gurevitch, and Janet Woollacott (eds.), *Mass Communication and Society*, London: Edward Arnold.

Alavi, Hamza, 1964, 'Imperialism Old and New', in Ralph Miliband and John Saville (eds.), *The Socialist Register 1964*, London: The Merlin Press.

Alavi, Hamza, 1965, 'Peasants and Revolution', in Ralph Miliband and John Saville (eds.), *The Socialist Register 1965*, London: The Merlin Press.

Alavi, Hamza, 1971, 'Bangla Desh and the Crisis of Pakistan', in Ralph Miliband and John Saville (eds.), *The Socialist Register 1971*, London: The Merlin Press.

Alavi, Hamza, 1973a, 'Peasant Classes and Primordial Loyalties', *The Journal of Peasant Studies*, Vol. 1, No. 1.

Alavi, Hamza, 1973b, 'The State in Postcolonial Societies: Pakistan and Bangladesh', in Kathleen Gough and Hari P. Sharma (eds.), *Imperialism and Revolution in South Asia*, New York: Monthly Review Press.

Alavi, Hamza, 1975, 'India and the Colonial Mode of Production', in Ralph Miliband and John Saville (eds.), *The Socialist Register 1975*, London: The Merlin Press.

Alavi, Hamza, 1976, *Las clases campesinas y las lealteades primordiales*, México: Anagrama.

Alavi, Hamza, 1982a, 'India: The Transition to Colonial Capitalism', in Hamza Alavi, P.L. Burns, G.R. Knight, P.B. Mayer and Doug McEachern, *Capitalism and Colonial Production*, London and Canberra: Croom Helm.

Alavi, Hamza, 1982b, 'State and Class Under Peripheral Capitalism', in Hamza Alavi and Teodor Shanin (eds.), *Introduction to the Sociology of 'Developing Societies' (first published in 1970)*, London: Macmillan.

Alavi, Hamza, 1988a, 'Peasantry and Capitalism: A Marxist Discourse', in Teodor Shanin (ed.), *Peasants and Peasant Societies* (second edition, first published in 1971), London: Penguin Books.

Alavi, Hamza, 1988b, 'Village Factions', in Teodor Shanin (ed.), *Peasants and Peasant Societies (second edition, first published in 1971)*, London: Penguin Books.

Albó, Xavier, 1972, 'Dinámica en la estructura intercomunitaria de Jesús de Machachaca', *América Indígena*, Vol. 32, No. 3.

Albó, Xavier, 1987, 'From MNRistas, to Kataristas, to Katari', in S. Stern (ed.) [1987].

Albó, Xavier, 1988, *Raices de América: el mundo Aymara*, Madrid: Alianza Editorial.

Albó, Xavier, 1993, 'Our Identity Starting from Pluralism in the Base', in Beverley and Oviedo (eds.) [1993].

Alegría, Ciro, 1941, *Broad and Alien is the World*, London: Nicholson and Watson.

Allina-Pisano, Jessica, 2004, 'Land Reform and the Social Origins of Private Farmers in Russia and the Ukraine', *The Journal of Peasant Studies*, Vol. 31, Nos. 3 & 4.

Almond, Gabriel A., 1989, 'The Intellectual History of the Civic Culture Concept', in Gabriel A. Almond and Sidney Verba (eds.) [1989].

Almond, Gabriel A., and Sidney Verba (eds.), 1989, *The Civic Culture Revisited*, London: Sage.

Amis, Kingsley, 1970, *What Became of Jane Austen?And Other Questions*, London: Jonathan Cape.

Amis, Kingsley, 1990, *The Amis Collection: Selected Non-Fiction 1954–1990*, London: Hutchinson.

Amis, Kingsley, 1991, *Memoirs*, London: Hutchinson.

Anderson, Benedict, 1983, *Imagined Communities: Reflections on the Origin and Spread of Nationalism*, London: New Left Books.

Anderson, Lindsay, 2004, *Never Apologise: The Collected Writings*, London: Plexus.

Anderson, Perry, 1966, 'Socialism and Pseudo-Empiricism', *New Left Review* No. 35.

Anderson, Perry, 1968, 'Components of the National Culture', *New Left Review* No. 50.

Anonymous, 1819, *Analyses of New Works of Voyages and Travels published during the last Six Months in Great Britain*, London: Printed for Sir Richard Phillips and Co., Bride-Court, Bridge-Street.

Asquith, Cynthia (ed.), 1931, *When Churchyards Yawn: Fifteen New Ghost Stories*, London: Hutchinson & Co.

Assessorato al Turismo, c. 1948, *Venice, Lake Garda and the Dolomites*, Milan: A. Pizzi S.A.

Baaz, Maria Erikson, 2005, *The Paternalism of Partnership: A Postcolonial Reading of Identity in Development Aid*, London: Zed Press.

Bacon, Francis, Lord Verulam, 1755 [1625], *Essays or Counsels, Civil and Moral*, London: A. Millar in the Strand.

Baedeker, Karl, 1911, *Handbook for Travellers – The Mediterranean: Seaports and Sea Routes including Madeira, the Canary Islands, the Coast of Morocco, Algeria, and Tunisia*, Leipzig: Karl Baedeker Publisher.

Bagehot, Walter, 1928 [1867], *The English Constitution*, Oxford: Oxford University Press.

Baird, Peter, and Ed McCaughan, 1979, *Beyond the Border: Mexico and the U.S. Today*, New York: NACLA.

Bakhtin, Mikhail, 1984, *Problems of Dostoevsky's Poetics*, Manchester: Manchester University Press.

Barabas, Alicia, and Miguel Bartolomé, 1974, 'Hydraulic Development and Ethnocide: The Mazatec and Chinantec People of Oaxaca, Mexico', *Critique of Anthropology*, Vol. 1, No. 1.

Baran, Paul, 1957, *The Political Economy of Growth*, New York: Monthly Review Press.

Baretti, Joseph, 1770, *A Journey from London to Genoa, through England, Portugal, Spain, and France* (in four volumes) – Vol. I, London: T. Davies, in Russell Street, Covent Garden, and L. Davies, in Holborn.

Barker, Francis, Peter Hulme and Margaret Iversen (eds.), 1990, *Postcolonial discourse/ postcolonial theory*, Manchester: Manchester University Press.

Barkin, David, 1995, 'Mexico's Integration into the North American Economy', in Antonio Callari, Stephen Cullenberg, and Carole Biewener (eds.), *Marxism in the Postmodern Age: Confronting the New World Order*, London and New York: The Guildford Press.

Barkin, David, 2002, 'The Reconstruction of a Modern Mexican Peasantry', *The Journal of Peasant Studies*, Vol. 30, No. 1.

Barnard, F.M., 1965, *Herder's Social and Political Thought: From Enlightenment to Nationalism*, Oxford: Clarendon Press.

Barnard, F.M. (ed.), 1969, *J. G. Herder on Social and Political Culture*, London: Cambridge University Press.

Barr, Charles, 1977, *Ealing Studios*, London: David and Charles.

Barrès, Maurice, 1970a [1894], 'From Hegel to the Workmen's Canteens of the North', in J.S. McClelland (ed.) [1970].

Barrès, Maurice, 1970b [1902], 'Scènes et Doctrines du Nationalisme', in J.S. McClelland (ed.) [1970].

Barthes, Roland, 1977, *Image, Music, Text*, London: Fontana.

Bartra, Roger, 1993, *Agrarian Structure and Political Power in Mexico*, London and Baltimore, MD: The Johns Hopkins University Press.

Bartra, Roger, and Gerardo Otero, 1987, 'Agrarian Crisis and Social Differentiation in Mexico', *The Journal of Peasant Studies*, Vol. 14, No. 3.

Baüer, Otto, 1978a [1907], 'Nationalities, Nationalism, and Imperialism', in Tom Bottomore and Patrick Goode (eds.) [1978].

Baüer, Otto, 1978b [1907], 'Socialism and the Principle of Nationality', in Tom Bottomore and Patrick Goode (eds.) [1978].

Baüer, Otto c., 1919, *El camino hacia el Socialismo*, Madrid: Editorial América (translation of *Der Weg zum Sozialismus*, Vienna: Wiener Volksbuchhandlung, 1919).

Bax, Ernest Belfort, 1967 [1918], *Reminiscences and Reflections of a Mid and Late Victorian*, New York: Augustus M. Kelley.

Baxter, John, 1996, *Steven Spielberg: The Unauthorized Biography*, London: HarperCollins Publishers.

Bear, William E., 1893, *A Study of Small Holdings* (Written for the Cobden Club), London: Cassell & Company Limited.

Bechhofer, Frank, and Brian Elliot (eds.), 1981, *The Petite Bourgeoisie: Comparative Studies of the Uneasy Stratum*, London: Macmillan.

Beerbohm, Max, 1993 [1928], *A Stranger in Venice*, London: The Winged Lion.

Bein, Peter, 1963, *L.P. Hartley*, London: Chatto and Windus.

Belloc, Hilaire, 1913, *The Servile State*, London and Edinburgh: T.N. Foulis.

Belloc, Hilaire, 1937, *The Crisis of Our Civilization*, London: Cassell and Company, Ltd.

Bendersky, Joseph W., 1983, *Carl Schmitt: Theorist for the Reich*, Princeton, NJ: Princeton University Press.

Berger, Mark T., 2001, 'Romancing the Zapatistas: International Intellectuals and the Chiapas Rebellion', *Latin American Perspectives*, Vol. 28, No. 2.

Bernstein, Henry, 1977, 'Notes on Capital and Peasantry', *Review of African Political Economy* No. 10.

Bernstein, Henry, 1981, 'Notes on State and Peasantry in Tanzania', *Review of African Politican Economy* No. 21.

Beverley, John, 2004, 'Subaltern Resistance in Latin America: A Reply to Tom Brass', *The Journal of Peasant Studies*, Vol. 31, No. 2.

Beverley, John, and José Oviedo (eds.), 1993, *The Postmodernism Debate in Latin America*, Durham, NC: Duke University Press.

Bhabha, Homi K., 1994, *The Location of Culture*, London and New York: Routledge.

Bierce, Ambrose, 1967, *The Enlarged Devil's Dictionary*, London: Victor Gollancz Ltd.

Birkenhead, The Earl of, 1973, 'Fiery Particles,' in David Pryce-Jones (ed.) [1973b].

Blake, Robert, 1966, *Disraeli*, London: Eyre and Spottiswoode.

Blake, Robert, 1972, *The Conservative Party from Peel to Churchill*, London: Fontana/Collins.

Bloom, Harold, Paul de Man, Jacques Derrida, Geoffrey Hartman, and J. Hillis Miller, 1979, *Deconstruction and Criticism*. London: Routledge & Kegan Paul.

Bluntschli, Johann Kaspar, 1885, *The Theory of the State*, Oxford: Clarendon Press.

Bourdieu, Pierre, 1986, *Distinction: A Social Critique of the Judgement of Taste*, London and New York: Routledge & Kegan Paul.

Boswell, James, 1933, *Boswell's Life of Johnson* (with an Introduction by Chauncey Brewster Tinker), London: Oxford University Press.

Botelho Gonsálvez Raúl, 1967 [1940], *Altiplano*, Lima: Ediciones Nuevo Mundo.

Bottomore, Tom, and Patrick Goode (eds.), 1978, *Austro-Marxism*, Oxford: Clarendon Press.

Boyson, Rhodes (ed.), 1975, *1985 – An Escape from Orwell's 1985: A Conservative Path to Freedom*, Enfield: Churchill Press.

Bradbury, Malcom, 1966, *Stepping Westward*, Boston, MA: Houghton Mifflin Company.

Bradbury, Malcom, 1973, 'America and the Comic Vision', in David Pryce-Jones (ed.), *Evelyn Waugh and his World*, London: Weidenfeld and Nicolson.

Brady, Frank, and Frederick A. Pottle (eds.), 1955, *Boswell on the Grand Tour: Italy, Corsica and France 1765–1766*, London: William Heinemann Limited.

Brailsford, H.N., 1961, *The Levellers and the English Revolution* (edited and prepared for publication by Christopher Hill), London: The Cresset Press.

Brass, Denis, 1960, *The Land and People of Portugal*, London: Adam and Charles Black.

Brass, Tom (ed.), 1995, *New Farmers' Movements in India*, London and Portland, OR: Frank Cass Publishers.

Brass, Tom (ed.), 2003, *Latin American Peasants*, London: Frank Cass Publisher.

Brass, Tom, 1986, 'The Elementary Strictures of Kinship: Unfree Relations and the Production of Commodities', *Social Analysis*, No. 20.

Brass, Tom, 1999, *Towards a Comparative Political Economy of Unfree Labour: Case Studies and Debates*, London and Portland, OR: Frank Cass Publishers.

Brass, Tom, 2000a, *Peasants, Populism and Postmodernism*, London and Portland, OR: Frank Cass Publishers.

Brass, Tom, 2000b, 'Unmasking the Subaltern, or Salamis without Themistocles', *The Journal of Peasant Studies*, Vol. 28, No. 1.

Brass, Tom, 2001, 'Reel Images of the Land (Beyond the Forest): Film and the Agrarian Myth', *The Journal of Peasant Studies*, Vol. 28, No. 4.

Brass, Tom, 2002, 'Latin American Peasants – New Paradigms for Old?', *The Journal of Peasant Studies*, Vol. 29, Nos. 3&4.

Brass, Tom, 2003, 'On Which Side of What Barricade? Subaltern Resistance in Latin America and Elsewhere', in Tom Brass (ed.) [2003].

Brass, Tom, 2005, 'The Journal of Peasant Studies: The Third Decade', *The Journal of Peasant Studies*, Vol. 32, No. 1.

Brass, Tom, 2006, 'Subaltern Resistance and the ("Bad") Politics of Culture: A Response to John Beverley', *The Journal of Peasant Studies*, Vol. 33, No. 2.

Brass, Tom, 2007a, 'Weapons of the Week, Weakness of the Weapons: Shifts and Stasis in Development Theory', *The Journal of Peasant Studies*, Vol. 34, No. 1.

Brass, Tom, 2007b, 'How Agrarian Cooperatives Fail: Lessons from 1970s Peru', *The Journal of Peasant Studies*, Vol. 34, No. 2.

Brass, Tom, 2010, 'Capitalism, Primitive Accumulation and Unfree Labour', in H. Veltmeyer (ed.), *Imperialism, Crisis and Class Struggle: The Enduring Verities of Capitalism*, Leiden: Brill.

Brass, Tom, 2011, *Labour Regime Change in the Twenty-First Century: Unfreedom, Capitalism and Primitive Accumulation*, Leiden: Brill.

Brass, Tom, 2012, 'Scott's "Zomia," or a Populist Post-modern History of Nowhere', *Journal of Contemporary Asia*, Vol. 42, No. 1.

Brass, Tom, 2013a [1991] 'Moral Economists, Subalterns, New Social Movements, and the (Re-) Emergence of a (Post-) Modernized (Middle) Peasant', in Vinayak Chaturvedi (ed.), *Mapping Subaltern Studies and the Postcolonial*, London and New York: Verso.

Brass, Tom, 2013b, 'Good companions or usual suspects?', *Capital & Class*, Vol. 37, No. 1.

Braudel, Fernand, 1982, *Civilization and Capitalism 15th –18th Century: Volume 2 – The Wheels of Commerce*, London: William Collins & Co.

Breman, Jan, 1974, *Patronage and Exploitation: Changing Agrarian Relations in South Gujarat, India*, Berkeley, CA: University of California Press.

Brenan, Gerald, 1950, *The Face of Spain*, London: Turnstile Press.

Brennan, Michael G., 2004, *The Origins of the Grand Tour: The Travels of Robert Montague, Lord Mandeville (1649–1658), William Hammond (1655–1658) and Banaster Maynard (1660–1663)*, London: The Hakluyt Society (Series III, Volume 14).

Bridges, E. Lucas, 1948, *Uttermost Part of the Earth*, London: Hodder & Stoughton.

Brittain, James J., 2005, 'A Theory of Accelerating Rural Violence: Lauchlin Currie's Role in Underdeveloping Colombia', *The Journal of Peasant Studies*, Vol. 32, No. 2.

Brown, Horatio F., 1884, *Life on the Lagoons*, London: Kegan Paul, Trench & Co.

Brown, Horatio F., 1887, *Venetian Studies*, London: Kegan Paul, Trench & Co.

Bruccoli, Matthew J. (ed.), 1976, *Raymond Chandler: The Blue Dahlia – A Screenplay* (with a Memoir by John Houseman), Carbondale, IL: Southern Illinois University Press.

Buck, Philip W., 1975, *How Conservatives Think*, London: Penguin Books.

Bulwer Lytton, Edward, 1836a [1833], *England and the English – Vol. I*, London: Richard Bentley, New Burlington Street.

Bulwer Lytton, Edward, 1836b [1833], *England and the English – Vol. II*, London: Richard Bentley, New Burlington Street.

Burbach, Roger, 1994, 'Roots of the Postmodern Rebellion in Chiapas', *New Left Review* No. 205.

Burbach, Roger, Orlando Núñez, and Boris Kagarlitsky, 1997, *Globalization and its Discontents: The Rise of Postmodern Socialisms*, London: Pluto Press.

Burgess, Anthony, 1984, *Ninety-nine Novels: The Best in English since 1939 (A personal choice by Anthony Burgess)*, London: Allison & Busby.

Burke, Kenneth, 1935, 'Revolutionary Symbolism in America', in Henry Hart (ed.) [1935].

Burke, Peter, 1981, 'The "discovery" of popular culture', in Raphael Samuel (ed.), *People's History and Socialist Theory*, London: Routledge & Kegan Paul.

Butler, Samuel, 1932 [1872], *Erewhon and Erewhon Revisited*, London and Toronto: J.M. Dent & Sons, Ltd.

Byron, Robert, 1926, *Europe in the Looking-Glass: Reflections of a Motor Drive from Grimsby to Athens*, London: George Routledge & Sons Ltd.

Byron, Robert, 1991, *Letters Home* (Edited by Lucy Butler), London: John Murray.

Cahill, Kevin 2001, *Who Owns Britain*, Edinburgh: Canongate.

Calia, Claudio, 2011, *Antonio Negri Illustrated: Interview in Venice* (translated by Jason Francis McGimsey), Ottowa: Quill Books.

Calvo Sotelo, José, 1938, *El Capitalismo Contemporáneo y su Evolución*, Valladolid: Cultura Española.

Cámara Barbachano, Fernando, 1979, 'The Influence of Sol Tax on Mexican Social Anthropology', in Robert Hinshaw (ed.), *Currents in Anthropology: Essays in Honour of Sol Tax*, The Hague: Mouton Publishers.

Campigotto, Luca, 2006, *Venice: The City by Night*, London: Thames & Hudson.

Cancian, Frank, 1965, *Economics and Prestige in a Maya Community: The Religious Cargo System in Zinacantan*, Stanford, CA: Stanford University Press.

Cancian, Frank, 1987, 'Proletarianization in Zinacantan', in Morgan D. Maclachlan (ed.), *Household Economies and their Transformations*, London and New York: University Press of America.

Cancian, Frank, 1989, 'Economic Behaviour in Peasant Communities', in Stuart Plattner (ed.), *Economic Anthropology*, Stanford, CA: Stanford University Press.

Cancian, Frank, 1992, *The Decline of Community in Zinacantan: Economy, Public Life, and Social Stratification, 1960–1987*, Stanford, CA: Stanford University Press.

Cannadine, David, 1990, *The Decline and Fall of the British Aristocracy*, London and New Haven, CT: Yale University Press.

Cannadine, David, 1994, *Aspects of Aristocracy: Grandeur and Decline in Modern Britain*, London and New Haven, CT: Yale University Press.

Cannadine, David, 1997, *The Pleasures of the Past*, London: Penguin Books.

Canning, George, 1820, *Speech of the Rt. Hon. George Canning delivered at the Liverpool Dinner, given in Celebration of his Re-election, 18th March, 1820*, London: The Guardian Office, 268 Strand, opposite St. Clement's Church.

Čapek, Karel, c. 1929, *Letters from Italy* (translated by Francis P. Marchant), London: Besant & Co., Ltd.

Cardoso, C.F.S., 1975, 'On the Colonial Modes of Production of the Americas', *Critique of Anthropology*, Nos. 4 & 5.

Carr, E.H., 1945, *Nationalism and After*, London: Macmillan.

Carrà, Carlo, 1925, *Giotto*, London: A. Zwemmer.

Carrigan, Ana, 2001, 'Afterword: Chiapas, the First Postmodern Revolution', in *Subcomandante Marcos* [2001].

Carter, April, 1971, *The Political Theory of Anarchism*, London: Routledge & Kegan Paul Ltd.

Carter, Ian, 1990, *Ancient Cultures of Conceit: British University Fiction in the Post-war Years*, London: Routledge.

Casasola, Agustín Victor, 1985, ¡Tierra y Libertad! Photographs of Mexico 1900–1935, from the Casasola Archive, Oxford: Museum of Modern Art.

Castells, Manuel, Shujiro Yazawa, and Emma Kiselyova, 1995/96, 'Insurgents Against the Global Order: A Comparative Analysis of the Zapatistas in Mexico, the American Militia and Japan's AUM Shinrikyo', Berkeley Journal of Sociology, Vol. 40.

Castro Pozo, Hildebrando, 1936, Del Ayllu al Cooperativismo Socialista, Lima: Biblioteca de la Revista de Economia y Finanzas.

Caute, David, 1994, Joseph Losey: A Revenge on Life, London and Boston, MA: Faber and Faber.

Chamberlain, The Right Hon. Joseph, M.P. 1885, The Radical Programme, London: Chapman and Hall.

Chatterjee, Partha, 1984, 'Gandhi and the Critique of Civil Society', in Ranajit Guha (ed.), Subaltern Studies III, Delhi: Oxford University Press.

Chayanov, A.V., 1966, The Theory of Peasant Economy (edited by Daniel Thorner, Basile Kerblay and R.E.F. Smith), Homewood, ILL: The American Economic Association.

Chetwode, Penelope, 1973, 'Recollections', in David Pryce-Jones (ed.), Evelyn Waugh and his World, London: Weidenfeld and Nicolson.

Chossudovsky, Michel, 1986, Towards Capitalist Restoration? Chinese Socialism after Mao, London: Macmillan.

Clark, Alan, 2002, The Last Diaries [1991–99], London: Weidenfeld and Nicolson.

Clark, Kenneth, 1977, The Other Half: A Self-Portrait, London: John Murray.

Cleaver, Harry, 1994, 'The Chiapas Uprising', Studies in Political Economy No. 44.

Cobden Unwin, Jane (ed.), 1904, The Hungry Forties – Life under the Bread Tax: Descriptive Letters and Other Testimonies from Contemporary Witnesses, London: T. Fisher Unwin.

Colgate, Isabel, 1980, The Shooting Party, London: Hamish Hamilton.

Colley, Linda, 1992, Britons: Forging the Nation, 1707–1837, London: Pimlico.

Collier, George A., and Jane F. Collier, 2007, 'The Zapatista Rebellion in the Context of Globalization', in Sarah Washbrook (ed.).

Collins, Jim, 1989, Uncommon Cultures: Popular Culture and Postmodernism, London and New York: Routledge.

Colton, C.C., 1835, Lacon, or Many Things in a Few Words, London: Longman, Rees, Orme, Green, & Longman.

Connolly, Cyril, 1931, 'The Art of Travel', The New Keepsake, London: Cobden-Sanderson.

Connor, Steven, 1989, Postmodernist Culture, Oxford: Basil Blackwell.

Cook, Juliet, and Julian Clarke, 1990, 'Racism and the Right', in Barry Hindess (ed.), Reactions to the Right, London: Routledge.

Cooper, Artemis, 2012, Patrick Leigh Fermor: An Adventure, London: John Murray.

Cooper, John M., 1917, *Analytical and Critical Bibliography of the Tribes of Tierra del Fuego and Adjacent Territory* (Smithsonian Institution, Bureau of American Ethnology, Bulletin 63), Washington, DC: Government Printing Office.

Coppola, Eleanor, 1995, *Notes on the Making of Apocalypse Now*, London: Faber and Faber.

Coquery-Vidrovitch, Catherine, 1975, 'Research on an African Mode of Production', *Critique of Anthropology*, Nos. 4 & 5.

Cornejo, Alberto, 1949, *Programas Políticos de Bolivia*, Cochabamba: Imprenta Universitaria.

Cory, Daniel (ed.), 1955, *The Letters of George Santayana*, London: Constable.

Covarrubias, Miguel, c. 1946, *Mexico South: The Isthmus of Tehuantepec*, London: Cassell and Co., Ltd.

Cowie, Peter, 2000, *The Apocalypse Now Book*, London: Faber and Faber.

Cowling, Maurice, 1978, 'The Present Position', in Maurice Cowling (ed.), *Conservative Essays*, London: Cassell.

Crovato, Giorgio, and Maurizio Crovato, 2008, *Isole abbandonate della laguna veneziana*, Teddington: San Marco Press.

Cunninghame, Patrick, and Carolina Ballersteros Corona, 1998, 'A Rainbow at Midnight: Zapatistas and Autonomy', *Capital & Class*, No. 66.

Curtis, Richard, 1994, *Four Weddings and a Funeral: The Screenplay*, London: Corgi Books.

Dahlberg, Edward, 1935, 'Fascism and Writers', in Henry Hart (ed.) [1935].

Dahrendorf, Ralf, 1967, *Conflict after class: New perspectives on the theory of social and political conflict* (Noel Buxton Lecture, University of Essex), London: Longmans, Green & Co, Ltd.

Damiani, Ludovica (ed.), 2010, *Set in Venice: Il cinema a Venezia scatti protagonisti racconti*, Milano: Electa.

Daniels, Stephen, 1994, *Fields of Vision: Landscape Imagery and National Identity in England and the United States*, Cambridge: Polity Press.

Davie, Michael (ed.), 1976, *The Diaries of Evelyn Waugh*, London: Weidenfeld and Nicolson.

Davies, Norman, 1999, *The Isles: A History*, London: Macmillan.

Davis, Robert C., 1991, *Shipbuilders of the Venetian Arsenal: Workers and Workplace in the Preindustrial City*, Baltimore, MA: The Johns Hopkins University Press.

De Angelis, Massimo, 2000, 'Globalization, New Internationalism and the Zapatistas', *Capital & Class*, No. 70.

de la Fuente, Julio, 1967, 'Ethnic Relationships', in Manning Nash (ed.) [1967b].

de la Peña, Guillermo, 2002, 'Anthropological Debates and the Crisis of Mexican Nationalism', in W. Lem and B. Leach (eds.), *Culture, Economy, Power*, New York: SUNY.

de León, Antonio García, 2007, 'From revolution to Transition: The Chiapas Rebellion and the Path to democracy in Mexico', in Sarah Washbrook (ed.).

de Madariaga, Salvador, 1958, *Democracy versus Liberty? The Faith of a Liberal Heretic*, London: Pall Mall Press Limited.

de Maeztu, Ramiro, 1937 [1931], 'Spain', *Colosseum*, Vol III, No. 16.

de Maeztu, Ramiro, 1941 [1934], *Defensa de la Hispanidad*, Madrid: Gráfica Universal.

Debray, Régis, 1967, *Revolution in the Revolution? Armed Struggle and the Political Struggle in Latin America* (translated by Bobbye Ortiz), New York and London: Monthly Review Press.

Debray, Régis, 1973, *Prison Writings* (translated by Rosemary Sheed), London: Allen Lane.

Debray, Régis, 2002, *Against Venice*, London: Pushkin Press.

Debray, Régis, 2007, *Praised Be Our Lords: A Political Education* (translated by John Howe), London: Verso.

Deere, C., Niurka Pérez, and Ernel Gonzales, 1994, 'The View from Below: The Cuban Agricultural Sector in the "Special Period in Peacetime"', *The Journal of Peasant Studies*, Vol. 21, No. 2.

Deutsch, Sandra McGee, 1986, *Counterrevolution in Argentina, 1900–1932: The Argentine Patriotic League*, Lincoln, NE: The University of Nebraska Press.

Deutsch, Sandra McGee, 1999, *Las Derechas: The Extreme Right in Argentina, Brazil, and Chile, 1890–1939*, Stanford, CA: Stanford University Press.

Deutsch, Sandra McGee, and Ronald H. Dolkart (eds.), 1993, *The Argentine Right: Its History and Intellectual Origins, 1910 to the Present*, Wilmington, DE: Scholarly Resources, Inc.

Dickinson, H.D., H.B. Acton, Henry Smith, Michael Polanyi, and G.D.N. Worswick, 1948, *Economic Problems in a Free Society*, London: Central Joint Committee on Tutorial Classes.

Dinerman, Alice, 2001, 'From "*Abaixo*" to "Chiefs of Production"; Agrarian Change in Nampula Province, Mozambique, 1975-87', *The Journal of Peasant Studies*, Vol. 28, No. 2.

Dixie, Lady Florence, 1880, *Across Patagonia*, London: Richard Bentley & Son.

Dovring, Folke, 1956, *Land and Labor in Europe 1900–1950: A Comparative Survey of Recent Agrarian History*, The Hague: Martinus Nijhoff.

Dovring, Karin, 1956, 'Land Reform as a Propaganda Theme', in Folke Dovring [1956].

Drazin, Charles, 1999, *In Search of The Third Man*, London: Methuen.

Drummond Wolff, Henry, 1853, *Pictures of Spanish Life*, London: Richard Bentley.

Dunn, Stephen P., 1975, 'New Departures in Soviet Theory and Practice of Ethnicity', *Dialectical Anthropology*, Vol. 1, No. 1.

Duveen, Sir Joseph, 1930, *Thirty Years of British Art*, London: The Studio.

Eccleshall, Robert, Vincent Geoghegan, Richard Jay, and Rick Wilford, 1986, *Political Ideologies*, London: Hutchinson.

Eden, Frederic, 2003 [1903], *A Garden in Venice*, London: Frances Lincoln Limited.

Eklof, Ben, and Stephen P. Frank (eds.), 1990, *The World of the Russian Peasant: Post-Emancipation Culture and Society*, Boston, MA: Unwin Hyman.

Engels, Frederick, 1976 [1847] 'Principles of Communism', *Marx and Engels Collected Works*, Vol. 6, London: Lawrence & Wishart.

Epstein, Klaus, 1966, *The Genesis of German Conservatism*, Princeton, NJ: Princeton University Press.

Esteva, Gustavo, 1999, 'The Zapatistas and People's Power', *Capital & Class* No. 68.

Evola, Julius, 1993 [1935], *René Guenon: A Teacher for Modern Times*, Edmonds, WA: Sure Fire Press.

Evola, Julius, 1995 [1934], *Revolt Against the Modern World*, Rochester, VT: Inner Traditions.

Evola, Julius, 2002, *Men Among the Ruins: Postwar Reflections of a Radical Traditionalist*, Rochester, VT: Inner Traditions.

Evola, Julius, 2003, *Ride the Tiger: A Survival Manual for the Aristocrats of the Soul*, Rochester, VT: Inner Traditions.

Fawcett, Henry, 1876 [1863], *Manual of Political Economy*, London: Macmillan & Co.

Fermor, Patrick Leigh, 1968 [1950], *The Traveller's Tree: A Journey through the Caribbean Islands*, London: John Murray.

Fermor, Patrick Leigh, 2003, *Words of Mercury* (edited by Artemis Cooper), London: John Murray.

Fermor, Patrick Leigh, 2004 [1966], *Roumeli: Travels in Northern Greece*, London: John Murray.

Field, Arthur J. (ed.), 1970, *City and Country in the Third World: Issues in the Modernization of Latin America*, Cambridge, MA: Schenkman Publishing Company, Inc.

Fine, Sidney, 1956, *Laissez Faire and the General-Welfare State: A Study of Conflict in American Thought, 1865–1901*, Ann Arbor, MI: The University of Michigan Press.

Fioravanti, Eduardo, 1974, *Latifundio y Sindicalismo Agrario en el Perú*, Lima: Instituto de Estudios Peruanos.

Fiore, Roberto, and Gabriele Adinolfi (eds.), 2004, *Noi Terza Posizione*, Rome: Settimo Sigillo.

Fischer, Ernst, 1974, *An Opposing Man*, London: Allen Lane.

Fletcher, Robert, 2001, 'What are We Fighting For? Rethinking Resistance in a Pewenche Community in Chile', *The Journal of Peasant Studies*, Vol. 28, No. 3.

Foner, Eric, 1998, *The Story of American Freedom*, New York: W.W. Norton.

Fontana, Giovanni, 2004, *Dedicato a Venezia*, Venice: Giugiaro.

Foot, Paul, 2005, *The Vote: How It was Won and How It was Undermined*, London: Penguin/Viking.

Fowler-Salamini, Heather, and Mary Kay Vaughan (eds.), 1994, *Women of the Mexican Countryside, 1850–1990*, London and Tucson, AZ: The University of Arizona Press.

Friedland, William H., 1964, 'Basic Social Trends', in William H. Friedland and Carl G. Rosberg, Jr. (eds.) [1964].

Friedland, William H., and Carl G. Rosberg, Jr. (eds.), 1964, *African Socialism*, Stanford, CA: Stanford University Press.

Friedman, Milton, 1962, *Capitalism and Freedom*, Chicago, IL: University of Chicago Press.

Froude, James Anthony, 1877, 'On the Uses of a Landed Gentry', in *Short Studies on Great Subjects*, New York: Scribner, Armstrong & Co.

Furniss, Edgar S., 1965 [1920], *The Position of the Labourer in a System of Nationalism: A Study in the Labour Theories of the Later English Mercantilists*, New York: Augustus M. Kelley.

Fussell, Paul, 1982, *Abroad: British Literary Travelling between the Wars*, Oxford: Oxford University Press.

Gamio, Manuel, 1966, *Consideraciones sobre el problema indígena*, México: Instituto Indigenista Interamericano.

Gamio, Manuel, 1971 [1930], *Mexican Immigration to the United States: A Study of Human Migration and Adjustment*, New York: Dover Publications, Inc.

García, Antonia, 1967, *Reforma Agraria y Economía Empresarial en América Latina*, Santiago de Chile: Editorial Universitaria, S.A.

García Canclini, Néstor, 2001, *Consumers and Citizens: Globalization and Multicultural Conflicts*, Minneapolis, MI: University of Minnesota Press.

Garland, Nicholas, 1983, *An Indian Journal*, Edinburgh: Salamander Press.

Gellner, Ernest, and John Waterbury (eds.), 1977, *Patrons and Clients*, London: George Duckworth & Co.

Genovese, Eugene D., 1994, *The Southern Tradition: The Achievement and Limitations of an American Conservatism*, Cambridge, MA: Harvard University Press.

Gibbon, Peter, and Michael Neocosmos, 1985, 'Some Problems in the Political Economy of "African Socialism"', in Henry Bernstein and Bonnie K. Campbell (eds.), *Contradictions of Accumulation in Africa: Studies in Economy and State*, London and Beverley Hills, CA: Sage Publications.

Giddens, Anthony, 1994, *Beyond Left and Right: The Future of Radical Politics*, Stanford, CA: Stanford University Press.

Gide, André, 1948, *The Journals – Volume II: 1914–1927* (translated by Justin O'Brien), London: Secker & Warburg.

Gilly, Adolfo, 1983, *The Mexican Revolution*, London: Verso.

Gilly, Adolfo, 1998, 'Chiapas and the Rebellion of the Enchanted World', in Daniel Nugent (ed.) [1998].

Gilroy, Paul, Lawrence Grossberg and Angela McRobbie (eds.), 2000, *Without Guarantees*, London: Verso.

Godechot, Jacques, 1972, *The Counter-Revolution: Doctrine and Action, 1789–1804* (translated by Salvator Attanasio), London: Routledge & Kegan Paul.

Goldring, Douglas, 1913, *Dream Cities: Notes of an Autumn Tour in Italy and Dalmatia*, London and Leipsic: T. Fisher Unwin.

Goldwater, Barry, 1964, *The Conscience of a Conservative*, London: Fontana Books.

Gombrich, E.H., 1965, 'Introduction' to *Heritage of Beauty: Architecture and Sculpture in Austria*, by S. Kruckenhauser, London: C.A. Watts & Co., Ltd.

Goodrich, Amanda, 2005, *Debating England's Aristocracy in the 1790s: Pamphlets, Polemics and Political Ideas*, Woodbridge: The Boydell Press for The Royal Historical Society.

Gordillo, Gustavo, 1988, *Campesinos al Asalto del Cielo: De la Expropiación Estatal a la Apropiación Campesina*, México, D.F.: Siglo Veintiuno Editores.

Gott, Richard, 1971, *Guerrilla Movements in Latin America*, London: Nelson.

Grahame, Georgina, 1909, *Under Petraia, with Some Saunterings*, London: John Lane, the Bodley Head.

Granado, Alberto, 2003, *Travelling with Che Guevara: The Making of a Revolutionary*, London: Pimlico.

Graves, Robert, 1960 [1934], *I, Claudius*, Harmondsworth: Penguin Books.

Graves, Robert, 1961 [1934], *Claudius the God*, Harmondsworth: Penguin Books.

Graves, Robert, 1969, 'The Phenomenon of Mass-tourism (1964)', in *The Crane Bag and Other Disputed Subjects*, London: Cassell & Company Ltd.

Gray, John, 1992, *The Moral Foundations of Market Institutions*, London: Institute of Economic Affairs.

Green, David G., 1993, *Reinventing Civil Society*, London: Institute of Economic Affairs.

Green, David G., 1996, *Community Without Politics: A Market Approach to Welfare Reform*, London: Institute of Economic Affairs.

Green, Russell, 1936, *Dreamers in Venice*, London: Thomas Nelson & Sons Ltd.

Greene, Graham, 1951, *The Lost Childhood and Other Essays*, London: Eyre & Spottiswoode.

Griffiths, Richard, 1983, *Fellow Travellers of the Right: British Enthusiasts for Nazi Germany, 1933–39*, London: Oxford University Press.

Grindle, Merilee S., 1988, *Searching for Rural Development: Labor Migration and Employment in Mexico*, Ithaca, NY: Cornell University Press.

Guevara, Ernesto Che, 1967, *Episodes of the Revolutionary War* (translated by Eduardo Bernat), Havana: Book Institute.

Guevara, Ernesto Che, 2004, *The Motorcycle Diaries: Notes on a Latin American Journey*, London and New York: Fourth Estate.

Guha, Ramachandra, 2007, *India after Gandhi: The History of the World's Largest Democracy*, London: Macmillan.

Guha, Ranajit (ed.), 1982–89, *Subaltern Studies I–VI*, New Delhi: Oxford University Press.

Guiton, Shirley, 1972, *No Magic Eden*, London: Hamish Hamilton.

Guiton, Shirley, 1977, *A World by Itself: Tradition and Change in the Venetian Lagoon*, London: Hamish Hamilton.

Gutelman, Michel, 1971, *Réforme et mystification agraires en Amérique latine: Le cas du Mexique*, Paris: François Maspero.

Hale, J.R. (ed.), 1979, *The Travel Journal of Antonio de Beatis: Germany, Switzerland, the Low Countries, France and Italy, 1517–1518* (translated from the Italian by J.R. Hale and J.M.A. Lindon), London: The Hakluyt Society.

Halpern, Joel M., and E.A. Hammel, 1969, 'Observations on the Intellectual History of Ethnology and Other Social Sciences in Yugoslavia', *Comparative Studies in Society and History*, Vol. 11, No. 1.

Hamilton, Alastair, 1971, *The Appeal of Fascism: A Study of Intellectuals and Fascism 1919–1945*, New York: The Macmillan Company.

Hardt, Michael, and Antonio Negri, 2000, *Empire*, Cambridge, MA: Harvard University Press.

Hardt, Michael, and Antonio Negri, 2005, *Multitude: War and Democracy in the Age of Empire*, London: Hamish Hamilton.

Hare, Augustus J.C., 1900, *Venice*, London: George Allen.

Harris, Ralph, 1978a, 'Can Confrontation be Avoided?', in Ralph Harris (ed.) [1978b].

Harris, Ralph (ed.), 1978b, *The Coming Confrontation: Will the Open Society Survive to 1989?*, London: Institute of Economic Affairs.

Hart, Henry (ed.), 1935, *American Writers' Congress*, New York: International Publishers.

Harte, Glynn Boyd, 1988, *Venice*, London: Hamish Hamilton.

Hartley, L.P., 1960, *Facial Justice*, London: Hamish Hamilton.

Hartley, L.P., 1985 [1953], *The Go-Between*, London: The Folio Society.

Hartley, L.P., 1986, *The Complete Short Stories*, New York: Beaufort Book Publishers.

Hartwell, R.M., 1995, *A History of the Mont Pelerin Society*, Indianapolis, IN: The Liberty Fund.

Harvey, Neil, 2007, 'Who Needs Zapatismo? State Interventions and Local Responses in Marqués de Comillas, Chiapas', in Sarah Washbrook (ed.).

Hayek, F., 1960, *The Constitution of Liberty*, London: Routledge & Kegan Paul.

Hayek, Friedrich A., 1944, *The Road to Serfdom*, Chicago, IL: Chicago University Press.

Hayek, Friedrich A., 1967 [1950], 'Full Employment, Planning and Inflation', in F.A. Hayek, *Studies in Philosophy, Politics and Economics*, London: Routledge & Kegan Paul.

Hayek, Friedrich A., 1973, *Economic Freedom and Representative Government*, London: Institute of Economic Affairs.

Heath, Dwight B., and Richard N. Adams (eds.), 1965, *Contemporary Cultures and Societies of Latin America*, New York: Random House.

Hecker, Julius F., 1934, *Russian Sociology: A Contribution to the History of Sociological Thought and Theory*, London: Chapman & Hall Ltd.

Hellman, Judith Adler, 1999, 'Real and Virtual Chiapas: Magic Realism and the Left', *Socialist Register 2000*, London: The Merlin Press.

Hellman, Judith Adler, 2000, 'Virtual Chiapas: A Reply to Paulson', *Socialist Register 2001*, London: The Merlin Press.

Helps, Arthur, 1872, *Thoughts Upon Government*, London: Bell and Daldy, York Street, Covent Garden.

Hernández, Hector, 1999, *The Sinarquista Movement, with special reference to the Period 1934–1944*, London: Minerva Press.

Herzen, Alexander, 1956, *From the Other Shore (1848)* (translated from the Russian by Moura Budberg), London: Weidenfeld and Nicolson.

Herzen, Alexander, 1995, *Letters from France and Italy, 1847–1851* (Edited and translated by Judith E. Zimmerman), Pittsburgh and London: University of Pittsburgh Press.

Hewitt de Alcántara, Cynthia, 1976, *Modernizing Mexican Agriculture: Socioeconomic Implications of Technological Change, 1940–1970*, Geneva: United Nations Research Institute for Social Development.

Hewitt de Alcántara, Cynthia, 1984, *Anthropological Perspectives on Rural Mexico*, London: Routledge & Kegan Paul.

Hitchcock, Alfred, 1984, *The Lady Vanishes* (screenplay by Frank Launder and Sidney Gilliat), London: Lorrimer Publishing Ltd.

Hobsbawm, Eric J., 1973, *Revolutionaries: Contemporary Essays*, London: Weidenfeld and Nicolson.

Hobsbawm, Eric J., 1981, 'The Forward March of Labour Halted?', in M. Jacques and F. Mulhern (eds.), *The Forward March of Labour Halted?*, London: Verso.

Hobsbawm, Eric J., 1990, *Nations and Nationalism since 1780: Programme, Myth, Reality*, Cambridge: Cambridge University Press.

Hochhuth, Rolf, 1963, *The Representative* (translated by Robert David Macdonald), London: Methuen & Co., Ltd.

Hoefle, Scott William, 2003, 'Beyond Cold War Pipedreams: What the West Was Not', *The Journal of Peasant Studies*, Vol. 30, No. 2.

Holloway, John, 2002a, 'Zapatismo and the Social Sciences', *Capital & Class*, No. 78.

Holloway, John, 2002b, *Change the World Without Taking Power: The Meaning of Revolution Today*, London: Pluto Press.

Holloway, John, and Eloína Peláez (eds.), 1998, *Zapatista! Reinventing Revolution in Mexico*, London: Pluto Press.

Huizer, Gerrit, 1970, 'Peasant Organizations in the Process of Political Modernization: The Latin American Experience', in Arthur J. Field (ed.) [1970].

Hume, David, 1817, *Essays and Treatises on Several Subjects – Volume I: Essays Moral, Political, and Literary*, Edinburgh: Bell & Bradfute, and W. Blackwood.

Hunt, John Dixon, and Peter Willis, 1975, *The Genius of the Place: The English Landscape Garden 1620–1820*, New York: Harper & Row.

Hussain, Athar, and Keith Tribe (eds.), 1984, *Paths of Development in Capitalist Agriculture: Readings from German Social Democracy, 1891–99*, London: Macmillan.

Hutton, Graham, 1960, *Inflation and Society*, London: George Allen & Unwin, Ltd.

Icaza, Jorge, 1973 [1953], *Huasipungo*, Buenos Aires: Editorial Losada, s.a.

Illife, John, 1983, *The Emergence of African Capitalism*, London: Macmillan.

Isherwood, Christopher, 1966, *Exhumations*, London: Methuen & Co., Ltd.

Jack, Ian, 2006, 'Introduction: too much travelling means the end of the road' (special issue: *On the Road Again: Where Travel Writing Went Next*), *Granta*, No. 94.

Jacobs, Lewis (ed.), 1977, *The Compound Cinema: The Film Writings of Harry Alan Potamkin*, New York and London: Teachers College, Columbia University Press.

James, Montague Rhodes, 1931, *The Collected Ghost Stories*, London: Edward Arnold.

James, Patricia (ed.), 1966, *The Travel Diaries of Thomas Robert Malthus*, London: Cambridge University Press.

Jameson, Fredric, 1988, *The Ideologies of Theory: Essays 1971–1986* (Volumes 1 and 2), London: Routledge.

Jameson, Fredric, 1992, *The Geopolitical Aesthetic: Cinema and Space in the World System*, Bloomington and Indianapolis, IN: Indiana University Press, and London: British Film Institute.

Jameson, Fredric, 1994, *The Seeds of Time,* New York: Columbia University Press.

Jebb, Richard, 1905, *Studies in Colonial Nationalism*, London: Edward Arnold.

Jebb, Richard, 1926, *The Empire in Eclipse*, London: Chapman and Hall, Ltd.

Jekyll, Gertrude, and Lawrence Weaver, 1913, *Gardens for Small Country Houses*, London: Country Life.

Jell-Bahlsen, Sabine, 1985, 'Ethnology and Fascism in Germany', *Dialectical Anthropology*, Vol. 9, Nos. 1–4.

Jerome, Jerome K., 1891, *The Diary of a Pilgrimage (and Six Essays)*, London and Bristol: Simpkin, Marshall, Kent & Co., Ltd./J.W. Arrowsmith, 11 Quay Street.

Jones, J.D.F., 2001, *Storyteller: The Many Lives of Laurens van der Post*, London: John Murray.

Joseph, Gilbert M., and Daniel Nugent (eds.), 1994, *Everyday Forms of State Formation: Revolution and the Negotiation of Rule in Modern Mexico*, Durham, NC: Duke University Press.

Jouvenel, Bertrand de, 1951, *The Ethics of Redistribution*, London: Cambridge University Press.

Kael, Pauline, 1970,*Going Steady*, London: Temple Smith.

Kaplan, Fred (ed.), 1994, *Travelling in Italy with Henry James*, London: Hodder & Stoughton.

Keates, Jonathan, 2011, *The Portable Paradise: Baedeker, Murray and the Victorian Guidebook*, London: Notting Hill Editions, Ltd.

Kemp, Philip, 2006, 'Royal Blues', *Sight and Sound*, Vol. 16, Issue 10 (NS).

Kingston-Mann, Esther, and Timothy Mixter (eds.), 1991, *Peasant Economy, Culture, and Politics of European Russia, 1800–1921*, Princeton, NJ: Princeton University Press.

Kipling, Rudyard, 1895, *Wee Willie Winkie, Under the Deodars, The Phantom Rickshaw, and Other Stories*, London: Macmillan and Co.

Kitchen, C.H.B., 1931, 'Beauty and the Beast', in Cynthia Asquith (ed.) [1931].

Kitchen, Martin, 1987, 'The Austrian Left and the Popular Front', in Helen Graham and Paul Preston (eds.), *The Popular Front in Europe*, London: Macmillan Press.

Klaren, P.F., 2000, *Peru: Society and Nationhood in the Andes*, New York: Oxford University Press.

Klinge, Gerardo, 1946, *Política Agrícola-Alimenticia*, Lima: Sociedad Nacional Agraria.

Knauerhase, R., 1972, *An Introduction to National Socialism, 1920 to 1939*, Columbus, OH: Charles E. Merrill Publishing Co.

Kneale, Nigel, 1949, *Tomato Cain and Other Stories*, London: Collins.

Kneale, Nigel, 1959, *The Quatermass Experiment*, London: Penguin Books.

Kneale, Nigel, 1960a, *Quatermass II*, London: Penguin Books.

Kneale, Nigel, 1960b, *Quatermass and the Pit*, London: Penguin Books.

Kneale, Nigel, 1973, 'Introduction' to *Ghost Stories of M.R. James*, London: The Folio Society.

Kneale, Nigel, 1976, *The Year of the Sex Olympics and Other TV Plays*, London: Ferret Fantasy.

Kneale, Nigel, 1979, *The Quatermass Conclusion*, London: Hutchinson.

Knight, Alan, 1986a, *The Mexican Revolution: Volume 1 – Porfirians, Liberals and Peasants*, Cambridge: Cambridge University Press.

Knight, Alan, 1986b, *The Mexican Revolution: Volume 2 – Counter-revolution and Reconstruction*, Cambridge: Cambridge University Press.

Knight, Alan, 1990, 'Racism, Revolution and *Indigenismo*: Mexico, 1910-1940', in Richard Graham (ed.), *The Idea of Race in Latin America, 1870–1940*, Austin, TX: University of Texas Press.

Kosinski, Jerzy, 1971, *Being There*, New York: Harcourt Brace Jovanovich.

Kracauer, Sigfried, 1960, *Theory of Film*, New York: Oxford University Press.

Král, Petr, 2011, *Loving Venice*, London: Pushkin Press.

KY and FE [Kate Young and Felicity Edholm], 1974, '*Todos Somos Mexicanos*, But Some Are More Mexican Than Others', *Critique of Anthropology*, Vol. 1, No. 1.

Lacroix, Paul, c.1876, *The XVIIIth Century – Its Institutions, Customs, and Costumes*: *France, 1700–1789*, London: Bickers and Son, 1 Leicester Square.

Laing, Samuel, 1850, *Observations on the Social and Political State of the European People in 1848 and 1849; Being the Second Series of The Notes of a Traveller*, London: Longman, Brown, Green, and Longmans, Paternoster-Row.

Lampert, Evgenii, 1965, *Sons against Fathers*: *Studies in Russian radicalism and Revolution*, Oxford: Clarendon Press.

Landsberger, Henry A., 1969, 'Chile: A Vineyard Workers' Strike – A Case Study of the Relationship between Church, Intellectuals, and Peasants', in Henry A. Landsberger (ed.), *Latin American Peasant Movements*, Ithaca, NY: Cornell University Press.

Lane, Frederic C., 1966, *Venice and History*: *The Collected Papers of Frederic C. Lane*, Baltimore, MD: The John Hopkins Press.

Lara, Jesús, 1965, *Llallipacha*: *Tiempo de Vencer*, Buenos Aires: Editorial Platina.

Larsen, Neil, 2001, *Determinations*: *Essays on Theory, Narrative and Nation in the Americas*, London: Verso.

Leader, Zachary (ed.), 2000, *The Letters of Kingsley Amis*, London: HarperCollins Publishers.

Lenin, V.I., 1963 [1912], 'In Memory of Herzen', *Collected Works*, Vol. 18, Moscow: Foreign Languages Publishing House.

Lenin, V.I., 1964 [1899], 'The Development of Capitalism in Russia', *Collected Works*, Vol. 3, Moscow: Foreign Languages Publishing House.

Lenin, V.I., 1964 [1914], 'The Rights of Nations to Self-Determination', *Collected Works*, Vol. 20, Moscow: Progress Publishers.

Lenin, V.I., 1965 [1920], 'A Publicist's Notes', *Collected Works*, Vol. 30, Moscow: Progress Publishers.

Lerner, Daniel, 1958, *The Passing of Traditional Society*: *Modernizing the Middle East*, New York: Free Press.

Lévi-Strauss, Claude, 1961, *A World on the Wane* (translated from the French by John Russell), London: Hutchinson & Co., Ltd.

Lewis, Norman, 1988, *The Missionaries*, London: Secker & Warburg.

Lewis, Norman, 1998, *The Happy Ant-Heap and Other Pieces*, London: Jonathan Cape.

Lewis, Oscar, 1951, *Life in a Mexican Village*: *Tepoztlán Restudied*, Urbana, ILL: University of Illinois Press.

Lewis, Oscar, 1965 [1952], 'Urbanization Without Breakdown: A Case Study', in Dwight B. Heath and Richard N. Adams (eds.) [1965].

Leys, Colin, 1996, *The Rise and Fall of Development Theory*, Oxford: James Currey.

Liebknecht, Wilhelm, 1908, *Karl Marx – Biographical Memoirs* (translated by Ernest Untermann), Chicago: Charles H. Kerr & Company.

Lippman, Walter, 1955, *The Public Philosophy*, London: Hamish Hamilton.

Lippmann, Walter, 1922, *Public Opinion*, New York: Harcourt Brace and Company.

Lodge, David, 1973, 'The Fugitive Art of Letters,' in David Pryce-Jones (ed.) [1973b].

Lodge, David, 1996, 'The Lives of Graham Greene', in *The Practice of Writing: Essays, Lectures, Reviews and a Diary*, London: Secker & Warburg.

Lodge, David, 2003, *Consciousness and the Novel*, London: Penguin Books.

Loomis, C.P., and J.A. Beegle, 1946, 'The Spread of German Nazism in Rural Areas', *American Sociological Review*, Vol. 11, No. 6.

López Alvez, Fernando, 2000, *State Formation and Democracy in Latin America, 1810–1900*, London and Durham, NC: Duke University Press.

Lopez y Fuentes, Gregorio, 1937, *El Indio*, New York: The Bobbs-Merrill Company.

Lora, Guillermo, 1970, *Documentos Políticos de Bolivia*, Cochabamba: Los Amigos del Libro.

Löwy, Michael (ed.), 1992, *Marxism in Latin America from 1909 to the Present*, London and New Jersey: Humanities Press.

Lucas, Kintto, 2000, *We Will Not Dance on Our Grandparents' Tombs: Indigenous Uprisings in Ecuador*, London: CIIR.

Lukács, Georg, 1971, *History and Class Consciousness: Studies in Marxist Dialectics*, London: Merlin Press.

Luxemburg, Rosa, 1976, *The National Question: Selected Writings*, London and New York: Monthly Review Press.

Lyttelton, Adrian (ed.), 1973, *Italian Fascisms: From Pareto to Gentile*, London: Jonathan Cape.

Lytton Sells, Arthur, 1964, *The Paradise of Travellers: The Italian Influence on Englishmen in the 17th Century*, London: George Allen & Unwin Ltd.

Mabey, Richard (ed.), 1967, *Class: A Symposium*, London: Anthony Blond.

Mabey, Richard, 1967, 'Not On Speaking Terms', in Richard Mabey (ed.) [1967].

Mabey, Richard, 1980, *The Common Ground: A Place for Nature in Britain's Future?*, London: Hutchinson/The Nature Conservancy Council.

Mabey, Richard, 1983, *In a Green Shade: Essays on Landscape, 1970–1983*, London: Hutchinson.

Mabey, Richard, 1990, *Home Country*, London: Century.

Mabey, Richard, 2000, 'A Village Voice', *Resurgence*, Issue 202.

MacCabe, Colin, 1985, *Theoretical Essays: Film, Linguistics, Literature*, Manchester: Manchester University Press.

Maine, Sir Henry Sumner, 1885, *Popular Government*, London: John Murray, Albermarle Street.

Mair, Lucy, 1963, *New Nations*, London: Weidenfeld and Nicolson.

Malinowski, Bronislaw, 1922, *Argonauts of the Western Pacific: An Account of Native Enterprise and Adventure in the Archipelagoes of Melanesian New Guinea*, London: Routledge & Kegan Paul Ltd.

Malinowski, Bronislaw, 1967, *A Diary in the Strict Sense of the Term*, London: Routledge & Kegan Paul.

Malinowski, Bronislaw, and Julio de la Fuente, 1982, *Malinowski in Mexico: The Economics of a Mexican Market System*, London: Routledge & Kegan Paul.

Mallock, W.H., 1924, *Democracy – The Limits of Pure Democracy*, London: Chapman and Hall, Ltd.

Malthus, Thomas Robert, 1890 [1798] *An Essay on the Principle of Population and its Effects on Human Happiness*, London: Ward, Lock & Co.

Mann, Thomas, 1940 [1911], 'Death in Venice', in *Stories and Episodes*, London: J.M. Dent & Sons Ltd.

Marcet, Jane, 1833, *John Hopkins's Notions on Political Economy*, Boston: Allen and Ticknor.

Marcus, George E. (ed.), 1997, *Cultural Producers in Perilous States*, London and Chicago, IL: The University of Chicago Press.

Mariátegui, José Carlos, 1968 [1928], *Siete Ensayos de Interpretación de la Realidad Peruana*, Lima: Biblioteca Amauta.

Marinetti, Filippo, 1972, *Selected Writings* (Edited by R.W. Flint, and translated with Arthur A. Coppotelli), London: Secker & Warburg.

Maritain, Jacques, 1957, *Existence and the Existent: An Essay on Christian Existentialism*, New York: Doubleday & Company, Inc.

Marshall, Peter, 1992, *Demanding the Impossible: A History of Anarchism*, London: Fontana Press.

Martins, José de Souza, 2003, 'Representing the Peasantry? Struggles for/about Land in Brazil', in Tom Brass (ed.) [2003].

Marx, Karl, 1971 [1861–63], *Theories of Surplus-Value – Volume IV of Capital* (Part III), Moscow: Progress Publishers.

Marx, Karl, 1973, *The First International and After* (edited by David Fernbach), London: Penguin Books.

Marx, Karl, 1976 [1867], *Capital: A Critique of Political Economy – Volume One*, Harmondsworth: Penguin Books.

Marx, Karl and Frederick Engels, 1976 [1848], 'The Communist Manifesto', *Marx and Engels Collected Works*, Vol. 6, London: Lawrence & Wishart.

Marzal, Manuel, 1990, 'Antropología e indigenismo en Perú', in Modesto Suárez (ed.) [1990].

Massingham, H.J. (ed.), 1945, *The Natural Order: Essays in The Return to Husbandry*, London: J.M. Dent & Sons Ltd.

McCarthy, Mary, 1956, *Venice Observed*, New York: Reynal & Co.

McClelland, J.S. (ed.), 1970, *The French Right: From de Maistre to Maurras*, London: Jonathan Cape.

McCulloch, J.R., 1830, *The Principles of Political Economy: With a Sketch of the Rise and Progress of the Science*, London: Longman, Rees, Orme, Brown, and Green.

McEwen, Ian, 2001, *Atonement*, London: Jonathan Cape.

McFarlane, Brian, 1997, *An Autobiography of British Cinema*, London: Methuen.

McHale, Brian, 1987, *Postmodernist Fiction*, London and New York: Methuen.

McKenzie, Robert, and Allan Silver, 1968, *Angels in Marble: Working Class Conservatives in Urban England*, London: Heinemann.

McNeish, John, 2003, 'Globalization and the Reinvention of Andean Tradition: The Politics of Community and Ethnicity in Highland Bolivia', in Tom Brass (ed.) [2003].

Medley, George W., 1885, *The Trade Depression: Its Causes and its Remedies*, London: Cassell & Company, Limited.

Meillassoux, Claude, 1981, *Maidens, Meal and Money: Capitalism and the Domestic Community*, Cambridge: Cambridge University Press.

Mendieta y Nuñez, Lucio, 1938, *La Economia del Indio*, Mexico, D.F.: n.p.p.

Metz, Christian, 1974, *Language and Cinema*, The Hague: Mouton.

Metz, Christian, 1982, *Psychoanalysis and Cinema: The Imaginary Signifier*, London: Macmillan.

Meyer, Jean, 1973–74, *La Cristiada: Vol. 1 – La guerra de los cristeros, Vol. 2 – El conflicto entre la iglesia y el estado (1926/29), Vol. 3 – Los cristeros, México*, DF: Siglo Veintiuno Editors, s.a.

Meyer, Jean, 1976, *The Cristero Rebellion: The Mexican People between Church and State, 1926–1929*, Cambridge: Cambridge University Press.

Meyer, Konrad, 1939, 'Discussion: The Social Implications of Economic Progress in Present-day Agriculture', *Proceedings of the Fifth International Conference of Agricultural Economists (1938)*, London: Oxford University Press.

Michael, M.A. (ed.), 1950a, *Traveller's Quest: Original Contributions towards a Philosophy of Travel*, London: William Hodge and Company Limited.

Michael, M.A., 1950b, 'What is Travel?', in M.A. Michael (ed.).

Mignolo, Walter D., 2002, 'The Zapatista's Theoretical Revolution: Its Historical, Ethical, and Political Consequences', *Review*, Vol. 25, No. 3.

Miles, David, 2005, *The Tribes of Britain: Who Are We? And Where Do We Come From?*, London: Weidenfeld and Nicolson.

Milius, John, and Francis Ford Coppola, 2001, *Apocalypse Now Redux – the Screenplay*. London: Faber and Faber Ltd.

Miller, Henry, 1980, 'Mother, China and the World Beyond', in *Sextet: Six Essays*, London: John Calder.

Miranda, Faustino, 1952, *La Vegetación de Chiapas*, Tuxtla Gutiérrez: Gobierno del Estado.

Mitford, Nancy, 1959, *Noblesse Oblige: An Enquiry into the Identifiable Characteristics of the English Aristocracy*, Harmondsworth: Penguin Books.

Mitrany, David, 1951, *Marx Against the Peasant: A Study in Social Dogmatism*, Chapel Hill, NC: University of North Carolina Press.

Moksnes, Heidi, 2007, 'Suffering for Justice in Chiapas: Religion and the Globalization of Ethic Identity', in Sarah Washbrook (ed.).

Montaigne, Michael, 1875, *The Essays of Michael Seigneur de Montaigne* (with notes and quotations and accounts of the author's life made English by Charles Cotton, Esq.), London: Ward, Lock, Bowden and Co.

Montaigne, Michael, 1903, *The Journal of Montaigne's Travels in Italy by way of Switzerland and Germany in 1580 and 1581* (translated and edited with an introduction and notes by W.G. Waters), 3 volumes, London: John Murray.

Morand, Paul, 1928, *Earth Girdled* (translated by Charles-Emile Roche), London: Alfred A. Knopf.

Morand, Paul, 1929, *Black Magic* (translated by Hamish Miles), London: William Heinemann Ltd.

Morand, Paul, 1932, *Orient Air Express*, London: Cassell & Co.

Morand, Paul, 1933, *Indian Air: Impressions of Travel in South America*, London: Cassell & Co.

Morand, Paul, 1937, *The Road to India*, London: Hodder & Stoughton.

Morand, Paul, 2002 [1971], *Venices*, London: Pushkin Press.

Morris, Jan, 2001, *Trieste and the Meaning of Nowhere*, London: Faber & Faber.

Mosca, Gaetano, 1939, *The Ruling Class* (translated by Hannah D. Kahn), New York: McGraw-Hill Book Company, Inc.

Mosk, Sanford A., 1965 [1954], 'Indigenous Economy in Latin America', in Dwight B. Heath and Richard N. Adams (eds.) [1965].

Mosley, Charlotte (ed.), 2009, *In Tearing Haste: Letters between Deborah Devonshire and Patrick Leigh Fermor*, London: John Murray.

Mosley, Oswald, 1932, *The Greater Britain*, London: British Union of Fascists.

Mosse, G., 1966, *Nazi Culture: Intellectual, Cultural and Social Life in the Third Reich*, London: W.H. Allen.

Municipality of Venice, Tourist Office, 1940, *Venice 1940 – XII Biennial International Art Exhibition*, Venezia: Ministero della Cultura Populare.

Munson, Arley, 1915, *Kipling's India*, New York: Doubleday, Page & Company.

Muraro, Michelangelo, and Paolo Marton, 1999, *Venetian Villas*, Cologne: Könemann.

Murra, John V., 1972, *El 'control vertical' de un máximo de pisos ecológicos en la economía de las sociedades Andinas*, Huanuco: Universidad Hermilio Valdizán.

Naipaul, V.S., 1957, *The Mystic Masseur*, London: André Deutsch.

Naipaul, V.S., 1967, *The Mimic Men*, London: André Deutsch.

Naipaul, V.S., 1979, *A Bend in the River*, London: André Deutsch.

Naipaul, V.S., 1980, *The Return of Eva Peron*, London: André Deutsch.

Naipaul, V.S., 1981, *Among the Believers: An Islamic Journey*, London: André Deutsch.

Naipaul, V.S., 1987, *The Enigma of Arrival*, London: Viking.

Naipaul, V.S., 1990, *India: A Million Mutinies Now*, London: Heinemann.

Naipaul, V.S., 1994, *A Way in the World*, New York: Alfred A. Knopf.

Naipaul, V.S., 1998, *Beyond Belief: Islamic Excursions among the Converted Peoples*, London: Little, Brown and Company.

Naipaul, V.S., 2002, *The Writer and the World – Essays* (edited by Pankaj Mishra), London: Picador.

Naipaul, V.S., 2007, *A Writer's People: Ways of Looking and Feeling*, London: Picador.

Naipaul, V.S., 2010, *The Masque of Africa: Glimpses of African Belief*, London: Picador.

Narayan, Uma, and Sandra Harding (eds.), 2000, *Decentering the Center: Philosophy for a Multicultural, Postcolonial and Feminist World*, Bloomington and Indianapolis, IN: Indiana University Press.

Nash, Manning (ed.), 1967b, *Handbook of Middle American Indians: Volume 6 – Social Anthropology*, Austin, TX: University of Texas Press.

Nash, Manning, 1967a, 'Indian Economies', in Manning Nash (ed.) [1967b].

Nehru, Jawaharlal, 1938, 'Nationalism and the Mass Struggle in India', *Labour Monthly*, Vol. 20, No. 8.

Nettl, J.P., 1966, *Rosa Luxemburg*, Volume II, London: Oxford University Press.

Newby, Eric, 1973, 'Lush Places', in David Pryce-Jones (ed.), *Evelyn Waugh and his World*, London: Weidenfeld and Nicolson.

Newby, Eric, 1984, *On the Shores of the Mediterranean*, London: Harvill Press.

Newman, Gerald, 1987, *The Rise of English Nationalism: A Cultural History 1740–1830*, New York: St. Martin's Press.

Nickeon, Nora, Michael J. Watts, and Wendy Wolford, 2004, *Peasant Associations in Theory and Practice*, Civil Society and Social Movements Programme Paper No. 8, UNSRID.

Nock, Albert Jay, 1935, *Our Enemy the State*, New York: W. Morrow & Company.

Nock, Albert Jay, 1991, *The State of the Union: Essays in Social Criticism* (edited by Charles H. Hamilton), Indianapolis, IN: Liberty Fund, Inc.

Nozick, Robert, 1975, *Anarchy, State and Utopia*, Oxford: Blackwell.

Nugent, Daniel (ed.), 1998, *Rural Revolt in Mexico: U.S. Intervention and the Domain of Subaltern Politics*, London and Durham, NC: Duke University Press.

O'Connor, Alan (ed.), 1989, *Raymond Williams on Television: Selected Writings*, London and New York: Routledge.

O'Sullivan, Noël, 1975, *Conservatism*, London: J.M. Dent and Sons, Ltd.

Olesen, Thomas, 2005, *International Zapatismo: The Construction of Solidarity in the Age of Globalization*, London: Zed Press.

Olivera, Mercedes, 2007, 'Subordination and Rebellion: Indigenous Peasant Women in Chiapas Ten Years after the Zapatista Uprising', in Sarah Washbrook (ed.).

Oorthuys, Cas, and A. den Doolaard, 1958, *This is Venice – Photobooks of the World*, London: Faber & Faber.

Orwell, George, 1937, *The Road to Wigan Pier*, London: Victor Gollancz Ltd.

Orwell, George, 1946, *Critical Essays*, London: Secker and Warburg.

Osborne, John, 1957, 'They call it cricket', in Tom Maschler (ed.), *Declaration*, London: MacGibbon & Kee.

Owen, Nicholas (ed.), 2003, *Human Rights, Human Wrongs: The Oxford Amnesty Lectures 2001*, Oxford: Oxford University Press.

Padmore, George, 1953, *The Gold Coast Revolution*, London: Denis Dobson.

Padmore, George, 1956, *Pan-Africanism or Communism? The Coming Struggle for Africa*, London: Denis Dobson.

Paige, Jeffery M., 1975, *Agrarian Revolution*, New York: The Free Press.

Palin, Michael, and Terry Jones, 1980, *More Ripping Yarns*, London: Eyre Methuen Ltd.

Palmier, Jean-Michel, 2006, *Weimar in Exile: The Anti-Fascist Emigration in Europe and America*, London and New York: Verso.

Pandey, Gyanendra, 1994, 'Nationalism and the Struggle over History', in Rob van den Berg and Ulbe Bosma (eds.) [1994].

Pandey, Gyanendra, 2006, 'The Subaltern as Subaltern Citizen', *Economic and Political Weekly*, Vol. 51, No. 46.

Paulson, Justin, 2000, 'Peasant Struggles and International Solidarity: The Case of Chiapas', *Socialist Register 2001*, London: The Merlin Press.

Paxman, Jeremy, 2006, *On Royalty*, London: Viking.

Payne, Leigh A., 2000, *Uncivil Movements: The Armed Right Wing and Democracy in Latin America*, Baltimore, OH: The Johns Hopkins University Press.

Pearse, Andrew, 1980, *Seeds of Plenty, Seeds of Want: Social and Economic Implications of the Green Revolution*, Oxford: Clarendon Press.

Petras, James, 1990, 'Retreat of the Intellectuals', *Economic and Political Weekly*, Vol. 25, No. 38.

Petras, James, 2002, 'A Rose by Any Other Name? The Fragrance of Imperialism', *The Journal of Peasant Studies*, Vol. 29, No. 2.

Petras, James, and Henry Veltmeyer, 2003, 'The Peasantry and the State in Latin America: A Troubled Past, an Uncertain Future', in Tom Brass (ed.) [2003].

Petras, James, and Steve Vieux, 1996, 'Myths and Realities of the Chiapas Uprising', *Economic and Political Weekly*, Vol. 31, No. 47.

Pfaff, Richard William, 1980, *Montague Rhodes James*, London: Scolar Press.

Pinter, Harold, 1971, 'The Go-Between,' in *Five Screenplays*. London: Methuen & Co., Ltd.

Pirie, David, 1973, *A Heritage of Horror*, London: Gordon Fraser.

Plekhanov, G.V., 1981 [1908], 'The Ideology of Our Present-Day Philistine', *Selected Philosophical Works*, Volume V, Moscow: Progress Publishers.

Pollock, Friedrich, 1984 [1932], 'Socialism and Agriculture', in Athar Hussain and Keith Tribe (eds.), *Paths of Development in Capitalist Agriculture: Readings from German Social Democracy, 1891–99*, London: Macmillan.

Pottle, Frederick A. (ed.), 1952, *Boswell in Holland, 1763–1764*, London: William Heinemann Limited.

Pottle, Frederick A. (ed.), 1953, *Boswell on the Grand Tour: Germany and Switzerland, 1764*, London: William Heinemann Limited.

Poulantzas, Nicos, 1975, *Classes in Contemporary Capitalism*, London: NLB.

Poulantzas, Nicos, 1977, 'The New Petty Bourgeoisie', in Alan Hunt (ed.), *Class and Class Structure*, Lawrence and Wishart.

Pryce-Jones, David (ed.), 1973, *Evelyn Waugh and his World*, London: Weidenfeld and Nicolson.

Pullan, Brian (ed.), 1968, *Crisis and Change in the Venetian Economy in the 16th and 17th Centuries*, London: Methuen & Co., Ltd.

Raban, Jonathan, 2011, 'Introduction', in Liz Jobey (ed.), *The New Granta Book of Travel*, London: Granta Books.

Rabasa, José, 1997, 'Of Zapatismo: Reflections on the Folkloric and the Impossible in a Subaltern Insurrection', in Lisa Lowe and David Lloyd (eds.), *The Politics of Culture in the Shadow of Capital*, Durham, NC: Duke University Press.

Rajadhyaksha, Ashish, and Paul Willemen (eds.), 1995, *Encyclopaedia of Indian Cinema*, New Delhi and London: Oxford University Press and British Film Institute.

Rama, Carlos M., 1981, *Nacionalismo e Historiografía en America Latina*, Madrid: Editorial Tecnos, S.A.

Ramos, Alcida Rita, 1998, *Indigenism: Ethnic Politics in Brazil*, Madison, WI: The University of Wisconsin Press.

Randall, Laura (ed.), 1996, *Reforming Mexico's Agrarian Reform*, Armonk, New York: M.E. Sharpe.

Rao, Nicola, 2006, *La fiamma e la celtica: Sessant'anni di neofascismo da Salò ai centri sociali de destra*, Milan: Sperling & Kupfer Editori.

Raphael, D.D. (ed.), 1967, *Political Theory and the Rights of Man*, London: Macmillan.

Redfield, Robert, 1930, *The Little Community*, Chicago, ILL: The University of Chicago Press.

Redfield, Robert, 1955, *Tepoztlán, a Mexican Village: A Study of Folk Life*, Chicago, ILL: The University of Chicago Press.

Redfield, Robert, 1956, *Peasant Society and Culture*, Chicago, ILL: The University of Chicago Press.

Redfield, Robert, and Alfonso Villa Rojas, 1934, *Chan Kom, a Maya Village*, Washington, DC: Carnegie Institution of Washington.

Redford, Bruce, 1996, *Venice and the Grand Tour*, London and New Haven, CT: Yale University Press.

Reed, J.-P., 2003, 'Indigenous Land Policies, Culture and Resistance in Latin America', *The Journal of Peasant Studies*, Vol. 31, No. 1.

Reinaga, Fausto, 1960, *El Sentimiento Mesianico del Pueblo Ruso*, La Paz – Bolivia: Ediciones SER (Sindicato de Escritores Revolucionarios).

Rey, Pierre-Phillipe, 1975, 'The Lineage Mode of Production', *Critique of Anthropology*, No. 3.

Richards, Jeffery, 1973, *Visions of Yesterday*, London: Routledge & Kegan Paul.

Richards, Jeffrey, 1977, *Swordsmen of the Screen*, London: Routledge & Kegan Paul.

Richards, Jeffrey, 1983, 'Pillars of a Society', in Philip French (ed.), *The Third Dimension*, London: The Stourton Press.

Richards, Jeffrey, 1988, *Happiest Days: The Public Schools in English Fiction*, Manchester: Manchester University Press.

Richards, Jeffrey, 1989, *The Age of the Dream Palace: Cinema and Society in Britain, 1930–1939*, London and New York: Routledge.

Roberts, David, 1979, *Paternalism in Early Victorian England*, London: Croom Helm.

Roberts, Field-Marshall Earl, 1912, *Lord Roberts' Message to the Nation*, London: John Murray, Albermarle Street, W.

Roberts, James, 1990, *The Counter-Revolution in France, 1787–1830*, London: Macmillan.

Rodríguez, Ileana (ed.), 2001, *The Latin American Subaltern Studies Reader*, Durham, NC: Duke University Press.

Rogers, Everett M., 1969, *Modernization among Peasants: The Impact of Communication*, New York: Holt, Rinehart and Winston, Inc.

Rogers, Samuel, 1830, *Italy, a Poem*, London: T. Cadell, The Strand.

Ronfeldt, David, 1973, *Atencingo: The Politics of Agrarian Struggle in a Mexican Ejido*, Stanford, CA: Stanford University Press.

Röpke, Wilhelm, 1948, *Civitas Humana*, London: William Hodge.

Röpke, Wilhelm, 1950, *The Social Crisis of Our Time*, Glasgow: William Hodge & Co.

Röpke, Wilhelm, 1960, *A Humane Economy: The Social Framework of the Free Market*, London: Oswald Wolff (Publishers) Ltd.

Rose, W.S., 1819, 'Letters from the North of Italy, addressed to Henry Hallam, esq.', in Anonymous (1919).

Ross, Alan (ed.), 1984, *The Penguin Cricketer's Companion*, Harmondsworth: Penguin Books.

Rothbard, M. 1982, *The Ethics of Liberty*, Atlantic Highlands, NJ: Humanities Press.

Rubin, Isaac Ilyich, 1979 [1929], *A History of Economic Thought* (translated and edited by Donald Filtzer), London: Ink Links.

Rus, Jan, 1994, 'The "Comunidad Revolucionaria Institucional": The Subversion of Native Government in Highland Chiapas, 1936-1968', in Gilbert M. Joseph and Daniel Nugent (eds.) [1994].

Rutherford, Jonathan (ed.), 1990, *Identity: Community, Culture, Difference*, London: Lawrence & Wishart.

Saavedra, Marco Estrada, 2007, 'The "Armed Community in Rebellion": Neo-Zapatismo in the Tojolab'al Cañadas, Chiapas (1988–96)', in Sarah Washbrook (ed.).

Sala, George Augustus, 1887, *A Journey due South: Travels in Search of Sunshine*, London: Vizetelly & Co.

Salomon, Sir Walter, 1983, *Fair Warning*, London: The Churchill Press Limited.

Salovesh, Michael, 1979, 'Looking Beyond the Municipio in Chiapas: Problems and Prospects in Studying Up', in Robert Hinshaw (ed.), *Currents in Anthropology: Essays in Honour of Sol Tax*, The Hague: Mouton Publishers.

Salvadori, Massimo, 1979, *Karl Kautsky and the Socialist Revolution 1880–1938*, London: New Left Books.

Sánchez, Rodrigo, 1977, 'The Model of Verticality in the Andean Economy: A Critical Reconsideration', *Bulletin of the Society for Latin American Studies* No. 27.

Sánchez, Rodrigo, 1982, 'The Andean Economic System and Capitalism', in A.D. Lehmann (ed.), *Ecology and Exchange in the Andes*, Cambridge: Cambridge University Press.

Sánchez-Jáuregui, María Dolores and Scott Wilcox (eds.), 2012, *The English Prize: The Capture of The Westmorland, An Episode of the Grand Tour*, New Haven, CT: Yale University Press.

Santayana, George, 1952, *Dominations and Powers: Reflections on Liberty and Government*, London: Constable and Company.

Sartre, Jean-Paul, 2000, 'Venice from My Window', in *Modern Times: Selected Non-Fiction* (translated by Robin Buss, edited by Geoffrey Wall), London: Penguin Books.

Saul, John S., 1976, 'African Peasantries and Revolutionary Change', in Joseph Spielberg and Scott Whiteford (eds.), *Forging Nations: A Comparative View of Rural Ferment and Revolt*, Michigan, MI: Michigan State University Press.

Schäffle, A., 1892, *The Impossibility of Social Democracy*, London: Swan Sonnenschein & Co.

Schuettinger, Robert (ed.), 1970, *The Conservative Tradition in European Thought*, New York: G.P. Putnam's Sons.

Scott, James C., 1976, *The Moral Economy of the Peasant: Rebellion and Subsistence in Southeast Asia*, London and New Haven, CT: Yale University Press.

Scott, James C., 1985, *Weapons of the Weak: Everyday Forms of Peasant Resistance*, London and New Haven, CT: Yale University Press.

Scott, James C., 1990, *Domination and the Arts of Resistance: Hidden Transcripts*, New Haven, CT: Yale University Press.

Scott, James C., 2009, *The Art of Not Being Governed: An Anarchist History of Southeast Asia*, London and New Haven, CT: Yale University Press.

Scruton, Roger, 2000, *England: An Elegy*, London: Chatto and Windus.

Scruton, Roger, 2001, 'A Conservative View of the Countryside', in Michael Sissons (ed.), *A Countryside for All: The Future of Rural Britain*, London: Vintage Books.

Seidler, David, 2010, *The King's Speech: The Shooting Script*, New York: Newmarket Press.

Seldon, Arthur, 1990, *Capitalism*, Oxford: Basil Blackwell.

Sender, John, and Sheila Smith, 1986, *The Development of Capitalism in Africa*, London and New York: Methuen.

Senior, Nassau W., 1863, *Biographical Sketches*, London: Longman, Green, Longman, Roberts, & Green.

Serge, Victor, 1963, *Memoirs of a Revolutionary 1901–1941* (translated and edited by Peter Sedgwick), London: Oxford University Press.

Serge, Victor, 2004, *Collected Writings on Literature and Revolution* (translated and edited by Al Richardson), London: Francis Boutle Publishers.

Shachtman, Max, 2003, *Race and Revolution*, London and New York: Verso.

Shakespeare, Nicholas, 1999, *Bruce Chatwin*, London: Harvill.

Shaw, George Bernard, 1931, 'The Apple Cart', *The Complete Plays*, London: Constable.

Shaw, George Bernard, 1934, 'The Apple Cart', *The Complete Prefaces*, London: Constable.

Shinn, William T. Jr., 1987, *Decline of the Russian Peasant Household*, Washington, DC: The Centre for Strategic and International Studies, Georgetown University.

Shonfield, Andrew, 1958, *British Economic Policy Since the War*, Harmondsworth: Penguin Books.

Siddiqa, Ayesha, 2007, *Military Inc.: Inside Pakistan's Military Economy*, London: Pluto Press.

Smith, Adam, 1812 [1776], *An Inquiry into the Nature and Causes of the Wealth of Nations*, Vol. III, London: Cadell and Davies.

Smuts, Jan Christian, 1930, *Africa and Some World Problems*, Oxford: Clarendon Press.

Snowman, Daniel, 2007, *Historians*, Basingstoke: Palgrave Macmillan.

Solomon, Susan Gross, 1977, *The Soviet Agrarian Debate: A Controversy in Social Science, 1923–1929*, Boulder, CO: Westview Press.

Sombart, Werner, 1937, *A New Social Philosophy*, Princeton, NJ: Princeton University Press.

Sorensen, Colin, 1996, *London on Film: One Hundred Years of Filmmaking in London*, London: Museum of London.

South American Missionary Society, 1890, *Missionary Magazine*, Vol. XXIV.

Spencer, Herbert, 1884, *Man versus the State*, London: Williams & Norgate.

Spender, Stephen, 1958, *Engaged in Writing*, London: Hamish Hamilton.

Spender, Stephen, 1985, *Journals 1939–1983* (edited by John Goldsmith), London and Boston, MA: Faber and Faber.

Spivak, Gayatri Chakravorty, 1994, 'How to Read a "Culturally Different" Book', in Francis Barker, Peter Hulme and Margaret Iversen (eds.) [1994].

Stallybrass, Peter, and Allon White, 1986, *The Politics and Poetics of Transgression*, London: Methuen.

Starr, Frederick, 1899, *Catalogue of a Collection of Objects illustrating the Folklore of Mexico*, London: The Folklore Society.

Stein, Maurice R., 1964, *The Eclipse of Community: An Interpretation of American Studies*, New York: Harper & Row, Publishers.

Stephen, Lynn, 2002, *Zapata Lives! Histories and Cultural Politics in Southern Mexico*, Berkeley, CA: University of California Press.

Stern, S. (ed.), 1987, *Resistance, Rebellion, and Consciousness in the Andean Peasant World*, Madison, WI: University of Wisconsin Press.

Stichter, Sharon, 1985, *Migrant Labourers* (African Society Today), Cambridge: Cambridge University Press.

Stoppard, Tom, 2012, *Parade's End – A television drama based on the novel by Ford Madox Ford*, London: Faber and Faber.

Stoye, John Walter, 1952, *English Travellers Abroad 1604–1667: Their Influence in English Society and Politics*, London: Jonathan Cape.

Strachey, John, 1934, 'The Education of a Communist', *Left Review*, 3 (December).

Strong, Roy, 1996, *Country Life 1897–1997: The English Arcadia*, London: Boxtree.

Suárez, Modesto (ed.), 1990, *Historia, Antropología y Política: Homenaje a Ángel Palerm*, (Vol. 1), México, D.F.: Alianza Editorial Mexicana.

Subcomandante Marcos, 2001, *Our Word is Our Weapon: Selected Writings*, London: Serpent's Tail.

Suetonius, Gaius, 1957, *The Twelve Caesars* (translated by Robert Graves), Harmondsworth: Penguin Books.

Swindell, Ken, 1985, *Farm Labour* (African Society Today), Cambridge: Cambridge University Press.

Tavanti, Marco, 2003, *Las Abejas: Pacifist Resistance and Syncretic Identities in a Globalizing Chiapas*, London and New York: Routledge.

Tax, Sol (ed.), 1952, *Heritage of Conquest: The Ethnology of Middle America*, Glencoe, ILL: The Free Press.

Taylor, John Russell, 1970, 'The Go-Between', *Sight and Sound*, Vol. 39, No. 4.

Taylor, John Russell (ed.), 1974, *Masterworks of the British Cinema (Brief Encounter, The Third Man, Kind Hearts and Coronets, Saturday Night and Sunday Morning)*, London: Lorrimer Publishing.

Terray, Emmanuel, 1972, *Marxism and "Primitive" Societies*, New York: Monthly Review Press.

Terray, Emmanuel, 1975, 'Classes and Class Consciousness in the Abron Kingdom of Gyaman', in Maurice Bloch (ed.), *Marxist Analyses and Social Anthropology*, London: Malaby Press.

Thackeray, William Makepeace, 1906, *The New Sketch Book: Being Essays Now Collected from "The Foreign Quarterly Review"* (edited/introduced by Robert S. Garnett), London: Alston Rivers, Ltd., Arundel Street, w.c.

Thakurdas, Sir Purshotamdas, J.D.R. Tata, G.D. Birla, Sir Ardeshir Dalal, Sir Shri Ram, Kasturbhai Lalbhai, A.D. Shroff, and John Matthai, 1945, *Memorandum Outlining a Plan of Economic Development for India (Parts 1 and 2)*, Harmondsworth: Penguin Books.

Theroux, Paul, 1998, *Sir Vidia's Shadow: A Friendship across Five Continents*, London: Hamish Hamilton.

Thesiger, Wilfred, 1988, *The Life of My Choice*, Glasgow: FontanaCollins.

Thesiger, Wilfred, 2005 [1964], *The Marsh Arabs*, London: The Folio Society.

Thomas, Christopher, 2012, *Venice in Solitude* (edited by Ira Stehmann, with poems by Albert Ostermaier, translated from the German by Kevin A. Perryman), Munich, London and New York: Prestel.

Thomas, Hugh (ed.), 1972, *José Antonio Primo de Rivera: Selected Writings*, London: Jonathan Cape.

Thompson, E.P., 1965, *The Making of the English Working Class*, London: Victor Gollancz, Ltd.

Thompson, F.M.L., 1963, *English Landed Society in the Nineteenth Century*, London: Routledge & Kegan Paul.

Thorner, Alice, 1982, 'Semi-Feudalism or Capitalism? Contemporary Debate on Classes and Modes of Production in India', *Economic and Political Weekly*, Vol. XVII, Nos. 49–51.

Tocqueville, Alexis de, 1959 [1835], *Democracy in America* (edited with an introduction by Henry Steele Commager), London: Oxford University Press.

Todorov, Tzvetan, 1984, *Mikhail Bakhtin: The Dialogical Principle*, Manchester: Manchester University Press.

Toor, Frances, 1947, *Mexican Folkways*, New York: Crown Publishers.

Torner, Eduardo M., 1924, *Cuarenta Canciones Españolas*, Madrid: La Residencia de Estudiantes.

Toynbee, Arnold, 1902, 'Industry and Democracy' [1881], in *Lectures on the Industrial Revolution of the 18th Century in England: Popular Addresses, Notes and Other Fragments*, London, New York and Bombay: Longmans, Green, and Co.

Traven, B., 1974, *The Rebellion of the Hanged*, New York: Hill and Wang.

Traven, B., 1981, *The Carreta*, London: Allison & Busby.

Traven, B., 1982, *March to the Monteria*, Allison & Busby.

Traven, B., 1994, *Trozas*, Allison & Busby.

Trotsky, Leon, 1930, *My Life*, London: Thornton Butterworth, Limited.

Trotsky, Leon, 1934, *The History of the Russian Revolution* (translated by Max Eastman), London: Victor Gollancz, Ltd.

Trotsky, Leon, 1936, *The Third International After Lenin*, New York: Pioneer Publishers.

Trotsky, Leon, 1953, *The First Five Years of the Communist International*, Volume II, New York: Pioneer Publishers.

Trotsky, Leon, 1975 [1934], *The Struggle Against Fascism in Germany*, Harmondsworth: Penguin Books, Ltd.

Turner, Michael, 2000, 'Corporate Strategy or Individual Priority? Land Management, Income and Tenure on Oxbridge Agricultural Land in the Mid-Nineteenth Century', *Business History*, Vol. 42, No. 4.

Tynan, Kenneth, 1975, 'The Judicious Observer will be Disgusted', in *The Sound of Two Hands Clapping*, London: Jonathan Cape.

van der Haar, Gemma, 2007, 'Land Reform, the State, and the Zapatista Uprising in Chiapas', in Sarah Washbrook (ed.).

Velasco, Adolfo, 1940, *La Escuela Indigenal de Warisata, Bolivia: Escuela de Recuperación Indígena de Caiza, Bolivia*, Mexico: Departamento de Asuntos Indigenas.

Venturi, Franco, 1960, *Roots of Revolution: A History of Populist and Socialist Movements in Nineteenth Century Russia* (translated from the Italian by Francis Haskell), London: Weidenfeld and Nicolson.

Verba, Sidney, 1989, 'On Revisiting The Civic Culture: A Personal Postscript', in Gabriel A. Almond and Sidney Verba (eds.) [1989].

Villafuerte Solís, Daniel, 2007, 'Rural Chiapas Ten Years after the Armed Uprising of 1994: An Economic Overview', in Sarah Washbrook (ed.).

Vio, Ettore (ed.), 2003, *St. Mark's: The Art and Architecture of Church and State in Venice*, New York: Riverside Book Company, Inc.

Vološinov, V.N., 1976, *Freudianism: A Marxist Critique*, New York: Academic Press.

von Mises, Ludwig, 1945, *Bureaucracy*, London: William Hodge & Company, Ltd.

Walicki, Andrzej, 1969, *The Controversy over Capitalism: Studies in the Social Philosophy of the Russian Populists*, Oxford: Clarendon Press.

Walicki, Andrzej, 1975, *The Slavophile Controversy: History of a Conservative Utopia in Nineteenth Century Russian Thought* (translated from the Polish by Hilda Andrews-Rusiecka), Oxford: Clarendon Press.

Walicki, Andrzej, 1980, *A History of Russian Thought from the Enlightenment to Marxism* (translated from the Polish by Hilda Andrews-Rusiecka), Oxford: Clarendon Press.

Walker, Pat (ed.), 1979, *Between Labour and Capital*, Brighton: The Harvester Press.

Walter, Nicholas, 1969, *About Anarchism*, London: Freedom Press.

Warman, Arturo, 1980, *'We Come to Object': The Peasants of Morelos and the National State*, Baltimore, MD: The Johns Hopkins University Press.

Warman, Arturo, 1983, 'Peasant Production and Population in Mexico', in Joan P. Mencher (ed.), *Social Anthropology of Peasantry*, Bombay: Somaiya Publications.

Warman, Arturo, 1988, 'The Political Project of Zapatismo', in Friedrich Katz (ed.), *Riot, Rebellion, and Revolution: Rural Social Conflict in Mexico*, Princeton, NJ: Princeton University Press.

Warriner, Doreen, 1948, *Land and Poverty in the Middle East*, London and New York: Royal Institute of International Affairs.

Warriner, Doreen, 1957, *Land Reform and Development in the Middle East*, London and New York: Royal Institute of International Affairs.

Warshow, Robert, 1964, *The Immediate Experience: Movies, Comics, Theatre and Other Aspects of Popular Culture*, New York: Anchor Books.

Washbrook, Sarah, 2004, 'Indígenas, exportación y enganche en el norte de Chiapas, 1876-1911', *Mesoamérica*, No. 46.

Washbrook, Sarah (ed.), 2007, *Rural Chiapas Ten Years after the Zapatista Uprising*, London: Routledge.

Watts, Michael J., 1983, *Silent Violence: Food, Famine and Peasantry in Northern Nigeria*, Berkeley, CA: University of California Press.

Watts, Michael J., 1984, 'The Demise of the Moral Economy: Food and Famine in a Sudano-Sahelian Region in Historical Perspective', in E. Scott (ed.), *Life before the Drought*, Boston, MA: Allen & Unwin.

Watts, Michael J., 2007, 'The Sinister Political Life of Community: Economies of Violence and Governable Space in the Niger Delta, Nigeria', at http://globetrotter .berkeley.edu/GreenGovernance/papers/Watts.

Waugh, Evelyn, 1931, *Remote People*, London: Duckworth.

Waugh, Evelyn, 1945, *Brideshead Revisited*, Boston, MA: Little, Brown and Company.

Waugh, Evelyn, 1951 [1946], *When the Going was Good*, Harmondsworth: Penguin Books.

Waugh, Evelyn, 1951a [1928], *Decline and Fall*, Harmondsworth: Penguin Books.

Waugh, Evelyn, 1951b [1930], *Vile Bodies*, Harmondsworth: Penguin Books.

Waugh, Evelyn, 1954 [1938], *Scoop*, Harmondsworth: Penguin Books.

Waugh, Evelyn, 1959, 'An Open Letter to the Hon Mrs Peter Rodd (Nancy Mitford) on a Very Serious Subject', in Nancy Mitford (ed.) [1959].

Waugh, Evelyn, 1962 [1932], *Black Mischief*, Harmondsworth: Penguin Books.

Waugh, Evelyn, 1977, 'Sinking, Shadowed and Sad – the Last Glory of Europe', in *Evelyn Waugh: A Little Order* (edited by Donat Gallagher), London: Eyre Methuen.

Waugh, Evelyn, 1980, *The Letters of Evelyn Waugh* (edited by Mark Amory), London: Weidenfeld and Nicolson.

Waugh, Evelyn, 2003, 'Labels' [1929], in *Waugh Abroad: Collected Travel Writing* (with an Introduction by Nicholas Shakespeare), London: Everyman's Library.

Weinberg, Bill, 2000, *Homage to Chiapas: The New Indigenous Struggles in Mexico*, London: Verso.

Weiner, Myron, 1967, *Party Building in a New Nation: The Indian National Congress*, Chicago, IL: The University of Chicago Press.

Whetten, Nathan L., 1948, *Rural Mexico*, Chicago, ILL: The University of Chicago Press.

White, Arnold, 1901, *Efficiency and Empire*, London: Methuen & Co.

White, Edmund, 2006 [1987], 'Venice Through the Looking Glass', in Lucretia Stewart (ed.),*Travelling Hopefully: A Golden Age of Travel Writing*, London: Theniju.

White, T.H., 1994, *The Age of Scandal*, London: The Folio Society.

Wiener, Antje, 1994, 'Institutionalizing Revolution, Rioting for Reform – Mexican Politics from Zapata to the Zapatistas', *Studies in Political Economy*, No. 44.

Wiener, Jon, 2007, '"Hell is Other People": Ted Turner's Two Million Acres', in Mike Davis and Daniel Bertrand Monk (eds.), *Evil Paradises: Dreamworlds of Neoliberalism*, New York: The New Press.

Wilkie, Raymond, 1971, *San Miguel: A Mexican Collective Ejido*, Stanford, CA: Stanford University Press.

Williams, Gavin, 1970, 'The Social Stratification of a Neo-colonial Economy: Western Nigeria', in Christopher Allen and R.W. Johnson (eds.), *African Perspectives: Papers in the History, Politics and Economics of Africa presented to Thomas Hodgkin*, London: Cambridge University Press.

Williams, Gavin, 1976, 'Taking the Part of Peasants: Rural Development in Nigeria and Tanzania', in Peter Gutkind and Immanuel Wallerstein (eds.), *The Political Economy of Contemporary Africa*, London and Beverley Hills, CA: Sage Publications.

Williams, Gavin, 1977, 'Class Relations in a Neo-colony: The Case of Nigeria', in Peter Gutkind and Peter Waterman (eds.), *African Social Studies*, London: Heinemann.

Williams, Raymond, 1958, 'Culture is ordinary', in Norman Mackenzie (ed.), *Conviction*, London: MacGibbon & Kee.

Wilson, Angus, Edwin Smith, and Olive Cook, 1971, *England*, London: Thames and Hudson.

Withey, Lynne, 1998, *Grand Tours and Cook's Tours: A History of Leisure Travel, 1750 to 1915*, London: Aurum Press, Ltd.

Wolf, Eric R., 1971, *Peasant Wars of the Twentieth Century*, London: Faber and Faber.

Wolf, Eric R., 2001, *Pathways of Power: Building an Anthropology of the Modern World*, London and Berkeley, CA: The University of California Press.

Wolff, Kurt H. (ed.), 1971, *From Karl Mannheim*, New York: Oxford University Press.

Womack, John Jr., 1969, *Zapata and the Mexican Revolution*, New York: Alfred A. Knopf.

Woodhouse, A.S.P. (ed.), 1938, *Puritanism and Liberty: Being the Army Debates (1647–9) from the Clarke Manuscripts*, London: J.M. Dent and Sons Limited.

Woolf, S.J., 1968, 'Venice and the Terraferma: Problems of the Change from Commercial to Landed Activities', in Brian Pullan (ed.), *Crisis and Change in the Venetian Economy in the 16th and 17th Centuries*, London: Methuen & Co., Ltd.

Zamosc, Leon, 1986, *The Agrarian Question and the Peasant Movement in Colombia*, Cambridge: Cambridge University Press.

Zangwill, Israel, 1917, *The Principle of Nationalities*, (Conway Memorial Lecture delivered at South Place Institute on 8th March) London: Watts & Co., Johnson's Court, Fleet Street, EC4.

Zapatista Army of National Liberation, 2002, 'EZLN Demands at the Dialogue Table', in Gilbert M. Joseph and Timothy J. Henderson (eds.), *The Mexico Reader: History, Culture, Politics*, London and Durham, NC: Duke University Press.

Zewde, Bahru, 2001, *A History of Modern Ethiopia, 1855–1991*, Oxford: James Currey.

Zimmerman, J.G., 1800, *Aphorisms and Reflections on Men, Morals and Things*, London: Thomas Maiden.

Zinkin, Maurice, 1956, *Development for Free Asia*, London: Chatto & Windus.

Subject Index

Abyssinia   307, 320–2, 329, 337
Acton, H.B.   92
Afghanistan   133, 208
Africa   11, 14, 20, 29, 56, 97, 134ff., 153–4,
    220, 241, 251, 292–3, 302, 309, 313ff., 321
    passim, 339ff., 380, 382, 392
African National Congress   14
agrarian myth
    African 'bush'   19, 309, 313–5, 321,
        325–7, 340ff., 391–2
    aristocratic/landlord   4, 5, 17, 19, 69, 71,
        73, 97, 103, 105–7, 114–5, 151, 161ff., 173,
        178, 189, 193, 203ff., 206, 217 *passim*, 233,
        242, 247, 260–1, 288, 291, 299, 300,
        310–11, 320, 335, 342, 350, 352ff., 358ff.,
        360, 384, 389ff.
    as Nature   4–5, 34, 42, 64, 67, 76, 95ff.,
        99, 102–4, 106–7, 114, 130–1, 134–5, 146,
        151ff., 181ff., 233–4, 237, 247, 250, 261,
        270, 273, 275, 277ff., 286, 289, 303,
        313ff., 318–9, 324, 333, 343, 351ff.,
        359, 373, 392
    Darwinian   4–5, 14, 18, 20, 157, 163,
        173–4, 178, 181ff., 191, 203–4, 206, 209,
        242, 247, 304, 310, 312ff., 342–3,
        382, 390ff.
    noble savage   14, 40, 151, 290, 308,
        313, 323
    pastoral   4–5, 15, 17, 19, 20, 67, 69, 71,
        105, 141, 151–2, 157, 163, 173, 189–90,
        203ff., 208–9, 217, 232–3, 242, 247,
        260–1, 278, 281, 288–9, 291, 293, 300,
        302, 304ff., 308–10, 312, 315, 320–1,
        332–3, 335, 342–3, 351ff., 360, 382,
        384, 390ff.
    plebeian/peasant   4–5, 17, 20, 23, 27,
        44, 67, 98, 103, 107, 114–5, 152, 174, 178,
        203ff., 206, 209, 217, 242, 247, 313, 335,
        342, 350
agrarian question   24, 65
    campesinista   24, 27, 37, 41–2, 52–3, 55,
        64 (see also Chayanov, *indigenismo*,
        peasantry, populism)
    descampesinista   24, 41, 55 (see also
        class, Lenin, Marxism)

agrarian reform   48, 53, 57, 100–2, 109,
    112–3, 127 (see also land tenure, the State)
Alavi, Hamza   127ff., 135
Albania   339, 374
Albó, Xavier   139–40
Allen, Woody   186
Amis, Kingsley   176, 194, 293ff., 306, 311,
    329ff., 343, 381
Anderson, Perry   198–200
anthropology   38–40, 199, 248ff., 317, 384
Argentina   109, 110ff., 151, 313, 315, 326ff.,
    339 (see also Tierra del Fuego)
aristocracy   12–3, 19, 68, 70, 72ff., 97–8, 114,
    162, 169 *passim*, 186 *passim*, 197–8, 201, 203
    passim, 220 *passim*, 235–6, 242, 257–8,
    264ff., 286, 305, 307, 320, 334, 359–60, 362,
    372, 378, 389–90 (see also agrarian myth,
    class, Grand Tour, land tenure, monarchy)
    Bedford, Duke of   172, 239
    Bolingbroke, Viscount   71
    cosmopolitanism   13, 19, 67–8, 97, 174,
        199, 247 *passim*, 262 *passim*, 284, 288,
        341, 359, 382, 390–1 (see also identity,
        Grand Tour)
    Devonshire, Duchess of   75, 338
    Devonshire, Duke of   74–5
    Marlborough, Duke of   239
    Northumberland, Duke of   172,
        239, 258
    Portsmouth, Earl of   104
    Westminster, Duke of   239
Australia   56, 74, 213, 318
Austria   30, 33–4, 126, 301, 330

Bacon, Francis   260–1
Bagehot, Walter   70, 166–7, 187
Baker, Kenneth   161
Bakhtin, Mikhail   162, 164, 188
Baldwin, Stanley   168
Baüer, Otto   30–5
BBC   195, 212–3, 240, 251, 365
Beerbohm, Max   364
Belgium   135, 313
Bergson, Henri   286
Berlin, Isaiah   282

Beveridge Report   236
Blair, Tony   72, 121, 214
Blanco, Hugo   41
Blunden, Edmund   104
Bluntschli, Johann Kaspar   29, 90
Bolivia   41, 42, 44, 49, 109–10, 115–6, 380
Bolshevism   33, 108, 111, 117, 120, 122,
     126–7, 154, 206, 217, 302, 335–6 (see also
     Communism, Russia, Socialism)
Boswell, James   248, 263, 273
Brass, Anna Luisa   iv, ix, 344, 351, 356, 361,
     371, 383
Brass, Denis   ix, 186
Brazil   16, 140, 210, 308, 337
Bridges, E. Lucas   151–2, 293, 310ff.,
     334–5, 343
British Honduras   309
Brown, Horatio   345, 347–8, 355, 359,
     363–4
Bulgaria   309, 338
Burke, Edmund   263, 269
Burke, Kenneth   142–3
Byron, Robert   252, 293–4, 302ff., 308, 317,
     320, 331, 335–6, 342–3
Byzantium   359, 373

Calvo Sotelo, José   102, 107
Cameron, David   72, 241
Canada   56, 84
Canning, George   72, 78–9, 81
Čapek, Karel   350, 366, 369–70
Capital
     finance   4, 33, 60, 75–6, 97ff., 102ff., 110,
          115, 216 passim, 247
     industrial   4, 9, 13, 24, 33, 60, 68, 73–4,
          82, 87, 97, 99ff., 112, 114, 126, 136, 145, 148,
          151, 168, 174, 285, 290, 293, 302, 304, 311,
          320ff., 330, 336–7, 342–3, 355, 357, 360,
          372, 375, 391 (see also colonialism,
          communism, imperialism)
capitalism   7, 11–2, 18, 23–4, 26–7, 30,
     32–3, 36–7, 40, 42–3, 48, 52, 55, 59, 62, 65,
     67–8, 73, 75, 85–7, 93–4, 100ff., 110, 114, 116,
     120–1, 127–8, 132, 135ff., 141, 144, 155–6, 170,
     229, 234, 236, 247, 286, 288, 315, 372, 374–5,
     380, 388ff. (see also class, communism,
     feudalism, socialism)
Caribbean   23, 308–9, 313, 315, 318, 339

Carpenter, Edward   145
cartoonists
     Garland, Nicholas   17, 295
     Gillray, James   161
     Searle, Ronald   187
Chatterjee, Partha   144–6, 148
Chatwin, Bruce   14
Chayanov, A.V.   41, 52, 126–7, 355
Chiapas   6, 18, 23 passim, 37 passim,
     45 passim, 64–6, 91, 118, 387 (see also
     Subcomandante Marcos, Zapatista Army
     of National Liberation)
Chile   62, 113, 151
China   30, 48, 53, 128–9, 141, 252, 302, 320,
     331, 363, 372
citizenship   44, 80, 86, 90ff., 119, 121, 130,
     131–2, 142ff., 147–8, 156, 203, 218, 274, 310,
     317, 388 (see also civil society, democracy,
     modernity)
civil society   18, 77–8, 95, 118ff., 125, 127,
     129, 130ff., 137, 140, 144, 145ff., 155–6, 388–9
civil war
     American   94, 163
     English   78, 123, 261
     Spanish   ix, 173, 337, 338
Class
     consciousness   1–3, 11–3, 30–1, 34, 66,
          86, 113, 116, 132, 137–8, 167–8, 196, 202,
          204, 243, 266 (see also capitalism,
          identity, nationalism, populism)
     formation   2, 4, 8, 12, 14, 99, 102, 118,
          125, 127, 168, 198, 218, 248, 253ff., 256
          passim, 265 passim, 288ff., 320, 322,
          353, 388 (see also mob-in-the-street,
          peasant differentiation)
     other-as-tourist   295–6, 302, 321,
          329–32, 349–50, 362–4, 366, 368, 375–7,
          380–3, 385, 390 (see also mass tourism,
          mob-in-the-streets)
     self-as-traveller   19, 247, 258–60, 264,
          266, 292, 294ff., 307, 321, 324–5, 328,
          329–31, 341, 343, 349, 364, 366, 370–1,
          383, 385, 390–1 (see also Grand Tour)
     struggle   2–5, 7 passim, 15, 17–20, 44,
          60, 69, 94, 100, 103, 109, 110, 113, 115,
          137–8, 155ff., 165 passim, 185 passim,
          204 passim, 243, 247 passim, 253
          passim, 266, 282, 288ff., 342, 358,

384, 388ff. (see also identity, populism, revolution)

Colgate, Isabel 215

Colombia 52, 132

colonialism 3, 15, 19, 28, 42, 44, 51, 56, 64–5, 127–9, 134, 145, 147, 153, 163, 165, 173–5, 185ff., 192ff., 199–201, 205, 207ff., 218, 221, 230–1, 233, 241ff., 259, 268, 293, 297–8, 301, 314, 316, 323, 327–8, 339, 389 (see also imperialism, nationalism)

post-colonialism 2, 51, 122, 127–8, 134

communism 11, 32, 53, 59–60, 92, 104, 108, 242, 283, 287, 336, 338, 355, 374

community, rural 25, 27–8, 31–2, 34, 38ff., 46, 50ff., 54, 65, 83, 95, 100ff., 104, 127, 139–40, 145, 155, 233, 266, 288, 290, 323, 363, 387

Congo 301–2, 313, 319, 326, 328, 341

Conrad, Joseph 313, 325–6

conservatism 1, 7, 14, 18, 45, 56, 59, 65, 67ff., 76ff., 81, 84 passim, 100 passim, 108 passim, 124, 131, 135, 140, 165, 168, 176, 178, 182, 189, 195, 198–9, 204, 212, 232, 236, 240–1, 243, 247, 264–5, 267, 281 passim, 305, 308, 324, 333, 337, 350, 373, 386ff. (see also agrarian myth)

Conservative Party 68–9, 71, 195, 212, 240–1

cooperatives 33, 38, 48–9, 53, 111, 136, 358

Crete 298–9, 308, 338

cricket 221, 223, 227ff., 297

crop
coffee 43, 45–6, 50, 54–5
maize 39, 45, 54, 325, 358
prices 33, 52–3, 55–7, 74, 82, 88, 104, 352, 355
viticulture 146, 351–2, 358, 359

cultural turn 3–4, 6, 11, 30–1, 118–9, 138, 141, 256, 388, 392 (see also agrarian myth, 'new' populist postmodernism)

culture
as education 32, 44, 130, 137, 180, 187, 257ff., 262, 264, 271–2, 275, 277, 282, 296, 322, 346, 381
as empowerment, disempowerment 1–2, 6, 18–9, 24–5, 29–31, 34, 44, 47, 51, 63–6, 106–7, 118–9, 122, 135, 137, 139, 144, 150ff., 154ff., 161 passim,

173 passim, 185 passim, 198ff., 203 passim, 219, 231, 233, 235ff., 240, 242–3, 257, 277, 386, 387, 388, 389ff. (see also agrarian myth, 'new' populist postmodernism, peasantry)

deferential 68, 105, 214, 219, 223, 235, 280–1, 285, 293, 360, 375
high 199
low 385

Darré, Richard Walther 99

Debray, Régis 346, 366, 370, 379ff., 385

democracy viii, 18, 25–7, 30, 48, 61ff., 68, 72, 74, 76, 78–81, 84, 86, 89, 92–4, 115, 121ff., 130ff., 135, 144–5, 147, 155–6, 284, 286–7, 316, 322–3, 327, 342, 379, 387–8 (see also capitalism, citizenship, civil society, class, nationalism)

redemocratization 12, 144, 156, 388 (see also agrarian myth)

development theory 14, 122, 130, 136–7, 143, 149 (see also modernity)

Disraeli, Benjamin 8, 10, 67ff., 78, 115, 217

Donoso Cortés, Juan 284–5

Dumont, Margaret 292

economic crisis 11, 13, 43, 45, 52, 55, 57–9, 74, 99–102, 109–10, 112, 168, 183, 193, 237, 297 (see also capitalism)

Ecuador 42, 61

Eden, Frederic 350ff., 356, 384

Edgar, David 105

egalitarianism 6, 8, 28, 40, 44, 72–3, 98, 115, 119, 124, 127, 155, 206, 213, 217, 237, 277 (see also democracy, populism, rural community)

Egypt 37, 83, 206, 369

empire 26, 30, 39, 56, 68–71, 89, 91–2, 96–7, 193, 206, 209, 211, 214, 238, 242, 249, 259, 261, 299, 334, 359, 366 (see also colonialism, imperialism, Multitude)

England 8, 16, 56, 66–7, 71ff., 75, 77ff., 85, 90ff., 94, 97, 105–6, 114–5, 124, 161, 168–9, 171, 177, 182, 184, 190, 192, 197, 215 passim, 232, 236, 238, 248, 254, 257, 259ff., 264, 269, 283, 295ff., 302, 304ff., 309–10, 312, 320ff., 335–6, 343, 355, 357, 389

Englishness   16, 69, 72, 105–6, 188, 192–3,
    197, 208, 256–7, 297, 317, 360 (see also
    identity, nationalism)
Enlightenment   2–3, 87, 95–6, 98, 109,
    146, 164, 174, 269 passim, 277–8, 286, 386
    (see egalitarianism, Herder, modernity,
    Romanticism)
Ethiopia   307–8, 321–2, 329, 337
Europe
    Common Agricultural Policy   239
    Eurocentrism   1, 3, 123, 150, 164, 271,
        277, 289, 341, 386, 392
Evelyn, John   261–2
Evola, Julius   76, 85, 120, 140–1
EZLN (see Chiapas, Subcomandante Marcos,
    Zapatista Army of National Liberation)

Falange
    Bolivian   109
    Chilean   113
    Spanish   100ff., 107–8, 113
fascism
    Argentine Patriotic League   110–2
    BUF   100
    Franco, Francisco   58
    Hitler, Adolf   58, 143, 186, 301
    Mussolini, Benito   58, 84, 112, 335, 371
    Salazar, Antonio   58
feudalism   8, 10, 13, 27, 33, 42, 52, 73, 96,
    99, 101, 105, 120, 127–9, 150, 170, 211, 263,
    275, 337, 388 (see also capitalism,
    communism, socialism)
    semi-feudalism   128
film directors
    Altman, Robert   204
    Anderson, Lindsay   190, 203
    Ashby, Hal   349
    Baker, Roy Ward   176
    Boulting, John   192, 195, 197, 201
    Boulting, Roy   195, 196–7, 201
    Bridges, Alan   212, 242
    Calvacanti, Alberto   192
    Capra, Frank   207
    Chaplin, Charlie   186
    Coppola, Francis Ford   210
    De Sica, Vittorio   365
    Fellini, Federico   365
    Fleming, Victor   206

Frears, Stephen   211
Gilbert, Lewis   184, 189
Griffiths, D.W.   206
Guest, Val   176
Hamer, Robert   190, 196
Heerman, Victor   292
Hitchcock, Alfred   296
Hooper, Tom   211
Hopper, Jerry   206
Houston, John   207
Jones, Terry   194
Launder, Frank   187–8
Lean, David   365
Losey, Joseph   212, 219, 242, 365
Madden, John   204
McLeod, Norman Z.   186
Minghella, Anthony   365
Mitchell, Roger   197
Montaldoa, Giuliano   365
Newell, Mike   197
Noyce, Philip   209
Radford, Michael   365
Reed, Carol   166
Roeg, Nicolas   365
Sen, Mrinal   203
Spielberg, Stephen   185, 201,
    206–7, 365
Tashlin, Frank   186
Thomas, Gerald   193
Tourneur, Jacques   176
Visconti, Luchino   365
Weir, Peter   184
Welles, Orson   365
Wright, Joe   219
film genres
    film noir   171–2
    horror   161 passim, 200–1, 205, 209, 231,
        242, 343, 380, 389
    humour   161 passim, 185 passim, 201,
        231, 297, 350
    science fiction   181ff.
    supernatural   166, 168, 173 passim,
        181ff., 201, 206, 231, 234–5, 242, 243
film images
    disempowering (see film genre/humour)
    empowering (see film genre/horror)
    'fiends'   18, 161 passim, 185 passim,
        200–5, 209, 242, 389

'fools' 19, 185 *passim*, 200–5, 226, 231, 242, 389, 390

'friends' 19, 69, 77, 201 *passim*, 211 *passim*, 226, 236, 241ff., 389ff.

Films

Animal Crackers (1930) 292

Apocalypse Now Redux (2002) 205, 209–11, 242

Atonement (2007) 219

Being There (1979) 349

Birth of a Nation (1915) 206

Blue Murder at St. Trinian's (1957) 187–8

Brothers in Law (1957) 195

Carleton-Browne of the FO (1958) 165, 192–3

Carry on Up the Khyber (1968) 165, 193

Casanova (1976) 365

Death in Venice (1971) 365

Don Giovanni (1979) 365

Don't Look Now (1973) 365

Duck Soup (1933) 117

Father Brown (1954) 196–7

Four Weddings and a Funeral (1994) 165, 197–8

Giordano Bruno (1973) 365

Gone With the Wind (1939) 206

Gosford Park (2001) 186, 204, 210–1, 242

Heavens Above! (1963) 195–7

HMS Defiant (1962) 184

Il Viaggio (1974) 365

Ill Met by Moonlight (1957) 298

I'm All Right Jack (1959) 195–6

Indiana Jones and the Last Crusade (1989) 365

Indiana Jones and the Temple of Doom (1984) 193, 205ff., 209, 211, 243

Kind Hearts and Coronets (1949) 161, 165, 190–92

Lost Horizon (1937) 207

Master and Commander (2003) 184

Monty Python and The Holy Grail (1975) 194

Monty Python's Life of Brian (1979) 194

Mrs Brown (1997) 204

Night of the Demon (1957) 176

Night Train to Munich (1940) 297

Notting Hill (1999) 197

Othello (1952) 365

Pure Hell of St. Trinian's (1960) 187–8

Quatermass and the Pit (1967) 176–7, 181ff.

Quatermass II (1956) 176–7

Quatermass Xperiment (1954) 176–7

Raiders of the Lost Ark (1981) 165, 185

Senso (1954) 365

Son of Paleface (1952) 186

Summertime (1955) 365

The Admirable Crichton (1957) 189

The Belles of St. Trinian's (1954) 187–8

The Go-Between (1970) 205, 212–3, 217 *passim*, 229 *passim*, 236, 241

The Great Dictator (1940) 186

The King's Speech (2011) 204–5, 211, 212–4, 236–7, 241

The Lady Vanishes (1938) 188, 296ff.

The Man Who Would Be King (1975) 205, 207ff.

The Merchant of Venice (2004) 365

The Paleface (1948) 186

The Queen (2006) 204–5, 211, 214–5, 236

The Quiet American (2002) 205, 209ff., 242

The Secret of the Incas (1954) 206–7

The Shooting Party (1985) 205, 212, 215–16

The Talented Mr Ripley (1999) 365

The Third Man (1949) 166

Went the Day Well? (1943) 192

Ford, Ford Madox 216

foundation myth 42, 44, 146–7, 166, 206 (see also agrarian myth, identity, nationalism, populism)

France 19, 37, 56, 72, 80, 85, 88–9, 97, 114–5, 139, 142, 146, 149, 221, 241, 248, 255–6, 260, 265, 267, 269–70, 280, 284, 290, 317, 322, 376–7, 380

franchise 1, 7, 62, 66, 69–70, 72, 76, 81–2, 84, 92, 100, 114, 124, 132, 251, 284 (see also class struggle, democracy, the State)

Futurism 372ff., 379, 384

Gandhi, M.K. 144–6
gangmaster system   94, 238–9 (see also
    migration)
García Canclini, Néstor   140
Gardiner, Rolf   104
Germany   4, 77, 79, 84, 90, 96, 98–100, 102,
    115–6, 126, 186, 192, 213–4, 260, 280, 297,
    300, 337, 368ff.
Giddens, Tony   121, 200
Goldring, Douglas   345, 347, 351, 367–9,
    372
governance, good   12
Grahame, Georgina   293, 305, 310, 322,
    329, 334, 348, 353, 358, 369
Grand Tour   13, 19, 174, 199, 247 passim,
    257 passim, 268 passim, 280, 284, 288–92,
    294, 300, 320, 341, 359–60, 381–2, 390ff.
    and aristocratic distinction   67–8, 174,
        257–8, 262ff., 267–8, 289, 291, 359, 383,
        391
    and classical antiquity   258–9, 261–2,
        266, 289, 359
Graves, Robert   188, 294–6, 329, 331, 333,
    343, 381
Greece   249, 262, 272, 302–3, 323ff., 330,
    338
Green, Russell   249–50, 345, 348ff., 360–1,
    367, 369–70
Guatemala   37, 43
Guenon, René   140–1
guerrillas   23, 55, 63, 117, 340, 380
Guiton, Shirley   351, 353ff., 356ff., 363, 384

Haiti   327
Harte, Glynn Boyd   344, 366, 368, 370
Hartley, L.P. 218 passim, 234 passim
Hayek, F.A. 6, 92–4, 103
Herder, Johann Gottfried   15, 19, 248,
    268 passim, 277–80, 286ff., 301, 317,
    384–5 (see also agrarian myth,
    nationalism)
Herzen, Alexander   15, 19, 248, 268, 270,
    279–80 passim, 317, 334, 384–5 (see also
    agrarian myth, peasants, populism)
Holland   259, 273, 317
Hope, Bob   186
human rights   18, 26, 50–1, 61–2, 65, 387
Hungary   84, 299, 338

Hyndman, H.M.   91
hypergamy   219–20

identity
    ethnic   2, 4, 11, 23, 28–31, 34–40, 42–4,
        46–7, 50, 59, 61–3, 65, 69, 84, 87, 91,
        101–2, 109, 113, 122, 133–5, 139–40, 144,
        149–50, 155, 157, 207, 221, 234, 247, 251,
        253, 256, 271, 285, 288, 302, 304, 307–8,
        316–8, 324, 335, 342–3, 366–7, 387 (see
        also agrarian myth, nationalism)
    gender   26, 34, 47, 50–2, 54–5, 65, 82,
        113–4, 168, 175, 182–3, 197, 219–20, 233–4,
        271, 303, 313, 358, 362, 365, 369,
        379–80, 382
    indianismo   43
    indigenismo   24, 37–8, 40ff., 44–5,
        51–2, 65, 140 (see also agrarian myth)
    kinship   4, 24, 41, 50, 52, 54, 79, 98, 100,
        102–3, 105, 106, 108–10, 113–4, 126–7, 130,
        140, 145, 149, 155, 190, 192, 196, 206, 210,
        216–8, 222, 225, 227, 234, 264, 269,
        273–4, 276, 278, 286, 289–90, 299–300,
        305–6, 313, 322, 324, 334, 338, 353–4,
        376, 378
    mestizo   44, 47, 292
    national   2, 4, 11, 29, 31, 34, 44, 65, 69,
        87, 91, 109, 122, 133, 149, 247, 253, 256,
        285, 316, 372
    regional   4, 32, 35, 48, 64, 76, 101, 118–9,
        134, 138, 140, 142, 152, 156, 208, 269, 272,
        309, 355, 358
    tribal   29, 40, 134, 151, 153–4, 208,
        249–51, 277, 305–6, 308, 311, 313, 316,
        322, 335, 366
imperialism   15, 19, 26, 30, 42, 56, 60, 64,
    70ff., 91, 104, 128–9, 145, 165, 173, 175, 192,
    204ff., 217, 230ff., 241ff., 323 (see also
    colonialism, nationalism)
India   17, 52, 55–6, 84, 90, 94, 112–3,
    122, 128, 131, 139, 141, 144ff., 149, 152, 175, 179,
    185, 193–4, 206ff., 211, 237, 243, 295, 318, 320,
    323, 378
    new farmers' movements   ix, 55ff., 144
Inkatha   14
internationalism   viii, 4, 12, 37, 65, 92, 115,
    184, 258ff., 270, 276, 289, 376, 382 (see also
    cosmopolitanism, socialism)

Iraq 252, 321
Isherwood, Christopher 16
Islam 141
Israel 37, 70
Italy 4, 84, 108, 121, 138, 258 *passim*, 269,
281, 290, 292–3, 300, 305, 322, 329, 334,
348, 352–3, 355, 360, 362, 374, 378
(see also Grand Tour, Venice)

James, Henry 252, 345–50, 360–4,
368, 381
James, M.R. 168, 176 *passim*, 201, 206, 231,
234–5, 242, 343
Japan 4, 43, 56–7, 84, 152, 318, 320, 366ff.,
370, 381, 383
Jews 69–70, 97, 102, 110–1, 114, 177, 179, 196,
221, 234, 382

Kenya 323, 329
Kipling, Rudyard 175–6, 179, 185, 201,
207–9
Kneale, Nigel 176 *passim*, 201, 231, 234,
343
Korea 209
Král, Petr 344–5, 363, 366, 370
Kreipe, General 259, 298, 299

labour
agricultural 26,35, 47, 66, 72, 79–81,
83, 85, 100, 120, 140, 148, 157, 162, 164,
354, 389 (see also class, poor peasants,
proletarianization)
industrial reserve army viii, 9, 136
reciprocal 50, 354, 384
unfree 45–6, 50, 73, 90, 94, 127, 136,
207, 213, 254, 274–5, 281, 285, 290
Labour Party 212
laissez-faire (see neo-liberalism)
land tenure
Cadogan Estate 239
collective 53, 120, 126, 127, 339
Cornwall, Duchy of 238, 239
Crown Estates 239
ejidos 48, 50, 53, 54
Grosvenor Estate 239
Howard de Walden Estate 239
latifundia 48, 112
minifundios 49, 54, 55, 112

plantations 45, 46, 50, 108, 207,
209, 210
sharecropping 57, 58, 161, 354,
358, 384
tenancy 5, 35, 55, 57, 69, 73, 83, 87, 98,
112, 113, 157, 161, 180, 205, 217 *passim*,
229–31, 233, 263, 301, 305, 310, 354,
357, 389
landscape 17, 105–6, 171, 174, 181, 232,
261–2, 289, 302, 304, 309, 332–3 (see also
agrarian myth)
language 3, 30–2, 36, 46, 61, 79, 101, 140,
164–5, 259–60, 264, 269, 271, 273, 276, 287,
295, 297, 299, 316, 327, 347, 375 (see also
culture, identity, nationalism)
Latin America 2, 11, 18, 23, 26–7, 35, 38, 40
passim, 49–50, 52, 55, 62, 64, 67, 94, 106
passim, 117, 122, 139–40, 144, 292, 305, 309,
315, 339–40, 380, 386
law 7, 11, 26, 31, 73, 76–83, 88–90, 92, 95,
101, 103–4, 108–9, 120, 169, 179, 195, 222,
229–30, 238, 240, 256, 272ff., 286–7, 313,
325, 334, 353, 359, 369, 372 (see also
human rights)
Corn Laws 82
Poor Laws 256
left, political viii, 18, 24, 29, 42, 91, 100, 120,
126, 131, 135–6, 141–2, 156, 379–80, 385, 387
(see also communism, Marxism, socialism)
Lenin, V.I. 30–1, 33, 127, 280, 288
liberalism 59–60, 62, 281, 287 (see also
neoliberalism)
Lippmann, Walter 81, 84
Lisbon 332

Mabey, Richard 106–7
Maine, Henry Sumner 66, 79–81, 84, 86
Mallock, W.H. 81, 84
Malthus, T.R. 183, 252ff.
Mandela, Nelson 14
Mariátegui, José Carlos 41, 379
Marinetti, Filippo 346, 371–5, 379, 384
Marx, Groucho 117, 292
Marx, Karl 8, 13–4, 31, 78, 88
Marxism 1–4, 7, 11, 13–5, 18, 24, 26, 27ff.,
31–3, 35, 37, 41, 43, 45, 51, 56, 60, 65, 78, 81,
86, 88, 99ff., 118, 120, 123, 125ff., 130 *passim*,
142–3, 147–9, 153, 156, 165, 173, 200, 219, 249,

271, 288, 334, 337, 374, 379, 381, 386, 388
(see also class, communism, socialism)
Austro-Marxism　　30, 31, 33
Stalinism　　42
Massingham, H.J.　　103–4
McCulloch, John Ramsey　　125
media, mass　　12, 132–3, 137, 187, 198–9, 211,
　215, 349 (see also film, television)
Mexico　　6, 12, 17, 23, 25 *passim*, 37 *passim*,
　48 *passim*, 91, 117–8, 128ff., 140, 209, 292,
　387 (see also Chiapas, the Zapatista Army
　of National Liberation)
Middle East　　11, 37, 123, 133, 241, 293, 342
migration　　5, 38, 45–6, 48, 51–2, 54–5, 71,
　79, 94, 111, 113, 152, 198–9, 239, 260, 326,
　339, 351
mob-in-the-streets　　12–3, 15–6, 19, 67, 71,
　76, 78, 80, 82, 86–9, 98–9, 103, 182, 230,
　243, 247–8, 255–6, 266–7, 279ff., 289–92,
　296, 300, 302, 306, 322, 329–30, 332ff.,
　337, 342–3, 345–6, 381–2, 385, 390–1
　(see also class, revolution, urbanization,
　workers)
Mobutu Sese Seko　　313, 326, 340–1
modernity　　17, 20, 36, 39, 45, 85, 117, 119,
　132–3, 135, 141, 144–5, 147–51, 157, 182–3, 197,
　217, 235, 250, 276, 293–5, 302, 306, 308, 311,
　313, 321, 323, 325, 327–8, 331, 335, 340ff.,
　345, 349, 355, 366, 373ff., 379, 384–6, 392
Mont Pelerin Society　　93
Montaigne, Michel de　　260, 378
Morand, Paul　　250, 253, 345–6, 348, 366–7,
　371 *passim*, 381, 384–5
Möser, Justus　　98–9
Mozambique　　49
Multitude　　26, 73 (see also 'new' populist
　postmodernism, subaltern studies)

NAFTA　　44, 54, 60
Naipaul, Vidia　　14, 251, 294, 304, 309–10,
　312 *passim*, 321, 325 *passim*, 339ff., 343
Napoleon　　184, 269, 376
national question　　7, 27 *passim*, 36, 56
　(see also capitalism, conservatism,
　Marxism, neoliberalism)
nationalism　　5–6, 9–10, 12, 14, 17, 19, 23
　passim, 33ff., 37, 42ff., 56, 58, 60, 64ff., 71ff.,
　77, 82, 86, 91, 96, 99, 101–2, 107ff., 114, 116,

121, 132ff., 139, 144ff., 155ff., 163, 165, 174–5,
　184–5, 198ff., 205, 207, 209–10, 218, 221, 226,
　230–1, 241ff., 247ff., 256–7, 265, 268ff.,
　274ff., 279–80, 284, 289ff., 294, 296, 304,
　316–7, 320, 341, 344, 359, 368, 372ff., 383,
　386, 389ff. (see also agrarian myth,
　colonialism, culture, internationalism,
　populism)
　hispanidad　　42, 58–60, 65, 107
　Mexicanidad　　42, 65
　patriotism　　30, 34, 71, 91, 97, 109–12,
　　221, 224, 233, 316–7, 372–4, 377
　self-determination　　29–30, 35
　Slavophilism　　270, 280–1, 284, 287–8,
　　317, 377
Nature　　4–5, 28, 34, 42, 64, 67, 76, 95–6,
　99, 102–4, 114, 130–1, 135, 146, 151ff., 181–3,
　233–4, 237, 247, 250, 261, 270, 273, 275,
　277ff., 286, 289, 303, 313–4, 318–9, 324,
　333, 343, 351–2, 355, 359, 373, 382, 392
　(see also agrarian myth, culture,
　peasant)
Negri, Antonio　　25–7, 37–8, 51, 379
neo-liberalism　　6, 11, 18, 23, 25–6, 29, 35ff.,
　48–9, 52, 56, 61ff., 76, 80, 87, 89, 92ff., 103,
　105, 119–20, 122, 129, 131, 133, 138–40, 150,
　155, 157, 164, 191 (see capitalism, class,
　the State)
　anarcho-capitalism　　6
New Guinea　　40, 249–50
New Labour　　11, 121, 214
New York　　302, 304
New Zealand　　56
Newby, Eric　　309, 339, 342, 345, 352, 368,
　376
NGOS　　53, 63, 130, 305
Nock, Albert Jay　　6, 81–2

oligarchs　　12, 129, 258
Ortega y Gasset, José　　107

Pakistan　　127–8, 130
Pandey, Gyanendra　　144, 147ff.
Paris　　88, 133, 141, 265, 280–83, 290, 299,
　317, 340, 368, 377, 385 (see also mob in the
　streets, revolution)
paternalism　　7ff., 19, 43, 73, 201–2, 205, 212,
　215, 308, 352, 383–4, 389–90

peasant
  differentiation   26, 28, 40, 46, 127, 136,
    285, 357 (see also class, Marxism,
    Lenin)
  economy   viii, 2, 24, 32–3, 41, 51ff., 60,
    64, 85, 87, 99–100, 102, 109, 112, 115,
    119–20, 126–7, 144, 355 (see also
    agrarian myth, Chayanov, petty
    commodity production, populism)
  essentialism   2, 4, 7, 18, 29, 149–50, 233,
    287, 315, 318, 328, 342, 373, 386, 391 (see
    also agrarian myth, culture, identity,
    populism)
  family   4, 24, 41, 50, 52, 57, 100,
    102–3, 109, 112, 127, 147, 149, 278, 286,
    324, 338
peasant movements
  Cristeros   18, 25, 57ff., 65
  Naxalites   29
  Sendero Luminoso   41
  Sinarquistas   18, 25, 57ff., 65
peasantry
  middle   24, 27, 48, 111, 128, 149, 288, 388
    (see also agrarian myth, petty
    commodity production)
  poor   3, 12, 17, 24, 27, 50, 76, 94, 100,
    120, 122, 127–8, 130, 139–40, 144, 148–9,
    155–7, 164, 288, 388 (see also agricul-
    tural labour, class, Marxism)
  rich   3, 13, 24, 26–7, 33, 47, 49–50, 55,
    106, 120, 127, 144, 148–9, 157, 254, 288,
    331, 388 (see also capitalism, class,
    new farmers' movements)
Peru   41, 42, 49–50, 107, 112, 136, 207, 379
petty bourgeoisie   35, 111–2, 134, 142, 148,
  186, 218, 225 passim, 280 (see also class,
  The Go-Between)
petty commodity production   2, 24, 40,
  45–6, 48, 51, 57, 100, 127, 136, 139, 148, 361,
  392–3 (see also agrarian myth, culture,
  identity, indigenismo, peasant economy,
  peasantry, populism)
Philippines   209
photography   117, 169, 305, 344, 364ff.,
  370, 385
Poland   260, 264, 299, 355
political economy   2, 9, 24, 52, 85, 93, 122,
  142, 303

popular culture   5, 7, 12–5, 40, 64, 107, 110,
  162, 164ff., 170ff., 185–6, 194, 199, 201, 203–4,
  212, 242–3, 247, 268ff., 279, 287, 291, 296,
  365, 386, 389–90 (see also film, identity,
  'new' populist postmodernism, television,
  travel writing)
  carnivalesque   162, 164, 172, 188
populism   1–3, 5, 6 passim, 18–9, 24
  passim, 41, 46, 55, 57, 59ff., 66 passim, 82ff.,
  86–7, 89ff., 98, 103ff., 107, 110, 114–16, 118ff.,
  126–7, 131–2, 134 passim, 164ff., 168, 171ff.,
  181, 184–5, 193, 198ff., 204ff., 209, 211, 217,
  236, 241, 243, 247–8, 256–7, 267–8, 270,
  279ff., 285, 288ff., 310, 320, 324, 326, 335,
  340–1, 367, 372–3, 381, 386, 388ff.
  noblesse oblige   69, 201–2, 204–5,
    216–7, 221, 233, 300, 352–3, 390
    (see also aristocracy)
  Third Way   103, 121
Portugal   ix, 42
postmodernism, 'new' populist   1–4, 6–8,
  11, 15–6, 18, 24ff., 28, 30–1, 35, 61, 64ff., 95,
  101, 118–9, 122–3, 125, 127, 131, 135, 137–8
  passim, 149ff., 155ff., 162, 164–5, 198, 200,
  236, 252–3, 256, 271, 277–8, 289–90,
  306, 317–8, 324, 341–2, 367, 372–3, 384,
  386ff. (see also agrarian myth,
  culture, identity, peasantry,
  subaltern studies)
Primo de Rivera, José Antonio   100–2, 107
  (see also Spanish Falange)
privatization   11, 52–4, 65, 129, 136, 237
proletarianization   45, 52, 58, 98, 102–3,
  136 (see also capitalism, class, peasant
  differentiation)
Putney Debates (see English civil war)

racism   44, 56, 71, 91, 99, 110, 142, 146, 163,
  169, 183, 191, 227, 248–9, 273, 287, 304, 306,
  309, 316, 320, 353, 372–4, 377 (see also
  conservatism, fascism, identity, migration,
  South Africa)
religion   4, 11, 25, 29, 34, 36–7, 49, 58ff., 63,
  71, 79, 84, 89, 91, 101, 108–9, 113–4, 121–2, 141,
  145, 156, 176, 179–80, 197, 207, 227, 237, 258,
  270, 272, 274ff., 289, 308, 314, 324, 341, 377,
  382 (see also culture, identity, popular
  culture)

revolution
    Algerian   48, 53
    Chinese   48, 53
    Cuban   23, 48, 53, 117, 128, 382
    French   59, 75, 80–1, 87–8, 161, 174, 232,
        248, 255, 265–6, 268, 271, 280ff., 289,
        300, 334, 376
    Green   52, 55, 129
    Mexican   48, 128
    Russian   27, 48, 81, 117, 122, 126,
        206, 299
    Vietnamese   128
right, political   4, 7, 18, 33, 81ff., 85ff., 91
    passim, 106 passim, 111 passim, 131, 138,
    141ff., 147, 149, 154, 176, 212, 371, 377, 379,
    384 (see also class, conservatism, fascism,
    nationalism, neoliberalism)
Romanticism   87, 147, 174–5, 269, 276, 369
Rome   188, 259, 265–6, 272, 281, 359, 374
Royalty
    Charles, Prince   14, 107, 186, 237, 238ff.
    Edward VIII   213
    Elizabeth I   353
    Elizabeth II   204–5, 211, 214–5, 236,
        238–9
    Frederick the Great   263, 269, 273
    George VI   214–5
    Haile Selassie   321, 337
Rumania   299, 301, 309, 338, 378
Ruskin, John   145
Russia   24, 27–8, 30, 33, 41, 48, 53, 62, 81,
    84, 97, 102, 104, 111, 117, 122, 126ff., 129, 145,
    192, 206, 264, 269–70, 272, 280 passim, 297,
    299, 302–3, 317, 335–6, 342

Sartre, Jean-Paul   95, 346, 379ff., 385
Scandinavia   252, 254–6
Schäffle, Albert   79–80, 126
Schmitt, Carl   76–7
schools, public   162, 168, 170–1, 173, 178,
    187, 194, 204, 231, 234, 265, 295, 305–6, 320
    (see also ancient universities, class)
Scott, J.C. 6, 27, 151ff., 164
Scott, Paul   207
Senior, Nassau William   87–9
servants   169, 182, 186, 189, 203, 208, 210–1,
    218, 228–9, 231, 235, 237, 275, 278, 281, 302,
    308, 331, 360, 379

sex   96, 176, 183, 197, 217, 220, 248–9, 278
Shiva, Vandana   107
Smith, Adam   125
Smuts, J.C.   154, 322
social movements, new   2, 24, 26, 137, 241
    (see also capitalism, class, new farmers'
    movements, 'new' populist
    postmodernism)
socialism   3, 4, 8, 13, 24, 26–7, 29ff.,
    35, 37–8, 52, 55, 59, 62, 65, 73, 76, 80,
    84, 87, 91ff., 102–3, 108, 110–1, 113, 115, 120ff.,
    126ff., 130 passim, 141, 144, 154ff., 164, 173,
    194–5, 234, 241, 280, 282, 285–6, 288, 290,
    293–4, 307, 324, 327, 334 passim, 346,
    372ff., 376 (see also capitalism,
    class, Marxism, mob in the streets,
    political left)
sociology   144, 199–200 (see also
    anthropology)
Sorel, Georges   286
South Africa   14, 29, 56, 97, 154, 220, 322
Spain   1, 16, 37, 42, 44, 59–60, 62, 100–2,
    107–8, 113, 115–6, 173, 264, 279, 285, 296,
    299, 304, 310, 318–9, 328–9, 331–2,
    337–8, 380
State, the   4–7, 9–11, 17–18, 25 passim, 39
    passim, 47 passim, 60ff., 66 passim, 87
    passim, 102 passim, 114 passim, 126 passim,
    138ff., 146, 150 passim, 162, 164, 199,
    206, 217, 234, 236–7, 260, 267, 279,
    285–6, 288, 304, 316, 326, 334, 337,
    377, 386, 387ff.
Stoppard, Tom   216–7, 242
strikes   9, 11, 111–3, 138, 334–5, 358
structuralism (see language, 'new' populist
    postmodernism)
Subaltern Studies   2–3, 18, 27–8, 31,
    65, 107–8, 116–7, 137, 139–40, 144ff., 148–49,
    155, 157, 164, 386, 388 (see also agrarian
    myth, culture, identity, 'new' populist
    postmodernism, popular culture,
    peasantry)
Subcomandante Marcos   23, 29, 118
    (see also Chiapas, culture, identity,
    Mexico, peasantry, Zapatista Army of
    National Liberation)
Switzerland   260
Syria   321

taxation   6, 11, 33, 75, 82, 93, 95, 104–6,
    169–70, 178, 214, 234, 236–9, 334,
    352 (see also neo-liberalism,
    the State)
television
    A Very British Coup (1988)   212
    All Gas and Gaiters (1966–71)   196
    Downton Abbey (2010–)   204
    House of Cards (1990–95)   204–5,
        211–4, 236–7
    Jewel in the Crown (1984)   207
    Parade's End (2012)   204–5, 212, 216–7
    Roger of the Raj (1979)   194
    The Quatermass Conclusion
        (1979)   176–7
    The Stone Tape (1972)   176, 181–3
    The Vicar of Dibley (1994–2007)   196
Thatcher, Margaret   14, 62, 94, 105, 161, 212
Thesiger, Wilfred   251–2, 293–4, 304ff.,
    312ff., 320ff., 329, 337, 343
Thompson, E.P.   198ff.
Tierra del Fuego   151–2, 293, 311–2, 334–5
    (see also E. Lucas Bridges)
Tolstoy, Leo   145
tourism, mass   13, 15–6, 19–20, 243, 250–1,
    291–2 *passim*, 328 *passim*, 341ff., 345, 349,
    361ff., 366, 376, 382–5, 390–1
trade unions   9, 46, 49, 76, 93, 108, 138–9,
    195–6, 322, 335–7, 352, 358
travel (see also Kingsley Amis, Max
    Beerbohm, E. Lucas Bridges, Horatio
    Brown, Robert Byron, Karel Čapek,
    Régis Debray, Patrick Leigh Fermor,
    Douglas Goldring, Georgina Grahame,
    Robert Graves, Petr Král, Russell Green,
    Norman Lewis, Paul Morand, V.S.Naipaul,
    Eric Newby, Wilfred Thesiger, Kenneth
    Tynan, and Evelyn Waugh; also, class,
    cosmopolitanism, Grand Tour, identity,
    mass tourism, nationalism)
    and anthropology   248–53, 317, 384
    and film/television   5, 12–7, 67, 247–8,
        253, 297, 319, 349, 364ff., 385, 390
    and home/abroad dichotomy   13, 16,
        19, 70, 255–6, 258, 260, 263, 265–6,
        268, 288–9, 294, 296, 301, 303–6, 308,
        315, 317–8, 321, 323, 329ff., 336, 342, 359,
        377, 389ff.

    and picturesque poverty   17, 29, 36, 38,
        59, 63, 123, 136, 156, 203, 324, 333, 337,
        350, 356ff., 383ff., 387
    and political exile   249
    and self/other (see identity, nationalism)
    travel guides   249–50, 264, 297–8, 339,
        346, 349, 369, 374, 380
Trieste   318, 377–8
Trotsky, Leon   13, 27–8, 31, 33, 41, 77, 120,
    249
Tynan, Kenneth   329, 331–3

United States   16ff., 35, 38ff., 54ff., 60, 67,
    69–70, 74, 79ff., 92, 94, 98, 103ff., 108, 110,
    112, 114, 115, 126, 142, 152, 163, 165–6, 185, 192,
    197, 205ff., 209ff., 241ff., 283, 296, 298,
    302ff., 308ff., 315–6, 318, 329, 339, 341–2,
    350, 364, 368, 370, 372, 375ff., 382–3
universities, ancient   10, 75, 178, 234, 257,
    298, 302, 305 (see also class, public
    schools)
urbanization   4, 13, 20, 36, 38, 40, 55, 60,
    87, 96ff., 103ff., 106, 110–1, 136, 138–9, 146,
    151, 156–7, 171, 182, 184, 217, 238, 278, 286–7,
    290, 293, 302, 306, 310ff., 322ff., 332, 335,
    342ff., 359, 382, 384 (see also class
    formation, industrialization, mob-in-the-
    streets, proletarianization)
Uruguay   315, 326, 327

van der Post, Laurens   14
Vatican   108–9
Venetian lagoon
    Burano   353, 356–8, 363
    fishing   357–8
    glass-making   358, 363
    lace-making   358
    Lido   253, 362, 365, 369, 379
    Mestre   345, 347, 377
    Murano   353, 363, 379
    San Francesco del Deserto   353–4
    Santa Cristina   353
    Sant'Erasmo   352
    Torcello   351, 353ff., 357, 369, 373
    villas, Palladian   359, 373
Venice
    aesthetics and   349, 351–2, 359–60,
        363, 367, 369, 371, 373, 383–4

Arsenale   356, 371, 375
authenticity of   343, 349, 363, 367, 370,
    373–4, 377–8, 381, 385–6, 392
Ducal Palace   iv, 349, 368, 382
exclusivity of   20, 343–5, 361ff., 366,
    376ff., 380–1, 384–5, 391
Giardini Eden and   350ff.
nostalgia for   344–5, 357, 378, 384
St. Mark's   367, 369, 372–4, 378
Vietnam   48, 128, 152, 209–10
Villa, Pancho   117
von Mises, Ludwig   92

war
    1914–18   56, 74–5, 84, 90, 111, 133, 180,
        215ff., 232, 249, 300, 302, 311
    1939–45   51, 84, 92, 105, 123, 130, 155, 171,
        213, 220, 224, 236, 309, 323, 334, 336ff.,
        356, 376–7
    Boer   97, 220, 224, 226, 230ff.
    Cold   37, 92, 104, 131–2
Waugh, Evelyn   16, 168–70, 173, 189, 192,
    293–4, 301ff., 306ff., 309, 321ff., 329, 334,
    346–7, 370ff., 375–6

Williams, Raymond   137, 345, 365
Wilson, Harold   72
Wodehouse, P.G. 189, 197
Wooster, Bertie   189, 197
workers   1, 3, 5, 7, 9, 11–2, 17–8, 30 passim,
    43, 46–7, 50ff., 58, 60 passim, 68 passim, 82
    passim, 102, 107 passim, 122, 130–1, 137
    passim, 155–6, 169, 175, 196, 205, 207, 209,
    223, 228ff., 236, 239, 243, 247–8, 254ff.,
    279 passim, 290, 301, 312, 315, 323, 333ff.,
    358, 360, 374, 384, 388ff. (see also class,
    labour, mob-in-the-streets,
    proletarianization)

Yugoslavia   133, 135, 318, 339

Zaïre (see Congo)
Zapata, Emiliano   29, 117
Zapatista Army of National Liberation   23
    passim, 37, 46 passim, 60ff., 66, 118, 157,
    386–7 (see also Chiapas, identity,
    indigenismo, Mexico, peasant movements,
    peasantry, Subcomandante Marcos)
Zomia   6, 7, 119, 152ff.

Author Index

A Foreign Resident   67, 69–70
Abelson, E.   103
Abercrombie, N.   225
About, E.   85
Abse, T.   137–8
Acton, H.B.   92
Adams, R.N.   41
Adinolfi, G.   121
Adorno, T.   161
Alavi, H.   127–8, 129, 135
Albó, X.   139–40
Alegría, C.   42
Allina-Pisano, J.   53
Almond, G.A.   130, 131
Amis, K.   176, 194, 293, 294, 295–6, 311, 329, 331–2, 333, 343, 381
Anderson, B.   257
Anderson, L.   190, 203
Anderson, P.   198ff.
Assessorato al Turismo   365

Baaz, M.E.   8
Bacon, F.   261
Baedeker, K.   297–8
Bagehot, W.   70, 166–7, 187
Baird, P.   51–2
Bakhtin, M.   162, 188
Ballersteros Corona, E.   29
Barabas, A.   40
Baran, P.   150
Baretti, J.   252, 259
Barkin, D.   53
Barnard, F.M.   269ff., 275ff., 317
Barr, C.   191–2
Barrès, M.   76, 139, 142–3, 146–7
Barthes, R.   3
Bartolomé, M.   40
Bartra, R.   52, 54
Baüer, O.   30ff.,
Bax, B.   91
Baxter, J.   207
Bear, W.E.   83
Bechhofer, F.   225
Beegle, J.A.   100
Beerbohm, M.   364

Belloc, H.   59, 92
Bendersky, J.W.   77
Berger, M.T.   29
Bernstein, H.   136–7
Beverley, J.   2, 35
Bhaba, H.K.   165
Bien, P.   226
Bierce, A.   1
Birkenhead, Earl of   173
Birla, G.D.   112–13
Blake, R.   68, 69, 70, 71, 73–4
Bloom, H.   3
Bluntschli, J.K.   29, 90
Botelho Gonsálvez, R.   42
Boyson, R.   92
Bradbury, M.   298, 307, 370, 376
Brady, F.   249, 263
Brailsford, H.N.   124
Brass, D.   ix
Brass, T.   2, 4, 5, 27, 28, 29, 35, 41, 50, 55, 94, 98, 110, 136, 140, 148, 152, 165, 175, 185, 215
Braudel, F.   359
Breman, J.   8
Brenan, G.   318
Brennan, M.G.   258, 260, 261
Bridges, E.L.   151, 293, 310ff., 334–5, 343
Brittain, J.J.   61
Brown, H.F.   345, 347, 355, 359, 363–4
Broccoli, M.J.   171
Buck, P.W.   71, 72
Bulwer Lytton, E.   170, 172, 257, 266, 267
Burbach, R.   27
Burgess, A.   220
Burke, K.   142–3
Burke, P.   279
Butler, S.   117–18
Byron, R.   252, 293, 294, 302ff., 308, 317, 320, 335–37, 342, 343

Cahill, K.   240
Calia, C.   379
Calvo Sotelo, J.   102
Cámara Barbachano, F.   40
Campigotto, L.   366
Cancian, F.   45

Canclini, N.G.   140
Cannadine, D.   74–5, 76, 171, 187
Canning, G.   78, 79
Čapek, K.   350, 366, 369–70
Cardoso, C.F.S.   135
Carr, E.H.   269
Carrà, C.   373–4
Carrigan, A.   27
Carter, A.   6
Carter, I.   170
Casasola, A.V.   117
Castells, M.   27
Castro Pozo, H.   41
Caute, D.   217ff., 231
Chamberlain, J.   85–6
Chatterjee, P.   144ff.
Chayanov, A.V.   24, 126, 127
Chetwode, P.   306
Chossudovsky, M.   53
Clark, A.   232
Clark, K.   318, 330
Clarke, J.   106
Cleaver, H.   28
Cobden Unwin, J.   82–3
Colgate, I.   215
Colley, L.   256, 257
Collier, G.A.   47, 61
Collier, J.F.   47, 61
Collins, J.   164, 165
Colton, C.C.   117
Connolly, C.   310
Connor, S.   165
Cook, J.   106
Cook, O.   190
Cooper, A.   249, 299ff., 305–6, 308, 309,
    318, 323–24, 330, 337–8
Cooper, J.M.   311
Coppola, E.   210
Coppola, F.F.   210
Coquery-Vidrovich, C.   135
Cornejo, A.   109
Cory, D.   84
Covarrubias, M.   40
Cowie, P.   210
Cowling, M.   94
Crovato, G.   366
Crovato, M.   366
Cunninghame, P.   29
Curtis, R.   197

Dahlberg, E.   143
Dahrendorf, R.   14
Dalal, A.   112–13
Damiani, L.   365
Daniels, S.   171
Davie, M.   169, 308
Davies, N.   257
Davis, R.C.   344, 375
De Angelis, M.   25
de Jouvenel, B.   93
de la Fuente, J.   39, 47
de la Peña, G.   43
de Leon, A.   25, 48, 63
de Madariaga, S.   1, 62
de Maeztu, R.   59–60, 108
de Man, P.   3
Debray, R.   346, 366, 370, 379ff., 385
Deere, C.   53
Derrida, J.   3
Deutsch, S.M.   109, 110, 111–12
Dickinson, H.D.   92
Dinerman, A.   49
Dixie, Lady F.   311
Dolkart, R.H.   109, 110
Doolaard, A. den   365
Dovring, K.   108–9
Drazin, C.   166
Dummond Wolff, H.   328
Dunn, S.P.   134
Duveen, J.   232

Eccleshall, R.   81
Eden, F.   350ff., 356, 384
Edgar, D.   105
Eklof, B.   127
Elliot, B.   225
Engels, F.   8, 13
Epstein, K.   98–99
Esteva, G.   63
Evola, J.   76, 85, 120, 141

Fawcett, H.   9–10
FE [Edholm, F.]   40
Fermor, P.L.   252, 259, 294, 298 passim,
    318, 321, 323ff., 330, 337–8, 342
Fine, S.   81, 92, 94
Fioravanti, E.   55
Fiore, R.   121
Fischer, E.   33

Fletcher, R.   113–14
Foner, E.   104
Fontana, G.   366
Foot, P.   124, 236
Fowler-Salamini, H.   54
Frank, S.P.   127
Friedland, W.H.   134
Friedman, M.   6
Froude, J.A.   68, 69
Furniss, E.S.   77, 78
Fussell, P.   15

Gamio, M.   51
García, A.   52
Garland, N.   17, 295
Gellner, E.   8
Genovese, E.D.   163
Geoghegan, V.   81
Gibbon, P.   136
Giddens, A.   121
Gide, A.   374
Gilly, A.   27–28, 44–45
Gilroy, P.   165
Godechot, J.   271
Goldring, D.   345, 347, 351, 367–8, 369, 372
Goldwater, B.   104
Gombrich, E.H.   330
Gonzales, E.   53
Goodrich, A.   266
Gordillo, G.   52
Gott, R.   55
Grahame, G.   293, 305, 310, 322, 329, 334, 348, 353, 358, 369
Granado, A.   382
Graves, R.   188, 294, 295, 296, 329, 331, 333, 342, 381
Gray, J.   95
Green, D.G.   95
Green, R.   249–50, 345, 348ff., 360–61, 367, 369, 370
Greene, G.   166, 175, 210
Griffiths, R.   104
Grindle, M.S.   51
Grossberg, L.   165
Guevara, E.   23, 292, 382
Guha, Ramachandra   144
Guha, Ranajit   27, 28
Guiton, S.   353ff., 356ff., 363, 384
Gutelman, M.   52

Hale, J.R.   260
Halpern, J.M.   133
Hamilton, A.   371
Hammel, E.A.   133
Harding, S.   165
Hardt, M.   25, 26, 27, 37–38, 51
Hare, A.J.C.   346, 348, 349
Harris, R.   87, 94
Hart, H.   143
Harte, G.B.   344, 366, 368, 370
Hartley, L.P.   218 passim, 234 passim
Hartman, G.   3
Hartwell, R.M.   93, 103
Harvey, N.   37, 47, 48, 50
Hayek, F.   6, 92, 93, 94
Hecker, J.F.   280
Hellman, J.A.   29
Helps, A.   10
Hernández, H.   57, 58, 59, 60
Herzen, A.   19, 280 passim, 289–90, 317
Hewitt de Alcántara, C.   41, 52
Hillis Miller, J.   3
Hitchcock, A.   296–7
Hobsbawm, E.J.   135, 257
Hochhuth, R.   196
Hoefle, S.W.   206
Holloway, J.   27
Horkheimer, M.   161
Huizer, G.   132
Hume, D.   262
Hunt, J.D.   261–2
Hussain, A.   126
Hutton, G.   93, 94

Icaza, J.   42
Illife, J.   136
Isherwood, C.   16

Jack, I.   333, 334
Jacobs, L.   165, 206
James, M. R.   168, 176 passim, 201, 206, 231, 234, 235, 242, 343
James, P.   252ff.
Jameson, F.   165
Jay, R.   81
Jebb, R.   56
Jekyll, G.   351
Jell-Bahlsen, S.   96
Jerome, J.K.   234

Jones, J.D.F.   14
Jones, T.   194

Kael, P.   366
Kagarlitsky, B.   27
Kaplan, F.   253, 345, 346, 347ff., 360ff., 364,
    368
Keates, J.   249
Kemp, P.   215
Kingston-Mann, E.   127
Kipling, R.   175, 176, 179, 185, 201, 207,
    208–9
Kiselyova, E.   27
Kitchen, C.H.B.   234
Kitchen, M.   30
Klaren, P.F.   107
Klinge, G.   112
Knauerhase, R.   100
Kneale, N.   176 passim, 201, 231, 234, 343
Knight, A.   41, 57
Kosinski, J.   349
Kracauer, S.   165
Král, P.   344, 345, 363, 366, 370
KY [Young, K.]   40

Lacroix, P.   265
Laing, S.   258
Lalbhai, K.   112–13
Lampert, E.   280, 285
Landsberger, H.A.   113
Lane, F.C.   344
Lara, J.   42
Larsen, N.   35
Leader, Z.   306, 333
Lenin, V.I.   30, 31, 33, 127, 280, 288
Lerner, D.   132
Lévi-Stauss, C.   247
Lewis, N.   294, 304, 305, 332, 342
Lewis, O.   38, 41
Leys, C.   131–2
Liebknecht, W.   316
Lippmann, W.   81, 84
Lodge, D.   168, 173, 210
Loomis, C.P.   100
López Alvez, F.   144
Lopez y Fuentes, G.   42
Lora, G.   109
Löwy, M.   35
Lucas, K.   42, 61

Lukács, G.   31
Luxemburg, R.   30
Lyttelton, A.   371, 373, 374
Lytton Sells, A.   259

Mabey, R.   106–7
Maine, H.S.   66, 79–81, 84, 86
Mair, L.   132
Malinowski, B.   39–40, 249, 250, 252
Mallock, W.H.   81, 84
Malthus, T.R.   256
Mann, T.   348
Marcet, J.   85
Marcos, Subcomandante   23, 29
Marcus, G.E.   165
Mariátegui, J.C.   41
Marinetti, F.   346, 371ff., 374–5, 379, 384
Maritain, J.   95
Marshall, P.   6
Martins, J. de S.   25
Marton, P.   359
Marx, K.   8, 13, 14, 31, 78, 88
Marzal, M.   140
Massingham, H.J.   103, 104
Matthai, J.   112–13
McCabe, C.   165
McCarthy, M.   344, 381
McCaughan, E.   51–2
McCulloch, J.R.   125
McEwen, I.   219–20
McFarlane, B.   195, 196
McHale, B.   164
McKenzie, R.   68–9, 70–71
McNeish, J.   49
McRobbie, A.   165
Medley, G.W.   83
Meillassoux, C.   136
Mendieta y Nuñez, L.   44
Metz, C.   165
Meyer, J.   57–58, 59
Meyer, K.   99–100
Michael, M.A.   295
Mignolo, W.D.   27
Miles, D.   257
Milius, J.   210
Miller, H.   320
Miranda, F.   55
Mitford, N.   170
Mitrany, D.   33–34

Mixter, T.   127
Moksnes, H.   25, 37, 45, 49, 63
Montaigne, M.   260
Morand, P.   250, 253, 345, 346, 348,
   366–67, 371 passim, 381, 384–5
Morris, J.   317–18
Mosca, G.   10, 72
Mosk, S.A.   43
Mosley, C.   338
Mosley, O.   100–101
Mosse, G.   99
Municipality of Venice   365
Munson, A.   208
Muraro, M.   359
Murra, J.V.   40–41

Naipaul, V.S.   14, 251, 294, 304, 309–10, 312
   passim, 321, 325 passim, 339ff., 343
Narayan, U.   165
Nash, M.   41, 42
Negri, A.   25, 26, 27, 37–38, 51
Nehru, J.   144–5
Neocosmos, M.   136
Nettl, J.P.   30
Newby, E.   309, 339, 342, 345, 352,
   368, 376
Newman, G.   262, 263, 264, 267
Nickeon, N.   137
Nock, A.J.   6, 81, 82
Nozick, R.   6
Núñez, O.   27

O'Connor, A.   345, 365
O'Sullivan, N.   81
Olesen, T.   25
Olivera, M.   50
Oorthuys, C.   365
Orwell, G.   170, 189, 196, 224, 225, 303
Osborne, J.   195
Otero, G.   52
Oviedo, J.   35
Owen, N.   50

Padmore, G.   134
Paige, J.M.   55
Palin, M.   194
Palmier, J.-M.   186
Pandey, G.   144, 147ff.
Paulson, J.   29

Paxman, J.   167, 169
Payne, L.A.   114
Pearse, A.   52
Peláez, E.   27
Pérez, N.   53
Petras, J.   26, 29, 35, 49, 126
Pfaff, R.W.   175ff., 178ff., 183
Pinter, H.   218, 223, 224, 225, 226, 227,
   228, 232
Pirie, D.   176
Plekhanov, G.V.   127, 288
Polanyi, M.   92
Pollock, F.   33
Pottle, F.A.   249, 263
Poulantzas, N.   225
Pryce-Jones, D.   173
Pullan, B.   344

Raban, J.   15
Rabasa, J.   27
Rajadhyaksha, A.   203
Ram, S.   112–13
Rama, C.M.   107
Ramos, A.R.   41, 140
Randall, L.   53
Rao, N.   121
Raphael, D.D.   50
Redfield, R.   38–9
Redford, B.   265, 266, 360
Reed, J.-P.   61
Reinaga, F.   41
Rey, P.-P.   136
Richards, J.   165, 168, 170, 172
Roberts, D.   8
Roberts, J.   271
Roberts, Lord   90–91, 92
Rodríguez, I.   35
Rogers, E.M.   132–33
Rogers, S.   300
Rojas, A.V.   38
Ronfeldt, D.   53
Röpke, W.   93, 103–4
Rosberg, C.G.   134
Rose, W.S.   292–3, 357
Ross, A.   227
Rothbard, M.   6
Rubin, I.I.   78, 88
Rus, J.   45, 46, 49
Rutherford, J.   165

Saavedra, M.   45, 49, 55
Sala, G.A.   295, 347–8, 363
Salomon, W.   94
Salovesh, M.   39
Salvadori, M.   126
Sánchez, R.   140
Sánchez-Jáuregui, M.D.   264
Santayana, G.   84
Sartre, J-P   95, 346, 379ff., 385
Saul, J.S.   129, 134
Schäffle, A.   79–80, 126
Schuettinger, R.   71
Scott, J.C.   6, 27, 151ff., 164
Scruton, R.   105, 106
Seidler, D.   213–14
Seldon, A.   81
Sender, J.   136
Senior, N.W.   87ff.
Serge, V.   249
Shachtman, M.   35
Shakespeare, N.   14
Shaw, G.B.   213
Shinn, W.T.   127
Shonfield, A.   11
Shroff, A.D.   112–13
Siddiqa, A.   130
Silver, A.   68–9, 70–71
Smith, Adam   125
Smith, E.   190
Smith, H.   92
Smith, S.   136
Smuts, J.C.   154
Snowman, D.   135
Solomon, S.G.   126–7
Sombart, W.   35
Sorensen, C.   196
South American Missionary Society   311
Spencer, H.   6
Spender, S.   249, 346, 348, 359
Spivak, G.C.   165
Stallybrass, P.   162
Starr, F.   39
Stein, M.R.   38–9
Stephen, L.   29
Stichter, S.   136
Stoppard, T.   216–17, 242
Stoye, J.W.   258, 260, 261, 264
Strachey, J.   232
Strong, R.   169

Suetonius, G.   188
Swindell, K.   136

Tata, J.D.R.   112–13
Tavanti, M.   49
Tax, S.   38, 40
Taylor, J.R.   161, 190, 191, 232
Terray, E.   136
Thackeray, W.M.   250, 254
Thakurdas, P.   112–13
Theroux, P.   339
Thesiger, W.   251, 252, 293, 294, 304ff.,
      312ff., 320ff., 329, 337, 343
Thomas, C.   366
Thomas, H.   100, 101–2
Thompson, E.P.   198ff.
Thompson, F.M.L.   75
Thorner, A.   135
Tocqueville, A. de   316
Todorov, T.   164
Toor, F.   40
Torner, E.M.   279
Toynbee, A.   139
Traven, B.   42
Tribe, K.   126
Trotsky, L.   28, 31, 33, 77, 120, 249
Turner, M.   75
Tynan, K.   329, 331–2, 333

Urry, J.   225

van der Haar, G.   48
Vaughan, M.K.   54
Velasco, A.   44
Veltmeyer, H.   49, 126
Venturi, F.   280
Verba, S.   130
Vieux, S.   29
Villafuerte, D.   48, 64
Vio, E.   373
Vološinov, V.N.   96
von Mises, L.   92

Walicki, A.   280
Walker, P.   225
Walter, N.   6
Warman, A.   52
Warriner, D.   123
Warshow, R.   203

Washbrook, S.   46
Waterbury, J.   8
Watts, M.J.   136–7
Waugh, E.   16, 168, 169, 170, 173, 189,
    192, 293, 294, 301ff., 306ff., 309,
    321ff., 329, 334, 346, 347, 370ff.,
    375–6
Weaver, L.   351
Weiner, M.   131
Whetten, N.L.   57
White, Allon   162
White, Arnold   97–8
White, E.   382
White, T.H.   236
Wiener, A.   61
Wiener, J.   152
Wilcox, S.   264
Wilford, R.   81
Wilkie, R.   54
Willemen, P.   203
Williams, G.   136

Williams, R.   137
Willis, P.   261–2
Wilson, A.   190
Withey, L.   15
Wolf, E.R.   48, 128
Wolff, K.H.   262
Wolford, W.   137
Womack, J.   117
Woodhouse, A.S.P.   124
Woolf, S.J.   359
Worswick, G.D.N.   92

Yazawa, S.   27

Zamosc, L.   52
Zangwill, I.   31
Zapatista Army of National
    Liberation   35–36, 50, 61
Zewde, B.   337
Zimmerman, J.G.   117
Zinkin, M.   113

A RESTATEMENT
OF RELIGION

Swami Vivekananda and the

Making of Hindu Nationalism

JYOTIRMAYA SHARMA

Yale UNIVERSITY PRESS

New Haven & London

First published in the United States in 2013 by Yale University Press.
First published in India in 2013 as *Cosmic Love and Human Apathy: Swami Vivekananda's Restatement of Religion.*

Copyright © 2013 by Jyotirmaya Sharma.

Yale University Press books may be purchased in quantity for educational, business, or promotional use. For information, please e-mail sales.press@yale.edu (U.S. office) or sales@yaleup.co.uk (U.K. office).

Set in 11/14.5 Book Antigua by R. Ajith Kumar
Printed in the United States of America.

Library of Congress Control Number: 2013933533
ISBN 978-0-300-19740-2 (cloth: alk. paper)

A catalogue record for this book is available from the British Library.

This paper meets the requirements of ANSI/NISO Z39.48-1992
(Permanence of Paper).

10 9 8 7 6 5 4 3 2 1

Contents

Preface   ix

Ramakrishna's One-Fourth   1

Whose Society, What Religion?   117

The Fly and the Syrup   191

Index   285

For
Meenakshi Mukherjee
Papiya Ghosh
Sabina Sehgal Saikia

Preface

The date is 21 February 1887. After the morning prayers, the disciples of Sri Ramakrishna are eating fruit and sweets for breakfast. Ramakrishna had died in August of the previous year. A monastic order in his name has been established and many of his disciples have renounced the world and assumed monastic names. On this February morning, Narendra, the future Swami Vivekananda, begins to playfully imitate Ramakrishna.[1] Putting a sweet in his mouth, with unblinking eyes, he stands still, enacting the state of going into *samadhi* or trance. A devotee pretends to hold his hand to prevent

---

1. *The Gospel of Sri Ramakrishna: Originally recorded in Bengali by M., a disciple of the Master,* Translated into English with an Introduction by Swami Nikhilananda, Ramakrishna-Vivekananda Center, New York, 2007 imprint, p. 979. This is a translation of Mahendranath Gupta's *Sri Sri Ramakrishna Kathāmrita,* originally published between 1897 and 1932 in five volumes in Bengali. Henceforth, all references to the English translation will be cited as *Gospel.*

him from falling down. Narendra closes his eyes for a few minutes. With the sweet still in his mouth, he then opens his eyes, and mimicking Ramakrishna's drawl says: 'I—am—all—right.'[2] Everyone present laughs loudly. Even during Ramakrishna's lifetime, Narendra always thought of his Master's trances as hallucinations, a figment of Ramakrishna's imagination.

Vivekananda's rejection of Ramakrishna's trances as hallucinations or a figment of his imagination is extremely significant. It marks a rupture that signifies two incompatible worlds, where the definitions of sanity and insanity are strikingly different. Ramakrishna's hallucinations are perfectly intelligible within the boundaries of Indian mysticism and would even be considered sane and normal.[3] Taking on feminine roles, enacting the part of Hanuman by tying a tail behind him, undergoing tantric spiritual practices, talking of ecstasy, longing, laughing, weeping, singing and dancing – all of these were part of Ramakrishna's mystical paths to attaining God. In a Tantra- and Bhakti-mediated universe, he could with effortless ease identify himself

---

2. Ibid., p. 979.
3. G.N. Devy, 'Silence, Insanity and Language', in *The G.N. Devy Reader*, Orient BlackSwan, Hyderabad, 2009, p. 17; for a detailed discussion on this point within the Vaishnava bhakti tradition, see Friedhelm Hardy, *Viraha-Bhakti: The Early History of Krsna Devotion in South India*, Oxford University Press, New Delhi, 1983, p. 6.

with 'the nature of a woman' while likening Narendra's temperament as 'manly'.[4] Kali, who Ramakrishna loved and worshipped as mother, could be called a Santhal woman and a valiant fighter by Dr Mahendra Sarkar, and the remark would merely invoke laughter from Ramakrishna. After all, he was inspired by Ramprasad Sen, the eighteenth-century mystic-poet and tantrik, who, in his poems, had the temerity to address Kali as 'crazy Kali' and say to her: 'Prasād says: find a half-wit/ And fool him if You want,/But if You don't save me/I'm going to get Shiva to spank you.'[5] For Ramakrishna, nationalism was maya and love of all countries and people and religions was daya or compassion, born only out of love of God.[6] Even renunciation was not just dispassion for the world but also longing for God.[7]

After Ramakrishna's death in 1886, Vivekananda shifted the devotional emphasis of the newly founded monastic order to the worship of the more masculine Shiva, and, quietly but decisively, exiled Kali into obscurity and insignificance. Ramakrishna's devotees began to identify themselves as the dānās and daityas (ghosts and demons) of Shiva and began to regularly

---

4. *Gospel*, p. 693.
5. Rāmprasād Sen, *Grace and Mercy in Her Wild Hair: Selected Poems to the Mother Goddess*, translated by Leonard Nathan and Clinton Seely, Hohm Press, Prescott, 1999, p. 24.
6. *Gospel*, p. 456.
7. Ibid., p. 506.

read and recite the Bhagavadgita. In his quest to create a European society with India's religion,[8] the world Vivekananda embraced was rational, scientific, masculine, 'sane', 'normal', orthodox and nationalistic. Ramakrishna's longing ecstasy for God and his simulation of Radha's love for Krishna would be dismissed by him as the weeping and moaning excesses of the 'women friends' of the Lord.[9] Instead, he would recommend beef, biceps and the Bhagavadgita as the way out for what he perceived were India's problems. Vivekananda's 'scientific' Ramakrishna would have to share space not with Chaitanya and Ramprasad, but with Kant, Schopenhauer, Paul Deussen and Max Müller. In Vivekananda's hands, Ramakrishna's 'catholicity' became a mere instrumental ploy to exhibit Hinduism's superiority. His frequent rejection of any relation Hinduism might have to external forms such as temples is also a rhetorical device that could be conveniently reversed to serve the purposes of religious nationalism. Rejection of temples, bhakti and the idea of worship of

---

8. *The Complete Works of Swami Vivekananda*, Vol. 4, Advaita Ashrama, Mayavati, Almora, Fourth edition, 1932, p. 313 (*The Complete Works of Swami Vivekananda* will henceforth be referred to as *CW*).

9. *Sri Sri Ramakrishna Lilaprasanga*, translated from Bangla as *Sri Ramakrishna: The Great Master* by Swami Jagadananda. See, Swami Saradananda, *Sri Ramakrishna: The Great Master*, Volume II, translated by Swami Jagadananda, Sri Ramakrishna Math, Madras, 2001 imprint, pp. 1241-2.

a Personal God had its own place, but the same rejection pragmatically turns into affirmation when rejoicing over the Hindu reappropriation of the Jagannath Temple in Puri, which he calls an old Buddhist temple. He goes a step further and lays forth the Hindu agenda: 'We took this and others over and re-Hinduised them. We shall have to do many things like that yet.'[10] His much-extolled idea of service too suffers from the flaw of proposing empathy without even a cosmetic pretence of altering either the orthodox social structure or the stranglehold of caste in society.

This book is the story of this rupture, of two worlds with a shared beginning which become increasingly incommensurable. It is also about the questions of Hindu identity seen through the prism of Hindu self-images. As part of what began as a trilogy and is now a quartet,[11] this volume affirms its objective of being more sceptical about our own tradition, questioning self-assumed identities and interrogating the voice and authority of traditionally privileged individuals, icons and texts. Following this objective, this volume looks

---

10. *The Complete Works of Swami Vivekananda*, Vol. 3, Advaita Ashrama, Mayavati, Almora, Fourth edition, 1932, p. 264.

11 The first two are *Hindutva: Exploring the Idea of Hindu Nationalism*, Penguin Books, New Delhi, 2011, revised edition; *Terrifying Vision: M.S. Golwalkar, the RSS and India,* Penguin/ Viking, February 2007. This volume is the third. The fourth will be an examination of Gandhi's restatement of Hinduism.

at the most definitive and influential restatement of Hinduism in the twentieth and twenty-first centuries by Vivekananda. Specifically, it examines his formulation of Hinduism as religion. In doing so, these essays critically examine the way Hindu self-images were sought to be created and justified as also the manner in which a Vedic-Vedantic primacy was sought to be privileged. Questions of caste, the primacy of the West in Vivekananda's vision for Hinduism and for India, and the systematic marginalization of other religions and heterodox religious thought in his formulation of 'India's religion' are central to understanding this restatement.[12] If Vivekananda's creation of Hinduism as India's religion is definitive, it also enforces the argument that forms the basis for this quartet: There is no distinction between Hinduism and Hindutva. If anything, Hindutva is the dominant expression of Hinduism in our times, though not the only way in which Hinduism articulates itself. Vivekananda's forceful and substantial articulation of

---

12. D.R. Nagaraj formulated a dimension of Vivekananda's thought in his inimitable fashion by calling it 'the notion of cosmic love but with it a perfected system of apathy'. The title of this book is inspired out of this formulation. I do not agree with several parts of Nagaraj's substantive argument regarding Vivekananda, but have nevertheless learned much from his essay. D.R. Nagaraj, *Listening to the Loom: Essays on Literature, Politics and Violence*, edited and with an introduction by Prithvi Datta and Chandra Shobhi, Permanent Black, Ranikhet, 2012, p. 320.

Hinduism as religion also makes him the father and preceptor of Hindutva. As an attempt to fabricate a longer and deeper genealogy of Hindu identity and its contemporary manifestation in the form of Hindutva, this volume rejects the claim that Hindu nationalists have appropriated Vivekananda's ideas to push their dark and diabolical political agenda. To paraphrase Vivekananda himself, the possibilities of a future tree are in the seed itself. The seed is what we today know by the composite term 'Hinduism' and Vivekananda's thought is just the tree at a certain stage of its growth.

If a critical study of Swami Vivekananda is written or read merely as a reason to intervene in the politics of Hindu nationalism, it is bound to have a very short breath. While correcting well-entrenched Hindu self-images is an important purpose of this book, challenging and questioning the atrophy of ideas connected with questions of Hindu identity is also an equally pre-eminent task. It is also reasonable to expect that the mystique and undeniable piety surrounding the figure of Vivekananda would always remain incommensurable, if not hostile, to any critical evaluation and reflection surrounding his ideas. Put differently, there is a tension between an entrenched nationalism that seeks to selectively deify individuals and the demands that an empirically rigorous and analytically unconventional interpretation makes. The only way to forge a dialogue between these two seemingly antagonistic positions is to delineate themes, concepts and categories that require further interrogation. A few examples and their implications would suffice to illustrate this point.

One such critical theme is that of the use of concepts such as *artha, dharma, kama* and *moksha,* together known as the *purusharthas.* As we will see in Chapter 2, Vivekananda disapproves of the Hindu preoccupation with moksha and privileges the West's quest after dharma. He interprets the Western pursuit of dharma as akin to the Mimāmsa system's use of the term to mean a hankering after worldly happiness. It has an even narrower connotation than anything suggested by the authoritative commentaries in the Mimāmsaka tradition: in Vivekananda's gloss, dharma is the singular pursuit of work leading to worldly happiness. It would be reasonable to suggest that artha in this instance has been conflated with dharma or subsumed under the role dharma ought to perform as per Vivekananda's understanding of the Mimāmsaka scheme of things. In doing so, there is little attention paid to the overall coherence of a philosophical system and its nuances. The subtle differences within a system of philosophy, in this instance the Mimāmsa system, are arbitrarily brushed aside. Ultimately, the attempt here is to construct a largely political and nationalist argument with the help of a philosophical concept masquerading as a quasi-religious argument. This raises questions about the way in which Vivekananda would have to reconcile a Mimāmsa-inspired notion of dharma, including the implications of such a borrowing on the meaning of the other three purusharthas, with his chosen brand of Advaita Vedanta. It further leads to the speculation if his unique brand of Practical Vedanta was born out of the compulsions of such a confusion of categories and concepts.

A similar exercise in the understanding of qualities or *gunas* such as *sattva*, *rajas* and *tamas* is necessary. Ramakrishna uses tamas in ways that suggest a conflation of qualities normally associated with rajas. In contrast, Vivekananda glorifies the rajasic element disproportionately while simultaneously diminishing the importance of sattva. While the pre-eminence of rajas tallies with his project of making Hindus more manly, the re-evaluation and reinterpretation of these seem random, discontinuous with philosophical traditions and lacking methodological justification. This arbitrary use of concepts and categories can be defended by arguing that Ramakrishna and Vivekananda were not systematic philosophers. In the case of Ramakrishna, it is possible to justify such randomness by taking into account his status as a mystic. However, the only way to rationalize Vivekananda's idiosyncratic use of concepts and categories is to view such an act as necessary to the compulsions of religious nationalism. Despite such disclaimers, it is important to understand the implications of these reinterpretations.

Firstly, the arbitrary use of concepts was entirely instrumental in nature and entailed no serious attempt at creating a heterodox system. In fact, creating a patchwork quilt of concepts only helped strengthen orthodoxy and reinstate an imagined Golden Age. Secondly, the incoherence built into an arbitrary reading of philosophical concepts led to an equally random selection of myths for proving a point and discarding them with alacrity if they failed to be in consonance with the dharmashastric tradition and its well-entrenched injunctions against myths in general and puranic myths in particular. Thirdly, philosophical schools and systems could be condemned as inferior or privileged as perfect without any systematic engagement with their arguments. Finally, an incoherence and arbitrariness in reading of concepts also affected the reading of texts. Devoid of context and historicity, texts could be read for fulfilling narrow political purposes[13] rather than for providing a fresh interpretation or for an imaginative leap into a new constellation of meanings.

Therefore, despite a conceptual continuity, the focus of the questions and the treatment of the theme in this volume do not overlap with an earlier essay

---

13. See Sanjay Palshikar's forthcoming volume on the nationalist readings of the Bhagavadgita. Sanjay Palshikar, *Bhagavadgita, Evil and the Practice of Finitude*, Routledge, New Delhi, 2013 (forthcoming).

on Vivekananda.[14] For instance, the popularly known speech by Vivekananda at the World's Parliament of Religions in 1893 in Chicago has been left out and so has the Kshir Bhavani episode. Nor is the intention here to enter into a discussion on already existing Vivekananda scholarship, especially on the question of Practical Vedanta. Paul Hacker's criticism of Vivekananda's formulation of Practical Vedanta continues to be debated to this day, with invaluable contributions from Wilhelm Halbfass, Andrew O. Fort, Stuart Elkman, Glyn Richards, Jeffrey J. Kripal, Loriliai Biernacki, Vrinda Dalmiya and Andrew J. Nicholson, to mention only a few.[15] There

---

14. Jyotirmaya Sharma, *Hindutva: Exploring the Idea of Hindu Nationalism*, Penguin Books, New Delhi, 2011, Second edition, pp. 73-126.

15. *Philology and Confrontation: Paul Hacker on Traditional and Modern Vedanta*, edited by Wilhelm Halbfass, State University of New York Press, Albany, 1995; Wilhelm Halbfass, 'Practical Vedānta', in *Representing Hinduism: The Construction of Religious Traditions and National Identity*, edited by Vasudha Dalmia, H Von Stietencron, Sage Publications, New Delhi, 1995, pp. 211-23; Wilhelm Halbfass, 'Research and Reflection: Responses to my Respondents', in *Beyond Orientalism: The Work of Wilhelm Halbfass and its Impact on Indian and Cross-Cultural Studies*, Edited by Eli Franco, Karin Preesendanz, Motilal Banarsidass, Delhi, 2007, pp. 587-94; Andrew O. Fort, 'Jīvanmukti and Social Service in Advaita and Neo-Vedanta', in *Beyond Orientalism*, op.cit., pp. 489-504; Stuart Elkman, 'Religious Plurality and Swami Vivekananda', in *Beyond Orientalism*, op.cit., pp. 505-11; Glyn Richards, 'Vivekananda and Essentialism', in *Swami Vivekananda and the Modernisation of Hinduism*, edited by

is much to learn from each of these interventions, as there are points of agreement and disagreement with each of these interpretations. Apart from these texts, the works of David Shulman, Don Handelman, Sarah Caldwell, Vasudha Narayanan, John Stratton Hawley, and Nathaniel Roberts have been indispensable for a better understanding of questions regarding Hindu self-images and Hindu identity.[16] Several controversies

William Radice, Oxford University Press, New Delhi, 1996, pp. 213-23; Jeffrey J. Kripal, *Kālī's Child: The Mystical and the Erotic in the Life and Teachings of Ramakrishna*, The University of Chicago Press, Chicago, 1995; Jeffrey J. Kripal, 'Why the Tāntrika is a Hero: Kālī in the Psychoanalytic Tradition', in *Encountering Kālī: In the Margins, at the Centre, in the West*, edited by Rachel Fell McDermott and Jeffrey J. Kripal, University of California Press, Berkeley, 2003, pp.196-222; Loriliai Biernacki, 'Towards a Tantric Nondualist Ethics through Abhinavagupta's Notion of Rasa', *The Journal of Hindu Studies*, 2011; 4: 258-73; Vrinda Dalmiya, 'The metaphysics of Ethical Love: Comparing Vedanta and Feminist Ethics', *SOPHIA* (2009) 48: 221-35; Andrew J. Nicholson, *Unifying Hinduism: Philosophy and Identity in Indian Intellectual History*, Columbia University Press, New York, 2010.

16. David Shulman, *More Than Real: A History of the Imagination in South India*, Harvard University Press, Cambridge, Massachusetts, 2012; Don Handelman, 'The Guises of the Goddess and the Transformation of the Male: Gangamma's Visit to Tirupati, and the Continuum of Gender', in *Syllables of Sky: Studies in South Indian Civilization In Honour of Velcheru Narayana Rao*, edited by David Shulman, Oxford University Press, Delhi, 1995, pp. 283-337; Sarah Caldwell, *Oh Terrifying Mother: Sexuality, Violence and Worship of the Goddess Kālī*, Oxford

pertaining to translation of texts from Bangla, especially those generated after the publication of Jeffrey J. Kripal's book, have also been left aside. Texts in Bangla crucial to the substantive argument have been closely studied. For the purposes of interpretation, the texts considered 'official' are good enough for building an argument. It does not matter, then, if Dr Mahendra Sarkar's calling Kali 'that santhal bitch' is either edited out of Swami Nikhilananda's translation or sanitized as 'that santhal hag'. Rather, reinstating Kali in a tantra- and bhakti-inspired tradition, inspired by the likes of Ramprasad Sen and Sri Ramakrishna is more significant, if only to delineate the manner in which Vivekananda sought to restate Hinduism as religion.

❦

In writing this book, many invaluable debts were incurred. The University of Hyderabad, and the then vice-chancellor of the university, Professor S.E. Hasnain,

University Press, New Delhi, 1999; Vasudha Narayanan, 'Diglossic Hinduism: Liberation and Lentils', *Journal of the American Academy of Religion*, December 2000, Vol. 68, No. 4, pp. 761-79; John Stratton Hawley, 'Who Speaks for Hinduism – and Who Against? *Journal of the American Academy of Religion*, December 2000, Vol. 68, No. 4, pp. 711-20; Nathaniel Roberts, 'Meanings of Monotheism: Ethnographic evidence and the intolerance thesis', Draft paper made available by the kind permission of the author.

granted me leave for a year and a half in order to take up various fellowships that were offered to me. I am very grateful for the university's decision to support my time away for research, a distinguishing mark of any good university. The current vice-chancellor, Professor Ramakrishna Ramaswamy, has been equally encouraging and supportive. I also thank all my colleagues in the Department of Political Science for supporting my absence away from teaching. I thank Professor I. Ramabrahmam, who as the then head of the department was very supportive. His successor, Professor Arun Patnaik, has been equally enthusiastic and encouraging.

This book was written during the Spring Semester I spent at the Swedish Collegium for Advanced Study (SCAS) in Uppsala. I thank Björn Wittrock, the principal of the Collegium, for this opportunity. Apart from his personal generosity, warmth and support, I am indebted to him for having invited me to an incomparable institution and for creating an almost perfect ambience for research and meaningful conversations. Though the home page of the SCAS carries a quote that calls it a 'scholar's utopia', one has to live there to realize that it far exceeds the epithet in being a warm, welcoming and ideal place for reading, writing, discussions and reflecting. The staff at the SCAS makes sure that the utopia is translated into reality every single day and no extent of formal expression of gratitude is enough to

pay back their various kindnesses. To Anna Svensson, Bjarne Graff, Kristina Lundgren, Maria Odengrund, Pia Hultgren, Linn Östman, Sandra Rekanovic, Ulrika Johansson and Martin Grentzelius – thank you for your magnificent generosity and all your help.

Professor Barbro Klien guided, encouraged and cheered me in ways only she can. I owe her an immense debt of gratitude for making my stay at SCAS memorable and fruitful. In Anders Hillborg, the composer-in-residence at SCAS, I found a warm and generous friend. Professor Mats Lundahl was equally generous with conversation, coffee and friendship. Professor Bernard Wasserstein was lavish with his inimitable banter, humour and deep wisdom. Dr Jyrki Ruohomäki, Dr Felicity Green and Dr Sanna Nyqvist were always a reassuring and warm presence. Professor Philippe Steiner brought great vivacity, intellectual energy and cheer for a month and his stay, though short, was memorable.

Professor Ali Ahmed made my stay at SCAS memorable for more reasons than I can recount. He not only strengthened my belief in the possibility of genuine friendship, but also laughed at all my jokes and shared my passion for Urdu poetry. His magnanimity, his large-heartedness and his lavish generosity will be difficult for me to repay. Neither do I have sufficiently appropriate words to express my gratitude. All I can say is that I am fortunate to have found a friend like Ali and hope that

I will have the opportunity of thanking him over the years to come.

I thank Professor Michael Puett for reading several of the chapters in this book and for his critical comments. I thank Professor Probal Dasgupta, Dr Anindita Mukhopadhyay, Dr Debjani Bhattacharyya and Mrs Chandana Chakraborti for helping me with translations of Bangla texts.

The theme of this book formed the basis of many of the elective courses I taught at the University of Hyderabad from 2007 to 2011. I thank all my students for their intellectual curiosity and their comments and suggestions.

During my time away from Hyderabad, Dr K.T. Mahi ensured that all my small worries were his and made sure that I remained unaffected by them. To him and his friendship I owe a deep debt of gratitude. Jasmine and Anoop Rao cheered and encouraged long-distance and it meant a lot to me. Ravita and Satyajai Mayor kept me connected to 'home' and updated me with all the news and gossip, for which I am very thankful.

A special word for Barbara de Saran. She helped in more ways than I can list. As long as I could turn to 'Barbie Auntie', I was assured that all was well with the world and that every issue would have a solution and would be sorted to everyone's satisfaction. A big 'thank you' for your help, support, but most of all, your friendship.

V.K. Karthika at HarperCollins proved once again that a book is ultimately a 'pact' between the publisher, the writer and the writer's friends. Her unstinting support, enthusiasm and faith in the book were gratifying and the source of immense encouragement. I owe her more than she may realize. I thank Shantanu Ray Chaudhuri for painstakingly editing the book and saving me from many errors and infelicities. Aditya Pratap Deo generously agreed to allow me the use of his photograph of a Kolkata street for the cover of the HarperCollins edition, for which I owe him great gratitude. Bipul Guha designed the cover, continuing an association and friendship that began fifteen years ago. I thank him for his magnificent kindness. I thank Shuka Jain for the overall cover design for the Indian edition and her painstaking attention to all design details.

Neelini Sarkar was instrumental in ensuring that the book reaches a bigger and wider audience for which I sincerely thank her. Jennifer Banks, senior editor at Yale University Press, showed tremendous enthusiasm for the book. The Yale University Press edition is a tribute to her faith in the worth of the book. I owe her a very genuine debt of gratitude for making this possible.

For me, any attempt to thank Professor Shalini Randeria will always remain incomplete and inadequate. Her support, encouragement, advice and generosity have been incomparable. I owe her innumerable debts that I could only falteringly and clumsily attempt to

repay; these defy ordinary expressions of gratitude available to us. All I can say is that I will keep trying by working hard and writing better, which would perhaps be the best way to thank her.

This book is dedicated to three remarkable women and three irreplaceable friends. The deaths of all the three were unnecessary, premature, and in the case of two of them, cruel. All three taught me a great deal, gave their affection generously, and demonstrated the finest instances of true friendship in the time I knew them. This book, then, is for Meenakshi Mukherjee, Papiya Ghosh and Sabina Sehgal Saikia.

A Restatement of Religion

Ramakrishna's One-Fourth

In 1901, Swami Vivekananda narrates a very significant story about himself and Sri Ramakrishna Paramahamsa. The conversation, recorded in the diary[1] of his disciple, Sharat Chandra Chakravarty, takes place in Belur Math a year before Vivekananda's death. The disciple asks after Vivekananda's health, who, despite various illnesses, had been travelling extensively. Vivekananda tells the disciple that his body might last for a few days more but he was determined to work till the end and die in harness. 'It is She who takes me here and there and makes me work without letting me remain quiet or allowing me to look to my personal comforts,'[2] says the Swami. The 'She' alluded to here is Goddess Kali. He further reveals

---

1. *The Complete Works of Swami Vivekananda*, Vol.7, Advaita Ashrama, Kolkata, Fourteenth impression, 2002, pp. 206-7 (*The Complete Works of Swami Vivekananda* will henceforth be referred to as *CW*).

2. Ibid., p. 206.

that a few days before Ramakrishna's death, 'She whom he [Ramakrishna] used to call "Kali" [the Goddess Kali] entered this [Vivekananda's] body,'[3] and it was She who made him work relentlessly. Was this metaphorical, asks the disciple. No, replies Vivekananda and begins to tell the story of Ramakrishna and himself a few days before Ramakrishna left his body. Ramakrishna summoned Vivekananda and looked at him 'steadfastly', and, then, fell into a samadhi or trance. On seeing this, Vivekananda too felt 'a subtle force like an electric shock'[4] passing through his body and soon lost what he calls outward consciousness. On regaining consciousness of his own body, he saw Ramakrishna crying. On being asked why he was weeping, Ramakrishna said to him: 'Today, giving you my all, I have become a beggar. With this power you are to do many works for the world's good before you will return.'[5] It was this power, concludes Vivekananda, that constantly directed him to keep on working.

To say that the story of Kali entering Vivekananda's body, his trance, a weeping Ramakrishna's passing on his powers to him is dramatic would be a gross understatement. Coming directly from Vivekananda, it bears the unmistaken imprimatur of legitimacy. But it also serves to establish clearly the line of succession

3. Ibid., p. 206.
4. Ibid., p. 207.
5. Ibid., p. 207.

from Master to chosen disciple. Words and phrases such as 'works' and 'world's good', crucially embedded in the story, also seek to establish the credibility of the future 'improvisation' of the Master's faith that Vivekananda would eventually undertake. For the devout and the faithful, this account stands beyond doubt and reproach. Swami Nikhilananda follows this path of devotion and fidelity to a fault. In the introduction to the English translation of Mahendranath Gupta's *Sri Sri Ramakrishna Kathāmrita*,[6] he reproduces Vivekananda's version of the story verbatim. Ironically, the volume for which he writes the introduction has a less dramatic account of the same story. The narrator of the story in this instance is also Vivekananda but the listener is Mahendranath Gupta himself, who not only records the conversation but also directly participates in it.

The date of the conversation between Vivekananda and Mahendranath is 9 April 1887. Ramakrishna had died in August the previous year. After dinner, the two men, sitting in the garden of the Baranagore Math, began to reminisce about Ramakrishna. At one point in the

6. *The Gospel of Sri Ramakrishna: Originally recorded in Bengali by M., a disciple of the Master*, Translated into English with an Introduction by Swami Nikhilananda, Ramakrishna-Vivekananda Center, New York, 2007 imprint, p. 72. This is a translation of Mahendranath Gupta's *Sri Sri Ramakrishna Kathāmrita*, originally published between 1897 and 1932 in five volumes in Bengali. Henceforth, all references to the English translation will be cited as *Gospel*.

conversation, Vivekananda says to Mahendranath that at Cossipore 'he [Ramakrishna] transmitted his power to me'.[7] His interlocutor is already aware of the story and indicates so. What follows in the course of the exchange between the two is crucial:

> *Narendra*: Yes. One day, while meditating, I asked Kali to hold my hand. Kali said to me, 'When I touched your body I felt something like an electric shock coming to my body.'
> But you must not tell this to anybody here. Give me your promise.
> *M*: There is a special purpose in his transmission of power to you. He will accomplish much work through you. One day the Master wrote on a piece of paper, 'Naren will teach people.'
> *Narendra*: But I said to him, 'I won't do any such thing.' Thereupon he said, 'Your very bones will do it.'[8]

Three elements stand out in this version of the story, a narrative separated from its 1901 telling by fourteen years. There is no mention, whatsoever, of Goddess Kali entering Vivekananda's body. The Kali in the story is Kaliprasad Chandra, later known as Swami

---

7.   Ibid., p. 985.
8.   Ibid., p. 985.

4

Abhedananda, a disciple of Ramakrishna. Neither are any details of the actual transmission of Ramakrishna's powers offered. In an earlier conversation with Mahendranath on 25 March 1887, Vivekananda mentions Ramakrishna offering to exercise his occult powers through him and his refusal to accept any such thing.[9] Between the conversations on 25 March and 9 April, an instance of Vivekananda going into deep meditation and samadhi is mentioned, but in both instances no direct transmission of occult powers occurs between Master and the chosen disciple. In fact, the burden of the 9 April dialogue shifts primarily to questions of Vivekananda teaching people and doing work.

While Ramakrishna had contempt for the idea of 'work' in the sense Vivekananda later sought to define and convey, a more detailed analysis of this tension between the two regarding the worth of work appears in the next chapter. What is equally intriguing, however, is Ramakrishna's offer to exercise occult powers through Vivekananda. Ramakrishna consistently believed that people who sought siddhis or occult powers were small-minded people.[10] He held in disdain people who acquired powers that enabled them to cure illnesses, win court cases or walk on water. Neither did he approve of genuine devotees working towards such goals and

---

9.   Ibid., pp. 980-1.
10.   Ibid., pp. 745, 459.

dreaded acquiring them even for his own self. Had he got for himself occult powers, Dakshineshwar, he felt, would have been transformed into a hospital or a dispensary.[11] To possess occult powers was troublesome. Once Hriday, Ramakrishna's nephew, egged him on to pray to Kali for bestowing Ramakrishna some occult powers. In his childlike gullibility, Ramakrishna did exactly that. Here is his account of the consequences of the prayer:

> The Divine Mother at once showed me a vision. A middle-aged prostitute, about forty years old, appeared and sat with her back to me. She had large hips and wore a black-bordered sāri. Soon she was covered with filth. The Mother showed me that occult powers are as abominable as the filth of that prostitute.[12]

Ramakrishna resolved to pray henceforth only for pure love, not occult powers, 'a love that does not seek any return'.[13]

Totapuri, the renunciate who had initiated Ramakrishna into sanyasa, taught him of the perils of possessing and holding siddhis through a couple of stories. A man in possession of occult powers was

---

11 Ibid., p. 459.
12. Ibid., p. 745.
13. Ibid., p. 308.

sitting on the seashore watching a great storm rising in front of him. This caused him great discomfort and so he decided to use his powers to quell the storm. A ship going full sail before the wind sank as a consequence of the storm's abrupt end. All the passengers on the ship died and the sin of causing their death fell upon him, resulting in loss of his occult powers. In another instance, God disguised as a holy man comes to a sage who has occult powers. God first encourages the sadhu to kill an elephant and then asks him to bring the elephant back to life. The sadhu manages to do both with the help of his siddhis. At this point, God, still in disguise, asks the sadhu what this act of killing and reviving the elephant had done for him. Was he uplifted by it? Did the act manage to help him realize God?[14]

Having narrated these stories, Ramakrishna comes to the conclusion that occult powers lead to pride and pride makes an individual forget God. A true seeker prays only for pure love of God, just as Radha did and just as the gopis did. There is no motive or desire for possessing occult powers beyond pure love of God. In a subtle restatement of the idea of acquiring and possessing occult powers, Ramakrishna plays with the conventional meaning of the words 'siddhi' and 'siddha'. For him, siddhi was not one of the normally understood eight occult powers that one could acquire but attainment of

---

14. Ibid., p. 547.

one's spiritual goal.[15] Following this, a siddha was one who has a firm conviction in the existence of God and in God being the sole instrument of all action. A higher category of siddha was one who had not merely seen God, but spoken intimately to God as Father, Son, or Beloved.[16] To underwrite his rejection of acquiring and possessing occult powers, Ramakrishna would often quote Krishna's words to Arjuna: 'Friend, if you want to realize Me, you will not succeed if you have even one of the eight occult powers'.[17]

If occult powers were instrumental in leading a true aspirant away from God and were comparable to the filth of a prostitute, it is incomprehensible why Ramakrishna would want to transfer his occult powers to Vivekananda. But the story of the transfer of Ramakrishna's powers to Vivekananda has acquired an indelible mystique in the popular imagination, especially so because the more familiar version of the story comes from Vivekananda himself. To quibble over its authenticity leads nowhere. But as a story, about Vivekananda and his Master, told directly to a disciple, and believed, absorbed and disseminated by other disciples and devotees, it remains a singularly important moment in the Ramakrishna-Vivekananda corpus. And it is crucial in understanding the manner in which Vivekananda distanced himself from

---

15. Ibid., p. 624.
16. Ibid., p. 624.
17. Ibid., p. 547.

the central core of Ramakrishna's teachings, remodelled Ramakrishna and then sought to build his model of Hinduism on the basis of his radical restatement of Ramakrishna.[18]

꧁꧂

Every element that constituted Vivekananda's creation of Hinduism as religion lies embedded in this narrative and requires careful unscrambling. Firstly, there is the element of Vivekananda's tortured, ambiguous and fraught relationship with the figure of Kali. While Kali was central to Ramakrishna's conception of what constituted faith and his ideal of bhakti, Vivekananda's attitude towards her iconic status remained ambivalent. Next, there is the emphasis on 'work', and more

---

18. In his extremely suggestive, brilliantly argued and indispensable essay titled, 'Kaliyuga, Chakri and Bhakti: Ramakrishna and His Times', Sumit Sarkar calls the process of Vivekananda's remodelling of Ramakrishna's teachings as an 'inversion', though he warns the reader that it would be a mistake to reduce Vivekananda's project as 'a mere series of inversions of Ramakrishna'. See Sumit Sarkar, *Writing Social History*, Oxford University Press, 2009 imprint, pp. 282-357. Also see, Narasingha P. Sil, 'Vivekananda's Ramakrishna: An Untold Story of Mythmaking and Propaganda', *Numen*, Vol. 40 (1993), pp. 38-62; Walter G. Neevel, Jr., 'The Transformation of Śrī Rāmakrishna', in *Hinduism: New Essays in the History of Religions*, edited by Bardwell L. Smith, E.J. Brill, Leiden, 1976, pp. 53-97.

significantly, the importance of 'work' for a sanyasi. Here, the sanyasi must not 'remain quiet' and must not look to his 'personal comforts'. Vivekananda not only seeks to restate the ideal of renunciation, but also attempts to redefine the role of religion in relation to the world. Another significant element is Vivekananda's unquestioned acceptance of the instance of Kali entering his body. As someone who rejected the prophetic and revelatory traditions within other religions and heralded his reading of Ramakrishna's Hinduism as scientific, this ready acceptance of Kali's entry into his body is surprising. While it is no surprise that Ramakrishna looked at him 'steadfastly' and fell into a trance, Vivekananda losing outward consciousness is unusual; Vivekananda had little sympathy for Ramakrishna's trances and often termed them as hallucinations. Also, having stated that 'She' whom Ramakrishna used to call Kali entered his body, he does not actually directly acknowledge Kali entering his body but equates that experience to a subtle force like an electric shock. Equally puzzling is why Ramakrishna, who was a sanyasi, would feel like a 'beggar' after having given his 'all' to Vivekananda. And having given his 'all', would Ramakrishna exhort Vivekananda to 'do many works for the world's good', especially when he consistently rejected even the slightest suggestion that a spiritual seeker and a sanyasi ought to have any role in directly alleviating misery in the world? Some of these questions require careful consideration for a better understanding of Vivekananda's definition of religion and his fashioning of Hinduism as religion.

Vivekananda was plagued to the end of his life by the question of Kali worship and its place in the religion that he sought to preach and disseminate. There was, indeed, an inherent tension between what Vivekananda preached and what he claimed to privately believe. Despite the fact that Kali had entered his body and was constantly pushing him to do good for the world, Kali's worship was not part of the religion that he preached to his disciples and audiences across the world. In a letter to Miss Mary Hale, dated 17 June 1900, Vivekananda is categorical in rejecting Kali worship as part of the religion he preached:

> Kali worship is not a necessary step in any religion. The Upanishads teach us all there is to religion. Kali worship is my special *fad*; you never heard me preach it, or read of my preaching it in India. I only preach what is good for universal humanity. If there is any curious method which applies entirely to me, I keep it a secret and there it ends. I must not explain to you what Kali worship is, as I never taught it to anybody.[19]

---

19. *The Complete Works of Swami Vivekananda*, Vol. 8, Advaita Ashrama, Calcutta, Twelfth impression, 1999, pp. 522-3 (Emphasis in original).

Kali worship, then, is reduced to a personal fad, a curious method, and a secret that is not to be shared with anyone. Nor is any explanation for nursing this secret fad to be entertained. More significantly, neither is Kali worship a necessary step in any religion that he preached or part of one that could be taught universally, nor is it something that could be for the good of humanity. But before Kali became his fad and secret, Vivekananda's relationship with the goddess was deeply fraught.

'How I used to hate Kali',[20] Vivekananda recalls in a conversation with a disciple. He hated her and hated 'all her ways'. This was what he calls the 'ground of my six years' fight – that I would not accept Her'.[21] The fight was with Kali and with Ramakrishna; any reconciliation with Kali would also mean accepting Ramakrishna. With Ramakrishna, the 'fight' lasted all the years Vivekananda had known him, between 1881, when he first met his future Master, and 1886, the year Ramakrishna died. Before going into the reasons for his initial hatred and eventual 'acceptance' of Kali, a word needs to be said about the dynamics that come into play between a Great Master and his disciples.

Vivekananda deified Ramakrishna but was never obliged to follow either his guru's life or thoughts. Following the example of charismatic religious

20. Ibid., p. 263.
21. Ibid., p. 263.

leaders in the past and their devotees, Vivekananda used his adoration of Ramakrishna to justify his own reformulation of religion and of what he believed to be Hinduism. He continued to claim that all he did and said was in the spirit of Ramakrishna's teachings and represented the Master's essential spirit. He gave Ramakrishna's faith a theological face and a preacher's energy, shedding all the intricate complexity and intense religious emotion that is the hallmark of Ramakrishna's pure devotionalism. When challenged by his brother monks about altering Ramakrishna's faith, he often got enraged and indulged in what can safely be called petulant and self-righteous outbursts:

What do you know? You are an ignorant man... Your study ended like that of Prahlada at seeing the first Bengali alphabet, Ka, for it reminded Prahlada of Krishna and he could not proceed further because of tears that came into his eyes... You are sentimental fools! What do you understand of religion? You are only good at praying with folded hands, 'O Lord! how beautiful is Your nose! How sweet are your eyes!' and all such nonsense... and you think your salvation is secured and Shri Ramakrishna will come at the final hour and take you by the hand to the highest heaven...Study, public preaching, and doing humanitarian works are, according to you, Maya, because he said to someone, 'Seek and find God first; doing good in the world is a presumption!' ...As if God is such an easy thing to be achieved! As if He is such a fool as to make Himself a plaything in the hands of an imbecile![22]

Bhakti and the primacy of attaining God as outlined by Ramakrishna are to be brushed aside. But Vivekananda also seems to know God's mind and even God's distaste for imbeciles. The outburst above is not merely one where Ramakrishna's idea of bhakti in its pure devotional form clashes with Vivekananda's credo of study, public preaching and doing humanitarian work; Vivekananda's religious nationalism appropriates and refashions Ramakrishna beyond recognition:

You think you have understood Shri Ramakrishna better than myself! You think Jnana is dry knowledge to be attained by a desert path, killing out the tenderest faculties of the heart! Your Bhakti is sentimental nonsense, which makes one impotent. You want to preach Ramakrishna as you have understood him, which is mighty little. Hands off! Who cares for your Ramakrishna? Who cares for your Bhakti and Mukti? Who cares what

---

22. Romain Rolland, *The Life of Vivekananda and the Universal Gospel*, Advaita Ashrama, Calcutta, 1975 impression, pp. 124-5.

your Scriptures say? I will go into a thousand hells cheerfully, if I can rouse my countrymen immersed in Tamas, to stand on their own feet and be *men* inspired with the spirit of Karma-Yoga...I am not a servant of Ramakrishna, or anyone, but of him only who serves and helps others, without caring for his own Bhakti or Mukti![23]

Familiar themes of making Indians more manly, the significance of raising Indians from tamas and making them self-reliant are all present in this second outburst. What is more significant is also the outright rejection of any possible version of Ramakrishna other than Vivekananda's own. Romain Rolland cites witnesses to such frequent outbursts and says that after these fulminations, Vivekananda would go to meditate. After he emerges from the meditation, he tells his brother monks of his unfinished work for his motherland and his undelivered message to the world. In the same breath, he speaks of being a slave of Ramakrishna; he was someone who was doing Ramakrishna's work and Ramakrishna was tirelessly making him do his work. What was Ramakrishna's 'work'? Could Vivekananda really do Ramakrishna's work? Answers to these questions have been attempted below. Still crucial is the need to ask if the 'six years' fight' between Ramakrishna and Vivekananda

---

23. Ibid., p. 125 (Emphasis in original).

ever resolved. Could any such reconciliation really happen without an acceptance of Kali?

I

For Ramakrishna, Shakti alone constitutes the universe. The world was Mahamaya or the Great Illusion. Ramakrishna describes the Divine Mother variously as the Shakti or Primal Energy, the 'Cosmic Power Itself' and the 'Great Illusion'. God had manifested in the form of the Divine Mother and through her had initiated the cycles of creation, preservation and destruction. In certain ways of looking at the world, God is perceived as the Absolute. For instance, the Vedanta way of perceiving reality suggests that only Brahman is real. Ramakrishna accepts all these views but suggests that there cannot be Absolute without the Relative and vice versa.[24]

---

24. *Gospel*, pp. 134-5. In Gaudiya Vaishnava tradition, Maya-Shakti is part of the infinite energies of the Bhagavat and is one of the three aspects of the Lord. Maya-Shakti is the external or Bahiranga aspect of the Bhagavat's Shakti. This Maya-Shakti is real and not the power of illusion as suggested by Advaitins and in the Vaishnava tradition the cause of the world. See *Caitanya Caritamrita of Krishnadasa Kaviraja*, a translation and commentary by Edward C. Dimock, Jr, Harvard University Press, Cambridge, Massachusetts, 1999, p. 174 (henceforth cited as *CC*). Also see, Sushil Kumar De, *Early History of the Vaisnava Faith and Movement in Bengal*, Firma K.L. Mukhopadhyay, Calcutta, 1961 edition, pp. 277-9.

The refrain, 'He who is Brahman is also Śakti',[25] appears throughout the *Kathāmrita* with consistency and regularity and constitutes an important element in shaping Ramakrishna's faith. His inspiration is the poet Ramprasad Sen, a mystic-poet and Tantrik of the eighteenth century. Take, for instance, this poem of Ramprasad, one which was a particular favourite of Ramakrishna:

> How are you trying, O my mind, to know the
> nature of God?
> You are groping like a madman locked in a dark
> room.
> He is grasped through ecstatic love; how can you
> fathom Him without it?
> Only through affirmation, never negation, can you
> know Him;
> Neither through Veda nor through Tantra nor the
> six darśanas.
>
> It is in love's elixir only that He delights, O mind;
> He dwells in the body's inmost depths, in
> Everlasting Joy.
> And, for that love, the mighty yogis practise yoga
> from age to age;
> When love awakes, the Lord, like a magnet, draws
> to Him the soul.

---

25. *Gospel*, p. 107.

He it is, says Rāmprasād, that I approach as
Mother;
But must I give away the secret, here in the market-
place?
From the hints I have given, O mind, guess what
that Being is![26]

Ramakrishna explains the meaning of the poem in the
following way:

Rāmprasād asks the mind only to guess the nature
of God. He wishes it to understand that what is
called Brahman in the Vedas is addressed by him
as the Mother. He who is attributeless also has
attributes. He who is Brahman is also Śakti. When
thought of as inactive, He is called Brahman, and
when thought of as the Creator, Preserver, and
Destroyer, He is called the Primordial Energy,
Kāli. Brahman and Śakti are identical, like fire
and its power to burn. When we talk of fire we
automatically mean also its power to burn. Again,
the fire's power to burn implies the fire itself. If you
accept one you must accept the other.[27]

---

26. Ibid., p. 107. For a short, but excellent, introduction to Ramprasad
Sen's life and work, see *The Oxford Anthology of Bhakti Literature*,
edited by Andrew Schelling, Oxford University Press, New
Delhi, 2011, pp. 216-8.
27. Ibid., pp. 107-8.

God is not to be attained through the mind or by using dry, formal logic. Only ecstatic love can draw an individual closer to God. Books and scriptures are meaningless if there is absence of love for God. Loving engagement and surrender to God will help us know God's true nature. Once that is known, the realization that there is no distinction between Brahman and Kali will become clear. These are the very contours of Ramakrishna's thought and the building blocks of his faith.

In suggesting that Brahman and Kali are the same, Ramakrishna also comes to the conclusion that differences are only in name and form, whereas Reality is one and undifferentiated.[28] When water is still, says Ramakrishna, it stands for an illustration of Brahman, but the same water moving in waves can be compared to Kali. Kali is one who

---

28. It has been suggested that Ramakrishna drew inspiration regarding his stance about God as both formless and with form from the Bengal School of Vaishnavism. In this version of Vaishnavism, it is called *Acintya-bhedābheda-vāda*, which translates as incomprehensible dualistic monism, indicating inconceivable existence of distinction and non-distinction. What follows is the idea that Bhagavata or the Lord is the perfect person, but he is not a formless entity but is an embodied substance in which infinite attributes and energies inhere. He is not unembodied, but possesses a blessed form, a Satchidananda-Vigraha. See Sushil Kumar De, op.cit., p. 284. On Bhedābheda, see an excellent exposition in Andrew J. Nicholson, *Unifying Hinduism: Philosophy and Identity in Indian Intellectual History*, Columbia University Press, New York, 2010.

communes with Maha-Kala, the Absolute. She is formless but she also has forms. She appears to be black because we only look at her from a distance. Greater proximity to Kali makes one realize that she has no colour. Again, to illustrate this point, Ramakrishna takes examples from daily life. For instance, the water in a lake might appear black from a distance, but take it in your hands and it is devoid of any colour. The water in the ocean might look blue from a distance but when held in one's hand it looks colourless. The important message here is to become intimate with God. The closer one comes to God, the greater the extent of lucidity that God has neither name nor form.[29] For a true devotee, it is important to meditate on Kali with firm conviction, coaxing Kali to reveal her true nature to him. For Ramakrishna, God is not a distant and intimidating figure. True devotion can impel God to come near a devotee and speak to him in ways that ordinary human beings talk to each other. But a few hurdles have to be crossed before such a conversation can actually take place.

Kali, the Divine Mother, destroys and creates the universe. After a cycle of creation and destruction completes, the time to create the universe arrives. In creating the universe, Kali 'garners the seeds for the next creation...like the elderly mistress of the house, who has a hotchpotch-pot in which she keeps different articles

---

29. *Gospel*, pp. 135, 271, 634.

for household use'.[30] Once the universe is created, the Primal Power dwells in the universe itself. In dwelling in the universe and pervading it, Kali is always 'playful and sportive', and the universe as a whole is 'Her play'.[31] Ramakrishna perceives Kali's play in the world in manifold ways and sees her manifest in a variety of forms. She is 'Mahā-Kāli, Nitya-Kāli, Śmaśāna-Kāli, Rakshā-Kāli and Śyāmā-Kāli'.[32] Of these forms, Mahā-Kāli and Nitya-Kāli are part of Tantra philosophy. As Mahā-Kāli, she is the formless one, existing in unison with the Mahā-Kāla, the Absolute. This is her state before the creation of the universe, before the beginning of the world as we know it. In an evocative phrase, Ramakrishna describes this moment as one 'when darkness was enveloped in darkness'. In other manifestations, she is the dispenser of boons and the dispeller of fear, and she protects in times of natural calamities. She is the embodiment of destruction as Śmaśāna-Kāli, residing in the cremation ground, surrounded by corpses, jackals and terrible female spirits, a stream of blood flowing from her mouth, a garland of human heads hanging around her neck and a girdle of human heads covering her waist.

Ramakrishna's Kali, 'my Divine Mother',[33] as he refers to her, is playful and sportive, but she is also 'self-willed

---

30. Ibid., p. 135.
31. Ibid., p. 136.
32. Ibid., p. 135.
33. Ibid., p. 135.

21

and must always have Her own way'.[34] She creates bondage in the world and she liberates. To play with her creation is for her a game of hide-and-seek. In the game, the eyes of the participants are covered, while the leader, called the 'granny' in the Indian version of the game, hides herself. One who manages to find the 'granny' and touch her gets to remove the cover from his eyes and is released from the game. Just as one participant is released from the game of hide-and-seek, only one out of a hundred thousand is liberated from the bondage of the world. When a Brahmo devotee asks the reason for Kali not liberating everyone, Ramakrishna's reply is interesting: 'In a game of hide-and-seek the running about soon stops if in the beginning all the players touch the "granny". If all touch her, then how can the game go on? That displeases her. Her pleasure is in continuing the game.'[35] As Mahamaya, this primal energy blinds us with ignorance. It was part of God's play to bind humans to the chains of illusion, or as Ramakrishna puts it, God had 'created the world in play'.[36] The magic of creation, preservation and destruction was part of the play. To realize God, these chains had to be broken. One had to enter the 'inner' chamber in order to transcend the world of objects and this could be done through the grace of Shakti alone. The only way to do that was to submit to

34. Ibid., p. 136.
35. Ibid., p. 136.
36. Ibid., p. 116.

the Divine Mother. Only when we get past the world of appearances do we encounter Eternal Being, described as Sachchidananda or the existence-knowledge-bliss idea of the absolute.

To go past the veil of ignorance and understand Mahamaya or the Great Illusion, it is important, suggests Ramakrishna, to come to grips with two aspects of Kali. These are vidya and avidya. Vidya or knowledge helps the devotee attain God through devotion, kindness, wisdom, and love. Avidya deludes, says Ramakrishna; it ensnares and casts a spell through 'kamini and kanchan', or 'woman and gold'.[37] In speaking about vidya and avidya, Ramakrishna is explicit in stating that Brahman is beyond vidya and avidya, both of which are 'the illusory duality of knowledge and ignorance' created by maya, which, in turn, is the illusion of duality.[38] But he is also categorical that the world is not illusory. He concedes to Narendra, the future Swami Vivekananda, that the whole world was a theatre where one sometimes saw the play of vidya and at other places the unfolding of avidya. Narendra contradicts him by suggesting that everything is the play of vidya alone. Ramakrishna does not entirely agree. For a man who has the knowledge of Brahman, he says, the world may be a play of vidya, but for those who follow the path of divine love both vidyamaya and

---

37. Ibid., p. 116.
38. Ibid., pp. 101-2.

avidyamaya exist.[39] When Mahendranath Gupta tells him that the body alone was the cause of all mischief, Ramakrishna has this to say: 'Why should you say such a thing? This world may be a "framework of illusion", but it is also said that it is a "mansion of mirth". Let the body remain. One can also turn this world into a mansion of mirth.'[40]

The phrases 'framework of illusion' and 'mansion of mirth' are from Ramprasad,[41] and Ramakrishna would refer to these frequently, as we will see subsequently. In the present context, it is important to understand that the world becomes a 'mansion of mirth' for Ramakrishna when one begins to see God in the whole universe and perceive the whole universe as permeated by God. Another time, Mahendranath Gupta records Ramakrishna saying this to him:

Why should the universe be unreal? This is a speculation of the philosophers. After realizing God, one sees that it is God Himself who has become the universe and all living beings.

The Divine Mother revealed to me in the Kāli temple that it was She who had become everything.

39. Ibid., pp. 704-5. The question of the path of knowledge and the path of divine love would be discussed in detail in the subsequent paragraphs.

40. Ibid., p. 298.

41. Ibid., p. 478.

> She showed me that everything was full of
> Consciousness. The Image was Consciousness, the
> altar was Consciousness, the water-vessels were
> Consciousness, the door-sill was Consciousness,
> the marble floor was Consciousness – all was
> Consciousness.[42]

To reach this stage of consciousness, however, a barrier
had to be crossed, a necessary leap was imperative.

In order to attempt this transition, it was crucial to
understand the nature of *ananda* or joy. Ramakrishna
suggests that ananda is of three kinds.[43] One is the joy of
worldly pleasures, consisting of the joys of 'woman and
gold'. This is the most common of all joys among people.
Chanting the name of God and his glories is the second
kind of joy. The 'joy of God-vision' or the joy of Brahman
is the third category of joy and attaining this joy helped
the sages of the past transcend all rules and conventions.
Of these joys, the enjoyment of 'woman and gold' alone is
maya.[44] While arguing that all women are the embodiments
of Shakti, an appearance of the Primal Power in the form

---

42. Ibid., p. 345.
43. Ibid., p. 478.
44. Ibid., p. 336. Within the framework of Bengal Vaishnavism,
    Ramakrishna's position would be closer to that of Chaitanya
    than later developments that welcomed women ascetics into
    the fold. See *CC*, op.cit., pp. 842-3. Here, Chaitanya says that
    he neither sees nor hears the name of a woman, and ordinary
    sexual desire is the illness of the heart.

of women is part of the play of Shakti as avidya. The first step to counter the spell of maya is to identify and name it. 'If māyā is once recognized,' says Ramakrishna, 'it feels ashamed of itself and takes to flight.'[45] This is more easily accomplished by practitioners of spiritual discipline than by householders. Householders seldom know whether their wives are vidyashakti or avidyashakti.[46] A wife embodying the characteristics of vidyashakti sleeps little, has no anger or lust, is affectionate, kind, devoted and modest. Such a woman pushes her husband away from herself and in the direction of God. She treats all men like her children. More than anything else, she spends little money, so that her husband doesn't have to work too hard and has all the leisure to aspire for the spiritual path. The traits of a woman who exemplifies avidyashakti are described by Ramakrishna as 'mannish', along with other bad traits as squint eyes, hollow eyes, catlike eyes, lantern jaw like a calf's jaw and pigeon breast.[47] It is remarkable that all the traits of wives who embody avidyashakti are physical unlike those who display the virtuous signs of vidyashakti.

For householders following the path of vidya or knowledge, enjoying conjugal happiness with their wives occasionally is part of satisfying a natural impulse,

---

45. *Gospel*, p. 336.
46. Ibid., pp. 701-2.
47. Ibid., p. 702.

a bit like enjoying 'a sweetmeat once in a while'.[48] But a householder also has to surmount impediments that lie in the way of practising spiritual discipline. Ramakrishna lists these as disease, grief, poverty, misunderstanding with one's wife, and disobedient, stupid, and stubborn children.[49] After producing one or two children, the ideal way forward for the husband and wife is to live like siblings. In doing so, they can continue to practise seven kinds of sexual intercourse.[50] Sitting with a woman, talking to a woman for a long time, listening and enjoying a conversation with a woman, to speak about a woman, to whisper to her privately, to keep something belonging to a woman, and enjoying it and touching a woman are the seven kinds of sexual intercourse Ramakrishna permits householders. The eighth kind is actual sexual intercourse resulting in coitus, which he recommends must stop after the birth of children.

In contrast, one is a sanyasi in the true sense only when he has renounced 'woman and gold' and does not regard women with the same gaze with which a worldly person would look at them. To know Brahman, it is important to be cautious about women. The company of young women can make a lustless man lusty – Ramakrishna likens this to staining one's body in a room filled with soot.[51]

48. Ibid., p. 387.
49. Ibid., p. 326.
50. Ibid., p. 701.
51. Ibid., p. 387.

But it [satisfying one's sexual impulse] is extremely harmful for a sannyāsi. He must not look even at the portrait of a woman. A monk enjoying a woman is like a man swallowing the spittle he has already spat out. A sannyāsi must not sit near a woman and talk to her, even if she is intensely pious. No, he must not talk to a woman even though he may have controlled his passion.

A sannyāsi must renounce both 'woman' and 'gold'. As he must not look even at the portrait of a woman, as also he must not touch gold, that is to say, money. It is bad for him even to keep money near him, for it brings in its train calculation, worry, insolence, anger, and such evils.[52]

Ramakrishna is clear on the question of women: they are a part of the Divine Mother, but as far as men are concerned, especially if they happen to be sanyasis and spiritual practitioners, they must shun women. For Ramakrishna, part of the reason is personal.

I am very much afraid of women. When I look at one I feel as if a tigress were coming to devour me. Besides, I find that their bodies, their limbs, and even their pores are very large. This makes

---

52. Ibid., p. 387. The phrase about a monk enjoying a woman being similar to licking one's own spittle after having spat it out once appears again on p. 701.

me look upon them as she-monsters. I used to be much more afraid of women than I am at present. I wouldn't allow one to come near me. Now I persuade my mind in various ways to look upon women as forms of the Blissful Mother.[53]

As a sanyasi, who also had a wife, the personal and the public easily get conflated in Ramakrishna in the form of the code of conduct desirable for a sanyasi. 'Don't let yourself touch the air near a woman's body,'[54] he advises, and counsels those engaged in spiritual practices to see women as a raging forest fire or a black cobra. It is only after one attains the state of perfection, which, in turn, comes only after attaining God-vision, that women appear as the Blissful Mother. The sanyasi must forgo 'woman and gold' in order to set an example for people wanting to practise renunciation as well as for his own good.

There were other reasons for Ramakrishna's injunctions against 'women and gold'. Three quarters of a man's mind is monopolized by a woman. After a child is born, the whole mind is 'frittered away' on the family and nothing or little is left for thinking about God. Some men shed the last drop of their blood in order to keep their wives out of mischief. Worldly men, concludes

---

53. Ibid., p. 593.
54. Ibid., p. 595.

Ramakrishna, get up and sit down on the orders of women and invariably speak highly of their wives.[55] It is difficult for a man to escape being stained, even if slightly, by 'woman and gold' if he lives in the midst of these two snares created by avidya. One way was to acknowledge that every man has two metaphorical wives, Dispassion and Worldliness.[56] He must only take Dispassion on the journey towards the knowledge of God, or as Ramprasad puts it, 'go for a walk' to Kali. But the walk was not an easy one and the sincere aspirant will have to ask help from Discrimination, who is Dispassion's son, and he is the one who will guide the genuine seeker towards God. Neither Ramakrishna nor Ramprasad tells their readers and listeners anything about the patrimony of Discrimination. Another way of avoiding the stain was maintaining physical distance: '[K]eep yourself eight cubits, two cubits, or at least one cubit away from all women except your mother.'[57]

A sanyasi, then, must always look upon a woman as his mother. If he happens to be near a woman, he must offer her his worship. This was the pure way of worshipping Adyashakti, who manifests also as avidya and has to be propitiated. Ramakrishna invokes an unusual metaphor to explain the 'pure' way of perceiving women. Drawing upon the tradition of

55. Ibid., p. 594.
56. Ibid., p. 327.
57. Ibid., p. 595.

observing a fast on ekadashi,[58] he lists the various ways in which the ekadashi fast could be observed. One was to eat only fruit and, perhaps, drink milk during the fast. Another way was to eat luchis and curries. His own way was to observe the fast without even drinking a drop of water, leave alone food: 'Looking on woman as mother is like fasting on the ekādaśi day without touching even a drop of water; in this attitude there is not the slightest trace of sensual enjoyment.'[59]

This was the way for the sanyasi to live. Enjoying what 'woman and gold' have to offer harms a sanyasi and also harms those who look up to him. Sanyasis ought not to sit with women devotees or even speak to them. Those who develop disinterest in the world from boyhood, reject the world of passion, and yearn for God are part of an 'unsullied aristocracy'.[60] To develop true renunciation, they keep themselves very far away from women and do not fall into the clutches of women. When a spiritual aspirant learns to meditate deeply, the objects of the senses do not any longer intrude but are left outside, just as looking at objects from the outside in a glass room. Having attained this exalted level of meditative depth, Ramakrishna saw 'the inside

---

58. The eleventh lunar day of the bright and dark fortnight of every lunar month.
59. *Gospel*, p. 701.
60. Ibid., p. 603.

31

and outside of the woman';[61] what he saw was 'entrails, blood, filth, worms, phlegm, and such things'.[62]

Despite the warnings to sanyasis regarding 'woman and gold', Ramakrishna was clear that it was Adyashakti who has assumed all female forms and had to be propitiated. While looking upon all women as mother was the pure way he had chosen, Ramakrishna was once a practitioner of another way of appeasing the avidya aspect of the Primal Energy, namely, Tantra. There are instances in the *Kathāmrita* when he rejects the efficacy of what he calls 'the path of the Vedas' in Kaliyuga for spiritual advancement and instead prescribes Tantra.[63] Admitting that the rites of Shakti worship are very difficult and that he had been initiated into performing these rites,[64] he also warns against the vamachara method prescribed in the Tantra. It was, he says, the 'dirty' method of spiritual discipline, a bit like 'entering a house through the back door by which the scavengers come'.[65] Vamachara inevitably led to a spiritual aspirant's downfall because of the proximity of 'an object of enjoyment', namely women.

⌒⌐

---

61. Ibid., p. 745.
62. Ibid., p. 745.
63. Ibid., p. 311.
64. Ibid., p. 116.
65. Ibid., p. 513.

In Tantra, then, a devotee can propitiate Shakti by assuming the attitude of a handmaid, or of a hero or of a child.[66] In the heroic attitude, the idea is to please Shakti in the same way as a man sexually pleases a woman, and in which instance a woman is seen to represent Shakti or Kali. Ramakrishna rejects the need for Tantric practices that involve the company of women. The *Kathāmrita* is generously interspersed with instances of Ramakrishna raising an eyebrow regarding certain sects, like the Ghoshpara, Kartabhaja and Panchanami,[67] and their enjoyment of sensuous pleasures in the name of conducting spiritual practices. In each of these instances, his objection is directed towards any man assuming the attitude of a 'hero', considering a woman as his mistress, in order to ritually appease Shakti. He recounts an instance when he was 'taken' to women of the Kartabhaja sect.[68] He addressed them as 'mother' and they, in turn, saw him as a beginner. In other words, he refused the posture of a hero and a lover and, instead, sought to perceive himself as a child.

But even in such cases, Ramakrishna stops short of

---

66. Ibid., p. 116.
67. Ibid., pp. 337, 513-14, 603. These are sects that were obscure and peripheral, drawing followers mostly from the lower castes. They also had a pronounced affinity with Tantra.
68. Ibid., p. 337. Also see, Jeffrey J. Kripal, *Kālī's Child: The Mystical and the Erotic in the Life and Teachings of Ramakrishna*, University of Chicago Press, 1998, second edition, pp. 123-4.

outright condemnation of these practices. Instead, he calls them 'the most difficult discipline'[69] and warns that this spiritual path may be one where maintaining the 'right attitude'[70] may not always be possible. But these were various paths leading to God, just as there were different roads to reach the Kali temple. For instance, in a conversation with Narendra, he rejects the 'hero' attitude without dismissing Tantra:

> *Narendra*: Isn't it true that the Tantra prescribes spiritual discipline in the company of women?
> *Master*: That is not desirable. It is a very difficult path and often causes the aspirant's downfall. There are three such kinds of discipline. One may regard woman as one's mistress or look on oneself as her handmaid or as her child. I look on woman as my mother. To look on oneself as her handmaid is also good; but it is extremely difficult to practise spiritual discipline looking on woman as one's mistress. To regard oneself as her child is a very pure attitude.[71]

When Achalananda, a tantrik, presses him to admit that the attitude of the 'hero' towards women was legitimate, especially so because it was so prescribed by Lord

---

69. *Gospel*, p. 572.
70. Ibid., p. 572.
71. Ibid., p. 123.

Shiva himself, the author of the Tantra, Ramakrishna politely, but firmly, rejects it. 'But, my dear sir, I don't know. I don't like these ideas,' he says, appending his well-known position on the issue by saying, 'To me every woman is a mother'.[72] Elsewhere, he calls this his 'natural attitude';[73] it helped him regard 'the breasts of any woman as those of my own mother'[74] and impelled him to worship all parts of the body of the Shorashi, a sixteen-year-old, in a tantric ritual as that of his mother.[75] As noted already, Ramakrishna thought of women as 'she-monsters' and found their bodies, limbs and pores very large. He also wonders what happiness could there be in sexlife with a woman. Instead, in ecstatic love of God 'all the pores of the skin, even the roots of the hair, become like so many sexual organs, and in every pore the aspirant enjoys the happiness of communion with the Ātman.'[76] In a unique and distinctive gloss on

72. Ibid., p. 284.
73. Ibid., p. 116.
74. Ibid., p. 116.
75. Ibid., p. 701. See also, p. 418.
76. Ibid., p. 346. A similar explanation given by Ramakrishna using the same expressions and the same phrases can be found in Swami Saradananda's *Sri Sri Ramakrishna Lilaprasanga*, translated from Bangla as *Sri Ramakrishna: The Great Master* by Swami Jagadananda. See, Swami Saradananda, *Sri Ramakrishna: The Great Master*, Volume I, translated by Swami Jagadananda, Sri Ramakrishna Math, Madras, 2001 imprint, p. 259. Henceforth referred in the text as *Lilaprasanga* and cited in footnotes as *Great Master*.

the purusha-prakriti dualism, Ramakrishna prescribes that spiritual aspirants cultivate 'the attitude of Prakriti in order to realize Purusha – the attitude of a friend, a handmaid, or a mother'.[77]

One way of conquering lust and sexual passion was to assume the guise and attitudes of a woman. Ramakrishna speaks of the time he spent as the handmaid of God.[78] He dressed in women's clothes, put on jewellery and covered the upper part of his body with a scarf. Explaining this by talking about the peacock feather in Lord Krishna's crest, he suggests that the feather bears the sign of the female sex. Its significance is that Krishna

---

77. *Gospel*, p. 346. On page 271, Ramakrishna offers a more conventional interpretation of the purusha-prakriti dualism. A discussion on the historical evolution of interpretations of the purusha-prakriti relationship is in the introduction.

78. Ibid., pp. 603-4. In the Bengal Vaishnava tradition, bhakti is classified as Samanya-bhakti, Sadhana-bhakti, Bhava-bhakti and Prema-bhakti. Sadhana-bhakti is further classified into Vaidhi-bhakti and Raganuga-bhakti. In Raganuga-bhakti, the aspirant attempts to meditate on the feelings of the people of Vraja towards Krishna and make efforts to live physically or mentally in the same state as the people of Vraja did for Krishna. They consider Krishna as the only male in Vraja and so their worship to him can only realize the ecstatic passion required to simulate the state of gopis in Vraja when they see themselves as females. This is further divided into perceiving Krishna as Kama-rupa, manifested as a desire for erotic-mystic enjoyment, and as Sambandha-rupa, where the devotee has a sense of relationship, that of father, mother or friend, with Krishna. See Sushil Kumar De, op.cit., pp. 173-85.

sports the female principle, Prakriti, on his head. When dancing with the gopis, Krishna dresses up as a woman. What does it all suggest? Ramakrishna is categorical that as long as a man does not assume a feminine nature and attitude, he is not entitled to be with a woman and enjoy her company.[79] But this can happen only after one realizes God, when the stage comes of seeing the Divine Mother in all women. For the spiritually naive, it is best to keep away from women as far as possible. It would be a mistake, however, to perceive Ramakrishna's anxiety to overcome passion by assuming the attitudes of a woman as a way of coming to terms with one aspect of avidya alone. On the contrary, it offers an opportunity to look at three important strands in Ramakrishna's religious universe, one that Vivekananda would eventually reject or ignore. The first is to explore the ways by which an individual can conquer fear, shame and aversion. No spiritual gain was possible without transcending this triad of fear, shame and aversion. Equally significant, and this is the second strand, was to construct a vocabulary and a methodology of transgression. Neither

---

79. *Gospel*, p. 604. 'Having abandoned his male body, he becomes *prakrti-svarupa*. Know therefore the *svarupa* of Radha; it can be known within the heart. When one becomes *prakrti* by union with *prakrti* it is not by means of his masculine body. God is hidden, but if one is purified, one can be saved my brother.' See Edward C. Dimock, Jr for discussion of the Sahajiya influence on Vaishnavism, op.cit., pp. 159-161.

of these elements could be attained without a careful and judicious restatement of Tantra and Bhakti, and this constitutes the third element in understanding Ramakrishna's faith.

∽◎

The *Kathāmrita* records several instances of Ramakrishna reminiscing about what he called his period of 'divine madness',[80] a period in which he followed the rigours of several spiritual disciplines and paths. The preliminary aim of these spiritual exercises was to overcome fear, shame and aversion in order to achieve the ultimate aim of seeing and realizing God.[81] Most remarkable among the *Kathāmrita* narratives connected to the period of 'divine madness' is the effortless ease with which Ramakrishna travels between accounts of his 'visions' and 'actual' incidents that happened during that time. Take, for instance, the following examples. Ramakrishna once had the vision of the non-dual and indivisible state in which he saw various sorts of men and animals. There were aristocrats, Englishmen, Muslims, scavengers and dogs. A bearded Muslim among these men and creatures had an earthen tray of rice in his hands and began to

---

80. *Gospel*, p. 491.
81. 'There are eight fetters. Shame, hatred, fear, caste, lineage, good conduct, grief and secretiveness – these are the eight fetters.' Ibid., pp. 243-4.

put a few grains in everyone's mouth, including that of Ramakrishna.[82] Another time, he saw rice, vegetables, filth and dirt lying around. The reader of the *Kathāmrita* is not sure in this instance whether what he 'saw' was a vision or a literal sighting of these objects. But more significant is what happens after Ramakrishna sees these things lying around: 'Suddenly the soul came out of my body and, like a flame, touched everything. It was like a protruding tongue of fire and tasted everything once, even the excreta.'[83]

Those who had transcended difference and had conquered fear, aversion and shame had also realized that everything was the same Substance, the same Consciousness. Real sages who had the knowledge of Brahman, the purnajnanis, were 'mad', and they did not follow any social conventions.[84] One such madman did, indeed, visit Dakshineshwar soon after the temple there was built, and was not allowed to eat at the guest house by Haladhari, a priest and cousin of Ramakrishna. Paying no

---

82. Ibid., p. 282. This is retold on page 746.
83. Ibid., p. 282. See Edward C. Dimock, Jr. on the Sahajiya idea of equality or sameness, op.cit., p. 108.
84. *Gospel*, p. 491. 'Following this advice, I take the name incessantly; and while taking the name, my mind becomes distracted. I am not able to hold myself in check; I become as mad: I laugh, I weep, I dance, I sing, as if drunk on wine. Then getting control of myself, I reflected in my mind, "My perception has become clouded by the name of Kṛṣṇa. I have become mad; I cannot hold my mind firm..." *CC*, op. cit., pp. 240-1.

heed to the slight, the madman started to push aside dogs rummaging in a rubbish heap eating crumbs and started to eat those crumbs from the leftovers in the leaf plates.[85] Before departing, the madman said: 'What else shall I say to you? When you no longer make any distinction between the water of this pool and the water of the Ganges, then you will know that you have Perfect Knowledge.'[86]

Ramakrishna categorizes spiritual discipline and its practise into three distinct categories: sattvic, rajasic and tamasic.[87] In the sattvic mode, the devotee does not seek any results but calls upon God with great longing and repeatedly. Many rituals are involved in the rajasic way of spiritual discipline. In the tamasic way, conventional purity is not observed and the devotee 'threatens' and 'coerces' the object of veneration to become visible and manifest. Which of these three categories did Ramakrishna himself follow? 'I vowed to the Divine Mother that I would kill myself if I did not see God. I said to Her: "O Mother, I am a fool. Please teach me what is contained in the Vedas, the Purānas, the Tantras, and the other scriptures".'[88]

---

85. In the *Kathāmrita*, recounting the same story another time, Ramakrishna says: 'Then he went up to a dog, held it by the ear, and ate some of its food. The dog didn't mind.' *Gospel*, p. 548.
86. Ibid., p. 491.
87. Ibid., p. 744.
88. Ibid., p. 544.

Having been so 'coerced', the Divine Mother reveals to him that the essence of Vedanta shows the Brahman to be real and the world to be illusory. But she also explains to him that the Sachchidananda Brahman of the Vedas is the Sachchidananda Shiva of the Tantra and the Sachchidananda Krishna of the Puranas. The point that Ramakrishna repeatedly makes is that all his subsequent spiritual experiences, as detailed by the scriptures, were a consequence of his 'direct perception of God'.[89] It was God who made him pass through various spiritual paths,[90] and it was God who made him behave 'like a child, like a madman, like a ghoul, and like an inert thing'.[91] Ramakrishna likens the quick succession of experiences to being propelled in a husking machine ('no sooner is one end down than the other goes up').[92]

The period of the 'divine madness' was one where Ramakrishna sometimes behaved like a child and at other times as a madman. This period lasted between 1856 and 1867. During the span of intense spiritual practice and divine madness, Ramakrishna was initiated into Shakti worship, Tantra, Vaishnava bhakti, Vedanta, Islam and Christianity. Ending discrimination between the real and the unreal, eliminating the distinction between pure and impure, overcoming fear, shame and aversion were steps

89. Ibid., p. 544.
90. Ibid., p. 543.
91. Ibid., p. 544.
92. Ibid., p. 544.

towards reaching the goal of seeing and knowing God. As part of these practices, Ramakrishna would place a handful of earth in one hand and a coin in the other and then throw it in the Ganga in order to show that both were equally devoid of value and that the 'love of gold' was worthless. He would clean excreta and toilets with his hands; placing excreta in one hand and sandal paste in another, he would come to the conclusion that both were equally part of the five elements. During this period of inflamed spiritual practice, he sometimes worshipped his own penis as a Shivalingam,[93] and while repeating Lord Rama's name, he got so 'God-intoxicated' that he assumed the role of Hanuman to experience the heightened level of devotion of a servant towards his master.[94] In the *Lilaprasanga*, this is how Ramakrishna narrates the experience of experiencing Hanuman's *dasya bhava*:

> 'At that time,' said the Master, 'I had to walk, take my food and do all other actions like Mahavir [Hanuman]. I did not do so of my own accord, but the actions so happened of themselves. I tied my cloth round my waist so that it might look like a tail and moved about jumping; I ate nothing but fruits and roots, which again I did not feel inclined to eat when skinned. I spent much of my time on

---

93. Ibid., p. 491.
94. Ibid., pp. 543-4.

trees and always cried, 'Raghuvir, Raghuvir!' with a deep voice. Both my eyes assumed a restless expression like those of the animal of that species, and strange to say, the lower end of the backbone (coccyx) lengthened at that time nearly an inch.'[95]

The elongation ceased to be what it became after the bhava or mood elapsed.

During the period when he practised Tantra, Ramakrishna lost sense of difference between the tulsi plant, considered sacred, and other plants. He would also eat leftovers from a jackal's food that had been exposed to other animals and poisonous creatures all night. There were other times when he would ride a dog and feed it luchis and also eat part of it himself.[96] While the Vedas and the Puranas have codes of what is considered impure, suggests Ramakrishna, the Tantra extols those very things as good and desirable.[97] Thus, he ate the greens cooked by the wife of a 'low-caste' man, touched his head and lips with the leaf plates left by beggars, felt the desire to eat the boatman's food[98] and enjoyed 'inhaling the smell of burning corpses, carried by the wind from the other side of the Ganges'.[99]

---

95. *Great Master*, pp. 182-3.
96. *Gospel*, p. 544.
97. Ibid., p. 564.
98. Ibid., p. 548.
99. Ibid., p. 564.

When the Bhairavi[100] initiates Ramakrishna into systematic tantric practices as prescribed in the sixty-four primary Tantras, Ramakrishna meditates and performs tantric rites sitting on 'skull-seats' made of the skulls of five dead beings including that of a man. Another 'ordeal' was to sit on the lap of a young, beautiful woman and meditate. Apart from this, Ramakrishna eats fish cooked in the skull of a dead body and overcomes aversion by putting a piece of rotten human flesh in his mouth. Finally, he worships a female figure in the 'heroic' form of Tantra worship, considering her throughout as a child would perceive its mother. His period of divine madness and practice of spiritual disciplines was a state when God himself becomes the entire universe and all its living beings, and the distinction between the inner world of Samadhi and the outer world is lost.

Eating for the tantrik is no ordinary act performed in order to continue life. For Kali, all living beings, dead or alive, are her children and also her food. She spares no one, not even Shiva. Ramakrishna recounts an instance when Mahamaya swallowed Shiva. As a consequence, the six centres in her were awakened and Shiva emerged out of her thigh, going on, then, to create Tantra philosophy.[101] For Ramakrishna, eating assumes a different dimension altogether, a path shown by the redoubtable Ramprasad.

---

100. *Great Master*, pp. 224-7. The Bhairavi has been sanitized as 'Brahmani' in the *Kathāmrita* and *Lilaprasanga* translations.
101. *Gospel*, p. 291.

44

To open one's mouth and eat, therefore, was symbolic of 'seizing' or 'eating' Kali, who had become the universe. In the *Kathāmrita*, Ramakrishna tells Narendra that the choice of what one eats depends on the aspirant's state of mind. A man who had attained the knowledge of Brahman does not himself eat but offers what is eaten to the Kundalini or the spiritual power coiled in each individual in the likeness of a snake.[102] There was a time, then, when Ramakrishna would open his mouth, 'touching, as it were, heaven and the nether world with my jaws, and utter the word "Mā"'.[103] Doing so, he would have the sense of seizing Kali just as a fisherman drags fish in his net. Once again, the inspiration for this symbolic act of 'eating' Kali is to be found in the songs and poems of Ramprasad. Ramakrishna recites one to illustrate his point:

This time I shall devour Thee utterly, Mother Kāli!
For I was born under an evil star,
And one so born becomes, they say, the eater of
    his mother.
Thou must devour me first, or I myself shall eat
    Thee up;
One or the other it must be.[104]

---

102. Regarding food and various states of mind of the aspirant, Ramakrishna says to Narendra in the same conversation cited: 'The present state of my mind is such that I cannot eat any food unless it is first offered to God by a brāhmin priest.' *Gospel*, p. 564.

103. Ibid., p. 564.

104. Ibid., p. 564.

This was not an empty threat. It was a way of claiming, against all odds, the exalted status of being Kali's son:

> O mother, I shall eat Thee up but not digest Thee;
> I shall install Thee in my heart
> And make Thee offerings with my mind.

> You may say that by eating Kāli I shall embroil myself
> With Kāla, Her Husband, but I am not afraid;
> Braving His anger, I shall chant my Mother's name.
> To show the world that Rāmprasād is Kāli's rightful son,
> Come what may, I shall eat Thee up – Thee and Thy retinue –
> Or lose my life attempting it.[105]

For Ramakrishna, this was genuine longing for God. If this longing was firmly in place, an aspirant would be blessed even though he was to eat pork. Conversely, despite eating ritually approved pure food, a person whose mind was focused on 'woman and gold' would scarcely find deliverance.

Overcoming fear, aversion and shame was only one part of the story in an aspirant's quest for God. While practising certain spiritual exercises and initiation into

---

105. Ibid., p. 565.

various spiritual disciplines could be a preliminary step in helping an aspirant inch closer to God, these were not enough for him to see, encounter and experience God and God's grace. Ramakrishna is categorical that in order to attain God one needed an 'intensely yearning heart'.[106] It required a heart that was capable of weeping for God, or as Ramakrishna puts it in his inimitable way, 'Cry to Him with a real cry'.[107] What was crucial, asserts Ramakrishna, was to seek and covet God with a 'longing heart'.[108] To love God with an intensely yearning heart had to have the combined force and an intensity that is akin to the love of a mother for her child, the love of a chaste wife for her husband and the love that a worldly man has for wealth.[109] The longing and love for God was no ordinary kind of love. The love that Sita had for Rama or the love that Parvati had for Shiva was on a different plane altogether: Ramakrishna calls it 'ecstatic love'.[110] It is a state when an individual becomes 'mad with love in order to realize God'.[111]

To develop ecstatic love for God demands complete surrender. In an evocative phrase, Ramakrishna calls upon the devotee who wants to cultivate an intensely

---

106. Ibid., p. 83.
107. Ibid., p. 83.
108. Ibid., p. 83.
109. Ibid., p. 83.
110. Ibid., p. 346.
111. Ibid., p. 346.

yearning heart to 'give God the power of attorney'.[112] It is a call to resign oneself to God and do whatever God wishes. In such a state, Ramakrishna assures, God undertakes to look after the concerns, worries and interests of that devotee, including matters that concern his family and other worldly affairs. All that is expected is praying to the Divine Mother with a longing heart and persisting in one's demand to see God with a yearning heart. But the longing and the yearning has to 'force your demand on the Divine Mother',[113] and that can happen only if the devotee thinks of her as his own mother. The child, says Ramakrishna, begs his mother for money to buy a kite. The mother is busy gossiping with another lady and fends off the demand by saying that she will have to ask the child's father, who is likely to disapprove. Hearing this, the child begins to cry and remains persistent. The mother interrupts her conversation to pacify the child by giving the child some money to buy his kite. Using this example, Ramakrishna derives a principle regarding his faith in the centrality of a longing heart and the need for persistence on part of the devotee:

I know that I know nothing. Sometimes I think of God as good, and sometimes as bad. What can I

112. Ibid., p. 628.
113. Ibid., p. 629.

know of Him?...Who can ever know God? I don't even try. I only call on Him as Mother. Let Mother do whatever She likes. I shall know Her if it is Her will; but I shall be happy to remain ignorant if She wills otherwise.[114]

In essence, no amount of reason and calculations can take a devotee nearer God. Ramakrishna wants true spiritual seekers wanting to develop a yearning for God to give up intellectual ideas like, for instance, karma being the cumulative result of one's actions.[115] Rather, the attitude of a child is the right one to emulate. The young child, explains Ramakrishna, only wants his mother. He doesn't know much about his mother, whether she is rich or poor. Neither does he know, nor does he want to know either. He is secure in the knowledge that he has a mother. 'My attitude, too, is that of a child,'[116] concludes Ramakrishna. Taking refuge in God, then, washes away the effects of karma.

Phrases like 'intensely yearning heart', 'ecstatic love', 'longing heart' and 'mad with love' were nothing but ways of expressing the nature of what Ramakrishna calls 'real bhakti'. Here is his expression of all the yearning, longing and madness for Kali, the Divine Mother:

---

114. Ibid., p. 299.
115. Ibid., p. 817.
116. Ibid., p. 299.

Here, Mother, take Thy sin; here, take Thy virtue. I don't want either of these; give me only real bhakti. Here, Mother, take Thy good; here, take Thy bad. I don't want any of Thy good or bad; give me only real bhakti. Here, Mother, take Thy dharma; here, take Thy adharma. I don't want any of Thy dharma or adharma; give me only real bhakti. Here, Mother, take Thy knowledge; here, take Thy ignorance. I don't want any of Thy knowledge or ignorance; give me only real bhakti. Here, Mother, take Thy purity; here, take Thy impurity. Give me only real bhakti.[117]

Real bhakti, then, entails cultivating devotion and love for God. In turn, God bestows his grace on such an individual. The path to real bhakti is not through discussions and opinions, and it is not about 'knowing many things'.[118] A real devotee who knows real bhakti cultivates love for God, attains God, and then leaves matters of knowing and understanding to God's grace and will. One of the most striking examples for illustrating real bhakti that Ramakrishna offers throughout the *Kathāmrita* is that of the kitten in relation with the mother cat. Sumit Sarkar refers to Ramakrishna's preference for the bhakti of a kitten as a 'startling

---

117. Ibid., p. 817.
118. Ibid., p. 506.

example'[119] and correctly traces it to the Sri Vaishnava Sampradaya in the city of Sri Rangam in the south of India. He also links it to the reception and assimilation of Vaishnava bhakti in Bengal, especially since the time of Chaitanya. On closer scrutiny, the example of the kitten and the mother cat constitutes the spiritual 'core' of Ramakrishna's faith and merits a more detailed explanation.

In the *Kathāmrita*, the kitten and mother cat example appears with striking regularity. It is used to portray the ideal relationship between the devotee and God but also distinguish between two distinct categories of spiritual aspirants:

> There are two classes of devotees. One class has the nature of the kitten. The kitten depends completely on its mother. It accepts whatever its mother does for it. The kitten only cries, 'Mew, mew!' It doesn't know what to do or where to go. Sometimes the mother puts the kitten near the hearth, sometimes on the bed...There is another class of devotees. They have the nature of the young monkey. The young monkey clings to its mother with might and main. The devotees who behave like the young monkey have a slight idea of being the doer. They feel: 'We must go to the sacred places; we must

---

119. Sumit Sarkar, op. cit., p. 316.

practise japa and austerity; we must perform worship with sixteen articles as prescribed by the śāstras. Only then shall we be able to realize God.' Such is their attitude.[120]

Ramakrishna considers both categories of aspirants as devotees of God, but clearly favours those who exhibit the attitude of the kitten. 'My nature is that of a kitten,' he emphatically declares. In making the distinction between the attitude of the kitten and the baby monkey, Ramakrishna not only presents his blueprint for real bhakti, but also harnesses the example in order to synthesize and reconcile various strands of his spiritual practices. For Ramakrishna, the model of the kitten and the baby monkey offers an invisible thread seamlessly connecting his private spiritual universe with seemingly public questions relating to religious tolerance, nationalism and philanthropy. A digression in order to understand the full implications of the kitten versus the baby monkey example, therefore, would be in order.

Nothing could better explain this than D. Dennis Hudson's remarkable essay titled 'By Monkey or by Cat? How is One Saved?'.[121] What follows is a summary of this essay. Sri Vaishnava thinkers and preceptors

---

120. *Gospel*, p. 843; see also, pp. 83, 369, 628.
121. D. Dennis Hudson, *Krishna's Mandala: Bhagavata Religion and Beyond,* edited and introduced by John Stratton Hawley, Oxford University Press, New Delhi, 2010, pp. 275-84.

of Sri Rangam and Kanchipuram, who followed a tradition drawn from the *Bhagavata Purana*, introduced distinctions in discussing the question of grace that have a striking visual metaphor. Grace is the 'experience of a freely given and undeserved gift'.[122] The visual metaphor they sought to convey was the difference between a mother monkey and a mother cat in the way they respond and carry their young when endangered. Borrowing from Buddhism, Hudson calls this distinction one between 'self-power' and 'other-power'; in the case of the baby monkey, who uses 'self-power', and the kitten, who uses other power, lies the 'difference in nature of the one seeking salvation and in the nature of the saving "mother"'.[123] In other words, the distinction seeks to delineate ways in which a spiritual aspirant could relate to God.

For the Bhagavatas, the consciousness of a sadhaka contained processes that could be represented by the monkey and cat example. More specifically, the example helps to understand the transformation a devotee undergoes on being given diksha or being consecrated by an acharya or a teaching-priest. On arrival for the consecration, the devotee was considered a refugee (*prapanna*) and had to be purified of sin and pollution. This was done through the Man-lion consecration or the

---

122. Ibid., p. 245.
123. Ibid., p. 276.

Narasimha-diksha. Once ritually purified, he had to be disciplined over several days and weeks and taught his rites and prayers, followed by several days of the diksha proper. All this culminated in the acharya imparting him a mantra and explaining to him its meaning. The *sadhaka* was now committed to a ritually pure and disciplined life of sadhana. Most Vaishnava devotees only underwent a single consecration that entitled them to the mantra worship of Narayana in a visible and material form. Called the Vibhava-diksha, it enabled them to perform a set of rites, rituals and devotions on their own and for themselves (*sva-artha-puja*). But highly evolved Bhagavata devotees could receive other consecrations for other purposes, such as the Vyuha-diksha and the Sukshma-diksha.

To understand the changes taking place within the devotee's consciousness and the significance of the various consecrations mentioned above, a deeper understanding of the monkey and cat example is imperative. In the South Asian literary tradition, the monkey who best illustrates 'self-power' is Hanuman. He is a model yogi, but with a difference. While yogis work on themselves in order to achieve specific goals, Hanuman is the supreme illustration of the manner in which 'self-power' ought to relate to 'other-power'.[124] In this instance, Rama represents 'other-power' for

---

124. Ibid., p. 278.

Hanuman, who is ever ready to spring to action as a devoted servant of Rama. On the other hand, cats symbolize 'other-power' but are secretive and deceptive. They live in forests and mountains as tigers and lions and are invisible till they emerge to kill their prey.

In the *Bhagavata Purana*, Nrisimha or Narasimha, a lion in a man's form, embodies, cat-like, the 'other-power'. The Man-lion story is about the asura king, Hiranyakashipu, whose name literally means, clothed in gold. The demon king had mastered the Samkhya system of philosophy and had practised self-discipline prescribed in the Yoga system. As a consequence, he had acquired a golden body and had taken over the rule of the world. To attain the pinnacle of worldly success, Hiranyakashipu had 'integrated Samkhya's perceived distinction between pure Awareness (purusha) and Matter (prakriti) with Yoga's self-discipline of body and mind'.[125] Hudson sees him as the paradigm of consecrated 'self-power' existing in isolation from 'other-power'.

The demon king has a son. His name is Prahlada, which means Delight. While the father and son share their asura nature, their consciousness is remarkably different. Having mastered Samkhya-Yoga, Hiranyakashipu sees himself as the master of the world, whereas Prahlada sees God at the centre of all things and the world being

---

125. Ibid., p. 279.

permeated by Vishnu. Prahlada, suggests Hudson, is not just 'delight' but 'Delight in Krishna' expressed through Bhakti-Yoga or the Yoga of devotion. In the Bhagavata tradition, Samkhya-Yoga gives birth to Bhakti-Yoga; the two are related as father and son. Despite this bond, they cannot live simultaneously in the consciousness of the same sadhaka or devotee, and so one has to be eliminated. The father, therefore, tries to kill the son. In the face of this threat, Prahlada relies on his passive faithfulness to the 'other-power' in the form of Vishnu to avert murderous assaults from his father. It is the same passive faithfulness that also prevents him from actively seeking to defend himself. The final solution lies in a cat-like act of deception, when the Man-lion emerges from a pillar and rips open the stomach of the asura father and kills him, providing Prahlada the same kind of protection that a mother cat provides her endangered kitten; the son watches as the Man-lion ends the life and rule of his demon father, who mastered Samkhya-Yoga and ruled the world.

Here lies the irony. The devotee in this case, the metaphorical Prahlada, 'Delight in Krishna', receives the cat-like protection only because he has employed 'self-power' in the form of highly ritualized worship of mandalas and mantras. In other words, like the baby monkey, he, in the initial stages of spiritual preparedness ritually clung onto God's power and readied himself for the Sukshma-diksha. It is this clinging that made the Man-lion act. For the devotee, the sound of the mantra at the time of the Vibhava-diksha was the embodiment of Vishnu himself in a visible and material form. Now, as the Man-lion appears as the 'other-power', the devotee has been cleansed completely of all possible remnants of defilement and has direct perception of Vishnu/Narayana/Krishna.

The Bhagavata tradition that existed till the eighth century saw a devotee move from the sleep of ignorance to the wakefulness of knowledge. In this process, the 'other-power' and the 'self-power' alternated and complemented each other rather than being seen as antagonistically opposed to each other. In Hudson's words, 'the mother monkey and the mother cat acted together in the same forest of consciousness'.[126] But by the fourteenth century, the acharyas of the Vaishnava Sampradaya made the question of grace and the distinctions in the manner in which it is received an either/or matter. The disagreement between the *Vatakalai* (Northern Division), who believe that a devotee must actively cooperate in God granting salvation, and the *Tenkalai* (Southern Division), who believe in being in the kitten-like state for God as the mother cat to come and grant them salvation, continues to this day.

Ramakrishna confessed that he was partial to the kitten-like attitude in relation to God, grace and salvation. But, as noted above, he does not reject the

---

126. Ibid., p. 280.

implications of the baby monkey example and the model of bhakti it represented. The frequency and enthusiasm with which Ramakrishna draws upon the kitten and mother cat example can mislead the reader of the *Kathāmrita* into assuming that Ramakrishna was partial to the *Tenkalai* view. On the contrary, drawing upon Hudson's insights, it would be safe to assume that like the early Vaishnava acharyas, Ramakrishna too saw 'other-power' and 'self-power' as alternating and complementing each other in the course of a spiritual aspirant's journey. He had himself undertaken such a journey and continued to endorse many elements that constituted the years of his 'mad sadhana' as desirable and worth emulation. Hence, he could reject the path of the Vedas as inappropriate for Kaliyuga and consider the path of Tantra to be efficacious,[127] but at the same time also say that 'In the Kaliyuga the best way is bhaktiyoga... The path of devotion alone is the religion of this age.'[128] Meditating on mantras and mandalas was, therefore, part of the same bhakti continuum, a form of Vibhava-diksha, which over a period of time matured into direct perception of God, comparable to the Sukshma-diksha. For Ramakrishna, what was non-negotiable for spiritual aspirants at every step on the way to realizing God was the sense of longing, the ecstatic and mad love of God.

---

127. *Gospel*, p. 311.
128 Ibid., p. 143; see also, p. 376.

There is, however, a set of ideas that complete, deepen, refine and add richness to our understanding of Ramakrishna's faith and these merit detailed and careful consideration. This is the distinction Ramakrishna makes between a *jnani* and a *vijnani*. In making this distinction, he is emphatic that the way of jnana or knowledge and the path of vijnana or bhakti are equally legitimate ways of attaining God. The difference between them lies elsewhere. Knowing and believing that God dwells in all beings is jnana, but knowing God intimately is vijnana or a form of richer knowledge.[129] In an aphoristic flourish, Ramakrishna constitutes the parameters through which this distinction becomes meaningful: 'To know many things is ajñāna, ignorance. To know only one thing is jnāna, Knowledge – the realization that God alone is real and that He dwells in all. And to talk to Him is vijnāna, a fuller Knowledge. To love God in different ways, after realizing Him, is vijnāna.'[130] In describing knowledge,

---

129. Ibid., p. 899. The terms 'jñāna' and 'vijñāna' have been used in philosophical texts from the Upanishads onwards to mean various things ranging from consciousness as distinguished from specific forms of cognitions. Vijñāna has been employed to indicate, as Ramakrishna does, a unique form of knowledge. The Buddhists and the Naiyayikas have used other terms to describe both of these terms or have coined terms that conflate the two ideas into one term. For an excellent account of the history of the use of jñāna and vijñāna, see Bina Gupta, *Cit: Consciousness*, Oxford University Press, New Delhi, 2003.

130. *Gospel*, pp. 598-9.

Ramakrishna is categorical that neither reasoning, nor knowledge of the scriptures could take anyone close to realizing God. For him, God was beyond the scriptures, beyond the Vedas and their prescriptions. In one instance, recorded in the *Kathāmrita*, Ramakrishna rejects the idea that God can be attained by reading the Vedas and the Vedanta, and, saying so, turns to Narendra and says: 'Do you understand this? The Vedas give only a hint.'[131] The scriptures might record many things but they were all useless without devotion and direct realization of God. He likens the scriptures to the almanac that forecasts the rain, but squeezing the almanac cannot produce even a drop of water. Texts, scriptures, and the reasoning about their content have a place only till such time a devotee has not realized God.

The jnani gives up the attachment of worldly things and begins a process of discrimination and elimination. Ramakrishna often describes this process as akin to climbing a roof, step by step, leaving each step behind. In undertaking this process of discrimination, a jnani is guided by scriptural injunctions.[132] Giving up identification with objects of sight, hearing and touch, he rejects the world as illusory. He discovers God by asking the question of the identity and source of the ego, the 'I'. Can the 'I' be reducible to the flesh, bones, marrow, mind

---

131. Ibid., p. 526.
132. Ibid., p. 476.

or intellect? Through the act of reasoning that results in saying 'Neti, neti' or 'Not this, not this' a jnani realizes that God or Brahman is his own inner consciousness, which is also his true identity. God for him is no longer a person, nor does he have the words to describe who or what God is. Why? Ramakrishna describes this state of speechlessness thus: 'And who will describe it? He who is to describe does not exist at all; he no longer finds his "I".'[133] Having attained such a state, God is experienced, not through the mind or the intelligence, but only as consciousness.[134]

Having experienced God-consciousness within himself, the jnani considers the universe illusory and thinks of it as a dream. Realizing Brahman, however, is not possible till an individual remains conscious of his ego, transcending the sense of 'I' and 'you' and of 'one' and 'many'. Once the knowledge of Brahman is attained, the ego is effaced and the devotee gets established in samadhi.[135] This is 'jada samadhi',[136] where the last trace of ego is erased. This is, of course, the ideal. In reality, there are only a few people who are able to shake off the 'I' by means of samadhi. 'You may indulge in thousands of reasonings,' says Ramakrishna, 'but still the "I" comes

---

133. Ibid., p. 859.
134. Ibid., p. 859.
135. Ibid., p. 416.
136. Ibid., p. 478.

back.'[137] Thus, having climbed the roof, an individual cannot stay there for long and has to come down. In the musical scale, one goes in the ascending order of the notes, sa, re, ga, ma, pa, dha, ni, but it is impossible to stay at ni for long.[138] Similarly, the ego has the tendency to reappear.

In the *Kathāmrita*, Ramakrishna uses the terms 'reasoning', 'Vedanta', 'path of discrimination', 'path of knowledge' and 'jnana/jnanayoga' interchangeably. While there is clear acknowledgement on his part that jnana is one way of reaching God, it is also unmistakeably clear that it is neither his preferred way nor is it a path he endorses enthusiastically. The reasons for this indifference to the path of discrimination are varied, but, together, they clearly set the stage for Ramakrishna's unreserved embracing of the way shown by vijnana. One reason for his reticence regarding jnana was the constraints Kaliyuga puts on following the difficult path of knowledge. Life of an individual in Kaliyuga is driven by food and, therefore, it is almost impossible to get rid of the consciousness of the body and the ego. An individual's claim of having attained the consciousness of Brahman, then, will sound hollow, especially when that individual cannot be above disease, grief, old age and death. 'However you may reason and

---

137. Ibid., p. 170.
138. Ibid., p. 104.

argue,' Ramakrishna asserts, 'the feeling that the body is identical with the soul will somehow crop up from an unexpected quarter.'[139] Ramakrishna goes a step further. He questions the Vedantin's utterance of 'I am He' or 'I am Brahman' in Kaliyuga, even after such an aspirant may have followed the path of knowledge and realized the non-dualistic nature of reality.

> The feeling, 'I am He', is not wholesome. A man who entertains such an idea, while looking on his body as the Self, causes himself great harm. He cannot go forward in spiritual life; he drags himself down. He deceives himself as well as others. He cannot understand his own state of mind.[140]

Even here, some exceptions had to be admitted. All devotees are not of the same level. Jnanis exhibit certain physical and behavioural features that distinguish them from ordinary people. Narendra, for instance, had big protruding eyes.[141] Further, a jnani does not injure anyone, and though might appear to be angry and egotistical, in reality he is not so; his anger and ego are a mere appearance. Neither does a man of knowledge have any attachment to anything worldly.[142] There were individuals

---

139. Ibid., p. 172. See also, p. 468.
140. Ibid., p. 172. See also, p. 103.
141. Ibid., p. 249.
142 Ibid., p. 417.

like Shankaracharya, Janaka, Narada, Hanuman, Sanaka, Sanatana, Sananda and Sanatkumara who had attained the knowledge of Brahman. In other words, they were Brahmajnanis. But they retained the 'ego of knowledge'[143] in order to do good to others and to teach others. They were unlike the sages of the old who attained knowledge for their own salvation and were timid.[144] The 'knowledge ego' retained after having attained Brahmajnana was the 'ripe' ego, unlike the man with an 'unripe' ego, who thinks that he is the doer rather than God who makes men do all things. Phrases like 'doing good to others' and 'teaching others', however, are not remotely connected to Swami Vivekananda's later formulation of Practical Vedanta. Neither are these in any manner of speaking the early intimation of what Vivekananda would formulate as Practical Vedanta. When Ramakrishna says that Shankaracharya retained the 'ego of knowledge' in order to teach and do good to others, he categorically means that the 'knowledge ego' was retained in order to teach spiritual life and nothing else.[145]

Leaving aside these exceptions, an individual who attains the knowledge and vision of Brahman goes silent. The process of reasoning and discrimination lasts only till he has not attained Brahman. Ramakrishna compares this state to butter sizzling on fire as long as the water

---

143. Ibid., pp. 416-17, 480, 103.
144. Ibid., p. 480.
145. Ibid., p. 860.

in it does not dry up or the buzzing of the bee till such time that it does not sit on a flower and sips nectar. His favourite example, however, is that of the husband of a young girl who comes to visit his father-in-law. The husband is seated in the drawing-room with other young men. The girl and her friends are watching them from the window. The girl's friends want her to identify her husband from among the young men gathered there. They point to many young men, one by one, and ask the girl if any of them is her husband. In each case, the girl smiles and answers in the negative. Finally, when her friends manage to correctly point to her husband and identify him, the girl neither says yes nor no, but smiles and keeps quiet.[146] In other words, realizing the true nature of Brahman makes the aspirant go silent. Why does he go silent? This is because Brahman cannot be described in words. Like food, everything in the world had been defiled by the tongue, including the Vedas, the Puranas, and the Tantras; they have been spoken about and uttered by the tongues of men.[147] Only the Brahman, says Ramakrishna, remains undefiled by the tongue.

Ramakrishna found jnanis to be monotonous people.[148] He had no use of mere reasoning and dry logic. In one of the more dramatic moments recorded in the *Kathāmrita*, Ramakrishna makes his view of jnana and endless

---

146. Ibid., p. 280.
147. Ibid., p. 900.
148. Ibid., p. 479.

reasoning amply clear: 'Mere dry reasoning – I spit on it! I have no use of it! (The Master spits on the ground.)'[149]

Instead, he wanted to be like the weaver woman who danced with both her hands held raised. Ramakrishna tells the story with great relish.[150] A weaver, who was spinning various kinds of silk thread, is visited by a woman friend. She is delighted to see her friend and goes inside the house to get her friend some refreshments. While she is away, her friend gets enticed by the different colours of the thread and steals one. She hides the bundle of thread under one arm. Returning after getting the refreshments, the weaver realizes that her friend has stolen a bundle of thread and decides upon a plan to get it back. She tells her friend that her happiness on seeing her was immense and she wanted to express that happiness by dancing with her. When the two began dancing, the weaver encouraged her friend to dance with both hands raised. She soon realized that her friend was dancing with only one hand raised, while pressing the other hand by her side. Despite much persuasion, the weaver failed to get her friend to dance with both hands raised. Her friend insisted that she only knew to dance with one hand raised and the other pressed by the side. Drawing from the story, Ramakrishna asserts that both his hands were free and he did not want to dance with one arm pressed to his side. In other words,

---

149. Ibid., p. 272.
150. Ibid., pp. 479-80.

he wished to accept the Nitya or the Absolute as well as the Lila or the relative. That is what a vijnani did and that is the reason why vijnana was richer and superior.

It is important at this juncture to capture the richness of Ramakrishna's delineation of the vijnani state before looking at the implications of the jnani-vijnani distinction. As noted earlier, the defining feature of a vijnani is his intimate knowledge of God, which, in turn, is a richer knowledge. Because of this intimacy, the vijnani, who also climbs the roof, does so incrementally, climbing step by step. But unlike the jnani, who discriminates, eliminates and rejects the steps, the vijnani realizes that the steps too are made of the same material as the roof.[151] The vijnani realizes that Brahman has become the universe, all living beings, mind, intelligence, love, knowledge and renunciation. Instead of being illusory and unreal, the world was, indeed, a 'mansion of mirth'. The realization dawns on him that whether one calls it Truth, Reality, God or Brahman, it is both *saguna* or with attributes and *nirguna* or without attributes. In truth, God is beyond form and formlessness, and it is churlish on our part to limit the idea of God by circumscribing him as formless or with form.[152] The Brahman is beyond speech and form, but the same Brahman is born in flesh and blood and performs various activities. 'From the one

---

151. Ibid., pp. 103-4.
152. Ibid., p. 192.

Om,' concludes Ramakrishna, 'have sprung "Om Śiva", "Om Kāli", and "Om Krishna".'[153]Endowed with this clarity, the vijnani discovers that there is no difference between Brahman and Bhagavan or the Personal God. Put differently, the vijnani is a bhakta and his ideal is a Personal God. For him, Brahman and Shakti are the same, like the gem and its lustre, where one cannot talk of one without speaking of the other. In other instances, he compares the oneness of Brahman and Shakti as fire and its power to burn, milk and its whiteness and water and its wetness. The vijnani, then, not just wants to know God, but he aspires to laugh, weep, dance, sing and sport in the ecstasy of God. 'In the Ocean of God-Consciousness,' says Ramakrishna, 'he sometimes swims, sometime goes down, and sometimes rises to the surface – like pieces of ice in the water.'[154] Bhakti also has a cooling influence on the Brahman and helps transform the Infinite into the finite and appear as God with form.[155]

Vijnana, then, is getting to know God in a 'special way',[156] though it is not the only way. A bhakta does not begin with the desire to attain the knowledge of Brahman.

---

153. Ibid., p. 366.
154. Ibid., p. 277.
155. Ibid., p. 859. 'Therefore people compare bhakti, love of God, to the cooling light of the moon, and jnāna, knowledge, to the burning rays of the sun.' See also, p. 218: 'The heat of the sun of Knowledge melts the ice-like form of the Personal God.'
156. Ibid., p. 288.

Rather, he wants to attain the Personal God who has form and wants to talk to that God. If God so desires, he will grant the devotee the love of God as well as the knowledge of Brahman. In the world of bhakti, pleased with the devotee's longing and ecstatic love, God himself may say to him,'You are the same as Myself.'[157] God runs after a devotee as a cow runs after the calf.[158] In another unique parable, Ramakrishna wants his interlocutors to imagine a king sitting on the throne in his court. If his cook were to enter and declare that he and the king were the same, it is certain that people would call the cook mad. On the contrary, if one day, pleased with the cook's services, the king were to ask him to come and sit next to him and tell the cook that there was no difference between them, no one will take this act of generosity coming from the king amiss.[159] Ramakrishna further simplifies the idea beautifully: The important thing was to reach Calcutta. Once there, one can see the maidan and the museum and many other places.[160] The awareness that fire exists

---

157. Ibid., p. 248.

158. Ibid., p. 157. This idea too is likely a slight modification of lines from Ramprasad: 'But I know too that salvation/Always follows worship around/Like a slave...'. See, Rāmprasād Sen, *Grace and Mercy in Her Wild Hair: Selected Poems To The Mother Goddess*, translated by Leonard Nathan and Clinton Seely, Foreword by Andrew Schelling, Hohm Press, Prescott, Arizona, 1999, p. 57.

159. *Gospel*, p. 248.

160. Ibid., p. 468.

in wood is jnana, while to cook rice on it, eat it and be nourished by it is vijnana.[161] To only have heard of milk is ajnana or ignorance, but to have seen it is jnana. But to drink milk and be nourished by it is vijnana.[162] Simply stated, the vijnani wants to enjoy God as a child, friend, master and beloved.[163] He does not want to become sugar, but wants to eat it.[164] He does so because he has the lucidity that it is extremely difficult in Kaliyuga to get rid of the 'I', the ego. To speak of the world as a dream is impossible as long as God keeps intact the awareness of 'I' and so long as one is conscious of the body and of sense objects. The body is a pot, while the mind and the intelligence stand for the water. Rice, potatoes and other vegetables are the objects of the senses. The Brahman or the Infinite is the fire. The 'I-consciousness' constantly makes the contents of the pot, identified with the objects of the senses, jump about, as if saying, 'We are here,' 'We are jumping.'[165] Instead of claiming perfect identification with the Brahman, like the Vedantin, and saying, 'I am He', Ramakrishna's constant refrain, therefore, is: 'Since this "I" must remain, let the rascal be God's servant.'[166]

---

161. Ibid., p. 288.
162. Ibid., p. 404.
163. Ibid., p. 288.
164. Ibid., p. 172. The phrase is from a poem by Ramprasad. The exact lines are: 'Sugar I love/But haven't the slightest desire/To merge with sugar.' See, Rāmprasād Sen, op. cit., p. 57.
165. *Gospel*, p. 243.
166. Ibid., p. 105.

Even after having attained samadhi, the bhakta retains the 'I-consciousness', but it takes the form of the 'servant ego' or the 'devotee ego'. Conversely, he opts for the attitude of the servant and the devotee and practises this kind of 'I-consciousness' in order to attain God. But the offer of Brahmajnana depends on the will and grace of God and the devotee does not actively seek it.[167] In his own case, Ramakrishna spoke of God changing the state of his mind from the Absolute to the Relative. In these changing states of mind, Ramakrishna realizes that the 'manifold has come from the One alone, the Relative from the Absolute'.[168] In other words, God as the non-dual, incomparable, unutterable One also becomes the creator, maya, the living beings and the universe. Ramakrishna describes the play between the absolute and the relative in terms of the two states of Shiva's mind. When he is satisfied in the Self and transfixed in samadhi, he is Atmarama. On descending from samadhi, he retains a trace of ego and dances and sings 'Rama, Rama' like a bhakta.[169] A devotee who has seen God retains his 'I-consciousness' only in name. That degree of 'I' is a mere appearance, like the mark left on a coconut tree by a fallen branch,[170] and through this 'I', the 'I' of

---

167. Ibid., p. 171.
168. Ibid., p. 307.
169. Ibid., p. 345.
170. Ibid., p. 405.

the devotee, he enjoys the infinite play of God.[171]

The argument this far: the way of the jnani was a legitimate path to follow in getting to know God. But knowing God through dry reasoning was not enough. The Vedantin gets to know God in a state of samadhi, but that state does not last long. In the play between the absolute and the relative, the persistence of the 'I-consciousness' inevitably brings an individual in that state to the world of living beings and the universe. God is Brahman, but is also Shakti, the Primordial Energy. While nothing can be said about the attributeless Brahman, Shakti manifests as the Primal Power, Mahamaya, which covers Brahman.[172] The relation between Brahman and Shakti is like the snake and its wriggling motion: one cannot think of the snake without its wriggling motion and vice versa. As long as Brahman remains wrapped in Mahamaya, God ought to be seen as Mother. Repeating 'Neti, neti', is, therefore, a waste of time. To say, 'I am He' also is incorrect. It is perfectly alright to reach the roof, but, having once reached the top of the roof, a true devotee must make an all-important transition, take a crucial leap. He must affirm that after having realized Brahman, it is the same Brahman that has become all living beings, the universe and the twenty-four cosmic principles.[173] Stated differently, it

---

171. Ibid., p. 479.
172. Ibid., p. 290.
173. Ibid., pp. 271-2.

is imperative to move to a stage beyond Brahmajnana, which is vijnana. To remove a thorn stuck in one's foot one needs another thorn. The first thorn is ajnana or ignorance and the second thorn that helps extract the first is jnana or knowledge. But to throw away both the thorns, that is, to go beyond knowledge and ignorance, vidya and avidya, is vijnana. After attaining the state of the vijnani, not only does the universe and all living beings appear as an extension of Brahman, but the meditation and the meditator as also bhakti and prema[174] appear to be part of the glory of that Absolute that the Vedantins call Brahman. In essence, the 'self power' of the baby monkey must travel the distance to make the transition to faith in the 'other-power' exemplified by the kitten and the mother cat.

ॐ

In the context of Ramakrishna's faith, it is abundantly clear that an all-embracing conception of bhakti held pride of place. It allowed for the spiritual seeker to embark on this journey through diverse paths, be it Tantra or Vedanta, but enjoined him to ultimately reach the goal of mature or ripe bhakti and become a vijnani. But indiscriminate bhakti does not help a devotee attain God. For bhakti to be meaningful, one had to assume

---

174. Ibid., p. 290.

the right bhava or attitude towards God. But the right attitude eludes an aspirant till such time he manages to acquire the right kind of bhakti. The equation for Ramakrishna is very straightforward: First one needs to inculcate and possess single-minded devotion to God, one in which one's mind and soul merge into God-consciousness.[175] It is the kind of devotion a wife feels for her husband. After bhakti matures, it becomes bhava.[176] Ramakrishna lists five such bhavas or attitudes:[177] the *shanta* (serene), *dasya* (of the servant towards the master), *sakhya* (friendship), *vatsalya* (of the mother towards her child), and, finally, and most important, the *madhura* (of the woman towards her lover). Radha had madhura-bhava for Krishna and so does a wife for her husband. For Ramakrishna, the madhura-bhava includes all the other four bhavas and is supreme. Assuming a bhava with the ordinary awareness of the physical body remaining intact is no great help in seeing God. The phrase 'seeing God' has a weight of its own where the word 'seeing' is not used unmindfully or casually. 'Better than reading is hearing,' maintains Ramakrishna, 'and better than hearing is seeing.'[178] If God, then, cannot be seen with physical eyes, something else would be needed for the devotee to see God. Ramakrishna calls this the

---

175. Ibid., p. 315.
176. Ibid., p. 255.
177. Ibid., p. 115.
178. Ibid., p. 476.

'love body', which, in turn, is endowed with 'love eyes', 'love ears' and sexual organs made of love. The devotee's intense longing and love for God makes the 'love body' help the soul commune with God.[179]

After bhava, therefore, comes mahabhava or divine ecstasy. Ramakrishna describes his own experience of mahabhava[180] as the joy he experienced that equalled the pain he suffered before attaining that exalted state of bliss. The experience shakes the body and the mind to the core: it is like an elephant entering a small hut. The elephant's entry can either shake the foundations or even destroy the hut. Ramakrishna speaks of the burning pain he felt on being separated from God. It made him unconscious for three days, and he lay in one place till the Bhairavi took him for a bath. The earth that stuck to his body had got baked as a result of his burning pain. Leading him to the bathing spot, she had to cover him in a thick sheet because his skin could not bear her touch. He describes his state as one where he felt as if 'a ploughshare were passing through my backbone'.[181] People around him thought he was going mad and he himself thought that he was either going mad or had fallen ill. The Bhairavi assured him[182] that he was not going mad and it was beyond ordinary mortals to

179. Ibid., p. 115.
180. Ibid., p. 747.
181. Ibid., p. 747.
182. *Great Master*, pp. 214-5.

recognize his state. She told him that his state was the same as that of Radha, Krishna's consort, and that of Chaitanya.[183] She identified his state to be one that a devotee experiences when he calls God with intense longing and earnestness.

The mahabhava is a state of samadhi, where an individual remains unconscious of the outer world, becomes speechless, a state in which his nerve currents and breath stop momentarily.[184] The stage after mahabhava is prema or ecstatic love, which is the prelude to attaining God. Again, it is rare for ordinary devotees to experience this state; Chaitanya jumped into the ocean thinking it was the River Jamuna when he was in this mood. With prema comes the detachment about one's own body, something that humans treasure above all else. To attain, realize and see God, ecstatic love and longing for God was the key. And the only way to inch towards that goal was prema-bhakti or raga-bhakti.[185] To some, raga-bhakti is innate. Others are not so lucky and they have to begin with japa or repeating God's name numerous times, fast, go on pilgrimages, make ritualistic

---

183. 'The essence of *hlādinī* is *prema*; the essence of *prema* is *bhāva*; the highest *bhāva* is called *mahābhāva*. The true form of *mahābhāva* is Rādhā Thākurāni, the treasure-house of all qualities, the crest-jewel among all the lovers of Krsna.' *CC*, op.cit., p. 193. Also note that Radha is identified with the Hlādini-śaktī of the Tantra philosophy.
184. *Gospel*, pp. 255, 315.
185. Ibid., pp. 172-3.

offerings and perform sacrifices. This is Vaidhi-bhakti or formal devotion. Ramakrishna describes it as using a hand-held fan to produce a semblance of breeze. The moment natural breeze starts flowing, one has to set aside the hand-held fan. Similarly, the moment one develops a spontaneous love and longing for God, japa, fasting and austerities 'drop away'.[186] Vaidhi-bhakti is 'green' bhakti or 'unripe' bhakti. Prema-bhakti and raga-bhakti are 'ripe' bhakti because they are instances of love of God, manifested as the mother's love for the child, the child's love for the mother or that of the wife for the husband. Ramakrishna categorically states that 'ripe' bhakti alone is sufficient in order to attain and see God. Radha, Ramakrishna tells his listeners,[187] saw Krishna within and without. When her friends could not see anything and thought Radha was delirious, Radha asked them to paint their eyes with the collyrium of divine love to be able to see Krishna everywhere. This was, for him, the highest embodiment of mature or 'ripe' bhakti as well as ecstatic, impatient longing for God.

Even within ecstatic love of God, Ramakrishna introduces a subtle distinction: 'I-ness' and 'my-ness'.[188] While positing them as distinctions, Ramakrishna suggests that the 'I-ness' flows into the 'my-ness' effortlessly, tied

---

186. Ibid., p. 173. See also, p. 659.
187. Ibid., p. 173.
188. Ibid., pp. 360, 229, 449.

by a common thread, namely, that the devotee does not look upon his object of adoration, the Personal God, as God. Yashoda, Krishna's mother, represents the passage from 'I-ness' aspect of love to the 'my-ness' attitude with effortless ease. Ramakrishna dramatizes this transition from 'I-ness' to 'my-ness' to show the remarkable quality that inheres in prema-bhakti and raga-bhakti:

> Yaśodā used to think: 'Who would look after Gopāla if *I* did not? He will fall ill if *I* do not serve Him.' She did not look on Krishna as God. The other element is 'my-ness'. It means to look on God as one's own — '*my* Gopāla'. Uddhava said to Yaśodā: 'Mother, your Krishna is God Himself. He is the Lord of the Universe and not a common human being.' 'Oh!' exclaimed Yaśodā. 'I am not asking you about your Lord of the Universe. I want to know how my Gopāla fares. Not the Lord of the Universe, but *my* Gopāla.'[189]

Yashoda, Radha and the gopis, continues Ramakrishna, had a single-minded devotion to Krishna. A yearning for Krishna that would produce divine madness in them at the sight of a black tree or make them place their subtle bodies under his feet to prevent the soles of his feet from getting hurt.[190] Krishna was their beloved, their

---

189. Ibid., p. 229.
190. Ibid., pp. 449, 361.

sweetheart and not their God. Radha's fire of anguish at being separated from Krishna would turn her tears into steam.[191] And even though Krishna was enshrined in her heart, she wanted 'to sport with Him in human form'.[192] Radha possessed one hundred and twenty-five per cent of the yearning and ecstatic love for Krishna, whereas very few possess even a 'particle of such prema'.[193] Attaining prema, concludes Ramakrishna, gives the devotee the rope to tie God.[194] Having attained prema-bhakti or raga-bhakti, a devotee becomes one of God's sincere devotees. It makes God responsible for them, just as a registered patient is never discharged by the doctor till he is fully cured.[195]

Prema-bhakti and raga-bhakti infused with madhura-bhava was for Ramakrishna not merely a way of seeing God, but, like Tantra, was a model for transgression leading to transcendence. The love that Radha and the gopis had for Krishna made them renounce 'husbands, children, family and propriety of conduct, honour and dishonour, shame and aversion, fear of public opinion and of society'.[196] But Radha's madhura-bhava cannot be understood just by reasoning. Rather, a devotee

---

191. Ibid., p. 449.
192. Ibid., p. 506.
193. Ibid., p. 449.
194. Ibid., p. 588.
195. Ibid., p. 659.
196. *Great Master*, p. 259.

had to lose himself completely in that mood, and as Ramakrishna puts it, 'become Radha'.[197] In the days of his 'divine madness', which was also the period of his intense spiritual practice, Ramakrishna sought to directly experience madhura-bhava. He elaborately dressed as a woman, including wearing a wig and gold ornaments. Losing complete consciousness of his body, he began to think, speak, smile, glance, gesture and move like one of Krishna's gopis. He remained in the guise of a woman for six months. During this period, he prayed for union with Krishna in the way that the gopis of Vrindavan did and expressed a heightened degree of sense of separation from Krishna. He soon realized that in order to attain Krishna, he had to please, pray and supplicate Radha. Having done so, soon he saw a vision of Radha, who disappeared into his own body. After that, Ramakrishna in moods of deep ecstasy began to feel as if he was Radha and his longing ended with the establishment of a relation of husband and wife between Krishna and himself.[198] Even in later life, any instance of a song being sung that would speak of the separation of Radha from Krishna would send Ramakrishna into a deep trance. The *Kathāmrita* records an instance in 1884, two years before his death, when Ramakrishna, hearing such a song, assumed the mood

---

197. Ibid., p. 259.
198. Ibid., pp. 273-5.

of Radha and in a voice full of sorrow began singing. 'O friend,' he sang, 'either bring my beloved Krishna here or take me to Him.'[199]

II

If there is one phrase in the popular consciousness that effortlessly invokes the name and memory of Ramakrishna, it is 'Ramakrishna's catholicity'. Vivekananda, more than anyone else, helped construct the elements that constituted this carefully edited, censored and wilfully misleading version of his master's 'catholicity'. He used it to mean what he thought was Ramakrishna's tolerance, generosity and inclusiveness in relation to other faiths while carefully glossing over the sources and influences that produced this 'catholicity'. The continued use of the term has had a longevity independent of Vivekananda's remoulding of Ramakrishna from a 'religious ecstatic to a religious eclectic',[200] and continues to be used even to this day by perceptive and critical readers of the Ramakrishna-

---

199. *Gospel*, p. 445. Ramakrishna visited Vrindavan, where an old woman, who lived alone in a hut, would look at his spiritual ecstasy and call him the very embodiment of Radha and began to address him as 'Dulaali'. See p. 129.

200. Narasingha P. Sil, 'Vivekānanda's Rāmakrishna: An Untold Story of Mythmaking and Propaganda', *Numen*, Vol. 40 (1993), p. 38.

Vivekananda story.[201] In speaking of Ramakrishna, Vivekananda refers to his 'highest catholicity'.[202] In a letter to Shivananda in 1894, Vivekananda calls Ramakrishna 'the latest and the most perfect'[203] among the incarnations of God. He was, argues Vivekananda, 'the concentrated embodiment of knowledge, love, renunciation, catholicity, and the desire to serve mankind'.[204] This is what the English translation offers. The term used in the Bangla original is *udarata*, which would normally translate as generosity or liberality or openness, but has been translated as catholicity in the official English translation.[205] The use of 'catholicity' fits better in Vivekananda's subsequent portrayal of Ramakrishna as the harbinger of a version of Vedantic universalism or as someone who attempted a synthesis of various sects and faiths. Ramakrishna, as we will see, had no such aim or intention. The other

---

201. For instance, Sumit Sarkar writes that 'Ramakrishna's catholicity was made into an argument for the essential superiority of an aggressive and muscular Hinduism'. See Sarkar, Op.cit., p. 291.

202. *CW*, Vol.7, pp. 412-3. See also, *The Complete Works of Swami Vivekananda*, Vol.1, Advaita Ashrama, Calcutta, Twenty-third impression, 2000, p. 19, for Vivekananda's use of the term in a speech in 1893 at the Parliament of Religions, where he talks about the 'catholicity' of the religious ideas of the Hindus.

203. Ibid., p. 483.

204. Ibid., p. 483.

205. I am indebted to Probal Dasgupta, Debjani Bhattacharyya, Chandana Chakraborti and Anindita Mukhopadhyaya for a better understanding of the Bangla original of this letter.

suggestion that Ramakrishna preached the idea of service to mankind will be taken up in the next chapter. However, it is crucial to understand Ramakrishna's attitude towards other sects and faiths, especially in order to map the breaks and departures in Vivekananda from his master's legacy.

Ramakrishna believed that God had created various forms of worship to suit men endowed with different stages of knowledge. To illustrate this point, he offers the example of a mother who cooks different kinds of food to suit the palates and digestive capacities of her various children.[206] He asks Mahendranath Gupta to imagine that the mother has five children and has fish as the main ingredient by which all the five have to be fed different things. She will, then, go ahead and make five different dishes to suit the needs of each of her children. This example is offered frequently throughout the *Kathāmrita*, though not always in the same context. But what ties all the various contexts together is Ramakrishna's assertion that despite different capacities of digestion, the mother loves all her children equally.[207] In this specific instance, Mahendranath has an argument with Ramakrishna about the suitability of worshipping a clay image. An exasperated Ramakrishna tells him to give up the habit of lecturing and teaching and stop to 'consider how to get the light himself'.[208] It is God whose job it is to teach

206. *Gospel*, p. 81.
207. Ibid., p. 559.
208. Ibid., p. 80.

everyone, says Ramakrishna, and it is God who will teach people the ways in which God himself wishes to be worshipped. All forms of worship, then, are devised by God, who also understands the need and rationale for them. All that was needed was to cultivate the love of God, surrender oneself and be open to the will of the 'other-power' powerfully illustrated by the relationship the kitten has with the mother cat.

All religions, then, were paths and forms devised by God. Ramakrishna attests[209] to having followed each of these faiths, which were different paths, and mentions Hinduism, Islam and Christianity. In the same breath, he also mentions the paths followed by the Shaktas, Vaishnavas and the Vedantists. All these paths led to one God despite their seeming differences. The Hindus call water 'jal', the Muslims call it 'paani' and the English call it 'water'. But it is the same water from various ends of the same lake. Note that Ramakrishna underlines the differences between the Hindus, Muslims and the English in terms of linguistic usage and not faith. The differences were, therefore, not of faith or belief but of the same Reality being called Allah, God, Brahman, Kali, Rama, Jesus, Durga and Hari.[210] In other words, difference lies in name and form, not in the nature of Reality. These differences do not exist because of greater

---

209. Ibid., p. 129.
210. Ibid., p. 135.

superiority or being more evolved. They exist because of differences in climate, temperament and language.

> I see people who talk about religion constantly quarrelling with one another. Hindus, Mussalmāns, Brāhmos, Śāktas, Vaishnavas, Śaivas, all quarrelling with one another. They haven't the intelligence to understand that He who is called Krishna is also Śiva and the Primal Śakti, and that it is He, again, who is called Jesus and Āllāh.[211]

Not only does Ramakrishna list all faiths without privileging any, but he also conflates the faiths and sects without singling any one out for special mention. He does the same with scriptures, when he lists the Vedas, the Puranas and the Tantra as instruments for seeking God and nothing more. After all, for him, the 'Satchidānanda Brahman in the Vedas is called Satchidānanda Śiva in the Tantra',[212] and, therefore, there was no inherent hierarchy that informed either faiths, or paths or even scriptures.

One of the sources of Ramakrishna's inclusiveness and universality lies in refusing to claim superiority for either a sect or school of thought or way of perception within the entity we know today as Hinduism. Neither did he entertain a defined, exclusive and sharply

---

211. Ibid., p. 423.
212. Ibid., p. 423. See also, p. 265.

delineated sense of Hindu identity. For him the Shaktas, the Vaishnavas and the Vedantins were all the same, each following a different path towards the same goal. God for him was described similarly in the Vedas, the Puranas and the Tantras, and could be formless or with form.[213] Ramakrishna recognized that it was in the nature of sects and faiths to magnify their views and claim superiority for them, but this was not to be his way. His bewilderment and anguish at people killing and shedding blood in the name of religion is beautifully captured in his citing an anonymous quote: 'The attributeless Brahman is my Father. God with attributes is my Mother. Whom shall I blame? Whom shall I praise? The two pans of the scales are equally heavy.'[214] For him, Shaktas, Vaishnavas and Vedantins harbouring malice against each other and quarrelling signified a lack of wisdom.[215]

Just as the mother who cooks different dishes for her children to suit their tastes and physical constitution and does so with love, all that faiths and sects require is sincere longing and an earnest yearning for God. Again, it is this element of longing, yearning and love that makes Ramakrishna's inclusiveness and universality stand apart from the 'empirical' and 'scientific' caricature of

213. Ibid., pp. 489-90.
214. Ibid., p. 490.
215. Ibid., p. 222.

it that Vivekananda sought to portray. Take, for instance, an example of a moment captured in the *Kathāmrita*. Ramakrishna is talking to Kali, his Divine Mother. He says:

> Mother, everyone says, 'My watch alone is right.' The Christians, the Brāhmos, the Hindus, the Mussalmāns, all say, 'My religion alone is true.' But Mother, the fact is that nobody's watch is right. Who can truly understand Thee? But if a man prays to Thee with a yearning heart, he can reach Thee, through Thy grace, by any path. Mother, show me some time how the Christians pray to Thee in their churches. But Mother, what will people say if I go in? Suppose they make a fuss! Suppose they don't allow me to enter the Kāli temple again! Well then, show me the Christian worship from the door of the Church.[216]

The yearning heart, however, is not a wandering and fickle heart. Having transcended name and form, having rejected the artificial distinction between the formless God and God with form, the sincere longing and the yearning heart must have an anchor. Ramakrishna calls this 'nishthaa', single-minded devotion, as contrasted with promiscuous devotion, which he likens to a tree

---

216. Ibid., pp. 93-94.

with five branches.[217] For Ramakrishna, his nishthaa to Kali opens for him the possibility of praying in a church. But he prays to Kali in the church, not any other form of God, and has no regrets if on account of entering the church, he is disallowed from entering the Kali temple again. For him, God manifests as Kali, and as a believer in the idea of a Personal God, his nishthaa is directed towards Kali. Hanuman and the gopis of Vrindavan were for him examples of nishthaa. When the gopis saw Krishna in the attire of a king in Mathura, they refused to recognize him till he would appear to them with a peacock feather in his crest wearing yellow clothes. In another epoch, Hanuman refused to acknowledge Krishna till Krishna appeared to him as Rama.[218] Liberal-minded devotees, argues Ramakrishna, accept all forms of God but at the same time direct their longing and yearning towards their chosen Personal God. Following one path with nishthaa tenaciously allows one to recognize the validity and truth of all other paths.[219]

Not only is it not desirable to characterize one's own faith as true and brand all others false, it is also entirely undesirable to point out flaws in one's own faith or in the faith of others. Ramakrishna, in suggesting this, goes far beyond any predictable model of tolerance, acceptance and fellow feeling among faiths. It is hubris, he suggests,

217. Ibid., p. 222.
218. Ibid., p. 307.
219. Ibid., p. 374.

that makes human beings think they can correct flaws in their own faith or in the faith of others.[220] Religions or systems of belief are just paths created by God, but are not remotely, in themselves, God.

Faith is a creation and gift of God and it is beyond the jurisdiction of humans to tamper with it: 'Suppose there are errors in the religion that one has accepted; if one is sincere and earnest, then God Himself will correct these errors...If there are errors in other religions, that is none of our business. God, to whom the world belongs, takes care of that.'[221] Ramakrishna does not stop at this, but goes further to warn against the triumphalism that sets in when individuals or faiths arbitrarily decide that they are right and all others are wrong. They think of faith in terms of winning and losing, where, invariably, they perceive that they and their faith alone have won and all others have lost. 'But a person who has gone forward may be detained by some slight obstacle,' warns Ramakrishna, 'and someone who has been lagging behind may then steal a march on him.'[222] God's ways are mysterious, and triumph and defeat too are in his hands.

If these are the foundations upon which Ramakrishna's inclusiveness, universality and doctrinal generosity rested, it is also true that there was a complete absence in the *Kathāmrita* of a clearly articulated Hindu identity.

---

220. Ibid., p. 559.
221. Ibid., p. 559.
222. Ibid., p. 578.

Even less so was the idea of a threatening, antagonistic 'Other' in the form of Islam or Christianity. Sumit Sarkar is right when he says that in Ramakrishna and in the pages of the *Kathāmrita* 'there is no developed sense of a sharply distinct "Hindu" identity – let alone any political use of it.'[223] There is, however, one exception within the *Kathāmrita* that causes a mild dissonance in our total and categorical rejection of the presence of a cohesive Hindu identity in Ramakrishna. It must also be said that this exception is vastly outweighed by the overwhelming evidence that points towards Ramakrishna's radical rejection of differences, hierarchies and claims of superiority among sects and faiths.

The exception can be traced to 20 October 1884.[224] Ramakrishna visits the Marwaris of Burrabazar, who are celebrating the Annakuta festival. While returning from the festival, Ramakrishna speaks admiringly of the devotion of the Marwaris, especially the joy with which they carried the image and lifted the throne of the deity on their shoulders. He calls this the 'real Hindu ideal' and also terms it 'Sanatana Dharma'. For Ramakrishna to be excited about expressions of bhakti is not unusual, and so the expression 'real Hindu ideal' can be understood in this context. What is more difficult to explain is the use of a politically charged neologism like 'Sanatana

---

223. Sumit Sarkar, op.cit., p. 324.
224. *Gospel*, pp. 641-2.

Dharma'. Not only does he mention the term, he, then, proceeds to explain it:

> The Hindu religion alone is the Sanātana Dharma. The various creeds you hear of nowadays have come into existence through the will of God and will disappear again through His will. They will not last forever. Therefore I say, 'I bow down at the feet of even the modern devotees.' The Hindu religion has always existed and will always exist.[225]

The coming together of the terms 'Sanatana Dharma' and 'Hindu religion' not just militates against the tone, tenor and spirit of the *Kathāmrita*, but the speech itself does not sound like Ramakrishna. If it does sound like anyone, it is Vivekananda, who considered only Hinduism to be worthy of the epithet 'religion' and thought of Islam and Christianity to be merely sects. As noted above, this exception takes little away from what is popularly known as Ramakrishna's 'catholicity'; that his inclusiveness and doctrinal generosity is much more radical and exceptional has been explained above.

Vivekananda's interpretation of Ramakrishna is a simultaneous act of fidelity and distortion. In every instance, the skeleton of Ramakrishna's thought is kept intact but the flesh and blood imposed on the skeleton often

---

225. Ibid., p. 642.

bear little resemblance to the original. Take, for instance, the moment when Vivekananda[226] is talking about the mistake Shankaracharya and other commentators made in thinking of the truth exemplified in the Vedas as having an overall coherence and unity. When faced with contradictions and conflicting voices within the Vedas, they tried to fit these contradictions forcefully within their own view and that of their philosophical system. As against this kind of attempt, contradictions do seem apparent between Vedic texts and between the doctrines they preach. Vivekananda suggests that Lord Krishna himself tried to partially harmonize these contradictions, and he himself had come in the form of Ramakrishna to show the right way in which to truly understand the Vedas and Vedanta. Ramakrishna, he suggests, had through his life and teachings made sense of the seeming contradictions in these scriptures. What did Ramakrishna do? Vivekananda concludes that Ramakrishna perceived the contradictions as indication that various texts and their teachings are 'meant for different grades of aspirants and are arranged in the order of evolution'.[227] We already know that Ramakrishna had little interest in scriptures, thought nothing of the Vedas, made little distinction between the Vedas and the Vedanta in a formal sense, and found such textual details boring and monotonous.

---

226. *CW*, Vol. 7, pp. 412-3.
227. Ibid., pp. 412-13.

Even the example of the mother cooking various dishes for her children with differing physical constitutions is an example of God offering various paths to his devotees, yet, like the mother, loving them all equally. Vivekananda imports the example from Ramakrishna and converts it into a hierarchy of aspirants and an evolutionary schema conspicuously absent in his master.

In July 1895, in a talk on Ramakrishna, Vivekananda paraphrases Ramakrishna and speaks of the way in which God, seen as the attributeless Brahman, manifests in the world covered under the spell of maya. The jnani, suggests Vivekananda, uncovers God by force, while the Dualist begs the Mother of the Universe to lend him the key that will help him uncover God.[228] Ramakrishna's view, as we have already seen, is the opposite. It is either the tamasic way, where a devotee forces and coerces God to reveal and become manifest, or it is the way of bhakti where Ramakrishna asks the devotee to 'force your demand on the Divine Mother'.[229] Note also the use of the word 'Dualist'. In the next chapter, it will become clear that for all practical purposes, the word is invariably used by Vivekananda in a pejorative sense. Further, Vivekananda celebrates Ramakrishna's tolerance and love of all sects. He mentions the fact that Ramakrishna had a place for all sects and he loved everyone, a fact

---

228. Ibid., p. 23.
229. *Gospel*, p. 629.

that all sects reciprocated in equal measure. He was, suggests Vivekananda, 'free in love, not in "thunder"'.[230] He explains that the mild type creates and the thundering type spreads. In other words, the juxtaposing of 'love' and 'mild' not merely distances Ramakrishna from Vivekananda but also increases the chasm between them, when in the next sentence Vivekananda identifies himself with Paul the Apostle, the influential missionary, 'who was the thundering type to spread the light'. It also undermines the centrality of love and bhakti in Ramakrishna by identifying it with the 'mild type', who are left to beg for the key in order to realize God.

More astounding is Vivekananda's claim that Ramakrishna had to 'go afresh to Nature'.[231] In Nature, Ramakrishna asked for facts. Through these facts, he 'got scientific religion which never says "believe", but "see"; "I see, and you too can see"'.[232] Having done that, Ramakrishna taught the constructive religion of today and not the destructive religion of the past. As is evident, Ramakrishna neither believed in facts as Vivekananda chooses to define the term in the modern scientific idiom, nor did he make the distinction between

230. *CW*, Vol. 7, p. 24.
231. Ibid., p. 24.
232. Ibid., p. 24.

believing and seeing. For Ramakrishna, to believe was to have a longing and yearning heart, and to see meant to see God, not just mentally, logically or even physically, but see God through the 'love eyes' which will be part of the 'love body'.[233] Instead, the 'seeing' in Ramakrishna is transformed by Vivekananda into an act of scientific verification and into an exercise of offering empirical proof for matters of belief that were based on facts. To call this an interpretation would be plainly incorrect; to call it an inversion would be excessively polite. It is, then, a distortion brought about to serve a purpose. In speaking of Ramakrishna's fashioning of a scientific religion, Vivekananda is quick to offer a disclaimer: 'Shri Ramakrishna's teachings are "the gist of Hinduism"; they were not peculiar to him."'[234] In one deft stroke, Vivekananda manages to fabricate an equation that would admirably serve his notion of Hinduism and the politically charged Hindu identity that he sought to create. This is how the equation was to be spelt out: Nature is essentially scientific – Vivekananda offers no explanation whether he was speaking of an objective physical nature or one's inner nature. Ramakrishna believed in the constructive religion of today, one that is based on facts. Belief is superstition until it is tempered by seeing. The act of seeing is verifying. One can only verify facts and not beliefs. Ramakrishna got facts from

233. *Gospel*, p. 115.
234. *CW*, Vol. 7, p. 24.

Nature in order to build a scientific religion. If we all use the scientific religion, we will all see the truth equally and this truth will be the same. Ramakrishna's religion was scientific. What Ramakrishna taught is the gist of Hinduism. If the religion Ramakrishna taught is scientific and is the gist of Hinduism, then Hinduism is scientific.

There is yet another instance where Vivekananda would need to refashion Ramakrishna as a scientist. Having acknowledged that Ramakrishna never taught Advaita and generally always taught dualism, Vivekananda claimed that Ramakrishna taught him Advaita. Why did he do so? That is because he was a scientist. He knew that different people needed different kinds of cures and treatment.[235] Again, the actual context from which this reference to Ramakrishna is taken is about three categories of physicians[236] corresponding to three types of religious teachers. In each of these categories, the superior physician as well as the superior religious teacher is one who shows signs of tamas and uses it to forcefully cure a patient or an unyielding student into good health or spiritual progress. Tamas in this context can hardly have the conventional import of inertia or dullness, but, rather, has the same connotation as Ramakrishna's term 'tāmasic bhakti',[237] which is a burning faith equipped

235. Ibid., p. 414.
236. *Gospel*, pp. 147-8.
237. Ibid., p. 147.

to extort boons from God in the manner of a robber grabbing an individual and divesting him of his money. Vivekananda knew well the tantric roots of this form of channelling tamas, and was contemptuous too of the excessive influence of Tantra in Vaishnavism. For him, Tantra as a practice was invariably Vamachara, which, in turn, he translated as 'immoral practices',[238] bhakti was frequently brushed aside as dualism, and modern Vaishnavism was condemned as 'the skeleton of the defunct Buddhism' saturated with Vamachara. Ignoring Tantra, giving bhakti a short shrift, and condemning Vaishnavism as it existed in Bengal during Ramakrishna's time effectively empties Ramakrishna's faith of meaning and relevance.

Instead of being the perfect synthesis of tantra and bhakti, Ramakrishna was transformed into the harbinger of modern India and of a Golden Age.[239] Ramakrishna's birth marked the beginning of the Satyayuga, argues Vivekananda, because he eliminated all distinctions, between man and woman, between the rich and the poor, between the literate and the illiterate and between the Brahmanas and the Chandāla, making everyone 'sharers in the Divine Love'.[240] He also brought about peace between Hindus and Muslims and between Hindus

---

238. *CW*, Vol. 7, p. 174.
239. *The Complete Works of Swami Vivekananda*, Vol. 6, Advaita Ashrama, Mayavati, Almora, Second edition, 1926, pp. 286-7.
240. Ibid., pp. 302-3.

and Christians. What brought this about was 'the tidal wave of Sri Ramakrishna's Love'.[241] This overwhelming and all-embracing love manifests itself, emphasizes Vivekananda, through Ramakrishna's rectifying the degenerate Sanatana Dharma, retrieving spirituality, upgrading the intellect and putting centre-stage the eclipsed spiritual ideal. What was this spiritual ideal? It was the Vedanta, the 'true religion of the Aryan race'.[242] Through upholding the spiritual ideal, he was able to reconcile sects, doctrinal differences and historical misunderstandings, bringing about unity of the Hindu religion.[243] Terms such as 'unity of the Hindu religion', and 'true religion of the Aryan race' would have bewildered Ramakrishna. But his retort to this unfamiliar caricature of himself would have been equally emphatic and decisive: '[T]o love one's own countrymen is māya. But to love the people of all countries, to love the members of all religions, is dayā. Such a love comes from love of God, from dayā.'[244]

᚛

241. Ibid., p. 303.
242. Ibid., p. 156.
243. Ibid., pp. 156-7.
244. *Gospel*, p. 456. Ramakrishna explains this clearly: 'Men like Śankarāchārya and Sukhadeva kept the "ego of knowledge". It is not for man to show compassion, but for God. One feels compassion as long as one has the "ego of knowledge". And it is God Himself who has become the "ego of knowledge".' See p. 460.

In 1896, Vivekananda gave two lectures in America and England on Ramakrishna.[245] At the outset, he confesses that he speaks on behalf of his Master, but the errors in interpreting the message are entirely his own. The bare bones of Ramakrishna's message are all there, beginning with renunciation, devotion, love and ending with Ramakrishna's love of all sects and religions. But the moment one unravels the details, a very carefully doctored picture emerges. The first thing that strikes any reader of these lectures is that they are placed entirely in the context of the glorious spiritual traditions of India as contrasted with the materialism of the West. Further, and, more importantly, they are placed within the context of the spiritual greatness of Hinduism. There are frequent references to Hinduism's capacity to withstand external shocks, including the coming of materialism in the guise of the West and the flashing of the Islamic sword. Despite all this, the national ideals remained intact because they were Hindu ideals. In turn, Hindu ideals are always painted as a deep quest for spirituality and the celebration of holiness.

Against this background, Ramakrishna's divine madness is explained away as the ordinary condition of things for people who have renounced the world. The Bhairavi, who is generally referred to as the Brahmani

---

245. *The Complete Works of Swami Vivekananda*, Vol. 4, Advaita Ashrama, Mayavati, Almora, Fourth edition, 1932, pp. 152-79.

in the hagiographic accounts of Ramakrishna, is called the Sanyasini by Vivekananda. Not a word is uttered about the Bhairavi teaching Ramakrishna Tantra or supervising his taking on some of the Vaishnava attitudes. Instead, she is held responsible for teaching Ramakrishna the forms of religions of India and different yogic practices. The only other instance of Ramakrishna's spiritual training that deserves a mention in the speech is Ramakrishna's initiation into the philosophy of the Vedas from Totapuri, who is referred to only as a learned, idealist philosopher and not by name. This constitutes the background for Vivekananda's explanation of Ramakrishna's 'catholicity'. Nothing is remotely mentioned about his tantric sadhana or his taking on various attitudes or bhavas, including living like a woman for almost six months.[246] Vivekananda tersely mentions that Ramakrishna was seized with the desire to find the truth of all religions.[247] He had only known his own religion till now. His listeners in 1896 and his readers today would, of course, understand Ramakrishna's religion to be Vivekananda's version

---

246. Vivekananda does mention Ramakrishna dressing up as a woman in the same speech, but the context is changed entirely. It no longer is part of the madhura-bhava or prema/raga bhakti. It becomes an exercise in rooting out the sex idea, especially so because the soul has no sex and so to reach the spirit, one needs to eliminate the various distinctions of sex. Ibid., p. 171-2.

247. Ibid., pp. 169-70.

of Hinduism, something that it was not even in a generously extended sense. The desire to know the truth about various faiths led Ramakrishna to get to know each first-hand. As the 'scientist' par excellence, Ramakrishna learns about Islam and Christianity.[248] After following these two faiths, he came to realize that these faith led him to the same goal he had already attained. The differences were only in name and form. All this was accomplished, Vivekananda tells us, from actual experience.

This is what Vivekananda claims he learned from his Master. Just as after learning about Islam and Christianity, Vivekananda's Ramakrishna comes to the conclusion that these faiths led to the same goal that Ramakrishna had already reached. Similarly, Vivekananda learnt from his Master that all religions in the world were phases of one eternal religion. Notice the dexterity with which the word 'phases' has been added and introduced. What was the parity and equality of all faiths becomes 'phases' of one 'eternal religion' in the hands of Vivekananda. In the last part of the lecture, Vivekananda would claim that Ramakrishna did not want to disturb the faith of any individual, not even a sect like the Muslims whom 'we always regard as the most exclusive'. [249] Again, Muslims and Islam are

---

248. By all accounts, Ramakrishna's sense of Islam and Christianity was slim and perfunctory. See Sumit Sarkar, op.cit., p. 324.
249. *CW*, Vol.4, p. 179.

reduced to a sect and condemned as 'exclusive'. But more crucially, and perhaps ironically, the idea that without disturbing a man's faith, one needs to 'get hold of a man where he stands and give him a push upwards'[250] is attributed to Ramakrishna. It also requires no great leap of imagination to know that 'eternal religion' translates as 'Sanatana Dharma'. Indeed, in the subsequent part of his lecture, the inference drawn becomes abundantly clear when Vivekananda argues that India was the soil to preach religion and the Hindus accept religion with effortless ease. The conflating of India, its soil and Hindu religiosity is accomplished with a flourish, something that would become part and parcel of Vivekananda's politically charged conception of Hinduism.

III

In the early years of knowing Ramakrishna, Vivekananda would taunt his Master about his devotion to Kali. As a follower of the Brahmo Samaj, he denied the idea that God could have form; to think of God with form would be to think of a mere idol. Ramakrishna would often talk about these taunts: 'He [Narendra] says further: "What? He [Ramakrishna] still goes to the Kāli temple!"'[251] The

---

250. Ibid., p. 179.
251. Gospel, p. 225; see also, p. 288.

year of the remark was 1883 and Ramakrishna's favourite disciple was then just twenty years old. Ramakrishna returned the favour by calling the Brahmos the modern Brahmajnanis, who had not tasted the sweet bliss of Kali, whose eyes and faces were dry. They lacked ecstatic love and were unlikely to make any great spiritual progress. Was the comment that Ramakrishna still goes to the Kali temple a sincere complaint or was it rightful indignation? Ramakrishna reveals what it exactly was. He says to Mahendranath Gupta on 26 September 1883: 'Have you seen Narendra lately? (With a smile) He said of me: "He still goes to the Kāli temple. But he will not when he truly understands".'[252] Despite such insolence, Ramakrishna continued to call Narendra 'my own'.[253] He knew that his favourite disciple was wedded to the idea of a formless God and this did not deter Ramakrishna, at least in the initial years, to show his fondness for Narendra and call him 'perfect from his very birth'.[254] Despite signs of deep affection, Ramakrishna also showed signs of exasperation in relation to Narendra as will be evident from the following:

Those who are my own will come here even if I scold them. Look at Narendra's nature! At first he used to abuse my Mother Kāli very much. One

252. Ibid., p. 296.
253. Ibid., p. 363.
254. Ibid., p. 364.

day I said to him sharply, 'Rascal! Don't come here any more.' He slowly left the room and prepared a smoke. He who is one's own will not be angry even if scolded. What do you say?[255]

A year later, in 1884, Ramakrishna is told the news of Vivekananda's involvement in a lawsuit. He responds by regretting the fact that Narendra refuses to believe in Shakti, the Divine Mother. As long as one has the human body, says Ramakrishna, one ought to recognize her. Pratap Hazra, a devotee, who has conveyed the news, then makes an astonishing claim on Narendra's behalf. He reports: 'Narendra says: "If I believed in Śakti, all would follow me. Therefore I cannot".' [256] Ramakrishna does not directly respond to the statement, but merely says that Narendra ought not to go to the extreme to deny Shakti. Was this a sense of destiny on part of the twenty-four-year-old Narendra or just plain hubris?

In 1887, a year after Ramakrishna's death, Vivekananda confesses to Mahendranath Gupta that during the years of his association with Ramakrishna, he used to 'follow my own whims in everything I did'[257] and Ramakrishna

---

255. Ibid., pp. 363-4.
256. Ibid., p. 505.
257. Ibid., p. 981.

never objected or interfered. Vivekananda also confesses to Mahendranath that in the beginning, he did not accept anything that Ramakrishna told him. His Master asked him, 'Then why do you come here?'[258] Vivekananda replied that he came to see Ramakrishna and not listen to him. Nevertheless, Ramakrishna continued to speak to him about Kali and the need for him to acknowledge Shakti. In 1885, after answering a question about Qualified Non-Dualism (Vishistadvaita of Ramanuja) posed by Narendra in the presence of other disciples, Ramakrishna turned to him and affectionately asked him about his health and personal welfare. Narendra's answer and Ramakrishna's response capture the full complexity of Vivekananda's attitude to Kali and to Ramakrishna:

> *Narendra (to the Master)*: Why, I have meditated on Kāli for three or four days, but nothing has come of it.
> *Master*: All in good time, my child. Kāli is none other than Brahman. That which is called Brahman is really Kāli. She is the Primal Energy. When that Energy remains inactive, I call it Brahman, and when It creates, preserves, or destroys, I call it Śakti or Kāli. What you call Brahman I call Kāli.[259]

---

258. Ibid., p. 984.
259. Ibid., p. 734.

Differences between Ramakrishna and Vivekananda were not only about choosing between Brahman and Kali, but spilt into sometimes fundamental and at other times peripheral issues. Ramakrishna often showed impatience about Narendra's fondness for the Brahmo Samaj, contemptuously calling the organization's members 'modern Brahmajnanis'. His attempts to convince Narendra that God was beyond the scriptures, and could not be found with the help of the Vedas and the Vedanta was another perennial source of irritation between the two. Narendra's financial problems after his father's death and worries about providing for his mother and brothers were also a sticky issue. Ramakrishna feared that these problems were pushing his chosen disciple into worldliness, the realm of 'women and gold', and turning him away from God. The *Kathāmrita* records one such conversation[260] where Ramakrishna tries to reason with a worried Narendra by telling him to go beyond his momentary grief. The way to do this, says Ramakrishna, is to recognize that just as knowledge and ignorance go together, similarly happiness and misery too come in pairs. Only by going beyond duality, beyond the binaries of knowledge and ignorance and pleasure and pain, does a seeker attain God. But he was also firm in the conviction that it is God who places people in happiness and in misery by turns. He wanted Narendra to surrender to

---

260. Ibid., p. 695.

God and not question God's inscrutable ways. Narendra was not prepared to do such a thing. He also expected Ramakrishna to help him, something Hazra clearly reports to Ramakrishna.[261] Ramakrishna, despite his deep and incomparable affection for Narendra, fails to comprehend the intellectual, spiritual and emotional turmoil of his twenty-one-year-old disciple. All he knows and does is to uphold the ideals of total, unquestioning submission to God and of complete renunciation of the world. Take, for instance, the following conversation between Ramakrishna and Mahendranath Gupta in Narendra's presence:

Master (to M): Well, I said to Keshab, 'One should be satisfied with what comes unsought.' The son of an aristocrat does not worry about his food and drink. He gets his monthly allowance. Narendra, too, belongs to a high plane. Then why is he in such straitened circumstances? God certainly provides everything for the man who totally surrenders himself to Him.

M: Narendra, too, will be provided for. It is not yet too late for him.

Master: But a man who feels intense renunciation within doesn't calculate that way. He doesn't say to himself, 'I shall first make an arrangement for

---

261. Ibid., p. 505.

the family and then practise sādhanā.' No, he doesn't feel that way if he has developed intense dispassion.[262]

Having said this, Ramakrishna offers a parable to illustrate the point. It makes everyone laugh. 'At these words Narendra felt as if stuck by an arrow,' records M, 'and lay down on the floor.'[263]

Notwithstanding encomiums heaped on Vivekananda, the Master and disciple constantly judged each other and openly discussed their differences. Ramakrishna often called Narendra a nityasiddha,[264] one who was exalted spiritually and eternally free, felt genuinely proud of his learning, and swore on more than one occasion about Narendra's lack of interest in 'woman and gold'. At the same time, as a devotee and a spiritual aspirant, Ramakrishna found his favourite disciple inadequate and incomplete. He believed that Narendra was among the 'partial knower' of God.[265] A partial knower limits God to one object and excludes all other possibilities of God's existence. This followed his threefold classification of devotees. The lowest one points to God residing somewhere is the skies or in the heaven. The mediocre devotee shows God's existence as an 'Inner Controller'.

262. Ibid., p. 896.
263. Ibid., p. 896.
264. Ibid., p. 279.
265. Ibid., p. 396.

The highest devotee sees God as having become the universe itself and all things, animate and inanimate, in the world. Having explained the nature of this classification, Ramakrishna says: 'Narendra used to make fun of me and say: "Yes, God has become all! Then a pot is God, a cup is God!"'[266] In another conversation, Vivekananda called the faith of those who believed that God has forms as blind faith. Ramakrishna's reaction is sharp and unambiguous:

> Well, can you explain to me what you mean by 'blind faith'? All faith is indeed blind. But then has faith any eye at all? Speak either of 'faith' or of 'knowledge'. But no, you will speak of someone's faith as blind and of some other's as having eyes; how is that?[267]

Neither did Ramakrishna mince words when it came to judging the intensity and depth of Vivekananda's spiritual quest: 'Narendra's devotion and enthusiasm are extraordinary indeed, but compared with the urge that came here (pointing to himself) at the time of Sadhana, his is most ordinary. It is not even one fourth of that.'[268]

Vivekananda was initially attracted to Ramakrishna and he found in him 'a man who dared to say that he

---

266. Ibid., p. 396.
267. *Great Master*, p. 431.
268. Ibid., p. 224.

saw God, that religion was a reality to be felt, to be sensed in an infinitely more intense way than we can sense the world'.[269] He began to go to Ramakrishna and came to the conclusion that 'religion could be given'.[270] It is evident that what Ramakrishna was offering was not what Vivekananda was looking for, and their self-understanding of terms like 'God', 'faith', 'devotion' and 'religion' was entirely founded on different premises.

In 1885, a year before his death, Ramakrishna encourages Girish Ghosh and Narendra to argue and engage in a verbal duel in English.[271] The two young men speak in Bangla instead but discuss the nature of God. Narendra says that God is Infinity and cannot be comprehended. More so, God dwells in every human being and does not manifest in just one person alone. Ramakrishna partially agrees with him, but adds that God's power is different in different beings, in some as avidyashakti and in some as vidyashakti. This makes all humans unequal, each manifesting in varying degrees the power of God. The conversation reverts again to the question of God assuming a human body. Narendra argues that this could not be the case because God was beyond words

269. *CW*, Vol. 4, pp. 174-5.
270. Ibid., p. 175.
271. *Gospel*, pp. 732-3.

or thought. Ramakrishna disagrees and says that God can be known through pure buddhi or the inner faculty of discrimination. When Narendra rejects a suggestion by Girish about God manifesting as teacher in a human incarnation and argues that God dwells in human hearts as an inner guide, Ramakrishna agrees. The discussion between Girish and Narendra becomes fraught, with references to Hamilton, Herbert Spencer, Tyndall and Huxley being thrown in for good measure. Ramakrishna puts an end to the debate saying that he did not enjoy such discussions, restating his position on God having become the universe and conveying to all present, including Narendra, that at the sight of his favourite disciple his mind loses itself in the consciousness of the Absolute.

Later, in the same year, a similar debate ensues.[272] Narendra demands proof that God incarnates as man, asks for proof of immortality of the gods, raises questions over the authenticity and legitimacy of the scriptures, points out contradictions within the Samkhya way of looking at various issues and expresses a sweeping scepticism about all questions relating to God, gods, scriptures and philosophy. Ramakrishna interjects now and again to offer examples of Narendra's doubts, disbelief and scepticism, something that created disbelief in his own mind. In the case of Ramakrishna, a conversation with Kali and, as a consequence of the

272. Ibid., pp. 771-3.

conversation, a vision, dispelled the doubts. 'Thereupon I said to Narendra: "You rogue! You created unbelief in my mind. Don't come here any more",' he informs the gathering.[273] The discussion continues. A part of the discussion, if only to show the chasm between Ramakrishna and Vivekananda, is worth reproducing in full.

> *A Devotee*: The Gītā contains the words of God.
> *Master*: Yes, the Gītā is the essence of all scriptures. A sannyāsi may or may not keep with him another book, but he always carries a pocket Gītā.
> *A Devotee*: The Gītā contains the words of Krishna.
> *Narendra*: Yes, Krishna or any fellow for that matter![274]

Mahendranath Gupta's remarks about the above exchange are equally revealing: 'Sri Ramakrishna was amazed at these words of Narendra.'[275] To this Ramakrishna himself only reiterates his firmly held and familiar position regarding not accepting anything till 'it agrees with the direct words of the Divine Mother'.[276]

In the last year of Ramakrishna's life, especially after he was diagnosed with cancer in July-August 1885, there

---

273. Ibid., p. 772.
274. Ibid., p. 772.
275. Ibid., p. 772.
276. Ibid., p. 773.

are several conversations recorded in the *Kathāmrita* that could be held as evidence to show Vivekananda's acceptance of Ramakrishna's views. Such 'concessions' on issues of faith could range between acceptance of pantheism[277] to conceding Ramakrishna's status as a godlike man. But the burden of evidence in the *Kathāmrita* and in the *Lilaprasanga* would suggest otherwise. In the months leading to Ramakrishna's death, when directly confronted by his Master on issues where they had serious disagreements, Vivekananda would invariably agree in order not to cause the ailing Ramakrishna any grief. But once removed from Ramakrishna's presence, he would affirm his own position clearly. For instance, on 15 March 1886, Ramakrishna, who, by now, is very ill, tells Narendra and other devotees that 'all things – everything that exists – have come from this'.[278] He, then, asks them to explain what they had understood by this statement. Narendra tells Ramakrishna, 'All created objects have come from you.'[279] Ramakrishna's face lights up with joy on hearing this and he can hardly believe that his rebellious disciple could have affirmed his status as an incarnation. A day earlier, Ramakrishna had clearly declared himself as an incarnation: 'I am seeing many forms of God. Among them I find this one also [meaning

---

277. Ibid. p. 966.
278. Ibid., p. 945.
279. Ibid., p. 945.

his own form].'[280] Just over a month later, on 21 April 1886, Narendra tells Mahendranath Gupta that there was no such thing as God.[281] Mahendranath was aware of Narendra's financial worries and the need to settle his family's affairs, and so, paraphrasing Ramakrishna, reassuringly tells him that scepticism would eventually lead him to realizing God. Narendra asks him if anyone he knows has seen God as clearly as he could see a tree at that point. Mahendranath replied that 'our Master has seen God that way'.[282] 'It may be his hallucination,' says Narendra. Alluding to 'a great argument'[283] with Ramakrishna himself, Narendra insists on knowing the truth; claims, proclamations and assertions were not even remote approximation of truth.

> He said to me, 'Some people call me God.' I replied, 'Let a thousand people call you God, but I shall certainly not call you God as long as I do not know it to be true.' He said, 'Whatever many people say is indeed truth; that is dharma.' Thereupon I replied, 'Let others proclaim a thing as truth, but I shall certainly not listen to them unless I myself realize it as truth.'[284]

---

280. Ibid., p. 941.
281. Ibid., p. 962.
282. Ibid., p. 962.
283. Ibid., p. 962.
284. Ibid., p. 962.

Ramakrishna and Vivekananda confronted the question of Ramakrishna being an incarnation even before Ramakrishna's illness. In March 1885, Narendra tells Ramakrishna that Girish Ghosh believed 'you to be an Incarnation of God'.[285] Having said this, he adds that 'I didn't say anything in answer to his remarks'.[286] On hearing this Ramakrishna wonders if Narendra did not notice Girish's great faith. The Master and disciple sit silently for a few minutes in front of each other after this exchange.

By November 1885, Ramakrishna's disciples had begun to worship him as Kali.[287] Narendra did not participate in this and little is known of what he thought of this iconic transformation of Ramakrishna into a deity. The farthest Narendra would go is to say that Ramakrishna was a 'godlike man'[288] and explain it in terms of 'a stage between the man-world and the God-world where it is extremely hard to say whether a person is a man or God'.[289] While Ramakrishna was alive, Vivekananda remained torn between his family problems and his spiritual quest. In a conversation with Mahendranath Gupta,[290] he talks about having gained

285. Ibid., p. 711.
286. Ibid., p. 711.
287. Ibid., pp. 928-9.
288. Ibid., p. 904.
289. Ibid., p. 904.
290. Ibid., p. 936.

a human birth, the desire for liberation and refuge with a great soul, something that Shankaracharya suggested one gains out of great effort and good fortune. The two remain silent for a while. Vivekananda breaks the silence and says to Mahendrananth: 'You have found peace, but my soul is restless.'[291]

---

291. Ibid., p. 936.

Whose Society, What Religion?

I

In a letter to a disciple from New York in 1894, Swami Vivekananda offers a blueprint for India's revival and ending its enslavement. The solution for him lies in unswerving fidelity to 'our religion'[1] and enhancing social freedom by removing priestcraft. Once this is achieved, the result will be the emergence of the best religion in the world. This was a step towards realizing the blueprint but was not the whole plan itself. Two sentences in the same letter, however, encapsulate the aim, purpose, mission and reasons for all that Vivekananda said and did in his life: 'Can you make a European

---

1. *The Complete Works of Swami Vivekananda,* Vol. 4, Advaita Ashrama, Mayavati, Almora, Fourth edition, 1932, p. 313. The letter was to Alasingha Perumal dated 19 November 1894, written from New York (*The Complete Works of Swami Vivekananda* will henceforth be referred to as *CW*).

society with India's religion? I believe it is possible and must be.'[2] Ambitious as it is, this plan required two very important components. The first was to have a clear conception of the elements that constitute Vivekananda's idea of 'European society', and, secondly, to have an unambiguous sense of what was entailed in the idea of 'India's religion'. The clue to the latter question lies in his demanding unwavering loyalty to 'our religion', in other words, Hinduism. But Vivekananda's Hinduism was not something even Sri Ramakrishna would have understood or approved. Ramakrishna never made the sharp and divisive distinction between the materialistic West and the spiritual East either. When a devotee suggested that the English, especially the intellectuals among the English people, no longer believed in the existence of God, Ramakrishna dismissed such atheism on their part as mere talk.[3] For him Christianity and Jesus were part of a saintly and spiritual world, represented by the picture of Jesus raising the drowning Peter hung amidst pictures of gods and saints in his own room. Pictures of rich men,

---

2. Ibid., p. 313.
3. *The Gospel of Sri Ramakrishna: Originally recorded in Bengali by M., a disciple of the Master*, Translated into English with an Introduction by Swami Nikhilananda, Ramakrishna-Vivekananda Center, New York, 2007 imprint, p. 457. This is a translation of Mahendranath Gupta's *Sri Sri Ramakrishna Kathāmrita*, originally published between 1897 and 1932 in five volumes in Bengali. Henceforth, all references to the English translation will be cited as *Gospel*.

kings and queens, and white men and women walking together were dismissed as 'English' pictures, hung on the walls of men with rajasic qualities rather than those who admired saints and holy men.[4] Vivekananda's project was very different. It was to create a society in India that resembled his conception of European society and to fabricate a religion for India that would be in harmony with this desirable model of society.

Given Vivekananda's predilection for contradicting himself and saying things that sound convincingly contrary to something he might himself have said elsewhere, it is important to chronicle these contradictions and make sense of them. If the above sets of interpretation are to hold, especially against the pietistical onslaught of the selectively chosen quote, such an exercise becomes inevitable. Take, for instance, Vivekananda's address at Ramnad on 25 January 1897.[5] He lists the old orthodoxy in India and the reception of the modern European civilization as the two inevitable fates from which a choice had to be made. He emphatically makes the choice in favour of the old orthodoxy for its manliness, faith, strength and self-reliance, despite its seeming ignorance and crudity. Contrasted with old orthodoxy is the modern European civilization, which, in the course of the speech is variously referred to as the Europeanized system, and

---

4. Ibid., p. 606.
5. *The Complete Works of Swami Vivekananda*, Vol. 3, Advaita Ashrama, Mayavati, Almora, Fourth edition, 1932, p. 151.

finally becomes an allusion to the Europeanized man. We finally know that Vivekananda is talking about the Europeanized man who has no backbone, who is a mass of heterogeneous ideas randomly picked, and that these ideas remain unassimilated, undigested and unharmonized. He, in other words, is the Indian reformer who, under European patronage, is prone to 'vehement vituperations against the evils of certain social customs...'.[6] In short, Vivekananda prefers the old Indian orthodoxy to the Europeanized reformer. He exhorts his listeners to subordinate their knowledge of European sciences, their wealth, position and name to spirituality and the purity of the race, elements that are inherent in every Hindu child. This for him also becomes the test of a true Hindu's character. It is not the place here to comment on such contentious notions as 'purity of the race' and 'true Hindu', but the confusion of categories and meanings in relation to Europe, European civilization, European system, European sciences and Europeanized reformers has to be carefully noted.

Subordination of European sciences to spirituality and to the purity of the race was important for Vivekananda because modern science and reason were akin to the existence of superstitions in the formative stages of religion.[7] While in the context of religion, such

6.   Ibid., p. 151.
7.   *The Complete Works of Swami Vivekananda*, Vol. 2, Advaita Ashrama, Mayavati, Almora, Fourth edition, 1932, p. 74.

superstitions eventually lead to birth of spirituality, modern science results in lust and greed; machines fulfilled desires by making desire keener. The foundation of European civilization, he argues, is the sword, while the Aryans built their idea of civilization on the basis of division of people on the basis of varnas. The varna system allowed people to 'rise higher and higher in proportion to one's learning and culture'.[8] In contrast, the West believed in matter alone and was 'addicted to the aggrandisement of self by exploiting others' countries, others' wealth by force, trick and treachery'.[9] From the Indian point of view, the westerner is an asura, concludes Vivekananda. Not only are they asuras, they are also bound by their worship of Shakti, the female principle, reminiscent of the manner in which the Vamachari worships women during tantric practice: 'As the Tantric says: "On the left side the woman...on the right, the cup full of wine; in front, warm meat with ingredients...the Tāntrika religion is very mysterious, inscrutable even to the Yogis." It is this worship of Shakti that is openly and universally practised.'[10] Given Vivekananda's rejection of Tantra, which he always sought to conflate with Vamachara, this indictment of the West, at face value, seems searing, categorical and final.

8. *The Complete Works of Swami Vivekananda*, Vol. 5, Advaita Ashrama, Mayavati, Almora, Fourth edition, 1936, p. 439.
9. Ibid., pp. 345-6.
10. Ibid., pp. 407-8.

Swearing his love for India, holding afloat his patriotism and affirming his veneration for the ancients, Vivekananda also wants Indians to learn from other nations.[11] He wants them to show a willingness to sit at the feet of all and learn valuable lessons. What are these lessons, if any? He wants the Indian to become 'an occidental of occidentals in your spirit of equality, freedom, work and energy...'.[12] While doing so, he also wants them to remain Hindu to the core in religious matters. After reading the epic Ramayana, Vivekananda finds the East and the West sharply divided in terms of representing two diametrically opposed ideals. Despite his grave reservations about contemporary European civilization and European science, not to mention their relentless pursuit of Shakti, Vivekananda does not utter the final word regarding the East and the West as representing two incompatible ideals. He begins, in fact, to express doubts regarding the individual merits of these ideals. Having created, affirmed and restated the binary between the East and the West, he now has second thoughts regarding this stereotypical, and predictably nineteenth-century, typology of the East and the West:

The West says, 'Do. Show your power by doing.' India says, 'Show your power by suffering.' The

---

11. *CW*, Vol. 3, p. 272.
12. *CW*, Vol. 5, p. 26.

> West has solved the problem of how much a man can have: India has solved the problem of how little a man can have. The two extremes, you see... Who knows which is the truer ideal? The apparent power and strength, as held in the West, or the fortitude in suffering, of the East?[13]

Vivekananda's dilemma was acute. To accept the modern West and European science was to indirectly accept the legitimacy of British rule in India. Moreover, to accept modern European ideas was to concur with the project of the social reformers in Bengal. Despite these obstacles, the energy, effort, freedom and equality of European civilization were admirable and worth emulating, only if it was to be the model of inspiration to create a European society in India with one's own religion. Put differently, the West had to be accommodated in India, but it had to be an edition of the West which was not materialistic, self-aggrandizing, exploitative, treacherous and asuric. Once admitted, this version of the West had to learn to live with his version of Hindu spirituality and Hindu orthodoxy. In other words, Vivekananda's reading of certain elements within contemporary European society and select features within contemporary India were equally incommensurable with his mission of creating for his country a European society with India's religion.

---

13. *CW*, Vol. 4, pp. 71-2.

Vivekananda surmounts this by drawing a parallel between the ancestors of modern Europe and of contemporary India. The history of ancient India, which was for Vivekananda the story of the Aryan civilization, was one of enormous energies, limitless spirit, a unique combination of forces of action and reaction, but, most of all, it manifested itself in 'the profound thoughtfulness of a godly race'.[14] Ancient India produced religious poetry, philosophies and scientific work, but the natural affinity of ancient India was for profound meditation, renunciation, quietness and a directing of all their energies inwards to knowledge of the Self. They looked for moksha or renunciation and cared little about the material world. While there are some in contemporary India still raring to claim the legacy of ancient India, 'the modern inhabitants of the land of Bharata are not the glory of the ancient Aryas'.[15] The latent embers of this glorious Aryan past had to be reignited and reclaimed. Vivekananda considers the elements from the past that could be recaptured but is bewildered by the diversity and complexity of customs and traditions existing in the country. Setting aside the question of retrieving the legacy of ancient India for the moment, Vivekananda is on surer ground when it comes to what he wants and what he approves.

---

14. Ibid., p. 332.
15. Ibid., p. 335.

Unlike modern India, which had spurned and wasted the glorious legacy of the Aryans, contemporary Europe was in all respects 'the disciple of ancient Greece, and her proper inheritor...'.[16] The Yavanas or the Greeks in antiquity had charming appearance, were perfectly formed, and had strong muscles and great vigour. They possessed steadiness and perseverance and managed to create unrivalled earthly beauties. Their contribution to earthly sciences like society, politics, war and sculpture remains unmatched and unsurpassed. Along with these achievements in earthly beauties and sciences, they also were blessed with extraordinary practicality and intellect. All this found a natural outlet in their constant expression of power, in their indomitable spirit in undertaking dexterous activities and in their quest for political independence. In contrast to the Aryans, the ancient Greeks directed their energies outwards, to gaining the knowledge of the not-Self or that of the perishable creation. In far antiquity, the Aryans and the Greeks – Vivekananda calls them two gigantic rivers – occasionally came into contact and created intellectual and spiritual fervour, enhanced human societies, elevated the idea of civilization and gave birth to great nations and, eventually, to the European civilization itself. This occasional coming together of Indian philosophy and Greek energy in the distant and hoary past has made Europe and America

---

16. Ibid., p. 334.

what they are, 'the advanced children of the Yavanas, a glory to their forefathers...'.[17]

For Vivekananda, modern Europe, the proud inheritors of the mantle of ancient Greece, had come in the form of the English. Their presence in India was nectar as well as poison. English laws in India were dismantling customs and traditions. At this juncture, Vivekananda makes two very significant observations. Firstly, he questions the desirability of some of the old customs in India being swept away by English rule, European technology and English laws and wonders if they were after all worth preserving. Secondly, he firmly believes that 'the power of stemming this tide is not in Hindu society'.[18] This powerlessness was a direct result of an excessive preoccupation with absolute purity of mind or the sattva guna. While sattva was not only desirable but the highest form of knowledge, it demanded a level of renunciation impossible among the multitude of people. Sattva and its glorification had led people to camouflage their laziness, stupidity and inactivity behind the so-called quest for transcendence and ultimate knowledge. The result was not an excess of sattva, but the country incrementally drowning in 'the ocean of Tamas or dark ignorance'.[19] Again, it is instructive to digress here in order to mark the discontinuity between Ramakrishna

17. Ibid., p. 335.
18. Ibid., p. 340.
19. Ibid., p. 338.

and Vivekananda in their understanding of the gunas and their respective roles. Ramakrishna calls sattva, rajas and tamas as three brothers and as three robbers.[20] They act in tandem to control humans. Sattva calls upon rajas for help, and, in turn, rajas gets assistance from tamas. Tamas, Ramakrishna believed, kills a person, and rajas binds us. Sattva has the quality to release a person from bondage but is powerless to take him closer to God. While tamas had the quality to kill, the tamasic quality could also be turned towards a version of bhakti represented by strength of mind and a burning faith.[21]

Returning to Vivekananda, he believed that the only way out of the debilitating spiral of being caught in the vortex of excessive sattva and drowning in the ocean of tamas was to preserve one's 'own ancestral property'[22] but also open the country to new ideas and fresh currents. For Vivekananda, while what constitutes for Indians the 'wealth of our own home'[23] varied and did lend itself to contradictions, there was no confusion or ambiguity in his mind about the way forward for India. This deep and profound clarity emerged out of the absence of any urgent need impelling him to solve the vexed question of India's ancient past and the elements from that past which could have salience of some sort in the present:

---

20. *Gospel*, p. 438.
21. Ibid., p. 494. See also, p. 147.
22. *CW*, Vol. 4, p. 339.
23. Ibid., p. 339.

What we should have is, what we have not, perhaps what our forefathers even had not; – that which the Yavanas had; that, impelled by the life-vibration of which, is issuing forth in rapid succession from the great dynamo of Europe, the electric flow of that tremendous power, vivifying the whole world. We want that. We want that energy, that love of independence, that spirit of self-reliance, that immovable fortitude, that dexterity in action, that bond of unity of purpose, that thirst for improvement. Checking a little the constant looking back to the past, we want that expansive vision infinitely projected forward; and we want, – that intense spirit of activity (Rajas) which will flow through our every vein, from head to foot.[24]

The enterprise, energy, vitality and love of independence of the Greeks had to be emulated. The ancient Greeks embodied rajas and it was rajas that ought to lead the way towards attaining sattva. In a subtle, but significant, inversion, Vivekananda argues that a man had to pass through a stage of possessing rajas in order to eventually aspire for the perfect sattvica state.[25] Bhoga or enjoyment had to come before yoga or the ultimate union with God: 'It is action with desire that leads to action without desire.

24. Ibid., p. 337.
25. Ibid., p. 338.

Is the renunciation of desire possible, if desire did not exist in the beginning? And what could it mean? Can light have any meaning if there is no darkness?'[26]

Vivekananda does create the usual binaries of the sattva-less West and the rajas-less India, arguing that nations that do not have sattva perish and ones that have sattva are immortal.[27] He also speaks of the judicious synthesis between the rajas of the West and the sattva of India. But the inevitability of importing the rajas as represented by ancient Greece and its heirs and inheritors was clear and categorical. Even English rule, which was described as a mixture of nectar and poison, was, after all, a great good for this very reason:

> [T]he great good of the English conquest is this: England, nay the whole of Europe, has to thank Greece for its civilization. It is Greece that speaks through everything in Europe. Every building, every piece of furniture has the impress of Greece upon it; European science and art are nothing but Grecian. To-day the ancient Greek is meeting the ancient Hindu on the soil of India.[28]

The blueprint was clear: ancient Greece and ancient India were the epitome of civilization. While modern

26. Ibid., pp. 424-5.
27. Ibid., p. 339.
28. *CW*, Vol. 3, p. 271.

Europe had inherited the mantle of ancient Greece, modern India had woefully failed to follow suit. Modern India's redemption lay in emulating ancient Greece, alive and palpable in modern Europe, and creating in India a European society with India's religion. What that religion would be and eventually resemble was something equally contentious, as we will see in the next chapter.

Incorporating the West within a blueprint for future India was not sufficient. Vivekananda had to convincingly articulate his celebration of ancient Greece and the continuity of its legacy in modern Europe in a language that was religious and recognizably 'Hindu'. The first step in this direction he takes is to identify and create a distinction between the core ideas in India and in the West: he called these the driving force and the operative impulses. In the case of India, he argues, the overwhelming desire is for mukti or liberation from the bondage of the world. But the West quests after dharma: 'Here the word "Dharma" is used in the sense of the Mimāmsakas. What is Dharma? Dharma is that which makes man seek for happiness in this world or the next. Dharma is established on work: Dharma is impelling man day and night to run after and work for happiness.'[29] Dharma, after all, had a meaning that resonated admirably with the Western idea of 'work'

---

29. *CW*, Vol. 5, p. 349.

and the desire for happiness in this world and the next, a meaning that had its foundation within the six orthodox systems of Hindu philosophy, namely, the Purva Mimamsa. But to the vast masses of Hindus that Vivekananda hoped to awaken and save from the brutal embrace of tamas, an esoteric and involved philosophical discussion alone was not adequate. To build an argument where dharma and work would be understood in tandem, Vivekananda turns to myths in order to push forward his formulation. At other times, he may have called myths in the Puranas grotesque, irrational and unhistorical, but their momentary usefulness in order to legitimize the need for absorbing the rajasic West in India was beyond doubt and dispute:

You certainly know the story of the Devas and the Asuras. The Devas have faith in their soul, in God, and in the after-life, while the Asuras give importance to this life, and devote themselves to enjoying this world and trying to have bodily comforts in every possible way. We do not mean to discuss here whether the Devas are better than the Asuras, or the Asuras than the Devas, but, reading their description in the Purānas, the Asuras seem to be, truth to tell, more like MEN, and far more manly than the Devas; the Devas are inferior, without doubt, to the Asuras, in many respects. Now, to understand the East and the West, we cannot do better than interpret the Hindus as the sons of the Devas and the Westerners as the sons of the Asuras.[30]

For Vivekananda, Hindu India was synonymous with the East, and Hindus synonymous with India. The West was, more often than not, a seamless, undifferentiated category. Perceived as asuras, the West was infinitely more manly; in fact, the West was the heir to 'the great hero Virochana',[31] the first king of the asuras. He also concedes that while India ought to, forever, remain teachers of the West in spiritual matters, 'they will remain our teachers in all material concerns'.[32] Despite the veneer of calmness and balance of the Sattvic state, people in India were inert, lazy and sensual like stock and stone, immersed in inactivity brought on by tamas. The West, in sharp contrast, was the very picture of enterprise, devotion to work, enthusiasm, a manifestation of rajas in every which way.[33]

---

30. Ibid., p. 373. For a detailed discussion on the nineteenth-century use of the Deva-Asura distinction, see 'Digesting the "Other": Hindu Nationalism and the Muslims in India', Jyotirmaya Sharma, *Hindutva: Exploring the Idea of Hindu Nationalism*, Penguin Books, New Delhi, 2011, revised edition.

31. *The Complete Works of Swami Vivekananda*, Vol. 6, Advaita Ashrama, Mayavati, Almora, Second edition, 1926, p. 403.

32. Ibid., p. 403.

33. *The Complete Works of Swami Vivekananda*, Vol. 7, Advaita Ashrama, Kolkata, Fourteenth impression, 2002, pp. 181-3.

Vivekananda's analysis of the state of Hindu India, its people and their degradation was always lyrical, though his prescription to rectify this was always direct and uncomplicated:

[I]n your country, it is as if the blood has become congealed in the heart, so that it cannot circulate in the veins – as if paralysis has overtaken the body and it has become languid. So my idea is first to make people active by developing their Rajas, and thus make them fit for the struggle for existence...I will rouse them through the infallible power of Vedic Mantras...With the help of Western science set yourself to dig the earth and produce food-stuffs – not by means of mean servitude of others – but by discovering new avenues to production, by your own exertions aided by Western science... Throw aside your scriptures in the Ganga and teach the people first the means of procuring their food and clothing, and then you will find time to read to them the scriptures. If their material wants are not removed by the rousing of intense activity, none will listen to words of spirituality.[34]

In his espousal of Western science as a means of removing servitude and poverty, Vivekananda is far

---

34. Ibid., pp. 181-3.

removed from any serious critique of the flip side of modern science and technology. As noted earlier, he does occasionally refer to the vicious cycle of desire and greed in the West, but subordinates it to an unequivocal approval of the activity, enterprise and the West's power to 'make the five elements play like puppets in their hands'.[35] This is a far cry from the same Vivekananda who after Ramakrishna's death was preaching the futility of worldliness and exhorting everyone else to give up women and gold.

As a religious nationalist, Vivekananda implicates the lack of attention to material civilization as the reason for all calamities and all misfortune for the Hindus. Conquest by Muslims is listed as one such calamity; so abject was the ignorance of material civilization that even the conquering Muslims managed to teach the Hindus to wear tailor-made clothes.[36] As we shall see, Vivekananda had one single model to measure material wealth and poverty, and that was America and Europe of his time. For him, this measure of affluence and poverty was absolute; it could be applied ahistorically to explain the fall of the Hindu civilization as he perceived it. Hence, the cultural particularity of not wearing tailor-made clothes could be seen as a shortcoming in his mind. In turn, this inadequacy could be conflated with

---

35. *CW*, Vol. 6, p. 403.
36. *CW*, Vol. 4, p. 313.

ubiquitous hunger in nineteenth-century Bengal and held as a universally valid proposition for India's lack of a material civilization. Vivekananda's explanation as to what stunted the growth of material civilization is equally complex: 'Bread! Bread! I do not believe in a God who cannot give me bread here, giving me eternal bliss in heaven!'[37] Put differently, religion, as it had existed to his day, was the reason for hunger, poverty and a lack of material well-being. He calls it the tyranny of the sages, of the spiritual, of the wise and of the intellectual – a tyranny, he suggests, more powerful than the tyranny of the ignorant.[38] These categories of men had forced their fellow human beings into accepting a view that rejected the goods of life and the importance of making money. Also, excess of religion and no sense of political power had led to India's slavery and poverty.[39] The sudden interpolation of political power as an element in a discussion on material civilization was for Vivekananda part of the same glorious rajas story, something that the ancient Greeks had gifted to the world and something that the liberation-loving Hindus did not have.

The story, then, was one of excess and shortage: excess of sattva and of religion and lack of rajas and of material well-being. A first step in order to rectify this imbalance,

---

37. Ibid., p. 313.
38. *The Complete Works of Swami Vivekananda*, Vol. 8, Advaita Ashrama, Calcutta, Twelfth impression, 1999, p. 76.
39. Ibid., p. 74.

urges Vivekananda, was to make all vain gods disappear, only to be replaced by another god. He calls this god, the Virāt.[40] He urges that all Indians purify their hearts by worshipping the Virat. Who, or, what is the Virāt?

> This is the only God that is awake, our own race, everywhere His hands, everywhere His feet, everywhere His ears, He covers everything. All other Gods are sleeping. What vain Gods shall we go after and yet cannot worship the God that we see all round us, the Virāt?...These are all our Gods, — men and animals, and the first Gods we have to worship, instead of being jealous of each other and fighting each other.[41]

Vivekananda creates a timeless abstraction that to this day has the ability to sweep aside vain and not so vain gods. At his rhetorical best, he often failed to notice the contradictions generated by his own evocative pronouncements. He could, therefore, speak of the laziness, inertia and inactivity of a vast majority of

---

40. The metaphor is taken from Krishna's revelation of his all-encompassing form, mentioned as the Vishvarupa in the eleventh chapter of the Bhagavadgita (see, for instance, verse 16). It is also called the virātrūpa, implying Krishna's vast and imposing form in which the entire universe could reside and manifest.

41. *CW*, Vol. 3, pp. 300-1.

Hindus, and, simultaneously speak of the people 'of our race' as the only god that was awake and worthy of worship. Did he really believe in the strength and the significance of his idea of the Virāt? In creating an enduring abstraction, Vivekananda added a dimension to it that lends a normative edge to the idea of the Virāt. The clue lies in the insistence on the word 'worship', a word not carelessly used in this context. 'Worship It', he insists, 'Worship is the exact equivalent of the Sanskrit word, and no other English word will do.'[42] The abstract idea of the Hindu masses had to be worshipped; Hindu masses alone because the Virāt is constituted by 'our own race'.

Except as an emotive abstraction, Vivekananda had little faith in the multitude of Indian masses, whether seen in purely racial terms, or conceived as the sum total of all people in India. Even the most humanitarian ideas in the hands of the multitude result in degradation, he argues.[43] The real custodians of religion and philosophy, perceived in their purest form, are the cultured, and it is learning and intellect that keep the intellectual and social capital of a community safe. Slavery over the centuries had accustomed Indians to covet power only to produce more slaves and not share one's liberty; freedom for the slave always translates into keeping some other people

42. Ibid., p. 301.
43. *CW*, Vol. 6, p. 124.

subjugated.[44] Neither did the people of India have any sense of the principles of self-government. Historically, whether under Hindu, Buddhist or Mughal rule, they were ruled by a godlike paternalistic king and did little for the common good or for self-defence.[45] The Buddhist period, the ascendency of the Rajputs and the eventual rise of the Mughal power had one thing in common: the decline of the priestly caste and that of the spiritual brilliance of the brahmins. Vivekananda had an idealized view of the priestly caste and of the brahmins and always held them as an ideal indispensable for India, a theme we will explore more fully in Section III.[46] All his diatribes against brahmins that are often quoted to argue that he was against the varna system are far off the mark in understanding his views on the subject. In fact, the converse is true: Vivekananda believed that the revival of the priestly power in India and the revival of India were inextricably linked.

As a votary of what he likened as the spiritual brilliance of the brahmins, Vivekananda strongly resented brahmins espousing more popular forms of religion, whether bhakti or Tantra. For him all non-Vedic and non-Vedantic forms of belief were to be condemned as dualism and branded as undesirable superstitions and rituals (as we will see in the next chapter). Attributing

---

44. *CW*, Vol. 4, p. 313.
45. Ibid., p. 374.
46. Ibid., pp. 376-8.

intensions of wanting to control the masses, he linked popular and ritualistic forms of brahminical practices to one form or the other of predatory exploitation. Of course, historically speaking, the proliferation of sects that preferred bhakti as the ideal way to reach God, or saw in Tantra a way of understanding the mysteries of life and the universe, also regularly rejected the straitjacket of caste and its fourfold division. In ignoring popular manifestations of heterodox Hindu sects, and in idealizing caste as well as the brahmins, Vivekananda brought together the existence of spiritual power among certain individuals with the priestly functions of the brahmins. But what is more fraught and highly contentious in this instance is the unequivocal location of spirituality within the ambit of the priestly caste. Here is an example of Vivekananda creating a double caricature. The portrait of the Muslim is unflattering and devoid of nuances,[47] but the exaggerated stress on the spiritual role of the brahmins defies historical scrutiny and common understanding:

> The Prophet Mahomet himself was dead against the priestly class in any shape, and tried his best for the total destruction of this power by formulating

47. For a detailed discussion on Vivekananda's portrayal of Islam and the Muslims, see, Jyotirmaya Sharma, *Hindutva: Exploring the Idea of Hindu Nationalism*, Penguin Books, New Delhi, 2011, revised edition.

rules and injunctions to that effect. Under the Mussulman rule, the king himself was the supreme priest; he was the chief guide in religious matters; and, when he became the emperor, he cherished the hope of being the paramount leader in all matters, over the whole Mussulman world. To the Mussulman, the Jew or the Christian is not an object of extreme detestation; they are, at the worst, men of little faith. But not so the Hindu. According to him the Hindu is idolatrous, the hateful Kafir; hence, in this life he deserved to be butchered; and in the next, eternal hell is in store for him. The utmost the Mussulman kings could do as a favour to the priestly class, — the spiritual guides of these Kafirs, — was to allow them to somehow pass their life silently and wait for the last moment. This was again considered too much kindness! If the religious ardour of any king was a little more uncommon, they would immediately follow arrangements for a great Yajna, by way of Kafir-slaughter![48]

Vivekananda regrets that after the waning of Mughal power, the Sikhs and the Marathas too did little to revive priestly power.[49]

---

48. *CW*, Vol. 4, p. 379. See also, p. 318.
49. Ibid., p. 380.

The brahmins, then, were the spiritual mentors of the Hindus. They were also the real custodians of learning and intellect. Having thus argued, Vivekananda goes a step further. He condemns all sectarian religions (in his list are included Islam, Christianity and all other forms of religion that believe in dualism) for believing in the essential equality of all human beings.[50] Not only is the proposition of equality of all humans untenable, it is also unscientific; differences in mind are greater than differences in bodies. People who preach doctrines that suggest God's descent on earth and the eventual equality of all humans are nothing more than sincere fanatics; he believed that fanatics among human beings are also the most sincere. Vivekananda squarely condemns any advocacy for the desirability of equality as just another millenarian idea; he does admit that equality could be a great motivation towards encouraging humans to put in greater effort and work in anticipation of a better tomorrow. Christianity grew, he argues, 'on the basis of the fascination of this fanaticism, and that is what made it so attractive to the Greek and the Roman slaves'.[51] Modern ideas of liberty, equality and fraternity also were modern versions of the same millenarian aspiration and reflected the same fanaticism. 'True equality has

---

50. *CW*, Vol. 6, p. 75.
51. *The Complete Works of Swami Vivekananda*, Vol. 1, Advaita Ashrama, Calcutta, Twenty-third impression, 2000, p. 113.

never been and never can be on earth,'[52] he emphasizes, and contrasts it with one of Hinduism's fundamental doctrines which believes that all men are different, only constituting a unity in variety. As we shall discover, the Aryan idea of caste embodied this notion of unity in variety.

If equality was a millenarian dream, was there an alternative in Vivekananda's view that was more desirable? Before considering the answer to this question, a word about Vivekananda's rejection of the modern idea of liberty is necessary. Since the words 'liberty' and 'freedom' appear in the Vivekananda corpus often, it is surprising that he rejects its modern variant. The precise reason for which he rejects the modern idea of liberty is its conjunction with equality and fraternity. Instead, the political liberty of the Greeks for him was worthy of emulation: in Vivekananda's reading of the political liberty of the Greeks,[53] which he erroneously identifies with social liberty, greater emphasis lay on protecting the nation, patriotism and primacy of the country. To return to the question of equality, Vivekananda believes that inequality is necessary for creation itself, that all the formative forces of nature manifest themselves through struggle, competition and conflict.[54] Equally, he believed that limiting inequality also entails a struggle.

52. Ibid., p. 113.
53. *CW*, Vol. 6, p. 52.
54. *CW*, Vol. 1, pp. 114-5.

If Hindus believed in humans being different and unequal, the question that needed an urgent answer was whether India had the appetite for conflict, struggle and competition to create as well as limit inequality.

Vivekananda's analysis of nineteenth-century Indian life is familiar and quoted often.[55] It speaks of the lack of mental activity, lifelessness among people, and absence of hope; it paints a picture where people lack will, enthusiasm, and are incapable even of expressing emotions. In the fashion of European writers on India in the eighteenth and the nineteenth centuries,[56] Vivekananda compares Indian society to

---

55. *CW*, Vol. 4, p. 422.

56. The early Indologists and orientalists contributed to a picture of India as despotic, stagnant and benighted. They all found Hinduism as it existed in the eighteenth and nineteenth centuries inadequate and degrading. Positing a Hindu Golden Age, they tried to find justification for a Hinduism that in their view was monotheistic, equalitarian and non-idolatrous. The attitude of the Indologists and orientalists finds its most comprehensive articulation in G.W.F. Hegel's writings on what he called the religion of the Indians: 'But what lions and oxen could not do, men themselves have done; the Indians and Egyptians, for example, had in animals their consciousness of the divine. Moreover they have had this consciousness in the sun, the stars, and ultimately in something still more trifling (this is where the Indians are especially conspicuous), in the most grotesque and deplorable products of an eccentric and ill-starred imagination.' See, G.W.F. Hegel, *Introduction to the Lectures on the History of Philosophy*, translated by T.M. Knox and A.V. Miller, Clarendon Press, Oxford, 1987, p. 36. Also see,

lumps of clay, lifeless machines and heaped-up pebbles.[57] He prefers people to make mistakes and commit errors as long as they are driven by their free will and intelligence rather than ending up as a mine of stupidity. The result, he avers, was for all to see: 'It never even occurs to this mind if there is any better state than this; where it does, it cannot convince; in the event of conviction, effort is lacking; and even where there is effort, lack of enthusiasm kills it out.'[58] This grim picture of Indian life essentially is Vivekananda's unflattering caricature of the state of Hindus in India in his time. This becomes even more evident when he rues the fact that despite the Upanishads being 'our scriptures',[59] weakness of every sort was the lot of the Hindus. One-third of this weakness was mental. Apart from a significantly greater proportion of physical weakness, Hindus were lazy, selfish, incapable of working in a group, devoid of love of each other and superstitious. But more than anything else, the physical weakness on their part also had an impact on the brain, rendering it incapable of work and action. He wants the young to realize that they will be 'nearer to Heaven through football than through

Bryan S. Turner, 'Asia in European Sociology', in *Handbook of Contemporary European Social Theory*, edited by Gerard Delanty, Routledge, London, 2006, pp. 395-404.

57. *CW*, Vol. 4, p. 423.
58. Ibid., p. 422.
59. *CW*, Vol. 3, p. 231.

the study of the Gita',[60] that they will understand the Gita better with biceps and muscles better developed. Inspired as he was from the model that ancient Greece presented to him, he wanted the young Hindus to relegate religion and concentrate on acquiring rajas. 'You will understand the Upanishads better and the glory of the Atman,' he says, 'when your body stands firm upon your feet, and you feel yourself as men.'[61]

Even the tremendous logical capacity of the Hindus had over a period of time degenerated into just an excess of logic without being accompanied by action, an effect that was felt in every sphere, from art to the sciences and even music.[62] Vivekananda calls India of his time the 'Kurukshetra (battle-field) of malady and misery, the huge cremation-ground, strewn with the dead bones of lost hope, activity, joy and courage...'.[63] This is what, he says, is visible to the European traveller visiting India. Though this dismal picture of India is presented from the perspective of the European traveller, it is as much Vivekananda's own view as it is of any outsider. For him, what compounds the malady and misery is the indifference of the yogin, 'sitting in august silence... absorbed in deep communion with the Spirit, with no

---

60. Ibid., p. 242.
61. Ibid., p. 242.
62. Ibid., p. 270.
63. *CW*, Vol. 5, pp. 344-5.

other goal in life than Moksha...'.[64] Even the English official who comes for the first time is greeted by three hundred million people 'swarming on the body of India, like so many worms on a rotten, stinking carcass...'.[65] India and China had become mummified civilizations as a result of poverty, where gathering together daily necessities itself was too great an effort to allow people to think about anything else.[66] Poverty leads to dehumanization, which, in turn, leads to slavery.

The reasons for poverty, dehumanization and slavery, Vivekananda elaborates, have been attributed to Hindu religion by social reformers, who feel that the only way out of this pathetic state of affairs is to crush religion. But religion was not to be blamed. Vivekananda calls Hinduism the 'grandest religion of the world'[67] and believes that the way out of misery and subjugation was to follow 'the great teachings of the Hindu faith'.[68] Nothing was wrong with the Hindu faith itself, but the error lay in lack of application and sympathy. Buddhism, which to Vivekananda was the logical development of Hinduism, had taught sympathy, and the Buddha's empathy for the poor, the miserable and the sinner was part of that faith. But this had been lost and Hinduism

---

64. Ibid., pp. 344-5.
65. Ibid., p. 345.
66. Ibid., p. 5.
67. Ibid., p. 11.
68. Ibid., p. 12.

had been reduced to a faith which, at once, preached the dignity of man on the one hand and also was a religion that, like no other faith, 'treads upon the necks of the poor and the low in such a fashion...'.[69] In arguing for empathy and for alleviating India's predicament, Vivekananda came up with some sentences that have cemented and perpetuated his mystique even to this day:

> I do not believe in a God or religion which cannot wipe the widow's tears or bring a piece of bread to the orphan's mouth. However sublime be the theories, however well-spun may be the philosophy – I do not call it religion so long as it is confined to books and dogmas.[70]

The problem lay precisely in Vivekananda's solution for Hindu India's woes in proposing an all-embracing idea of religion. It sometimes manifested in statements where he reduced and shrunk Hindu identity to an exclusively religious one: 'The Hindu man drinks religiously, sleeps religiously, walks religiously, marries religious, robs religiously.'[71] To wipe a widow's tears or to provide food for the orphan need not always be a religious act, nor does even Buddhism, understood properly, make a claim to performing or recommending

69. Ibid., pp. 12-3.
70. Ibid., p. 39.
71. *CW*, Vol. 8, p. 74.

such practical activities. Further, organized religions are often beholden to books and dogmas, and Vivekananda himself would often name the Vedas and the Upanishads as the Hindu scriptures. But the rhetorical flourish was a necessary methodological component to constructing his distinctive brand of Hinduism as will be evident in the next chapter.

If Buddha taught sympathy, he also 'ruined us, so did Christ ruin Greece and Rome!' [72] Vivekananda squarely blames the Buddha and Christ for their preoccupation with moksha or salvation, without suggesting a middle course.[73] They promoted tamas, in fact, the lowest form of tamas, by nurturing the idea of not protesting even if one were kicked. Under the influence of the Jains and the Buddhists, the Hindus too had become a tamasic lot, good only at praying and having these prayers unanswered. God does not hear them, says Vivekananda, because the cries of a fool go unattended by man and God alike.[74] Europe was saved from what Christ did by the Protestant reformation, while Hindus were shown the way out by Kumarilla, Shankara and Ramanuja by showing, not the path of devotion, but of karma or action. These men restated 'the Eternal Vedic religion, harmonising and balancing in due proportions Dharma,

---

72. *CW*, Vol. 5, p. 357.
73. Ibid., pp. 355-7.
74. Ibid., p. 356.

Artha, Kama, Moksha'.[75] All that the Hindus had to do in order to overcome tamas and emerge out of their inertia and servitude was to follow the path shown by the sages. The masses and the nation as a whole had lost their individuality, their progress vitiated in equal measure by Hindus, Muslims and Christians. Compounding this was jealousy among the Hindus. In fact, Hindus were not a nation like the British. Why was this so? It was because people in the villages had 'forgotten their manhood, their individuality'.[76] The inspiration for raising the masses and restoring to them their sense of individuality, however, must come from within. It must come, he emphatically states, from religion, and, especially from the orthodox Hindus.[77] Coming full circle, while Vivekananda argues for a synthesis of the East and the West, he is equally insistent that the energy, inspiration and motivation for any reform of old Hinduism can only come through Hinduism[78] and not currently fashionable reform movements. Similarly, old Hinduism is not to be confused with ancient Hinduism, but contemporary Hinduism that had gone decrepit and degenerate.

A major factor for the loss of masculinity, loss of individuality, lack of effort and absence of will was

75. Ibid., p. 357.
76. *CW*, Vol. 8, pp. 306-7.
77. *CW*, Vol. 6, pp. 225-6.
78. *CW*, Vol. 8, p. 308.

Chaitanya and his ideal of Radha-prema.[79] In emulating Radha's love to Krishna, the whole nation had been made effeminate. Bengal and Orissa had been reduced to a land of cowards. Four hundred years of Chaitanya and Radha-prema had resulted in a complete loss of the sense of manliness among Hindus. Just as Radha wept and cried when estranged from Krishna, so have the Hindus made crying and weeping into a national trait. This had also influenced Bengali literature of the past four hundred years, which was nothing but a chronicle of moaning and crying, and gave birth to no heroic poetry. Vivekananda uses terms like 'effeminate' and links moaning and crying to a feminine temperament. His writings, conversations and speeches are replete with instances where 'women and eunuchs' is not only used as a term to express anger, loathing and disgust[80] against people who are inactive, inert, and not rajasic, but also contrast the state of being 'women and eunuchs' to the more coveted ideal of manliness. Yet, Vivekananda fails to grasp the contradiction when he bemoans the inequality between men and women in his time and glorifies women like Maitreyi and Gargi in ancient India. Is there a way to understand this inherent paradox in Vivekananda?

Vivekananda held the view that the Vedanta rejects distinction between men and women and perceives

79. *CW*, Vol. 5, pp. 260-1.
80. Ibid., p. 68.

them to be participating in the same conscious Self. Women like Gargi and Maitreyi took the place of sages, read the Vedas and the Upanishads and were capable of discussing the mysteries and intricacies of the Brahman.[81] If they were accorded this privilege, so should the women of the present age. He does concede that historically the priests, in order to further their privileges, had prohibited lower castes and women from reading the Vedas, but that injunction was untenable. The equation for Vivekananda, then, is simple enough: women who read the Vedas and the Upanishads and discuss the complexities of the idea of Brahman were to be seen as equal to men. After all, the Vedas and the Upanishads were masculine, robust and activity-oriented texts, unlike bhakti-inspired texts which only encouraged limitless prayers, singing, dancing, weeping and moaning. Those men who were under the influence of the Bhakti texts and the ideas they promoted were like women. This model of femininity had to be despised and condemned.

In every district and village you may visit, you will find only the sound of the Khol and Kartāl! Are not drums made in the country? Are not trumpets and kettle-drums available in India? Make the boys hear the deep-toned sound of these

---

81. *CW*, Vol. 7, pp. 214-5.

instruments. Hearing from boyhood the sound of these effeminate forms of music and listening to the kirtana, the country is well-nigh converted into a country of women. What more degradation can you expect?[82]

In idealizing women, Vivekananda was ready to respect them as living images of Shakti, and even accept what he considered as the uncontaminated Tantra view of worshipping women in the spirit of divinity.[83] At the same time he could write to Sister Nivedita that India was not yet ready to produce great women and so it must 'borrow them from other nations'.[84] What were the features he saw in Sister Nivedita that made her a great woman? Her education, sincerity, purity, immense love, determination, and 'above all, the Celtic blood'[85] made her 'a real lioness',[86] suitable even more than men to work for India and Indian women. Never one to strike a balance between the ideal and the rhetorical, Vivekananda often lends himself to seeming contradictions. For instance, he condemns Hinduism for allowing girls to become mothers before attaining puberty and prescribing their marriage at a very young age. He castigates scriptures

82. Ibid., p. 232.
83. Ibid., pp. 215-6.
84. Ibid., p. 511.
85. Ibid., p. 511.
86. Ibid., p. 511.

such as the Grihya Sutras, the Vedic Asvamedha sacrifice and even the Brāhmanas for sanctioning undesirable practices affecting women.[87] Having thus argued, he goes on to say that child marriage also has a positive side: it breeds chastity and 'chastity is the life of a nation'.[88]

II

In order to create 'India's religion', isolating and privileging stray elements like caste, masculinity and the Vedas and the Upanishads was not sufficient. Vivekananda needed a skeleton that would act as the necessary scaffold to support all the details of his conception of 'our religion'. It was easy enough for him to reject popular forms of faiths and sects that existed during his time in favour of orthodox Hinduism. Doing so would, to an extent, explain the degeneration and slavery of India. A part of the blame could also be shared with other faiths like Jainism and Buddhism. The coming of the Muslims and Islam could substantially be held responsible for Hindu India's degeneration and Vivekananda does so regularly. Further, the English rule too could be held accountable. But Vivekananda

87. *CW*, Vol. 6, pp. 286-7.
88. *CW*, Vol. 2, pp. 100-1.

knew that neither the picture of India's degeneration, with the exception of poverty and localized instances of starvation, nor his indictment of popular forms of worship could ever pass the test of historical scrutiny. The skeleton he needed to fabricate, therefore, had to be ahistorical, emotive and durable. What Vivekananda created in the end was a Hindu self-image that endures in its self-righteousness, revels in its ahistoricity, and remains smug in its designer victimhood. It informs and irrigates versions of Hindu identity, especially as a smokescreen to politically dominant and assertive manifestations of that identity. To investigate it is to invite scorn, invective and, more often than not, retributive violence.

For Ramakrishna, virtues such as kindness, empathy and mercy were not national, religious or racial traits but come from a love of God. Contrary to Ramakrishna's rejection of love for the nation or the race or of one's own countrymen as mere maya,[89] the first major component of this Hindu self-image Vivekananda puts in place is the idea of the Hindu as gentle, generous, mild, calm, introspective and spiritually inclined. For that reason alone, India, the land of the Hindus, was Punya Bhumi. Unlike Savarkar later, Vivekananda does not translate Punya Bhumi as holy land, but as the land of karma or action. Every soul inclined towards God and spirituality

---

89. *Gospel*, p. 456.

ought to find in this land his 'last home'[90] and it was the land where one's actions would be judged and accounted for in the final analysis. The world owed much to the patient and mild Hindu and he was 'the blessed child of God'.[91] The mild, patient and calm Hindu never preached his spirituality through fire and sword; he preached and practised through toleration and sympathy. The maxim, 'That which exists is One; sages call It by various names', had seeped deep into the bloodstream of the Hindu nation and helped the Hindus welcome and nurture all other religions and sects into their fold. In constructing Hindu tolerance as the second bit of scaffolding on which Vivekananda's Hindu self-image rests, he remains unconcerned about obvious contradictions and easy caricatures. On other occasions he could effortlessly date the beginning of India's decline with the invention of the word 'mlechchha',[92] the ritual and geographical outsider; but in creating the picture of the tolerant Hindu, this was just another detail that could be glossed over. He often speaks of those faiths that consider their way to be the only way and their truth to be the only version of truth, contrasting it with the Hindu ideal of welcoming all faiths so long as the Hindu is allowed to follow his own way.[93] In fact, he proposes to travel the extra mile

---

90. *CW*, Vol. 3, p. 105.
91. Ibid., p. 105.
92. *CW*, Vol. 5, p. 40.
93. *CW*, Vol. 3, p. 132.

by elevating the idea of tolerance, which could seem condescending and patronizing, to one of fellow feeling, mutual esteem and mutual respect.[94] Rhetoric apart, it is extremely significant to note the way in which he builds the idea of the religiously tolerant Hindu by drawing a negative comparison with other faiths.

> It is here that Indians build temples for Mohammedans and Christians; nowhere else. If you go to other countries and ask Mohammedans, or people of other religions to build a temple for you, see how they will help. They will instead try to break down your temple and you too, if they can. The one great lesson therefore that the world wants most, that the world has yet to learn from India, is the idea, not only of toleration, but of sympathy.[95]

Indians in this instance are Hindus, as contrasted with Muslims and Christians. The meek, tolerant and generous Hindus construct mosques for Muslims and churches for Christians 'in spite of their [Muslim and Christian] hatred, in spite of their brutality, in spite of their tyranny, and in spite of the vile language they are given to uttering...'.[96] In other words, the gentle and the loving Hindu will, in course of time, conquer all hostile

---

94. *CW*, Vol. 2, p. 68.
95. *CW*, Vol. 3, p. 114.
96. Ibid., pp. 187-8.

faiths through love. The world must, therefore, learn from the Hindus. A real lover of Shiva, for example, must forget the distinctions of name and form and see him as the 'one Lord of all, the one Soul of all souls'.[97] Such a keen devotee of Shiva acknowledges all 'knees bending towards the Kaaba, or kneeling in a Christian Church, or in a Buddhist Temple'[98] as prayers being offered to Shiva-seen-as-the-One. The Muslim or the Christian or the Buddhist may not even be aware of it or conscious of this fact. Is the reverse true? While Vivekananda is silent on this point, as we shall see in the next chapter, he believed that Hinduism had evolved into being the mother and teacher of all religions and other faiths were mere sects with inadequate notions of God.

A third element that forms a major component of the self-image is the theme of 'eternal India'. In warming up to this idea, Vivekananda momentarily discards the entire constellation of arguments that only a moment ago had condemned the inert, inactive and lifeless Hindus to lumps of clay and pebbles. Rather, the outward signs of passivity are misleading, he argues, for all activity among the Hindus takes place in the realm of religious activity.[99] This is the reason why India was imperishable and eternal. If Manu were to return, he would find the same laws, with thoughtful adjustments, and the

97. Ibid., p. 115.
98. Ibid., p. 115.
99. Ibid., pp. 137-8.

same customs having survived thousands of years. No amount of misfortune has altered this eternal and constant character of Hindu India.[100] Eternal India for Vivekananda was religious India. It was also Hindu India. Also, since fostering self-images requires neither empirical evidence nor historical accuracy, he elaborates on the theme by asserting that there was always absolute religious freedom in India. There was no body of priests, he continues, that prevented people from telling the truth and allowed for the free expression of religious opinion. Such religious freedom was not a thing of the past, but something that flourished till the present times.

> [I]n religion, we find atheists, materialists, and Buddhists, creeds, opinions, and speculations of every phase and variety, some of a most startling character, living side by side. Preachers of all sects go about teaching and getting adherents, and at the very gates of the temples of gods, the Brāhmanas – to their credit it be said – allow even the materialists to stand and give forth their opinions.[101]

If this seems bewildering and unreal, if not also exaggerated, it helped lay the foundation for a contrast

---

100. Ibid., p. 107.
101. *CW*, Vol. 2, p. 114. See also, *CW*, Vol. 1, pp. 348-9.

between religious freedom in India as against the social freedom in the West. Vivekananda pits Hindu India's religious freedom against the freedom in social matters in Europe.[102] In social matters, India was cramped, strict, shackled and bound. Europe, in contrast, had imposed its religious beliefs through sword and fire, and, as a result, remained religiously and spiritually backward. In short, the dream of building future India as a judicious mix of European society and India's religion was well under way: India could borrow the European model of society and the West could do with a dose of religious freedom.

Eternal India's strength was also meekness. Vivekananda drives the point home with the zeal of a preacher, eager to convert a weak argument into a strong one. Struggle, conflict and competition, which were once recommended, were now to be dropped and made subservient to the idea of meekness. 'Dash, pluck, fight,' says Vivekananda, 'all these things are weakness.'[103] Neither football nor muscles are abandoned in favour of meekness but kept apart and suspended in order to provide the necessary filigree for the conception of eternal India. The word 'meekness', otherwise used pejoratively by Vivekananda, is employed in order to serve a set of other arguments: the idea that India never conquers by force, war or arms, and, flowing from this, it

---

102. *CW*, Vol. 2., pp. 114-5.
103. *CW*, Vol. 5, p. 120.

usually conquers its conquerors through its spirituality. Predictably, the narrative offers a picture of perfect peace and amity, a spiritual idyll even for the heterodox Jains, who did not believe in a god, till the Muslims 'brought murder and slaughter in their train, but until their arrival peace prevailed.'[104] Having painted the Muslims as the villains who disrupted this peaceful equilibrium, Vivekananda turns to converting the fact of conquests and slavery to his advantage.

It was India's Karma, her fate, to be conquered, and in her turn, to conquer her conqueror. She has already done so with her Mohammedan visitors: Educated Mohammedans are Sufis, scarcely to be distinguished from Hindus. Hindu thought has permeated their civilisation; they assumed the position of learners. The great Akbar, the Moghul Emperor, was practically a Hindu. And England will be conquered in her turn. Today she has the sword, but it is worse than useless in the world of ideas.[105]

Hindu spirituality converts its conquerors as long as they become pupils and sit at the feet of the teacher. The idea that was Hindu India's gift to the world, one that

---

104. Ibid., p. 120.
105. Ibid., p. 120.

it continues to distribute generously, was the ideal of a non-aggressive, non-threatening spirituality. The Hindu race, asserts Vivekananda, is not a race of dreamers and philosophers. Neither should its repeated conquests and enslavement be seen as a sign of passivity: rather, Hindu India continues to conquer the world in the spiritual realm.[106]

Having created the unlikely, but formidable, self-image of the Hindu as gentle, calm, generous, mild, introspective, meek and spiritually driven, Vivekananda adds another element to his long list of Hindu virtues. He speaks about the way in which Islam, Christianity and Buddhism spread by converting people, but asserts that Hindus do not convert. Yet, given the richness of the virtues offered, as Hinduism comes into contact with other faiths and races, they begin to adopt 'the manners and customs of the Hindus and falling in line with them'.[107] They begin to see the path shown by Hinduism and its rejection of such trivialities as the idea of an anthropomorphic god, ideas of heaven and earth, scriptures and doctrines; other faiths and sects see the light and start 'coming within Hinduism'.[108] In saying this, Vivekananda glides through ignoring caste hierarchy as one of the defining reasons for Hindus not converting, the deeply entrenched ideas of caste and ritual purity and the longevity of the

---

106. *CW*, Vol. 1, p. 383; See also, *CW*, Vol. 4, pp. 152-3.
107. *CW*, Vol. 2, p. 360.
108. Ibid., p. 360.

term *mlechchha* to denote the outsider. For the sake of the argument, India was Hindu India and it had produced two great ideas: renunciation and spirituality. Of the two, Vivekananda marks spirituality as the national ideal.[109] As an ideal to be held afloat for the purposes of marking the difference between Europe and India, spirituality as the cumulative outcome of the mild, introspective and tolerant Hindu's unbroken legacy served its intended purpose. But for the purposes of furthering a distinctive brand of religious nationalism as also imparting the idea of 'our religion' greater content than could be offered by a fragile abstraction like spirituality, Vivekananda further had to arbitrarily push and alter conceptual boundaries.

If the European traveller and chronicler often found the staggering plurality of Indian religions, sects, rituals and customs understandably bewildering, Vivekananda saw in this complexity a source of conflict, chaos and absence of clarity. It also was an impediment in the way of fostering his political agenda of religious nationalism as the basis for national unity. In dealing with the intractable question of diversity, Vivekananda begins by acknowledging the diversity of races, languages, manners and customs that had the potential for creating 'more differences between two Indian races than between the European and the Eastern races'.[110] Amidst this diversity

---

109. Ibid., p. 370.
110. *CW*, Vol. 3, p. 286.

and complexity, he identifies religion as the common ground around which national unity could be built. But a fragmented religion could hardly be the basis for national unity. The first step towards the future of India, says Vivekananda, was to ensure unity of religion, a conscious and deliberate 'recognition of one religion throughout the length and breadth of this land'.[111] He believed that, despite differences, enough common ground could be found between various sects and their own individual goals and narrowly defined ambitions; in its natural course, Hinduism entertained enough religious liberty and allowed for sufficient variations.

> Therefore, the first plank in making of a future India, the first step that is to be hewn out of that rock of ages, is this unification of religion. All of us have to be taught that we are Hindus – Dualists, qualified Monists, or Monists, Shaivas, Vaishnavas, or Pashupatas, — to whatever denomination we may belong, have certain common ideas behind us, and that the time has come when for the well-being of our race, we must give up all our little quarrels and differences.[112]

Note that the idea of a unified Hinduism does not exist

---

111. Ibid., p. 287.
112. Ibid., pp. 287-8.

at this point but has to be created in order to serve the putative idea of 'our religion'. Vivekananda, however, believed that there was something called the 'Indian mind'[113] and this unified, monolithic entity recognized nothing higher than religion. All difficulties of race, language, society, he concludes, 'melt away before this unifying power of religion'.[114] The way to unify religion, then, was to find a common ground acceptable to all sects and denominations. That Hinduism as a religion can be unified and that a common ground between sects and religious practices exists are borne by historical examples, according to Vivekananda. The examples offered follow a familiar trajectory of Hindu victimhood against the aggression of foreign conquerors, with Hindu resilience and religious fervour emerging triumphant after facing death, pillage, and desecration of temples.[115] When Vivekananda speaks of national unity and unity of religion, it means nothing more than the unity of the Hindu nation and the unity of Hinduism. From the vantage point of real and presumed victimhood, religion was the repository of this history of ruin and regeneration, especially in the face of barbarian onslaught, with 'barbarians bringing barbarous religions...'.[116] This instance of threat and religion's

---

113. Ibid., p. 287.
114. Ibid., p. 287.
115. Ibid., p. 289.
116. Ibid., pp. 370-1.

tenaciousness to withstand various outrageous assaults constituted for Vivekananda the national mind and the national life-current. Nations are like individuals: every individual has specific characteristics and a destiny to fulfil. Similarly, the destiny of the Hindu nation and the Hindu race lies in the realm of religion. Religion was where the nation's centre lay, it was where the nationality of the nation was to be located, it was the core, and was where the vitality of the race rested.[117] The implications of this view of nationality defined purely in religious terms are far-reaching: no arena of human life would be left free from the stranglehold of religion. Neither was Vivekananda's definition of religion open-ended. He not only conflated the subtle, but significant, distinction between spirituality and religion, but also sought to demand allegiance to his idea of religious nationalism in categorical terms: 'If a Hindu is not spiritual I do not call him a Hindu...National union in India must be a gathering up of its scattered spiritual forces. A nation in India must be a union of those whose hearts beat to the same spiritual tune.'[118] For him, there was no room to choose between alternative modes of nationality or even reject his ideal of unified Hinduism. Religion, he declared, was the Hindu's second nature. Even more dramatically, he would announce that 'the

---

117. Ibid., pp. 369-1.
118. Ibid., p. 371.

name of religion and Hindu have become one'.[119] To reject religion was to reject the nation itself.

෴

Before filling in the details of Vivekananda's conception of unified Hinduism, let us return briefly to his idea of tolerance. In another of those rhetorical flourishes, Vivekananda calls the idea of tolerance blasphemous. He is appalled by the idea that someone could exist on the basis of someone else's sufferance and declares that he accepts all religions, worships every conception of God, and was ready to pray in all varieties of places of worship.[120] Toleration was the product of conceit and condescension; the need was to become many-sided, protean in character, and see ourselves as fellow-travellers of other faiths in the common quest after God.[121] Vivekananda raises the bar further: tolerance is conceit but fighting even in self-defence is wrong.[122] Though fighting in self-defence might be marginally superior to fighting out of aggression, such retaliatory violence ultimately takes place because of the inability to see the 'sameness in all things'.[123] Non-resistance, he argues, is a great

---

119. Ibid., pp. 370-1.
120. *CW*, Vol. 2, p. 372.
121. *CW*, Vol. 6, pp. 103-4.
122. *CW*, Vol. 7, p. 49.
123. Ibid., p. 49.

strength; in meekness, mildness and suffering lie great strength. This is the ideal, he adds, the Hindu race has always upheld.[124] Vivekananda's mystique firmly rests on the selective dissemination of such sentences culled from his works. Again, the thin line that divides the ideal from the practical, the actual from the rhetorical is, indeed, very thin. Let us examine the evidence:

> The Hindu scriptures say, 'No doubt, Moksha is far superior to Dharma; but Dharma should be finished first of all.' The Bauddhas were confounded just there and brought about all sorts of mischief. Non-injury is right. 'Resist not evil' is a great thing – these are indeed grand principles; but the Shāstras say, 'Thou art a householder; if anyone smites thee on thy cheek, and thou dost not return him an eye for an eye, a tooth for a tooth, thou wilt verily be a sinner.' Manu says, 'When one has come to kill you, there is no sin in killing him, even though he is a Brāhmana.'(Manu, VIII.350). This is very true, and this is a thing which should not be forgotten.[125]

Notice that there is little offered here in terms of an ethical debate on the question of non-injury versus retaliatory

---

124. *The Complete Works of Swami Vivekananda*, Vol. 9, Advaita Ashrama, Kolkata, Fourth impression, 2004, p. 255.
125. *CW*, Vol. 5, p. 351.

violence except quoting from scriptures, shastras and from Manu. He acknowledges that non-resistance and non-injury were part of the Buddha's teaching, but this method hides a 'dreadful weakness'.[126] The way of the Upanishads was better since the emphasis there is on strength: 'I do not think of punishing or escaping from a drop of sea-spray. It is nothing to me. Yet to the mosquito it would be serious. Now I would make all injury like that.'[127] Earlier, Vivekananda had argued that retaliation would be undesirable because the act failed to see the sameness in all things. The same idea now is employed to argue in favour of strength and fearlessness: 'My own ideal is that saint whom they killed in the Mutiny and who broke his silence, when stabbed to the heart, to say, "And thou also art He!"'[128] But non-injury and non-resistance are just that, a set of ideal. Those who hunger after righteousness and perfection are free to follow these ideals, but turning the other cheek is otherwise impossible and impracticable.[129]

Vivekananda's rejection of non-injury and non-resistance rests on the premise that resisting evil would be cowardice. Yet there is little attempt to discuss what constitutes evil. Is it possible to arbitrarily designate an individual or a group as evil on the basis of an ideology,

---

126. *CW*, Vol. 8, p. 267.
127. Ibid., p. 267.
128. Ibid., p. 267.
129. *CW*, Vol. 6, p. 75.

a superstition or a misunderstanding? Vivekananda does not entertain this doubt and its ramifications. The idea of evil, by and large, remains a physical and material conception, manifest in the idea that 'the wicked would take possession of our properties and our lives, and do whatever they liked with us'.[130] Resistance too is reduced mostly to mere physical resistance. Vivekananda goes a step ahead and reduces all human actions to the act of ultimately resisting evil.[131] Not surprisingly, the inspiration for this conception of resisting evil comes from the Battle of Kurukshetra and the dialogue between Krishna and Arjuna. For Vivekananda, Krishna does not represent cunning but 'exemplified the idea that once you are in a thing, do not retreat'.[132] Retreating would be cowardice and in the normal order of things, a 'man's duty is to resist evil; let him work, let him fight, let him strike straight from the shoulder'.[133] The consideration that the idea of a just war in the Mahabharata could have been a pretext for justifying fratricidal violence as also a device for legitimating violence in order to maintain caste hierarchy has to wait for the revisionist accounts of Gandhi and Ambedkar; it certainly forms no part of Vivekananda's mental universe.

---

130. *CW*, Vol. 1, p. 37.
131. Ibid., p. 40.
132. Ibid., p. 40.
133. Ibid., p. 39.

Even forgiveness, if weak and passive, is not true: fight is better. Forgive when you could bring legions of angels to victory. Krishna, the charioteer of Arjuna, hears him say, 'Let us forgive our enemies', and answers, 'You speak the words of a wise man, but you are not a wise man, but a coward.'[134]

Non-resistance and non-injury are not always about meekness and cowardice, but about the need to forget, the need to erase memories of the past in order not to end up settling scores. Vivekananda firmly rejects the idea that too great an emphasis on the memory of the past is undesirable. On the contrary, he feels that Hindu India's woes were compounded because of forgetting the past. Not only does he believe that the future has to be moulded from the past, but hopes that 'this past will become the future'.[135] In consonance with the nineteenth-century obsession with linear history, Vivekananda feels that a nation is nothing but its historical memory. It is the memory of a noble descent, and as long as this memory is kept intact, a nation does not sink low.[136] Hindu India had lost its historical memory and the degradation and degeneration were for all to witness.

---

134. *CW*, Vol. 8, p. 227.
135. *CW*, Vol. 4, p. 270.
136. *CW*, Vol. 5, p. 281.

III

If India's past had to become its future, especially if this past had anything to do with the 'centre' or 'core' of Hindu India's life, namely religion, the question of caste had to be confronted. Another pillar on which Vivekananda's mystique rests is his views on caste, especially his strong and vocal criticism of brahmins and of untouchability. But even the criticism is not always categorical. For instance, he speaks of the brahmins being good and moral, holding no property, but beset with one weakness.[137] This was their fondness for power. They perceive themselves as 'twice-born', the sons of God, and view themselves as above all law and punishment. If his views on the brahmins, at first sight, are ambiguous, even more perplexing are his pronouncements on the lower castes; he often calls them lower classes, thus, combining the ideas of caste and class. A conversation with a disciple in 1898 is signally representative of this strand in Vivekananda.[138]

He tells the disciple that the lower classes of India, the peasants, the shoemaker and the sweeper have a greater capacity for work, industry and a sense of self-reliance than the upper castes and classes. Uncomplaining, they have produced, over the centuries, the entire wealth

---

137. *CW*, Vol. 7, p. 72.
138. Ibid., pp. 148-50.

of the nation. They are the backbone of the nation. The upper castes and classes have oppressed them and taken for granted their forbearance. But the situation was fast changing. These oppressed individuals had now begun to unite, ask for their legitimate dues, and were going to seek retribution. He warns that the upper classes will cease to get their food and clothing if the lower orders were to stop working. They had already started to go on strikes more frequently and a day would come when the upper classes will not be in a position to repress them. 'Gradually capital is drifting into their hands,' he warns, 'and they are not so much troubled with wants as you are.'[139]

Further, fashions and attitudes among the upper castes had changed and they lacked the inventive genius to create new wealth. Searching for employment was increasingly becoming the ultimate aim of the upper castes. The disciple doubts Vivekananda's analysis. He is sceptical of the lower classes acquiring power and culture to supplant the upper castes and classes, especially because the lower classes were 'guided by our intelligence'.[140] Vivekananda brands this view as one coming from someone who had read a few books and acquired a tailor-made civilization. Instead of flaunting their culture at the lower castes and classes, he

139. Ibid., p. 148.
140. Ibid., p. 148.

wants the upper castes and classes to spread education among the lower orders and convince them that they are 'part and parcel of our bodies, and we love you and never hate you'.[141] Once the lower castes and classes receive this sympathy, 'their enthusiasm for work will be increased a hundredfold'.[142] The disciple interjects to wonder if after receiving education, the lower classes will become idle and inactive, exploiting, in turn, the classes below them, even though their minds may become fertile. Vivekananda's answer is, at once, naive as well as illustrative of his deeply entrenched faith in the idea of caste.

Why shall it be so? Even with the awakening of knowledge, the potter will remain a potter, the fisherman a fisherman, the peasant a peasant. Why should they leave their hereditary calling? 'सहजं कर्म कौन्तेय सदोषमपि न त्यजेत् — Don't give up the work to which you are born, even if it be attended with defects.' If they are taught in this way, why should they give up their respective callings? Rather they will apply their knowledge to the better performance of the work to which they have been born. A number of geniuses are sure to arise from among them in course of time.

141. Ibid., p. 149.
142. Ibid., p. 149.

You (the higher classes) will take these into your fold. The Brahmins acknowledged the valiant King Vishvāmitra as a Brahmin, and think how grateful the whole Kshatriya race became to the Brahmins for this act! By such sympathy and co-operation even birds and beasts become one's own – not to speak of men![143]

The lower castes must get an education in order to do what they have done as hereditary vocations better. All that needed to be given to them after education had supplemented and enhanced their traditional skills were sympathy, assurance, and, most importantly, the possibility of the few geniuses among them being accorded brahminical status. Vivekananda believed so and he could always quote the Gita, as he does above, in order to lend weight to his contention.

Brahmins, as long as they remained within the limits of orthodoxy, were to be looked upon as the spiritual mentors of the Hindus. Any trace of deviation from the path of the Vedas was immoral and unreasonable.[144] This is what the brahmins did: because of their greed for power and in order to keep their privileged positions intact, they introduced non-Vedic doctrines into Hinduism. Vivekananda detests Vamachara of the Tantra for this

143. Ibid., pp. 149-50.
144. Ibid., pp. 173-4.

reason alone: it was against the spirit of the Vedas. His frequently quoted diatribe against brahmins is directed against those among them who deviated from the path of Vedic orthodoxy. Apart from the brahmins, Vivekananda also offers insights into what he thinks of other castes.[145] The rule of the kshatriyas is tyrannical and cruel, but also marked by a flourishing of arts and social culture. While the vaishyas are less exclusive than the kshatriyas, their ascendency heralds a 'silent crushing and blood-sucking power'.[146] During the period of their prominence, culture begins to decay. The shudra rule introduces a marked equality in distribution of physical comforts and ordinary education, but it also signals the lowering of culture and fewer geniuses. Vivekananda's utopian state would keep intact the benefits of all essential caste characteristics while erasing their perceived disadvantages. But he admits that such an ideal state may be a dream, and, in the meantime the rule of the shudras had come to stay and their power would be irresistible.

Vivekananda finds efforts to designate caste as a religious institution deeply flawed. For him, all reformers from the Buddha to Ram Mohan Roy had committed this error and, as a consequence, tried to 'pull down religion and caste altogether, and failed'.[147] Having thus stated, he goes on to offer his views on caste that are often

145. *CW*, Vol. 6, p. 343.
146. Ibid., p. 343.
147. *CW*, Vol. 5, p. 19.

mistakenly held as examples of Vivekananda's antipathy towards caste combined with his equally misunderstood liberality in wanting to do away with it: 'But in spite of all the ravings of the priests, caste is simply a crystallised social institution, which after doing its service is now filling the atmosphere of India with its stench, and it can only be removed by giving back to the people their lost social individuality.'[148]

The operative words and phrases here are 'crystallised', 'after doing its service', and 'lost social individuality', rather than 'stench' and 'removed'. A close reading of Vivekananda helps explain the meaning of these words and phrases, but also encourages a search for clues regarding the emerging contours of the unified version of 'our religion'. To begin with, Vivekananda's explanation of the idea of caste and its tried and tested virtues:

In Sanskrit, Jāti i.e., species, — now this is the first idea of creation. 'I am One, I become many' (various Vedas). Unity is before creation, diversity is creation. Now if this diversity stops, creation will be destroyed. So long as any species is vigorous and active it must throw-out varieties. When it ceases or is stopped from breeding varieties, it dies. Now the original idea of Jati was this freedom of the individual to express his nature, his Prakriti,

---

148. Ibid., p. 19.

his Jati, his caste, and so it remained for thousands of years. Not even in the latest books is inter-dining prohibited; nor in any of the older books is inter-marriage forbidden. Then what was the cause of India's downfall? – the giving up of this idea of caste.[149]

Expressing one's caste was freedom; its loss is what is alluded to as the lost social individuality that caste had for centuries engendered. As an institution that helped an individual to express his Jati, in its current state that institution and that idea had got crystallized, failed to produce variations and had died. Its death was also for Vivekananda an explanation for India's downfall.

The present caste is not the real Jati, but a hindrance to its progress. It really has prevented the free action of Jati, i.e., caste or variation. Any crystallised custom or privilege or hereditary class in any shape really prevents caste (Jati) from having its full sway, and whenever any nation ceases to produce this immense variety, it must die. Therefore what I have to tell you, my countrymen, is this: — That India fell because you prevented and abolished caste. Every frozen aristocracy or privileged class is a blow to caste and is not-caste.

---

149. *CW*, Vol. 4, p. 317.

Let Jati have its sway; break down every barrier in
the way of caste and we shall rise.[150]

In practical terms, caste designated individuals to perform
certain actions according to their natures, their prakriti.
As long as they continued to perform those without
locating their actions or varna-prescribed vocation in
custom, privilege or heredity, caste functioned smoothly.
So, the cobbler, the peasant and the sweeper, despite
an education will continue to do their jobs and do them
even better as long as they got the sympathy of the upper
castes. This, in sum, is Vivekananda's argument till now.

India was a mad confluence of races. Vivekananda
wants to find a way of bringing about a fusion between
races and tribes, especially so because he finds them to
be unequal in culture. Similarly, a profusion of languages
ought to have a common link. In Sanskrit, 'a great sacred
language of which all others would be considered as
manifestations',[151] he located and found the most viable
linguistic solution. The common rubric under which he
attempts to club all the races and tribes was found in
the term 'Arya'. Even the distinction between Aryan
and Dravidian was casually brushed aside as merely
a philological one and not of race and blood.[152] Once
language and race were unified, the asymmetry between

---

150. Ibid., p. 317.
151. Ibid., p. 255.
152. Ibid., pp. 244-5.

178

cultures had to be rectified: 'Just as Sanskrit has been the linguistic solution, so the Arya the racial solution. So the Brāhmanhood is the solution of the varying degrees of progress and culture as well as that of all social and political problems.'[153]

Once the supremacy and the primacy of the Aryan race were established, he could now readily pronounce brahminhood as 'the great ideal of India'.[154] It was true that the degradation of brahminhood and kshatriyahood was prophesied in the Puranas;[155] in the Kaliyuga, they claimed, there would only be non-brahmins. Vivekananda regrets that this was becoming increasingly true, though a few brahmins remained, and did so only in India. Any vision of bringing about order to the diversity of races and languages, then, can only be brought about by a superior culture. The Aryans, Vivekananda asserts, provided such a culture and this culture expressed itself through the caste system: 'It put, theoretically at least, the whole of India under the guidance – not of wealth, nor of the sword – but of intellect, — intellect chastened and controlled by spirituality. The leading caste in India is the highest Aryans – the Brāhmans.'[156]

References can be traced in Vivekananda's works where he speaks about brahmins and kshatriyas as

153. Ibid., p. 255.
154. Ibid., p. 255.
155. Ibid., p. 256.
156. Ibid., p. 243.

ideals rather than fixed or designated castes: 'Whatever caste has the power of the sword, becomes Kshatriya; whatever learning, Brahman; whatever wealth, Vaishya.'[157] He also describes caste as a status achieved or acquired, where individuals having attained the status of learning, wealth or sword worked towards preserving the privileges of that caste. Was it then possible for a shudra to acquire learning and become a brahmin? Vivekananda's answer is emphatically in the negative: 'If you want to rise to a higher caste in India, you have to elevate all your caste first, and then there is nothing in your onward path to hold you back.'[158] The lower castes had to aspire, en masse, to rise to the level of a higher caste. It did not really matter whether caste was seen as an ideal or perceived as a social institution in operation. For Vivekananda, the rules to aspire for a higher status were already put in place by the Aryan and brahmin superior culture inaugurated in ancient India.

India's ancestors had the brahmins as their racial ideal. Vivekananda describes this ideal in terms of representing renunciation and spirituality.[159] If a country were to be governed by men of such selflessness and spiritual excellence, no police, laws or even government would be needed in any way. Following this Platonist ideal, he quotes the

157. Ibid., p. 244.
158. Ibid., p. 244.
159. *CW*, Vol. 3, pp. 196-8.

Mahabharata to suggest that in the Satyayuga, there were only brahmins. Their eventual degeneration led to proliferation of other castes. It was a cycle and there would come a day when everyone would return to these brahminical origins.[160] The law of the ancestors has to be obeyed: all races and castes must aspire to become brahmins and attain the brahminical ideal. It was a law not only for Hindus and Indians but for the entire world: to attain the brahminical ideal of non-resistance, calmness, steadiness, worshipfulness, purity and introspection. Cursing and vilifying the brahmins are futile and fruitless, since bringing down what is already up is against the dictates of the Vedantic religion. Neither the brahmin nor caste as an institution ought to be condemned or be subjected to reform.

> I have seen castes in almost every country in the world, but nowhere is their plan and purpose so glorious as here. If caste is thus unavoidable, I would rather have a caste of purity and culture and self-sacrifice, than a caste of dollars. Therefore utter no words of condemnation. Close your lips and let your hearts open.[161]

---

160. Ibid., p,293.
161. Ibid., p. 199.

The brahminical ideal of purity, culture and self-sacrifice was, at once, the caste ideal, the race ideal and the national ideal. Whenever Vivekananda condemns caste, he has in mind the economic and social idea of class privilege and exclusivity. Questions of power and its arbitrary use by the upper castes are relegated to the whimsical and naive belief that all human beings will unquestioningly accept the brahmin ideal as the highest that Hinduism's ancestors in India and Vedantic religion could offer. His fondness for caste, however, is total and not entirely innocent. Neither can it be supported by arguing that in glorifying the brahmins and the caste, Vivekananda was only speaking of an ideal of spirituality and renunciation.

> Caste is a natural order. I can perform one duty in social life, and you another; you can govern a country, and I can mend a pair of shoes, but that is no reason why you are greater than I, for can you mend my shoes? Can I govern the country? I am clever in mending shoes, you are clever in reading Vedas, but that is no reason why you should trample on my head; why if one commits murder should he be praised, and if another steals an apple why should he be hanged! This will have to go. Caste is good. That is the only natural way of solving life. Men must form themselves into groups, and you cannot get rid of that. Wherever

you go there will be caste. But that does not mean
that there should be these privileges. They should
be knocked on the head.[162]

Knocking privilege on the head sounded good and
eminently desirable, but could not go hand in hand
with differentiation and inequality that was deemed
natural and desirable. The example of reading Vedas
and mending shoes is equally disingenuous. Having
privileged the Vedas, Vedanta and the brahmins, a
comparison between reading the Vedas and mending
shoes does not hold. Moreover, when it came to practical
solutions for rectifying what Vivekananda perceived as
privilege within the caste institutions, there was never a
call for the brahmin to learn to mend shoes. Rather, the
demand always is for the lower-castes to learn Sanskrit.

Thinkers and spiritual masters such as Ramanuja,
Chaitanya and Kabir tried to raise the lower castes but
failed. Vivekananda attributes this failure to their not
spreading Sanskrit among the masses. This was not
merely their error: it was a flaw they shared with the
Buddha, 'when he stopped the Sanskrit language from
being studied by the masses'.[163] Vivekananda wants the
lower castes to desist from being critical of the higher
castes; they must accept that all of India is nothing but

162. Ibid., p. 245.
163. Ibid., pp. 290-1.

Aryan, the brahmins are the ideal and Sanskrit is the sacred language.

> The only safety, I tell you men who belong to the lower castes, the only way to raise your condition is to study Sanskrit, and this fighting and writing and frothing against the higher castes is in vain, it does no good, and it creates fight and quarrel, and this race, unfortunately already divided, is going to be divided more and more.[164]

In other words, if the Hindus remain divided, the onus of such a division would lie with the lower castes and their refusal to accept the superior culture of the upper castes. 'The ideal at one end is the Brahman and the ideal at the other end is the Chandala,' states Vivekananda, 'and the whole work is to raise the Chandala up to the Brahman.'[165] The idea is not to bring down the higher, he elaborates, but to raise the lower to the level of the higher. The brahmins must work towards this goal in order to justify that name and epithet. It is the brahmins' refusal to share this superior culture with the lower castes that made the Muslim invasions possible.[166] Yet, because of caste, a semblance of Hindu intellectuality and learning remained for Europeans to study, something that in

---

164. Ibid., p. 291.
165. Ibid., p. 295.
166. Ibid., p. 298.

the absence of caste would have been smashed by the Muslim invaders.[167] But the blame was not entirely that of the brahmins. Vivekananda, once again, chastises the lower castes for not looking up to the brahmins and spurning the superior culture embodied by the brahmins: 'Do not seize every opportunity of fighting the Brahman...Who told you to neglect spirituality and Sanskrit learning?...Why do you fret and fume because somebody else had more brains, more energy, more pluck and go, than you?'[168] The warning is clear and direct. Not even a trace of the Buddha's followers remains in India, he concludes, because the Buddha refused to recognize caste.[169] Caste was good; it was the plan Vivekananda wanted to follow for India's future. All it needed was an occasional readjustment.[170]

Vivekananda's plan of readjustment of caste was not mere expression of pious intention or a romantic dream. He wanted caste reinstated and strengthened. Regretting that the original fourfold division of castes, the chaturvarnya, was not to be found in India any longer, Vivekananda proposes that the entire Hindu population be redivided and grouped under the original

---

167. *CW*, Vol. 5, p. 144.

168. *CW*, Vol. 3, p. 298.

169. *CW*, Vol. 7, p. 39. 'One sect wanted to destroy and they were thrown out of India: they were the Buddhists.' Volume 5, p. 147.

170. *CW*, Vol. 7, p. 145.

division of the castes.[171] All subdivisions of individual castes, say of the brahmins, had to be abolished and united under a single caste rubric. This was the Vedic ideal and also the concrete reality during the Vedic times and had to be restored. If Jati dharma, which was the very basis of Vedic religion and Vedic society, could be 'rightly and truly preserved,' the nation shall never fall.[172] At another time, Vivekananda wants the three upper castes alone to be 'produced' in future India; the 'Sudra caste will exist no longer – their work being done by machinery.'[173]

In 1898, Vivekananda was celebrating Ramakrishna's birthday. He wanted every brahmin to be given the sacred thread, even lapsed brahmins. He instructed non-brahmins to be given the Gayatri Mantra.[174] In the conversation recorded on that day by Sharat Chandra Chakravarty, a disciple, Vivekananda wanted all Hindus to be united, shun untouchability based on ritual purity and wanted all the people of the land lifted to the position of brahmins. Note that non-brahmins have not been given the sacred thread, but only the Gayatri Mantra. In the same set of conversations, he rejects Shankara's 'specious argument'[175] of the non-brahmins

---

171. Ibid., p. 322.
172. Ibid., p. 359.
173. Ibid., p. 240.
174. Ibid., pp. 107-8.
175. Ibid., pp. 117-8

not being entitled to attain the supreme knowledge of the Brahman. Irritated by Shankara's illiberality and his brahminical pride, Vivekananda poses the question: 'The Vedas have entitled anyone belonging to the three upper castes to a study of the Vedas and the realisation of Brahman, haven't they? So Shankara had no need whatsoever of displaying this curious bit of pedantry on this subject, contrary to the Vedas.'[176] Denying non-brahmins the sacred thread, yet granting them the realization of the Brahman was not seen by Vivekananda as a contradiction that needed resolution.

Did Ramakrishna share Vivekananda's views on caste? Ramakrishna endorsed the Brahmo Samaj's sentiment regarding abolishing caste but felt that the only way to remove caste was by love of God: 'Lovers of God have no caste.'[177] Through love of God, he argues, the untouchable becomes pure and the outcaste no longer remains one. For him, the great example of how the love of God transcended caste was Chaitanya, who embraced one and all in his sect. Love of God is enough to achieve liberation. The Puranas clearly state that this path of loving devotion does not entail worship, sacrifice, tantric

---

176. Ibid., pp. 117-8.
177. *Gospel*, pp. 157-8. See also, p. 591.

rituals or reciting mantras. Conversely, the way shown by the Vedas for human liberation required a more rigid adherence to caste: 'But the teachings of the Vedas are different. According to the Vedas none but a brāhmin can be liberated. Further, the worship is not accepted by the gods unless the mantras are recited correctly. One must perform sacrifice, worship, and so on, according to scriptural injunction.'[178]

Unlike Vivekananda, caste was not part of Ramakrishna's spiritual world. Neither were the Vedas helpful in achieving liberation; they were a positive impediment in the path towards realizing God. For him, ecstatic love of God and genuine bhakti mattered more than any significance that scriptures or tradition might attach to caste. Yet, despite his categorical denial of caste in matters of faith, Ramakrishna had a mild, ordinary and generalized sense of caste in personal matters. He would, for instance, sometimes not eat food from the hands of a *dome*[179] and would in later life insist that his food be cooked by a brahmin observing ritual purity. As a tantric practitioner, he had already gone beyond the binaries of purity and impurity mandated by caste. But the tantric period was designated by him as 'that mood'[180] and he no longer felt bound by it. But he would consistently reject outright the suggestion that liberation

178. Ibid., p. 584.
179. Ibid., p. 597.
180. Ibid., p. 549.

was possible only for those born in a brahmin body.[181] Neither was any caste held as an ideal for the Hindus or for the future Indian nation.

❧

Vivekananda's project was essentially one where nationalism, religion and politics are made to cohabit. These lines of demarcation in his case are often blurred and often defy neat conceptual categorization. Indeed, the thousands of books and pamphlets that depend on partial quotes from Vivekananda's writings, letters and speeches have painted a picture of him that does not remotely tally with a closer reading of his works. A few examples would suffice. While Vivekananda swears by the Vedas and the Upanishads, upholds the original varna classification, he also speaks of the 'eternal subjection of the individual to society and forced self-sacrifice by dint of institutions and discipline'.[182] He condemns the smothering of individual lives by the shastras, and yet wants to uphold the brahminical ideal of spirituality and renunciation as circumscribed by the shastras. Being someone who regularly condemned customs and rituals, he could vehemently argue that the shraddha ceremony 'appeases the departed beings'.[183] But a careful reading

---

181. Ibid., p. 591.
182. *CW*, Vol. 4, pp. 421-2.
183. *CW*, Vol. 7, p. 132.

of his thought suggests coherence and integrity in his vision of future India, brilliantly captured by the phrase 'European society with India's religion'. Now that the scaffolding on which 'our religion' is to be created is in place, the next chapter will attempt to understand the complexity and deft manoeuvres that went into making of a modern religion, Hinduism.

The Fly and the Syrup

I

In December 1884, Ramakrishna meets Bankim Chandra Chatterji.[1] As soon as they have been introduced, Ramakrishna puns on Bankim's name which means 'bent' or 'twisted'. 'What has made you bent?' asks Ramakrishna, to which Bankim replies that the boots of the white masters had bent his body. Ramakrishna ignores the politically pregnant remark and begins to speak of the ecstatic love of Krishna for Radha that made his body

---

1. *The Gospel of Sri Ramakrishna: Originally recorded in Bengali by M., a disciple of the Master*, Translated into English with an Introduction by Swami Nikhilananda, Ramakrishna-Vivekananda Center, New York, 2007 imprint, pp. 666-76. This is a translation of Mahendranath Gupta's *Sri Sri Ramakrishna Kathāmrita*, originally published between 1897 and 1932 in five volumes in Bengali. Henceforth, all references to the English translation will be cited as *Gospel*.

bend in three places. Soon the conversation veers towards matters of faith. At one point, Ramakrishna asks Bankim about the duties of an individual. Eating, sleeping and sex, replies Bankim. Ramakrishna calls him saucy and unforgivingly chastises him for possessing knowledge without discrimination and renunciation. The crow thinks he is a clever bird, says Ramakrishna, but the moment he wakes up, his mind turns to filling his stomach with other people's filth. The swan, in sharp contrast, leaves the water aside and drinks the milk. The crow struts about, but the swan walks straight in one direction. The difference between the crow and the swan is one between worldliness and love of God alone. Humans who are enmeshed in matters of the world are crow-like and those who think only of the love of God are like the swan.

Soon the conversation moves in the direction of Ramakrishna's familiar denunciation of 'woman and gold'. Bankim agrees with Ramakrishna that money is nothing but a lump of clay, but suggests that money sometimes can help the poor and do good to others. Ramakrishna is appalled by the suggestion. For him charity and the idea of doing good to others are sheer arrogance. It is a form of hubris born out of lack of faith in the idea that kindness belongs to God alone. Every form of charity and philanthropy, whether done by a sanyasi or a householder, is ultimately just doing good to oneself and not to others. Ramakrishna is familiar with the idea of serving and helping all beings without a trace of attachment, but even this form of karmayoga ultimately helps only the individual. Conceding that selfless and dispassionate service could be a way of attaining God, Ramakrishna rejects its suitability for Kaliyuga. Ramakrishna wants faith in God and God's will reinstated clearly; for him the ambiguity regarding the source of charity and mercy had to be removed. Put differently, for humans to claim merit for doing good to others was nothing but pride and misplaced selfishness.

> Helping others, doing good to others – this is the work of God alone, who for men has created the sun and moon, father and mother, fruits, flowers, and corn. The love that you see in parents is God's love: He has given it to them to preserve His creation. The compassion that you see in the kind-hearted is God's compassion: He has given it to them to protect the helpless. Whether you are charitable or not, He will have His work done somehow or other. Nothing can stop His work.
>
> What then is man's duty? What else can it be? It is just to take refuge in God and pray to Him with a yearning heart for His vision.[2]

Ramakrishna's insistence on God as the source of all kindness and compassion is not just the pronouncements

---

2. *Gospel*, p. 671.

of a bhakta or the predictable outpourings of a sanyasi. Not only does his argument flow from the idea of the impermanence of the world and the ultimate reality only of God, it significantly introduces in modern Indian thought a theory of modesty. The contrast to his theory of modesty lay in the modern idea of first studying the world and its creatures through science and then attempting to understand God. Bankim subscribes to this view and Ramakrishna acknowledges that many of his devotees too are beholden to this view. Ramakrishna, instead, relentlessly asks the question, 'Which comes first, "science" or God?'[3]

In proposing the primacy of God before scientifically knowing the universe, Ramakrishna adds a subtle layer to his theory of modesty. As seen above, he begins by positing that God comes first and then the world. Merely acknowledging God was not enough but attaining God through ecstatic love was the next step. To this he adds a third element. After attaining God, one can know everything else 'if it is necessary'.[4] The worldly man thinks about the world all the time and reproduces the world, or in Ramakrishna's words, a man belches what he eats. To be worldly is to be calculating and deceitful. The argument this far is: God has to be privileged before the impermanent world. After attaining God, one can

---

3.   Ibid., p. 672.
4.   Ibid., p. 672.

know the world if there be a compelling necessity to know it. The quest for knowing the world excessively arises from altering the order of what is to be known as a result of deceit and calculation, a direct consequence of human pride and arrogance. If there is still a residual longing to know the world after knowing God, one can do so only if such knowing becomes necessary. In other words, knowing the world before knowing God is a sign of immaturity; to want to know the world after attaining God may be a necessity. Two ideas consistently run through Ramakrishna's thought: first, a human individual cannot really help the world and second, that even an act done selflessly is an action that only does good to the doer.[5] To illustrate Ramakrishna's disdain for performing acts of charity and social service, his conversation with Sambu Mallick is often cited. Sambu Mallick wanted to establish hospitals, schools, dispensaries and make roads and dig reservoirs. Ramakrishna had advised him to limit the number of activities or he would otherwise be in danger of losing sight of God, like those who came to Kalighat and spent their entire time giving alms without bothering to have a glimpse of Kali in the temple.

Sambu Mallick's example is strewn all across the pages of the *Kathāmrita*, and is also cited by Ramakrishna in his conversation with Bankim to demystify the excessive

---

5.   Ibid., pp. 108, 452, 142-43, 378-9.

importance attached to doing good deeds. As a parable used to illustrate human arrogance and selfishness as also to correct the imbalance of priorities between attaining God and scientifically knowing the world, it works well. But Sambu Mallick's penchant for charity does not fully reflect the sharp distinction between the primacy of ecstatic love of God and the secondary importance attached to acts of charity and merit. To love God was to get deranged by the love of God and lose one's head. It was not a question of rationally choosing and calculating one's next action with respect to either one's own self or with respect to others.

> Once I said to Narendra: 'Suppose there were a cup of syrup and you were a fly. Where would you sit to drink the syrup?' Narendra said, 'I would sit on the edge of the cup and stretch out my neck to drink it.' 'Why?' I asked. 'What's the harm of plunging into the middle of the cup and drinking the syrup?' Narendra answered, 'Then I should stick in the syrup and die.' 'My child,' I said to him, 'that isn't the nature of the Nectar of Satchidānanda. It is the Nectar of Immortality. Man does not die from diving into It. On the contrary he becomes immortal.'[6]

---

6. Ibid., p. 675.

Not only does the above quote reflect the deep schism between two contentious views about faith in its relation to the world, but it also portrays something more significant. Ramakrishna kept the realm of faith distant from the pulls and pressures of ordinary life, whereas Vivekananda sought to perceive the whole gamut of human activities through religious bifocals. Ramakrishna sought to protect faith from being contaminated by worldly things, while Vivekananda circumscribed every aspect of human life with his brand of religiosity. The Master plunged into the syrup, while his favourite disciple sat on the edge straining his neck to drink it. Vivekananda wanted religion to be a practical science and could quote Bishop Berkeley on the question of the existence of God.

❧

One way of understanding Ramakrishna's rejection of work in general and his indifference to acts of charity and philanthropy is to acknowledge the considerable influence of Bengal Vaishnavism in his life and his thought. The *Caitanya Caritamrita of Krishnadasa Kaviraja* is full of instances where Chaitanya rejects jnana (knowledge), yoga (union of the individual with the Infinite), karma (action) and mukti (liberation) categorically in favour of prema-bhakti, the highest form of loving devotion to Krishna, and reciting Krishna's name (nama-samkirtana).

These form part of the *Caritamrita*'s list of the highest truths: Krishna, Krishna-bhakti, prema and nama-samkirtana. No scripture, it argues, was greater than this designated set of activities and there are specific injunctions that discourage pursuit of knowledge, action and liberation. Several verses in it point to the futility of jnana and karma in attaining the state of prema-bhakti.

- The abandonment of karma and the vilification of karma – this the śāstras attest; there is never any prema-bhakti of Kṛṣṇa from karma.[7]
- Those who follow karma and jñāna are both devoid of Bhakti...[8]

Work, then, is a prelude to faith and an unavoidable step before an individual becomes ready for renunciation. The *Bhagavata Purana* (11.20.9) makes this abundantly clear in saying: 'You shall work until a condition of renunciation arises, or until faith, in listening, etc., to my story, is born in the heart.'[9] Karma is not merely an impediment in attaining the highest form of devotion but is also a positive hindrance in the worship of Krishna.

---

7. *Caitanya Caritamrita of Krishnadasa Kaviraja*, a translation and commentary by Edward C. Dimock, Jr., Harvard University Press, Cambridge, Massachusetts, 1999, p. 476, (henceforth cited as CC).
8. Ibid., pp. 477-8.
9. Ibid., p. 477.

To consider karma as the dharma was 'the darkness of ignorance of the solitary jīva'.[10] The status of jnana and yoga was no different: they were powerless without Krishna-bhakti.[11] The *Caritamrita* goes a step further. Quoting the *Bhagavata Purana*, it argues that even selfless and unattached action is meaningless if it is empty of emotion for God.[12] Neither can jnana alone help reach the goal of liberation without bhakti, but mukti without jnana is possible if there is sincere and loving devotion.

For Ramakrishna, the legacy of Chaitanya's distinctive brand of Vaishnavism was not merely a way of establishing the primacy of following the path of ecstatic love of God. It went beyond the demands of reciting Krishna's name and expressing love of Krishna. As the *Caritamrita* clearly delineates, the way of bhakti was also a ruse to become indifferent to the world and its socio-political realities. The first step in this process was to reject the classification of life based on the fourfold division of human beings into castes, namely, the varnashramadharma: 'Abandoning all this [association of unholy people and those who are restless in desire, especially desire of women] and the varnāśrama-dharma, one should become indifferent to the world and take refuge only in Kṛṣṇa.'[13]

---

10. Ibid., p. 163.
11. Ibid., p. 685.
12. Ibid., p. 686.
13. Ibid., p. 694.

Indifference to the world also implies rejecting the nature and consequences of actions and their intended effect on the established social hierarchy and political power structure: 'He who abandons the dharma of injunctions and worships the feet of Kṛṣṇa, there is never in his mind wrong or forbidden actions.'[14] Therefore, actions performed as part of the caste duty in order to keep intact the social and political order are circumspectly, but firmly, rejected by elevating the worship and love of Krishna. Indeed, the imperative of worshipping and loving Krishna robs all other activities of their sacredness and legitimacy. In a spectacular revision of the central thesis of the Bhagavadgita, which sanctifies and legitimizes the varnashramadharma, the *Caritamrita* quotes a familiar verse from the eighteenth chapter of the Bhagavadgita to argue in favour of its indifference to the world. The verse where Krishna asks Arjuna to 'Abandon all the Laws and instead seek shelter with me alone'[15] and Krishna's simultaneous assurance that he will set Arjuna

---

14. Ibid., p. 701.
15. Ibid., p. 695. The translation of 18:66 from the Bhagavadgita is as per the *Caritamrita* and so the stress and inflections in the translation are of the *Caritamrita* and not of this author. For a similar treatment of the ways in which Chaitanya's legacy perceived the Bhagavadgita, see Joseph T. O'Connell, 'Caitanya's Followers and the *Bhagavad-gītā*:A Case Study in Bhakti and the Secular', in *Hinduism: New Essays in the History of Religions*, edited by Bardwell L. Smith, E.J. Brill, Leiden, 1976, pp. 33-52.

free from all evils is cited to strengthen the argument in favour of abandoning varna-inspired activity. Elsewhere in the *Caritamrita*, a conversation between Ramananda Raya, who calls himself a lowly Shudra,[16] and Chaitanya is cited. Here Chaitanya categorically rejects as superficial[17] the import of a verse from the *Vishnu Purana* that suggests following the varnashramadharma as the only way of attaining Vishnu. Following this rejection, Chaitanya also rejects the necessity of following one's ordinary caste duties and personal obligations,[18] svadharma, as superficial and not deep enough.

Far removed from this world of intense love of Krishna, Vivekananda discovers the ideal for creating his version of 'our religion' as the absolute monarch in the pages of the Upanishads. Tenets of religion, he argues, are not born from retiring into the forest nor from indifference to the world, but are crafted in the hands of those who were most involved in the world, namely, the kshatriya kings.[19]

---

16. *CC*, pp. 432-3.
17. Ibid., pp. 434-5.
18. Ibid., p. 435.
19. *The Complete Works of Swami Vivekananda*, Vol. 2, Advaita Ashrama, Mayavati, Almora, Fourth edition, 1932, pp. 289-90, 311 (*The Complete Works of Swami Vivekananda* will henceforth be referred to as *CW*).

His world is not Ramakrishna's mansion of mirth but an ideal from the past whose importance needs to be restated and its bygone glory restored. The story of Śvetaketu, his father and teacher Gautama and Pravāhaṇa Jaivali, the king, narrated in the *Chandogya Upanishad*, underscores the centrality of the kshatriya ideal for Vivekananda, a story which this essay will have an opportunity to revisit. In similar fashion, the Bhagavadgita's affirmation of the varna-oriented ideal of rectitude also constitutes an indispensable element in the composition of 'our religion'. Calling the Bhagavadgita the best commentary on Vedanta philosophy, Vivekananda extols the text's message of 'intense activity in the midst of calmness...the calmness that cannot be ruffled, the balance of mind which is never disturbed, whatever happens'.[20] Arguing that it is 'the calm, forgiving, equable, well-balanced mind that does the greatest amount of work',[21] Vivekananda's vision of 'India's religion' steadily undervalues and demotes emotions, feelings, imagination and passions. Like several of his contemporaries in the nineteenth century, Vivekananda's preoccupation with brahminical Hinduism and its carefully crafted world of order, discipline and control, with masculinity and kshatriyahood being simultaneously and unequivocally celebrated alongside, often led to condemning feelings, emotions, imagination

20. Ibid., p. 290-91.
21. Ibid., p. 291.

and passions as feminine, unscientific or deviant. Among the likes of Vivekananda, operating from within the anachronistic framework of the Bhagavadgita's definition of dharma or right conduct, there is a singular absence of discovering valuable links between feelings, emotions, anger and passions to questions of justice, injustice, pain and freedom.

Take for instance the story of Jabālā and Satyakāma Jābāla from the *Chandogya Upanishad* that Vivekananda narrates on 12 November 1896 as part of the second lecture on Practical Vedanta. First, the brief outline of the story:[22] Satyakāma goes to his mother Jabālā and wants to know his lineage in order to become a vedic student. His mother tells him that when she was young, she worked as a maid and had many relationships, and, hence it was impossible for her to tell him his lineage. She says to him: 'But my name is Jabālā, and your name is Satyakāma. So you should simply say that you are Satyakāma Jābāla.'[23] Hearing this, Satyakāma goes to Hāridrumata Gautama and asks to be accepted as a vedic student. Hāridrumata asks Satyakāma his lineage. Satyakāma narrates his earlier conversation with his mother and accordingly identifies himself as Satyakāma Jābāla. On hearing this, Hāridrumata says to him: 'Who but a Brahmin could speak like that!

---

22. This summary is based on Patrick Olivelle's translation. See *Upaniṣads, A new translation by Patrick Olivelle*, Oxford University Press, New York, 2008 impression, pp. 130-31.
23. Ibid., p. 130.

Fetch some firewood, son. I will perform your initiation. You have not strayed from the truth.'[24] Vivekananda uses the story to illustrate a principle hidden in it but otherwise finds it 'very crude'.[25] The principle that he teases out from it was that the Vedanta always reconciled the actual to the ideal. But other than this, he remains impervious to the layers of meaning inherent in it. The remarkable sexual freedom that Jabālā so nonchalantly speaks about and exhibits, the clear evidence of the Vedas being the exclusive privilege of the brahmins and those of correct lineage, the association of being a brahmin and fearlessly speaking the truth, and the rendering of truth as the almost exclusive preserve of the brahmins are entirely glossed over by Vivekananda. But more than anything else, while Hāridrumata neither comments on Jabālā's numerous relationships nor is he censorious about them, it is safe to assume that Vivekananda's selective misogyny led him to the conclusion that the story was very crude.

The first step, then, towards recreating Vivekananda's version of a masculine, rational and scientific brahminical Hinduism as the core of the nation was to posit control, power, dominance and stability as the constitutive elements.[26] These elements were essential for any

---

24. Ibid., p. 130.
25. *CW*, Vol. 2, p. 307.
26. See Sarah Caldwell's brilliantly suggestive essay titled 'Margins at the Center: Tracing Kālī through Time, Space, and Culture', in *Encountering Kālī: In the Margins, at the Center, in*

conception of 'our religion' to synchronize with the proposed establishment of a European society in India. But to bring about the unlikely synthesis in India between a projected European society and an Indian religion, the non-Sanskritic, bhakti, tantric, tribal, folk, low-caste, vernacular and all other non-elite and politically marginal perspectives had to be sidelined and discredited. In redefining the centre/core and the marginal, Vivekananda was forsaking an idea of the 'centre' that existed in India which signified movement, ambiguity, doubt and transformation.[27] His arguments in favour of the centrality of the Upanishads and the unquestioned perfection of Vedanta were ways of surmounting European colonial censure against everything that did not conform to a non-threatening, but largely moribund, indigenous brahminical elite tradition. He hoped that his reading of the Upanishads and the Vedanta would effectively re-establish religious orthodoxy in India, inaugurating a version of faith and belief that would be in consonance with the rational and scientific ideals represented by ancient Greece and

the West, edited by Rachel Fell McDermott and Jeffrey J. Kripal, University of California Press, Berkeley, 2003.

27. David Shulman's formulation cited in Don Handelman, 'The Guises of the Goddess and the Transformation of the Male: Gangamma's Visit to Tirupati, and the Continuum of Gender', in *Syllables of Sky: Studies in South Indian Civilization In Honour of Velcheru Narayana Rao*, edited by David Shulman, Oxford University Press, Delhi, 1995, p. 286

contemporary Europe. Had not Schopenhauer, after all, taken recourse to reason alone and rationalized the Vedas?[28] For him, as we shall see, movement, ambiguity, transformation and doubt were signs of weakness, superstition and irrationality.

Vivekananda rejects every philosophical system and every strand of thought as unorthodox if they did not 'obey the Upanishads'.[29] The soil of India, he argues, had rejected Jainism and Buddhism for this very reason: they did not bear allegiance to the Upanishads. Despite his regular fulminations against books and scriptures, he singles out the Upanishads as 'our scriptures',[30] much in the way the Bible is for the Christians, the Qur'an is to the Muslims, the Tripitaka are for the Buddhists and the Zend Avesta for the Parsis. The laws of Manu, the Grihya and Shrauta Sutras, and all the Puranas had to agree with the authority and primacy of the Vedas and the Upanishads. When they did not conform, they had to be 'rejected without mercy'.[31] Contemptuous of popular Hinduism and any strand of heterodoxy, Vivekananda establishes the supreme authority of the Vedas and the Upanishads as the only criterion by

---

28. *The Complete Works of Swami Vivekananda*, Vol. 7, Advaita Ashrama, Kolkata, Fourteenth impression, 2002, p. 50-1.

29. *The Complete Works of Swami Vivekananda*, Vol. 3, Advaita Ashrama, Mayavati, Almora, Fourth edition, 1932, p. 323.

30. Ibid., p. 323.

31. Ibid., pp. 332-3.

which a Hindu ought to deserve the name. To deny the Vedas and the Upanishads would render such an individual in the category of a nāstika or non-believer.[32] Any form of religion that promoted 'conflictual models of divinity, immanent, embodied powers and a deep concern with death and sexuality'[33] had to be rejected or made subordinate to the authority of the Vedas and the Upanishads.

> A petty village custom seems now the real authority and not the teachings of the Upanishads. A petty idea current in a wayside village in Bengal seems to have the authority of the Vedas, and even something better. And that word 'orthodox,' how wonderful its influence! To the villager, the following of every bit of the karma-kanda is the height of 'orthodoxy,' and one who does not do it is told, — 'Go away, you are no more a Hindu.'[34]

Petty village customs that did not bend before 'our scriptures' had to be mercilessly rejected and their influence purged. But Vivekananda's crusade for subservience to the Vedas and the Upanishads extends beyond the wayside villages of Bengal. He belittles the Christian, Muslim and Buddhist scriptures as mere

---

32. Ibid., p. 333.
33. Sarah Caldwell, op.cit., p. 258.
34. *CW*, Vol. 3, pp. 332-3

Puranas and not worthy of being called scriptures. A true scripture does not record historical detail, either of events or of individuals, and the Bible and the Qur'an fell short on this count. In contrast, the Vedas were never written and they never came into existence in a historical sense. He concedes that other scriptures may have moral teachings within their pages, but their acceptance or rejection must pass the test of being compatible with the Vedas. If they do not agree with the Vedas, they had to be rejected. Would they be accepted as scriptures if they more or less agreed with the Vedas and the Upanishads? While Vivekananda brushes aside such overwhelming compatibility as unlikely, he concedes that a greater level of agreement with the Hindu scriptures could make them eligible to 'have the authority of the Puranas, but no more'.[35] Having unremittingly argued with Ramakrishna about the historical veracity of the existence of Radha and Krishna in Vraj, Vivekananda now questions the soundness of a religion inspired by the lives of founders of that faith. Jainism, Buddhism, Christianity and Islam are all called into question, and disputes regarding the historicity of their founders are shown as examples of their inherent weakness.[36] Hinduism, in contrast, is characterized as a universal religion and its tolerance explained in terms of its lack of reliance on historical

---

35. Ibid., pp. 333-4.
36. Ibid., p. 249.

figures of sages, prophets and heroes. For any individual to be called a Hindu, affirming the supreme authority of the Vedas was enough. He goes on to claim that all Hindu sects, despite their differences, affirm the authority of the Vedas as their scriptures,[37] an assertion historically inaccurate and philosophically misleading.

The petty village custom that dares to supplant the supreme authority of the Vedas and the Upanishads does so because it is ensnared by the charms of Dualism. Vivekananda admits that Dualists constituted the largest number of people in India but the reason for these large numbers was self-evident: 'Dualism naturally appeals to less educated minds.'[38] If Vivekananda's Vedic-Vedantic Hinduism had an identifiable enemy, it was Dualism.[39] There was not one Dualistic religion, he argues, that is not exclusive. It was in their nature to fight and quarrel and they have been doing so since time immemorial. Their popularity is due to their insidious appeal to the vanity of the uneducated. The masses, who have been persecuted for ever, feel that the Dualist morality based on punishment is the only way to salvation. He considers teaching Dualism in India and everywhere else in the world as a tremendous mistake; he concedes that in many of its forms, he had no objection to Dualism, but a substantial part of Dualist teaching inculcated weakness

37. Ibid., p. 228.
38. *CW*, Vol. 2, p. 141.
39. Ibid., p. 142.

of the mind. This weakness and its effects are dangerous because it 'makes one superstitious, makes one mope, makes one desire all sorts of wild impossibilities, mysteries, and superstitions'.[40] Put differently, anything that was not abstract, detached, rational and masculine was a result of weakness brought about by Dualism.

> The vast mass of Indian people are Dualists. Human nature ordinarily cannot conceive of anything higher. We find that ninety per cent of the population of the earth who believe in any religion are Dualists. All the religions of Europe and Western Asia are dualistic; they have to be. The ordinary man cannot think of anything which is not concrete...This is the religion of the masses all over the world. They believe in a God who is entirely separate from them, a great king, a high, mighty monarch, as it were. At the same time they make Him purer than the monarchs of the earth; they give Him all good qualities and remove the evil qualities from Him.[41]

Dualists are also guilty of thinking that their way was the only way. Vivekananda brands the Vaishnavas, who are Dualists, as the most intolerant among Hindu sects.[42]

---

40. Ibid., p. 201.
41. Ibid., p. 241.
42. *CW*, Vol. 7, pp. 27-8.

Among the Shaivas, he gives the example of a sect that refuses even to hear the name of Vishnu. He is appalled by Madhva's Dualist philosophy and his insistence that salvation can come only through worship of Vishnu.[43] Again, the reason for these instances of intolerance is explained by the allegiance of these sects to the Puranas rather than to the Vedas and the Upanishads. An almost categorical rejection of Dualism also amounts to Vivekananda's denial of everything that Ramakrishna's faith signified: the place of the divine in this world, the idea of ecstatic, sensual love of God, the primacy of emotions, especially prema-bhakti, and the centrality of the feminine in matters of faith. All these characteristic features of Ramakrishna's faith were derived in one way or the other from Dualism and not Vivekananda's ideal of Advaita Vedanta's transcendental abstraction.

Vivekananda's ire against Dualism was just that: it ignored ultimate principles.[44] He acknowledges that among the ultimate principles, their 'tremendous philosophical and logical propositions were alarming'[45] to the uneducated masses. But the consequence was a neglect of Advaita Vedanta, 'the fairest flower of philosophy and religion that any country in any age has produced, where human thought attains its highest expression, and even goes beyond the mystery which

---

43. Ibid., p. 37.
44. *CW*, Vol. 2, p. 199.
45. Ibid., p. 199.

seems to be impenetrable'.[46] Unlike the Dualists, Advaita denies individuality because everybody and everything always changes. Neither body nor mind, not even thoughts remain the same. The only thing there is is the Atman, and there is perfect identity between Atman and Brahman. In fact, the Atman, argues Vivekananda, is the Brahman itself. Therefore, there is only one individual, and that is the Infinite or the Brahman: 'In plain words, we are rational beings, and we want to reason. And what is reason? More or less of classification, until you cannot go on any further. And the finite can only find its ultimate rest when it is classified into the Infinite.'[47]

Creating a universal model of an undifferentiated Hindu identity, Vivekananda speaks of the 'Hindu mind' rejecting the idea of a personal and external God; rather the Hindu worships the God within.[48] The perfect identity between the Atman and the Brahman makes this withdrawal into oneself possible. Hindu religious thought achieves this perfect harmony through accomplishing three steps. The first in this is the idea of a personal or extra-cosmic God. Then the idea moves to the internal cosmic body or the God immanent in the universe. Finally, the identification of the soul with that of God, firmly bound as one soul and a seamless union

---

46. Ibid., p. 247.
47. *CW*, Vol. 3, p. 347.
48. *CW*, Vol. 2, pp. 29-30.

into one of all the manifestations in the universe.[49] The three steps are Dualism, qualified Monism and, finally, perfect Monism. The 'Hindu mind', claims Vivekananda, does not care for the particular but always hankers after the general and the universal.[50]

Religion, then, was not of this world. It was essentially 'heart-cleansing' and it is folly to privilege its effects on the world. The world was full of people like Ramakrishna who insisted on nishtha or single-minded devotion, a pure recipe in Vivekananda's eyes for fanaticism, superstition and intolerance. In Hinduism and in Islam, such people often came from the 'lower planes of Bhakti'.[51] Following Kant's idea of religion and his distinction between religion as cult versus religion as moral action,[52] Vivekananda sought to model 'our

49. Ibid., pp. 252-3.
50. Ibid., p. 263.
51. *CW*, Vol. 3, p. 32.
52. In his *Religion Within the Limits of Reason Alone*, the German philosopher, Immanuel Kant, makes a distinction between religion as cult (asking God for material benefits and other tangible good to those who sought favours through prayer) and religion as moral action (implores people to change their moral and ethical stance in order to live a better and more meaningful life, seen mostly in spiritual clarity and inner salvation and enlightenment). He further elaborates the idea of religion as moral action by elaborating the idea of 'reflecting faith', where inner faith, rather than religious dogma and its knowledge, led to salvation. See Immanuel Kant, *Religion Within the Limits of Reason Alone*, Translated with an Introduction and Notes by

religion' on these very lines. Lower forms of Bhakti had to be supplanted with something that was higher and less in partaking of the details of this world.

> That love of God grows and assumes a form which is called Para-Bhakti, or supreme devotion. Forms vanish, rituals fly away, books are superseded, images, temples, churches, religions and sects, countries and nationalities, all these little limitations and bondages fall off by their own nature from him who knows this love of God. Nothing remains to bind him or fetter his freedom.[53]

Among the many reasons for people not being able to attain to the exalted state of Para-Bhakti was the hold myths had on people. Vivekananda's stark vision of the faith that he was beginning to outline had no place for myths except for his own use as explanatory tools. In the austere world that he chose as his ideal and as the ideal for future India, myths were to be ridiculed and caricatured.

> In our mythology it is said there are demons, who sometimes trouble the gods. In all mythologies, you read how these demons and the gods fought,

---

Theodore M. Greene and Hoyt H. Hudson, Harper Torchbooks, New York, 1960 edition.

53. *CW*, Vol. 3, p. 72.

and the demons sometimes conquered the gods, although many times, it seems, the demons did not do so many wicked things as the gods. In all mythologies, for instance, you find the Devas fond of women. So after their reward is finished, they fall down again, come through the clouds, through the rains, and thus get into some grain or plant and find their way into the human body, when the grain or plant is eaten by men. The father gives them the material out of which to get a fitting body. When the material suits them no longer, they have to manufacture other bodies. Now there are the very wicked fellows, who do all sorts of diabolical things; they are born again as animals, and if they are very bad, they are born as very low animals, or become plants, or stones.[54]

As we have already seen, Vivekananda conveniently uses the deva-asura typology elsewhere to portray the difference between the East and the West. Not only does his condemnation of myths betray a sneaking Victorian attitude reflected in his censure of the devas' fondness for women and fear of the power of feminine sexuality, but it also borrows heavily from the Lutheran-Protestant worldview of Kant in establishing the pre-eminence of

---

54. *The Complete Works of Swami Vivekananda*, Vol. 1, Advaita Ashrama, Calcutta, Twenty-third impression, 2000, p. 399.

a 'reflecting faith'. Given this aridity of imagination, Vivekananda expressed a personal disinterest in mythical stories; they remained for him a symbol of the tools used by Christian missionaries to ridicule Hinduism. He never saw in the stories the opportunity to creatively interpret them in order to create an alternative to the rational and linear narratives of the West or to use them in order to weaken the stranglehold of an entrenched Sanskritic-brahminical view: Krishna was a married man. There are thousands of books about him. They do not interest me much. The Hindus are great in telling stories, you see. '[If] Christian missionaries tell one story from their Bible, the Hindus will produce twenty stories.'[55] The Upanishads, Vivekananda contends, have little to do with the stories of any individual. Unlike other scriptures, the Vedas and the Upanishads deal almost entirely with philosophy. 'Religion without philosophy runs into superstition,' he concludes, 'philosophy without religion becomes dry atheism.'[56]

As a non-dualist and an idealist, Vivekananda argues that societies ought to be moulded upon truth rather than truth being made to adjust to the details and vagaries of societal diversity and plurality.[57] He wants the highest truth in society to be practical, but the determination of truth and its relevance to any society

---

55. Ibid., p. 456.
56. *CW*, Vol. 7, p. 36.
57. *CW*, Vol. 2, pp. 84-5.

were not matters of debate or even doubt. He became increasingly convinced that Advaita was that system which preached principles rather than focusing on a person, though allowing both human and divine persons to have their full play.[58] Advaita's superiority lay in not disturbing even those faiths that were attached to what Vivekananda considers 'lower forms of worship'.[59] It was Advaita's business to raise everyone to a higher plane. All other world religions and all Dualist sects in India can never aspire to reach Advaita's lofty perfection for one reason alone: 'They are all parts equally struggling to attain to the whole.'[60] In such circumstances, they could not seek the epithet of being a universal religion. Not merely is Advaita not fragmentary but it also has the added advantage of including within itself all stages and degrees of religious development.

At this juncture, the trajectory of Vivekananda's thought needs careful mapping: he begins by establishing the unquestioned primacy of the Vedas and the Upanishads, followed by a denunciation of Dualism as errant, deviant and disruptive for not pledging uncompromising allegiance to the Vedas and the Upanishads. The natural corollary to this is to establish simultaneously the supremacy of Vedanta. After accomplishing this, the

---

58. *The Complete Works of Swami Vivekananda*, Vol. 4, Advaita Ashrama, Mayavati, Almora, Fourth edition, 1932, p. 257.

59. *CW*, Vol. 2, p. 141.

60. Ibid., p. 141.

fairest flower ever of religion and philosophy, namely, Advaita Vedanta, is brought in to counter the arguments of the Dualists. Soon enough, Advaita Vedanta is rendered as the finest expression of Vedanta. Put differently, Vedanta is reduced to Vivekananda's version of Advaita Vedanta: 'Monism or absolute oneness is the very soul of Vedanta.'[61] The idealist, privy to the mysteries of Advaita Vedanta, had transcended limitations of this world and could now soar to unchartered metaphysical heights.

> The only explanation [of how the One becomes many] must come from beyond the sense-plane; we must rise to the superconscious, to a state entirely beyond sense-perception. That metaphysical power is the further instrument that the idealist alone can use. He can experience the Absolute; the man Vivekananda can resolve himself into the Absolute and then come back to the man again...Thus religion begins where philosophy ends. The 'good of the world' will be that what is now superconscious for us will in ages to come be the conscious for all. Religion is therefore the highest work the world has; and because man has unconsciously felt this, he has clung through all the ages to the idea of religion.[62]

---

61. *CW*, Vol. 7, pp. 27-8.
62. Ibid., p. 44.

This is a significant passage. Once risen to the superconscious state, Vivekananda the man can become Vivekananda the Absolute and return to being Vivekananda the man again. It was, as he suggests, a question of going beyond sense-perception. This is, more or less, the non-dualist position. While there could be debate regarding the absolute unreality of the world as contrasted with the eventual or ultimate denial of the world of name and form,[63] most non-dualists would admit to a transient and conditional existence of the world where humans had to perform various duties and follow certain moral and ethical rules. This is captured by the distinction between vyavaharika or conventional truths and paramarthika or ultimate truths. At the vyavaharika level, the normative order Vivekananda creates is brahminical, Vedic, Vedantic, Advaitic, rational, male and Hindu. Despite ultimate fidelity to the principle of oneness, Vivekananda was explicit in his injunction that all individuals without fail ought to follow their svadharma. To jump the stages designated by the varnadharma and the ashramadharma was not only undesirable but was a form of mischief perpetrated by the Buddhists.[64] It is only by following the normative

---

63. For an excellent summary of these debates, see, Andrew J. Nicholson, *Unifying Hinduism: Philosophy and Identity in Indian Intellectual History,* Columbia University Press, New York, 2010.

64. *The Complete Works of Swami Vivekananda*, Vol. 5, Advaita Ashrama, Mayavati, Almora, Fourth edition, 1936, p. 351.

code approved and established by Vivekananda that one could begin contemplating transcending the world of sense-perception and arrive at the superconscious state. Once an individual attains this superconscious stage, the imperatives of the vyavaharika normative code are no longer applicable; he has been able to reach this state, in fact, by scrupulously following the moral and ethical code designated as desirable. As the Absolute, however, the individual is neither bound by social mores nor ordinary moral and ethical codes. Is he to abandon performing any actions on reaching this stage? Is karma or ritual action superfluous on reaching this superconscious state? Was the only way out of this dilemma one where the Bhagavadgita's recommendation of performing actions without a thought about their consequence, even if performing karma might mean fratricidal violence and socially sanctioned murder, is accepted without a challenge? Vivekananda's rhetorical claim of his brand of absolute oneness being the soul of Vedanta had to be grounded in arguments that were more substantial; they had to be intelligible as 'India's religion' and also fulfil the test of universality.

II

The primacy of the Vedanta for Vivekananda was not negotiable. It was also his notion of the Vedanta that had to take precedence over all other historically valid interpretations of the Upanishadic legacy that constituted the Vedanta corpus. The Vedantic seers had seen the truth. It was not a relative truth but one that had existed from time immemorial and one that would continue to exist in times to come.[65] For Vivekananda, these were not merely truths that the sages had stumbled upon which they had not understood as was in the case of Prophet Muhammad.[66] These truths were religious laws as well as the grand truths of spirituality. Their status as eternal truths and laws rested on the absence of their not having either a beginning or an end. More so, their supremacy was further enforced because of their independence from texts and prophets.

> The sublimity of the law propounded by Ramayana or Bharata does not depend upon the truth of any personality like Rama or Krishna, and one can even hold that such personages never lived, and at the same time take these writings as high authorities in respect of the grand ideas which they place before mankind. Our philosophy does not depend upon any personality for its truth. Thus Krishna did not teach anything new or original to the world, nor does Ramayana profess anything

---

65. *The Complete Works of Swami Vivekananda*, Vol. 6, Advaita Ashrama, Mayavati, Almora, Second edition, 1926, p. 7.

66. *CW*, Vol. 1, p. 184.

which is not contained in the Scriptures. It is to be noted that Christianity cannot stand without Christ, Mohammadenism without Mohammed, and Buddhism without Buddha, but Hinduism stands independent of any man...[67]

Calling it the impersonal nature of truth, Vivekananda goes on to argue that the 'Vedanta is the *rationale* of all religions,'[68] and, therefore, for instance, Christians could never understand the New Testament without understanding the Vedanta. Understanding and acknowledging Vedanta was what made any religion worthy of the nomenclature. Failing to do so rendered them to the status of mere superstitions. Establishing the superiority of the Vedanta and proclaiming its universal authenticity as the only true, eternal and tenable moral law was for Vivekananda only a first step. The debunking of the prophetic and revelatory traditions had to be taken to its logical conclusion.

Vivekananda no longer wanted prophets selected by society or by chance. Neither did he believe in prophets being anointed through acts of will or claims of superior intelligence. Instead, the truths of the Vedas and the Upanishads had to be realized and disseminated in society. This could be done only by training people to

---

67. *CW*, Vol. 5, p. 137.
68. Ibid., p. 142.

become prophets. He proposes that to become religious was the act of becoming a prophet and no one could be called religious till he or she turned into a prophet. To study religion was to train people into becoming prophets; he proposes that schools and colleges ought to be training grounds for manufacturing prophets. In characteristic Vivekananda hyperbole, he proposes the universalizing and democratizing of the prophetic tradition: 'The whole universe must become prophets; and until a man becomes a prophet, religion is a mockery and a by-word unto him. We must see religion, feel it, realise it in a thousand times more intense a sense than that in which we see the wall.'[69]

For an unsuspecting moment, it might seem that Vivekananda seems to be proposing a return to the mystic intensity of Ramakrishna's faith in proposing a religion that is based on seeing, feeling and realizing God. But this is not remotely the case. For him, religion is a scientifically demonstrable entity. To be religious and to know religion is to use one's reason. Those who believe through non-rational ways are worthy of being compared to beasts. Mystical flights, ecstatic love, talking to Kali and hearing her talk back was just an individual attribute of being peculiar and having this special gift by chance. In the modern world, Vivekananda concludes, no one ought to believe in anything that is left to chance

---

69. *CW*, Vol. 6, pp. 8-10.

and not mediated through modern scientific rationality.[70] The peculiar and the particular were characteristic features of Dualism: they ignored the principle. Religion for Vivekananda was destruction of peculiarity.

Having chipped away at the claims of the Dualists as well as those following the prophetic-revelatory traditions, Vivekananda introduces into the argument a note that seems to contradict all that he seems to have argued till this moment. It is, in fact, a celebration of a plurality of standpoints, religions, scriptures and prophets in the world. But this plurality on close examination is welcome only in order to apply to it the scientific method. At no point does Vivekananda ask questions regarding the correctness or viability of the scientific method. Nor does his entrenched belief in it go beyond demonstrable verification of things through what he called reasoning, which for him consisted of starting from the particular and moving towards a principle. The sense in which he uses reason is, however, purely instrumental: it helps him debunk everything else other than the Vedanta and his interpretation of Advaita Vedanta. He is conscious that he could argue for seeming plurality in the world of religious symbols and forms while simultaneously reducing these to insignificance by arguing in favour of the Vedantic idea of a unity that permeates and circumscribes the universe. Take

---

70. Ibid., pp. 9-10.

for instance this passage: 'The Mohammedans want to have the whole world Mohammedan; the Christians, Christian; the Buddhists, Buddhist; but the Vedanta says: "Let each person in the world be separate, if you will; the one principle, the unity will be behind".'[71]

It is only when humans have name, form and histories that the question of any moral and ethical engagement with each other arises. Vivekananda pushes the idea of oneness as the core of Vedanta in order to forestall a debate regarding ethical questions: after all, the abstraction called the immortal soul as contrasted to the perishable body in the Bhagavadgita was a response to Arjuna's ethical dilemma. Vivekananda takes the argument further. Nothing perishes but is just a single continuum. There is no diversity or plurality but everything is myself. If I am a leaf and I die, the life of the tree continues. If one tree dies, the idea of the tree continues because every tree is part of the whole called universe. Therefore, there is one mind, one body and one soul that really exist. Universal oneness and not universal brotherhood, then, was the central thought conveyed by the Upanishads.[72] Having stated his view of the Vedanta, Vivekananda gives short shrift to the question of human action and its consequences: 'I am the same as any other man, as any animal - good, bad,

71. Ibid., p. 14.
72. *The Complete Works of Swami Vivekananda*, Vol. 8, Advaita Ashrama, Calcutta, Twelfth impression, 1999, pp. 128-9.

anything.'[73] Having recommended transformation of all humans into prophets, he now wants every living being metamorphosed into the divine: 'You are all Gods. One God is not sufficient. You are all Gods, says the Vedanta.'[74] While ethical dilemmas are hardly the stuff of prophets and gods, the question of action and its consequences is also neatly relegated to the recesses of the inner realm. The Vedanta, after all, teaches that one need not step out of oneself in order to discover the truth, which is within oneself.

The God of the Vedanta, Vivekananda emphasizes, is an impersonal principle and not a person. There is no Personal God, but 'You and I, the cat, rat, devil, and ghost, all these are Its persons – all are Personal Gods'.[75] The human body is the temple inside which resides this 'Lord of souls and the King of kings.'[76] The Hindus, laments Vivekananda, are wedded to the idea of God as the king of the earth rather than the king of souls. Vedanta for this reason cannot flourish in India. The concept of all living beings as prophets and gods, he elaborates, is a democratic idea and can flourish only in America.[77] Hindus, on the other hand, were busy building temples and seeking the truth elsewhere.

---

73. Ibid., pp. 128-9.
74. Ibid., pp. 124-5.
75. Ibid., pp. 133-4.
76. Ibid., pp. 135-6.
77. Ibid., p. 126.

We do not see that, so we make stone images of Him and build temples over them. Vedanta has been in India always, but India is full of these temples but also caves containing carved images. 'The fool, dwelling on the bank of the Gangā, digs a well for water!' Such are we! Living in the midst of God – we must go and make images. We project Him in the form of the image, while all the time He exists in the temple of our body. We are lunatics, and this is the great delusion.[78]

In other words, the Vedanta proposes that all living beings are prophets and personal gods. It also situates truth within the human body rather than as an object to be discovered externally. At no point in the argument does Vivekananda pause to consider if the truth of the Upanishads, which for him was also a rational and scientific truth, verifiable by moving from the particular to the principle, was also applicable to the rat and the cat. It is perfectly possible that this truth was merely a moment of realization and had little to do with human action. But even if specific actions had to be accounted for, it was impossible to do so if every rational individual was also simultaneously a prophet and a god. Neither was the truth that one was being goaded and impelled to discover within the temple of the body a disembodied and value-neutral entity: it was

---

78. Ibid., pp. 135-6.

a reading of the Vedantic truth as embodied in the realm of brahminical Hinduism. Vivekananda takes recourse here to a reading of the Mahabharata and the character of Krishna in it. The question of action and its consequences is dexterously sidestepped: 'Krishna shows the way how to do this, — by being non-attached: do everything but do not get identified with anything. You are the Soul, the pure, the free, all the time; you are the Witness. Our misery comes, not from work, but by getting attached to something.'[79] The Hindus, he explains, had discovered the concept of the Atman or the universal soul. It was this discovery that was the basis of ethics for the Hindus.

> Though all religions have taught ethical precepts, such as, 'Do not kill, do not injure; love thy neighbour as yourself,' etc., yet none of these has given the reason. Why should I not injure my neighbour? To this question there was no satisfactory or conclusive answer forthcoming, until it was evolved by the metaphysical speculations of the Hindus who could not rest satisfied with mere dogmas.[80]

Note carefully, first, the dismissal of Christian ethics as dogma. Next, the question of injuring one's neighbour,

---

79. *CW*, Vol. 4, p. 92.
80. *CW*, Vol. 1, pp. 384-5.

assuming that the injury is physical, is resolved through the metaphysical speculations as they evolved among the Hindus.

> So the Hindus say that this Atman is absolute and all-pervading, therefore infinite. There cannot be two infinities, for they would limit each other and would also become finite. Also each individual soul is a part and parcel of that Universal Soul, which is infinite. Therefore in injuring his neighbour, the individual actually injures himself. This is the basic metaphysical truth underlying all ethical codes.[81]

The injury is to the body most times, and at other times to the emotions, to one's self-esteem and to an individual's basic existence as one. Vivekananda's refusal to grant any legitimacy to the world of appearances, and the body as one such tangible object among many, is what a perceptive modern commentator has called 'the refusal of the body as a site of any experience, any tragedy, any remorse, and, above all, any politics'.[82] The emphasis, as we have seen earlier, on the superconscious state was to transcend the body, which could be a site of contestation, argument, and, above all, history: 'In all religions the superconscious state is identical. Hindus, Christians, Mohammedans,

---

81. Ibid., pp. 384-5.
82. Aishwary Kumar, 'Ambedkar's Inheritances', *Modern Intellectual History*, 7,2,(2010), p. 397.

Buddhists, and even those of no creed, all have the very same experience when they transcend the body.'[83] Injury to the neighbour is, then, not a real injury, but only something that is part of metaphysical speculation that can, at best, be understood and rationalized. All that it serves is the claim that the truth of the universal Atman enables the Hindus to understand the religious truth of all religions, from the lowest to the highest.

In establishing the sovereign authority of Vedanta, Vivekananda posits three stages in the spiritual growth of every individual. These three stages correspond to the evolution of all other faiths.[84] The Vedanta, he argues, contains and reflects all these three stages. It is a process of evolution, beginning with Dvaita or Dualism, Vishishtadvaita or qualified Monism and Advaita or absolute Monism. Vedanta had to be applied according to needs, locale and nationality, but it was also important to remember that there was no difference, whatsoever, between the idea of religion and Vedanta. The only religion in the universe was Vedanta and Vedanta was the only religion worthy of the name. In a passage that is self-assured as it is breathtakingly presumptuous, but also historically and philosophically inaccurate, Vivekananda dismisses Jainism and Buddhism as mere clones of Vedanta.

---

83. *CW*, Vol. 7, p. 43.
84. *CW*, Vol. 5, p. 64.

This is what I mean by the word Vedanta, that it covers the ground of Dualism, of Qualified Monism and Advaitism in India. Perhaps we may even take in parts of Buddhism, and of Jainism too, if they would come in, — for our hearts are sufficiently large. But it is they that will not come in; we are ready; for upon severe analysis you will always find that the essence of Buddhism was all borrowed from the same Upanishads; even the ethics, the so-called great and wonderful ethics of Buddhism, were there word for word, in some one or the other of the Upanishads, and so all the good doctrines of the Jains were there, minus their vagaries.[85]

It is worth noting the phrasing of the above quote: the essence of Buddhism was 'all borrowed' and it only had a 'so-called' great and wonderful ethics. Elsewhere, while maintaining that Vedanta was the foundation of Buddhism, Vivekananda does concede that 'what we call Advaita philosophy of the modern school has a great many conclusions of the Buddhists'.[86] He also makes a distinction between the Northern Buddhists and the Southern Buddhists; his quarrel seems to be with the Southern Buddhists for their denial of a noumenal

---

85. *CW*, Vol. 3, p. 230.
86. *CW*, Vol. 5, pp. 206-7.

world and their avowal of a phenomenal world.[87] For Vivekananda, there is just one world and it is the noumenal world.

≈

Much of Vivekananda's mystique rests on his perceived liberality with respect to other faiths. There is a clear identification between Vivekananda and the view that religions might differ in word, ritual, doctrine and emphasis but all faiths are ultimately paths to the same God. In many of his public pronouncements, he explicitly seeks to convey that his message was one of peace and a united religion and not of antagonism.[88] Having studied comparative religions, he finds all faiths to have had the same foundations as his own faith. If there were differences, these were in the realm of the non-essential[89] elements within faiths. Going a step further, he wants a plurality of faiths in the world to suit a variety of contexts. In a world that constantly has to contend with religious strife and the violence that is the inevitable consequence of such conflict, such words and thoughts can be seductively reassuring. This is especially

---

87. Ibid., p. 207. Kant makes the distinction between phenomenon and noumenon as indicating the difference between 'thing as appearance' and 'thing in itself'.

88. *CW*, Vol. 1, p. 317.

89. Ibid., p. 318.

so when quoted out of context, selectively and without attention to the fine print. An example would illustrate the point better. Here, Vivekananda is talking about the desirability of different faiths:

> I do not deprecate the existence of sects in the world. Would to God there were twenty million more, for the more there are, there will be a greater field for selection. What I do object to is trying to fit one religion to every case. Though all religions are essentially the same, they must have the varieties of form produced by dissimilar circumstances among different nations.[90]

This sounds perfectly reasonable. It is worth marking that he calls them 'sects' and not religions. But the overall tone and tenor is one of remarkable liberality. Now read the last line of the quote: 'We must each have our own individual religion, individual *so far as the externals of it go*.'[91] The plurality of faiths, then, is limited to the externals. Remove the externals and what will emerge is a universal faith defined by Vivekananda, based entirely on his reading of the Vedanta. The Vedantic ideal of Oneness and the Universal Soul would ultimately prevail.

---

90. Ibid., pp. 325-6.
91. Ibid., pp. 325-6 (author's emphasis).

When we shall feel that oneness, we shall be immortal. We are physically immortal even, one with the universe. So long as there is one that breathes throughout the universe, I live in that one. I am not this limited little being, I am the universal. I am the life of all the sons of the past. I am the soul of Buddha, of Jesus, of Mohammed.[92]

When the argument for a single universal faith had to be made strenuously, Vivekananda abandons even the 'We must each have our own individual religion' rhetoric with alacrity: 'There never was my religion or yours, my national religion or your national religion; there never existed many religions, there is only the one. One Infinite Religion existed all through eternity and will ever exist, and this Religion is expressing itself in various countries, in various ways.'[93] What, then, about the argument that promised to accommodate even twenty million or more sects in the world, even if this acceptance of plurality was only based on the acknowledgement of a multitude of external forms of religion? The above quote ends with the following sentence: Therefore we must respect all religions and we must try to accept them all *as far as we can*.[94]

---

92. Ibid., p. 341.
93. *CW*, Vol. 4, p. 176.
94. Ibid., p. 176 (author's emphasis).

The respect for other religions was, therefore, conditional. It depended on phrases like 'so far as the externals of it go' and 'as far as we can'.

The refrain of not judging others and not being contemptuous towards other faiths occurs regularly within the Vivekananda corpus. It is also always invariably accompanied by the argument that differences are only of a degree and that there are people who are not as developed as 'we' are.[95] Differences and variations were only the 'externals', they were part of the phenomenal world. Invoking biological and naturalistic metaphors, Vivekananda argues that Nature always represents unity in variety, that '...through all these variations of the phenomenal runs the Infinite, the Unchangeable, the Absolute Unity'.[96] What was true of Nature is also true for humans: '...the microcosm is but a miniature repetition of the macrocosm.'[97] This is the reason, affirms Vivekananda, why no man's faith ought to be disturbed. While this too sounds utterly reasonable, it also is part of the same trajectory where other faiths are limited and inadequate and require getting 'hold of a man where he stands and giving him a push upwards'.[98] Oneness, Absolute Unity and the necessary push upwards were possible, though, only

---

95. *CW*, Vol. 2, p. 297.
96. *CW*, Vol. 4, p. 177.
97. Ibid., p. 177.
98. Ibid., p. 179.

if a set of preconditions were met and unambiguously affirmed.

∽

Having pronounced his version of the Vedanta as the only religion in the world, Vivekananda wants every 'narrow, limited, fighting ideas of religion'[99] to be eliminated. Sects, tribes and nations have their own ideas of religion and of God and this caused them to quarrel over claims to superiority. Such ideas of a Personal God were the scourge brought about by Dualism, which was another name for superstition. To move to the future, this deadweight of the past had to be abandoned. Vivekananda says very little why other ideas of religion are narrow and limited except to offer Vedanta and its vision of oneness as the superior alternative. Indeed, grand abstractions were seemingly always preferable to disturbing historical details and philosophical nuances. The influence of German philosophy is starkly visible here, as is in the rest of his philosophical edifice. A few months before Ramakrishna's death in 1886, Vivekananda asks Mahendranath for a history of philosophy to read. Mahendranath offers one by Lewis. 'No, Überweg. I must read a German author,'[100] says

---

99. *CW*, Vol. 2, p. 67.
100. *Gospel*, p. 963.

Vivekananda. While no reference to Überweg is recorded in subsequent conversations or in his writings, there is a marked influence of nineteenth-century German philosophical tradition on the structure as well as content of his thought. Hence, echoing Hegel, but more so Schopenhauer's principle of the sufficient reason of becoming, Vivekananda proceeds to define a religion that must leave behind all specificity; the German inspiration also synchronizes well with Krishna's advice of doing everything but not getting identified with anything.

> Religion is not in doctrines, in dogmas, nor in intellectual argumentation; it is being and becoming; it is realisation. We hear so many talking about God and the soul, and all the mysteries of the universe, but if you take them one by one, and ask them, 'Have you realised God? Have you seen your Soul?' how many can say they have. And yet they are all fighting with one another![101]

Denying intellectual argumentation is ironical because during the years he had known his young pupil, Ramakrishna despaired of Vivekananda's relentless discussion and debate on matters that, for the Master, could only be resolved through sincere longing and ecstatic love. In his exposition of religion, Vivekananda stacks

---

101. *CW*, Vol. 2, p. 43

'doctrines', 'dogmas' and 'intellectual argumentation' as the antagonistic opposites of 'becoming', realisation', as well as of realizing God and seeing one's soul. More importantly, he likens expressing oneself about God, the soul and the mysteries of the universe to 'fighting' and diminished as legitimate forms of human activity.

In order to explain his conception of universal religion, Vivekananda proposes yet another fourfold classification of humans.[102] The active man is the worker, the emotional man is the lover of the sublime and the beautiful, the mystic is one whose mind wants to analyse its own self, and finally the philosopher who weighs everything with the use of his intellect. Any religion attempting to claim universality ought to satisfy all these natures. Having arrived at this classification, Vivekananda claims that the plan of the universe exhibits unity in variety. What is this ultimate unity? It is God, he says. But the reality and existence of this ultimate unity do not mean that differences have to be obliterated. Neither does it mean that one set of doctrines should be believed by all mankind; just as all faces cannot be the same, so can there be no single set of doctrines that

---

102. Ibid., pp. 383-4.

are shared by all humanity.[103] Variation, he elaborates, is a natural necessity just as unity is equally a natural necessity. To apologists of Vivekananda, this would be clinching evidence of his broad-mindedness, empathy and tolerance, especially towards other forms of belief and religious practices. Closely examined, Vivekananda's argument is clear and straightforward: Unity and variation are natural necessities. Translated in theological terms, this merely means that 'truth may be expressed in a hundred thousand ways, and that each of these ways is true as far as it goes'.[104] Put differently, while a thousand ways of expressing truth could be allowed, truth itself was what the Vedantic seers had propounded in the pages of the Upanishads. The liberality attributed to Vivekananda is only in name: it is, in fact, the space he creates for others to acknowledge the truth designated by him as ultimate and universal. As seen above, he argues that religion is Vedanta and Vedanta is religion. Hence, after arguing that there can be no single set of doctrines in the world, he offers a Vedanta-inspired definition of religion that neutralizes the concession granted to differences in favour of unity. The 'hundred thousand ways' of expressing truth are merely ways by which inadequate notions of religion attempt to approximate to the idea of the Vedantic truth.

---

103. Ibid., pp. 379-80.
104. Ibid., pp. 380-1.

Equally compelling in the Vivekananda corpus are quotes like this: 'Religion is realisation; not talk, nor doctrine, nor theories, however beautiful they may be. It is being and becoming, not hearing or acknowledging; it is the whole soul becoming changed into what it believes. That is religion.'[105] In the *Kathāmrita*, Ramakrishna asks Narendra if he intended to continue with his studies. This is recorded on 4 January 1886, the year Ramakrishna died. To this query, Narendra's reply is significant. He says: 'I shall feel greatly relieved if I find a medicine that will make me forget all I have studied.'[106] In line with Vivekananda's argument that religion does not consist of theories, doctrines and dogmas, it does not seem unusual. But on 17 April 1886, Narendra is arguing with Mahendranath in Ramakrishna's presence regarding the question of the existence of God. He says: 'How can you say that God exists? It is you who have created this universe. Don't you know what Berkeley says about it?'[107] In May 1887, after Ramakrishna's death, one finds Vivekananda finding similarities between John Stuart Mill and the Vedas on the question of God's kindness.[108] Theories, then, were important as much as rhetorical denial of their usefulness. These examples do not include Vivekananda's considerable debt to the

---

105. Ibid., p. 394.
106. *Gospel*, p. 935.
107. Ibid., p. 960.
108. Ibid., p. 999.

thought of Immanuel Kant and Arthur Schopenhauer, not to mention such obvious influences as Paul Deussen and Max Müller. Vivekananda saw no apparent contradiction in this: after all, truth could be expressed in many ways as long as it conformed to the truth of the Upanishads as he perceived it.

III

Any critical evaluation of Vivekananda has to contend with scattered islands of reasonableness periodically emerging in the vast ocean of a singular, uncompromising and stridently Vedic-Vedantic vision. One such question is the act of judging others. If a small selection of quotations from him about the ways in which we ought to judge, if judge we must, were to be reproduced, they would seem to show us the ideal way forward on this topic. Of course, by now we know something of Vivekananda's views on religion, on caste, and about his uncompromisingly unequivocal privileging of his version of the Vedanta. But it is still useful to see what he has to say on the critical issue of judging, if only to subsequently seek answers to two questions: First, did Vivekananda judge, and, second, if he did, to what end? In this context, let us examine the following quotes from Vivekananda:

- The great lesson to learn is that I am not the standard by which the whole universe is to be judged; each man is to be judged by his own idea, each race by its own standard and ideal, each custom of each country by its own reasoning and conditions. American customs are the result of the environment in which Americans live, and Indian customs are the result of the environment in which the Indians are; and so of China, Japan, England and every other country.[109]

- We are always making this mistake in judging others; we are always inclined to think that our little mental universe is all that is; our ethics, our morality, our sense of duty, our sense of utility, are the only things that are worth having.[110]

- Everyone must be judged according to his own ideal, and not by that of anyone else. In our dealings with our fellow-beings we constantly labour under this mistake, and I am of opinion that the vast majority of our quarrels with one another arise simply from this one cause, that we are always trying to judge others' gods by our own, others' ideals by our own ideals, and others' motives by our own motives.[111]

---

109. *CW*, Vol. 5, pp. 168-9.
110. *CW*, Vol. 2, p. 24.
111. Ibid., p. 106.

There is very little in the above quotes that seems explicitly unreasonable or objectionable. While unequivocally rejecting the right of anyone to judge the gods, customs, motives and ideals, he goes to the extent of suggesting that one earned the right to criticize individuals like the Buddha and Christ only if one could emulate the breadth and scope of their work and their suffering. Having stated his position on the thorny question of judgement, Vivekananda is quick to judge. A few examples will illustrate the point better. Did Vivekananda do enough and suffer enough to judge the Buddha? His judgements on the Buddha and on Buddhism are categorical and often seem contradictory. These contradictions, however, arise out of Vivekananda's familiar inability to distinguish between text, person, doctrine, practice and the historical evolution of a faith and any set of beliefs and practices. Following this trajectory, he faults the Buddha and Buddhism for their negative iconoclasm and their rejection of Sanskrit. This had serious consequences: it led to alienation of the Hindus from the Vedas and disturbed the ancient equilibrium between brahmins and kshatriyas.[112] Buddhism was nothing but a sect. The Buddha was selfless but he was also 'perfectly agnostic about metaphysics or theories about God'.[113] He clearly states that he differs with the Buddha on many issues

---

112. *CW*, Vol. 4, pp. 272-3.
113. Ibid., p. 131.

but also aspires for a heart equal to that of the Buddha, not to mention his selflessness. But contrary to the Buddha's indifference to metaphysics, he wants a 'good deal of metaphysics'.[114] Was disinterest in metaphysics the Buddha's only flaw? Buddhism, contrary to popular perception, he imputes, did not destroy brahminical idolatry, but created both brahminism[115] and idolatry.

Vivekananda's judgement of Buddhism, then, falls into three distinct lines of argument. First is the acknowledgement of the Buddha's empathy, his courage, his sincerity and offering the world a comprehensive system of morality.[116] After acknowledging the Buddha as a person and, in a qualified sense, his original message, there comes a thorough indictment of 'the hideousness that came in the wake of Buddhism'.[117] Modern Hinduism had borrowed a great deal from this degraded Buddhism of hideous ceremonies, obscene books and bestial forms masquerading as religion: 'I am perfectly convinced that what they call modern Hinduism with all its ugliness is only stranded Buddhism. Let the Hindus understand this clearly, and then it would be easier for

114. Ibid., p. 132.
115. Ibid., p. 264. See also, *CW*, Vol. 7, pp. 21-2. Brahminism is not to be confused with brahminhood. The latter is Vivekananda's ideal for future India whereas by brahminism he means ritualistic priestcraft. This has been explained in detail in the previous chapter.
116. *CW*, Vol. 7, pp. 40-1.
117. *CW*, Vol. 3, pp. 264-5.

them to reject it without murmur.'[118]

Vivekananda often describes the Buddha as a reformer of Hinduism, who denied the Vedas because of the Vedic sanction to various forms of violence. Did the Buddha do anything wrong in opposing the ritualistic violence supported by the Vedas? Vivekananda is categorical here: the Buddha had no authority to do so.[119] Worse still, the Buddha, says Vivekananda, compounded his error of opposing the Vedas by not understanding the idea of harmony of religions and by introducing sectarianism.[120] For wanting to destroy the Vedic religion, Buddhism paid the price and was thrown out of India. Finally, the only way to understand the Buddha and his teachings that would make them acceptable was to do so from a Hindu standpoint. Once the supremacy of the Hindu point of view was established, Vivekananda declares that the Buddha 'taught the gist of the philosophy of the Vedas to one and all and without distinction'[121] and was no longer the destroyer of the Vedic religion. In so doing, he imparted his great message of equality to the world. Vivekananda was no champion of equality as ordinarily understood. In interpreting the message of the Buddha in the Hindu way, he returns to the Upanishads and his version of oneness of the world:

---

118. *CW*, Vol. 7, p. 505.
119. *CW*, Vol. 6, p. 86.
120. Ibid., p. 86.
121. *CW*, Vol. 8, pp. 97-8.

There is another way of looking at the truth we have been discussing: the Hindu way. We claim that Buddha's great doctrine of selflessness can be better understood if it is looked at in our way. In the Upanishads there is already the great doctrine of the Atman and the Brahman. The Atman, Self, is the same as Brahman, the Lord. This Self is all that is; It is the only reality. Māyā, delusion, makes us see It as different. There is one Self, not many. That one Self shines in various forms. Man is man's brother because all men are one. A man is not only my brother, say the Vedas, he is myself. I am the universe. It is a delusion that I think I am Mr. So-and-So – that is delusion.[122]

Vivekananda liked the Buddha's kindness, mercy and charity but not his doctrine.[123] If the doctrine had to be understood, it could be so done only in the Hindu way prescribed by Vivekananda. The gulf between Vivekananda's injunction not to judge and his willingness to do the opposite can hardly be overstated. In the case of Islam, this chasm is even more obvious and deeper. While this has been discussed in some detail elsewhere,[124] an example here would suffice.

---

122. Ibid., pp. 100-1.

123. Ibid., p. 103.

124. Jyotirmaya Sharma, *Hindutva: Exploring the Idea of Hindu Nationalism*, Penguin, New Delhi, 2011 edition.

In a letter written on 10 June 1898 to Mohammed Sarfaraz Husain, a Muslim resident of Nainital, Vivekananda attempts one of the most complex and astonishingly perplexing definitions of religion. He begins with the assertion that Vedantism, and more specifically Advaitism, was the 'last word of religion and thought'.[125] He introduces no element of the variety of views and attitudes expressed in the Upanishads, nor does he entertain the differences between the purva mimamsa and uttara mimamsa. In conflating Vedantism and Advaitism, little is done to clarify distinctions between the two main streams of Vedantic interpretation.[126] Not only was Advaitism the last word in religion and thought but it was 'the only position from which one can look upon all religions and sects with love'.[127] The Hindus could get the credit of arriving at it earlier than the Jews and the Muslims, and Advaitism was the religion of the future enlightened humanity. But practical Advaitism was another matter altogether. It was that Advaitism that dared look upon and treat all humanity as one's own soul. The Hindus had not embraced this universally, whereas the only religion that approximated to this ideal of equality in any manner in

---

125. *CW*, Vol. 6, p. 375.
126. G.C. Pande, *Foundations of Indian Culture: Spiritual Vision and Symbolic Forms in Ancient India*, Volume I, Motilal Banarsidass, Delhi, 2005 edition, pp. 141-2.
127. *CW*, Vol. 6, p. 375.

the realm of everyday life in a practical sense was Islam. Therefore, 'without the help of practical Islam, theories of Vedantism, however fine and wonderful they may be, are entirely valueless to the vast mass of mankind'.[128] The great religious texts, the Vedas, the Bible and the Qur'an would have to be harmonized and mankind will have to be taught that all faiths are manifestations of the only religion that taught oneness, something that the Hindus first arrived at and which manifests in the form of Advaita. Vivekananda's endorsement of Islam's practice of equality in ordinary life might seem fulsome and categorical, but it is not. He only grants Islam the primacy of action, but not of thought. Hence, the equality that practical Advaita preaches and Islam practices 'may be quite unconscious generally of the deeper meaning and the underlying principle of such conduct, which the Hindus, as a rule, so clearly perceive'.[129] The India of the future had to be founded, therefore, on the basis of a synthesis: 'Vedanta brain and Islam body'.[130] Yet, there are instances when Vivekananda argues that the body divides people and is the cause of separation among people, especially if there is no knowledge of the spirit.[131] Less than a year before the letter to Mohammed Sarfaraz Husain, in another letter dated 10 October 1897,

---

128. Ibid., p. 376.
129. Ibid., p. 376.
130. Ibid., p. 376.
131. *CW*, Vol. 2, p. 84.

written to Akhandananda, Vivekananda enjoins him to accept Muslim boys in the newly formed sect, asks him not to tamper with their religion, but also advices that the 'only thing you will have to do is to make separate arrangements for their food, etc., and teach them so that they may be moral, manly, and devoted to doing good'.[132] While he is emphatic that Hindu, Muslim and Christian boys ought to be admitted, he is insistent that 'they get their food and drink a little separately'.[133]

Ramakrishna believed that God alone would rectify any errors that a faith might have and such correction was God's business alone. He did not also believe in the idea of faiths evolving at different speeds and paces. There is no place in Ramakrishna's thought for the idea of a perfected faith having first realized the truth, one that all other evolving faiths had perforce to emulate. Vivekananda rejected Ramakrishna's non-hierarchical view of other faiths and he had unconcealed contempt for the idea that it was longing, ecstatic faith in a Personal God that alone accounted for the equality of all faiths, belief systems and sects. Vivekananda's Ramakrishna was a 'scientist' who had rationalized all the scriptures,

---

132. *CW*, Vol. 6, p. 371.
133. Ibid., p. 371.

especially the Vedas and the Upanishads, and all other seemingly contradictory doctrines to create a scientific Hinduism. In Vivekananda's hands, the faith that emerged had the following features:[134]

- The Vedas alone know and teach the idea of the real absolute God;
- The absolute, also called the Brahman, was alone true;
- All other ideas of God are nothing more than minimized and limited visions of the absolute truth;
- Different religions and sects in India and in the world represent different manifestations of the Brahman or the absolute God and so are true;
- Other sects and religions, however, exhibit various stages of being manifest in unprogressive and crystallized form;
- Therefore, other religions and sects are true as they are manifestations of Brahman, but some are higher than the others.
- There is only one perfect religion, the nameless, limitless and eternal Vedic religion. All the minimized, limited, unprogressive and crystallized forms of religion in the world were included in the Vedic religion.

---

134. *CW*, Vol. 4, p. 289.

In the evolutionary schema that Vivekananda devises, humanity is a vast organism that slowly moves from darkness to light. In doing so the first tentative steps are through the help of matter and rituals.[135] In order to find light, which is God, every religion proceeds to worship, firstly, forms or symbols, names next, and finally, god-men. This also becomes the source of all religious strife and dissension. Each religion, then, claims that its forms, names and god-men are true to the exclusion of all others.

In itself, the evolutionary progression towards light suggests that other sects and faiths would one day transcend the preliminary stages of being beholden to forms, names and god-men and reach the perfection attained by the Vedic religion. At this stage of the argument, there is little indication whether having attained the perfection of the Vedic religion other faiths would retain their distinctiveness and individuality or merge into the idea of the real absolute God. But there are enough instances where Vivekananda seems to suggest that other faiths could progressively move towards the Vedic conception of absolute truth. He does, however, say that '…every religion, is true, as each is but a different stage in the journey, the aim of which is the perfect conception of the Vedas'[136] but also admits 'that all the religions, from the lowest fetishism to the highest

---

135. *CW*, Vol. 2, pp. 41-2.
136. *CW*, Vol. 1. pp. 331-2.

absolutism, mean so many attempts of the human soul to grasp and realise the infinite, each determined by the conditions of its birth and association, and each of them marking a stage of progress'.[137] Here there is not even a scant allusion to the earlier formulation of other faiths being unprogressive and crystallized. There is relentless exhortation for others to recognize and affirm the perfection of the Vedic religion, but, at the same time, enough ambiguity to substantially doubt the capacity of other faiths to attain the absolute ideal. To continue to argue in this fashion was to make the evolutionary schema and its inherent hierarchy among faiths redundant. It would eventually also render superfluous the entire project of establishing the supremacy of the Vedic religion. Vivekananda ruthlessly thwarts even the momentary illusion that other faiths and sects might have harboured of ever attaining the real absolute God. This is accomplished by introducing the idea of involution as a necessary precondition for evolution in any manner of speaking to take place in the first instance.

All the possibilities of a future tree are in that seed; all the possibilities of a future man are in the little baby; all the possibilities of any future life are in the germ. What is this? The ancient philosophers of India called it involution. We find then, that every

137. Ibid., pp. 331-2.

evolution presupposes an involution. Nothing can
be evolved which is not already there.[138]

The message is clear and direct: Vedic religion has in its
seed the intimations of future perfection. Other faiths
could, indeed, be sincere efforts on the path of realizing
God and truth, but would never attain the real absolute
God; they would, for ever, remain hostage to only limited
and minimized versions of the truth. Inevitably, this
would raise questions about what was 'already there'
in Vedic religion that paved the way for involution,
evolution and perfection. Vivekananda dismisses even
a remote semblance of scepticism about the perfect seed
and the perfect future tree by identifying the one thing
that makes Vedic religion perfect: the idea of the soul.

There were two ways to study religions, suggests
Vivekananda, in order to understand the idea of
involution. One is the Semitic idea of religion, where
the idea of God comes prior to the idea of the human
individual. In the Semitic group of religions, the idea
of God emerges 'strangely enough, without any idea of
soul'.[139] In sharp contrast, the Aryan idea of religion was

138. *CW*, Vol. 2, p. 227.
139. *CW*, Vol. 6, p. 1.

to start with the human individual and progressively move towards the idea of God: 'All the knowledge they got of God was through the human soul; and, as such, the peculiar stamp that has been left upon their whole cycle of philosophy is that introspective search after Divinity. The Aryan man was always seeking Divinity inside his own self.'[140]

This introspective search, claims Vivekananda, led the Aryan man towards the ideal of unity and non-separateness. This was the foundation of all ethics and all morality and was also found in all religions and among all other prophets. What marked Aryans as distinctive and led to their perfection was the idea of the soul that was already interred in the seed in the first instance. Explaining it differently, Vivekananda singles out Vedanta as the only religion where the principles take precedence over the mythology. Without exception, in all other faiths, 'the principles are so interwoven with the mythology, that it is very hard to distinguish one from the other'.[141] The mythology swallows the principles and, over a period of time, the principles are lost altogether. Christianity cannot explain the principles of its faith as distinct from Christ and neither can Islam preach its principles independent of Prophet Muhammad.

---

140. Ibid., p. 1.
141. Ibid., p. 5.

In Vedanta the chief advantage is that it was not the work of one single man; and therefore, naturally, unlike Buddhism, or Christianity, or Mohammedanism, the prophet or teacher did not entirely swallow up or overshadow the principles. The principles live, and the prophets, as it were, form a secondary group, unknown to Vedanta.[142]

Prophets were people who appealed to emotions and not to 'something higher, to our calm judgement'.[143] Emotions drag people to the level of animals;[144] emotions have a greater connection to the senses than the capacity to reason. When emotions rather than reason prevail, religion slides into fanaticism and sectarianism. Principles, rather than emotions, must triumph in the final analysis. In so arguing, Vivekananda forestalls the possibility of Vedanta ever degenerating into sectarianism and fanaticism. Nor could Vedanta ever have scope for emotions that were irrational. The seed, even before it had begun to evolve, was perfect. All other faiths, however sincere, were always in the danger of sliding to the level of animals.

Degeneration of religions to the level of beasts happens because principles often spill over into mythology. Vivekananda delineates mythologies as

142. Ibid., p. 5.
143. Ibid., p. 5.
144. Ibid., pp. 5-6; see also, CW, Vol. 1, p. 460.

consisting of lives of saints or heroes, demigods, or gods, and divine beings, but all mythologies shared a common feature, namely, the expression of power. In the primitive category of mythologies, he elaborates, the emphasis is usually on portraying their heroes as strong and gigantic. After this stage has been crossed, the higher mythologies have great moral men as their heroes, men whose actual strength lies in becoming moral and pure. The final stage in the development of religions is even lower than creation of myths. He calls it the invention of symbolism. This manifests in the form of rituals and ceremonials. It is an expression of the lowest minds where symbolism works as the 'kindergarten of religion'.[145] Religions that rely excessively on myths and symbols discover that 'all that is left to them is but an empty shell, a contentless frame of words and sophistry'.[146] In his relentless and systematic demolition of all other faiths and sects, Vivekananda now adds another element. He wonders if the methods of modern science can at all be applied to the science of religion, and, unsurprisingly, answers in the affirmative: 'Not only will it be made scientific – as scientific, at least, as any of the conclusions of physics or chemistry – but will have greater strength, because physics or chemistry has no internal mandate to vouch for its truth, which religion has.'[147]

---

145. *CW*, Vol. 6, p. 4.
146. *CW*, Vol. 3, p. 44.
147. *CW*, Vol. 1, p. 367.

Till this moment in the narrative, Vivekananda seems to propose that the Vedic religion was the only perfect religion, that the Vedas alone disseminate the idea of the real absolute God, and that the Aryan man alone was capable of an introspective search for divinity. There were various grades and levels of religion and other religions could evolve and chart their own course towards attaining God. If they evolved enough to recognize the perfection of the Vedic religion, they would sooner than later be in communion with the absolute truth. If they remained true to their name and form, they would evolve but eventually fail to attain the perfection of the Vedic religion because of the absence of involution. Face-to-face with the dazzling brilliance and perfection with which Vivekananda endows his version of the Vedic religion, clearly no other faith, sect, prophet or doctrine could remotely stand and be counted in comparison. The only sliver of hope now rested in seeking refuge in science. Having mentioned the possibility of applying methods of modern science to the science of religion, would Vivekananda relent and allow other faiths and sects to at least appropriate the methods of science and become scientific?

Characteristically, Vivekananda begins with an imaginary conversation between a Christian and a Muslim, both claiming the inherent superiority of their respective faiths. It quickly moves to the question of conversion in Islam, invoking well-known stereotypes as the use of force, and the killing of infidels if conversion was resisted. At the conclusion of this conversation, Vivekananda lays the blame for this conflict on the Christian and Islamic preoccupation with sacred books, a conflict that the sacred books themselves cannot resolve. He then moves to elaborate the operative part of his argument: there ought to be an outside agency, something higher than all ethical codes to resolve such conflict. He demands something that is higher than the claims of every set of individual inspirations, an external agency that would arbiter between 'inspiration and inspiration'.[148] Scientific reason, he concludes, was to be that external agency to arbiter between rival claims made by different faiths. Scientific reason has this edge because, firstly, 'the particular is explained by the general, the general by the more general, until we come to the universal'.[149] But this was not enough. A second way of looking at the principles of reason was to seek the explanation of a thing from the inside and not the outside. 'In one word, what is meant by science,' he explains, 'is that the explanations of things are in their own nature, and that no external beings or existences are required to explain what is going on in the universe.'[150] For Vivekananda, the idea that the explanation of everything comes from inside the thing itself tallies

148. Ibid., p. 369.
149. Ibid., p. 369.
150. Ibid., pp. 370-1.

with the modern law of evolution as well. Evolution is nothing but a thing reproducing its own nature, 'that the effect is nothing but the cause in another form, that all the potentialities of the effect were present in the cause, that the whole of creation is but an evolution and not a creation'.[151]

Having established the two principles upon which scientific reason was to arbiter between claims of superiority put forth by various sects and religions, Vivekananda finds only one religion fulfilling the requirements of these principles:

Can there be a religion satisfying these two principles? I think there can be. In the first place we have seen that we have to satisfy the principle of generalisation. The generalisation principle ought to be satisfied along with the principle of evolution. We have to come to an ultimate generalisation, which not only will be the most universal of all generalisations, but out of which everything else must come. It will be of the same nature as the lowest effect; the cause, the highest, the ultimate, the primal cause, must be the same as the lowest and most distant of its effects, a series of evolutions. The Brahman of the Vedanta fulfils that condition, because Brahman is the last

151. Ibid., pp. 371-2.

generalisation to which we can come. It has no
attributes but is Existence, Knowledge, and Bliss
– Absolute.[152]

Modern science, then, proves the Vedantic ideal of unity
and oneness. The Brahman, the God of the Vedanta, is
everything. There is nothing external to him. The only
religion that can stand the test of modern reasoning is the
Advaita Vedanta. All other faiths and sects entertain the
idea of a Personal God, which is not a true generalization;
the real absolute God is impersonal: 'The Self is the
essence of this universe, the essence of all souls; He is the
essence of your own life, nay, "Thou art That". You are
one with this universe. He who says he is different from
others, even by a hair's breadth, immediately becomes
miserable.'[153]

The Impersonal God is, therefore, not a relative God.
If he is so, he is beyond good and evil. Vivekananda was
conscious of the pitfalls of his version of the Advaita
Vedanta. Having painstakingly sketched the nature of
this Impersonal God, one who is beyond attributes, and
who transcends the ordinary realm of ethics, he concedes
that 'Good, however, is a nearer manifestation of It than
evil'.[154] The ethical implications of this view will be
examined in Section IV of this essay. But it would suffice

---

152. Ibid., p. 372.
153. Ibid., p. 374.
154. Ibid., p. 377.

to say here that the identification of the Brahman with principles of modern science completes Vivekananda's attempt to demote other faiths, sects and arguments in comparison with his perceived perfection of the Vedic religion.

Despite drawing upon science, among other things, to painstakingly create the idea of an impersonal God, Vivekananda would continue to wrestle with ethical questions regarding religion and its place in the world. There are instances when he says that all religions show a way out of this world and never aspire to reconcile the world and religion as an ideal.[155] It was also not sects and societies but the relation between the soul and God; it consisted in realization.[156] But there are equally compelling examples in Vivekananda where he explicitly hands over the mantle of helping humans to religion, not merely in liberating them from the illusions of the world but in concrete ways.[157] In one of the most frequently quoted passage from Vivekananda, the demands made on religion are not books, dogmas, philosophy or even God, but to 'to wipe the widow's tears or to bring a piece of bread to the orphan's mouth'.[158] But elsewhere he argues that 'religion has to do only with the soul and

---

155. *CW*, Vol. 2, p. 124.
156. *CW*, Vol. 4, p. 175.
157. *CW*, Vol. 2, pp. 24-5.
158. *CW*, Vol. 5, p. 39.

has no business to interfere in social matters.'[159] Also, far from wiping tears and giving bread, Vivekananda could also denounce the body and the pain it might feel as something grossly shameful and perceive it as a sign of slavery to the body.[160] In putting forth his ideas on Practical Vedanta, Vivekananda would insist on removing the 'fictitious differentiation between religion and the life of the world'.[161]

IV

Despite emphatic assertions about not disturbing anyone's faith, Vivekananda rarely saw anything worthwhile in other religions. He was sceptical of the Islamic idea of universal brotherhood, a concept whose operation he saw as one that was inextricably linked to the actual fact of being a Muslim. If an individual did not conform to Islam, not only would he remain outside the pale of universal brotherhood, but 'he will more likely have his throat cut'.[162] The same conditions applied to being accepted as part of the Christian idea of universal brotherhood, and any deviation from the prescribed path could send an individual 'to that place where he will be

---

159. *CW*, Vol. 4, p. 304.
160. *CW*, Vol. 1, p. 463.
161. *CW*, Vol. 2, p. 289.
162. Ibid., p. 378.

eternally barbecued'.[163] Islam and Christianity were, after all, primitive religions where there was first the idea of the universe created by a 'certain Being'.[164] Only much later did they develop an equally primitive idea of the soul encased in the body which was not the same as the body but distinct from it. The Christians also entertained ideas and doctrines like the world coming into existence because Adam ate an apple or escaping the wrath of an angry God, or even founding the basis of faith on the death of one man, in this instance, Jesus Christ.[165] For Vivekananda, there can be only one religion. The moment one names another religion with its own truth, it ceases to be a religion and becomes a sect. A religion has to be eternal, not the creation of a historically identifiable individual and unattached to any sacred book. Only the Vedas could ever satisfy all the three parameters.

More than damning other faiths and making them seem incomplete and inadequate, Vivekananda still had the task of fabricating 'our religion', 'India's religion', a faith that would happily resonate with the plan of establishing a European society in India. As religion, this entity had to permeate every aspect of human life, invade all arenas of thought, and, above all, be increasingly practical. Having identified Vedanta as the only religion in the world, a faith not only confined to India, but one whose

---

163. Ibid., p. 378.
164. *CW*, Vol. 1, p. 393.
165. Ibid., p. 468.

salience ultimately transcended culture, geography and nationality, Vivekananda wanted Vedanta to be 'intensely practical'.[166] Any proposed model of religion had to have Rajas driving individuals and nations towards sattva and, hence, be imbued with the kind of energy and activity exemplified by the ancient Greeks, the modern Europeans and the kshatriyas in India. For Vivekananda, the tenets of such a faith could only come from such people who were actively involved in the world, the ruling monarchs from among the kshatriyas, and not from those who gave up the world to retire into the forest to contemplate. Practical Vedanta, as Vivekananda chose to call this 'new' religion,[167] had to learn from the inspired example of an exchange between Śvetaketu, a brahmin and Pravāhaṇa Jaivali, a king, cited in the Chandogya Upanishad.

The original story itself has a straightforward narrative structure.[168] Āruṇi's son and disciple, Śvetaketu, happens to be in the court of Pañcāla, where he is asked several questions by Pravāhaṇa Jaivali, the king, who is also one of the three men who had mastered the High Chant.[169] Despite being tutored by his father, Śvetaketu

166. *CW*, Vol. 2, p. 289.
167. Vivekananda's own formulation in describing Practical Vedanta. Ibid., p. 299.
168. The summary presented here is based on Patrick Olivelle's translation of the Upanishads. Patrick Olivelle, op.cit., pp. 140-3.
169. Udgītha, the High Chant among the Sāmavedic chant in the Soma Sacrifice, called the Sāmana. Patrick Olivelle, op.cit., p. 95.

fails to answer these questions. The king questions the very fact of his being educated. Śvetaketu returns to his father and expresses his deep misgivings about the education he had received. He tells his father about the five questions 'That excuse for a prince'[170] had asked him. His father confesses that he did not know the answer to those questions, otherwise the question of withholding this knowledge from his son and pupil would not have arisen. Āruṇi, also mentioned in the text as Gautama, decides to go to the king's palace, where Pravāhaṇa Jaivali receives him with great courtesy and asks him to choose material gifts. Gautama rejects the offer of the material gifts and instead asks the king to tell him what he had asked Śvetaketu. The king gets worried hearing Gautama and orders him to stay a while longer in the court. The king, after a certain lapse of time, tells him: 'As to what you have asked me, Gautama, let me tell you that before you this knowledge had never reached the Brahmins. As a result in all the worlds government has belonged exclusively to royalty.'[171]

Pravāhaṇa Jaivali then answers Gautama's questions.

---

170. Ibid., p. 140. The five questions were: 'Do you know where people go from here when they die?', 'Do you know how they return again?', 'Do you know how the two paths – the path to the gods and the path to the fathers – take different turns?', 'Do you know how that world up there is not filled up?', 'Do you know how at the fifth offering the water takes on a human voice?'

171. Ibid., p. 140.

He talks about five fires, various paths and states and their relation to humans. In short, a human is born out of a fire. Once born, he lives a certain allotted lifespan, and after he dies, he is taken to the fire from which he was born. People in the wilderness who practise austerities are led by a 'person who is not human' to Brahman after they die; this is the path that leads to the gods. Those following the path of the fathers return to earth after a certain period. There is a third category or state of people who follow neither of these two paths and are condemned to encircle the earth and endlessly be born only to die. Pravāhaṇa Jaivali comes to two very significant generalizations in the course of revealing the answers to the five questions he had asked Śvetaketu. The first is a certain privileging of individuals who know about the five fires (that correspond to the five questions and their answers), who, as a result of this knowledge, remain pure and untainted and attain a good world. The second is even more significant.

> Now people here whose behaviour is pleasant can expect to enter a pleasant womb, like that of a woman of the Brahmin, the Kshatriya, or the Vaiśya class. But people of foul behaviour can expect to enter a foul womb, like that of a dog, a pig, or an outcaste woman.[172]

---

172. Ibid., p. 142.

The social code of ethics that is sketched by the king is equally pertinent. Stealing gold, drinking liquor, killing a brahmin, fornicating with the wife of one's teacher, and keeping the company of those who do these acts will confine a man to the third state of encircling the earth in a ceaseless cycle of births and deaths. It is also equally important to note that the story of the exchange between Śvetaketu, Pravāhaṇa Jaivali and Gautama appears in the Brihadaranyaka Upanishad. The broad outline of the narrative is the same as the one in the Chandogya Upanishad, but differs in some significant details. In the Brihadaranyaka Upanishad gloss on the story, the king asks Gautama not to ask for a boon that is 'in the category of divine wishes', but asks him to make a wish that is 'of a human sort'.[173] Gautama's reply is even more significant: 'As you know, I have my share of gold, cows, horses, slave girls, blankets and clothes.'[174] Gautama wants the knowledge of the infinite and the boundless. Pravāhaṇa Jaivali wants Gautama to ask for this in the right manner and commands him to become his pupil. In the Brihadaranyaka version, the king only alludes to this knowledge not being in the possession of brahmins but no reference is made to it being the sole preserve of rulers. Jaivali's reasons for parting with the knowledge, despite Gautama having become his pupil, are also

---

173. Ibid., p. 82.
174. Ibid., p. 82.

significantly different. Jaivali fears that if he does not admit Gautama to the knowledge of the infinite and the boundless, Gautama or his ancestors might cause him harm. Also, in describing the five fires, the two paths and the states, there is no direct reference to the Varna classification nor are the low outcastes listed along with dogs and pigs in describing the third state.

Vivekananda never cites the Brihadaranyaka Upanishad version of the story. In search of the kshatriya ideal of activity and practicality, his recounting of the story is always, inevitably, from the Chandogya Upanishad version. Neither does he seem to find the close affinities between privilege, power, wealth and the varna stratification in the narrative anachronistic and inappropriate. The existence of only two paths, the path of the gods and the path of the fathers, does not bother him, especially so because the one path is of renunciation and life in the forest and the other one was of ritual, both of which he often overtly seems to reject. The constant reference in the Upanishads to sacrifice and rituals is also conveniently ignored. The picture of Gautama as the rich brahmin, with slave girls as part of his wealth, did not fit the picture of brahminhood Vivekananda had sought to create; we know little of what King Pravāhaṇa Jaivali does of a practical nature other than expounding on the eternal and boundless mysteries, not to mention the recitation of the Samavedic High Chant. In truth, Vivekananda draws only two inferences from the story:[175] that a certain kind of practical knowledge always lay with kings and not brahmins and this was the reason why the kshatriyas ruled the world, and that the human body was the highest symbolism for worship of God. The first of these inferences helps his argument that Vedanta could be intensely practical, the second inference is puzzling. All that the Chandogya Upanishad story says is this: 'Once he is born, he lives his allotted lifespan. When he has departed, when he has reached his appointed time – they take him to the very fire from which he came, from which he sprang.'[176] In other words, the human body as the symbolism for worship of God is Vivekananda's own inflection to the Chandogya Upanishad story.

For Vivekananda, the Upanishads were the guides to realizing the truth and the foundations upon which Practical Vedanta stood. In his reading of the truth of the Upanishads, the word 'Truth' is capitalized and stands for the absolute truth. Realizing truth was not a choice between good and bad, but knowing that everything emerges from the Self, which alone is everything.[177] It also means shunning and denying the Universe and

---

175. *CW*, Vol. 2, pp. 289-90, 295, 311.
176. Patrick Olivelle, op.cit., p. 141.
177. *CW*, Vol. 2, p. 316.

shutting one's eyes to it. More so, it means seeing the Lord or Brahman in life and in death. The Upanishads introduce the idea of a living God. This is an impersonal idea, always difficult for people to understand, but the idea of God here is that he is an angel, a man or an animal and yet he is something more. The Impersonal God is the sumtotal of everything in the universe; he is also more than this sumtotal.[178] Practical Vedanta was for Vivekananda the distilled essence of the Upanishads.

Therefore I will ask you to understand that Vedanta, though it is intensely practical, is always so in the sense of the ideal. It does not preach an impossible ideal, however high it be, and it is high enough for an ideal. In one word this ideal is that you are divine. 'Thou art that.' This is the essence of Vedanta; after all its ramifications and intellectual gymnastics you know the human soul to be pure and omniscient; you see that such superstitions as birth and death would be entirely nonsense when spoken in connection with the soul...All such ideas as we can do this, or cannot do this, are superstitions. We can do everything. The Vedanta teaches men to have faith in themselves first. As certain religions of the world say that a man who does not believe in a Personal God outside

---

178. Ibid., p. 317.

of himself is an atheist, so the Vedanta says, a man who does not believe in himself is an atheist... There is neither man nor woman nor child, nor difference of race or sex, nor anything that stands as a bar to the realisation of the ideal, because Vedanta shows that it is realised already, it is already there.[179]

Reiterating the core idea in the Vedanta, Vivekananda emphasizes the uncompromising centrality of 'One Life, One World, One Existence, Everything is that One'.[180] To recognize the salience of the idea of oneness is not to condemn others but also recognize that there are people who are not as developed as the followers of the Vedanta.[181] No sooner does he explicitly make claims for the oneness of the universe, moral and ethical questions begin to demand answers. For instance, he condemns any idea of God who is partial to humans and cruel to beasts. Any religion where a god suggests that animals were there for human consumption is no God but a veritable demon.[182] This is in the context of the suggestion that Vedanta, unlike other creeds, does not make a distinction between humans and beasts.

The question of eating meat is an interesting one

179. Ibid., pp. 292-3.
180. Ibid., p. 295.
181. Ibid., p. 297.
182. Ibid., pp. 295-6.

especially because it tests Vivekananda's claims of Vedantic oneness. There are several instances when Vivekananda argues that eating meat was far preferable to centuries of slavery.[183] His advice to young men in India to eat beef in order to develop muscles and get a rajasic temperament hardly merits repetition. In the context of a discussion on changing customs, he even explains the way in which in ancient India beef was central to the brahmin's way of life.[184] But even in a more contemporary context, he was unambiguous regarding the desirability of eating meat.

But he who has to steer the boat of his life with strenuous labour through the constant life-and-death struggles and the competition of this world must of necessity take meat. So long as there will be human society such a thing as the triumph of the strong over the weak, animal food is required, or some other suitable substitute for it has to be discovered; otherwise the weak will naturally be crushed under the feet of the strong.[185]

---

183. *CW*, Vol. 4, p. 419.
184. 'There was a time in this very India when, without eating beef, no Brahman could remain a Brahman; you read in the Vedas how, when a Sannyasin, a king, or a great man came into a house, the best bullock was killed…'. *CW*, Vol. 3, p. 174.
185. *CW*, Vol. 5, p. 387.

Having elaborated the Practical Vedanta ideal and its radical restatement of oneness and unity of the entire universe, meat eating would require a defence that would serve two purposes. The first is to uphold the formulation of 'One Life, One World, One Existence, Everything is that One', but also, and this is the other requirement, uphold his condemnation of religions that justify killing animals for human consumption as part of religious sanction.

> I myself may not be a very strict vegetarian, but I understand the ideal. When I eat meat I know it is wrong. Even if I am bound to eat it under certain circumstances, I know it is cruel. I must not drag my ideal down to the actual and apologise for my weak conduct in this way. The ideal is not to eat flesh, not to injure any being, for all animals are my brothers. If you can think of them as your brothers, you have made a little headway towards the brotherhood of all souls, not to speak of the brotherhood of man![186]

Practical Vedanta was, then, to be perceived as just an ideal for an individual to aspire, emulate and realize. Practical Vedanta was meant to make humans free, not impel them to give up the world and go to the forest or live

186. *CW*, Vol. 2, p. 296.

in a cave. It required those who understood its real import to be where they were and just 'understand the whole thing'.[187] Vivekananda calls this understanding freedom. Face-to-face with this notion of freedom, every human being will know what he or she really is and see himself as the manifested God. In doing so, he will also worship other humans as gods. To put it differently, Practical Vedanta was a way of attaining clarity and lucidity.

> And this is the real, practical side of Vedanta. It does not destroy the world, but it explains it; it does not destroy the person, but explains him; it does not destroy the individuality but explains it, by showing the real individuality. It does not show that this world is vain, and does not exist, but it says, 'Understand what this world is, so that it may not hurt you...' The theme of the Vedanta is to see the Lord in everything, to see things in their real nature, not as they appear to be.[188]

In his formulation of Practical Vedanta, terms such as 'real nature' are not accidental. They serve a very important purpose in becoming the arbiter of all actions. Vivekananda is emphatic that all actions that constitute and exemplify oneness are good and all actions that

---

187. Ibid., p. 323.
188. Ibid., p. 310.

lend themselves to diversity are not good.[189] The world as diversity is a sign of humans not understanding their 'real nature' and going against the grain of the ideal of oneness that Practical Vedanta offers.

If the question of eating meat lays bare the moral and ethical claims of Practical Vedanta, Vivekananda was acutely conscious of other similar inadequacies in his formulation. It would be pertinent to look at Vivekananda's formulation of one such question and also carefully follow his attempts to address it.

> Everyone of us will think, 'I am God, and whatever I do or think must be good, for God can do no evil.' In the first place, even taking this danger of misinterpretation for granted, can it be proved that on the other side the same danger does not exist?[190]

Instead of providing an explanation of how the Impersonal idea would work better, Vivekananda's initial reaction is a predictable attack on the ideas of Dualism, Personal God and sectarianism 'deluging the world with blood and causing men to tear each other to pieces'.[191] But he ventures to confront the question more squarely after rhetorically invoking the inadequacies of the 'other side'.

---

189. Ibid., pp. 302-3.
190. Ibid., p. 320.
191. Ibid., p. 320.

How can you expect morality to be developed through fear? It can never be. 'Where one sees another, where one hurts another, that is Maya. Where one does not see another, where one does not hurt another, when everything has become the Atman, who sees whom, who perceives whom?' It is all He, and all I, at the same time. The soul has become pure.[192]

Till this point, the argument is pitched at two distinct levels. At a high level of abstraction, Practical Vedanta is an ideal, it is the ultimate recognition of oneness and unity, it is self-purification, it is understanding, it is realization and it is also shunning the universe of name and form. Another level of explanation restores the place and role of the world, of individuality and personality as long as humans remain aware of oneness rather than diversity. In the latter explanation, the only requirement is to see the Lord in all things, shun appearances and discover our 'real nature'.

Borrowing concepts and categories from Kantian philosophy, Vivekananda likens the arguments proffered against Practical Vedanta's espousal of oneness to a fight between the phenomenon and the noumenon.[193] The phenomenal world, he explains, was the universe

---

192. Ibid., p. 320.
193. Ibid., pp. 330-1.

of continuous change, and the noumenal world was something beyond the phenomenal world that does not change. There were people like the Dualists who in their folly believed that both these worlds were true and had a more or less independent existence. Vedanta alone, he asserts, gives a satisfactory answer to this division of reality into the phenomenal and the noumenal. Vedanta explains that there cannot be two worlds, one changing and the other unchanging. Rather, it clarifies that 'it is the one and the same thing which appears as changing, and which is in reality unchangeable'.[194] Other than Kantian philosophy, Vivekananda introduces several scientific metaphors to explain the reasons for radical oneness as the centrepiece of his Practical Vedanta ideal. Describing the relationship of the Impersonal to the Personal, or the phenomenal to the noumenal, he speaks of atoms in flux in relation to an unchangeable universe.

> So the whole is the Absolute; but with It every particle is in a constant state of flux and change. It is unchangeable and changeable at the same time, Impersonal and personal in one. This is our conception of the universe, of motion and of God, and that is what is meant by 'Thou art That.'[195]

---

194. Ibid., p. 330.
195. Ibid., p. 336.

Soon enough a biological metaphor is added to the armoury of explanations: 'The gigantic intellect, we know, lies coiled up in the protoplasmic cell, and why should not the infinite energy?...Each one of us has come out of one protoplasmic cell, and all the powers we possess were coiled up there.'[196]

The point Vivekananda tries to convey is clear: the Impersonal goes beyond the Personal and the relative and 'explains it [the personal and the relative] to the full satisfaction of our reason and heart'.[197] The phenomenal world, with its names and forms, is merely the Being, as he chooses to call it, perceived through the prism of our little minds and personalities. Once this narrow and restricted idea of identity is given up, 'we shall become one with It. That is what is meant by "Thou art That".'[198] Using another scientific metaphor, he rejects the proposition that the substance could ever be separate from the qualities of that substance. In fact, the relation between substance and qualities is one where the unchangeable appears as the changeable. Following this argument, human feelings, perceptions and even the awareness of the body are nothing but the soul.

∽

---

196. Ibid., pp. 337-8.
197. Ibid., pp. 336-7.
198. Ibid., pp. 336-7.

If there is a clinching example of the ethical and moral vacuum at the heart of Vivekananda's formulation of Practical Vedanta, it is the story of the actor and the beggar that he himself offers. The picture that Vivekananda paints is one where the contrast is between an actor playing the part of a beggar and the life of a real beggar. It would be interesting to look at this example and carefully examine its implications.

> The one enjoys his beggary while the other is suffering misery from it. And what makes this difference? The one is free and the other is bound. The actor knows his beggary is not true, but that he has assumed it, for play, while the real beggar thinks that it is his too familiar state and that he has to bear it whether he wills it or not. This is the law. So long as we have no knowledge of our real nature, we are beggars, jostled about by every force in nature, and made slaves of by everything in nature...[199]

The simple assumption that the actor enjoys playing the beggar's role and the real beggar finds only misery in begging is erroneous. As individuals with different motives and perspectives, this may not strictly be true. The actor may be free from the state of being a beggar,

---

199. Ibid., pp. 321-2.

but may not be free in a larger sense. The beggar, on the contrary, could be a free and liberated soul, especially if he has rejected material attachments and begging for him is simply a way of keeping himself alive. If the beggar is, indeed, miserable, there is no guarantee that he does not want to get out of this state or does not have enough will to help himself out of his abject state. Vivekananda's suggestion that the beggar has to bear his misery, whether he wills it or not, because his state is a consequence of an unspecified, but inevitable, law renders Practical Vedanta into another meaningless abstraction.

Though Vivekananda repeatedly enjoins his interlocutors to approach the idea of oneness with the heart, wants their hearts to feel God in itself and in others,[200] he continues to hold on to the limiting, fixed and regressive idea of 'real nature'. Begging and feeling miserable is the law for the beggar and is inevitable. He cannot escape from it, just as in Vivekananda's scheme of things, the cobbler will continue to mend shoes despite learning Sanskrit. He is free, however, to realize his 'real nature', whether or not such a realization alters his condition or lessens his humiliation and misery, if he so suffers from these states in his present condition. Vivekananda's Practical Vedanta would, however, help him in one respect: he will, perhaps, cease to hope for

---

200. Ibid., p. 305.

help from the outside. Vivekananda was contemptuous of Dualists and all believers in a Personal God for offering a religion that offered hope. Religion for him had to be moral and manly.

> [T]hey want a consoling religion and we understand that it is necessary for them. The clear light of truth very few in this life can bear, much less live up to. It is necessary, therefore, that this comfortable religion should exist; it helps many souls to be a better one. Small minds whose circumference is very limited and which require little things to build them up, never venture to soar high in thought.[201]

Small minds directed their energies in the misguided deployment of love. This is Vivekananda's stark conclusion. A man murders another man for the love of his child, limiting his love only for his progeny, but excluding millions from that love.[202] Selfish and limited love is misdirected love: only evil comes out of such a misdirected love. A love that does not involve any sense of one's ego or corporeal existence is true renunciation, and hence, selfless and genuine love.

∽

---

201. Ibid., p. 335.
202. Ibid., p. 252.

After Ramakrishna's death, Narendra tells Mahendranath of an instance when the Master asked Annada Guha to help his favourite disciple financially. Narendra and his family were in deep financial difficulties and were starving. After Annada left, Narendra scolded the Master for having asked for help on his behalf. Tearful from the rebuke received from his disciple, Ramakrishna said: 'Alas! For your sake I could beg from door to door.'[203] Having narrated the incident, Narendra makes one of the most significant remarks to be found in the Ramakrishna-Vivekananda corpus: 'He tamed us by his love. Don't you think so?'[204] Mahendranath's reaction to this is equally important: 'There is not the slightest doubt about it. His love was utterly unselfish.'[205] Narendra also recounts the number of times Ramakrishna prayed 'to the Divine Mother to give me money'.[206] There are several other occasions when Narendra would exclaim about Ramakrishna: 'He loved me so much!'[207] During this period, after Ramakrishna's passing away, a member of the monastery suggests that 'one person cannot give love to another person'.[208] Narendra immediately claims that the Master had, indeed, given him such love. The

---

203. *Gospel*, p. 980.
204. Ibid., p. 980.
205. Ibid., p. 980.
206. Ibid., p. 987.
207. Ibid., p. 987.
208. Ibid., p. 1007.

brother disciple expresses scepticism over Narendra's claim. Narendra's reaction is worth recounting: 'What can you understand about love? You belong to the servant class. All of you must serve me and massage my feet. Don't flatter yourself by thinking you have understood everything. Now go and prepare a smoke for me.'[209] Hearing this everyone laughed.

This anecdote nearly brings to a close the substantive part of Swami Nikhilananda's translation of Mahendranath Gupta's *Kathāmrita*. Having heard Vivekananda's response to the question of Ramakrishna's love, Mahendranath says something extremely significant to himself: 'Sri Ramakrishna has transmitted mettle to all the brothers of the math. It is no monopoly of Narendra's.'[210] This instance of expressing scepticism was, perhaps, a rare challenge to not merely Vivekananda's position as the 'inheritor' of Ramakrishna's mantle, but also offers the first methodological hint towards challenging Vivekananda's claims about Hinduism as religion. While his mystique endures, it survives in the absence of a self-reflective tradition that clings to his version of Hinduism in the form of pamphlets and in the guise of partially cited quotations from the corpus of his work. Any serious study of Vivekananda, then, is also a step towards delineating the themes crucial for

---

209. Ibid., p. 1008.
210. Ibid., p. 1008.

creating a genealogy of Hindu identity and questioning Hindu self-images. Perhaps we do not know enough; perhaps we will never know enough. But it is time now to stop serving and massaging the feet of the version of Hinduism that he offered. The servant class must now question, challenge and disturb. In doing so lies hope for the survival of India's democracy.

Index

Abhedananda, Swami (Kaliprasad Chandra), 4–5

Absolute, 16, 67, 71, 73, 218, 219, 220, 260

Achalananda, 34

Acintya-bhedabheda-vada, 19n

action without desire, 128–29

adharma, 50

Advaita Vedanta. *See* Vedanta

Adyashakti, 30, 32

ajnāna, 59, 70, 73

Akbar, 160

Akhandananda, 249

Ambedkar, B.R., 169

ananda (joy), 25

ancestors
of modern Europe and contemporary India, 124
Brahmins, Indian racial ideal, 180–82

Arjuna, 8, 169–70, 200, 225

Artha, xvi, 149

Āruni, 264, 265

Aryan(s), 98, 121, 124–25, 179–80, 254, 257
idea of caste, 142
and Dravidian, distinction, 178
and the Greeks, 125
idea of religion, 253

ashramadharma. *See* varnashramadharma

Asura(s), 131, 132

Ātman, 35, 145, 228–30, 276
and Brahman, 212
avidya, 23, 26, 30, 32, 37, 73, 110
Awareness (purusha) and Matter (prakriti), 55

Baranagore Math, 3
beliefs and practices, belief systems, 89, 95, 205, 243, 249
Belur Math, 1
Berkeley, Bishop, 197, 240
Bhagavadgita, xii, 112, 145, 174, 200, 202–03, 220, 225
Bhagavata Purana, 53, 55, 57, 198, 199
Bhagavatas, 53–54, 56–57
Bhairavi, 44, 75, 99–100
bhakti, bhakti-yoga, 15, 36n, 38, 41, 49–50, 56, 58, 69, 73–74, 90, 93–94, 138–39, 151, 188, 198, 213
and bhava, 74
and primacy of attaining God, 14
prema-bhakti or raga-bhakti, 76–78, 197
tāmasic, 96–97
vaidhi-bhakti, 36, 77

bhava(s), 74–75, 79–80
Bhoga, 128
Bible, 206, 208, 216, 248
bliss, 23, 75, 135, 260
Body, 62–63
as Self, 63
and sense objects, 70
and soul, 278–80
bondage of the world, 22, 127, 130, 214
Brahmajnana, 64, 71, 73
Brahman, 25, 39, 41, 45, 61–64, 67, 68, 70, 72, 105–6, 151, 179–80, 187, 212, 259
and Kali, 16–20
is beyond vidya and avidya, 23
Brāhmanas, 97, 153, 158
Brahmins, Brahminhood, 153, 158, 167, 174, 175, 179–85, 188–89, 266, 268
ritualistic forms of brahmanical practices, 139
Brahmo Samaj, Brāhmos, 85, 87, 102, 103, 106, 187
Brihadaranyaka Upanishad, 267–68
British rule in India, 123, 126, 129–30, 153

Buddha, 146, 148, 168, 175, 183, 185, 222, 234, 243–46
    refusal to recognize caste, 185
Buddhism, 53, 97, 146, 147, 153, 161, 206, 208, 222, 230–31, 243–45, 255

Caitanya Caritamrita of Krishnadasa Kaviraja, 197, 199–201
caste, xiv, 139, 153, 161, 171–72, 179, 180–81, 184–85, 188–89
    and classes, 172–73
    designated individuals, 178
    hierarchy, 161
    institutions, privilege within, 183
    is a natural order, 182–83
    as a religious institution, 175
Chaitanya, xii, 51, 76, 108–09, 150, 183, 187, 197, 199, 201
Chakravarty, Sharat Chandra, 1, 186
Chandāla, 97, 184
Chandogya Upanishad, 202,
    203, 264, 267–69
charity and philanthropy, 192
chaturvarnya. *See* varna system
Christ, 148, 243, 254, 263

Christian ethics, Christianity, 41, 84, 87, 90, 91, 98, 101, 118, 141, 149, 206, 207, 222, 228
compassion (dayā), 98, 193
consciousness, 25, 39, 54, 56, 61, 62, 80, 81
conversion in Islam, 257–58
cosmic principles, Cosmic Power, 16, 72
creation, preservation and destruction, cycles, 16, 18, 20–22
culture, 172, 179, 182
customs and traditions, 189
    diversity and complexity, 124

Dakshineshwar, 6, 39
dasya (of servant towards the master), 42, 74
deceit and calculation, 195
desire and greed, 134

Deussen, Paul, xii, 241
devas, 131, 132
    and asuras in mythologies, 214–15
dharma (right conduct), xvi, 50, 114, 130–31, 148, 167, 199, 200, 203
differentiation and inequality, 183
discrimination, 30, 41, 60, 62, 64, 67, 111, 192
disease, 27
dispassion and worldliness, 30
diversity of races, languages and customs, 162, 176, 275
dualism, 19n, 138, 141, 209–13, 217–18

East and West
    difference, 215
    synthesis, 149
economic and social idea of class privilege and exclusivity, 182
ego, 60, 61–62, 64, 71, 281
equality, freedom, work and energy, 122
Eternal Being, 23

ethics and morality, 254, 267
European(s), 264
    civilization, 119–23, 125
    sciences, 120, 122–23, 129
    society, 118–19, 123, 130, 159, 190, 205, 263
evil, idea of, 120, 167–69, 260, 275, 281
evolution principle, 92, 230, 243, 251–53, 259
existence-knowledge-bliss idea of the absolute, 23, 260

faith and belief. See beliefs and practices
fanaticism, 141, 213
forgiveness, 170
freedom, notion of, 274

Gandhi, M.K., 169
Gargi, 150, 151
Gautama, 202, 265, 267–68
Gayatri Mantra, 186
Ghosh, Girish, 110–11, 115
Ghoshpara, 33
God, 18–19, 24–25, 40–42, 59–60, 67, 69, 72–76, 79, 87–88, 91, 94–95, 128, 193–94, 237, 251, 271

God-consciousness, 61, 68

gopis of Vrindavan, 7, 80, 88

Greece, 129–30, 205

Greeks, 125, 128, 142, 264

Grihya Sutras, 153, 206

Guha, Annada, 282

Gupta, Mahendranath, xxi, 3–5, 24, 83, 103–05, 107, 112, 114–16, 236, 240, 282
  Sri Sri Ramakrishna Kathāmrita, 3, 17, 32, 33, 38, 39, 45, 50, 51, 58, 60, 62, 65, 80, 83, 87, 89–91, 106, 113, 195, 240, 283

Hacker, Paul, xix

Haladhari, 39

Hale, Mary, 11

Hamilton, 111

Hanuman, 54–55, 64, 88
  dasya bhava, 42–43

Hāridrumata Gautama, 203–04

Hazra, Pratap, 104, 107

Hegel, G.W.F., 237

Hindu(s), 84–85, 87, 97, 132, 137, 141, 143–45, 149, 157, 174, 181
  divided, 184
  identity, xiii, xv, xix, 86, 89, 90, 95, 130, 147
  intellectuality, 184
  orthodoxy, 123, 149
  religiosity, 102
  self-image, xiii, xix, 154–55, 157–58
  spirituality, 123, 160

Hinduism, xxi, 13, 84, 85, 91, 98, 99, 101, 118, 142, 146, 182, 190, 206, 222
  fundamental doctrines, 142
  as religion, xiv–xv, 11, 9, 98
  a scientific religion, 94–96
  superiority, xii
  tolerance, 208
  universal religion, 208, 217, 220

Hiranyakashipu, 55–56

householders, 26–27, 29

Hriday (Ramakrishna's nephew), 6

Hudson, D. Dennis, 52–53, 55, 57–58

human action and its consequences, 225–27

human arrogance and selfishness, 196

humanitarian work, 14–15
humans, fourfold classification, 238
Husain, Mohammed Sarfaraz, 247, 248
Huxley, Aldous, 111

I-consciousness, 70–72
I-ness and my-ness, 77–78
identity, 61, 278
ignorance veil, 23, 59, 70, 119, 199
impermanence of the world, 194
individuality, 149, 176, 177, 212, 251, 274, 276
Infinite, 68
intellect, 179
introspection, 181
Islam, 41, 84, 90, 91, 99, 101, 141, 153, 161, 208, 213, 246, 248, 254, 257–58, 262–63

Jabālā, 203
Jagannath Temple, Puri, xiii
Jainism, Jains, 153, 160, 206, 208, 230, 231
Janaka, 64
japa and austerity, 52, 77

Jāti, Jati dharma, 176, 177–78, 186
Jnāna (knowledge), 14, 59, 62, 70, 197–99
and karma, 198
jnani, 59–61, 63, 72, 93
and vijnani, distinction, 59, 67

Kabir, 183
Kafirs, 140
Kāla, 46
Kali, xi, xxi, 1–2, 4, 9, 44, 45, 88, 102–3, 105, 106, 112, 195, 223
Brahman and, 17–20
Divine Mother, 16, 20–21, 24, 40–41, 48–49, 87, 93–94, 104, 112, 282
forms, 21
formless, 21
playful and supportive, 21–22
worship as part of religion, rejected by Vivekananda, 11–12
Kaliyuga, 32, 58, 62, 63, 179, 193
Kama, xvi, 149

Kanchipuram, 53
Kant, Immanuel, xii, 241, 277
    Lutheran-Protestant worldview, 215–16
    idea of religion and his distinction between religion and cult, 213
karma (action), 160, 197–99
    effects, 49
    karma-kanda, 207
    Karma-Yoga, 15, 193
Kartabhaja, 33
kirtana, nama-samkirtana, 152, 197–98
knowledge, 59–60, 67, 109, 126, 173, 198, 260
    ego, 64
    and renunciation, 67
    of self, 124
    wakefulness, 57
Krishna (Krsna), xii, 8, 36–37, 41, 56, 57, 74, 76, 77–81, 85, 88, 92, 112, 150, 170, 191, 197–201, 208, 216, 221, 228, 237
Kshatriya, 174, 175, 179–80, 243, 264, 266, 269
    degradation, 179
    ideal for Vivekananda, 202

Kshir Bhavani episode, xix
Kumarila Bhatt, 148
Kundalini, 45
Kurukshetra battle, 169

liberation from bondage (mukti), 130, 187–88, 197–99
liberty, equality and fraternity, 141–42
Sri Sri Ramakrishna Lilaprasanga, 42–43, 113

madhura bhava (of the woman towards her lover), 74, 79, 80, 100n
Madhva, 211
Mahabharata, 169, 181, 221
mahabhava (divine ecstasy), 74, 76
Maha-Kala, the Absolute, 20–21
Mahamaya, 23, 44, 72
Maitreyi, 150, 151
Mallick, Shambhu, 195–96
man-lion consecration, 53
Manu, 157, 167, 206
Marathas, 140
masculinity, 153, 202

material well-being, 134–35
materialistic West and spiritual East, 99, 118
Māyā, Maya-Shakti, 16n, 13, 26, 71, 98, 246, 276
meat eating, 271–73, 275
meditation, 58, 124
meekness, 159, 167
metaphysical speculations, 229–30
Mill, James Stuart, 240
Mimāmsakas, Mimamsa system, xvi–xvii, 130–31
    purva, 131, 247
    uttara, 247
mlechchha, 155, 162
Mohammedanism, 255
Moksha, xvi, 146, 148–49
Monism, 213, 218, 230–31
Mughal power, 138, 140
Muhammad, Prophet, 221, 222
mukti. *See* liberation from bondage
Müller, Max, xii, 241
Muslims, 85, 87, 97, 101, 134, 149, 153, 160–61, 185, 206, 207, 247

Narada, 64

Narasimha, 55–56
Narasimha-diksha, 54
Narayana, 54
nationalism, xi, 52, 189
neologism, 90
Neti, neti, 61, 72
Nikhilananda, Swami, xxi, 3, 283
nirguna, 67
nishthaa (single-minded devotion), 87–88, 213
Nitya, 67
Nivedita, Sister, 152
non-injury versus retaliatory violence, 167–70
non-resistance, 166, 168, 170, 181

occult powers, 5–8
Om, 68
orthodoxy, 119–20, 174, 207

Pañcāla, 264
Panchanami, 33
pantheism, 113
Pashupatas, 163
Perfect Knowledge, 40
Personal God, 68–69, 78, 88, 226, 227, 236, 249, 260–61, 270, 275, 278

phenomenon and noumenon, 276–77
philanthropy, 52
political power structure, politics, 125, 189, 200
poverty, 27, 154
    dehumanization and slavery, 146
practicality and intellect, 125
Prahalada, 55–56
Prakriti, 36, 37, 55, 176
Pravāhana Jaivali, 201, 202, 264–68
prema, 73, 76, 198
priestcraft, 117
Primordial Energy, 72
protestant reformation, 148
Puranas, 40, 41, 65, 86, 131, 179, 206, 208
purity, 181
    and impurity mandated by caste, 188
    of race, 120
Purusha, 36, 55
purusha-prakriti dualism, 36

Qur'an, 208

race(s), racial
    language and society, 164
    purity, 161
    traits, 154
    and tribes, fusion, 178
Radha, xii, 7, 37n, 74, 76, 77, 79, 80–81, 150, 191, 208. See also Krishna; gopis
rajas, xvii, 40, 119, 127–29, 131–33, 135, 145, 150, 264, 272
    of the West and the sattva of India, 129
Rajputs, 138
Rama, 54, 88, 221
Ramakrishna Paramahamsa, in conversation with Bankim Chandra Chatterjee, 191–95
    ideal of bhakti, 9, 14, 76–77, 90, 94, 188
    sense of caste, 188
    catholicity, 81–82, 91, 100
    diagnosed with cancer, 113
    death, ix, xi, 2–3, 104, 113, 134, 236, 240, 282
    devotionalism, 13
    disciples worship as

Kali, 115

divine madness, 38, 41, 44, 78, 80, 99

on gunas (sattva, rajas and tamas), 40, 127–28

preached the idea of service, 83

stance about God, 16–20, 46–49, 72–76, 84, 86, 88–89, 94–95, 106–11, 113–15, 154, 193–94, 223

transition from I-ness to myness, 77–78

inclusiveness and universality, 85–86, 91

perceived Kali, 16–22, 111

mansion of mirth, 201

theory of modesty, 194

powers passed to Vivekananda, 2, 4–5

on religion, 223

into sanyasa, 6

faith in Shakti, 16–18

spiritual practices, 41, 42, 52, 80

symbolic act of eating

Kali, 45–46

Tantra practice, 32–33, 43–44, 100

tolerance, 81, 88, 93

initiation into Vedas, 100

denunciation for woman and gold, 23, 25, 27, 29, 30, 31, 32, 46, 106, 108, 134, 192

perceived woman, 26–31

Ramanuja, 105, 122, 148, 183, 221

Reality, 67, 84, 110, 186, 194, 238, 246, 277

Vedanta way (non-dualistic nature), 16, 19, 63

reasoning and discrimination, 61–62, 64–66

religion(s), 86, 89, 135, 165, 171, 189, 190, 213, 218, 223, 237, 247, 251, 253, 256;

and cult, distinction, 213–14

degeneration, 255

and philosophy, 137

and Vedanta, 230

religiosity, 197

religious

beliefs and practices, 159, 239

fragmentation, 163

freedom in India, 158–59

nationalism of Vivekananda, xii, xvii, 14, 134, 162

orthodoxy in India, 205

symbols and forms, 224

tolerance, 52, 156–57

renunciation, 10, 31, 67, 99, 107, 124, 126, 129, 182, 189, 192, 198

ritual purity, 161, 186, 188

Rolland, Romain, 15

Roy, Ram Mohan, 175

sadhaka, 54

sadhana, 54, 58, 108

sakhya bhava (friendship), 74

Samadhi, 44, 61, 71, 76

Sambandha-rupa, 36n

Samkhya yoga, 55–56, 111

Sanaka, 64

Sananda, 64

Sanatana, 64

Sanatana Dharma, 90–91, 98, 102

Sanatkumara, 64

Sanskrit language, 179, 183–87, 243

sanyasi, 10, 28, 30–31

should refrain from woman and gold, 23, 25, 27, 29, 30, 31, 32, 46, 106, 108, 134, 192

Sarkar, Mahendra, xi

Satchidānanda, 23, 85, 196

Satchidananda-Vigraha, 19n

sattva guna, xvii, 40, 126–29, 135, 264. *See also* rajas; tamas

Satyakāma Jābāla, 203

Satyayuga, 181

Savarkar, Vinayak Damodar, 154

Schopenhauer, Arthur, xii, 206, 237, 241

science, 260

and reason, 120–21, 258–59

and technology, 134

scientific rationality, 224

scriptures, doctrines and dogmas, 60, 92, 98, 133, 141, 161, 168, 174, 206–08, 222, 231, 232, 237–40, 243, 246, 250, 257, 263

authenticity and legitimacy, 111
sectarianism and fanaticism, 245, 255, 275
sects and faiths, 82–83, 84, 86, 90, 101–02, 162, 261
Self, 71, 124, 151, 246, 269
self-discipline, 55
self-government, 138
selflessness and spiritual excellence, 180
self-power, 54, 55
self-reliance, 119, 128, 171
self-righteousness, 154
self-sacrifice, 181, 182, 189
Sen, Rāmprasād, xi, xii, xxi, 17–18, 24, 30, 44–46
sense-perception, 220
servitude and poverty, 133
sexual freedom, 204
Shaivas, 85, 163
Shaktas, 84, 85, 86
Shakti, 16–18, 22, 25, 32, 33, 41, 68, 72, 104, 105, 121, 122, 152; as avidya, 26
Shankaracharya, 64, 92, 116, 148, 186–87
shanta bhava (serene), 74
Shastras (sāśtras), 52, 167
Shiva, xi, 35, 41, 44, 71, 85, 157
Shivananda, 82
Shorashi, 35
shraddha ceremony, 189
Shrauta Sutra, 206
shudra, 175, 180, 201
siddhi and siddha, 6–8
Sikhs, 140
slavery, 137, 146, 160
social
  culture, 175
  diversity and plurality, 216
  freedom in the West, 117, 159
  hierarchy, 200
  individuality 177
  institution, 180
  structure, xiii
soul and God, 261, 278
speechlessness, 61
Spencer, Herbert, 111
spiritual discipline, 26, 27, 32–34, 38, 40, 44, 47
spirituality, spiritual practices, x, 28, 29, 33, 41, 42, 52, 80, 98–99, 139, 160, 179, 182, 189, 221
  subordination of European sciences,

120–21
Sri Rangam, 53
substance and qualities, 278
Sufis, 160
Sukshma-diksha, 54, 56, 58
super-conscious state, 218–20, 229
superstitions, 169, 213, 216
    in formative stages of religion, 120–21
    and irrationality, 206
sva-artha-puja, 54
Śvetaketu, 202, 264–67
symbolism, 256

tamas, xvii, 15, 40, 93, 96, 97, 126–27, 131–32, 148–49
Tantras, xxi, 17, 21, 32–35, 40, 41, 43, 44, 58, 65, 73, 79, 85, 86, 121
    and Bhakti, x, 38, 97, 138, 139, 152
    influence in Vaishnavism, 97
Vamachara, 32, 97, 121, 174
temples, rejection by Vivekananda, xii
tolerance and sympathy, 155–56, 162, 166, 208,

210, 239
Totapuri, 6, 100
truth(s), 67, 216, 226–28, 238
    of the Upanishads, 241
    Vyavaharika and paramarthika, 219–20
twice-born, 171
Tyndall, 111

Überweg, Friedrich, 236–37
unity and variation, 238–39
universal brotherhood, 262
untouchability, 171, 186
Upanishads, 11, 144, 145, 148, 151, 153, 168, 189, 201, 205–09, 211, 216, 217, 221, 222, 225, 227, 231, 239, 241, 245–47, 250, 267–70
Vaishnavism, Vaishnavas, 41, 51, 52, 54, 57, 84, 85, 86, 97, 100, 163, 199
    Bengal School, 19n, 36n, 197
    Gaudiya tradition, 16n
    Vatakalai (Northern Division) and Tenkalai (Southern Division), disagreement, 57–58
Vaiśya, 180, 266

varna system, varnadharma, 121, 138, 178, 219

chaturvarnya, 185

varnashramadharma, 199, 201, 219

vatsalya (of the mother towards her child), 74

Vedanta, Vedantin(s), 16, 41, 60, 62–63, 70, 72–73, 82, 84, 86, 92, 98, 106, 150, 181–82, 193, 202–05, 209, 217–22, 224–33, 236, 239, 241, 247, 254–55, 259, 263, 271–72

Advaita, xvii, 96, 211–12, 217–18, 224, 230–31, 248, 260

religion, 182

idea of Universal Soul, 233

universalism, 82

Vivekananda's formulation of Practical Vedanta, xix, 64, 203, 262, 264, 269–70, 273–77, 279–80

Vedas, Vedic, xiv, 18, 32, 40, 41, 43, 58, 60, 65, 85–86, 92, 106, 133, 148, 151, 183, 187–89, 208, 209, 211,

216, 248, 251

on God, 240

orthodoxy, 175

religion, 148, 186, 245, 250–53, 257, 261

society, 186

Vibhava-diksha, 54, 57, 58

vidya and avidya, 23, 73

vijnāna, 59, 62, 67, 68, 70, 73

vijnani, 67, 68, 73

Virāt, 136–37

Virochana, 132

Vishistadvaita, 105

Vishnu Purana, 201

Vishnu, 56, 57, 201

Vishwamitra, 174

Vivekananda, Swami (Narendra)

on Advaita Vedanta, xix, 64, 96, 211–12, 217–31, 236, 248, 260

on Ātman, 212, 228–30

on bhakti, xii, 214

on Buddha and Buddhism, 230–31, 244–45

on caste, 173–77, 180–85

dilemma, 123

doubts and disbelief, 111–12

on dualism, 209–13, 218–
19, 224, 236, 275
idea of 'European society',
118–26, 129–30
formulation of practical
Vedanta, 203, 262,
264, 269–70, 273–77,
279–80
influence of German
philosophy, 236–37
on God, 197, 212, 226–27,
232, 233, 236–8
analysis of Hindu India,
Hinduism, xiv–xv,
xxi, 102, 132–33, 147–
55, 158–62, 170, 171,
202, 204, 209, 212–13,
216, 220, 222, 226–30,
245–46, 283
on Islam, 248
Kali entered his body, 2,
4, 9–12
claim of oneness, 218–20,
225, 233–36, 245, 248,
260, 271–77, 280
rejection of non-injury
and non-resistance,
168
and his master
Ramakrishna, 10, 12–

16, 23, 34, 45, 82, 93–
95, 99, 101–161, 126–
27, 211, 237, 283
address at Ramnad
(1897), 119–20
on religion, 14, 118–30,
165, 218–19, 223–24,
231–34, 237–40, 244,
281
respect to other faiths,
232–35
in samadhi and
meditation, 5
selective misogyny, 204
rejection of Tantra, 121
on tri-gunas, xvii, 126–
29, 131–33, 135, 145,
148, 264, 272
utopian state, 175
on Vaishnavas, 210
on Vedas and
Upanishads, 209, 211,
217, 222, 224, 227, 231,
245–46
idealized women, 152–53
Vyuha-diksha, 54

war and sculpture, 125
western science, 133
woman and gold, 23, 25, 27,

29, 30, 31, 32, 46, 106, 108, 134, 192

Woman, 30–32, 150–52

as Divine Mother, 28, 30–31, 37

traits, 26–30: Great Illusion, 16; mansion of mirth, 24

World's Parliament of Religions, Chicago, 1893, xix

worldliness, 134

worship, xii, 30, 32, 35, 41, 42, 44, 52, 54, 56, 83–84, 115, 121, 136–37, 152, 154, 166, 181, 187–88, 198, 211–12, 217, 251, 269, 274; Christian, 87; of Kali, 11–12

Yavanas, 125, 126, 128

yoga (union of the individual with the Infinite), yogis, yogic practices, 54, 55, 128, 145, 197